The Game Design Reader

The Game Design Reader

A Rules of Play Anthology

Katie Salen and Eric Zimmerman

The MIT Press
Cambridge, Massachusetts
London, England

book design and photography | Douglas Diaz and Katie Salen

This book was set in 9-point DIN by Douglas Diaz and Katie Salen and was printed and bound in the United States of America.

Library of Congress Cataloging-in-Publication Data

The Game design reader: a rules of play anthology / edited by Katie Salen and Eric Zimmerman
        p.cm.
ISBN 978-0-262-19536-2 (hc. : alk. paper)
1. Computer games—Programming. 2. Computer games—Design. 3. Video games—Design. I. Salen, Katie. II. Zimmerman, Eric.

QA76.76.C672G357 2005
794.8_1536—dc22   2005043879

10 9 8 7 6 5 4

To Hampton Fancher, for everything.—Katie

To Gil, Enid, Laura, and Zach, for teaching me how to be me.—Eric

Contents

x   **Foreword**

Warren Spector

xvi   **Preface**

Katie Salen and Eric Zimmerman

interstitial: How to Win "Super Mario Bros"

1   **Topic Essays**

Katie Salen and Eric Zimmerman

      3   The Player Experience

      9   The Rules of a Game

      15   Gaming the Game

      21   The Game Design Process

      27   Player and Character

      33   Games and Narrative

      39   Game Communities

      45   Speaking of Games

      53   Game Design Models

      59   Game Economies

      65   Game Spaces

      71   Cultural Representation

      77   What Is a Game?

      83   What Is Play?

interstitial: Cosplay

91   **Texts: Bibliography**

93   **Chart of Texts and Topics**

interstitial: Urban Invasion

96   **Nature and Significance of Play as a Cultural Phenomenon** (1955)
Johan Huizinga

122   **The Definition of Play: The Classification of Games** (1962)
Roger Caillois

156   **Shoot Club: The DOOM 3 Review** (2004)
Tom Chick

interstitial: Collateral Romance

172   **Construction of a Definition** (1990)
Bernard Suits

192   **I Have No Words & I Must Design** (1994)
Greg Costikyan

212   **The Cabal: Valve's Design Process for Creating Half-Life** (1999)
Ken Birdwell

interstitial: Urban Games

228   **Semiotic Domains: Is Playing Video Games a "Waste of Time?"** (2003)
James Gee

268   **The Evil Summoner FAQ v1.0: How to Be a Cheap Ass** (2001)
Mochan

296   **Play and Ambiguity** (2001)
Brian Sutton-Smith

314   **A Theory of Play and Fantasy** (1972)
Gregory Bateson

330   **"Complete Freedom of Movement": Video Games as Gendered Play Spaces** (1998)
Henry Jenkins

interstitial: DDR Step Charts

366   **Formal Abstract Design Tools** (1999)
Doug Church

382   **Game Theory** (1992)
William Poundstone

410   **Games and Design Patterns** (2005)
Staffan Björk and Jussi Holopainen

438   **Tools for Creating Dramatic Game Dynamics** (2005)
Marc LeBlanc

460   **Game Analysis: Centipede** (2001)
Richard Rouse III

interstitial: Indie Game Jam

476   **Unwritten Rules** (1999)
Stephen Sniderman

504   **Beyond the Rules of the Game: Why Are Rooie Rules Nice?** (1983)
Linda Hughes

518   **Changing the Game** (1978)
Bernard DeKoven

538   **The Design Evolution of Magic: The Gathering** (1993 | 2004)
Richard Garfield

interstitial: Blast Theory

558   **Eyeball *and* Cathexis** (1983)
David Sudnow

578   **Frames and Games** (1983)
Gary Alan Fine

602   **Bow, Nigger** (2004)
always_black

610   **Cultural Models: Do You Want to Be the Blue Sonic or the Dark Sonic?** (2003)
James Gee

interstitial: Red vs. Blue

642 **Interaction and Narrative** (2000 | 2005)
Michael Mateas and Andrew Stern

670 **Game Design as Narrative Architecture** (2004)
Henry Jenkins

690 **Adventure as a Video Game: Adventure for the Atari 2600** (1983–84)
Warren Robinett

714 **Eastern Front (1941)** (2003)
Chris Crawford

interstitial: Serious Games

728 **The Lessons of Lucasfilm's Habitat** (1990)
F. Randall Farmer and Chip Morningstar

754 **Hearts, Clubs, Diamonds, Spades: Players Who Suit MUDs** (1996)
Richard Bartle

788 **Declaring the Rights of Players** (2000)
Raph Koster

814 **Virtual Worlds: A First-Hand Account of Market and Society
on the Cyberian Frontier** (2001)
Edward Castronova

interstitial: Painstation

866 **Coda: Piercing the Spectacle** (2005)
Brenda Laurel

interstitial: Le Parkour

872 **Interstitial Credits**

876 **Index**

924 **Final Word**
Katie Salen and Eric Zimmerman

Foreword

Warren Spector

As I write this, games are poised to take a leap forward—or, rather, many leaps forward.

There's the leap the industry takes every 4–6 years, whenever a new generation of hardware emerges, forcing us to reevaluate what is possible in this still infant medium struggling to find its true nature.

But this isn't just an ordinary transition. This time, we're at the precipice of another cliff, a cultural one. This is a big moment, a moment that sees gaming drifting. And the direction of that drift will determine our future.

Sometimes we drift, unknowing and seemingly uncaring, in the direction of rampant commercialism. We pander to our audiences, feeding them a concoction that is equal parts pablum and violence. Rather than striving for something new and wonderful, we go with the tried and true, making assumptions about what players want and need based on what they've wanted in the past—what they've told us they want with their dollars.

And yet, we sometimes drift in another direction, offering players the opportunity to explore aspects of themselves and the world in a way no other medium allows. And we do it with what can only be described as, well, artistry. In addition, we are this close—*this* close—to being a true cultural force, our influence far exceeding the size of our audience.

To date, we've drifted in these various directions without a paddle, rudderless, going wherever the currents of commerce took us. This isn't good enough. If we're going to succeed, change, grow, reach new audiences, and offer them more compelling works—and more compelling ways to interact with those works—in other words, if we're going to take our place among the successful, influential media and art forms, we need to find a rudder and to learn to use our paddles more effectively. That's where games criticism, and books like this one, come in.

There have been many books written about games. Most are dry histories or even drier discussions of how one makes games (often by people who don't seem ever to have come within a hundred yards of a development team!). Books of games criticism—what makes games work or not work, how games make meaning, what place games have in world culture—are few and far between. Of these, Katie Salen and Eric Zimmerman's *Rules of Play* is the best, the first Important Book about electronic games.

Now, I have to confess, I'm not a completely impartial observer. I've known the authors for a long time—shared panels with them, listened to them lecture in classes and at conferences, and enjoyed their work as practitioners of the art of making games.

The fact that they are both critics and creators is part of what sets them apart from, well, nearly everyone else working or writing about the field. But my affection for the authors notwithstanding, I'll stand by my assessment of their last book.

Quite simply, *Rules of Play* covered more ground than any earlier offering—enough ground that its utility extended beyond the classroom and into industry. *Rules of Play* was a book that offered game developers as much as it did students and players.

It did this, at least in part, by offering an astonishingly wide variety of perspectives. Yes, it offered the authors' views, but it was largely structured around the work of others. *Rules of Play* is filled with countless quotes and citations from academics, critics, designers, producers, you name it. Rather than simply pontificate, the authors offered competing views, saying in essence, "We don't know it all. Here's what some other folks have to say about this."

This approach—author as moderator of discussion—allowed others to step up, virtually, and offer their opinions. To ensure the success of this approach, the authors provided a thematic structure and interstitial material that gave all those disparate voices coherence. *Rules of Play* was really quite a virtuosic performance, not unlike the experience of attending a concert and seeing what a great conductor can make of sheet music and a room full of musicians. To my astonishment, reading the book elicited some rather strong emotions in me.

I found that odd because it isn't often that textbooks elicit any kind of emotion—that's not their job, after all. Yet I found *Rules of Play* exhilarating in its enthusiasm for its subject, awe-inspiring in its breadth, fulfilling in its respect for a medium that gets far too little, and entertaining in its every word. I finished the book with the undeniable idea that the medium in which I have chosen to work is Important, Influential, and filled with unrealized Potential.

But just as there is potential in the games medium to be more than it is today, I also saw potential in the book *Rules of Play* that was unrealized. As impressed as I was with *Rules of Play*, I couldn't help feeling the book lacked something.

Or, more to the point, *I* lacked something...

Nearly every turn of the page introduced me to a concept I hadn't considered before, an author or critic I'd never heard of (or whose work I had never had the opportunity to read).

The authors cast their net so widely and so well I was surprised at how much had been written about games over the years and at the same time, overwhelmed by the breadth of knowledge I lacked. And I like to think I'm pretty well read when it comes to games criticism.

The breadth of games scholarship as revealed in the pages of *Rules of Play* was impressive and daunting. And while I felt exhilarated at having been exposed to so many new ideas, so many impressive works of scholarship, I wondered how I'd ever get my hands on half the works cited in the book—and getting my hands on them seemed critical if I were going to reach the deeper level of understanding *Rules of Play* promised to reveal to me.

Therefore, as I read *Rules of Play,* I found myself mentally constructing a companion piece, a "Games Criticism Reader," keyed to the sections in the original book. It seemed vital to offer students, players, parents, and practitioners a selection of works that would offer them the opportunity to explore in *depth* the incredible *breadth* of information provided in *Rules of Play.*

And, now, here's that reader come to life.

With *The Game Design Reader,* the authors have put together a selection of essays, some of them difficult to find, spanning fifty years of game analysis and criticism. These pieces connect in pleasantly surprising ways the electronic marvels of today's gaming world with "face-to-face" games that have for millennia provided diversion, entertainment, and education. The "platform agnosticism" of the book is one of its greatest strengths, reminding us all that games have a rich heritage, a long-standing tradition of enriching and informing human experience.

In addition, the authors have sought out contributions from the denizens of several different gaming-related worlds—represented in the pages that follow are game developers, game journalists, gamers, and academics. These contributors bring with them the unique perspectives of their respective disciplines.

Represented here are fields as diverse as psychology, sociology, anthropology, linguistics, cultural theory—and, of course, game development. The fact that Huizinga, Bateson, Sutton-Smith or Caillois fit comfortably in a book also featuring Garfield, Crawford, Church, Costikyan and LeBlanc is testament to the authors' desire to appeal to, and educate, a diverse audience.

I've often described game development as the most intensely collaborative, cross-disciplinary endeavor I can imagine. The authors reflect that belief in the wide range of contributors to *The Reader*. But they also reflect an even more fundamental truth about gaming: games are a medium that demands the participation of users—players must act, and *re-act* or nothing happens.

Without player input and player reaction, a game comes to a standstill. No story, no victory, no loss, no cultural significance, no nothing. Perhaps the most elegant thing about *The Reader* is that the authors' clear intent is to allow players...er, I mean, readers...to chart their own course through the material. Thus the structure of the book elegantly mirrors the subject being studied!

I hope all readers—whether game development professionals, teachers, parents, students, players, or politicians—heed the call to action implicit in this book. Dive in. Choose what to read, in what order... See how a cultural theorist writing in the '60s enhances your understanding of a first-person shooter released in 2004. Participate. Think. Understand.

This book is a roadmap to understanding (particularly in conjunction with *Rules of Play*); the authors are your native guides, pointing you to interesting sights along the way. Ultimately, though, the journey, as in a great game, is yours. So get going.

Warren Spector, a 20-year game industry veteran, has worked on several games in the *Ultima* series as well as *Underworld*, *System Shock* and others. As studio director at Ion Storm, he oversaw the creation of the critically acclaimed *Deus Ex* in 2000 and, more recently, *Deus Ex: Invisible War,* released in 2003, and *Thief: Deadly Shadows,* released in 2004. He has since left Ion Storm to pursue other interests.

Preface

Katie Salen and Eric Zimmerman

Our primary problem is that we have little theory on which to base our efforts. We don't really know what a game is, or why people play games, or what makes a game great... We need to establish our principles of aesthetics, a framework for criticism, and a model for development... We computer game designers must put our shoulders together so that our successors may stand on top of them.

—Chris Crawford

Radicals and Refugees

In 1982, game designer Chris Crawford threw down the gauntlet in one of the first books written on the design of digital games, *The Art of Computer Game Design.* The questions he asked then still ring true today. Do we know what games are, why people play them, or what makes a game great? Perhaps not, but we're getting closer. Twenty-three years later, we've picked up the gauntlet. For today, we stand on the shoulders of giants.

Giants of play theory like Johan Huizinga, Roger Caillois, Bernard DeKoven, and Brian Sutton-Smith. Gurus of game design such as Richard Garfield, Raph Koster, Marc LeBlanc, and Warren Robinett. Pioneering writers and philosophers like David Sudnow, William Poundstone, Bernard Suits, Stephen Sniderman.

Chris Crawford saw the future, took note of it, and stood waiting for others to join him. One by one, these writers, thinkers, players, and designers arrived, from expected and unexpected places. *Game Design: Theory and Practice; From Barbie to Mortal Kombat; Shoot Club.* They came: pioneers, radicals, and malcontents in their own fields, writing into a tradition that didn't yet exist, struggling to find the words for concepts that no one knew yet how to convey. They came, stood, and waited—often alone.

They wrote in zines, blogs, journals, and books, taking games and play, design and technology, players and culture as the subjects of their impassioned study. And while these essays were read, photocopied, downloaded, and passed hand to hand among an increasingly hungry community of readers, a sense of the collective whole remained elusive. Writers and readers shared joint status as videogame refugees, waiting to discover a place they could call home.

The road has been long and a little bit bumpy—like all new paths through an untamed wilderness. But today the refugees have joined rank, and stand shoulder to shoulder before you, bound together in the 33 texts that make up *The Game Design Reader.* This book is, above all else, a historical document of an emerging set of disciplines, an ensemble of unique responses generated by those who love games and all that is made possible through play.

The Reader is also a response to our own status as refugee game designers, teachers, players, and industry advocates. For years, we dreamed about a book that would collect the best writing on games into a single volume. Something to make our students rant and rave, something we could beg game publishers to read, a book to pass around at late-night game conference hotel rooms, a book to show to our skeptical non-gamer friends who doubted games were worthy of such loving attention.

This book *is* that book. We feel privileged to make available the work of fellow game designers struggling against the commercial constraints of the game industry and academics risking tenure to fuel their passion for games. We are inspired by provocative game journalists bucking tired commercial formats, and humbled by historical figures refining their fascination with play. *The Reader* is their book, their testament to what is possible when people get serious about games. This book is something we are truly proud of, because of who and what it contains, and for what it may mean to the future of games.

More than One Way to Play

Don't call us unambitious. *The Game Design Reader,* as well as its textbook predecessor, *Rules of Play: Game Design Fundamentals,* takes on a truly challenging set of questions. What are games and how do they function? How do they interact with culture at large? What critical approaches can game designers take to create meaningful experiences for players? Our audience includes students, game developers, game scholars, game critics, fans, and players.

This is not a book about how to make games, or how to study them from the point of view of one particular field. Instead, it is a collection of perspectives that can be put to use in many different ways. How you use this book is entirely dependent on why you are interested in games in the first place. More than a themed set of texts, *The Game Design Reader* is a snapshot of evolving thinking about games as a subject of study and design. It is a living history of what it means to play a game. Not surprisingly, the wide diversity of its writers mirrors that of its intended readers, and testifies to the vast number of ways that games can be studied.

What's the best way to understand a game? From a formal perspective, we could study probability and logic, systems theory and cybernetics. We could refine our sensibilities in art and design, and explore the aesthetics of sound and space. We could invite sociologists and psychologists, instructional technologists and educators to weigh in. We could include media theorists and semioticians, marketers and entrepreneurs—just to name a few. That's to say nothing of game design, game programming, and other fields that contribute to the actual creation of games. In fact, if you wanted to study everything that might relate in some direct or indirect way to games and play, you could easily spend many lifetimes reading.

There is, obviously, no single approach that covers all of these fields. Add the fact that computer and electronic games are relatively new, critical writings about them even newer, and the vast scope of the problem becomes clear. To say that putting together an anthology of writings like this one is an enormous undertaking is something of an understatement.

So what is one to do in the face of such a daunting task? We planned and improvised, pulling in pieces from every quarter. We deferred to history by drawing from an existing landscape of writing we felt to be essential reading. We polled friends and colleagues incessantly about the best game writing in a variety of fields. We researched and ransacked conference proceedings, journals, syllabi, blogs, and bibliographies (including our own). We looked for the obvious and hidden spaces where writing on games and play was taking place. And somehow, through this frenetic dance of discovery, the structure and content of this book emerged.

Writing Game Writing

Good writing—important writing—on games does exist. More writing than you might think. But a book only has so many pages. Our aim in gathering this collection of texts was not to fulfill the impossible quest of including exhaustive examples from every possible discipline connected to games. Instead, we sought out what we thought to be the most broadly useful types of game writing, and drilled down to find a range of perspectives in each.

Within games journalism, for example, we discovered examples of early and innovative game writing, like those contributed by William Poundstone and David Sudnow. We also included samples of "New Games Journalism," by game-native writers like Tom Chick and Ian Shanahan. Each of these authors pioneered a mode of writing about games we felt was important to include.

We also identified other strong sets of voices within player culture, academia, and game development. What will become immediately apparent in reading the essays included in the collection are the radical differences in approach taken by each. From tone to language to subject matter, the concerns of each are quite distinct. As a taste of the book to come, the following examples demonstrate the range of writing included.

Game journalist:

"Third-person allows you to fully appreciate the acrobatics of the sabre fighting animations. You can swing away in one of three 'styles,' fast, medium, and heavy, all of which allow you to wrestle mouse movement and direction key presses to produce jaw-dropping combinations of slashes, chops, and stabs that risks you forgetting any question of your actual opponent as you stare in disbelief and whisper 'Did I just do that?'."—always_black on Jedi Knights II

Card game designer:

"Sometimes seemingly innocuous cards would combine into something truly frightening. A good part of playtest effort was devoted to routing out the cards that contributed to so-called 'degenerate' decks—the narrow, powerful decks that are difficult to beat and often boring to play with or against."—Richard Garfield on Magic: The Gathering

Computer game developer:

"The goal of this group was to create a complete document that detailed all the levels and described major monster interactions, special effects, plot devices, and design standards. ...As daunting as that sounds, this is exactly what we did."—Ken Birdwell on Half-Life

Sociologist:

"Slippages of awareness indicate the fragility of the role-playing enterprise—it can easily be subverted. I emphasize, however, that although this subversion damages the nature of the role-playing, it does not destroy the game."—Gary Alan Fine on Empire of the Petal Throne

Player:

"I'll let you in on a secret: swords SUCK. Yes, it's true! Although the swords *LOOK* like they have better stats than the blunt weapons, don't be misled. Most creatures in this game take more damage from blunt weapons than slashing or piercing."—Mochan on Summoner

Selecting the Texts

In the face of so much good writing, how did we choose what to include? As our search began to unearth textual treasures, we established five primary criteria to guide the selection process.

Seminal

Each essay should be a "classic" text, representing the first of its kind (initiating a new approach, form of writing, method, or way of thinking) and having an impact on the analysis or practice of games. Each should be broadly acknowledged as a basic core text for anyone studying games.

Teachable

Every essay should raise enough issues to act as a springboard for an important discussion, a class assignment, or a design project. Each should stand on its own, without needing expert knowledge or surrounding chapters to make sense. *The Game Design Reader* is, among other things, an educational reader and we needed to imagine each text being used in a classroom seminar, industry workshop, or other instructional context.

Significant

In addition to being "classic" and teachable, texts should introduce key issues and approaches, summarize a set of methods, or question dominant attitudes and assumptions. Furthermore, every contribution should concentrate squarely on games. We were tempted by texts that looked at interactive narrative, complex systems, software development, or other parallel fields—but we included only those having games as their explicit focus.

Relevant

With so broad an audience, the book's essays should have relevance and value to a variety of readers. They should address both game designers and game scholars, and be of concern to readers on both sides of the "theory/practice" divide—or for those (like us) who are caught in the middle. Thus we avoided essays that were theoretically tied to a narrow academic field, as well as essays that were primarily concerned with solving practical game development problems.

Diverse

Lastly, each essay should be distinct from the others, staking out a unique territory of ideas. We sought diversity on many levels. Our search extended to a range of disciplines and authors, garnering a rich texture of writing styles.

While these five criteria guided us, we did leave ourselves some wiggle room. For example, a text might be somewhat obscure (and therefore not "seminal"), but if it succeeded in strongly fulfilling most or all of the other criteria, we included it. Some criteria we managed to meet nearly all of the time: for example, we think all of the texts are highly teachable.

But others were not so well met. Most obviously, we had trouble putting together a collection of truly diverse authors. The writers we ended up including are mostly American, and overwhelmingly male. This was in part because of translation issues for non-English writing, but also because the game industry, and even game-related academia, is not yet represented by a truly diverse set of voices. There are many more women writing on games today then there were fifty—or even five—years ago, and it is our belief that their work will soon make its way into future editions of anthologies such as this one.

It should also be noted that we were not always able to get permission to publish the works we had hoped to include. This is of course a challenge and frustration in any anthology of this scale.

In the end, while these selection criteria helped us make some hard decisions about what to include and what to leave out, the process was still highly subjective. When in doubt, we returned to our own goal of making a collection that was useful to a wide audience interested in games, a collection that we ourselves would enjoy reading, and one that would do its best to mark this unique moment in the history of writing on games.

One Book, Many Topics

The process of selecting essays and putting them together led to the book you are now holding in your hands. But this process was merely preliminary to something more important: determining how the collection would be used by you, our readers. How would you discover which texts are most relevant to your interests? Would it be easy to find themes running through the essays or to see connections between ideas? These questions are important to anyone developing game design curriculums, working through research agendas in game studies programs, or simply looking more deeply into games. In any case, it was our goal to create a book that could inspire new bodies of knowledge by sharing existing ones.

While we could simply suggest that you begin at the beginning and work your way through to the end, given our diverse audience, this may not be the best approach. Luckily, we do have an answer to the challenge of using this book, something to help game theorists, game writers, game designers, design educators, game critics, and fans find what they need.

As a kind of "strategy guide" to reading this book, we have created a series of broad subject areas—Topics—that can be used as skeleton keys to unlock the volume at hand. Some Topics represent an idea fundamental to the study of games, such as *Game Design Models* or *The Player Experience.* Others cover emerging areas of research, such as *Game Communities* or *Game Spaces.* There are fourteen Topics in all:

The Player Experience	Speaking of Games
The Rules of a Game	Game Design Models
Gaming the Game	Game Economies
The Game Design Process	Game Spaces
Player and Character	Cultural Representation
Games and Narrative	What Is a Game?
Game Communities	What Is Play?

Each Topic is linked to several of the texts that make up the book. Most of the texts, in turn, appear in more than one Topic. For example, Richard Garfield's detailed case study "The Design Evolution of Magic: The Gathering" appears in the Topics *The Game Design Process* and *Game Economies.* Reading Garfield's essay within two distinct Topics brings out different aspects of his analysis, highlighting specific facets of his core concerns.

Each of the fourteen Topics is summarized in a brief Topic Essay that identifies a set of key ideas and questions, and links that Topic's essays together. After each Topic Essay, suggestions for additional resources, including chapters from our previous book, *Rules of Play,* are listed. The Topic Essays can be found in the section following this introduction.

We developed the Topics as a way to create connective tissue between contributions, highlight common themes, and give readers a place to begin. There are, of course, many ways to organize the texts in this collection. The linear organization of the book, for example, was designed with a certain internal logic. Other approaches will emerge as you bring in your own interests. Feel free to mix and match Topics and essays to structure a range of game-related courses, target specific areas of learning for students and professionals, or otherwise reveal hidden connections between contributions. Ultimately it is up to each reader to discover the best way of using *The Game Design Reader,* and it is our hope that the Topics will act as jumping off points for more intricate and sophisticated approaches to come.

The Book Awaits

Following the Topic Essays comes the true soul of the book: its anthology of 33 texts. Each begins with a short author biography and a statement of context, written in most cases by the authors themselves, addressing the why, when, and how the essay was written.

Between groups of essays are a number of "interstitials"—visual essays, game documentation, or other cultural ephemera that work between and around the main essays. These interstitials [designed by Katie] are meant to provide a visual break, and often act in counterpoint to the group of essays that follow.

The Game Design Reader has been a long time in the making. It is a first-of-a-kind anthology, a testament to the brilliance of our young field, a book with the feeling of a truly great party, where all of the guests, despite themselves, wind up mixing with everyone else like old friends.

We'd love for you to come and mix it up, too. It is our hope that *The Reader* works not just as a historical document, but also as a future catalyst for new thinking, new writing, and better yet, lots and lots of new games. We think the view from the shoulders of giants is glorious indeed. It is time for the refugees to come in from out of the storm: we have found a home at last.

A Note on Consistency

This volume includes texts from a range of sources, each with its own approach to referencing games (capitalized vs. uncapitalized, italic vs. nonitalic), the spelling of popular terms (gameplay vs. game play; videogame vs. video game, etc.), and bibliographic format. In remaining true to the voices of the authors, we chose to preserve the texts as they originally appeared.

In addition, essays that exist as book chapters sometimes reference the books from which they were taken. If the chapter piques your interest, we heartily recommend you read the entire book!

Web Resources

Beyond the texts collected between these covers, we recommend the following websites as starting resources for learning more about game design, game scholarship, the game industry, and game culture.

Industry

www.igda.org

www.gamasutra.com

www.theesa.com

Academic

www.digra.org

www.seriousgames.org

www.educationarcade.com

www.gamestudies.org

Journalism

www.gamegirladvance.com

www.extra-life.org.uk/wiki

http://blogs.guardian.co.uk/games

Blogs

www.designersnotebook.com

www.ludology.org

http://terranova.blogs.com

www.costik.com/blog

www.grandtextauto.org

www.deepfun.com

www.quartertofour.com

www.gamedevblog.com

www.game-research.org

www.GameMatters.com

www.thegameblog.com

www.playcube.org

Acknowledgments

Computer games don't affect kids; I mean if Pac-Man affected us as kids, we'd all be running around in darkened rooms, munching magic pills and listening to repetitive electronic music.
—Kristian Wilson, Nintendo Inc., 1989

Darkened rooms lit by the solitary glow of a monitor and repetitive electronic music (tinged with a bit of punk rock) were just a few of the things that made work on this book possible. While there were no magic pills, we did rely on the support and friendship of the many authors included within this volume, the patience and love of our friends and families, the mentorship of our teachers, students, and collaborators, and the play of the games that continue to inspire us.

We are indebted to Doug Sery and Valerie Geary at MIT Press for their guidance and assistance in editing and securing permissions, to Staffan Björk and Jussi Holopainen, Brenda Laurel, Marc LeBlanc, and Warren Spector, who contributed new texts to this volume, to Espen Aarseth, Marc "the Jinx" Anderson, Eric "el penguin" Aujero, Jonathan Blow, Alex Galloway, Justin Hall, Chris Hecker, Robin Hunicke, Jesper Juul, Miodrag Mitrasinovic, Nancy Nowacek, Jane Pinkard, Harvey Smith, and Randy Smith, for their recommendations, encouragement, and insights. Most of all, we want to thank all of the authors and publishers who graciously granted permission for the publication of their work in this collection.

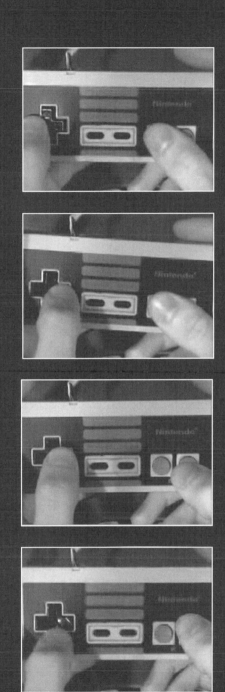

```
← OOOOOOOOOOOOOOOOOOOOOOOOOOOOOOOOOOOOOOOOOOOOOOOOOOOOOOOOOOOOOOOOOOOOOOOOOOOO
→ -------------------------------------------------------------------
^ -------------------------------------------------------------------
v -------------------------------------------------------------------
B -----------------------------OOOOOOOOOOOOOOOOOOOOOOOOOOOOOOOOOOOOOOOOO
A -------------------------------------------------------------------


← OOOOOOOOOOOOOOOOOOOOOOOOOOOOOOOO----------------------------------------
→ ----------------------------------------OOOOOOOOOOOOOOOOOOOOOOOOOOOO
^ -------------------------------------------------------------------
v -------------------------------------------------------------------
B OOOOOOOOOOOOOOOOOOOOOOOOOOOOOOOOOOOOOOOOOOOOOOOOOOOOOOOOOOOOOOOOOOOOOOOOOOOO
A -------------------------------------------------------------------



← -------------------------------------------------------------------
→ OOOOOOOOOOOOOOOOOOOOOOOOOOOOO-OOOOOO-OOOOOOOOOOOO-OOOOOO-OOOOOOOOOOOO-OOOOO
^ -------------------------------------------------------------------
v -------------------------------------------------------------------
B OOOOOOOOOOOOOOOOOOOOOOOOOOOOO-OOOOOO-OOOOOOOOOOOO-OOOOOO-OOOOOOOOOOOO-OOOOO
A -----------------------OOOOOO-OOOOOOOOOOOO-OOOOOO-O-OOOOOOOOOOO-OOOOO



← -------------------------------------------------------------------
→ OOOOOOOOOOOOOOOOOOOOOOOOOOOOOOOOOOOOOOOOOOOOOOOOOOOOOOOOOOOOOOOOOOOOOOOOOOOO
^ -------------------------------------------------------------------
v -------------------------------------------------------------------
B OOOOOOOOOOOOOOOOOOOOOOOOOOOOOOOOOOOOOOOOOOOOOOOOOOOOOOOOOOOOOOOOOOOOOOOOOOOOOO
A O-----------------------------------------------------------------



← -------------------------------------------------------------------
→ OOOOOOOOOOOOOOOOOOOOOOOOOOOOOOOOOOOOOOOOOO------------------------------
^ -------------------------------------------------------------------
v -------------------------------------------------------------------
B OOOOOOOOOOOOOOOOOOOOOOOOOOOOOOOOOOOOOOOOOOOOOOOOOOOOOOOOOOOOOOOOOOOOOOOOOOOOOO
A -------------------------------------------------------------------
```

Topic Essays

Katie Salen and Eric Zimmerman

3   The Player Experience

What kinds of play experiences do games provide?

9   The Rules of a Game

What are rules and how do they relate to play?

15   Gaming the Game

How and why do players bend, break, and remake rules?

21   The Game Design Process

How do designers approach the process of making games?

27   Player and Character

What is the complex relationship between game player and game character?

33   Games and Narrative

What are the relationships between story, game, and narrative play?

39   Game Communities

What are the forms and meanings of social interaction in a game?

45   Speaking of Games

What ideologies inform the discourse of games?

53   Game Design Models

What are formal ways of understanding how games work?

59   Game Economies

How do game experiences emerge through systems of exchange?

65   Game Spaces

What does space contribute to the experience of play?

71   Cultural Representation

What aspects of culture do games model and represent?

77   What is a Game?

How can we define what makes a game a game?

83   What is Play?

What are the forms and meanings of play?

The Player Experience

What kinds of play experiences do games provide?

The Definition of Play; The Classification of Games 122
Roger Caillois

Shoot Club: The DOOM 3 Review 156
Tom Chick

"Complete Freedom of Movement": 330
Video Games as Gendered Play Spaces
Henry Jenkins

Tools for Creating Dramatic Game Dynamics 438
Marc LeBlanc

Game Analysis: Centipede 460
Richard Rouse III

Eyeball; Cathexis 558
David Sudnow

Hearts, Clubs, Diamonds, Spades: 754
Players Who Suit MUDs
Richard Bartle

GAMEING is an enchanting witchery, gotten betwixt Idleness and Avarice: An itching Disease, that makes some scratch the Head, whilst others, as if they were bitten by a Tarantula, are laughing themselves to death....—Charles Cotton

Games have long been hardwired to the pleasure center of a gamer's brain, turning play into an act of nearly religious devotion. Who among us has not been snared in the spell of a Tetris, Zelda, or Snood? Yet, when it comes to describing just how games make us feel, even magical words fall short. How does one describe the joy of mastering a six-finger controller scheme in less than an hour, or the thrill of spinning out of control down a virtual race track, brakes shot and the engine running wide open? What words characterize the social and strategic flow of *Texas Hold'em* or the feeling of envy and pride when your Starcraft clanmate bumps you down on the leader boards? How does one capture such itchy witchery?

Understanding the variety and intensities of player experiences produced by games is of great import to both game designers and those studying player behavior. What aspects of a game produce particular forms of experience? How do game mechanics influence player behavior? What constitutes an aesthetic of player pleasure? Of conflict? Or drama? The essays in this Topic begin to address these questions, each offering a unique rumination on what we feel when we play.

David Sudnow's spellbinding descriptions in *Eyeball* and *Cathexis* launch us directly into the eye of the pleasure storm. Writing from the perspective of his own addiction to the game Breakout, Sudnow focuses on the physiological and psychological pleasures of play.

> Forget about placement, a score, elegance as an end in its own right. Forget about a model of good play to motivate practice. Here's all the motivation you'd ever want: get that action again, those last few bricks left and that eerie lobbing interim as the ball floats about so you never know when it'll hit and you don't dare try placing a shot because you're more than happy just to hold on with your eyes glued to the ball.

Sudnow is lost in the pattern of play, held hostage by three bricks of light snuggled tightly against the uppermost edge of a TV screen. Each move takes place within the context of an unfolding drama fueled by an uncertain outcome.

Richard Rouse III picks up on the pleasure found in such situations in his analysis of the classic arcade game Centipede. While Sudnow writes in the spirit of a case study—a journalist visiting the world of games—game designer Rouse is truly a native practitioner. Particularly incisive is his analysis of how the formal mechanics of Centipede create waves of escalating tension.

> Many waves into the game, the increased mushroom density makes shooting poisoned mushrooms all but impossible, and with these poisoned mushrooms in place, the player is bombarded by centipedes hurtling toward him in every single wave. Thus, a player is almost relieved when his shooter is destroyed and all those poisoned mushrooms are removed from the top of the screen. This causes the player's game to be much more relaxed, at least for the time being.

These moments of rhythmic flow—the escalating tension of *Centipede,* or the hypnotic pulse of *Breakout*—contribute to a feeling of drama and tension within a game, and are never accidental. They arise as the result of careful decisions made by the game's designer. Attention to drama is precisely the subject of Marc LeBlanc's essay, "Tools for Creating Dramatic Game Dynamics." LeBlanc is a game designer who has long been concerned with developing a conceptual toolkit to help designers build better, more engaging games. An advocate of games imbued with a sense of drama, LeBlanc outlines how the *dynamics* of a game—its patterns of play—result in the game's *aesthetics*—its experience of fun:

> A game's aesthetics are its "emotional content," the desirable emotional responses we have when we play—all the kinds of "fun" that result from playing the game.... A game's aesthetics emerge from its dynamics; how the game behaves determines how it makes the player feel.

LeBlanc's essay links particular design choices on the level of game rules and mechanics with the experiences those dynamics create for the player. The bottom line is that designers have it within their control to determine the dramatic quality of the game experiences they produce. Knowing how to trigger specific kinds of "fun"—from social camaraderie to physical challenges to improvisational narrative play—is one of the great challenges game designers face.

Drama, uncertainty, and the visceral engagement of play are just some of the many experiences generated by games. What other kinds exist? "Shoot Club: The DOOM 3 Review," is a gem of reporting from the player trenches, in which writer Tom Chick takes aim at the purported pleasures offered by the overhyped and underwhelming PC game DOOM 3. The essay broadens traditional concepts of what constitutes the player experience, by expanding it to include all of the experiences that take place around the game itself. For players, this might mean obsessively scouring John Carmack's .plan, waiting in line for hours to buy the game on the day of its launch, and seeking clues as to yet unreleased details and features. For Trevor, the hapless subject of Chick's essay, this meant rifling through a world exclusive first interview in a coveted copy of *PC Gamer*:

> He thumbed through the six pages repeatedly, holding the screenshots close to his face and peering at them as if looking for clues. "I think there are some new kinds of monsters," he noted.

New monsters or not, the game ultimately failed to live up to expectations. But even if the game itself was disappointing, "Shoot Club" points out that player experience can begin far in advance of a game's release, and be deeply satisfying on its own. Recognizing the numerous moments of player engagement, whether it is reading about, purchasing, or exchanging information about a game, can extend the game experience. These are spaces, too, that can be made meaningful for players.

No exploration of player experience would be complete without a nod to Roger Caillois, one of the first scholars to identify the forms of experience produced through play. "The Definition of Play: The Classification of Games" contains Caillois's typology of play forms. He identifies four elemental play rubrics—*agôn, alea, mimicry,* and *illinx*—each based on a different kind of player pleasure. The pleasure of agônistic (competitive) play is the feeling of superiority, as when a boxer vanquishes his opponent in record time. In alea (chance-based) play such as dice games, pleasure is discovered in a player's surrender to destiny and fate. Within mimicry (make-believe) play, there is pleasure in pretending to be another, while the pleasure of illinx (vertigo) is located in the physical sensation of spinning and whirling.

Caillois doesn't argue that one rubric presents more pleasurable play than any other, and game designers should take this lesson to heart. More than the scientific accuracy of his four categories, Caillois's contribution is found in his celebration of the diversity of forms that play experience can take. Richard Bartle takes on a parallel project in his now-classic essay "Hearts, Clubs, Diamonds, Spades: Players Who Suit MUDs." As a pioneering game designer, Bartle is interested in creating well-balanced player communities. His insight is that what people enjoy doing in a MUD—the kinds of pleasure they seek—is embodied in the way they play. Bartle designates four main player types:

> **Achievers** are proud of their formal status in the game's built-in level hierarchy, and how short a time they took to reach it;

> **Explorers** are proud of their knowledge of the game's finer points, especially if new players treat them as founts of all knowledge;

> **Socializers** are proud of their friendships, their contacts and their influence;

> **Killers** are proud of their reputation and of their oft-practiced fighting skills.

As Bartle makes clear, *how* players interact with a game world, be it with spaces, objects, rules, or other players, offers insight into the *kinds* of pleasures they seek. Understanding more about possible modes of interaction, styles of play, and their associated rewards can lead to innovative game forms that support multiple desires and new ways of playing. Bartle's model is designed to address MUDs, but there is a wealth of work to be done in examining and classifying play styles in other kinds of games.

The final essay in this Topic takes on the crucial issues of genre and gender. While Bartle made no distinction between male and female players in his study, recent research has asked whether boys and girls play differently and therefore desire different kinds of games. Henry Jenkins contributes to this discussion in his essay "'Complete Freedom of Movement': Video Games as Gendered Play Spaces" by focusing on the kinds of play traditionally associated with "boy culture" and "girl culture," as well as those pleasures enjoyed by both, including freedom of movement, intensity of experience, escape from adult regulation, and spaces on which to map fantasies of empowerment and escape. Jenkins is a proponent of videogames as places that offer children rich contexts in which to exert developmental and social mastery. He argues that mastery for boys and girls often takes very different forms, and is reflective of what a child likes to do when given the simple freedom to play. Ultimately, Jenkins makes a point that is echoed in many of the readings in this Topic: game designers craft particular kinds of experiences for particular kinds of players, experiences that emerge from the design choices they make.

Player experience can take many forms, be framed in many guises, and is always expressed in a diversity of social and cultural contexts. In studying player experience, we are exploring truly fundamental questions about games, play, and design. And in acknowledging the complexity of these questions, we can appreciate the many, many games still left to be created, played and ultimately, understood.

Further Reading on this Topic

Rules of Play: Game Design Fundamentals, Katie Salen and Eric Zimmerman.
Cambridge: MIT Press, 2004.

> *Recommended:*
> Chapter 23: Games as the Play of Experience
> Chapter 24: Games as the Play of Pleasure

"The Conditions of Flow," Mihaly Csikszentmihalyi.
Flow: The Psychology of Optimal Experience.
New York: HarperCollins Publishers, 1991.

Creating Emotion in Games: The Craft and Art of Emotioneering, David Freeman.
Berkeley: New Riders Publishing, 2003.

A Theory of Fun, Raph Koster.
Scottsdale: Paraglyph Press, 2005.

"Videogames and Computer Holding Power," Sherry Turkle.
The Second Self: Computers and the Human Spirit.
New York: Simon & Schuster, 1984, p.64–92.

The Rules of a Game

What are rules and how do they relate to play?

Construction of a Definition 172
Bernard Suits

I Have No Words & I Must Design 192
Greg Costikyan

Games and Design Patterns 410
Staffan Björk and Jussi Holopainen

Unwritten Rules 476
Stephen Sniderman

Declaring the Rights of Players 788
Raph Koster

Knowing the rules of the game is not nearly as simple as committing the relevant passages to memory, because memorization does not bring understanding. It is not only important to know what is written in the rules but also to perceive how the parts of the rules fit together and work in harmony with each other. This latter task is certainly achievable, but it is not easy.—Gary Gygax

Rules are a fundamental part of any game. If you purchase a board game, you are purchasing, in essence, a set of rules. It's true that you are also purchasing materials that let you play the game—a board, a pair of dice, a set of tokens—all of which have aesthetic, interactive, and narrative trappings. But to the extent that they embody the game rules and enable them to be followed, the materials are in some ways mere extensions of the rules. A game is, in this sense, nothing more and nothing less than a set of rules. In this Topic, five essays examine the nature of game rules, untangling their paradoxes and dilemmas, strategizing ways to create better rule sets, and linking rules to larger questions regarding games, play, and design.

For philosopher Bernard Suits, rules are the fundamental element of games that make play possible. As Suits outlines in his book *Grasshopper: Games, Life and Utopia,* to play a game is to follow the rules because the rules demarcate what players can and can't do to achieve the goal of the game. Rules, in this sense, define the activities players adopt in order to play, and the guidelines they obey to make the game move forward.

Suits argues that rules provide both ends and means. Rules specify the aim of the game, such as to be the first to cross the finish line. They also identify the accepted ways that the goal can be accomplished. To cross the finish line, you must line up with the other runners, begin running at the starting signal, and stay on the course for the duration of the race. The unique and frustrating pleasure of games, according to Suits, arises from the tension between the goal of the game and the "inefficient" ways that players are permitted to achieve these ends. Means are inefficient because there are often better ways of reaching the goal: a runner could make a short cut across the race course, but that—of course—would be against the rules.

Greg Costikyan's approach to rules in his essay "I Have No Words & I Must Design," is an applied version of Suits's means and ends. As a game designer, Costikyan is less concerned with defining what rules are and more concerned with explaining how they shape player experience. While rules aren't the overt subject of his essay, Costikyan implicitly explores rules by listing aspects of games and game design strategies.

> At every point, he [the player] considers the game state. That might be what he sees on the screen. Or it might be what the gamemaster has just told him. Or it might be the arrangement of the pieces on the board. Then, he considers his opposition, the forces he must struggle against. He tries to decide on the best course of action. And he makes a decision. What's key here? Goals. Opposition. Resource management. Information.

Throughout his essay, Costikyan stresses how game designers must carefully structure a game through the rules they create. For example, he makes the point that play can become more meaningful when the rules give a player multiple resource trade-offs within a given decision:

> If the game has more than one "resource," decisions suddenly become more complex. If I do this, I get money and experience, but will Lisa still love me? If I steal the food, I get to eat, but I might get caught and have my hand cut off.... These are not just complex decisions; these are interesting ones. Interesting decisions make for interesting games.

In linking rules with "interesting decisions," Costikyan emphasizes how rules cannot be considered apart from the particular moments of play they create. As his examples demonstrate, interesting decisions emerge from complex relations among rules, situations in which players are caught in cross-currents of decision-making that result from careful rule design.

Digging even deeper into the form and function of games, Staffan Björk and Jussi Holopainen undertake a detailed explication of rules in "Games and Design Patterns."

> Rules dictate the flow of the game and have been a central aspect of most definitions of games. Although rules have a distinct place in the framework, they are also embedded in every other component: there are rules that govern what the game elements are, how they behave, what actions players can perform, and so on.

In their careful cataloging of a game's essential elements, Björk and Holopainen spin out a dense web of structural relations. They describe how rules relate to other formal game elements, such as goals and subgoals, how rules enable actions by the players and result in game events, and how a game interface allows interaction between players and the form of a game. All of these structures, born out of designed rules, create moments of play for players. Rules are the "material" with which a game designer crafts a game. Björk and Holopainen's detailed taxonomy makes plain just how intricate is the task of constructing or analyzing a set of game rules.

But is every rule under the direct control of the game designer? In the essay "Unwritten Rules," we find a very different point of view. For Stephen Sniderman, the "official" rules of a game constitute only a fraction of the story. In any game, there are a host of "unwritten rules"—the normally unspoken behaviors that players adopt in order to play, such as spending a reasonable amount of time to take a turn in Tic-Tac-Toe. These unwritten rules are never explicitly stated, but players seem to agree on them nevertheless.

Sniderman lists eight things we must know and do to play the simplest game. What Bernard Suits calls the "constitutive rules"—the logical rules of play—is only one item on the list, which also includes everything from the etiquette and ethos of a game to the intuitive cultural notion about what it means to "play." For Sniderman, a game is fundamentally a social contract. He is less interested in game rules in and of themselves, instead prying open the relationships between rules and the real-life contexts that surround them.

Raph Koster, in "Declaring the Rights of Players," takes the idea of rules as a social contract to its logical extreme. Koster is a designer of massively multiplayer games, and his essay offers a set of "rules" for the social behavior of game players and the staff that administrate their virtual worlds. For example, one of the rights he asserts is that

> No avatar shall be accused, muzzled, toaded, jailed, banned, or otherwise punished except in the cases and according to the forms prescribed by the code of conduct.

Ironically mimicking an eighteenth-century political document, Koster's Declaration forcefully asserts a set of "metarules"—rules of game-playing behavior to be observed, regardless of the particular virtual world at hand. In this sense, the essay codifies Sniderman's unwritten rules, translating implicit social behavior into explicitly stated guidelines. In his essay, Koster not only lists his rules, but also includes questions and comments submitted by readers in response to his original Declaration. By sharing the dialogue and debate generated by his document, Koster's work points to the fact that these kinds of social contracts are likely to be under constant negotiation and redesign.

Can we ever grasp all the rules of a game? It depends on your point of view. It can be said that rules are limited and knowable, the underlying mathematical structures that define a game. But perhaps game rules only come into being when they ramify into play, as the structures experienced by players as they interact with a game. Or maybe, the secret to understanding rules lies in unwritten regulations, the social codes that link the artificial worlds of games to the cultural contexts they inhabit.

Rules are, of course, all of these things. Despite the authority that game rules sometimes exude, remember that rules are never as stable as they may seem. Rules are made not only to be followed, but also to be broken, uncovered, negotiated, and refashioned into entirely new kinds of play.

Further Reading on this Topic

Rules of Play: Game Design Fundamentals, Katie Salen and Eric Zimmerman.
Cambridge: MIT Press, 2004.

> *Recommended:*
> Chapter 11: Defining Rules
> Chapter 12: Rules on 3 Levels
> Chapter 13: The Rules of Digital Games

Game Design Workshop: Designing, Prototyping, and Playtesting Games,
Tracy Fullerton, Steven Hoffman, and Christopher Swain.
Recommended, chapter 3: Working with Formal Elements.
San Francisco: CMP Books, 2004.

The Moral Judgment of the Child, Jean Piaget.
Recommended, "The Rules of the Game," p.13–29
New York: Free Press, 1997.

New Rules for Classic Games, R. Wayne Schmittberger.
New York: Random House, 1994.

RE:PLAY: Game Design + Game Culture, Amy Scholder and Eric Zimmerman, eds.
Recommended, Module 1: Games as Structure
New York: Walter Lang, 2004.

Gaming the Game

How and why do players bend, break, and remake rules?

The Evil Summoner FAQ v1.0: 268
How to Be a Cheap Ass
Mochan

Unwritten Rules 476
Stephen Sniderman

Beyond the Rules of the Game: 504
Why Are Rooie Rules Nice?
Linda Hughes

Changing the Game 518
Bernard DeKoven

The Lessons of Lucasfilm's Habitat 728
F. Randall Farmer and Chip Morningstar

If you can't play it, change it. If it helps, cheat.—Bernard DeKoven

Counterstrike mods; "home rules" for playing Monopoly; artists hacking The Sims: it's clear that playing *by* the rules and playing *with* the rules of a game go hand in hand. As anyone who has spent any time at all around games will be quick to tell you, it is impossible to predict just what a player will do once play begins. Kenneth Goldstein notes that the "official" rules of a game are merely the rules by which people *should* play, rather than the ones by which they *do* play. The "real rules" of a game, the ones actually used by players, are often something else entirely. The tension between these two kinds of rules, *ideal* and *real* rules, is at the center of this Topic: a series of essays exploring how players bend, break, and change game rules through play.

Players break rules: this is a simple fact. But instead of viewing this behavior as negative, destructive cheating, we see it as one of the most fascinating and creative aspects of play. What are the creative impulses behind rule-reinvention? What are the social codes that drive players to cheat? What is put at play when player-created rules trump the "official" ones? This is an area of inquiry drawn along both formal and social lines, encompassing notions of community, laws governing behavior in virtual worlds, and hacks and mods and cheats. Understanding the impulse for "gaming the game" can help designers harness and redirect this transgressive energy. Sometimes this means offering cheat codes or tools players can use to modify the game system; at others, designing flexible rule-sets that accommodate alteration, or making "house rules" an official feature of a game. From a design perspective, gaming the game cuts both ways.

In his essay "Unwritten Rules," Stephen Sniderman makes a distinction between explicit rules (what we generally understand to be the rules of a game) and implicit rules, the unrecorded rules that affect a player's behavior without the player being aware of them. Implicit rules include formal structures such as the amount of time players should take between turns, or social structures like an unspoken agreement to play more gently when little kids are present. Sniderman goes into detail about his own group of tennis players:

...the "casual" game of tennis that my buddies and I play is really based on an enormously complex set of "rules"—assumptions, traditions, and conventions—that govern our behavior on the court (whether we are consciously aware of it or not). My contention is that no one could ever "fully" describe those rules or those governing the players of any other game.

Obviously it is impossible to state every implicit and explicit rule of a game. But surprisingly, this doesn't destroy play—in fact, as Sniderman points out, "almost all games are taken very 'seriously' by almost all players almost all of the time."

If the play of a game stems not from a fixed set of logical rules, but instead from a constantly shifting, unspoken set of assumptions, how is it that we manage to play a game at all? Playing a game relies on a shared understanding between participants, an understanding that is always ripe for negotiation. Rules, as a result, are under the control of players. A game is a kind of social contract between them, maintained and modified through their ongoing interaction.

Gaming as a social contract between players is also at the heart of Linda Hughes's study of playground Foursquare. "Beyond the Rules of the Game: Why Are Rooie Rules Nice?" offers an enlightening and often comical glimpse into the difference between game rules and the rules of gaming. In her study, Hughes discovered that children modified rule sets as a way of maintaining existing social relationships on the playground. The rule sets invented by the children rarely stipulated specific game actions. Instead, the rules provided general frameworks for social interaction. As Hughes notes about a set of rule variants named after a player called "Rooie":

> Despite the fact that play regularly proceeds after a call of "Rooie Rules," no player, including Rooie and the "king" who calls them, can supply a complete list of rules encompassed by this call.... What allows the game to proceed with such apparent ambiguity concerning the precise rules of the game is the tacit understanding that Rooie Rules are "nice" and "nice" is perhaps the paramount concern among these players. It is far more important to understand "nice" play than to understand the rules.

Rooie Rules are an instance of Sniderman's implicit rules. These rules lack explicit representation yet offer an interpretive framework for player interaction that binds together game rules and player actions. The "real" rules of Foursquare (as opposed to the "ideal" rules) don't just hold the game together—they maintain the social status quo.

The playground players that Hughes studied were wonderfully inventive with their game. In her essay, she lists dozens of rule variations on Foursquare created by the children through their multileveled play. These players make up an instance of what Bernard DeKoven, in his essay "Changing the Game" calls a "play community." In his essay, DeKoven brings together ideas of rule change and social interaction. To "play well" is to play well together, to bend, break, or invent new rules that change the game in ways that strengthen the play community.

> ...we cannot even begin to explore ways of changing the game until we are certain that we share the intention to play well together... this is something not embodied in the rules but is found and maintained through the conventions of the play community.

Like Sniderman and Hughes, DeKoven sees a game as a social contract between players. "Playing well" is the result of an ongoing process of negotiation and renegotiation of the rules. Play changes as we do.

In moving from the playground to the world of digital games, we discover whole new ways of gaming the game. Mochan's "The Evil Summoner FAQ v1.0: How to be a Cheap Ass" takes the RPG game Summoner, released in 2001, as its victim. This cheeky FAQ uses the standard format of a game guide to share exploits, cheats, and degenerate strategies of play—all methods of playing a game in unintended ways.

> If you pause the game, you will notice certain commands, like Rosalind's Assess, can be used indefinitely even with time stopped! It's stupid, but that's what happens when you rip-off the Diablo system and give it a pause feature, without knowing what you're doing (shame on you Volition [the company that developed Summoner]).

Players can come to know a game even better than its designers, which is one reason why they can exploit game features in such creative and detailed ways. By sharing hints, tips, and other resources online, players game the game. In doing so, more than just cheat codes are revealed. The values, attitudes, and motivations of the players themselves also come to light. We learn what players want to be able to do and are informed about the way they were able to do so by changing the rules.

17

Gaming the game is not just a quaint player phenomenon, but constitutes the very heart and soul of play. Through their collective activity of gaming the game, Summoner fans and Foursquare cliques create their own player communities—socially-rich subcultural groups that express themselves through the ways they play with their chosen games.

Sometimes players choose to transgress rules just because the rules are there. Understanding and predicting player behavior can often feel like a lost cause, especially in massively multiplayer online systems where players spend large chunks of time playing in (and with) the world. In the case of the Habitat project, wonderfully chronicled in Randall Farmer and Chip Morningstar's essay "The Lessons of Lucasfilm's *Habitat*," players never behaved in the way their designers expected:

> It was clear we were not in control. The more people we involved in something, the less in control we were. We could influence things, we could set up interesting situations, we could provide opportunities for things to happen, but we could not dictate the outcome. Social engineering is, at best, an inexact science (or, as some wag once said, "in the most carefully constructed experiment under the most carefully controlled conditions, the organism will do whatever it damn well pleases").

Rather than take this seemingly inherent desire to game the system as an obstacle, the designers of Habitat allowed this behavior to drive the ongoing design of the world. The example of Habitat points to a new paradigm for game design, one in which gaming the game is part of the process of game creation, in which players are encouraged to play well together by deconstructing and reconstructing the very games that they play. It is a remarkable shift in thinking to see rule-breaking as just another form of iterative design. Who better to tweak and tune a system than those for whom the game was made?

Further Reading on this Topic

Rules of Play: Game Design Fundamentals, Katie Salen and Eric Zimmerman.
Cambridge: MIT Press, 2004.

> *Recommended:*
> Chapter 21: Breaking the Rules
> Chapter 28: Social Play
> Chapter 31: Games as Open Culture
> Chapter 32: Games as Cultural Resistance

"Strategies in Counting Out," Kenneth Goldstein.
The Study of Games, ed. Elliott Avedon and Brian Sutton-Smith.
New York: John Wiley & Sons Inc., 1971, p. 172–77.

"Gaming the System: Multi-player Worlds Online," J. C. Herz.
Game On: The History and Culture of Video Games, ed. Lucien King.
London: Laurence Ling Publishing Ltd., 2002.

"Game Patch: the Son of Scratch?" Eric Huhtamo.
Cracking the Maze, curator Anne-Marie Schleiner, July 16, 1999.
www.switch.sjsu.edu/CrackingtheMaze.

"Telefragging Monster Movies," Katie Salen.
Game On: The History and Culture of Video Games, ed. Lucien King.
London: Laurence Ling Publishing Ltd., 2002.

The Game Design Process

How do designers approach the process of making games?

The Cabal: 122
Valve's Design Process for Creating Half-Life
Ken Birdwell

Changing the Game 314
Bernard DeKoven

The Design Evolution of Magic: The Gathering 578
Richard Garfield

Eastern Front (1941) 602
Chris Crawford

The Lessons of Lucasfilm's Habitat 642
F. Randall Farmer and Chip Morningstar

Much good design evolves: the design is tested, problem areas are discovered and modified, and then it is continually retested and re-modified...—Donald Norman

Many people play games. But how many know anything about how games actually *get made?* By exploring the game design process, we can better know how game designers work, how play emerges out of designed structures, the complex relationships between player and designer, and the culture of game development itself.

While every game designer or design team has a unique process, all five essays in this Topic stress the importance of *iterative design,* a methodology based in playtesting. The game is prototyped during its development, and then played by the designers, as well as by outside testers. Design decisions are based on the results of the playtests, and a new prototype is created, which is playtested again. As board game designer Renier Knizia has written, "The fun and excitement of playing cannot be calculated in an abstract fashion: it must be experienced." A game must be played as it is created.

Iterative design and testing is more than just informal play—it is a rigorous design process. Knizia writes about the design process of The Lord of the Rings Boardgame, in the following excerpt from a case study he wrote about the game for our book *Rules of Play:*

> I prepare each of my playtest sessions in great detail—I plan the exact issues I want to monitor and test. During play, I record relevant data about the game flow. Afterwards, I analyze the results and then make necessary or exploratory changes. This becomes the preparation for the next playtest session, during which I can find out how the changes will affect the game. The revolving process usually continues for many months, sometimes years. With experienced playtesters, we spend much time after each test discussing how it went—what worked and what didn't. Often we make changes on the spot and play again.

Most of the essays included in this Topic are game design case studies, in which designers write about and reflect on their own process. Case studies offer critical insights into the challenges, solutions, and strategies that led to the design of a successful—or unsuccessful—game. (What doesn't work properly in a game is often more illuminating than what does.) For those who both make and study games, case studies are one of the most valuable forms of game design writing.

Inspiration for a game can come from anywhere. In the case of Chris Crawford's title Eastern Front (1941), the technology of a scrolling map guided much of his initial thinking. Crawford's first playable prototype was not very enjoyable—a common occurrence with early versions of new kinds of games. However, Crawford responds by clearly identifying problems in the design and making necessary adjustments. He solicits feedback from playtesters, but is careful to filter their ideas into categories that make sense for his process: "Most suggestions are additions; some are embellishments, some are corrections, and some are consolidations."

One danger of an iterative process is that it can lead to a never-ending list of tweaks and adjustments. Particularly in commercial videogames, the time and effort required to implement changes must always be taken into account. Smaller embellishments are more easily considered than wholesale overhauls. Too much iteration and the entire process can run amok. In the course of his essay, Crawford finds a balance between accepting outside input and following his internal design sense.

In his case study "The Design Evolution of Magic: The Gathering," game designer Richard Garfield also begins with an idea for a new game form. But in this case, the technology is paper, not software. From his initial inspiration (games like Cosmic Encounter), to game balancing and rule-writing early prototypes, through the final commercial release, Garfield keeps a sharp focus on the players' experience. Focusing on a consistent design goal—giving the game "a feeling of infinite size and possibility"—allows him to successfully navigate the trials and tribulations of the iterative process.

Magic was the first trading card game, in which players trade, wager, and win new cards in between matches. Thus Garfield had to design not just the core dueling mechanics of Magic, but also the surrounding metagame. As his case study reveals, sometimes he directly guided the evolution of the card economy, by banning cards that could overbalance the game. Other times, he let the players police themselves. An important aspect of the iterative process is releasing control of the game design just enough to let the players surprise you.

However, sometimes the process itself provides the surprise. Ken Birdwell's case study for the blockbuster first-person shooter Half-Life begins at a crisis point in the game's development. As with Crawford's initial prototype, the game just wasn't enjoyable:

By late September 1997, nearing the end of our original schedule, a whole lot of work had been done, but there was one major problem—the game wasn't any fun.... There were some really wonderful individual pieces, but as a whole the game just wasn't working.

The obvious answer was to work a few more months, gloss over the worst of the problems and ship what we had. For companies who live and die at the whim of their publishers, this is usually the route taken—with predictable results.... At this point we had to make a very painful decision—we decided to start over and rework every stage of the game.

In response, the *Half-Life* team had to invent new ways of thinking about game design, as well as a new methodology for game development, which they called the "Cabal" process. The team also generated their own player-centric game design theories and methods, such as how to measure the experience of the player and how to arrange and structure events for maximum enjoyment. Throughout, playtesting and iterative design were central. Playtesting served a number of purposes for the *Half-Life* team, such as providing an "objective" way of resolving differences of opinion among team members about how the design should proceed.

In contrast to the processes of Crawford and Garfield, the *Half-Life* team lacked a single "game designer" figure. Instead, the role of the game designer was distributed among the team of level designers, visual designers, and programmers, resulting in a process in which everyone was, as Birdwell puts it, "invested in the design as a whole." (Game design work need not be limited to just "official" game designers.)

Because iterative design is an open-ended process, a strong vision for the player's experience helps to structure the process. At any moment in the cycle of iteration, a game designer might try out thousands of different rule tweaks and variations—why choose *this* modification over *that* one? In Half-Life, the notion of a thrilling, single-player experience guided the development team through the thicket of possible design directions. In the case of Magic, Richard Garfield pushed his initial idea about a game of infinite possibilities through to the very end.

Randy Farmer and Chip Morningstar, in their case study of the online community game Habitat, also maintained a strong design focus throughout their iterative process. Engendering social play and interaction was their goal: as they note, the idea of "a multiuser environment is central." Similar to Magic, the Habitat designers released the game and let the design evolve, using the initial play experience as a playtest for the design as a whole.

Instead of trying to push the community in the direction we thought it should go, an exercise rather like herding mice, we tried to observe what people were doing and aid them in it. We became facilitators as much as we were designers and implementers.

This approach pushes the experimentation of iterative design to greater heights. Rather than going through cycles of testing prior to launch, Farmer and Morningstar relied on player input. In so doing, they relaxed their roles as the sole authors of the world, letting player activity guide the design process.

A more extreme proponent of exploration through iteration is designer and philosopher Bernard DeKoven. In "Changing the Game," a chapter from his book *The Well-Played Game,* DeKoven outlines his ideas about the design process, in which players directly control the evolution of a game. For DeKoven, play itself is a form of iteration. Why keep players under the thumb of professional game designers? Let them create the games they want to play! Although DeKoven's essay isn't a case study of a single game, it does offer concrete playtesting tips. For example, DeKoven advises his player/designers to make only small modifications in each iteration, so that it is easier to see how the changes affected play.

In some measure, all iterative design partakes of this spirit, of sharing design decisions with an engaged audience, of mixing play and design. For example, the design processes of Magic and Habitat gave players tremendous power over the way the game designs evolved—in a very DeKovian fashion. But, as a clear advocate of blurring the roles of player and designer, DeKoven certainly assumes the most radical stance.

Perhaps DeKoven can take this position because he has the luxury of not shipping a product for a publisher on a limited budget and schedule. As Crawford and Birdwell both point out, the restrictions of commercial development play a very strong role in determining what direction a game design takes. We'd be hard pressed to find a working game designer who would disagree.

But we wonder: how might DeKoven's ideas translate to a commercial context? What if a game could perpetually evolve, giving players the role of designers, a game in which the iterative design process was simply *how the game was played?* Perhaps, considering the cutthroat game industry, this is a vision of starry-eyed optimism. Or a game design impossibility. Or maybe, just maybe, it's that no game designer has been brave enough to fully live up to DeKoven's utopian vision for the future of play.

Further Reading on this Topic

Rules of Play: Game Design Fundamentals, Katie Salen and Eric Zimmerman.

Cambridge: MIT Press, 2004.

> *Recommended:*
> Chapter 2: The Design Process
> Commissioned Essay: Renier Knizia
> Commissioned Games: Richard Garfield, Frank Lantz, Kira Snyder, James Ernest

Designing Virtual Worlds, Richard Bartle.

Berkeley: New Riders Games, 2003.

Recommended, chapter 2: How to Make Virtual Worlds.

"Chapter 5: The Game Design Sequence," Chris Crawford.

The Art of Computer Game Design.

www.vancouver.wsu.edu/fac/peabody/game-book/Coverpage.html.

Game Design Workshop: Designing, Prototyping, and Playtesting Games,
Tracy Fullerton, Steven Hoffman, and Christopher Swain.

Recommended, *chapter 7: Prototyping; chapter 8: Playtesting.*

San Francisco: CMP Books, 2004.

*Postmortems from Game Developer: Insights from the Developers of Unreal
Tournament, Black and White, Age of Empires, and Other Top-Selling Games,*
Austin Grossman, ed.

San Francisco: CMP Books, 2003.

Masters of Doom: How Two Guys Created an Empire and Transformed Pop Culture,
David Kushner.

New York: Random House, 2003.

"Play as Research," Eric Zimmerman.

Design Research: Methods and Perspectives, ed. Brenda Laurel.

Cambridge: MIT Press, 2003.

Player and Character

What is the complex relationship between
game player and game character?

WINS: 7

The Definition of Play; The Classification of Games 122
Roger Caillois

A Theory of Play and Fantasy 314
Gregory Bateson

Frames and Games 578
Gary Alan Fine

Bow, Nigger 602
always_black

Interaction and Narrative 642
Michael Mateas and Andrew Stern

What is the transaction that takes place between the player and the character that they inhabit to play the game?.... How are identities absorbed and played out? What skins do we take with us when play ends? If you could exchange your current world to become any character in your lexicon of game identities, who would you be?
—Sara Diamond

Power up a videogame and prepare to enter a realm of false idols. Who has not relinquished their soul to a mustachioed hero named Mario, or lain quietly in wait for a chance encounter with the White Mage? Games are identity factories where characters are constructed and put to work, often with little more fanfare than the choice of a name, or the selection of an outfit, vehicle, or weapon. From Pac-Man to Donkey Kong, Max Payne to Solid Snake, UuLaLa to Jak and Daxter, there is no shortage of opportunities to wear the skin of another. Who will you become—Human, Elf, Dwarf, Orc—when the game begins? Better yet, who will you be when given the chance to play again?

The relationship between game player and game character is immensely complex, despite the ease with which each identity is assumed. We think nothing of picking up a controller, toggling through a few menu screens, and pretending to be another. We might be a plastic token on a game board, a 3D figure blowing up enemies on a PC, or an imagined persona taken up and acted out in a tabletop role-playing game. In every case, games give us permission to play with identity because they give us *characters to play.* No other medium can make the same claim. Television, film, and books can't, despite their narrative richness. Games can and do—which is one reason why the territory of player and character is such an important topic of study. How do players relate to their game characters? How are identities absorbed and played out? What skins do we take with us when play ends?

These questions point to important lines of inquiry regarding how players relate to games, how games are experienced on cognitive, psychological, and emotional levels, and how designers can tap into these relationships to produce deeper and more engaging play. The essays in this Topic focus on the point of intersection between player and character, that fulcrum of self upon which game identity hinges.

These issues of player and character echo concepts developed by play theorist Roger Caillois in "The Definition of Play: The Classification of Games." Caillois' famous taxonomy includes the category of *mimicry*—play activities that center on make-believe. According to Caillois, the player's relationship to the activity of making believe is more than simple faith in the game's story. It also embodies a complex play of truth and fiction:

> The pleasure [of mimicry] lies in being or passing for another. But in games the basic intention is not that of deceiving the spectators. The child who is playing train may well refuse to kiss his father while saying to him that one does not embrace locomotives, but he is not trying to persuade his father that he is a real locomotive.

More than just casually miming a representation, players actively shape their status as game characters as they become caught up in a game. Only when players give themselves over to the give-and-take flow of game play can the representation of character most effectively take place. Games not only allow players to pretend at being another, but also support their engagement in the illusion by encouraging players to work at moving deeply into the fiction of play.

But what is the nature of this work? Significantly, Caillois notes that games are *not* about deceiving spectators. A father watching his son play at being a locomotive is in no way convinced that the boy is a train. What he does know, however, is that the boy is *playing* at being a train, and is engaged in the fiction of this effort. The father and the boy both recognize the truth and the fiction of the play activity. This same idea is at the heart of the essay "A Theory of Play and Fantasy," in which anthropologist Gregory Bateson explores play as a complex and double-edged act of communication.

Play, argues Bateson, is part of our developmental history, not just from the perspective of biology, but also from that of language. Someone at play is constantly signaling the fact that that he or she is "just playing," so that playful actions won't be taken as "real." (A dog that wags its tail as it barks communicates play, not aggression.) Bateson calls this signaling of play "metacommunication," a special kind of communication *about communication*—or, as Bateson explains, when "the subject of the discourse is the relationship between speakers." In Caillois's example, the child playing at being a train and refusing to kiss his father is not just miming a train, but is taking part in a complex conversation *about* the act of make-believe—and at the very same time, both participants enjoy the fictional play itself.

In *Rules of Play,* we took a stand against what we call the "immersive fallacy": the idea that the primary or sole pleasure of a game is its ability to deceive players into believing that what they are experiencing is real. While sensory illusion is part of the experience of some games, it is certainly not how all people relate to every game. Games are *not* merely watered-down versions of the Star Trek holodeck. To play a game is also to enjoy the artifice, to engage with the game through the frame of metacommunication.

Michael Mateas and Andrew Stern, in "Interaction and Narrative," tie these concepts to a larger history of ideas. Within a broad analysis of several theoretical approaches to narrative and interactivity, Mateas and Stern discuss the relationship between *agency* and *immersion,* two terms borrowed from interactive narrative theorist Janet Murray. By "agency," they refer to the player's sense of being able to make meaningful actions in a fictional world. By "immersion," Mateas and Stern mean the feeling of being taken up into the narrative world: "when a participant is immersed in an experience, they are willing to accept the internal logic of the experience, even though this logic deviates from the logic of the real world." This willing suspension of disbelief feeds a player's ability to immerse him- or herself in a character, and to take meaningful action through character agency. Triangulating the ideas of Brenda Laurel, Janet Murray, and Aristotle, Mateas and Stern emphasize how designers must find a balance between agency and immersion, a balance between passively accepting a fictional world and actively gaming it in order to advance the story.

When metacommunication, immersion, and agency collide, the result is a complex lamination of player and character identity, clearly evident in a genre of games known as "RPGs," or role-playing games. In an RPG, a player literally assumes the identity of a game character in a narrative world, and performs as that character throughout the game. *Shared Fantasies,* a book by folklorist Gary Allen Fine, is a thoughtful ethnography of tabletop roleplayers. The centerpiece of his analysis, outlined in "Frames and Games" is a three-layer model of player identity:

First, is the *person:* the real-world social being as defined by outside contexts.

Next, the *player:* the participant as someone who is playing a game.

Finally, the *character:* the fictional persona depicted by the player through the mechanisms of the game.

These three layers all coexist simultaneously. Thus Caillois's child, playing with his daddy at being a train, is at once the *character* of the locomotive, the giggly *player* taking on a fictional identity, and a *person* in a real-world family. To take another example: booting up World of Warcraft, a player is simultaneously the orc warrior *character* named Scarzan, an experienced World of Warcraft *player* with several characters and a set of online game-playing buddies, as well as a *person* in the real world, with values, ideas, and knowledge that comes from outside the game—such as the pop cultural intuition about what makes an orc different from an elf.

Moving through and among this lamination of identity is part of what it means to play a game. When Fine describes players trying to role-play medieval characters *as if* they did not know about twentieth-century science and technology, or mocking each other *in character* for slipping into contemporary slang, what he is really observing are instances of this playfully layered negotiation.

The final essay in this Topic, "Bow, Nigger," is a marvelously detailed case study of player-character engagement. always_black, playing Jedi Knights II: Jedi Outcast, writes from a player's perspective, recounting the emotional roller coaster of a particularly memorable duel. always_black's account exemplifies many of the concepts developed by Caillois, Mateas, and Fine:

> He has agency: *You can swing away in one of three "styles," fast, medium and heavy, all of which allow you to wrestle mouse movement and direction key presses to produce jaw-dropping combinations of slashes, chops, and stabs...*
>
> He is immersed: *My concentration was absolutely intense and never before have I tried so hard to "be the mouse." I felt a trickle of wet run down from my under my right armpit.*
>
> He is a character: *I crouch and duck my head, a "bow."*
>
> A player: *Five health points remain and I know I haven't hit him yet.*
>
> And a person: *I'm a big boy now and I don't want to be a Jedi when I grow up.*

always_black paints a complex picture of the player-character construct as he weaves and shifts identities through his avatar name and appearance, style of game play and communication, observance and breach of game etiquette, immersive projection into the game, and identification with the larger *Star Wars* universe.

The player-character construct is one of the most complicated aspects of studying games, partly because a game does not define the relationship so much as *mediate* it. Players are ultimately the ones in control of their status as characters, and the degree to which they engage in this complex choreography of truth and fiction. The special status of players as both active and willing participants in character creation and recreation makes them ideal subjects for design. Who could ask for a more captive audience?

Further Reading on this Topic

Rules of Play: Game Design Fundamentals, Katie Salen and Eric Zimmerman.
Cambridge: MIT Press, 2004.

> *Recommended:*
> Chapter 25: Games as the Play of Meaning
> Chapter 27: Games as the Play of Simulation

Remediation: Understanding New Media, Jay David Bolter and Richard Grusin.
Recommended, Introduction; Immediacy, Hypermediacy, and Remediation; Computer Games.
Cambridge: MIT Press, 1999.

"A Rape in Cyberspace," Julian Dibbel.
http://www.juliandibbell.com/texts/bungle.html.

The Fantasy Role-Playing Game: A New Performing Art, Daniel Mackay.
Recommended, chapter 2: Formal Structure.
London: McFarland & Company, Inc., 2001.

Life on the Screen: Identity in the Age of the Internet, Sherry Turkle.
Recommended, chapter 7: Aspects of the Self.
New York: Simon & Schuster, 1995.

Games and Narrative

What are the relationships between story, game, and narrative play?

Tools for Creating Dramatic Game Dynamics 438
Marc LeBlanc

Frames and Games 578
Gary Alan Fine

Interaction and Narrative 642
Michael Mateas and Andrew Stern

Game Design as Narrative Architecture 670
Henry Jenkins

As questions go, this is not a bad one: Do games tell stories?
—Jesper Juul

One of the most contested terrains in the study of games is that of games and narrative. For the past decade or more, the debate has been sometimes fiery, other times pleasantly cordial. Today, however, the situation can only be characterized as a tangled mess of intersecting positions, counterpositions, retractions, qualifications, sidesteps, and reframings. Which is all to say that while there is much to be said regarding the narrative possibilities (or impossibilities!) of games, it will be some time before it is all sorted out.

Each of the four texts included in this Topic is a stellar example of writing being done on the subject of games and stories. There are many aspects of the larger debate left untouched—the territory is simply too vast for such a small collection to cover. Instead, each of the included texts occupies a particular, strategic niche. Michael Mateas and Andrew Stern's essay, for example, includes a terrific summary of several major figures—Brenda Laurel, Janet Murray, Jesper Juul, Gonzalo Frasca, Marie-Laure Ryan, and Henry Jenkins. For his part, Henry Jenkins gives a concise and highly diplomatic description of the Narratology vs. Ludology debate, which alone makes his essay worth reading.

Although many approaches to narrative and games, including those of Mateas and Jenkins, take a strongly theoretical stance, game designer Marc LeBlanc offers a refreshingly practical slant on the subject. In "Tools for Creating Dramatic Game Dynamics," he presents a handful of specific game design strategies for producing "dramatic uncertainty." For LeBlanc, a model of the dramatic arc (conflict, climax, resolution) is the foundation for crafting drama in games.

LeBlanc's dramatic arc is a formal model of game behavior, where dramatic tension is defined as "a kind of quality that can accumulate and discharge, increase or decrease as time passes." While dramatic tension cannot be exactly measured, games can be designed to increase or decrease its value at different moments, by manipulating uncertainty and inevitability. LeBlanc goes on to describe in detail several conceptual tools available to game designers, tools with names like "the fog of war," "hidden energy," and "cashing out." Each tool represents a formal game dynamic that can be tuned to manipulate and control the drama of a game.

This conceptualization of game drama is not a typical way of framing games and narrative. Rather than the certain trajectory of a three-act story, Leblanc's model embraces uncertainty as a catalyst for ongoing moments of drama, which end up being resolved in a number of different ways.

"Interaction and Narrative," an excerpt taken from Michael Mateas and Andrew Stern's paper "Interactive Drama, Art, and Artificial Intelligence," presents a more story-centric approach. Their theoretical work on the subject stems from Façade, an interactive drama driven by natural language recognition. Because of this, rather than trying to develop an overall theory of interactive drama, Mateas and Stern are here primarily interested in providing an approach to the design of emergent and player-constructed narrative, "a rich framework within which individual players can construct their own narratives, or groups of players can engage in the shared social construction of narratives."

As programmers, Mateas and Stern took a high-level approach to the operation of narrative within an interactive space, and translated it into working algorithms that model this behavior. "Interaction and Narrative" offers insight into how this was accomplished and leaves open the door for continued research in this area. If you find these ideas of interest, we recommend you read the rest of their original paper, which contains a further elaboration on their approach to game design and technology.

In "Game Design as Narrative Architecture," Henry Jenkins makes an important conceptual leap: game designers, he argues, are less storytellers than narrative architects. In taking this position, Jenkins shifts the debate about games and narrative into the realm of spatiality. Connecting games to the historical tradition of spatial storytelling, he defines four approaches to creating immersive narrative experiences:

> ...spatial stories can evoke pre-existing narrative associations (evocative spaces); they can provide a staging ground where narrative events are enacted (enacting stories); they may embed narrative information within their mise-en-scène (embedded narratives); or they provide resources for emergent narrative (emergent narratives).

Although not a designer himself, Jenkins is a forceful and thoughtful advocate of design. His theoretical work on games offers conceptual tools to strengthen the craft of game design. Jenkins's work also demonstrates that there is more than one way to skin the cat of games and narrative. By questioning long-held assumptions he is able to make new inroads into that well-trod territory.

Gary Alan Fine's essay "Frames and Games" takes a theoretical leap of another sort, into the complex realm of fantasy role-playing games, chronicled in his book *Shared Fantasy: Role-Playing Games as Social Worlds.* Tabletop RPGs are inherently narrative, as players interact with one another inside fantasy worlds they help to build and maintain. An RPG gamemaster must carefully craft the narrative dimensions of these worlds to accommodate and respond to unexpected player action. Developing a narrative structure that is episodic, open to change, supportive of emergent possibilities, and engaging for everyone involved is no simple task. It requires a tremendously sophisticated understanding of game rules and mechanics, dramatic structure, and player behavior. It is no wonder that researchers like Fine find fantasy role-playing a rich context for study.

Fine's method differs from that of the other authors included in this Topic. Trained as a folklorist, Fine closely *observes* the way that game players act and interact, constructing his theory in retrospect as a way to explain his observations. His focus is primarily on the construction of player identity in a game, the way that role-players constantly shift between frames of experience. A player of Dungeons & Dragons is simultaneously a person in the real world, a player in the game space, and a character in the fictional world of the game. In each of these frames a person/player/character must manage information known to some, but not others, in the frame, all the while remaining engrossed in the fantasy experience.

Players must not only know what their character should (or shouldn't) know, but must also discern *who* they are dealing with (a real person or a character?) in each exchange of the game. Fine offers an example of the potential confusions such a situation evokes:

> Jerry said that "I" [my character] had gone over to the king's capital city, and on the docks "I" [my character] had met "Barry" [Barry's character]. "Barry" [the person] shakes my hand [my real hand] and says, "Nice to meet you [the character]." "I" [in character] say, "Nice to meet you [Barry's character] to him. Jerry seems surprised and asks, "Don't the two of you know each other?" Barry comments, "Not in this game." [Field notes]

Maintaining the narrative of the game is contingent on the players' abilities to manage this frame complexity. While this process seems complicated, Fine discovers that players achieve the transition between frames quite easily. As Bateson's work on play and fantasy in *Steps to an Ecology of Mind* has shown us, knowing that one is at play is all part of the game. Metacommunication clearly plays an important role in fantasy role-playing games: without it, access into and out of the fictionalized worlds created by players would be impossible. Fine's essay is a delightful report on what it *means to play* a character in a narrative game.

In this Topic, we find a game designer inventing formal tools for game creation, a pair of programmer-theorists designing emergent player narratives, a media studies scholar reframing game design as narrative architecture, and an ethnographer recording the metacommunicative aspects of role-playing games. This wealth of perspectives helps us to see some, but not all, of the ways to tackle the question posed by ludologist Jesper Juul in the epigraph to this Topic essay.

As with many complicated questions, discovering answers to the slew of uncertainties surrounding games and narrative is very much a function of what questions are asked. Perhaps it is time to invent new ways of looking at the problem by asking new kinds of questions. Rather than "Do games tell stories?" we might ask, "*How* do games tell stories?" Or, "What kinds of stories can *only* be told in a game?" There's no limit to the questions we might ask, once we are willing to change our own perspective.

Further Reading on this Topic

Rules of Play: Game Design Fundamentals, Katie Salen and Eric Zimmerman.
Cambridge: MIT Press, 2004.

> *Recommended:*
> Chapter 26: Games as the Play of Meaning
> Chapter 26: Games as Narrative Play
> Chapter 27: Games as the Play of Simulation

Cybertext: Perspectives on Ergodic Literature, Espen Aarseth.
Baltimore: The Johns Hopkins University Press, 1997.
Recommended, chapter 5: Intrigue and Discourse in the Adventure Game.

Half-Real: Video Games between Real Rules and Fictional Worlds, Jesper Juul.
Cambridge: MIT Press, 2005.
Recommended, chapter 4: Fiction; chapter 5: Rules and Fiction.

Computers as Theater, Brenda Laurel.
Reading, MA: Addison-Wesley Publishing Company, 1993.

Hamlet on the Holodeck: The Future of Narrative in Cyberspace, Janet Murray.
Cambridge: MIT Press, 1998.
Recommended, Part II: The Aesthetics of the Medium.

Possible Worlds, Artificial Intelligence, and Narrative Theory, Marie-Laure Ryan.
Bloomington: Indiana University Press, 1991.

First Person: New Media as Story, Performance, and Game, Noah Wardrip-Fruin and
Pat Harrigan, eds.
Cambridge: MIT Press, 2004.

Game Communities

What are the forms and meanings of social interaction in a game?

Shoot Club: The DOOM 3 Review 159
Tom Chick

Beyond the Rules of the Game: 504
Why Are Rooie Rules Nice?
Linda Hughes

The Lessons of Lucasfilm's Habitat 728
F. Randall Farmer and Chip Morningstar

Hearts, Clubs, Diamonds, Spades: 754
Players Who Suit MUDs
Richard Bartle

Declaring the Rights of Players 788
Raph Koster

Virtual Worlds: 814
A First-Hand Account of Market and Society on the Cyberian Frontier
Edward Castronova

I thought it was silly, the first time I saw it. Then I saw everybody was doing it. And then I felt silly not doing it. It's strange how much weight the actions of your peers can bring to bear, even when your social medium is only a bunch of maths on a German server.

—always_black

Game behavior is impossible to predict. Players do things they are not supposed to do. They are transgressive. They break rules, cause grief, and often behave very, very badly. But they also are wonderfully inventive and surprisingly generous. They share knowledge with new players. They build tools for each other, create forums, and often compete in fair and honorable ways. Usually, players do all of this without rules explicitly demanding that they do so. These collective actions occur because the players are part of a *game community*, a group of individuals who all buy into a shared desire to play together.

Each of the six essays included in this Topic on game communities shares a strong emphasis on player behavior. This is not a coincidence: players are a key in understanding how community operates in games. While this may seem obvious, it reminds us that player communities are not abstract entities with generalized behavior, but are instead heterogeneous groups composed of individuals with their own unique motivations and desires.

Take Tom Chick, who chronicles his experience in "Shoot Club: The DOOM 3 Review." Chick stands in line for seven hours to buy a copy of a game he's already played (and hated) because his friend hasn't (but will).

> ...I've long since learned that what we're waiting for doesn't matter. We're in it for the thrill of the communal wait, that shared moment where fellow victims of hype come together for the moment of truth.

Standing in line with eighty-six other guys at midnight outside the neighborhood Best Buy is reason enough to cause Chick to wax poetic about the power of shared experience. Game communities need not form only around online virtual worlds. Membership in the hallowed clan of DOOM addicts and hardcore gamers represents its own distinctive kind of player community.

Joining a game community means entering into a shared social culture. In games like Jedi Knights II, Lineage, and EverQuest, not to mention staples of the playground like Dodgeball and Foursquare, playing well means playing well together. Membership in a community requires that players know not only what the game rules allow, but also what the etiquette of the play community requires. Newbies to any multiplayer game are quick to discover that the best way to learn about what is going on is to watch what other players are doing, and to not take things too personally the first few times they slip up.

In "Virtual Worlds: A First-hand Account of Market and Society on the Cyberian Frontier," Ed Castronova writes about his entry into EverQuest:

> Suddenly my chat box lights up with [a] message from a Being named "Deathfist Pawn" to the effect that I will not be allowed to ruin this land. Then: *"Deathfist Pawn hits YOU for 2 points of damage."* I hear myself grunt in pain. Flustered, I peer out and see no one. *"Deathfist Pawn hits YOU for 3 points of damage."* He is behind me of course. I learn that you can be attacked here. Why is this person attacking me? What have I done? I guess I have to fight.... I fumble for my sword. The chat box reports *"You have been slain by Deathfist Pawn."* The screen freezes. I am dead.

Castronova is primarily interested in studying the economy of Norrath, one of the worlds that make up the MMORPG (massively multiplayer online role-playing game) Ever-Quest. He does so by becoming one of its citizens, observing how and why people (including himself) spend their time there. By documenting actual player behaviors, Castronova is able to make judgments about what is socially valuable and meaningful in Norrath, as well as to explore the implications of these values and meanings.

What Castronova discovers is rather remarkable. Norrath is not only a world in which a player "faces the same sort of social reward systems as are found in Earth Society," but it is one that a surprising number of people call "home":

> Perhaps the most striking finding is that a significant fraction, 20 percent, view them-selves as people who "live" in Norrath. A similar fraction, 22 percent, express the desire to spend all of their time there.

A game community, in other words, can transcend its status as a play space to become a human community in its own right. One of the earliest documents from such communities comes from F. Randall Farmer and Chip Morningstar's classic case study "The Lessons of Lucasfilm's Habitat." Designed in the late 1980s for the Commodore 64 (!), Habitat was a large-scale, multiplayer environment, considered a precursor to virtual worlds like The Sims, Habbo Hotel, and Second Life. Habitat was a self-governing community that allowed players to chat, play games, go on scavenger hunts, build businesses, collect and exchange goods, and experiment with a range of social practices.

Farmer and Morningstar were on the design team of Habitat and focus their case study on lessons they learned from the experience of building the world. Some of these lessons concern approaches to platform and technology; others address administrating and managing the world. But the following lesson is one all game developers should take to heart: Habitat, as a designed experience, was primarily defined by the interactions among the players, rather than by the technology with which it was implemented. Time and again Farmer and Morningstar point out that, despite their best efforts to speculate on possible new features, it was only when they focused on players and player interaction that Habitat truly came alive.

> It seems to us that the things that are important to the inhabitants of such an environment are the capabilities available to them, the characteristics of the other people they encounter there, and the ways these various participants can affect one another.

Community emerges from relationships between people, places, and activities. By designing a range of player spaces and actions into Habitat, Farmer and Morningstar were simultaneously fostering the growth of community. Good community design comes from understanding how the elements within the system of a game are valued and made meaningful by its participants. Richard Bartle expands on this premise in "Hearts, Clubs, Diamonds, Spades: Players Who Suit MUDs." Bartle is well known for his classification of player types, developed as a tool to help designers of text-based virtual worlds (called "multiuser domains," or "MUDs") balance the dynamics of player population.

Any community consists of players with a range of playing styles. Bartle's simple taxonomy equates player interest in four primary activities (achieving, exploring, socializing, and player-killing) with player categories (Achiever, Explorer, Socializer, and Killer). The taxonomy itself is an extremely useful design tool for thinking about how any particular game experience might support one or more player type. But Bartle's further contribution is in arguing that player styles represent parts within the system of a community, a system that can be carefully balanced and manipulated. Having more or fewer of one type of player has a ripple effect among the others:

> The most volatile group of people is that of the socialisers. Not only is it highly sensitive to the number of killers, but it has both positive and negative feedback on itself, which amplifies any changes. An increase in the number of socialisers will lead to yet more socialisers, but it will also increase the number of killers; this, in turn, will reduce the number of socialisers drastically, which will feed back into a yet greater reduction.

Ultimately, game communities live or die, grow or change based on the people who take part in them. Who are these players? What do they want? And what "rights" do they have? Massively multiplayer game designer Raph Koster meditates on these questions in a mock Bill of Rights known as "A Declaration of the Rights of Avatars." A provocation aimed at virtual world players and game administrators, the essay takes on the critical debate over who really should have control over a player's rights.

> There's at least one theory of rights, which says that rights aren't "granted" by anyone. They arise because the populace decides to grant them to themselves. On the other hand, the creators of game communities often feel differently: Many MUD admins are of the belief that their MUDs are their private playgrounds. That they have discretion on who enters and who gets to stay...can delete a character at a whim, can play favorites and choose to grant administrative favors to their friends.

Koster cleverly find the common ground between these two groups by focusing his Bill of Rights not on players, or on game administrators, but on game *avatars,* the player-controlled game characters that link the two groups. While Farmer and Morningstar concentrate on designing player actions for Habitat, Koster proposes a set of metarules, guidelines for game design and player behavior that could be carried across games. In this way, Koster reminds us to look beyond the bounds of any individual game when considering the nature of a play community. His essay is an attempt to reformulate the "rules" by which online community games are played.

As long as there have been games, there have been communities of players making the games their own. And as they do so, they strengthen the bonds of the group. One of the most well-documented examples of such player behavior comes from "Beyond the Rules of the Game: Why Are Rooie Rules Nice?" In this essay, folklorist Linda Hughes looks at the way children manipulate the game rules of Foursquare as a means of maintaining the subtle social order of a playground community.

Hughes argues that the rules of any game are subject to constant negotiation and reinterpretation. The set of rules that results from this process of negotiation describes more than a list of allowable actions. Instead, it represents a "framework for player interaction, and encompasses a complex matrix of social rights and obligations." In Foursquare, for example, "Hitting the ball into a competitor's square" merely describes an action. Hitting the ball "nicely" is the social rule that *really* matters when it comes time to play.

In playing with others, game rules only go so far in determining the nature of this participation. As Hughes points out, game play is often predicated on the social exclusion of non-players. And we know that any game that pits player against player in unproductive ways has the potential for negative conflict. Yet despite these tendencies, game communities continue to thrive, grow, and teach us new ways of playing and being with one another. Maybe in playing together, we learn to play well after all.

Further Reading on this Topic

Rules of Play: Game Design Fundamentals, **Katie Salen and Eric Zimmerman.**
Cambridge: MIT Press, 2004.

> *Recommended:*
> Chapter 20: Games as Systems of Conflict
> Chapter 28: Games as Social Play

Designing Virtual Worlds, **Richard Bartle.**
Berkeley: New Riders Games, 2003.
Recommended, chapter 5: Life in the Virutal World.

My Tiny Life: Crime and Passion in a Virtual World. **Julian Dibbel.**
Henry Holt & Company, 1999.

http://terranova.blogs.com; www.legendmud.org/raph

Word Freak: Heartbreak, Triumph, Genius, and Obsession in the World of Competitive Scrabble Players, **Stefan Fatsis.**
Boston: Houghton Mifflin, 2001.

Speaking of Games

What ideologies inform the discourse of games?

Nature and Significance of Play as a Cultural Phenomenon 96
Johan Huizinga

Semiotic Domains: 228
Is Playing Video Games a "Waste of Time?"
James Gee

Play and Ambiguity 296
Brian Sutton-Smith

Unwritten Rules 476
Stephen Sniderman

Cultural Models: 610
Do You Want to Be the Blue Sonic or the Dark Sonic?
James Gee

As extensions of the popular response to the workaday stress, games become faithful models of a culture. They incorporate both the actions and the reactions of whole populations in a single dynamic image.
—Marshall McLuhan

How do we speak of games? What hopes and fears color our descriptions? What images are evoked, what ideologies are uncovered, as we act and react to games? The language of the American political right is replete with references to the devil (and heavy metal) when it comes to the ill-found virtues of videogames, while a growing movement in K-12 education casts them as a Holy Grail in the uphill battle to keep kids learning. Games "empower" players, say some; games "waste time," say others. Are games "frivolous," "vital," "safe" or "dangerous?" It all depends on whom and how you ask.

Games are expressions of culture. As a result they embody ideas, narratives, and ideologies that, as part of a larger cultural landscape, shape our understanding of games and give us a language with which to speak about them. This Topic engages this rich cultural terrain to address the varied perspectives, vocabularies, and rhetorics that underlie and inform the way we speak about games.

According to James Gee, linguist by profession and gamer at heart, games take part in what he calls "cultural models:" sets of values embodied in "images, story lines, principles, or metaphors that capture what a particular group finds 'normal' or 'typical' in regard to a given phenomenon." As Gee notes in "Cultural Models: Do You Want to Be the Blue Sonic or the Dark Sonic?"

> ...if someone thinks war is heroic, *Return to Castle Wolfenstein* will not disabuse him or her of this viewpoint. If someone thinks that the quality of life is integrally tied to one's possessions, *The Sims* (a best-selling game where you build and maintain whole families and neighborhoods) will not disabuse him or her of this perspective, either.

Cultural models capture the ways people see the world. Because games are part and parcel of larger cultural models, understanding how games get caught up in cultural structures—the words used, the arguments employed, and the cultural values subsequently

45

granted—can shed light on the diversity of meanings attributed to games and play. Doing so is incredibly important both to those who make games and to those who are working to make an argument *for* games. The debate surrounding violence in videogames, for example, employs a range of competing cultural models around the effects of interactivity, "good" vs. "bad" content, and the inherent value of play. When we write and speak about games, we are not simply describing them; we are also making a case for how and why they should or shouldn't be played.

Prolific and polydisciplinary scholar Brian Sutton-Smith also engages play in a cultural context. In *The Ambiguity of Play,* Sutton-Smith doesn't study play in and of itself, but instead explores the differences in perspective which define what play means, how it is valued, and who should (and should not) play. In "Play and Ambiguity," the introductory chapter of his book, he identifies seven "rhetorics of play," each rhetoric a different way that play is represented and re-presented within culture.

> What is talked about here as rhetoric [is] the way in which the underlying ideological values attributed to these matters are both subsumed by the theorists and presented persuasively to the rest of us.

The rhetorics include both ancient and modern forms: the rhetoric of play as progress, as fate, as power, as identity, as the imaginary, as self, and as frivolous. Although similar in intent, Sutton-Smith and Gee take inverse approaches. Gee's cultural models represent broad sets of cultural values that end up affecting how games are made, played, and interpreted. Sutton-Smith, on the other hand, looks first at instances of play and extrapolates outward in order to understand how particular conceptions of play reside within culture at large. Significantly, Sutton-Smith focuses not just on these ideological constructs as representations of underlying values, but also on how they are *spoken*—rhetorics are embodied in game forms, in game scholarship, and in popular discourse. As distillations of culture's ideas about play, his seven rhetorics are tremendously useful, helping us see often hidden ideological grammars in games and the discourse around them.

Brian Sutton-Smith and James Gee are both working out of a contemporary, comparative approach to cultural analysis. Earlier writers seem less self-conscious about making bold statements regarding play. Case in point: historian and philosopher Johan Huizinga, who doesn't just write about what play is, but who also makes a passionate argument that play is central to culture.

In play as we conceive it the distinction between belief and make-believe breaks down. The concept of play merges quite naturally with that of holiness. Any Prelude of Bach, any line of tragedy proves it.

To speak of games is to speak in a particular way. Knowing how to decode the discourse can offer clues about the cultural models being employed. Recognizing that Johan Huizinga formulated his argument for play in the midst of a work-oriented, Marxist intellectual climate is critical to understanding the new perspective he introduced. Rather than framing play as a wasteful pastime, Huizinga saw it as essential to key components of culture, from religion and art to law and war. Significantly, unlike Gee and Sutton-Smith, Huizinga does not see play as something that partakes in cultural values: "Play lies outside the antithesis of wisdom and folly, and equally outside those of truth and falsehood, good and evil...it has no moral function." Rather than treating play as part and parcel of cultural values, Huizinga sees it as ultimately transcendent. But this perspective, of course, expresses its own set of particular cultural values.

It is one thing to make grand statements about culture. But how can we connect the way we speak about games to the practice of designing them? In "Semiotic Domains: Is Playing Video Games a 'Waste of Time?'" James Gee demonstrates that videogames offer deep learning spaces that require their own form of literacy to decode and design. Like Stephen Sniderman, he achieves this agenda by looking not at play per se, but instead at what is required *in order to play.* Rather than employing the term *rhetoric,* Gee introduces the concept of semiotic domains:

> By semiotic domain I mean any set of practices that recruits one or more modalities (e.g., oral or written language, images, equations, symbols, sounds, gestures, graphs, artifacts, etc.) to communicate distinctive types of meanings.

Gee articulates two crucial aspects of a semiotic domain. The first is that individuals can become *literate* in a domain, whether it be physics, Hip-Hop, organic gardening, or videogames, by learning to read the signs of that domain, to become fluent in its meanings. Players become literate within a game when they "learn the rules" that make actions meaningful in that system, and not necessarily in any other.

The second crucial aspect of a semiotic domain is that it is, in fact, *designed*. As Gee notes, "I want us to think about the fact that for any semiotic domain, whether it is first-person shooter games or theoretical linguistics, that domain, internally and externally, was and is designed by someone." Each domain, like any game, is composed of a set of rules, or what Gee calls "design grammars," which organize elements within the system in specific ways. These grammars allow participants to act within the domain ("read") as well as produce ("write"). This ability to produce meaning within a domain is one of the keys connecting literacy to learning.

> Therefore, if we are concerned with whether something is worth learning or not, whether it is a waste of time or not—videogames or anything else—we should start with questions like the following: What semiotic domain is being entered through this learning? Is it a valuable domain or not? In what sense? Is the learner learning simply to understand ("read") parts of the domain or also to participate more fully in the domain by learning to produce ("write") meanings in the domain?

Ultimately Gee is making a case against those who consider videogame play a waste of time. By framing games as semiotic spaces that can be acted within and produced by participants, he forces us to see play in an entirely different light. But his concepts have broader relevance. What exactly does it mean to "write" game meanings in a cultural space? How do the rules of games intersect with their cultural values? This is a largely unexplored area of inquiry, but a clue to how such questions might be answered is found in philosopher Stephen Sniderman's essay "Unwritten Rules."

Sniderman looks at the structures that make play possible: not just the designed structures of rules, but also the social structures that determine what it means to play. Unwritten rules are the implicit rules that often emerge out of respect for social convention. These rules of "etiquette or ethos" are generally hidden from us, in the same way that our feelings about the value of games or play are camouflaged by the cultural models we employ. In identifying these "unwritten rules," Sniderman finds a missing link between formal and cultural aspects of games: the cultural codes manifest in the actual regulations of play.

Unwritten rules gain their potency because of their connection to the world outside the game. As Sniderman notes, "All play activities exist in a 'real-world' context, so that to play the game is to immerse yourself in that context, whether you want to or not. In fact, it is impossible to determine where the 'game' ends and 'real life' begins." In other words, any game is tied up in knots of convention that govern not only what may be done in the game (kill monsters) but also how one is to behave while doing so (trash-talking is okay; racial slurs are not). The need to "play fair," for example, is rarely stated explicitly at the beginning of a game, but it is a rule followed by all who would invest it with a spirit of honorable competition. In looking closely at the cultural end of Gee's "design grammars," Sniderman points out how speaking of games never occurs in a vacuum. Belief systems are always bubbling up, informing our grammars and coloring our actions.

These kinds of belief systems are always with us when we speak about, write about, create, and even play games. Ideologies appear where we least expect them. Take game journalism. Popular writing on games is perhaps the most dominant way that games—especially computer games—are spoken about today. Game magazines like *Edge, PC Gamer, Game Developer* and online sites like Gamespot, Gamasutra, Planetquake, and Old Man Murray spawn thousands of words daily about historical, newly released, and upcoming games.

But despite the wealth of coverage, even professional writers struggle with what it means to speak about games. According to independent journalist Kieron Gillen in his manifesto "The New Games Journalism," most industry writing has too narrow an agenda, spinning a tradition that takes the mechanics of the form as its focus:

> No matter what the precise form this tradition takes, it works of a single assumption; that the worth of a videogame lies in the videogame, and by examining it like a twitching insect fixed on a slide, we can understand it.

Gillen points out that the underlying cultural model of such writing places value on the game, not the gamer. Conventional game journalism often overlooks the experience of the player, focusing on the mechanics of the game, on features, polygon counts, and rating systems designed to pique player purchases. If there is an ideology at work in mainstream writing on games, it is the sheer power of consumerism.

What gets lost in all this is a more personal, often critical, voice: the voice of the player. Players are not concerned with what a game is *supposed* to do based on technological wizardry or radical new game features. Their focus is on the actual experience of the game, on what they feel when they play. So why not create a new way of speaking about games within games journalism? It's hard to fight entrenched voices of the establishment, but it can be done. One benefit to identifying the ideologies implicit in the ways we write about games is that it helps us to incorporate new kinds of actions and reactions into the games, criticism, and scholarship we make.

It is time to reinvent the language of play. As this book demonstrates, writing on games has hit critical mass. Is there something in and among this Topic's essays—each speaking about games in a different way—which points to a larger movement, a new strategy for dialogue and discussion? Perhaps. We don't know what it is, but we believe it's out there. So plug in, play on, and speak up!

Further Reading on this Topic

Rules of Play: Game Design Fundamentals, Katie Salen and Eric Zimmerman.
Cambridge: MIT Press, 2004.

> *Recommended:*
> Chapter 29: Defining Culture
> Chapter 30: Games as Cultural Rhetoric

"Videogames of the Oppressed. Videogames as a Means for Critical Debate and Debate,"
Gonzalo Frasca.
http://www.ludology.org.

Handbook of Computer Game Studies, Jeffrey Goldstein and Joost Raessens, eds.
Cambridge: MIT Press, 2005.

"The Heresy of Zone Defense," Dave Hickey.
Air Guitar: Essays on Art and Democracy.
Art Issues Press, 1997.

"Testimony Before the U.S. Senate Commerce Committee, May 4, 1999," Henry Jenkins.
www.senate.gov/~commerce/hearings/0504jen.pdf.

*Playing With Power in Movies, Television, and Video Games: From Muppet Babies to Teenage
Mutant Ninja Turtles,* Marsha Kinder.
Berkeley: University of California Press, 1993.

"The St. Louis Court Brief: Debating Audience 'Effects' in Public,"
Particip@tions 1, no.1, (November 2003).
http://www.participations.org/volume%201/issue%201/1_01_amici_contents.htm.

"The New Games Journalism," Kieron Gillen.
State.com, March 2004.
www.extra-life.org.uk/wiki/?ViewStateItem&item=a95.

Game Design Models

What are formal ways of understanding how games work?

Formal Abstract Design Tools 366
Doug Church

Game Theory 382
William Poundstone

Games and Design Patterns 410
Staffan Björk and Jussi Holopainen

Tools for Creating Dramatic Game Dynamics 438
Marc LeBlanc

Game Analysis: Centipede 460
Richard Rouse III

Adventure as a Video Game: 690
Adventure for the Atari 2600
Warren Robinett

Videogames are nerd poetry.—Ernest Adams

Games are mathsex.—Frank Lantz

If you want to understand something, try building a model. It could be a model of the solar system, of brain cognition, or of presidential election voting patterns. Respectively, astronomers, neuroscientists, or political analysts might use these models. Designers use models, too—as tools for analysis, modification, and design. An architectural model, for instance, might be a small-scale cardboard version of a building that helps to visualize the way it will look in context. Certainly, design models don't have to be physical: the same architectural project might use an algorithmic model of pedestrian flow to determine the size and location of doorways inside the building.

Designers create systems. Games, when we consider them in all their mathematical, psychological, and cultural intricacy, are infinitely complicated systems. Models are abstractions—simplified representations—that isolate a particular facet of a game system so that a designer can focus on solving one part of a much bigger problem. Why are game design models important? Models provide a vocabulary and set of concepts for thinking about games and for solving problems as they emerge in the design process. As game designer Doug Church writes, models give us a way to

> talk about the underlying components of a game. Instead of just saying, "That was fun," or "I don't know, that wasn't much fun," we could dissect a game into its components, and attempt to understand how these parts balance and fit together.

Over the last few years, a significant amount of attention has been given to game design models. Ludology theorist Steffen P. Walz has elaborated a model that compares game structures to classical forms of rhetoric. Veteran game designers Hal Barwood and Noah Falstein have undertaken the 400 Rules Project, which seeks to define the underlying mechanisms by which games operate. Both initiatives share a focus on developing models for how rules and game structures function.

Game designer Doug Church is a progenitor of this formal tradition. The first section of his essay "Formal Abstract Design Tools" is a call to arms that eloquently articulates

53

a need for game design concepts and a model based in a shared vocabulary. Such a model would be a "tool kit to pick apart games and take the parts which resonate with us to realize our own game vision, or refine how our own games work." The "Formal" part in "Formal Abstract Design Tools" refers to the fact that Church's is a rigorous analytical model, one that has been *formalized* into a set of ideas and methods, and one that looks at the essential, inner *forms* of games.

His model takes the form of a set of "design tools," modular concepts that can be used to analyze a game. In his essay, Church takes a stab at identifying some of these concepts, such as *intention, perceivable consequence,* and *story.* Church intended other designers to pick up where he left off, adding more formal abstract design tools and eventually building a complete language for understanding games.

A different approach is taken by game theory, a branch of economics born in the 1940s that looks at decision-making in gamelike situations. The reading included here comes from "Prisoners Dilemma," a nontechnical introduction to the subject written by William Poundstone. While Church's model abstracts simple features from complex computer and video games, game theory uses an inverse approach. It takes as its subject extremely simple two-player games, analyzing these limited games to a high level of detail.

Does game theory represent a game design model? Yes and no. On one hand, game theory was not developed for game designers, and, truth be told, the kinds of games it analyzes are not that much fun to play. Yet game theory is fantastically useful for analyzing certain kinds of player decisions. It is the source of many commonly used game design concepts, including decision trees, minimax strategies, and zero-sum games. And the rigor of game theory analysis reminds us that designing and balancing games often comes down to math.

Two writers working in the spirit, though not the letter, of game theory, are Staffan Björk and Jussi Holopainen. For several years, inspired by the design patterns work of architect Christopher Alexander, they have pursued a project they call "game design patterns," a systematic examination of the "commonly reoccurring parts of the design of a game that concern gameplay." According to Björk and Holopainen, game design patterns can be used to identify and classify games, to analyze how they function, to diagnose problems in a game design, and to solve those problems as well.

For example, the game design pattern "Producer-Consumer" occurs when resources in a game are produced by one game element and consumed by another. New units in the computer game Civilization are *produced* in cities, only to be *consumed* at a later time in battle. While game design patterns may seem abstract, there is no doubt that the work of Björk and Holopainen represents some of the most rigorous formal modeling of games. Game design patterns are, in many ways, the best example we have found of Church's formal abstract design tools.

A major challenge in creating a game design model is to conceptualize games on an abstract level, while also providing more specific rubrics for solving concrete game design problems. Game designer Marc LeBlanc, in his essay "Tools for Creating Dramatic Game Dynamics," has his cake and eats it, too. He offers a general theory for understanding the operation of games, and provides highly specific ways to implement his theory in design practice. LeBlanc elegantly embeds model within model: his model of *dramatic tension* (between *uncertainty* and *inevitability*) itself resides within a larger framework of *mechanics/dynamics/aesthetics*. And within his model of dramatic tension, LeBlanc provides concepts like *escalation, fog of war,* and *the decelerator,* game design tools that model particular game dynamics.

Because the design process is iterative, models are useful as a first step for understanding a game design problem. But they can never provide a complete solution. In practice, game designers rarely utilize a design model in an orthodox fashion. Instead, they use models in a more general sense, to dissect their game as a system, taking it apart to figure out why some aspect is or isn't working. That's why we included two formal case studies in this Topic. Each case study analyzes a game by describing the rule-structures unique to the game, creating a formal model specific to the individual game at hand.

The first is an analysis of the Atari 2600 game Adventure, written by its designer Warren Robinett. Because Adventure is somewhat simpler than contemporary video games, the structures that constitute its formal system can be rigorously mapped. For example, Robinett describes the relations among the parts that create the game's goals:

> One single treasure, the Enchanted Chalice, must be located and brought home. Thus, the tool-objects must contribute somehow to the overall goal of the quest. For example, if the chalice is locked inside the Black Castle, then finding the Black Key becomes a

subgoal, subordinated to the primary goal of getting to the chalice. If the Black Key is found, but is inaccessible because of the dragon guarding it, then another subgoal is spawned—find the sword so as to get past the dragon. Each tool-object is a means of getting past a certain kind of barrier. Since needed objects may be behind barriers, which, in turn, require other objects, a hierarchy is created of goals and subgoals.

From the player's point of view, Adventure's formal system of goals and barriers becomes a flow of tasks that must be completed in order to finish a game. Robinett's incisive analysis shows that these structures are embedded within other structures—each of the game objects is, itself, a yet smaller system. The "barrier" object of the dragon, for example, is a structure composed of smaller subsets of behavioral states. As Robinett reports in his essay, these states and their relationships were tweaked many times until the timing of the dragon's behavior turned out just right.

Game designer Richard Rouse similarly undertakes a systemic analysis of Centipede, looking at how its many elements interrelate:

> Though not a very complex game by today's standards, the marvel of Centipede is how all of the different gameplay elements work together to create a uniquely challenging game. Nothing in Centipede is out of place, nothing is inconsistent, nothing is unbalanced.

He concludes that the appeal of Centipede lies in the way that the centipede, mushrooms, spiders, scorpions, fleas, and other elements relate to each other within the system of the game, a situation he terms "interconnectedness." Spiders, for example, present a dangerous threat to the player. But they also eat the mushroom obstacles, forcing the player into a difficult choice about whether or not to keep the spider onscreen. Like a word in a sentence, each part gains its meaning and significance by virtue of its relationships to the others. When this kind of systemic thinking is generalized to cover many games—or all games—it becomes a game design model.

In a certain sense, all of the essays in this book represent some model or another. There are narrative game models, models of player experience, even models for games as agents of social change. Every model builds a solid understanding of some aspect of games, even while leaving others out. Building models—creating a representation of a particular aspect of a game—remains one of the most important tools we have for understanding them.

Further Reading on this Topic

Rules of Play: Game Design Fundamentals, **Katie Salen and Eric Zimmerman.**

Cambridge: MIT Press, 2004.

      Recommended:

      Chapter 14: Games as Emergent Systems

      Chapter 15: Games as Systems of Uncertainty

      Chapter 16: Games as Information Theory Systems

      Chapter 17: Games as Systems of Information

      Chapter 18: Games as Cybernetic Systems

      Chapter 19: Games as Game Theory Systems

Patterns in Game Design, **Staffan Björk and Jussi Holopainen.**

Hingham, MA: Charles River Media, 2005.

The 400 Rules Project, Hal Barwood and Noah Falstein.

www.theinspiracy.com/400_project.htm.

"The Open and the Closed: Games of Emergence and Games of Progression," Jesper Juul.

Computer Games and Digital Cultures: Conference Proceedings, Frans Mäyrä, ed.

Tampere, Finland: Tampere University Press, 2002.

"Game Design Methods: A 2003 Survey," Bernd Kreimeier.

www.gamasutra.com/features/20030303/kreimeier_01.shtml.

Game Economies

How do game experiences emerge through systems of exchange?

The Evil Summoner FAQ v1.0: 212
How to Be a Cheap Ass
Mochan

The Design Evolution of Magic: The Gathering 538
Richard Garfield

Hearts, Clubs, Diamonds, Spades: 518
Players Who Suit MUDs
Richard Bartle

Virtual Worlds: 714
A First-Hand Account of Market and Society on the Cyberian Frontier
Edward Castronova

The way to make choices meaningful is to give players resources to manage. "Resources" can be anything: Panzer divisions. Supply points. Cards. Experience points. Knowledge of spells. Ownership of fiefs. The love of a good woman. Favors from the boss. The good will of an NPC. Money. Food. Sex. Fame. Information.—Greg Costikyan

We (Katie and Eric) once designed a social card game for an academic conference. The game was called "Buzzwords," and was played during and between sessions at the first DiGRA conference, at the University of Utrecht. Each Buzzwords game card featured a keyword from the title of a paper presented at the conference. At the opening session of the conference, each attendee was given three cards. When a player heard someone say a buzzword that corresponded to one of that player's cards, he or she could say "Sting!" and hand the card over to whoever had said the word. The goal for each player was to get rid of all their game cards by the end of the conference.

Even though money never changed hands in the game of Buzzwords, it created a *game economy.* The word *economy* does not necessarily refer to currency, but to any collection of pieces, points, cards, creatures, or other items that form the system of a game. An economy is a set of parts that are won and lost, traded and brokered, hidden and revealed, hoarded and stolen away by players as they play. In *Buzzwords,* we created an economy of language, facilitated via another economy of cards, circulated among the economy of conference attendee players.

Economies are an important way to think about games that grows directly from considering games as *systems.* A system is a set of parts that interrelate to form a whole. A systems-based approach to games is absolutely essential for any kind of deep analysis, whether it is a designer struggling with a game in development, a scholar comparing aspects of different games across genres, or a journalist dissecting a recently published game to figure out why it isn't as fun as it ought to be.

In thinking about systems of game economies, we have to consider both the formal makeup of the economy and how players interact with it. Are the unused Scrabble tiles visible to both players, or hidden? Do monsters respawn every hour, or only when they are killed? Can players customize their decks or units before the game starts, or does each player have an identical starting state? And in each case, how do players come to know how the game economy works? These kinds of questions have a direct impact on the experience and operation of a game, as well as on the way the game relates to outside contexts.

The subject of Richard Garfield's essay "The Design Evolution of Magic: The Gathering" is a game in which economies are utterly central. Magic is constituted as a vast and complex economy of cards. There are thousands of different cards that can be collected, exchanged, played, and wagered by players. From a personal collection of dozens, hundreds, or thousands of these cards, a player creates a "deck" of about 60—a designed subset of his or her overall collection. In a Magic duel, each player pits his or her own deck against an opponent's.

Any card game automatically has some kind of economy (the set of cards and the game actions they afford), but in Magic, Garfield took the notion of cards as an economy and extended it to its logical extreme. Magic has an economy that is far larger than any individual player's own set of cards. As Garfield puts it, in Magic "players are exploring a world rather than knowing all the details to start. I view Magic as a vast game played among all the people who buy decks, rather than just a series of little duels. It is a game for tens of thousands in which the designer acts as the gamemaster." Magic's game economy is utterly central to its play.

To collect cards, design decks, and duel Magic is to explore the game's economy. In his essay, Garfield highlights how the game design achieves this result. The variable rarity of cards, the relation of a card's scarcity to its game play power, special cards that undermine dominant strategies, "colors" that encourage players to specialize their decks—all are ways that Magic celebrates the idea of game *as economy*. To say nothing of the real-world economics of buying and selling the cards in hobby stores and online auction sites.

The growing sophistication of digital and electronic games has ushered in an era of increasingly complex game economies. It only makes sense that eventually these economies would come to the attention of bona fide economists. Edward Castronova is one such economist who studies the economics of multiplayer persistent-world games, a game genre he calls "virtual worlds" (also known as "massively multiplayer online role-playing games" or "MMORPGs"). Castronova applies economic ideas and theories to games—such as determining a virtual world's GNP or calculating the value of a virtual unit of money relative to real-world currencies.

In addition to his purely economic observations, Castronova has some wonderful insights about designing game economies. For example, he points out that "somewhat shockingly, scarcity is what makes the VW [virtual world] so fun," naming three ways in which virtual world games have scarcity. There is scarcity in deciding how to create and evolve an avatar's skills, abilities, and appearance; there is the scarcity and difficulty of acquiring goods and services; and lastly, there is scarcity and competition for social roles. The reason Castronova finds this "shocking" is that many economists assume that the most pleasurable world is one in which resources are plentiful, so that everyone can partake of whatever they want. However, Castronova finds that such worlds (usually less game-oriented social worlds) do not command the same degree of participation as games in which scarcity and inequality run rampant.

Castranova's writing details how he, playing an EverQuest character, was able to get involved in the game economy. In the course of playing the game, Castronova and players he observed slew rats to sell their furs, foraged for acorns and sold them at a profit, killed and looted other players, and even went online to buy and sell virtual currency on eBay. Part of the richness of a game economy comes not just from its scale and activity, but also from the numerous ways to engage with it.

The ways that players interact with the system of a game is exactly the subject of Richard Bartle's essay, "Why Players Suit MUDS." MUDS, or multi-user domains, are the text-based precursors of the MMORPGs that Castronova studies. But in this case, the economy that Bartle uncovers and analyzes is not virtual money, but instead the players themselves— the system of MUD player styles.

He identifies an economy of four player types: Killers, Explorers, Achievers, and Socializers. Every game has a different balance of these types, and according to Bartle, a healthy mix of all four makes for a rich player pool and a long-lived game community. But Bartle goes beyond merely listing each type. He enumerates how to grow and change the economy of players over time: How each group relates, in positive and negative effects, to the others.

To increase the number of achievers:
—reduce the number of killers, but not by too much
—if killer numbers are high, increase the number of explorers

To decrease the number of achievers:
—increase the number of killers
—if killer numbers are low, reduce the number of explorers

And so on. Bartle's complex matrix of causes and effects is an exciting articulation of a game system as interconnected economy, an economy described in practical design terms.

The three games mentioned thus far are multiplayer games. But game economies appear in single-player games as well. Mochan's "The Evil Summoner FAQ," a humorously critical player-written guide to the PC role-playing game Summoner, reveals a game bristling with economies. Skill points, hit points, damage points, skill levels, characters, monsters, items, actions, commands: Summoner is a tightly woven web of numbers and levels, parts and relationships.

Summoner isn't unusual in this regard—any detailed FAQ will reveal similar game complexities. But Mochan's essay is also evidence of game economies outside the game proper. The essay notes the timing of the release of Summoner, placing it within an economy of competing product launches. It mentions the differences between PC and console games, and between Japanese and American role-playing titles. The essay itself represents a commodity, a FAQ within a larger economy of fan-created FAQs, walkthroughs and strategy guides; of game websites, fan fiction, and online blog reviews.

Game economies and systems, whether they are actual virtual currencies, or dynamically interrelated sets of parts, present a fundamental perspective for analyzing games. This Topic, focusing on games as complex systems, opens up into many of the other Topics. Game systems that players can break and remake connects to *Gaming the Game;* games as systems of parts that can be fiddled and tweaked by designers points to *Game Design Models* and *The Game Design Process;* games as sets of cultural relationships to be created, explored, and undermined brings us to *Cultural Representation.*

Upon first glance, game economies can seem rather dry. But as several of the essays included here point out, game economies are the underlying structures that give rise to rich game experiences. From the social intrusion of Buzzwords to the customized dueling decks of Magic to the characters, commands, and creatures of EverQuest, game economies play a huge role in giving any game its particular flavor. Carefully balance the ingredients, choose just the right spice, and hungry players will keep coming back for more.

Further Reading on this Topic

Rules of Play: Game Design Fundamentals, Katie Salen and Eric Zimmerman.
Cambridge: MIT Press, 2004.

> *Recommended:*
> Chapter 5: Systems
> Chapter 14: Games as Emergent Systems

Synthetic Worlds: The Business and Culture of Online Games, Edward Castronova.
Chicago: University of Chicago Press, 2006.

"Metagames," Richard Garfield.
Horsemen of the Apocalypse: Essays on Roleplaying, ed. Jim Dietz.
Sigel: Jolly Rogers Games, 2000, p. 16–22.

"Game Systems, Parts I, II, III," Ron-Evans Hale.
www.thegamesjournal.com/articles/GameSystems1.shtml;
www.thegamesjournal.com/articles/GameSystems2.shtml;
www.thegamesjournal.com/articles/GameSystems3.shtml.

Emergence: The Connected Lives of Ants, Brains, Cities, and Software, Steven Johnson.
Recommended, chapter 5: Control Artist.
New York: Scribner, 2001.

RE:PLAY: Game Design + Game Culture, Amy Scholder and Eric Zimmerman, eds.
Recommended, Module 4: Games as Exchange.
New York: Walter Lang, 2004.

Game Spaces

What does space contribute to the experience of play?

"Complete Freedom of Movement": 330
Video Games as Gendered Play Spaces
Henry Jenkins

Eyeball; Cathexis 558
David Sudnow

Game Design as Narrative Architecture 670
Henry Jenkins

Adventure as a Video Game: 690
Adventure for the Atari 2600
Warren Robinett

Eastern Front (1941) 714
Chris Crawford

You are in a maze of twisty little passages, all alike.—*Adventure*

The design and organization of space is a concern central not only to game designers but also to those studying player behavior. What kinds of activities and interactions does the game space encourage or discourage? Do players hang out, trade goods, or race through at break-neck speed? What strategic or storytelling opportunities does the space afford, and what forms of navigation does it support? As D.B. Weiss notes in the videogame-inspired novel *Lucky Wander Boy,* games offer an entirely new kind of spatial frontier:

> When a Pac-Man disappears into one of the off-screen mid-maze tunnels, there is a lag of about a half second before he reemerges on the other side. Assuming his speed remains constant, we can extrapolate some other-dimensional space of approximately six dots' length that the Pac-Man must traverse each time he goes through the off-screen tunnel.... In its evocation of an unseen world beyond the rectangle of the seen screen, *Pac-Man* forces us to reckon with a space that is real, yet never experienced directly, empirically.

Game spaces allow for and restrict player action, whether the wide-open cityscapes of *Grand Theft Auto,* or the grooved tracks of *Frequency* and *Amplitude.* As representational systems with spatial dimensions, games give players a chance to build meaning through spatialized interaction. Pass Go, collect $200. Type "N" to move North. Use the D-Pad to control the camera. B-7, hit: You sunk my battleship! The essays included in this Topic are dedicated to understanding the narrative, interactive, informational, strategic, imaginative, and experiential qualities of the spaces found in videogames.

Technology plays a large role in determining the nature and qualities of these spaces. From text-based adventure games and vector-drawn space fields to real-time rendered, physics-enabled 3D, the affordances and limitations of technology determine a great deal about how game spaces are depicted and inhabited. Technology informs space informs design.

In the essay "Eastern Front (1941)," veteran game designer Chris Crawford discusses his use of a revolutionary new scrolling map technology (circa 1980) as the basis for his game Eastern Front (1941). Because the technology allowed Crawford to run a map offscreen, he designed a game space that extended up to four screens in each direction, giving players the chance to scroll into these hidden areas during game play. The extension of the game map opened up many new strategic possibilities for the player, and inspired Crawford to invent a form of A.I. specifically for the kinds of spatial movement afforded by the map.

Although scrolling 2D spaces have since become extremely common in games (from Earthworm Jim to Starcraft), a tremendous amount can be learned from the ways designers originally wrestled with these new challenges. Take Adventure, for example, a game chronicled in "Adventure as a Video Game: Adventure for the Atari 2600," by Warren Robinett. The impossible spaces that make up the mazes of Adventure are remarkable pieces of networked architecture. Players use a joystick to move a cursor through a complicated series of screens connected edge to edge, doing their best not to get lost while avoiding a trio of hungry dragons. Although there are plenty of tasks to complete—finding keys, unlocking castles, and sword fighting dragons—players spend most of their time navigating, exploring, and interacting with Adventure's remarkably intricate spaces.

Unlike a scrolling map, Adventure uses a spatial configuration of discrete rooms, connected in both predictable and surprising ways. At the time, this form of videogame space was revolutionary. As Robinett notes, "The action of the game could therefore take place in a much larger and more interesting space than the single screen of most of the then-current video games."

Inspired directly by the early text adventure also called "Adventure," Robinett gave himself the task of turning textually represented space into the televised space of a videogame. The representational implications were immense:

> In a text adventure, a room is a single location. Although there are passages to other rooms, the room itself has no internal structure. A video adventure, by comparison, allows the player to have a position within a room, shown on the screen by the cursor's position.

By allowing the player to have a position within the room (depicted through graphics), an abstract space described only in words had to be made concrete, and each pixel explicitly defined. Not content with an ordinary spatial simulation, Robinett created spaces in his game that defied the logic of the real world. For example, the four mazes of Adventure rely on an inconsistent geometry that makes the topology of the map impossible to depict in flat form.

Players must abandon their normal assumptions about how space works, in order to navigate the wraparound and nonretraceable paths of which Adventure's mazes were made.

Adventure's spatial design makes clear that game space is more than just the perception of pixels on a screen, pieces on a gameboard, or athletes on a field. As these spaces are perceived, entered, navigated, and inhabited by players, they grow to include the perceptual and cognitive apparatuses of the players themselves. For example, spaces that seem simple or small upon first glance can grow in complexity and size as players gain fluency in the actions such spaces afford. Space, it seems, is in the eye of the beholder. As David Sudnow notes of his experience with the 8-bit game Breakout in "Eyeball" (taken from his marvelous book *Pilgrim in a Microworld*):

> Of course size is relative, the more competent you become the more these lights take on a sort of environmental density and you're pulled by the fingertips onto a full-scale playing field whose dimensions aren't found on rulers.

Sudnow, writing from the perspective of neither a game designer nor an academic, but from that of a player, reveals the process by which players learn to read the space of a game, authoring their own responses through strategic play:

> ...I began getting off on the action, building control and precision in these gentle little calibrations. With slow shots my gaze could lift a bit off from the finer details of the ball's path to roam the court analytically, to glance at my paddle, then where the ball would hit the barricade, and then ahead to predict where it'd hit the side so I could position myself in advance.

The space of Breakout demands an instant geometry of response. Players must scrutinize the interlocking structure of bricks, learning to feel their way through them in accord with a careful timing of shots. The form of the space must be discovered through play if the player is to ever move successfully through it. Game spaces are systems, and become known only through interaction.

But the space of digital games goes beyond technology and coordinate geometry, beyond the perception and cognition of space, to include social and cultural structures as well. The final two essays in this Topic are from a series written by Henry Jenkins, director of the Comparative Media Studies program at MIT. In them, Jenkins argues that "game consoles should be regarded as machines for generating compelling spaces...and that the core narrative behind many games centers around the struggle to explore, map, and master contested spaces." For example, in "Game Design as Narrative Architecture," Jenkins discusses the ways that game space facilitates narrative experience. More than a container for player action, the space of a game is *a space of representation* that helps a player build meaning.

Jenkins's second contribution, "'Complete Freedom of Movement': Video Games as Gendered Play Spaces" connects spaces found in videogames to traditional play areas like backyards and back lots. By their very design, such spaces empower different forms of imaginative play, which can be categorized along gendered lines. The spaces of SuperMario Bros., for example, parallel the kinds of spaces depicted in nineteenth- and early-twentieth-century boy's adventure stories, like *Treasure Island* and *The Jungle Book*. Characters in both book and game must race across unknown frontiers, encounter and vanquish enemies, and map uncharted territories. "Girl spaces," on the other hand, encourage different forms of spatial exploration:

> ...play spaces for girls adopt a slower pace, are less filled with dangers, invite gradual investigation and discovery, foster an awareness of social relations and a search for secrets, center around emotional relations between characters... [they] allow for the exploration of physical environments, but are really about the interior world of feelings and fears.

As Jenkins and others point out, digital game space needs to be understood as more than a series of polygons or pixelated images experienced on a screen. It is something bounded by technology, processed by the hand, eye, and mind, and embodied in the real and imagined identities of players. Too often, the design of digital game space is taken for granted and the results are flat-footed attempts at "realistic" 3D environments. For all of their real-time-rendered, texture-mapped geometry, there are few contemporary videogames that demonstrate the sheer spatial imagination of Adventure's mind-bending mazes.

By rediscovering the technological, experiential, and cultural possibilities of space, we can look at game design in new ways, and construct spaces undreamed of in other media. Perhaps inventive spatial models will emerge as we become tired of the same 3D game spaces. Or perhaps they will grow from mixed-reality games like I Love Bees, Majestic, or Can You See Me Now? Or from groundbreaking historical precedents like Cubism, Fluxus, or Surrealist collage. But perhaps tomorrow's game spaces simply cannot be visualized today. The limitations of one generation's game spaces may become the defining feature of another. Space is indeed a final frontier.

Further Reading on this Topic

Rules of Play: Game Design Fundamentals, **Katie Salen and Eric Zimmerman.**
Cambridge: MIT Press, 2004.
   Recommended:
   Chapter 26: Games as Narrative Play
   Chapter 27: Games as the Play of Simulation
   Chapter 33: Games as Cultural Environment

"Theory of the Derive," Guy Debord.
http://library.nothingness.org

The Practice of Everyday Life, **Michel De Certeau.**
Berkeley: University of California Press, 1984.
Recommended, p. 11–32: General Introduction; 91–110: Spatial Practices: Walking in the City.

"The Art of Contested Spaces," Henry Jenkins and Kurt Squire.
Game On: The History and Culture of Video Games, Lucien King, ed.
London: Laurence Ling Publishing Ltd., 2002.

"'This is Not a Game': Immersive Aesthetics and Collective Play," Jane McGonigal.
Digital Arts & Culture 2003 Conference Proceedings, Melbourne. May 2003.

"The Geography of a Non-Place," Torill Mortensen.
http://www.dichtungdigital.de/2003/issue/ 4mortens/index.htm

"Space in the Video Game," Mark J. P. Wolf.
The Medium of the Video Game.
Austin: University of Texas Press, 2002, p. 53–70.

Cultural Representation

What aspects of culture do games model and represent?

"Complete Freedom of Movement": 330
Video Games as Gendered Play Spaces
Henry Jenkins

Frames and Games 578
Gary Alan Fine

Bow, Nigger 602
always_black

Cultural Models: 610
Do You Want to Be the Blue Sonic or the Dark Sonic?
James Gee

Fanciful words can speak about make-believe places, but these words can only be spoken in the real world.—Erving Goffman

Games are not only spaces of strategic possibility—places to battle, puzzle, explore, and socialize, but are also spaces of *representation,* of things both real and make-believe. The Sims 2, for example, contains thousands of representations: of people, objects, actions, attitudes, behaviors, and emotions...you name it. Sometimes these representations depict things known to us from the real world, like hot tubs and toasters that can be put inside a house. At other times, game representations model made-up things, such as a house with walls that become invisible. In either case, the game is a complex representational system, one made meaningful through designed player interaction. Like a sheet of music sitting on a music stand, a game's potential for representation is not fully realized until it is played.

Gameplay always already operates on a level of representation. Beyond physical engagement with an input device, players also interact with the representations of a game on an interpretive level, bringing knowledge, assumptions, and expectations drawn from the real world to bear on determining what depictions in a game might *mean.* A "king" in Chess has certain meanings within the game (it is more valuable than a pawn, for example). Because the concept of a "king" also exists outside of the game, however, we bring additional real-world understanding to our reading of the representation within the game. Thus if a Chess "king" were renamed a "pimp," the meaning of that particular piece would trigger an entirely different set of symbolic associations—even if its in-game abilities remained unchanged.

A system of game representations—whether depictions of gender, race, class, power, history, religion, or politics—forms a whole "universe of discourse" that can be interpreted and read in a number of ways. The representation of "battle" in a military simulation like Battlefield 1942, for example, certainly means something different from what it would mean in a game like Pokèmon. We could go through a similar exercise by looking at representations of female game characters, or at how notions of the Other are constructed in American games about Japan. To "read" the representation of a game, we can bring whole armies of interpretive theories to bear, from Marxism and Feminism to Post-stucturalist literary criticism. Yet let's not forget that the important question is not how we understand just any cultural representation, but the specific ways that *game* representations are made, read, and played.

71

The idea that games are unique spaces of both representation and interpretation is at the heart of the four diverse essays included within this Topic. "Frames and Games" tackles the problems of simulation, player identity, and representation. "Cultural Models: Do You Want to Be the Blue Sonic or the Dark Sonic?" addresses the issue of player representation and the belief systems that shape game play. "'Complete Freedom of Movement': Video Games as Gendered Play Spaces" takes gender representation as its subject, discussing how certain types of game spaces express traditional notions of "boy" and "girl" culture. Finally, "Bow, Nigger" offers a compelling and sometimes uncomfortable walk through the cultural minefield of player-character representation.

In "Frames and Games," ethnographer Gary Alan Fine situates a discussion of representation and interpretation within the realm of fantasy role-playing games. In games where players must act within a fantasy world, there is a particular kind of representational ambiguity. Participants constantly shift representations of their own identities between their status as a person in the real world, a player in the game, and a character being played by that player. As Fine explains,

> In fantasy gaming, players not only manipulate characters, they are characters. The character identity is separate from the player identity. In this, fantasy gaming is distinct from other games. It makes no sense in chess to speak of "black" as being distinct from Karpov the player.... The pieces in chess ("black") have no more or less knowledge than their animator. However, Sir Ralph the Rash, the doughty knight, lacks some information that his player has, (for example, about characteristics of other characters, and spheres of game knowledge outside his ken such as clerical miracles) and has some information that his player lacks.... To speak of a chess knight as having different knowledge from its animator might make for good fantasy but not for meaningful chess.

As players manipulate their own identities and those of their characters, they are at the same time manipulating the representational space of the game. A fantasy role-player must be aware of his or her own status as a character within the game, and model the representation of that character in an appropriate manner. If Sir Ralph the Rash were to suddenly start acting on knowledge he couldn't possibly have, confusion in the representational fidelity of the character would occur. It is this very ambiguity, spurred on by the status of players as beings in the real world that makes role-playing games so fascinating from a representational perspective.

While Fine looks at the complex way identity is created during a game, literacy and education scholar James Gee widens his lens to look at how games sit within culture at large. Gee's contribution, "Cultural Models: Do you want to be the Blue Sonic or the Dark Sonic?" uses several case studies to outline the kinds of cultural baggage players bring to the interpretation of games. In the Syrian game Under Ash, for example, the player is cast as a young Palestinian resisting Israeli soldiers and settlers. The game posits a political and cultural perspective different from that presented by many games native to the United States. As Gee writes, determining who did and did not count as a "civilian" in the game was something of a revelation.

> I was originally surprised...that settlers (since they are not in the army) didn't count as civilians. But then I realized that this game accepts a cultural model in terms of which the settlers are seen as the "advance" troops of the occupation army.

Players must understand not only the logical "rules of play," but also the cultural framework informing its representation. Knowing who does and does not constitute a civilian in a military shooter affects the ability of a player to follow the rules of the game and to play well. In a game like America's Army, designed for the U.S. military, players must interpret character action, characteristics, and game mechanics through a particular cultural lens. Players of Under Ash must also employ an interpretive lens, albeit one with a radically different political ideology.

When games model some aspect of culture, as does a first-person shooter like Under Ash or a historical simulation like Civilization III, players must be aware of the kinds of meanings the game space supports. If they are not, there is a chance that their performance in the game will be affected, for, as Gee points out, they will not understand the "rules" that guide their action in the world. At the same time, a game designer must be deeply aware of the cultural system his or her game is modeling, the degree to which it is drawing on outside references, and how much of the game depends on a player's understanding of these references. Players who are well versed in the social etiquette of elves and dwarves will do much better in a game dependent on such knowledge than players who are blind to these hidden cultural codes.

Cultural representations can be a conscious or unconscious part of a game's design. Regardless of designer intention, games can be powerful spaces for players to learn about, play with, and even transform culture. In "'Complete Freedom of Movement': Video Games as Gendered Play Spaces," Henry Jenkins discusses the way certain games serve to support traditional notions of "boy" and "girl" culture. Connecting videogames and late-nineteenth-century children's literature, Jenkins makes a thoughtful reading of the cultural geography of videogame spaces. Rather than looking only at the images games employ, he instead turns his attention to the design of game spaces and the kinds of activities they encourage or deny. Some game spaces, such as Mario-style platform scrollers, support interactions and behaviors consistent with traditional ideas of "boy culture."

> The central virtues of the nineteenth-century "boy culture" were mastery and self-control. The boys set tasks and goals for themselves, which required discipline in order to complete. Through this process of setting and meeting challenges, they acquired the virtues of manhood.

The core of Jenkins's analysis goes against the common preconception that videogames are a form of media culture without precedent, removed from more historically traditional forms of play. At the same time, Jenkins concludes his essay by speculating on how games might evolve to engender different and more progressive play spaces. While Jenkins's essay focuses solely on the geography of space and gender, his approach to looking for representational biases within games could also be applied to research around race, class, ethnicity or other similar issues.

In an essay mined from the increasingly sophisticated body of writing authored by gamers and designers, and posted to blogs and fan forums, always_black tells us that "...my screen name has nothing to do with my ethnicity." "Bow, Nigger" is a small, sharp piece of writing, a case study in the representational twists and turns of identity online. The essay gives a blow-by-blow description of a duel between the author and another player in Jedi Knights II: Outcast. The language cuts like a knife.

> "Are you really a black nigger?" he types.
>
> "Why?" I replied.
>
> "Because it matter," he says.

What is significant about this essay—beyond the insight it offers into gamer subculture and the representational ambiguity inherent in any online interaction, particularly as performed along cultural lines—is the way the writer seamlessly shifts voice between player and character. In the spirit of Fine's essay, always_black negotiates the terrain of cultural representation as he slips on and off identities that depict his real-world persona, his status as player, his role as a Jedi in the game, and the meaning of all these in relation to the culture of *Star Wars*. It is a remarkable piece of writing that highlights the many layers of symbolic exchange that must be negotiated by players acting within fictionalized worlds.

Games reflect the values of the society in which they are played because they are part of the fabric of that society. Any game designer or game scholar who doesn't engage with games on the level of cultural representation is missing out on a very important part of the picture. As "Bow, Nigger" reminds us, hiding behind theoretical discussions of player identity and cultural representation are the very real bodies and minds of players. In representing aspects of culture—from depictions of good and evil in Black and White to representations of race and class in GTA San Andreas—games create profound and often visceral experiences for players.

Further Reading on this Topic

Rules of Play: Game Design Fundamentals, Katie Salen and Eric Zimmerman.
Cambridge: MIT Press, 2004.

    Recommended:
    Chapter 31: Games as Open Culture
    Chapter 32: Games as Cultural Resistance

From Barbie to Mortal Kombat: Gender and Computer Games, Justine Cassell and Henry Jenkins, eds.
Cambridge: MIT Press, 1998.

Killing Monsters: Why Children Need Fantasy, Superheroes, and Make-Believe Violence, Gerard Jones.
New York: Basic Books, 2002.

"Lara Croft: Feminist Icon or Cyberbimbo?" H. W. Kennedy.
Game Studies: The International Journal of Computer Game Research 2: 1-12.

Trigger Happy: Videogames and the Entertainment Revolution, Steven Poole.
New York: Arcade Publishing, 2000.

What Is a Game? ⌒

How can we define what makes a game a game?

The Definition of Games: The Classification of Games 122
Roger Caillois

Construction of a Definition 172
Bernard Suits

I Have No Words & I Must Design 192
Greg Costikyan

Games and Design Patterns 410
Staffan Björk and Jussi Holopainen

Consider, for example, the proceedings that we call "games." I mean board-games, card-games, ball-games, Olympic games, and so on. What is common to them all?—Don't say: "There must be something common, or they would not be called 'games'"—but look and see whether there is anything common to all.—For if you look at them you will not see something that is common to all, but...a complicated network of similarities overlapping and criss-crossing: sometimes overall similarities, sometimes similarities of detail.

—Ludwig Wittgenstein

In *Philosophical Investigations,* the philosopher Ludwig Wittgenstein uses "games" as an example of why it is impossible to arrive at a precise definition of any real-world phenomenon. Perhaps philosophers can afford such radical skepticism. But for those of us involved with games, it is important to understand what it is we are studying, designing, or analyzing.

Definitions can be slippery creatures, and we're certainly not trying to assert that there is just one absolute definition of games, lurking out there somewhere, waiting to be found. Many great definitions exist today, illuminating concepts that can aid in research, theory, and design. A definition of "game" that helps a game designer to create a new genre of commercial product will be very different from a definition that helps a sociologist to construct a new research problem about player behavior. At the same time, both designer and sociologist might learn something unexpected by looking at their own work through the definitions of the other. This is the spirit of the Topic at hand, which brings different points of view to bear on the wonderfully troublesome task of defining games.

What is a Game? What indeed. Defining "games" is a formidable challenge, if we consider all of the activities and objects, both on and off the computer, which might be considered a game. The scope of inclusion—the range of what is and what is not considered a game—is one important feature of the four diverse definitions we examine in this Topic. Perhaps even more important is not just what each author considers a game, but the very nature of how they approach the task of constructing a definition.

Anthropologist Roger Caillois, one of the earliest authors to try and define games, casts his definitional net wide. The second chapter of *Man, Play and Games,* "The Definition of Play: The Classification of Games," attempts to typologize all of the diverse phenomena that he considers to be a game. Building on the concept of play established in the first chapter of his book, Caillois considers a wide gamut of playful behaviors. These range from rule-bound *ludus* pursuits, such as playing Chess, to free-wheeling, improvisational paida activities, like spinning around to get dizzy. Caillois adds a second axis to the ludus/paida continuum, composed of four general categories of games: *agôn* (competition), *alea* (chance), *illinx* (vertigo), and *mimicry* (make-believe).

Can such a model be understood as a definition of games? Certainly, but one presented in an atypical format. Caillois presents his definition *by taxonomy,* identifying what games are through a rigorous system of classification. The strength of his descriptive approach is that it builds directly on real-world play phenomena. However, some of the activities Caillois includes, such as ballroom dancing and mountain climbing, indicate that he may have been overly inclusive in constructing his definition of game. Perhaps this is because in French, as in many languages, the words for "play" and "game" are quite close. In French, to play a game is *"jouer à un jeu."*

Philosopher Bernard Suits, in his book *Grasshopper: Games, Life and Utopia,* takes a different approach: he offers a brief, definitional statement. In its shortest form, his definition of playing a game is "the voluntary effort to overcome unnecessary obstacles." Suits's definition differs from Caillois's not only in structure, but also in focus. Rather than identifying the *form* of a game, Suits defines the state of mind of the game player—an agenda linked to the knotty philosophical problems of playing and reality he attacks in the rest of his book. His definition is less useful for determining what is and isn't a game, but is quite helpful in identifying what is unique about playing them. Suits's concept of the game player's "lusory attitude" is a cornerstone of our own thinking about games.

Greg Costikyan, in contrast to Caillois and Suits, is a game designer, and his definition of games reflects his disciplinary point of view:

> A game is a form of art in which participants, termed players, make decisions in order to manage resources through game tokens in the pursuit of a goal.

Here is yet a different approach: the bulk of Costikyan's definition concerns itself with the way players take action in a game. Costikyan's definition reads like a laundry list of game design ingredients: players, decisions, resources, tokens, and a goal. Significantly, Costikyan considers games a form of art, and he spends the first part of his essay emphasizing what games are *not* (toys, stories, or puzzles). For Costikyan, games are a form of culture, and it is important to carve out a unique space for them, separating them from phenomena that are similar to but ultimately distinct from games. As a producer of games, Costikyan has a very real stake in defining their unique cultural status.

Staffan Björk and Jussi Holopainen have a very different point of view about definitions, and they state it quite clearly in their work on game design patterns:

> We, however, rejected the possibility to start from one specific definition in order to create tools for understanding and designing games.... We are not saying that definitions are not useful, for a definition lets us know what a game is.... However, a definition of a game does not help us make design decisions within the design space of all possible games. Just as having a definition of a house does not provide more than vague guidelines of how to build a house (it should have walls and a roof), having a definition of what a game is does not give us more than the most basic ideas of what a game should contain.[1]

This is a powerful argument against the utility of definitions. Yet Björk and Holopainen do end up creating a definition, despite what they say. Much of their work on game patterns focuses on identifying the atomic elements of games, the constituent parts that make up the form, structure, and experience of games. Their approach provides an alternate model for creating a definition—one that is not top-down, but instead arises bottom-up from an investigation of the elements common to all games. This approach may not be very useful for those engaged in a philosophical debate about what is or is not a game, but their flexible concepts are quite handy for understanding and solving game design problems. And as Björk and Holopainen make abundantly clear, this is ultimately what they aim to achieve in their work.

What makes these four essays so delightful is not only the richness of their proposed definitions, but the wide range of approaches taken. A definition does not have to assume the form of a dictionary-style sentence. For Caillois, a definition takes the shape of a grid of characteristics; for Björk and Holopainen, an open list of formal attributes. And there are other approaches as well. In *Rules of Play,* we compare several definitions and synthesize our own. So does game designer and theorist Jesper Juul, who in his essay "The Game, the Player, the World: Looking for a Heart of Gameness" boils down several definitions into one:

> A game is a rule-based system with a variable and quantifiable outcome, where different outcomes are assigned different values, the player exerts effort in order to influence the outcome, the player feels attached to the outcome, and the consequences of the activity are optional and negotiable.

Is that *the* definition of game? Does it matter? The real question is not *what* the definition is, but *why* games require such definitions and *how* they can be utilized. For Björk and Holopainen, a definition is a design tool. For Suits, defining a game is a philosophical device for raising issues about the nature of truth, lying, and social interaction. For Costikyan, a definition justifies a creative practice. For Jesper Juul and Roger Caillois, definitions are ways to identify new fields of study. In fact, in some way, every essay in *The Game Design Reader* contains an implicit definition of the term "game."

Definitions are not perfect creatures. They have weaknesses, holes, and exceptions. And while we might know a game when we see one, the details are always open for debate. There may never be a definitive answer to the question, "What is a game?" but that's perfectly all right with us. Definitions are concepts that do work: they are, to quote MIT scientist Marvin Minsky, "things to think with." In identifying what games are and what they are not, in using definitions to refashion our preconceptions of games, we can open up new spaces to see what games are, what they should be, and what they might become.

End Note

1. *Patterns in Game Design,* Staffan Björk and Jussi Holopainen. Hingham, MA: Charles River Media, 2005.

Further Reading on this Topic

Rules of Play: Game Design Fundamentals, Katie Salen and Eric Zimmerman.

Cambridge: MIT Press, 2004.

> *Recommended:*
>
> Chapter 7: Defining Games
>
> Chapter 8: Defining Digital Games
>
> Chapter 33: Games as Cultural Environment

The Study of Games, E. M. Avedon and Brian Sutton-Smith, eds.

Recommended: "The Structural Elements of Games," E. M. Avedon and Brian Sutton-Smith.

New York: Wiley, 1971.

"Chapter 1: What is a Game?" Chris Crawford.

The Art of Computer Game Design.

www.vancouver.wsu.edu/fac/peabody/game-book/Coverpage.html.

Half-Real: Video Games between Real Rules and Fictional Worlds, Jesper Juul.

Cambridge: MIT Press, 2005.

Recommended, chapter 2: Videogames and the Classic Game Model.

What Is Play?

What are the forms and meanings of play?

Nature and Significance of Play as a Cultural Phenomenon 96
Johan Huizinga

The Definition of Play; The Classification of Games 122
Roger Caillois

Play and Ambiguity 296
Brian Sutton-Smith

A Theory of Play and Fantasy 314
Gregory Bateson

The most irritating feature of play is not the perceptual incoherence, as such, but rather that play taunts us with its in accessibility. We feel that something is behind it all, but we do not know, or have forgotten how to see it.—Robert Fagen

A woman rushing to work notices a chalk grid scrawled on the sidewalk beneath her feet: nine squares brimming with slashed Xs and wobbly Os. She smiles as she hurries past, imagining a group of young children huddled in a conspiratorial circle, strategizing their moves in what she takes as nothing more than a simple game. But to the players of the game, the experience is far less than simple. There is the psychological intensity of the conflict, the turn-based rhythm of the sidewalk choreography, the bragging rights wagered, and won—or lost. Play happens all around us. Yet truly understanding play demands something more.

Games create play: of that there is no doubt. But there is much more to this relationship, as four texts from Johan Huizinga, Roger Caillois, Gregory Bateson, and Brian Sutton-Smith point out. Navigating a web of competing definitions, this Topic asks: Where is play found? What forms does it take? And why does it matter anyway?

"Nature and Significance of Play as a Cultural Phenomenon" is the opening chapter of *Homo Ludens,* one of the most important and influential texts ever written on the study of play. Johan Huizinga looks at play, not in terms of biology or psychology, but in *social and cultural* terms, writing, "We shall not look for the natural impulses and habits conditioning play in general, but shall consider play in its manifold concrete forms as itself a social construction. We shall try to take play as the player himself takes it: in it primary significance." Huizinga chooses to deal fundamentally with "what play is *in itself* and what it means for the player."

The significance of Huizinga's chapter lies not so much in the accuracy of his ideas, which are still being debated today, but in his radical attempt to tackle the problem of play as a function of culture. Rather than defining play within the Marxist ideology popular at the time of its writing (work, not play, was considered central to society), *Homo Ludens* recasts play in experiential terms. In exploring the nature and significance of play, Huizinga not only puts forth an exacting definition, but also argues that play is essential to all aspects of culture—from art and religion to law and war. In subsequent decades, many play scholars have taken up this challenge to frame play as not just a wasteful pastime, but as the complex product of formal, social, and cultural patterns.

Following closely on the theoretical heels of Huizinga is Roger Caillois, whose book *Man, Play, and Games* is a direct response to *Homo Ludens.* Caillois critiques Huizinga for not attempting to classify games themselves. He calls *Homo Ludens* "not the study of games, but an inquiry into the creative quality of the play principle in the domain of culture." In "The Definition of Play: The Classification of Games," Caillois not only constructs a modified version of Huizinga's definition of play, but also provides a concrete taxonomy of play forms.

Expanding Huizinga's focus on play as competition, Caillois offers four play rubrics—*agôn* (competition), *alea* (chance), *illinx* (vertigo), and *mimicry* (make-believe). Each describes a type of game based on fundamental experiential qualities of play. For example, games that fall under the category of illinx, such as Ring-Around-the-Rosy, involve instability of perception and a physical surrender to vertigo, seizure, or shock. Because Caillois's categories are based on the player's *experience,* they offer game designers a surprisingly useful conceptual toolbox with which to toy and tinker. Caillois's four rubrics can be used to analyze game experience, tune game designs in progress, or generate new game ideas.

Whereas Huizinga and Caillois focus on the essential qualities of play, Gregory Bateson's "A Theory of Play and Fantasy" shifts attention to the significance of play as an act of communication. In his essay, Bateson argues that play was an important step in the evolution of how animals communicate. His imagination was sparked during an afternoon at the zoo:

> What I encountered at the zoo was a phenomenon well known to everybody: I saw two young monkeys playing, i.e., engaged in an interactive sequence of which the unit actions or signals were similar but not the same as those of combat. It was evident, even to the human observer, that the sequence as a whole was not combat, and evident to the human observer that to the participant monkeys this was "not combat."

Bateson goes on to argue that play is an act of *metacommunication,* a form of communication about communication. Play is a kind of metacommunication because any act of play carries the message, "this is play." In the same way that the monkeys' play-fighting communicates that they are "not really fighting," Spin the Bottle players know that their kisses do not mean the same thing as a real, romantic kiss, since they are "just playing." Players perform actions that reference real-world activities. But, at the same time, these same actions communicate the fact that the players are merely "at play." Metacommunication has huge implications for anyone studying or designing games. The fact that a player is always actively aware of being at play provides a fresh way of looking at issues such as game immersion, player-avatar identification, the effects of media, and the way people relate to games in general.

Bateson's idea that play both is and is not what it appears to be is echoed by Brian Sutton-Smith in his essay, "Play and Ambiguity," the introductory chapter to his book *The Ambiguity of Play.* Sutton-Smith is an interdisciplinary scholar and theorist who has spent many years investigating not only play itself, but also the way play is defined and described within discourse. Like Bateson, he is interested in exploring how our understanding of play is constructed—just what do we take play to "mean?" Yet, unlike Bateson, Caillois, or even Huizinga, Sutton-Smith undertakes a metastudy of play by identifying a set of "play rhetorics" or ideological discourses that shape the way we speak about play. As Sutton-Smith writes, "the rhetorics of play express the way play is placed in context within broader value systems."

In other words, Sutton-Smith is interested in exploring the way the concept of play has been studied, used, and constructed across disciplines and cultures. His analysis not only offers insight into what can and cannot be considered play, but also describes an immense cornucopia of play forms and experiences. "Play and Ambiguity" briefly introduces all seven rhetorics: *play as progress, fate, power, identity, the imaginary, the self, and frivolity;* in the rest of his book, he explores each rhetoric in detail.

Any definition of play will be a bit fuzzy at best. But this fuzziness points to the fact that there is something fundamentally unknowable and ephemeral about play, something mysterious and exciting. Play surprises and delights us, moves and transforms us. There is, after all, something *playful* about play. It is this exacting ambiguity that makes play so rich, and potentially so valuable to a range of disciplinary communities. Can a theory of play speak to fields and ideas outside game design and game studies? We think so. The study of play is gaining momentum through the invention of new models, taxonomies, and perspectives. With them, of course, comes the design of potentially revolutionary ways to play.

The essays that follow provide the foundation on which these new experiences will be built, and pave the way for change. Whether these changes will be radical reinventions or incremental shifts of alignment remains to be seen. What will actually come to pass all depends on what we choose to make of it. Take these pages not only as a historical document, but as the first bold steps in defining the legacy of games for the twenty first-century. Make it elegant. Design for innovation. And above all, play like you mean it.

Further Reading on this Topic

Rules of Play: Game Design Fundamentals, Katie Salen and Eric Zimmerman.
Cambridge: MIT Press, 2004.

> *Recommended:*
> Chapter 9: The Magic Circle
> Chapter 22: Defining Play
> Chapter 25: The Play of Meaning

A Book of Surrealist Games, Alastair Brotchie and Mel Gooding.
Boston: Shambhala Press, 1995.

"Deep Play: Notes on the Balinese Cockfight," Clifford Geertz.
Interpretation of Cultures.
New York: Basic Books, 1977.

Situationist Texts.
online at www.nothingness.org.

Child's Play, Brian Sutton-Smith and R. E. Herron, eds.
Malabar: Warrior Books, 1971.

"The Toy As Machine: The Video Game," Brian Sutton-Smith.
Toys as Culture.
New York: Gardner Press, Incorporated, 1986.

Texts: Bibliography

Source of Original Publication

always_black. "Bow, Nigger." www.alwaysblack.com/blackbox/bownigger.html, 2004.

Bartle, Richard. "Hearts, Clubs, Diamonds, Spades: Players Who Suit MUDs." http://www.mud.co.uk/richard/hcds.htm, 1996.

Bateson, Gregory. "A Theory of Play and Fantasy." In *Steps to an Ecology of Mind*. Chicago: The University of Chicago Press, 1972.

Birdwell. Ken. "The Cabal: Valve's Design Process for Creating Half-Life."www.gamasutra.com, December 10, 1999.

Björk, Staffan and Jussi Holopainen. "Games and Design Patterns." Excerpts from *Patterns in Game Design*. Boston: Charles River Media, 2005.

Caillois, Roger. "The Definition of Play": "The Classification of Games." In *Man, Play and Games*. Free Press of Glencoe, Inc., 1961.

Castronova, Edward. "Virtual Worlds: A First-Hand Account of Market and Society on the Cyberian Frontier." CESifo Working Paper Series No. 618, *SSRN* (social Science Research Network), http://papers.ssrn.com, December 2001.

Chick, Tom. "Shoot Club: The DOOM 3 Review." www.quartertothree.com/inhouse/columns/86/, August 5, 2004.

Church, Doug. "Formal Abstract Design Tools," www.gamasutra.com, July 16, 1999.

Costikyan, Greg. "I Have No Words & I Must Design." In *Interactive Fantasy #2*. www.costik.com/nowords.html, 1994.

Crawford, Chris. "Eastern Front (1941)." In *On Game Design*. Berkeley: New Riders Games, 2003.

DeKoven, Bernard. "Changing the Game." In *The Well-Played Game*. New York: Doubleday, 1978.

Garfield, Richard. "The Design Evolution of Magic: The Gathering." In *Game Design Workshop: Designing, Prototyping, and Playtesting Games*, Tracy Fullerton, Steven Hoffman, and Christopher Swain. Manhasset: CMP Books, 2004.

Farmer, F. Randall and Chip Morningstar. "The Lessons of Lucasfilm's Habitat." In *Cyberspace: First Steps*, Michael Benedikt, ed. Cambridge: MIT Press, 1990.

Fine, Gary Alan. "Frames and Games." In *Shared Fantasy*. Chicago: University of Chicago, 1983.

Gee, James Paul. "Semiotic Domains: Is Playing Video Games a "Waste of Time?" In *What Video Games Have to Teach Us About Learning and Literacy*. New York: Palgrave/MacMillan, 2003.

Gee, James Paul. "Cultural Models: Do You Want to Be the Blue Sonic or the Dark Sonic?" In *What Video Games Have to Teach Us About Learning and Literacy.* New York: Palgrave/MacMillan, 2003.

Hughes, Linda. "Beyond the Rules of the Game: Why Are Rooie Rules Nice?." In *The World of Play*, ed. Frank E. Manning. Proceedings of the 7th Annual Meeting of the Association of the Anthropological Study of Play. New York: Leisure Press, 1983.

Huizinga, Johann. "Nature and Significance of Play as a Cultural Phenomenon. "In *Homo Ludens: A Study of the Play Element in Culture.* Boston: Beacon Press, 1955.

Jenkins, Henry. "Complete Freedom of Movement': Video Games as Gendered Play Spaces." In *From Barbie to Mortal Kombat: Gender and Computer Games,* Justine Cassell and Henry Jenkins (eds.). Cambridge: MIT Press, 1998.

Jenkins, Henry. "Game Design as Narrative Architecture." In *First Person: New Media as Story, Performance, and Game,* Noah Windrip-Fruin and Pat Harrigan (eds.). Cambridge: MIT Press, 2004.

Koster, Raph. "Declaring the Rights of Players."www.legendmud.org/raph/gaming/player-rights.html, 2000.

Laurel, Brenda. "Piercing the Spectacle." Original essay, 2005.

LeBlanc, Marc. "Tools for Creating Dramatic Game Dynamics." Original essay, 2005.

Mateas, Michael and Andrew Stern. "Interaction and Narrative." Portions of the essay based on Michael Mateas' Ph.D. Dissertation, *Interactive Drama, Art, and Artificial Intelligence.* Carnegie Mellon. 2000.

Mochan. "The Evil Summoner FAQ v1.0: How to Be a Cheap Ass." dlh.net/cheats/ps2/english/summoner/faq_walkthrough3.html, May 28, 2001.

Poundstone, William. "Game Theory." In *Prisoner's Dilemma.* New York: Doubleday, 1992.

Robinett, Warren. "Adventure as a Video Game: Adventure for the Atari 2600." In *Inventing the Adventure Game.* Unpublished manuscript.

Rouse, Richard III. "Game Analysis: Centipede." *Game Design: Theory and Practice.* Plano, TX: Wordware Publishing, 2004.

Sniderman, Stephen. "Unwritten Rules." *The Life of Games,* No. 1, October 1999. www.gamepuzzles.com/tlog/tlog2.htm.

Sudnow, David. "Eyeball;" "Cathexis." In *Pilgrim in the Microworld.* New York: Warner Books, 1983.

Suits, Bernard. "Construction of a Definition." In *Grasshopper: Games, Life and Utopia.* Boston: David R. Godine, 1990.

Sutton-Smith, Brian. "Play and Ambiguity." In *The Ambiguity of Play.* Boston: Harvard University Press, 2001.

Topics:

Texts:	The Player Experience	The Rules of a Game	Gaming the Game	The Game Design Process	Player and Character	Games and Narrative	Game Communities	Speaking of Games	Game Design Models	Game Economies	Game Spaces	Cultural Representation	What Is a Game?	What Is Play?
Huizinga								x						x
Caillois	x				x								x	x
Chick	x						x							
Suits		x											x	
Costikyan		x											x	
Birdwell				x										
Gee (Semiotic Domains)								x						
Mochan			x						x					
Sutton-Smith								x						x
Bateson					x									x
Jenkins (Complete Freedom)	x										x	x		
Church									x					
Poundstone									x					
Björk | Holopainen		x							x				x	
LeBlanc	x					x			x					
Rouse III	x								x					
Sniderman		x	x					x						
Hughes		x					x							
DeKoven			x	x										
Garfield				x						x				
Sudnow	x										x			
Fine				x		x						x		
always_black				x								x		
Gee (Cultural Models)								x				x		
Mateas | Stern					x	x								
Jenkins (Game Design)					x						x			
Robinett									x		x			
Crawford				x							x			
Farmer | Morningstar		x	x				x							
Bartle	x						x			x				
Koster		x					x							
Castronova							x			x				

10 POINTS

INVASION OF TOKYO > SUCCESSFUL

 × 75   SCORE = 0950

3

INVASION OF AUSTRALIA

PERTH	👾 × 26	SCORE	= 400
MELBOURN	👾 × 26	SCORE	= 440
TOTAL	👾 × 52	SCORE	= 800

I 👾 NY

INVASION OF LOS ANGELES

WAVE 01	👾 × 41	SCORE	= 0670
WAVE 02	👾 × 24	SCORE	= 0480
WAVE 03	👾 × 28	SCORE	= 0480
WAVE 04	👾 × 11	SCORE	= 0180
TOTAL	👾 × 104	SCORE	= 2070

Nature and Significance of Play as a Cultural Phenomenon

Johan Huizinga

Context

*The title of **Homo Ludens: A Study of the Play Element in Culture,** the book for which this essay serves as the opening chapter, is a play on **Homo sapiens** meaning "Man, the player." A wide-ranging work that touches on numerous aspects of the influence of play on culture, it was first published in 1938.*

Speaking of Games

What Is Play?

Johan Huizinga (1872–1945) has been called the greatest Dutch cultural historian. Huizinga held a number of distinguished academic posts during his lifetime, including chairman of the Division of Letters of the Royal Dutch Academy of the Sciences. He published a number of books on a wide range of political, historical, and cultural subjects, including *The Autumn of the Middle Ages*, the biography *Erasmus and the Age of Reformation*, and *Men and Ideas: History, the Middle Ages, the Renaissance*, a book of essays.

Johan Huizinga, *Homo Ludens,* 1955. Reprinted by permission of Beacon Press.

Play is older than culture, for culture, however inadequately defined, always presupposes human society, and animals have not waited for man to teach them their playing. We can safely assert, even, that human civilization has added no essential feature to the general idea of play. Animals play just like men. We have only to watch young dogs to see that all the essentials of human play are present in their merry gambols. They invite one another to play by a certain ceremoniousness of attitude and gesture. They keep to the rule that you shall not bite, or not bite hard, your brother's ear. They pretend to get terribly angry. And—what is most important—in all these doings they plainly experience tremendous fun and enjoyment. Such rompings of young dogs are only one of the simpler forms of animal play. There are other, much more highly developed forms: regular contests and beautiful performances before an admiring public.

Here we have at once a very important point: even in its simplest forms on the animal level, play is more than a mere physiological phenomenon or a psychological reflex. It goes beyond the confines of purely physical or purely biological activity. It is a *significant* function— that is to say, there is some sense to it. In play there is something "at play" which transcends the immediate needs of life and imparts meaning to the action. All play means something. If we call the active principle that makes up the essence of play, "instinct," we explain nothing; if we call it "mind" or "will" we say too much. However we may regard it, the very fact that play has a meaning implies a non-materialistic quality in the nature of the thing itself.

Psychology and physiology deal with the observation, description and explanation of the play of animals, children, and grown-ups. They try to determine the nature and significance of play and to assign it its place in the scheme of life. The high importance of this place and the necessity, or at least the utility, of play as a function are generally taken for granted and form the starting-point of all such scientific researches. The numerous attempts to define the biological function of play show a striking variation. By some the origin and fundamentals of play have been described as a discharge of superabundant vital energy, by others as the satisfaction of some "imitative instinct," or again as simply a "need" for relaxation. According to one theory play constitutes a training of the young creature for the serious work that life will demand later on. According to another it serves as an exercise in restraint needful to the individual. Some find the principle of play in an innate urge to exercise a certain faculty, or in the desire to dominate or compete. Yet others regard it as an "abreaction"—an outlet for harmful impulses, as the necessary restorer of energy wasted by one-sided activity, as "wish-fulfilment," as a fiction designed to keep up the feeling of personal value, etc.[1]

All these hypotheses have one thing in common: they all start from the assumption that play must serve something which is *not* play, that it must have some kind of biological purpose. They all enquire into the why and the wherefore of play. The various answers they give tend rather to overlap than to exclude one another. It would be perfectly possible to accept nearly all the explanations without getting into any real confusion of thought—and without coming much nearer to a real understanding of the play-concept. They are all only partial solutions of the problem. If any of them were really decisive it ought either to exclude all the others or comprehend them in a higher unity. Most of them only deal incidentally with the question of what play is *in itself* and what it means for the player. They attack play direct with the quantitative methods of experimental science without first paying attention to its profoundly aesthetic quality. As a rule they leave the primary quality of play as such, virtually untouched. To each and every one of the above "explanations" it might well be objected. "So far so good, but what actually is the *fun* of playing? Why does the baby crow with pleasure? Why does the gambler lose himself in his passion? Why is a huge crowd roused to frenzy by a football match?" This intensity of, and absorption in, play finds no explanation in biological analysis. Yet in this intensity, this absorption, this power of maddening, lies the very essence, the primordial quality of play. Nature, so our reasoning mind tells us, could just as easily have given her children all those useful functions of discharging superabundant energy, of relaxing after exertion, of training for the demands of life, of compensating for unfulfilled longings, etc., in the form of purely mechanical exercises and reactions. But no, she gave us play, with its tension, its mirth, and its fun.

Now this last-named element, the *fun* of playing, resists all analysis, all logical interpretation. As a concept, it cannot be reduced to any other mental category. No other modern language known to me has the exact equivalent of the English "fun." The Dutch "aardigkeit" perhaps comes nearest to it (derived from "aard" which means the same as "Art" and "Wesen"[2] in German, and thus evidence, perhaps, that the matter cannot be reduced further). We may note in passing that "fun" in its current usage is of rather recent origin. French, oddly enough, has no corresponding term at all; German half makes up for it by "Spass" and "Witz" together. Nevertheless it is precisely this fun-element that characterizes the essence of play. Here we have to do with an absolutely primary category of life, familiar to everybody at a glance right down to the animal level. We may well call play a "totality" in the modern sense of the word, and it is as a totality that we must try to understand and evaluate it.

Since the reality of play extends beyond the sphere of human life it cannot have its foundations in any rational nexus, because this would limit it to mankind. The incidence of play is not associated with any particular stage of civilization or view of the universe. Any thinking person can see at a glance that play is a thing on its own, even if his language possesses no general concept to express it. Play cannot be denied. You can deny, if you like, nearly all abstractions: justice, beauty, truth, goodness, mind, God. You can deny seriousness, but not play.

But in acknowledging play you acknowledge mind, for whatever else play is, it is not matter. Even in the animal world it bursts the bounds of the physically existent. From the point of view of a world wholly determined by the operation of blind forces, play would be altogether superfluous. Play only becomes possible, thinkable and understandable when an influx of *mind* breaks down the absolute determinism of the cosmos. The very existence of play continually confirms the supra-logical nature of the human situation. Animals play, so they must be more than merely mechanical things. We play and know that we play, so we must be more than merely rational beings, for play is irrational.

In tackling the problem of play as a function of culture proper and not as it appears in the life of the animal or the child, we begin where biology and psychology leave off. In culture we find play as a given magnitude existing before culture itself existed, accompanying it and pervading it from the earliest beginnings right up to the phase of civilization we are now living in. We find play present everywhere as a well-defined quality of action which is different from "ordinary" life. We can disregard the question of how far science has succeeded in reducing this quality to quantitative factors. In our opinion it has not. At all events it is precisely this quality, itself so characteristic of the form of life we call "play," which matters. Play as a special form of activity, as a "significant form," as a social function—that is our subject. We shall not look for the natural impulses and habits conditioning play in general, but shall consider play in its manifold concrete forms as itself a social construction. We shall try to take play as the player himself takes it: in its primary significance. If we find that play is based on the manipulation of certain images, on a certain "imagination" of reality (i.e. its conversion into images), then our main concern will be to grasp the value and significance of these images and their "imagination." We shall observe their action in play itself and thus try to understand play as a cultural factor in life.

The great archetypal activities of human society are all permeated with play from the start. Take language, for instance—that first and supreme instrument which man shapes in order to communicate, to teach, to command. Language allows him to distinguish, to establish, to state things; in short, to name them and by naming them to raise them into the domain of the spirit. In the making of speech and language the spirit is continually "sparking" between matter and mind, as it were, playing with this wondrous nominative faculty. Behind every abstract expression there lie the boldest of metaphors, and every metaphor is a play upon words. Thus in giving expression to life man creates a second, poetic world alongside the world of nature.

Or take myth. This, too, is a transformation or an "imagination" of the outer world, only here the process is more elaborate and ornate than is the case with individual words. In myth, primitive man seeks to account for the world of phenomena by grounding it in the Divine. In all the wild imaginings of mythology a fanciful spirit is playing on the border-line between jest and earnest. Or finally, let us take ritual. Primitive society performs its sacred rites, its sacrifices, consecrations and mysteries, all of which serve to guarantee the well-being of the world, in a spirit of pure play truly understood.

Now in myth and ritual the great instinctive forces of civilized life have their origin: law and order, commerce and profit, craft and art, poetry, wisdom and science. All are rooted in the primaeval soil of play.

The object of the present essay is to demonstrate that it is more than a rhetorical comparison to view culture *sub specie ludi*. The thought is not at all new. There was a time when it was generally accepted, though in a limited sense quite different from the one intended here: in the 17th century, the age of world theatre. Drama, in a glittering succession of figures ranging from Shakespeare and Calderon to Racine, then dominated the literature of the West. It was the fashion to liken the world to a stage on which every man plays his part. Does this mean that the play-element in civilization was openly acknowledged? Not at all. On closer examination this fashionable comparison of life to a stage proves to be little more than an echo of the Neo-platonism that was then in vogue, with a markedly moralistic accent. It was a variation on the ancient theme of the vanity of all things. The fact that play and culture are actually interwoven with one another was neither observed nor expressed, whereas for us the whole point is to show that genuine, pure play is one of the main bases of civilisation.

To our way of thinking, play is the direct opposite of seriousness. At first sight this opposition seems as irreducible to other categories as the play-concept itself. Examined more closely, however, the contrast between play and seriousness proves to be neither conclusive nor fixed. We can say: play is non-seriousness. But apart from the fact that this proposition tells us nothing about the positive qualities of play, it is extraordinarily easy to refute. As soon as we proceed from "play is non-seriousness" to "play is not serious," the contrast leaves us in the lurch—for some play can be very serious indeed. Moreover we can immediately name several other fundamental categories that likewise come under the heading "non-seriousness" yet have no correspondence whatever with "play." Laughter, for instance, is in a sense the opposite of seriousness without being absolutely bound up with play. Children's games, football, and chess are played in profound seriousness; the players have not the slightest inclination to laugh. It is worth noting that the purely physiological act of laughing is exclusive to man, whilst the significant function of play is common to both men and animals. The Aristotelian *animal ridens* characterizes man as distinct from the animal almost more absolutely than *homo sapiens*.

What is true of laughter is true also of the comic. The comic comes under the category of non-seriousness and has certain affinities with laughter—it provokes to laughter. But its relation to play is subsidiary. In itself play is not comical either for player or public. The play of young animals or small children may sometimes be ludicrous, but the sight of grown dogs chasing one another hardly moves us to laughter. When we call a farce or a comedy "comic," it is not so much on account of the play-acting as such as on account of the situation or the thoughts expressed. The mimic and laughter-provoking art of the clown is comic as well as ludicrous, but it can scarcely be termed genuine play.

The category of the comic is closely connected with *folly* in the highest and lowest sense of that word. Play, however, is not foolish. It lies outside the antithesis of wisdom and folly. The later Middle Ages tended to express the two cardinal moods of life—play and seriousness—somewhat imperfectly by opposing *folie* to *sense*, until Erasmus in his *Laus Stultitiae* showed the inadequacy of the contrast.

All the terms in this loosely connected group of ideas—play, laughter, folly, wit, jest, joke, the comic, etc.—share the characteristic which we had to attribute to play, namely, that of resisting any attempt to reduce it to other terms. Their rationale and their mutual relationships must lie in a very deep layer of our mental being.

The more we try to mark off the form we call "play" from other forms apparently related to it, the more the absolute independence of the play-concept stands out. And the segregation of play from the domain of the great categorical antitheses does not stop there. Play lies outside the antithesis of wisdom and folly, and equally outside those of truth and falsehood, good and evil. Although it is a non-material activity it has no moral function. The valuations of vice and virtue do not apply here.

If, therefore, play cannot be directly referred to the categories of truth or goodness, can it be included perhaps in the realm of the aesthetic? Here our judgement wavers. For although the attribute of beauty does not attach to play as such, play nevertheless tends to assume marked elements of beauty. Mirth and grace adhere at the outset to the more primitive forms of play. In play the beauty of the human body in motion reaches its zenith. In its more developed forms it is saturated with rhythm and harmony, the noblest gifts of aesthetic perception known to man. Many and close are the links that connect play with beauty. All the same, we cannot say that beauty is inherent in play as such; so we must leave it at that: play is a function of the living, but is not susceptible of exact definition either logically, biologically, or aesthetically. The play-concept must always remain distinct from all the other forms of thought in which we express the structure of mental and social life. Hence we shall have to confine ourselves to describing the main characteristics of play.

Since our theme is the relation of play to culture we need not enter into all the possible forms of play but can restrict ourselves to its social manifestations. These we might call the higher forms of play. They are generally much easier to describe than the more primitive play of infants and young animals, because they are more distinct and articulate in form and their features more various and conspicuous, whereas in interpreting primitive play we immediately come up against that irreducible quality of pure playfulness which is not, in our opinion, amenable to further analysis. We shall have to speak of contests and races, of performances and exhibitions, of dancing and music, pageants, masquerades and tournaments. Some of the characteristics we shall enumerate are proper to play in general, others to social play in particular.

First and foremost, then, all play is a voluntary activity. Play to order is no longer play: it could at best be but a forcible imitation of it. By this quality of freedom alone, play marks itself off from the course of the natural process. It is something added thereto and spread out over it like a flowering, an ornament, a garment. Obviously, freedom must be understood here in the wider sense that leaves untouched the philosophical problem of determinism. It may be objected that this freedom does not exist for the animal and the child; they *must* play because their instinct drives them to it and because it serves to develop their bodily faculties and their powers of selection. The term "instinct," however, introduces an unknown quantity, and to presuppose the utility of play from the start is to be guilty of a *petitio principii*. Child and animal play because they enjoy playing, and therein precisely lies their freedom.

Be that as it may, for the adult and responsible human being play is a function which he could equally well leave alone. Play is superfluous. The need for it is only urgent to the extent that the enjoyment of it makes it a need. Play can be deferred or suspended at any time. It is never imposed by physical necessity or moral duty. It is never a task. It is done at leisure, during "free time." Only when play is a recognized cultural function—a rite, a ceremony—is it bound up with notions of obligation and duty.

Here, then, we have the first main characteristic of play: that it is free, is in fact freedom. A second characteristic is closely connected with this, namely, that play is not "ordinary" or "real" life. It is rather a stepping out of "real" life into a temporary sphere of activity with a disposition all of its own. Every child knows perfectly well that he is "only pretending," or that it was "only for fun." How deep-seated this awareness is in the child's soul is strikingly illustrated by the following story, told to me by the father of the boy in question. He found his four-year-old son sitting at the front of a row of chairs, playing "trains." As he hugged him the boy said: "Don't kiss the engine, Daddy, or the carriages won't think it's real." This "only pretending" quality of play betrays a consciousness of the inferiority of play compared with "seriousness," a feeling that seems to be something as primary as play itself. Nevertheless, as we have already pointed out that consciousness of play being "only a pretend" does not by any means prevent it from proceeding with the utmost seriousness, with an absorption, a devotion that passes into rapture and, temporarily at least, completely abolishes that troublesome "only" feeling. Any game can at any time wholly run away with the players. The contrast between play and seriousness is always fluid. The inferiority of play is continually being offset by the corresponding superiority of its seriousness. Play turns to seriousness and seriousness to play. Play may rise to heights of beauty and sublimity that leave seriousness far beneath. Tricky questions such as these will come up for discussion when we start examining the relationship between play and ritual.

As regards its formal characteristics, all students lay stress on the *disinterestedness* of play. Not being "ordinary" life it stands outside the immediate satisfaction of wants and appetites, indeed it interrupts the appetitive process. It interpolates itself as a temporary activity satisfying in itself and ending there. Such at least is the way in which play presents itself to us in the first instance: as an intermezzo, an *interlude* in our daily lives. As a regularly recurring relaxation, however, it becomes the accompaniment, the complement, in fact an integral part of life in general. It adorns life, amplifies it and is to that extent a necessity both for the individual—as a life function—and for society by reason of the meaning it contains, its significance, its expressive value, its spiritual and social associations, in short, as a cultural function. The expression of it satisfies all kinds of communal ideals. It thus has its place in a sphere superior to the strictly biological processes of nutrition, reproduction and self-preservation. This assertion is apparently contradicted by the fact that play, or rather sexual display, is predominant in animal life precisely at the mating-season. But would it be too absurd to assign a place *outside* the purely physiological, to the singing, cooing and strutting of birds just as we do to human play? In all its higher forms the latter at any rate always belongs to the sphere of festival and ritual—the sacred sphere.

Now, does the fact that play is a necessity, that it subserves culture, or indeed that it actually becomes culture, detract from its disinterested character? No, for the purposes it serves are external to immediate material interests or the individual satisfaction of biological needs. As a sacred activity play naturally contributes to the well-being of the group, but in quite another way and by other means than the acquisition of the necessities of life.

Play is distinct from "ordinary" life both as to locality and duration. This is the third main characteristic of play: its secludedness, its limitedness. It is "played out" within certain limits of time and place. It contains its own course and meaning.

Play begins, and then at a certain moment it is "over." It plays itself to an end. While it is in progress all is movement, change, alternation, succession, association, separation. But immediately connected with its limitation as to time there is a further curious feature of play: it at once assumes fixed form as a cultural phenomenon. Once played, it endures as a new-found creation of the mind, a treasure to be retained by the memory. It is transmitted, it becomes tradition. It can be repeated at any time, whether it be "child's play" or a game of chess, or at fixed intervals like a mystery. In this faculty of repetition lies one of the most essential qualities of play. It holds good not only of play as a whole but also of its inner structure. In nearly all the higher forms of play the elements of repetition and alternation (as in the *refrain*), are like the warp and woof of a fabric.

More striking even than the limitation as to time is the limitation as to space. All play moves and has its being within a play-ground marked off beforehand either materially or ideally, deliberately or as a matter of course. Just as there is no formal difference between play and ritual, so the "consecrated spot" cannot be formally distinguished from the play-ground. The arena, the card-table, the magic circle, the temple, the stage, the screen, the tennis court, the court of justice, etc., are all in form and function play-grounds, i.e. forbidden spots, isolated, hedged round, hallowed, within which special rules obtain. All are temporary worlds within the ordinary world, dedicated to the performance of an act apart.

Inside the play-ground an absolute and peculiar order reigns. Here we come across another, very positive feature of play: it creates order, *is* order. Into an imperfect world and into the confusion of life it brings a temporary, a limited perfection. Play demands order absolute and supreme. The least deviation from it "spoils the game," robs it of its character and makes it worthless. The profound affinity between play and order is perhaps the reason why play, as we noted in passing, seems to lie to such a large extent in the field of aesthetics. Play has a tendency to be beautiful. It may be that this aesthetic factor is identical with the impulse to create orderly form, which animates play in all its aspects. The words we use to denote the elements of play belong for the most part to aesthetics, terms with which we try to describe the effects of beauty: tension, poise, balance, contrast, variation, solution, resolution, etc. Play casts a spell over us; it is "enchanting," "captivating." It is invested with the noblest qualities we are capable of perceiving in things: rhythm and harmony.

The element of tension in play to which we have just referred plays a particularly important part. Tension means uncertainty, chanciness; a striving to decide the issue and so end it. The player wants something to "go," to "come off"; he wants to "succeed" by his own exertions. Baby reaching for a toy, pussy patting a bobbin, a little girl playing ball—all want to achieve something difficult, to succeed, to end a tension. Play is "tense," as we say. It is this element of tension and solution that governs all solitary games of skill and application such as puzzles, jig-saws, mosaic-making, patience, target-shooting, and the more play bears the character of competition the more fervent it will be. In gambling and athletics it is at its height. Though play as such is outside the range of good and bad, the element of tension imparts to it a certain ethical value in so far as it means a testing of the player's prowess: his courage, tenacity, resources and, last but not least, his spiritual powers—his "fairness"; because, despite his ardent desire to win, he must still stick to the rules of the game.

These rules in their turn are a very important factor in the play-concept. All play has its rules. They determine what "holds" in the temporary world circumscribed by play. The rules of a game are absolutely binding and allow no doubt. Paul Valéry once in passing gave expression to a very cogent thought when he said: "No scepticism is possible where the rules of a game are concerned, for the principle underlying them is an unshakable truth...." Indeed, as soon as the rules are transgressed the whole play-world collapses. The game is over. The umpire's whistle breaks the spell and sets "real" life going again.

The player who trespasses against the rules or ignores them is a "spoil-sport." The spoil-sport is not the same as the false player, the cheat; for the latter pretends to be playing the game and, on the face of it, still acknowledges the magic circle. It is curious to note how much more lenient society is to the cheat than to the spoil-sport. This is because the spoil-sport shatters the play-world itself. By withdrawing from the game he reveals the relativity and fragility of the play-world in which he had temporarily shut himself with others. He robs play of its *illusion*—a pregnant word which means literally "in-play" (from *inlusio*, *illudere* or *inludere*). Therefore he must be cast out, for he threatens the existence of the play-community. The figure of the spoil-sport is most apparent in boys' games. The little community does not enquire whether the spoil-sport is guilty of defection because he dares not enter into the game or because he is not allowed to. Rather, it does not recognize "not being allowed" and calls it "not daring." For it, the problem of obedience and conscience is no more than fear of punishment. The spoil-sport breaks the magic world, therefore he is a coward and must be ejected. In the world of high seriousness, too, the cheat and the hypocrite have always had an easier time of it than the spoil-sports, here called apostates, heretics, innovators, prophets, conscientious objectors, etc. It sometimes happens, however, that the spoil-sports in their turn make a new community with rules of its own. The outlaw, the revolutionary, the cabbalist or member of a secret society, indeed heretics of all kinds are of a highly associative if not sociable disposition, and a certain element of play is prominent in all their doings.

A play-community generally tends to become permanent even after the game is over. Of course, not every game of marbles or every bridge-party leads to the founding of a club. But the feeling of being "apart together" in an exceptional situation, of sharing something important, of mutually withdrawing from the rest of the world and rejecting the usual norms, retains its magic beyond the duration of the individual game. The club pertains to play as the hat to the head. It would be rash to explain all the associations which the anthropologist calls "phratria"—e.g. clans, brotherhoods, etc.—simply as play-communities; nevertheless it has been shown again and again how difficult it is to draw the line between, on the one hand, permanent social groupings—particularly in archaic cultures with their extremely important, solemn, indeed sacred customs—and the sphere of play on the other.

The exceptional and special position of play is most tellingly illustrated by the fact that it loves to surround itself with an air of secrecy. Even in early childhood the charm of play is enhanced by making a "secret" out of it. This is for *us*, not for the "others." What the "others" do "outside" is no concern of ours at the moment. Inside the circle of the game the laws and customs of ordinary life no longer count. We are different and do things differently. This temporary abolition of the ordinary world is fully acknowledged in child-life, but it is no less evident in the great ceremonial games of savage societies. During the great feast of initiation when the youths are accepted into the male community, it is not the neophytes only that are exempt from the ordinary laws and regulations: there is a truce to all feuds in the tribe. All retaliatory acts and vendettas are suspended. This temporary suspension of normal social life on account of the sacred play-season has numerous traces in the more advanced civilizations as well. Everything that pertains to saturnalia and carnival customs belongs to it. Even with us a bygone age of robuster private habits than ours, more marked class-privileges and a more complaisant police recognized the orgies of young men of rank under the name of a "rag." The saturnalian licence of young men still survives, in fact, in the ragging at English universities, which the *Oxford English Dictionary* defines as "an extensive display of noisy and disorderly conduct carried out in defiance of authority and discipline."

The "differentness" and secrecy of play are most vividly expressed in "dressing up." Here the "extra-ordinary" nature of play reaches perfection. The disguised or masked individual "plays" another part, another being. He *is* another being. The terrors of childhood, open-hearted gaiety, mystic fantasy and sacred awe are all inextricably entangled in this strange business of masks and disguises.

Summing up the formal characteristics of play we might call it a free activity standing quite consciously outside "ordinary" life as being "not serious," but at the same time absorbing the player intensely and utterly. It is an activity connected with no material interest, and no profit can be gained by it. It proceeds within its own proper boundaries of time and space according to fixed rules and in an orderly manner. It promotes the formation of social groupings which tend to surround themselves with secrecy and to stress their difference from the common world by disguise or other means.

The function of play in the higher forms which concern us here can largely be derived from the two basic aspects under which we meet it: as a contest *for* something or a representation *of* something. These two functions can unite in such a way that the game "represents" a contest, or else becomes a contest for the best representation of something.

Representation means display, and this may simply consist in the exhibition of something naturally given, before an audience. The peacock and the turkey merely display their gorgeous plumage to the females, but the essential feature of it lies in the parading of something out of the ordinary and calculated to arouse admiration. If the bird accompanies this exhibition with dance-steps we have a performance, a *stepping out of* common reality into a higher order. We are ignorant of the bird's sensations while so engaged. We know, however, that in child-life performances of this kind are full of imagination. The child is *making an image* of something different, something more beautiful, or more sublime, or more dangerous than what he usually is. One is a Prince, or one is Daddy or a wicked witch or a tiger. The child is quite literally "beside himself" with delight, transported beyond himself to such an extent that he almost believes he actually is such and such a thing, without, however, wholly losing consciousness of "ordinary reality". His representation is not so much a sham-reality as a realization in appearance: "imagination" in the original sense of the word.

Passing now from children's games to the sacred performances in archaic culture we find that there is more of a mental element "at play" in the latter, though it is excessively difficult to define. The sacred performance is more than an actualization in appearance only, a sham reality; it is also more than a symbolical actualization—it is a mystical one. In it, something invisible and inactual takes beautiful, actual, holy form. The participants in the rite are convinced that the action actualizes and effects a definite beatification, brings about an order of things higher than that in which they customarily live. All the same this "actualization by representation" still retains the formal characteristics of play in every respect. It is played or performed within a playground that is literally "staked out," and played moreover as a feast, i.e. in mirth and freedom. A sacred space, a temporarily real world of its own, has been expressly hedged off for it. But with the end of the play its effect is not lost; rather it continues to shed its radiance on the ordinary world outside, a wholesome influence working security, order and prosperity for the whole community until the sacred play-season comes round again.

Examples can be taken from all over the world. According to ancient Chinese lore the purpose of music and the dance is to keep the world in its right course and to force Nature into benevolence towards man. The year's prosperity will depend on the right performance of sacred contests at the seasonal feasts. If these gatherings do not take place the crops will not ripen.[3]

The rite is a *dromenon*, which means "something acted," an act, action. That which is enacted, or the stuff of the action, is a *drama*, which again means act, action represented on a stage. Such action may occur as a performance or a contest. The rite, or "ritual act" represents a cosmic happening, an event in the natural process. The word "represents," however, does not cover the exact meaning of the act, at least not in its looser, modern connotation; for here "representation" is really *identification*, the mystic repetition or *re-presentation* of the event. The rite produces the effect which is then not so much *shown figuratively* as *actually reproduced* in the action. The function of the rite, therefore, is far from being merely imitative; it causes the worshippers to participate in the sacred happening itself. As the Greeks would say, "it is *methectic* rather than *mimetic*."[4] It is "a helping-out of the action."[5]

Anthropology is not primarily interested in how psychology will assess the mental attitude displayed in these phenomena. The psychologist may seek to settle the matter by calling such performances an *identification compensatrice*, a kind of substitute, "a representative act undertaken in view of the impossibility of staging real, purposive action."[6] Are the performers mocking, or are they mocked? The business of the anthropologist is to understand the significance of these "imaginations" in the mind of the peoples who practise and believe in them.

We touch here on the very core of comparative religion: the nature and essence of ritual and mystery. The whole of the ancient Vedic sacrificial rites rests on the idea that the ceremony—be it sacrifice, contest or performance—by representing a certain desired cosmic event, compels the gods to effect that event in reality. We could well say, by "playing" it. Leaving the religious issues aside we shall only concern ourselves here with the play-element in archaic ritual.

Ritual is thus in the main a matter of shows, representations, dramatic performances, imaginative actualizations of a vicarious nature. At the great seasonal festivals the community celebrates the grand happenings in the life of nature by staging sacred performances, which represent the change of seasons, the rising and setting of the constellations, the growth and ripening of crops, birth, life and death in man and beast. As Leo Frobenius puts it, archaic man *plays* the order of nature as imprinted on his consciousness.[7] In the remote past, so Frobenius thinks, man first assimilated the phenomena of vegetation and animal life and then conceived an idea of time and space, of months and seasons, of the course of the sun and moon. And now he plays this great processional order of existence in a sacred play, in and through which he actualizes anew, or "recreates," the events represented and thus helps to maintain the cosmic order. Frobenius draws even more far-reaching conclusions from this "playing at nature." He deems it the starting-point of all social order and social institutions, too. Through this ritual play, savage society acquires its rude forms of government. The king is the sun, his kingship the image of the sun's course. All his life the king plays "sun" and in the end he suffers the fate of the sun: he must be killed in ritual forms by his own people.

We can leave aside the question of how far this explanation of ritual regicide and the whole underlying conception can be taken as "proved." The question that interests us here is: what are we to think of this concrete projection of primitive nature-consciousness? What are we to make of a mental process that begins with an unexpressed experience of cosmic phenomena and ends in an imaginative rendering of them in play?

Frobenius is right to discard the facile hypothesis which contents itself with hypothecating an innate "play instinct." The term "instinct," he says, is "a makeshift, an admission of helplessness before the problem of reality."[8] Equally explicitly and for even better reasons he rejects as a vestige of obsolete thinking the tendency to explain every advance in culture in terms of a "special purpose," a "why" and a "wherefore" thrust down the throat of the culture-creating community. "Tyranny of causality at its worst," "antiquated utilitarianism" he calls such a point of view.[9]

The conception Frobenius has of the mental process in question is roughly as follows. In archaic man the experience of life and nature, still unexpressed, takes the form of a "seizure" — being seized on, thrilled, enraptured. "The creative faculty in a people as in the child or every creative person, springs from this state of being seized." "Man is seized by the revelation of fate." "The reality of the natural rhythm of genesis and extinction has seized hold of his consciousness, and this, inevitably and by reflex action, leads him to represent his emotion in an act." So that according to him we are dealing with a necessary mental process of transformation. The thrill, the "being seized" by the phenomena of life and nature is condensed by reflex action, as it were, to poetic expression and art. It is difficult to describe the process of creative imagination in words that are more to the point, though they can hardly be called a true "explanation." The mental road from aesthetic or mystical, or at any rate meta-logical, perception of cosmic order to ritual play remains as dark as before.

While repeatedly using the term "play" for these performances the great anthropologist omits, however, to state what exactly he understands by it. He would even seem to have surreptitiously re-admitted the very thing he so strongly deprecates and which does not altogether fit in with the essential quality of play: the concept of purpose. For, in Frobenius' description of it, play quite explicitly serves to represent a cosmic event and thus bring it about. A quasi-rationalistic element irresistibly creeps in. For Frobenius, play and representation have their *raison d'être* after all, in the expression of something else, namely, the "being seized" by a cosmic event. But the very fact that the dramatization is *played* is, apparently, of secondary importance for him. Theoretically at least, the emotion could have been communicated in some other way. In our view, on the contrary, the whole point is the *playing*. Such ritual play is essentially no different from one of the higher forms of common child-play or indeed animal-play. Now in the case of these two latter forms one could hardly suppose their origin to lie in some cosmic emotion struggling for expression. Child-play possesses the play-form in its veriest essence, and most purely.

We might, perhaps, describe the process leading from "seizure" by nature to ritual performance, in terms that would avoid the above-mentioned inadequacy without, however, claiming to lay bare the inscrutable. Archaic society, we would say, plays as the child or animal plays. Such playing contains at the outset all the elements proper to play: order, tension, movement, change, solemnity, rhythm, rapture. Only in a later phase of society is play associated with the idea of something to be expressed in and by it, namely, what we would call "life" or "nature." Then, what was wordless play assumes poetic form. In the form and function of play, itself an independent entity which is senseless and irrational, man's consciousness that he is embedded in a sacred order of things finds its first, highest, and holiest expression. Gradually the significance of a sacred act permeates the playing. Ritual grafts itself upon it; but the primary thing is and remains play.

We are hovering over spheres of thought barely accessible either to psychology or to philosophy. Such questions as these plumb the depths of our consciousness. Ritual is seriousness at its highest and holiest. Can it nevertheless be play? We began by saying that all play, both of children and of grown-ups, can be performed in the most perfect seriousness. Does this go so far as to imply that play is still bound up with the sacred emotion of the sacramental act? Our conclusions are to some extent impeded by the rigidity of our accepted ideas. We are accustomed to think of play and seriousness as an absolute antithesis. It would seem, however, that this does not go to the heart of the matter.

Let us consider for a moment the following argument. The child plays in complete—we can well say, in sacred—earnest. But it plays and knows that it plays. The sportsman, too, plays with all the fervour of a man enraptured, but he still knows that he is playing. The actor on the stage is wholly absorbed in his playing, but is all the time conscious of "the play." The same holds good of the violinist, though he may soar to realms beyond this world. The play-character, therefore, may attach to the sublimest forms of action. Can we now extend the line to ritual and say that the priest performing the rites of sacrifice is only playing? At first sight it seems preposterous, for if you grant it for one religion you must grant it for all. Hence our ideas of ritual, magic, liturgy, sacrament and mystery would all fall within the play-concept. In dealing with abstractions we must always guard against overstraining their significance. We would merely be playing with words were we to stretch the play-concept unduly. But, all things considered, I do not think we are falling into that error when we characterize ritual as play. The ritual act has all the formal and essential characteristics of play which we enumerated above, particularly in so far as it transports the participants to another world. This identity of ritual and play was unreservedly recognized by Plato as a given fact. He had no hesitation in comprising the *sacra* in the category of play. "I say that a man must be serious with the serious," he says (*Laws*, vii, 803). "God alone is worthy of supreme seriousness, but man is made God's plaything, and that is the best part of him. Therefore every man and woman should live life accordingly, and play the noblest games and be of another mind from what they are at present.... For they deem war a serious thing, though in war there is neither play nor culture worthy the name (οὔτ οὖν παιδια ... οὔτ αὖ παιδεία), which are the things *we* deem most serious. Hence all must live in peace as well as they possibly can. What, then, is the right way of living? Life must be lived as play, playing certain games, making sacrifices, singing and dancing, and then a man will be able to propitiate the gods, and defend himself against his enemies, and win in the contest."[10]

The close connections between mystery and play have been touched on most tellingly by Romano Guardini in his book *The Spirit of the Liturgy* (Ecclesia Orans 1, Freiburg, 1922), particularly the chapter entitled "Die Liturgie als Spiel." He does not actually cite Plato, but comes as near the above quotation as may be. He ascribes to liturgy more than one of the features we held to be characteristic of play, amongst others the fact that, in its highest examples, liturgy is "zwecklos aber doch sinnvoll"—"pointless but significant."

The Platonic identification of play and holiness does not defile the latter by calling it play, rather it exalts the concept of play to the highest regions of the spirit. We said at the beginning that play was anterior to culture; in a certain sense it is also superior to it or at least detached from it. In play we may move below the level of the serious, as the child does; but we can also move above it—in the realm of the beautiful and the sacred.

From this point of view we can now define the relationship between ritual and play more closely. We are no longer astonished at the substantial similarity of the two forms, and the question as to how far every ritual act falls within the category of play continues to hold our attention.

We found that one of the most important characteristics of play was its spatial separation from ordinary life. A closed space is marked out for it, either materially or ideally, hedged off from the everyday surroundings. Inside this space the play proceeds, inside it the rules obtain. Now, the marking out of some sacred spot is also the primary characteristic of every sacred act. This requirement of isolation for ritual, including magic and law, is much more than merely spatial and temporal. Nearly all rites of consecration and initiation entail a certain artificial seclusion for the performers and those to be initiated. Whenever it is a question of taking a vow or being received into an Order or confraternity, or of oaths and secret societies, in one way or another there is always such a delimitation of room for play. The magician, the augur, the sacrificer begins his work by circumscribing his sacred space. Sacrament and mystery presuppose a hallowed spot.

Formally speaking, there is no distinction whatever between marking out a space for a sacred purpose and marking it out for purposes of sheer play. The turf, the tennis-court, the chess-board and pavement-hopscotch cannot formally be distinguished from the temple or the magic circle. The striking similarity between sacrificial rites all over the earth shows that such customs must be rooted in a very fundamental, an aboriginal layer of the human mind. As a rule people reduce this over all congruity of cultural forms to some "reasonable," "logical" cause by explaining the need for isolation and seclusion as an anxiety to protect the consecrated individual from noxious influences—because, in his consecrated state, he is particularly exposed to the malign workings of ghosts, besides being himself a danger to his surroundings. Such an explanation puts intellection and utilitarian purpose at the beginning of the cultural process: the very thing Frobenius warned against. Even if we do not fall back here on the antiquated notion of a priestcraft inventing religion, we are still introducing a rationalistic element better avoided. If, on the other hand, we accept the essential and original identity of play and ritual we simply recognize the hallowed spot as a play-ground, and the misleading question of the "why and the wherefore" does not arise at all.

If ritual proves to be formally indistinguishable from play the question remains whether this resemblance goes further than the purely formal. It is surprising that anthropology and comparative religion have paid so little attention to the problem of how far such sacred activities as proceed within the forms of play also proceed in the attitude and mood of play. Even Frobenius has not, to my knowledge, asked this question.

Needless to say, the mental attitude in which a community performs and experiences its sacred rites is one of high and holy earnest. But let it be emphasized again that genuine and spontaneous play can also be profoundly serious. The player can abandon himself body and soul to the game, and the consciousness of its being "merely" a game can be thrust into the background. The joy inextricably bound up with playing can turn not only into tension, but into elation. Frivolity and ecstasy are the twin poles between which play moves.

The play-mood is *labile* in its very nature. At any moment "ordinary life" may reassert its rights either by an impact from without, which interrupts the game, or by an offence against the rules, or else from within, by a collapse of the play spirit, a sobering, a disenchantment.

What, then, is the attitude and mood prevailing at holy festivals? The sacred act is "celebrated" on a "holiday"—i.e. it forms part of a general feast on the occasion of a holy day. When the people foregather at the sanctuary they gather together for collective rejoic-ing. Consecrations, sacrifices, sacred dances and contests, performances, mysteries—all are comprehended within the act of celebrating a festival. The rites may be bloody, the probations of the young men awaiting initiation may be cruel, the masks may be terrifying, but the whole thing has a festal nature. Ordinary life is at a standstill. Banquets, junketings and all kinds of wanton revels are going on all the time the feast lasts. Whether we think of the Ancient Greek festivities or of the African religions to-day we can hardly draw any sharp line between the festival mood in general and the holy frenzy surrounding the central mystery.

Almost simultaneously with the appearance of the Dutch edition of this book the Hungarian scholar Karl Kerényi published a treatise on the nature of the festival which has the closest ties with our theme.[11] According to Kerényi, the festival too has that character of primacy and absolute independence which we predicated of play. "Among the psychic realities," he says, "the feast is a thing in itself, not to be confused with anything else in the world." Just as we thought the play-concept somewhat negligently treated by the anthropologist, so in his view is the feast. "The phenomenon of the feast appears to have been completely passed over by the ethnologist." "For all science is concerned it might not exist at all." Neither might play, we would like to add.

In the very nature of things the relationship between feast and play is very close. Both proclaim a standstill to ordinary life. In both mirth and joy dominate, though not necessarily—for the feast too can be serious; both are limited as to time and place; both combine strict rules with genuine freedom. In short, feast and play have their main characteristics in common. The two seem most intimately related in dancing. According to Kerényi, the Cora Indians inhabiting the Pacific coast of Mexico call their sacred feast of the young corn-cobs and the corn-roasting the "play" of their highest god.

Kerényi's ideas about the feast as an autonomous culture-concept amplify and corroborate those on which this book is built. For all that, however, the establishment of a close connection between the spirit of play and ritual does not explain everything. Genuine play possesses besides its formal characteristics and its joyful mood, at least one further very essential feature, namely, the consciousness, however latent, of "only pretending." The question remains how far such a consciousness is compatible with the ritual act performed in devotion.

If we confine ourselves to the sacred rites in archaic culture it is not impossible to adumbrate the degree of seriousness with which they are performed. As far as I know, ethnologists and anthropologists concur in the opinion that the mental attitude in which the great religious feasts of savages are celebrated and witnessed is not one of complete illusion. There is an underlying consciousness of things "not being real." A vivid picture of this attitude is given by Ad. E. Jensen in his book on the circumcision and puberty ceremonies in savage society.[12] The men seem to have no fear of the ghosts that are hovering about everywhere during the feast and appear to everyone at its height. This is small wonder, seeing that these same men have had the staging of the whole ceremony: they have carved and decorated the masks, wear them themselves and after use conceal them from the women. They make the noises heralding the appearance of the ghosts, they trace their footprints in the sand, they blow the flutes that represent the voices of the ancestors, and brandish the bull-roarers. In short, says Jensen, "their position is much like that of parents playing Santa Claus for their children: they know of the mask, but hide it from them." The men tell the women gruesome tales about the goings-on in the sacred bush. The attitude of the neophytes alternates between ecstasy, feigned madness, flesh-creeping and boyish swagger. Nor, in the last resort, are the women wholly duped. They know perfectly well who is hiding behind this mask or that. All the same they get fearfully excited when a mask comes up to them with minatory gestures, and fly shrieking in all directions. These expressions of terror, says Jensen, are in part quite genuine and spontaneous, and in part only acting up to a part imposed by tradition. It is "the done thing." The women are, as it were, the chorus to the play and they know that they must not be "spoil-sports."

In all this it is impossible to fix accurately the lower limit where holy earnest reduces itself to mere "fun." With us, a father of somewhat childish disposition might get seriously angry if his children caught him in the act of preparing Christmas presents. A Kwakiutl father in British Columbia killed his daughter who surprised him whilst carving things for a tribal ceremony.[13] The unstable nature of religious feeling among the Loango negroes is described by Pechuel-Loesche in terms similar to those used by Jensen. Their belief in the sanctities is a sort of half-belief, and goes with scoffing and pretended indifference. The really important thing is the mood, he concludes by saying.[14] R. R. Marett, in his chapter on "Primitive Credulity" in *The Threshold of Religion*, develops the idea that a certain element of "make-believe" is operative in all primitive religions. Whether one is sorcerer or sorcerized one is always knower and dupe at once. But one chooses to be the dupe. "The savage is a good actor who can be quite absorbed in his role, like a child at play; and, also like a child, a good spectator who can be frightened to death by the roaring of something he knows perfectly well to be no 'real' lion." The native, says Malinowski, feels and fears his belief rather than formulates it clearly to himself.[15] He uses certain terms and expressions, and these we must collect as documents of belief just as they are, without working them up into a consistent theory. The behaviour of those to whom the savage community attributes "supernatural" powers can often be best expressed by "acting up to the part."[16]

Despite this partial consciousness of things "not being real" in magic and super-natural phenomena generally, these authorities still warn against drawing the inference that the whole system of beliefs and practices is only a fraud invented by a group of "unbelievers" with a view to dominating the credulous. It is true that such an interpretation is given not only by many travellers but sometimes even by the traditions of the natives themselves. Yet it cannot be the right one. "The origin of any sacred act can only lie in the credulity of all, and the spurious maintaining of it in the interests of a special group can only be the final phase of a long line of development." As I see it, psychoanalysis tends to fall back on this antiquated interpretation of circumcision and puberty practices, so rightly rejected by Jensen.[17]

From the foregoing it is quite clear, to my mind at least, that where savage ritual is concerned we never lose sight of the play-concept for a single moment. To describe the phenomena we have to use the term "play" over and over again. What is more, the unity and indivisibility of belief and unbelief, the indissoluble connection between sacred earnest and "make-believe" or "fun," are best understood in the concept of play itself. Jensen, though admitting the similarity of the child's world to that of the savage, still tries to distinguish in principle between the mentality of the two. The child, he says, when confronted with the figure of Santa Claus, has to do with a "ready-made concept," in which he "finds his way" with a lucidity and endowment of his own. But "the creative attitude of the savage with regard to the ceremonies here in question is quite another thing. He has to do not with ready-made concepts but with his natural surroundings, which themselves demand interpretation; he grasps their mysterious daemonism and tries to give it in representative form."[18] Here we recognize the views of Frobenius, who was Jensen's teacher. Still, two objections occur. Firstly, when calling the process in the savage mind "quite another thing" from that in the child-mind, he is speaking of the *originators* of the ritual on the one hand and of the child of *to-day* on the other. But we know nothing of these originators. All we can study is a ritualistic community which receives its religious imagery as traditional material just as "ready-made" as the child does, and responds to it similarly. Secondly, even if we ignore this, the process of "interpreting" the natural surroundings, of "grasping" them and "representing" them in a ritual image remains altogether inaccessible to our observation. It is only by fanciful metaphors that Frobenius and Jensen force an approach to it. The most we can say of the function that is operative in the process of image-making or imagination is that it is a poetic function; and we define it best of all by calling it a function of play—the *ludic* function, in fact.

So that the apparently quite simple question of what play really is, leads us deep into the problem of the nature and origin of religious concepts. As we all know, one of the most important basic ideas with which every student of comparative religion has to acquaint himself is the following. When a certain form of religion accepts a sacred identity between two things of a different order, say a human being and an animal, this relationship is not adequately expressed by calling it a "symbolical correspondence" as *we* conceive this. The identity, the essential oneness of the two goes far deeper than the correspondence between a substance and its symbolic image. It is a mystic unity. The one has *become* the other. In his magic dance the savage is a kangaroo. We must always be on our guard against the deficiencies and differences of our means of expression. In order to form any idea at all of the mental habits of the savage we are forced to give them in our terminology. Whether we will or not we are always transposing the savage's ideas of religion into the strictly logical modes of our own thought. We express the relationship between him and the animal he "identifies" himself with, as a "being" for him but a "playing" for us. He has taken on the "essence" of the kangaroo, says the savage; he is playing the kangaroo, say we. The savage, however, knows nothing of the conceptual distinctions between "being" and "playing"; he knows nothing of "identity," "image" or "symbol." Hence it remains an open question whether we do not come nearest to the mental attitude of the savage performing a ritual act, by adhering to this primary, universally understandable term "play." In play as we conceive it the distinction between belief and make-believe breaks down. The concept of play merges quite naturally with that of holiness. Any Prelude of Bach, any line of tragedy proves it. By considering the whole sphere of so-called primitive culture as a play-sphere we pave the way to a more direct and more general understanding of its peculiarities than any meticulous psychological or sociological analysis would allow.

Primitive, or let us say, archaic ritual is thus sacred play, indispensable for the well-being of the community, fecund of cosmic insight and social development but always play in the sense Plato gave to it—an action accomplishing itself outside and above the necessities and seriousness of everyday life. In this sphere of sacred play the child and the poet are at home with the savage. His aesthetic sensibility has brought the modern man closer to this sphere than the "enlightened" man of the 18th century ever was. Think of the peculiar charm that the mask as an *objet d'art* has for the modern mind. People nowadays try to feel the essence of savage life. This kind of exoticism may sometimes be a little affected, but it goes a good deal deeper than the 18th century *engouement* for Turks, "Chinamen" and Indians. Modern man is very sensitive to the far-off and the strange. Nothing helps him so much in his understanding of savage society as his feeling for masks and disguise. While ethnology has demonstrated their enormous social importance, they arouse in the educated layman and art-lover an immediate aesthetic emotion compounded of beauty, fright, and mystery. Even for the cultured adult of to-day the mask still retains something of its terrifying power, although no religious emotions are attached to it. The sight of the masked figure, as a purely aesthetic experience, carries us beyond "ordinary life" into a world where something other than daylight reigns; it carries us back to the world of the savage, the child and the poet, which is the world of play.

Even if we can legitimately reduce our ideas on the significance of primitive ritual to an irreducible play-concept, one extremely troublesome question still remains. What if we now ascend from the lower religions to the higher? From the rude and outlandish ritual of the African, American or Australian aborigines our vision shifts to Vedic sacrificial lore, already, in the hymns of the *Rig-Veda*, pregnant with the wisdom of the Upanishads, or to the profoundly mystical identifications of god, man, and beast in Egyptian religion, or to the Orphic and Eleusinian mysteries. In form and practice all these are closely allied to the so-called primitive religions even to bizarre and bloody particulars. But the high degree of wisdom and truth we discern, or think we can discern in them, forbids us to speak of them with that air of superiority which, as a matter of fact, is equally out of place in "primitive" cultures. We must ask whether this formal similarity entitles us to extend the qualification "play" to the consciousness of the holy, the faith embodied in these higher creeds. If we accept the Platonic definition of play there is nothing preposterous or irreverent in doing so. Play consecrated to the Deity, the highest goal of man's endeavour—such was Plato's conception of religion. In following him we in no way abandon the holy mystery, or cease to rate it as the highest attainable expression of that which escapes logical understanding. The ritual act, or an important part of it, will always remain within the play category, but in this seeming subordination the recognition of its holiness is not lost.

Notes

1. For these theories see H. Zondervan, *Hèt Spel bij Dieren, Kinderen en Volwassen Menschen* (Amsterdam, 1928), and F. J. J. Buytendijk, *Het Spel van Mensch en Diel als openbaring van levensdriften* (Amsterdam, 1932).

2. Nature, kind, being, essence, etc. Trans.

3. M. Granet, *Festivals and Songs of Ancient China; Dances and Legends of Ancient China; Chinese Civilization* (Routledge).

4. Jane Harrison, *Themis: A Study of the Social Origins of Greek Religion* (Cambridge, 1912), p. 125.

5. R. R. Marett, *The Threshold of Religion*, 1912, p. 48.

6. Buytendijk, *Het Spel van Mensch en Dier als openbaring van levensdriften* (Amsterdam, 1932), p. 70–71.

7. *Kulturgeschichte Afrikas, Prolegomena zu einer historischen Gestaltlehre; Schicksalskunde im Sinne des Kulturwerdens* (Leipzig, 1932).

8. *Kulturgeschichte*, pp. 23, 122.

9. *Ibid.* p. 21.

10. Cf. Laws, vii, 796, where Plato speaks of the sacred dances of the Kouretes of Crete, calling them ενόπλια παίγνια

11. *Vom Wesen des Fesles*, Paideuma, Mitteilungen zur Kulturkunde 1, Heft 2 (Dez., 1938), p. 59–74.

12. *Beschneidung und Reifezeremonien bei Naturvölkern* (Stuttgart, 1933).

13. F. Boas, *The Social Organisation and the Secret Societies of the Kwakiutl Indians*, Washington, 1897, p. 435.

14. *Volkskunde von Loango*, Stuttgart, 1907, p. 345.

15. The Argonauts of the Western Pacific, London, 1922, p. 339.

16. Ibid. p. 240.

17. Jensen, *op. cit.* p. 152.

18. *Op. cit.* p. 149 f.

The Definition of Play *and* The Classification of Games

Roger Caillois

Context

The ideas that reached fruition in **Man, Play and Games** *began as an appendix to Caillois' 1959 book* **Man and the Sacred**. *Much of Caillois' work on play and games is a direct critique of Johan Huizinga's* **Homo Ludens**. *In* **Man, Play and Games,** *he expands Huizinga's more contest-oriented notion of play to include a range of cultural forms. Driven by a desire to study play in and of itself, during the two chapters included here Caillois establishes his well-known taxonomy of play forms. In the rest of the book, Caillois applies this taxonomy to play activities from a range of world cultures. "The Definition of Play," and "The Classification of Games" come from* **Man, Play and Games,** *copyright 1958 by Librairie Gallimard. English translation by Meyer Barash, copyright 1961 by the Free Press of Glencoe, Inc. Used with permission of the University of Illinois Press.*

The Player Experience

Player and Character

What Is a Game?

What Is Play?

Roger Caillois (1913–1978) was a French writer and philosopher whose books ranged on topics from psychoanalysis and sociology to anthropology and art. He was the founding editor of *Diogenes*, the journal of the International Council for Philosophy and Humanistic Studies, and is considered by many to be one of the most influential thinkers on games and play.

The Definition of Play

In 1933, the rector of the University of Leyden, J. Huizinga, chose as the theme of an important oration, "The Cultural Limits of Play and the Serious." He took up and developed this topic in an original and powerful work published in 1938, *Homo Ludens*. This work, although most of its premises are debatable, is nonetheless capable of opening extremely fruitful avenues to research and reflection. In any case, it is permanently to J. Huizinga's credit that he has masterfully analyzed several of the fundamental characteristics of play and has demonstrated the importance of its role in the very development of civilization. First, he sought an exact definition of the essence of play; second, he tried to clarify the role of play present in or animating the essential aspects of all culture: in the arts as in philosophy, in poetry as well as in juridical institutions and even in the etiquette of war.

Huizinga acquitted himself brilliantly in this task, but even if he discovers play in areas where no one before him had done so, he deliberately omits, as obvious, the description and classification of games themselves, since they all respond to the same needs and reflect, without qualification, the same psychological attitude. His work is not a study of games, but an inquiry into the creative quality of the play principle in the domain of culture, and more precisely, of the spirit that rules certain kinds of games—those which are competitive. The examination of the criteria used by Huizinga to demarcate his universe of discourse is helpful in understanding the strange gaps in a study which is in every other way remarkable. Huizinga defines play as follows:

> Summing up the formal characteristics of play we might call it a free activity standing quite consciously outside "ordinary" life as being "not serious," but at the same time absorbing the player intensely and utterly. It is an activity connected with no material interest, and no profit can be gained by it. It proceeds within its own proper boundaries of time and space according to fixed rules and in an orderly manner. It promotes the formation of social groupings which tend to surround themselves with secrecy and to stress their difference from the common world by disguise or other means.[1]

Such a definition, in which all the words are important and meaningful, is at the same time too broad and too narrow. It is meritorious and fruitful to have grasped the affinity which exists between play and the secret or mysterious, but this relationship cannot be part of the definition of play, which is nearly always spectacular or ostentatious. Without doubt, secrecy, mystery, and even travesty can be transformed into play activity, but it must be immediately pointed out that this transformation is necessarily to the detriment of the secret and mysterious, which play exposes, publishes, and somehow *expends*. In a word, play tends to remove the very nature of the mysterious. On the other hand, when the secret, the mask; or the costume fulfills a sacramental function one can be sure that not play, but an institution is involved. All that is mysterious or make-believe by nature approaches play: moreover, it must be that the function of fiction or diversion is to remove the mystery; i.e. the mystery may no longer be awesome, and the counterfeit may not be a beginning or symptom of metamorphosis and possession.

In the second place, the part of Huizinga's definition which views play as action denuded of all material interest, simply excludes bets and games of chance—for example, gambling houses, casinos, racetracks, and lotteries—which, for better or worse, occupy an important part in the economy and daily life of various cultures. It is true that the kinds of games are almost infinitely varied, but the constant relationship between chance and profit is very striking. Games of chance played for money have practically no place in Huizinga's work. Such an omission is not without consequence.

It is certainly much more difficult to establish the cultural functions of games of chance than of competitive games. However, the influence of games of chance is no less considerable, even if deemed unfortunate, and not to consider them leads to a definition of play which affirms or implies the absence of economic interest. Therefore a distinction must be made.

In certain of its manifestations, play is designed to be extremely lucrative or ruinous. This does not preclude the fact that playing for money remains completely unproductive. The sum of the winnings at best would only equal the losses of the other players. Nearly always the winnings are less, because of large overhead, taxes, and the profits of the entrepreneur. He alone does not play, or if he plays he is protected against loss by the law of averages. In effect, he is the only one who cannot take pleasure in gambling.

Property is exchanged, but no goods are produced. What is more, this exchange affects only the players, and only to the degree that they accept, through a free decision remade at each game, the probability of such transfer. A characteristic of play, in fact, is that it creates no wealth or goods, thus differing from work or art. At the end of the game, all can and must start over again at the same point. Nothing has been harvested or manufactured, no masterpiece has been created, no capital has accrued. Play is an occasion of pure waste: waste of time, energy, ingenuity, skill, and often of money for the purchase of gambling equipment or eventually to pay for the establishment. As for the professionals—the boxers, cyclists, jockeys, or actors who earn their living in the ring, track, or hippodrome or on the stage, and who must think in terms of prize, salary, or title—it is clear that they are not players but workers. When they play, it is at some other game.

There is also no doubt that play must be defined as a free and voluntary activity, a source of joy and amusement. A game which one would be forced to play would at once cease being play. It would become constraint, drudgery from which one would strive to be freed. As an obligation or simply an order, it would lose one of its basic characteristics: the fact that the player devotes himself spontaneously to the game, of his free will and for his pleasure, each time completely free to choose retreat, silence, meditation, idle solitude, or creative activity. From this is derived Valéry's proposed definition of play: it occurs when *"l'ennui peut délier ce que l'entrain avait lié."*[2] It happens only when the players have a desire to play, and play the most absorbing, exhausting game in order to find diversion, escape from responsibility and routine. Finally and above all, it is necessary that they be free to leave whenever they please, by saying: "I am not playing any more."

In effect, play is essentially a separate occupation, carefully isolated from the rest of life, and generally is engaged in with precise limits of time and place. There is place for play: as needs dictate, the space for hopscotch, the board for checkers or chess, the stadium, the racetrack, the list, the ring, the stage, the arena, etc. Nothing that takes place outside this ideal frontier is relevant. To leave the enclosure by mistake, accident, or necessity, to send the ball out of bounds, may disqualify or entail a penalty.

The game must be taken back within the agreed boundaries. The same is true for time: the game starts and ends at a given signal. Its duration is often fixed in advance. It is improper to abandon or interrupt the game without a major reason (in children's games, crying "I give up," for example). If there is occasion to do so, the game is prolonged, by agreement between the contestants or by decision of an umpire. In every case, the game's domain is therefore a restricted, closed, protected universe: a pure space.

The confused and intricate laws of ordinary life are replaced, in this fixed space and for this given time, by precise, arbitrary, unexceptionable rules that must be accepted as such and that govern the correct playing of the game. If the cheat violates the rules, he at least pretends to respect them. He does not discuss them: he takes advantage of the other players' loyalty to the rules. From this point of view, one must agree with the writers who have stressed the fact that the cheat's dishonesty does not destroy the game. The game is ruined by the nihilist who denounces the rules as absurd and conventional, who refuses to play because the game is meaningless. His arguments are irrefutable. The game has no other but an intrinsic meaning. That is why its rules are imperative and absolute, beyond discussion. There is no reason for their being as they are, rather than otherwise. Whoever does not accept them as such must deem them manifest folly.

One plays only if and when one wishes to. In this sense, play is free activity. It is also uncertain activity. Doubt must remain until the end, and hinges upon the denouement. In a card game, when the outcome is no longer in doubt, play stops and the players lay down their hands. In a lottery or in roulette, money is placed on a number which may or may not win. In a sports contest, the powers of the contestants must be equated, so that each may have a chance until the end. Every game of skill, by definition, involves the risk for the player of missing his stroke, and the threat of defeat, without which the game would no longer be pleasing. In fact, the game is no longer pleasing to one who, because he is too well trained or skillful, wins effortlessly and infallibly.

An outcome known in advance, with no possibility of error or surprise, clearly leading to an inescapable result, is incompatible with the nature of play. Constant and unpredictable definitions of the situation are necessary, such as are produced by each attack or counterattack in fencing or football, in each return of the tennis ball, or in chess, each time one of the players moves a piece. The game consists of the need to find or continue at once a response *which is free within the limits set by the rules*. This latitude of the player, this margin accorded to his action is essential to the game and partly explains the pleasure which it excites. It is equally accountable for the remarkable and meaningful uses of the term "play," such as are reflected in such expressions as the *playing* of a performer or the *play* of a gear, to designate in the one case the personal style of an interpreter, in the other the range of movement of the parts of a machine.

Many games do not imply rules. No fixed or rigid rules exist for playing with dolls, for playing soldiers, cops and robbers, horses, locomotives, and airplanes—games, in general, which presuppose free improvisation, and the chief attraction of which lies in the pleasure of playing a role, of acting *as if* one were someone or something else, a machine for example. Despite the assertion's paradoxical character, I will state that in this instance the fiction, the sentiment of *as if*, replaces and performs the same function as do rules. Rules themselves create fictions. The one who plays chess, prisoner's base, polo, or baccara, by the very fact of complying with their respective rules, is separated from real life where there is no activity that literally corresponds to any of these games. That is why chess, prisoner's base, polo, and baccara are played *for real*. *As if* is not necessary. On the contrary, each time that play consists in imitating life, the player on the one hand lacks knowledge of how to invent and follow rules that do not exist in reality, and on the other hand the game is accompanied by the knowledge that the required behavior is pretense, or simple mimicry. This awareness of the basic unreality of the assumed behavior is separate from real life and from the arbitrary legislation that defines other games. The equivalence is so precise that the one who breaks up a game, the one who denounces the absurdity of the rules, now becomes the one who breaks the spell, who brutally refuses to acquiesce in the proposed illusion, who reminds the boy that he is not really a detective, pirate, horse, or submarine, or reminds the little girl that she is not rocking a real baby or serving a real meal to real ladies on her miniature dishes.

Thus games are not ruled and make-believe. Rather, they are ruled *or* make-believe. It is to the point that if a game with rules seems in certain circumstances like a serious activity and is beyond one unfamiliar with the rules, i.e. if it seems to him like real life, this game can at once provide the framework for a diverting make-believe for the confused and curious layman. One easily can conceive of children, in order to imitate adults, blindly manipulating real or imaginary pieces on an imaginary chessboard, and by pleasant example, playing at "playing chess."

This discussion, intended to define the nature and the largest common denominator of all games, has at the same time the advantage of placing their diversity in relief and enlarging very meaningfully the universe ordinarily explored when games are studied. In particular, these remarks tend to add two new domains to this universe: that of wagers and games of chance, and that of mimicry and interpretation. Yet there remain a number of games and entertainments that still have imperfectly defined characteristics—for example, kite-flying and top-spinning, puzzles such as crossword puzzles, the game of patience, horsemanship, seesaws, and certain carnival attractions. It will be necessary to return to this problem.

But for the present, the preceding analysis permits play to be defined as an activity which is essentially:

1. **Free:** in which playing is not obligatory; if it were, it would at once lose its attractive and joyous quality as diversion;

2. **Separate:** circumscribed within limits of space and time, defined and fixed in advance;

3. **Uncertain:** the course of which cannot be determined, nor the result attained beforehand, and some latitude for innovations being left to the player's initiative;

4. **Unproductive:** creating neither goods, nor wealth, nor new elements of any kind; and, except for the exchange of property among the players, ending in a situation identical to that prevailing at the beginning of the game;

5. **Governed by rules:** under conventions that suspend ordinary laws, and for the moment establish new legislation, which alone counts;

6. **Make-believe:** accompanied by a special awareness of a second reality or of a free unreality, as against real life.

These diverse qualities are purely formal. They do not prejudge the content of games. Also, the fact that the two last qualities—rules and make-believe—may be related, shows that the intimate nature of the facts that they seek to define implies, perhaps requires, that the latter in their turn be subdivided. This would attempt to take account not of the qualities that are opposed to reality, but of those that are clustered in groups of games with unique, irreducible characteristics.

The Classification of Games

The multitude and infinite variety of games at first causes one to despair of discovering a principle of classification capable of subsuming them under a small number of well-defined categories. Games also possess so many different characteristics that many approaches are possible. Current usage sufficiently demonstrates the degree of hesitance and uncertainty: indeed, several classifications are employed concurrently. To oppose card games to games of skill, or to oppose parlor games to those played in a stadium is meaningless. In effect, the implement used in the game is chosen as a classificatory instrument in the one case; in the other, the qualifications required; in a third the number of players and the atmosphere of the game, and lastly the place in which the contest is waged. An additional over-all complication is that the same game can be played alone or with others. A particular game may require several skills simultaneously, or none.

Very different games can be played in the same place. Merry-go-rounds and the diabolo are both open-air amusements. But the child who passively enjoys the pleasure of riding by means of the movement of the carousel is not in the same state of mind as the one who tries as best he can to correctly whirl his diabolo. On the other hand, many games are played without implements or accessories. Also, the same implement can fulfill different functions, depending on the game played. Marbles are generally the equipment for a game of skill, but one of the players can try to guess whether the marbles held in his opponent's hand are an odd or even number. They thus become part of a game of chance.

This last expression must be clarified. For one thing, it alludes to the fundamental characteristic of a very special kind of game. Whether it be a bet, lottery, roulette, or baccara, it is clear that the player's attitude is the same. He does nothing, he merely awaits the outcome. The boxer, the runner, and the player of chess or hopscotch, on the contrary, work as hard as they can to win. It matters little that some games are athletic and others intellectual. The player's attitude is the same: he tries to vanquish a rival operating under the same conditions as himself. It would thus appear justified to contrast games of chance with competitive games. Above all, it becomes tempting to investigate the possibility of discovering other attitudes, no less fundamental, so that the categories for a systematic classification of games can eventually be provided.

* * * * *

After examining different possibilities, I am proposing a division into four main rubrics, depending upon whether, in the games under consideration, the role of competition, chance, simulation, or vertigo is dominant. I call these *agôn, alea, mimicry,* and *ilinx,* respectively. All four indeed belong to the domain of play. One *plays* football, billiards, or chess (*agôn*); roulette or a lottery (*alea*); pirate, Nero, or Hamlet (*mimicry*); or one produces in oneself, by a rapid whirling or falling movement, a state of dizziness and disorder (*ilinx*). Even these designations do not cover the entire universe of play. It is divided into quadrants, each governed by an original principle. Each section contains games of the same kind. But inside each section, the different games are arranged in a rank order of progression. They can also be placed on a continuum between two opposite poles. At one extreme an almost indivisible principle, common to diversion, turbulence, free improvisation, and carefree gaiety is dominant. It manifests a kind of uncontrolled fantasy that can be designated by the term *paidia*. At the opposite extreme, this frolicsome and impulsive exuberance is almost entirely absorbed or disciplined by a complementary, and in some respects inverse, tendency to its anarchic and capricious nature: there is a growing tendency to bind it with arbitrary, imperative, and purposely tedious conventions, to oppose it still more by ceaselessly practicing the most embarrassing chicanery upon it, in order to make it more uncertain of attaining its desired effect. This latter principle is completely impractical, even though it requires an ever greater amount of effort, patience, skill, or ingenuity. I call this second component *ludus*.

I do not intend, in resorting to these strange concepts, to set up some kind of pedantic, totally meaningless mythology. However, obligated as I am to classify diverse games under the same general category, it seemed to me that the most economical means of doing so was to borrow, from one language or another, the most meaningful and comprehensive term possible, so that each category examined should avoid the possibility of lacking the particular quality on the basis of which the unifying concept was chosen. Also, to the degree that I will try to establish the classification to which I am committed, each concept chosen will not relate too directly to concrete experience, which in turn is to be divided according to an as yet untested principle.

In the same spirit, I am compelled to subsume the games most varied in appearance under the same rubric, in order to better demonstrate their fundamental kinship. I have mixed physical and mental games, those dependent upon force with those requiring skill or reasoning. Within each class, I have not distinguished between children's and adults' games, and wherever possible I have sought instances of homologous behavior in the animal world.

The point in doing this was to stress the very principle of the proposed classification. It would be less burdensome if it were perceived that the divisions set up correspond to essential and irreducible impulses.

1. Fundamental Categories

Agôn. A whole group of games would seem to be competitive, that is to say, like a combat in which equality of chances is artificially created, in order that the adversaries should confront each other under ideal conditions, susceptible of giving precise and incontestable value to the winner's triumph. It is therefore always a question of a rivalry which hinges on a single quality (speed, endurance, strength, memory, skill, ingenuity, etc.), exercised, within defined limits and without outside assistance, in such a way that the winner appears to be better than the loser in a certain category of exploits. Such is the case with sports contests and the reason for their very many subdivisions. Two individuals or two teams are in opposition (polo, tennis, football, boxing, fencing, etc.), or there may be a varying number of contestants (courses of every kind, shooting matches, golf, athletics, etc.). In the same class belong the games in which, at the outset, the adversaries divide the elements into equal parts and value. The games of checkers, chess, and billiards are perfect examples. The search for equality is so obviously essential to the rivalry that it is re-established by a handicap for players of different classes; that is, within the equality of chances originally established, a secondary inequality, proportionate to the relative powers of the participants, is dealt with. It is significant that such a usage exists in the *agôn* of a physical character (sports) just as in the more cerebral type (chess games for example, in which the weaker player is given the advantage of a pawn, knight, castle, etc.).

As carefully as one tries to bring it about, absolute equality does not seem to be realizable. Sometimes, as in checkers or chess, the fact of moving first is an advantage, for this priority permits the favored player to occupy key positions or to impose a special strategy. Conversely, in bidding games, such as bridge, the last bidder profits from the clues afforded by the bids of his opponents. Again, at croquet, to be last multiplies the player's resources. In sports contests, the exposure, the fact of having the sun in front or in back; the wind which aids or hinders one or the other side; the fact, in disputing for positions on a circular track, of finding oneself in the inside or outside lane constitutes a crucial test, a trump or disadvantage whose influence may be considerable. These inevitable imbalances are negated or modified by drawing lots at the beginning, then by strict alternation of favored positions.

The point of the game is for each player to have his superiority in a given area recognized. That is why the practice of *agôn* presupposes sustained attention, appropriate training, assiduous application, and the desire to win. It implies discipline and perseverance. It leaves the champion to his own devices, to evoke the best possible game of which he is capable, and it obliges him to play the game within the fixed limits, and according to the rules applied equally to all, so that in return the victor's superiority will be beyond dispute.

In addition to games, the spirit of *agôn* is found in other cultural phenomena conforming to the game code: in the duel, in the tournament, and in certain constant and note-worthy aspects of so-called courtly war.

In principle, it would seem that *agôn* is unknown among animals, which have no conception of limits or rules, only seeking a brutal victory in merciless combat. It is clear that horse races and cock fights are an exception, for these are conflicts in which men make animals compete in terms of norms that the former alone have set up. Yet, in considering certain facts, it seems that animals already have the competitive urge during encounters where limits are at least implicitly accepted and spontaneously respected, even if rules are lacking. This is notably the case in kittens, puppies, and bear cubs, which take pleasure in knocking each other down yet not hurting each other.

Still more convincing are the habits of bovines, which, standing face to face with heads lowered, try to force each other back. Horses engage in the same kind of friendly dueling: to test their strength, they rear up on their hind legs and press down upon each other with all their vigor and weight, in order to throw their adversaries off balance. In addition, observers have noted numerous games of pursuit that result from a challenge or invitation. The animal that is overtaken has nothing to fear from the victor. The most impressive example is without doubt that of the little ferocious "fighting" willow wrens. "A moist elevation covered with short grass and about two meters in diameter is chosen for the arena," says Karl Groos.[3] The males gather there daily. The first to arrive waits for an adversary, and then the fight begins. The contenders tremble and bow their heads several times. Their feathers bristle. They hurl themselves at each other, beaks advanced, and striking at one another. *Never is there any pursuit or conflict outside the space delimited for the journey.* That is why it seems legitimate for me to use the term *agôn* for these cases, for the goal of the encounters is not for the antagonist to cause serious injury to his rival, but rather to demonstrate his own superiority. Man merely adds refinement and precision by devising rules.

In children, as soon as the personality begins to assert itself, and before the emergence of regulated competition, unusual challenges are frequent, in which the adversaries try to prove their greater endurance. They are observed competing to see which can stare at the sun, endure tickling, stop breathing, not wink his eye, etc., the longest. Sometimes the stakes are more serious, where it is a question of enduring hunger or else pain in the form of whipping, pinching, stinging, or burning. Then these ascetic games, as they have been called, involve severe ordeals. They anticipate the cruelty and hazing which adolescents must undergo during their initiation. This is a departure from *agôn*, which soon finds its perfect form, be it in legitimately competitive games and sports, or in those involving feats of prowess (hunting, mountain climbing, crossword puzzles, chess problems, etc.) in which champions, without directly confronting each other, are involved in ceaseless and diffuse competition.

Alea. This is the Latin name for the game of dice. I have borrowed it to designate, in contrast to *agôn*, all games that are based on a decision independent of the player, an outcome over which he has no control, and in which winning is the result of fate rather than triumphing over an adversary. More properly, destiny is the sole artisan of victory, and where there is rivalry, what is meant is that the winner has been more favored by fortune than the loser. Perfect examples of this type are provided by the games of dice, roulette, heads or tails, baccara, lotteries, etc. Here, not only does one refrain from trying to eliminate the injustice of chance, but rather it is the very capriciousness of chance that constitutes the unique appeal of the game.

Alea signifies and reveals the favor of destiny. The player is entirely passive; he does not deploy his resources, skill, muscles, or intelligence. All he need do is await, in hope and trembling, the cast of the die. He risks his stake. Fair play, also sought but now taking place under ideal conditions, lies in being compensated exactly in proportion to the risk involved. Every device intended to equalize the competitors' chances is here employed to scrupulously equate risk and profit.

In contrast to *agôn, alea* negates work, patience, experience, and qualifications. Professionalization, application, and training are eliminated. In one instant, winnings may be wiped out. *Alea* is total disgrace or absolute favor. It grants the lucky player infinitely more than he could procure by a lifetime of labor, discipline, and fatigue. It seems an insolent and sovereign insult to merit. It supposes on the player's part an attitude exactly opposite to that reflected in *agôn*. In the latter, his only reliance is upon himself; in the former, he counts on

133

everything, even the vaguest sign, the slightest outside occurrence, which he immediately takes to be an omen or token—in short, he depends on everything except himself.

Agôn is a vindication of personal responsibility; *alea* is a negation of the will, a surrender to destiny. Some games, such as dominoes, backgammon, and most card games, combine the two. Chance determines the distribution of the hands dealt to each player, and the players then play the hands that blind luck has assigned to them as best they can. In a game like bridge, it is knowledge and reasoning that constitute the player's defense, permitting him to play a better game with the cards that he has been given. In games such as poker, it is the qualities of psychological acumen and character that count.

The role of money is also generally more impressive than the role of chance, and therefore is the recourse of the weaker player. The reason for this is clear: *Alea* does not have the function of causing the more intelligent to win money, but tends rather to abolish natural or acquired individual differences, so that all can be placed on an absolutely equal footing to await the blind verdict of chance.

Since the result of *agôn* is necessarily uncertain and paradoxically must approximate the effect of pure chance, assuming that the chances of the competitors are as equal as possible, it follows that every encounter with competitive characteristics and ideal rules can become the object of betting, or *alea*, e.g. horse or greyhound races, football, basketball, and cock fights. It even happens that table stakes vary unceasingly during the game, according to the vicissitudes of *agôn*.[4]

Games of chance would seem to be peculiarly human. Animals play games involving competition, stimulation, and excess. K. Groos, especially, offers striking examples of these. In sum, animals, which are very much involved in the immediate and enslaved by their impulses, cannot conceive of an abstract and inanimate power, to whose verdict they would passively submit in advance of the game. To await the decision of destiny passively and deliberately, to risk upon it wealth proportionate to the risk of losing, is an attitude that requires the possibility of foresight, vision, and speculation, for which objective and calculating reflection is needed. Perhaps it is in the degree to which a child approximates an animal that games of chance are not as important to children as to adults. For the child, play is active. In addition, the child is immune to the main attraction of games of chance, deprived as he is of economic independence, since he has no money of his own. Games of chance have no power to thrill him. To be sure, marbles are money to him. However, he counts on his skill rather than on chance to win them.

Agôn and *alea* imply opposite and somewhat complementary attitudes, but they both obey the same law—the creation for the players of conditions of pure equality denied them in real life. For nothing in life is clear, since everything is confused from the very beginning, luck and merit too. Play, whether *agôn* or *alea*, is thus an attempt to substitute perfect situations for the normal confusion of contemporary life. In games, the role of merit or chance is clear and indisputable. It is also implied that all must play with exactly the same possibility of proving their superiority or, on another scale, exactly the same chances of winning. In one way or another, one escapes the real world and creates another. One can also escape himself and become another. This is *mimicry*.

Mimicry. All play presupposes the temporary acceptance, if not of an illusion (indeed this last word means nothing less than beginning a game: *in-lusio*), then at least of a closed, conventional, and, in certain respects, imaginary universe. Play can consist not only of deploying actions or submitting to one's fate in an imaginary milieu, but of becoming an illusory character oneself, and of so behaving. One is thus confronted with a diverse series of manifestations, the common element of which is that the subject makes believe or makes others believe that he is someone other than himself. He forgets, disguises, or temporarily sheds his personality in order to feign another. I prefer to designate these phenomena by the term *mimicry*, the English word for mimetism, notably of insects, so that the fundamental, elementary, and quasi-organic nature of the impulse that stimulates it can be stressed.

The insect world, compared to the human world, seems like the most divergent of solutions provided by nature. This world is in contrast in all respects to that of man, but it is no less elaborate, complex, and surprising. Also, it seems legitimate to me at this point to take account of mimetic phenomena of which insects provide most perplexing examples. In fact, corresponding to the free, versatile, arbitrary, imperfect, and extremely diversified behavior of man, there is in animals, especially in insects, the organic, fixed, and absolute adaptation which characterizes the species and is infinitely and exactly reproduced from generation to generation in billions of individuals: e.g. the caste system of ants and termites as against class conflict, and the designs on butterflies' wings as compared to the history of painting. Reluctant as one may be to accept this hypothesis, the temerity of which I recognize, the inexplicable mimetism of insects immediately affords an extraordinary parallel to man's penchant for disguising himself, wearing a mask, or *playing a part*—except that in the insect's case the mask or guise becomes part of the body instead of a contrived accessory. But it serves the same purposes in both cases, viz. to change the wearer's appearance and to inspire fear in others.[5]

Among vertebrates, the tendency to imitate first appears as an entirely physical, quasi-irresistible contagion, analogous to the contagion of yawning, running, limping, smiling, or almost any movement. Hudson seems to have proved that a young animal "follows any object that is going away, and flees any approaching object." Just as a lamb is startled and runs if its mother turns around and moves toward the lamb without warning, the lamb trails the man, dog, or horse that it sees moving away. Contagion and imitation are not the same as simulation, but they make possible and give rise to the idea or the taste for mimicry. In birds, this tendency leads to nuptial parades, ceremonies, and exhibitions of vanity in which males or females, as the case may be, indulge with rare application and evident pleasure. As for the oxyrhinous crabs, which plant upon their carapaces any alga or polyp that they can catch, their aptitude for disguise leaves no room for doubt, whatever explanation for the phenomenon may be advanced.

Mimicry and travesty are therefore complementary acts in this kind of play. For children, the aim is to imitate adults. This explains the success of the toy weapons and miniatures which copy the tools, engines, arms, and machines used by adults. The little girl plays her mother's role as cook, laundress, and ironer. The boy makes believe he is a soldier, musketeer, policeman, pirate, cowboy, Martian,[8] etc. An airplane is made by waving his arms and making the noise of a motor. However, acts of mimicry tend to cross the border between childhood and adulthood. They cover to the same degree any distraction, mask, or travesty, in which one participates, and which stresses the very fact that the play is masked or otherwise disguised, and such consequences as ensue. Lastly it is clear that theatrical presentations and dramatic interpretations rightly belong in this category.

The pleasure lies in being or passing for another. But in games the basic intention is not that of deceiving the spectators. The child who is playing train may well refuse to kiss his father while saying to him that one does not embrace locomotives, but he is not trying to persuade his father that he is a real locomotive. At a carnival, the masquerader does not try to make one believe that he is really a marquis, toreador, or Indian, but rather tries to inspire fear and take advantage of the surrounding license, a result of the fact that the mask disguises the conventional self and liberates the true personality. The actor does not try to make believe that he is "really" King Lear or Charles V. It is only the spy and the fugitive who disguise themselves to really deceive because they are not playing.

Activity, imagination, interpretation, and *mimicry* have hardly any relationship to *alea*, which requires immobility and the thrill of expectation from the player, but *agôn* is not excluded. I am not thinking of the masqueraders' competition, in which the relationship is obvious. A much more subtle complicity is revealed. For nonparticipants, every *agôn* is a spectacle. Only it is a spectacle which, to be valid, excludes simulation. Great sports events are nevertheless special occasions for *mimicry*, but it must be recalled that the simulation is now transferred from the participants to the audience. It is not the athletes who mimic, but the spectators. Identification with the champion in itself constitutes *mimicry* related to that of the reader with the hero of the novel and that of the moviegoer with the film star. To be convinced of this, it is merely necessary to consider the perfectly symmetrical functions of the champion and the stage or screen star. Champions, winners at *agôn*, are the stars of sports contests. Conversely, stars are winners in a more diffuse competition in which the stakes are popular favor. Both receive a large fan-mail, give interviews to an avid press, and sign autographs.

In fact, bicycle races, boxing or wrestling matches, football, tennis, or polo games are intrinsic spectacles, with costumes, solemn overture, appropriate liturgy, and regulated procedures. In a word, these are dramas whose vicissitudes keep the public breathless, and lead to denouements which exalt some and depress others. The nature of these spectacles remains that of an *agôn*, but their outward aspect is that of an exhibition. The audience are not content to encourage the efforts of the athletes or horses of their choice merely by voice and gesture. A physical contagion leads them to assume the position of the men or animals in order to help them, just as the bowler is known to unconsciously incline his body in the direction that he would like the bowling ball to take at the end of its course. Under these conditions, paralleling the spectacle, a competitive *mimicry* is born in the public, which doubles the true *agôn* of the field or track.

With one exception, *mimicry* exhibits all the characteristics of play: liberty, convention, suspension of reality, and delimitation of space and time. However, the continuous submission to imperative and precise rules cannot be observed—rules for the dissimulation of reality and the substitution of a second reality. *Mimicry* is incessant invention. The rule of the game is unique: it consists in the actor's fascinating the spectator, while avoiding an error that might lead the spectator to break the spell. The spectator must lend himself to the illusion without first challenging the decor, mask, or artifice which for a given time he is asked to believe in as more real than reality itself.

*Ilinx.*The last kind of game includes those which are based on the pursuit of vertigo and which consist of an attempt to momentarily destroy the stability of perception and inflict a kind of voluptuous panic upon an otherwise lucid mind. In all cases, it is a question of surrendering to a kind of spasm, seizure, or shock which destroys reality with sovereign brusqueness.

The disturbance that provokes vertigo is commonly sought for its own sake. I need only cite as examples the actions of whirling dervishes and the Mexican *voladores.* I choose these purposely, for the former, in technique employed, can be related to certain children's games, while the latter rather recall the elaborate maneuvers of high-wire acrobatics. They thus touch the two poles of games of vertigo. Dervishes seek ecstasy by whirling about with movements accelerating as the drumbeats become ever more precipitate. Panic and hypnosis are attained by the paroxysm of frenetic, contagious, and shared rotation.[7] In Mexico, the *voladores*—Huastec or Totonac—climb to the top of a mast sixty-five to one hundred feet high. They are disguised as eagles with false wings hanging from their wrists. The end of a rope is attached to their waists. The rope then passes between their toes in such a way that they can manage their entire descent with head down and arms outstretched. Before reaching the ground, they make many complete turns, thirty according to Torquemada, describing an ever-widening spiral in their downward flight. The ceremony, comprising several flights and beginning at noon, is readily interpreted as a dance of the setting sun, associated with birds, the deified dead. The frequency of accidents has led the Mexican authorities to ban this dangerous exercise.[8]

It is scarcely necessary to invoke these rare and fascinating examples. Every child very well knows that by whirling rapidly he reaches a centrifugal state of flight from which he regains bodily stability and clarity of perception only with difficulty. The child engages in this activity playfully and finds pleasure thereby. An example is the game of teetotum[9] in which the player pivots on one foot as quickly as he is able. Analogously, in the Haitian game of *maïs d'or* two children hold hands, face to face, their arms extended. With their bodies stiffened and bent backward, and with their feet joined, they turn until they are breathless, so that they will have the pleasure of staggering about after they stop. Comparable sensations are provided by screaming as loud as one can, racing downhill, and tobogganing; in horsemanship, provided that one turns quickly; and in swinging.

Various physical activities also provoke these sensations, such as the tightrope, falling or being projected into space, rapid rotation, sliding, speeding, and acceleration of vertilinear movement, separately or in combination with gyrating movement. In parallel fashion, there is a vertigo of a moral order, a transport that suddenly seizes the individual. This vertigo is readily linked to the desire for disorder and destruction, a drive which is normally repressed. It is reflected in crude and brutal forms of personality expression. In children, it is especially observed in the games of hot cockles, "winner-take-all," and leapfrog in which they rush and spin pell-mell. In adults, nothing is more revealing of vertigo than the strange excitement that is felt in cutting down the tall prairie flowers with a switch, or in creating an avalanche of the snow on a rooftop, or, better, the intoxication that is experienced in military barracks—for example, in noisily banging garbage cans.

To cover the many varieties of such transport, for a disorder that may take organic or psychological form, I propose using the term *ilinx*, the Greek term for whirlpool, from which is also derived the Greek word for vertigo (*ilingos*).

This pleasure is not unique to man. To begin with, it is appropriate to recall the gyrations of certain mammals, sheep in particular. Even if these are pathological manifestations, they are too significant to be passed over in silence. In addition, examples in which the play element is certain are not lacking. In order to catch their tails dogs will spin around until they fall down. At other times they are seized by a fever for running until they are exhausted. Antelopes, gazelles, and wild horses are often panic-stricken when there is no real danger in the slightest degree to account for it; the impression is of an overbearing contagion to which they surrender in instant compliance.[10]

Water rats divert themselves by spinning as if they were being drawn by an eddy in a stream. The case of the chamois is even more remarkable. According to Karl Groos, they ascend the glaciers, and with a leap, each in turn slides down a steep slope, while the other chamois watch.

The gibbon chooses a flexible branch and weighs it down until it unbends, thus projecting him into the air. He lands catch as catch can, and he endlessly repeats this useless exercise, inexplicable except in terms of its seductive quality. Birds especially love games of vertigo. They let themselves fall like stones from a great height, then open their wings when they are only a few feet from the ground, thus giving the impression that they are going to be crushed. In the mating season they utilize this heroic flight in order to attract the female. The American nighthawk, described by Audubon, is a virtuoso at these impressive acrobatics.[11]

Following the teetotum, *maïs d'or*, sliding, horsemanship, and swinging of their childhood, men surrender to the intoxication of many kinds of dance, from the common but insidious giddiness of the waltz to the many mad, tremendous, and convulsive movements of other dances. They derive the same kind of pleasure from the intoxication stimulated by high speed on skis, motorcycles, or in driving sports cars. In order to give this kind of sensation the intensity and brutality capable of shocking adults, powerful machines have had to be invented. Thus it is not surprising that the Industrial Revolution had to take place before vertigo could really become a kind of game. It is now provided for the avid masses by thousands of stimulating contraptions installed at fairs and amusement parks.

These machines would obviously surpass their goals if it were only a question of assaulting the organs of the inner ear, upon which the sense of equilibrium is dependent. But it is the whole body which must submit to such treatment as anyone would fear undergoing, were it not that everybody else was seen struggling to do the same. In fact, it is worth watching people leaving these vertigo-inducing machines. The contraptions turn people pale and dizzy to the point of nausea. They shriek with fright, gasp for breath, and have the terrifying impression of visceral fear and shrinking as if to escape a horrible attack. Moreover the majority of them, before even recovering, are already hastening to the ticket booth in order to buy the right to again experience the same pleasurable torture.

It is necessary to use the word "pleasure," because one hesitates to call such a transport a mere distraction, corresponding as it does more to a spasm than to an entertainment. In addition, it is important to note that the violence of the shock felt is such that the concessionaires try, in extreme cases, to lure the naive by offering free rides. They deceitfully announce that "this time only" the ride is free, when this is the usual practice. To compensate, the spectators are made to pay for the privilege of calmly observing from a high balcony the terrors of the cooperating or surprised victims, exposed to fearful forces or strange caprices.

It would be rash to draw very precise conclusions on the subject of this curious and cruel assignment of roles. This last is not characteristic of a kind of game, such as is found in boxing, wrestling, and in gladiatorial combat. Essential is the pursuit of this special disorder or sudden panic, which defines the term vertigo, and in the true characteristics of the games associated with it: viz. the freedom to accept or refuse the experience, strict and fixed limits, and separation from the rest of reality. What the experience adds to the spectacle does not diminish but reinforces its character as play.

2. From Turbulence to Rules

Rules are inseparable from play as soon as the latter becomes institutionalized. From this moment on they become part of its nature. They transform it into an instrument of fecund and decisive culture. But a basic freedom is central to play in order to stimulate distraction and fantasy. This liberty is its indispensable motive power and is basic to the most complex and carefully organized forms of play. Such a primary power of improvisation and joy, which I call *paidia*, is allied to the taste for gratuitous difficulty that I propose to call *ludus*, in order to encompass the various games to which, without exaggeration, a civilizing quality can be attributed. In fact, they reflect the moral and intellectual values of a culture, as well as contribute to their refinement and development.

I have chosen the term *paidia* because its root is the word for child, and also because of a desire not to needlessly disconcert the reader by resorting to a term borrowed from an antipodal language. However, the Sanskrit *kredati* and the Chinese *wan* seem both richer and more expressive through the variety and nature of their connotations. It is true that they also present the disadvantages of overabundance—a certain danger of confusion, for one. *Kredati* designates the play of adults, children, and animals. It applies more specifically to gamboling, i.e., to the sudden and capricious movements provoked by a superabundance of gaiety and vitality. It applies equally to illicit sex relationships, the rise and fall of waves, and anything that undulates with the wind. The word *wan* is even more explicit, as much for what it defines as for what it avoids defining, i.e. specifying games of skill, competition, simulation, and chance. It manifests many refinements of meaning to which I will have occasion to return.

In view of these relationships and semantic qualifications, what can be the connotations and denotations of the term *paidia?* I shall define it, for my purposes, as a word covering the spontaneous manifestations of the play instinct: a cat entangled in a ball of wool, a dog sniffing, and an infant laughing at his rattle represent the first identifiable examples of this type of activity. It intervenes in every happy exuberance which effects an immediate and disordered agitation, an impulsive and easy recreation, but readily carried to excess, whose impromptu and unruly character remains its essential if not unique reason for being. From somersaults to scribbling, from squabble to uproar, perfectly clear illustrations are not lacking of the comparable symptoms of movements, colors, or noises.

This elementary need for disturbance and tumult first appears as an impulse to touch, grasp, taste, smell, and then drop any accessible object. It readily can become a taste for destruction and breaking things. It explains the pleasure in endlessly cutting up paper with a pair of scissors, pulling cloth into thread, breaking up a gathering, holding up a queue, disturbing the play or work of others, etc. Soon comes the desire to mystify or to defy by sticking out the tongue or grimacing while seeming to touch or throw the forbidden object. For the child it is a question of expressing himself, of feeling he is the *cause*, of forcing others to pay attention to him. In this manner, K. Groos recalls the case of a monkey which took pleasure in pulling the tail of a dog that lived with it, each time that the dog seemed to be going to sleep. The primitive joy in destruction and upset has been notably observed by the sister of G. J. Romanes in precise and most meaningful detail.[12]

The child does not stop at that. He loves to play with his own pain, for example by probing a toothache with his tongue. He also likes to be frightened. He thus looks for a physical illness, limited and controlled, of which he is the cause, or sometimes he seeks an anxiety that he, being the cause, can stop at will. At various points, the fundamental aspects of play are already recognizable, i.e. voluntary, agreed upon, isolated, and regulated activity.

Soon there is born the desire to invent rules, and to abide by them whatever the cost. The child then makes all kinds of bets—which, as has been seen, are the elementary forms of *agôn*—with himself or his friends. He hops, walks backwards with his eyes closed, plays at who can look longest at the sun, and will suffer pain or stand in a painful position.

In general, the first manifestations of *paidia* have no name and could not have any, precisely because they are not part of any order, distinctive symbolism, or clearly differentiated life that would permit a vocabulary to consecrate their autonomy with a specific term. But as soon as conventions, techniques, and utensils emerge, the first games as such arise with them: e.g. leapfrog, hide and seek, kite-flying, teetotum, sliding, blindman's buff, and doll-play. At this point the contradictory roads of *agôn, alea, mimicry,* and *ilinx* begin to bifurcate. At the same time, the pleasure experienced in solving a problem arbitrarily designed for this purpose also intervenes, so that reaching a solution has no other goal than personal satisfaction for its own sake.

This condition, which is *ludus* proper, is also reflected in different kinds of games, except for those which wholly depend upon the cast of a die. It is complementary to and a refinement of *paidia*, which it disciplines and enriches. It provides an occasion for training and normally leads to the acquisition of a special skill, a particular mastery of the operation of one or another contraption or the discovery of a satisfactory solution to problems of a more conventional type.

The difference from *agôn* is that in ludus the tension and skill of the player are not related to any explicit feeling of emulation or rivalry: the conflict is with the obstacle, not with one or several competitors. On the level of manual dexterity there can be cited games such as cup-and-ball, diabolo, and yo-yo. These simple instruments merely utilize basic natural laws, e.g. gravity and rotation in the case of the yo-yo, where the point is to transform a rectilinear alternating motion into a continuous circular movement. Kite-flying, on the contrary, relies on the exploitation of a specific atmospheric condition. Thanks to this, the player accomplishes a kind of auscultation upon the sky from afar. He projects his presence beyond the limits of his body. Again, the game of blindman's buff offers an opportunity to experience the quality of perception in the absence of sight.[13] It is readily seen that the possibilities of *ludus* are almost infinite.

Games such as solitaire or the ring puzzle, although part of the same species, already belong to another group of games, since they constantly appeal to a spirit of calculation and contrivance. And lastly, crossword puzzles, mathematical recreations, anagrams, olorhymes[14] and obscure poetry, addiction to detective stories (trying to identify the culprit), and chess or bridge problems constitute, even in the absence of gadgets, many varieties of the most prevalent and pure forms of *ludus*.

It is common knowledge that what to begin with seems to be a situation susceptible to indefinite repetition turns out to be capable of producing ever new combinations. Thus the player is stimulated to emulate himself, permitting him to take pride in his accomplishment, as against those who share his taste. There is a manifest relationship between *ludus* and *agôn*. In addition, it can happen that the same game may possess both, e.g. chess or bridge.

The combination of ludus and alea is no less frequent: it is especially recognizable in games of patience, in which ingenious maneuvers have little influence upon the result, and in playing slot machines in which the player can very crudely calculate the impulsion given to the ball at various points in directing its course. In both these examples, chance is still the deciding factor. Moreover, the fact that the player is not completely helpless and that he can at least minimally count on his skill or talent is sufficient reason to link *ludus* with *alea*.[15]

Ludus is also readily compatible with *mimicry*. In the simplest cases, it lends aspects of illusion to construction games such as the animals made out of millet stalks by Dogon children, the cranes or automobiles constructed by fitting together perforated steel parts and pullies from an Erector set, or the scale-model planes or ships that even adults do not disdain meticulously constructing. However, it is the theater which provides the basic connection between the two, by disciplining mimicry until it becomes an art rich in a thousand diverse routines, refined techniques, and subtly complex resources. By means of this fortunate development, the cultural fecundity of play is amply demonstrated.

In contrast, just as there could be no relationship between *paidia*, which is tumultuous and exuberant, and *alea*, which is passive anticipation of and mute immobility pending the outcome of the game, there also can be no connection between *ludus*, which is calculation and contrivance, and *ilinx*, which is a pure state of transport. The desire to overcome an obstacle can only emerge to combat vertigo and prevent it from becoming transformed into disorder or panic. It is, therefore, training in self-control, an arduous effort to preserve calm and equilibrium. Far from being compatible with *ilinx*, it provides the discipline needed to neutralize the dangerous effects of *ilinx*, as in mountain climbing or tightrope walking.

Ludus, in itself, seems incomplete, a kind of makeshift device intended to allay boredom. One becomes resigned to it while awaiting something preferable, such as the arrival of partners that makes possible the substitution of a contest for this solitary pleasure. Moreover, even in games of skill or contrivance (e.g. patience, crossword and other puzzles) which exclude or regard as undesirable the intervention of another person, *ludus* no less inspires in the player the hope of succeeding the next time when he may obtain a higher score. In this way, the influence of *agôn* is again manifested. Indeed, it enriches the pleasure derived from overcoming an arbitrarily chosen obstacle. In fact, even if each of these games is played alone and is not replaced by an openly competitive one, it can easily and quickly be converted into a contest, with or without prizes, such as newspapers organize on occasion.

There is also an aspect of *ludus* that, in my opinion, is explained by the presence of *agôn* within it: that is, that it is strongly affected by fashion. The yo-yo, cup-and-ball, diabolo, and ring puzzle appear and disappear as if by magic and soon are replaced by other games. In parallel fashion, the vogues for amusements of a more intellectual nature are no less limited in time; e.g. the rebus, the anagram, the acrostic, and the charade have had their hours. It is probable that crossword puzzles and detective stories will run the same course. Such a phenomenon would be enigmatic if *ludus* were an individual amusement, as seems superficially to be the case. In reality, it is permeated with an atmosphere of competition. It only persists to the degree that the fervor of addicts transforms it into virtual *agôn*. When the latter is missing, *ludus* cannot persist independently. In fact, it is not sufficiently supported by the spirit of organized competition, which is not essential to it, and does not provide the substance for a spectacle capable of attracting crowds. It remains transient and diffuse, or else it risks turning into an obsession for the isolated fanatic who would dedicate himself to it absolutely and in his addiction would increasingly withdraw from society.

Industrial civilization has given birth to a special form of *ludus*, the hobby, a secondary and gratuitous activity, undertaken and pursued for pleasure, e.g. collecting, unique accomplishments, the pleasure in billiards or inventing gadgets, in a word any occupation that is primarily a compensation for the injury to personality caused by bondage to work of an automatic and picayune character. It has been observed that the hobby of the worker-turned-artisan readily takes the form of constructing *complete* scale models of the machines in the fabrication of which he is fated to cooperate by always repeating the same movement, an operation demanding no skill or intelligence on his part. He not only avenges himself upon reality, but in a positive and creative way. The hobby is a response to one of the highest functions of the play instinct. It is not surprising that a technical civilization contributes to its development, even to providing compensations for its more brutal aspects. Hobbies reflect the rare qualities that make their development possible.

In a general way, *ludus* relates to the primitive desire to find diversion and amusement in arbitrary, perpetually recurrent obstacles. Thousands of occasions and devices are invented to satisfy simultaneously the desire for relaxation and the need, of which man cannot be rid, to utilize purposefully the knowledge, experience, and intelligence at his disposal, while disregarding self-control and his capacity for resistance to suffering, fatigue, panic, or intoxication.

What I call *ludus* stands for the specific element in play the impact and cultural creativity of which seems most impressive. It does not connote a psychological attitude as-precise as that of *agôn, alea, mimicry* or *ilinx*, but in disciplining the *paidia*, its general contribution is to give the fundamental categories of play their purity and excellence.

Besides, *ludus* is not the only conceivable metamorphosis of *paidia*. A civilization like that of classical China worked out a different destiny for itself. Wisely and circumspectly, Chinese culture is less directed toward purposive innovation. The need for progress and the spirit of enterprise generally seem to them a kind of compulsion that is not particularly creative. Under these conditions the turbulence and surplus of energy characteristic of *paidia* is channelized in a direction better suited to its supreme values. This is the place to return to the term *wan*. According to some, it would etymologically designate the act of indefinitely caressing a piece of jade while polishing it, in order to savor its smoothness or as an accompaniment to reverie. Perhaps this origin clarifies another purpose of *paidia*. The reservoir of free movement that is part of its original definition seems in this case to be oriented not toward process, calculation, or triumph over difficulties but toward calm, patience, and idle speculation. The term wan basically designates all kinds of semiautomatic activities which leave the mind detached and idle, certain complex games which are part of *ludus*, and at the same time, nonchalant meditation and lazy contemplation.

Tumult and din are covered by the expression *jeou-nao*, which means literally "passion-disorder." When joined to the term *nao*, the term *wan* connotes any exuberant or joyous behavior. But this term *wan* must be present. With the character *tchouang* (to pretend), it means "to find pleasure in simulating." Thus *wan* coincides fairly exactly with the various possible manifestations of *paidia*, although when used alone it may designate a particular kind of game. It is not used for competition, dice, or dramatic interpretation. That is to say, it excludes the various kinds of games that I have referred to as institutional.

The latter are designated by more specialized terms. The character *hsi* corresponds to games of disguise or simulation, covering the domain of the theater and the spectacle. The character *choua* refers to games involving skill and ability; however, it is also used for contests involving jokes or puns, for fencing, and for perfection in practicing a difficult art. The character *teou* refers to conflict as such, cock fighting or dueling. It is also used for card games. Lastly, the character *tou*, not to be applied to children's games, covers games of chance, feats of daring, bets, and ordeals. It also is the name for blasphemy, for to tempt chance is considered a sacrilegious wager against destiny.[16]

The vast semantic area of the term *wan* makes it even more deserving of interest. To begin with, it includes child's play and all kinds of carefree and frivolous diversion such as are suggested by the verbs to frolic, to romp, to trifle, etc. It is used to describe casual, abnormal, or strange sex practices. At the same time, it is used for games demanding reflection and *forbidding haste*, such as chess, checkers, puzzles (*tai Kiao*), and the game of nine rings.[17] It also comprises the pleasure of appreciating the savor of good food or the bouquet of a wine, the taste for collecting works of art or even appreciating them, voluptuously handling and even fashioning delicate curios, comparable to the Occidental category of the hobby, collecting or puttering. Lastly, the transitory and relaxing sweetness of moonlight is suggested, the pleasure of a boat ride on a limpid lake or the prolonged contemplation of a waterfall.[18]

The example of the word *wan* shows that the destinies of cultures can be read in their games. The preference for *agôn, alea, mimicry,* or *ilinx* helps decide the future of a civilization. Also, the channeling of the free energy in *paidia* toward invention or contemplation manifests an implicit but fundamental and most significant choice.

Table I. Classification of Games

	AGÔN (Competition)	ALEA (Chance)	MIMICRY (Simulation)	ILINX (Vertigo)
PAIDIA Tumult Agitation Immoderate laughter	Racing Wrestling } not Etc. } regulated Athletics	Counting-out rhymes Heads or tails	Children's initiations Games of illusion Tag, Arms Masks, Disguises	Children "whirling" Horseback riding Swinging Waltzing
	Boxing, Billiards Fencing, Checkers Football, Chess	Betting Roulette		Volador Traveling carnivals Skiing Mountain climbing Tightrope walking
LUDUS Kite-flying Solitaire Patience Crossword puzzles	Contests, Sports in general	Simple, complex, and continuing lotteries*	Theater Spectacles in general	

N.B. In each vertical column games are classified in such an order that the *paidia* element is constantly decreasing while the *ludus* element is ever increasing.

* A simple lottery consists of the one basic drawing. In a complex lottery there are many possible combinations. A continuing lottery (e.g. Irish Sweepstakes) is one consisting of two or more stages, the winner of the first stage being granted the opportunity to participate in a second lottery. [From correspondence with Caillois. M.B.]

Notes

1. J. Huizinga, *Homo Ludens* (English translation; New York: Roy Publishers, 1950, p. 13). On p. 28 there is another definition not quite as eloquent, but less restricted: "Play is a voluntary activity or occupation executed within certain fixed limits of time and place, according to rules freely accepted but absolutely binding, having its aim in itself and accompanied by a feeling of tension, joy, and consciousness that it is different from ordinary life."

2. Paul Valéry, *Tel quel*, II (Paris, 1943), p. 21.

3. Karl Groos, *The Play of Animals* (English translation; New York: D. Appleton & Co., 1898, p. 151).

4. For example, in the Balearic Islands for jai-alai, and cockfights in the Antilles. It is obvious that it is not necessary to take into account the cash prizes that may motivate jockeys, owners, runners, boxers, football players, or other athletes. These prizes, however substantial, are not relevant to *alea*. They are a reward for a well-fought victory. This recompense for merit has nothing to do with luck or the result of chance, which remain the uncertain monopoly of gamblers; in fact it is the direct opposite.

5. Terrifying examples of mimicry or structural dissimulation among insects (the spectral attitude of the mantis and the fright offered by *Smerinthus ocellata*) will be found in my study entitled "*Mimétisme et psychasténie*," in *Le Mythe et L'Homme* (Paris, 1938), pp. 101–143. Unfortunately, this study treats the problem with a perspective that today seems fantastic to me. Indeed I no longer view mimetism as a disturbance of space perception and a tendency to return to the inanimate, but rather, as herein proposed, as the insect equivalent of human games of simulation. The examples utilized in *Le Mythe et L'Homme* nevertheless retain their value [translated by M. B. from French text]:

"In order to protect itself, an inoffensive animal assumes the appearance of a ferocious animal; for example the bee-shaped butterfly *Trochilium* and the wasp *Vespa crabro*: even to the smoky wings, brown feet and antennae, yellow-and-black striped abdomens and thoraxes, and the same impressive noisy flight in broad day. Sometimes the mimetic animal has a further goal. The caterpillar *Choerocampa elpenor*, for example, has two eyelike black-bordered spots on its fourth and fifth segments. When disturbed it retracts its anterior segments. The fourth swells enormously. The effect obtained is the illusion of a snake's head, a frightening apparition to lizards and small birds (L. Cuénot, *La génèse des espèces animales*, Paris, 1911, pp. 470 and 473). According to Weismann (*Vorträge über Descendenztheorie*, Vol. 1, pp. 78–79) *Smerinthus ocellata*, which like all sphinxes at rest hides its lower wings, when in danger suddenly masks them with two large blue eyes on a red background, thus unexpectedly frightening the aggressor. [This terrifying transformation is automatic. It is approximated in cutaneous reflexes which, although they do not extend as far as a change of color designed to transform the animal, sometimes result in lending it a terrifying quality. A cat, confronted by a dog, is frightened; its hair stands on end, thus causing the cat to become frightening. Le Dantec by this analogy (*Lamarckiens et Darwiniens,* 3rd ed.; Paris, 1908, p. 139) explains the human phenomenon known as "goose pimples," a common result of extreme fright. Even though rendered dysfunctional by the comparative hairlessness of man, the reflex still persists.] This act is accompanied by a kind of nervousness. At rest, the animal resembles a thin, dessicated leaf. When disturbed, it clings to its perch, extends its antennae, inflates its thorax, retracts its head, exaggerates the curve of its abdomen, while its whole body shakes and shivers. The crisis past, it slowly returns to immobility. Standfuss' experiments have demonstrated the efficacy of this behavior in frightening the tomtit, the robin, the common nightingale and frequently the grey nightingale. [Cf. Standfuss, "Beispiel von Schutz and Trutzfärbung," *Mitt. Schweitz. Entomol. Ges.,* XI (1906), 155–157; P. Vignon, *Introduction a la biologie expérimentale,* Paris, 1930 (*Encycl. Biol.,* Vol. VIII), p. 356]. The moth, with extended wings, seems in fact like the head of an enormous bird of prey....

"Examples of homomorphism are not lacking: the *calappes* and round pebbles, the *chlamys* and seeds, the *moenas* and gravel, the prawns and fucus. The fish *Phylopteryx* of the Sargasso Sea is only an 'alga cut into the shape of a floating lanner' (L. Murat, *Les merveilles du monde animal,* 1914, pp. 37–38) like *Antennarius* and *Pterophryne* (L. Cuénot, *op. cit.,* p. 453). The polyp retracts its tentacles, crooks its back, and adapts its color so that it resembles a pebble. The white and green lower wings of *catocala nupta* resemble the umbelliferae. The embossments, nodes, and streaks of the pieridine, *Aurora,* make it identical with the bark of the poplars on which it lives. The lichens of *Lithinus nigrocristinus* of Madagascar and the Flatides cannot be distinguished (*ibid.,* Fig. 114). The extent of mimetism among the mantidae is known. Their paws simulate petals or are rounded into corollae, which resemble flowers, imitating the effects of the wind upon the flowers through a delicate mechanical balance (A. Lefèbvre, *Ann. de la Soc. entom. de France,* Vol. IV; Léon Binet, *La vie de la mante religieuse,* Paris, 1931; P. Vignon, *op. cit.,* pp. 374 ff.). *Cilix compressa* resembles a type of bird dung, and the *Ceroxeylus laceratus* with its foliated, light olive-green excrescences resembles a stick covered with moss. This last insect belongs to the phasmidae family which generally hang from bushes in the forest and have the bizarre habit of letting their paws hang irregularly thus making the error even easier (Alfred R. Wallace, *Natural Selection and Tropical Nature,* London: Macmillan, 1895, p. 47). To the same family belong even the bacilli which resemble twigs. *Ceroys* and *Heteropteryx* resemble thorny dessicated branches; and the *membracides,* hemiplera of the Tropics, resemble buds or thorns, such as the impressive thorn-shaped insect, *Umbonia orozimbo.* Measuring worms, erect and rigid, can scarcely be distinguished from bush sprouts, equipped as they are with appropriate tegumentary wrinkles. Everyone is familiar with the insect of the genus *Phyllium* which resembles leaves. From here, the road leads to the perfect homomorphism of certain butterflies: *Oxydia,* above all, which perches perpendicularly from the tip of a branch, upper wings folded over, so that it looks like a terminal leaf. This guise is accentuated by a thin, dark line continuing across the four wings in such a way that the main vein of a leaf is simulated (Rabaud, *Éléments de biologie générale,* 2nd ed., Paris, 1928, p. 412, Fig. 54).

"Other species are even more perfected, their lower wings being provided with a delicate appendix used as a petiole, thus obtaining 'a foothold in the vegetable world' (Vignon, *loc. cit.*). The total impression of the two wings on each side is that of the lanceolate oval characteristic of the leaf. There is also a longitudinal line, continuing from one wing to the other, a substitute for the median vein of the leaf; 'the organic driving force has had to design and cleverly organize each of the wings so that it should attain a form not self-determined, but through union with the other wing' (*ibid.*). The main examples are *Coenophlebia archidona* of Central America (Delage and Goldsmith, *Les théories de l'évolution,* Paris, 1909, Fig. 1, p. 74) and the various types of *Kallima* in India and Malaysia."

Additional examples: *Le Mythe et L'Homme,* pp. 133–136.

6. As has been aptly remarked, girls' playthings are designed to imitate practical, realistic, and domestic activities, while those of boys suggest distant, romantic, inaccessible, or even obviously unreal actions.

7. O. Depont and X. Coppolani, *Les confréries religieuses musulmanes* (Algiers, 1887), pp. 156–159, 329–339.

8. Description and photographs in Helga Larsen, "Notes on the Volador and Its Associated Ceremonies and Superstitions." *Ethnos.* 2, No. 4 (July, 1937), 179–192, and in Guy Stresser-Péan, "Les origines du volador et du comelagatoazte," *Actes du XXVIIIe Congres International des Américanistes* (Paris, 1947), 327–334. I quote part of the description of the ceremony from this article [translated by M. B. from French text]:

"The chief of the dance or *K'ohal,* clad in a red and blue tunic, ascends in his turn and sits on the terminal platform. Facing east, he first invokes the benevolent deities, while extending his wings in their direction and using a whistle which imitates the puling of eagles. Then he climbs to the top of the mast. Facing the four points of the compass in succession, he offers them a chalice of calabash wrapped in white linen just like a bottle of brandy, from which he sips and spits some more or less vaporized mouthfuls. Once this symbolic offering has been made, he puts on his headdress of red feathers and dances, facing all four directions while beating his wings.

"These ceremonies executed at the summit of the mast mark what the Indians consider the most moving phase of the ritual, because it involves mortal risk. But the next stage of the 'flight' is even more spectacular. The four dancers, attached by the waist, pass underneath the structure, then let themselves go from behind. Thus suspended, they slowly descend to the ground, describing a grand spiral in proportion to the unrolling of the ropes. The difficult thing for these dancers is to seize this rope between their toes in such a way as to keep their heads down and arms outspread just like descending birds which soar in great circles in the sky. As for the chief, first he waits for some moments, then he lets himself glide along one of the four dancers' ropes."

9. [*Toton* in the French text. M. B.]

10. Groos, *op. cit.*, p. 208.

11. *Ibid.*, p. 259.

12. Observation cited by Groos, *ibid.*, pp. 92–93:

"I notice that the love of mischief is very strong in him. Today he got hold of a wine-glass and an egg cup. The glass he dashed on the floor with all his might and of course broke it. Finding, however, that the egg cup would not break when thrown down, he looked round for some hard substance against which to dash it. The post of the brass bedstead appearing to be suitable for the purpose, he raised the egg cup high above his head and gave it several hard blows. When it was completely smashed he was quite satisfied. He breaks a stick by passing it down between a heavy object and the wall and then hanging onto the end, thus breaking it across the heavy object. He frequently destroys an article of dress by carefully pulling out the threads (thus unraveling it) before he begins to tear it with his teeth in a violent manner.

"In accordance with his desire for mischief he is, of course, very fond of upsetting things, but he always takes great care that they do not fall on himself. Thus he will pull a chair toward him till it is almost overbalanced, then he intently fixes his eyes on the top bar of the back, and when he sees it coming over his way, darts from underneath and watches the fall with great delight; and similarly with heavier things. There is a washstand, for example, with a heavy marble top, which he has with great labor upset several times, but always without hurting himself." (G. J. Romanes, *Animal Intelligence*, New York, D. Appleton & Co., 1897, p. 484.)

13. This had already been observed by Kant. Cf. Y. Hirn, *Les jeux d'enfants* (French translation; Paris, 1926), p. 63.

14. [Olorimes (in French) are two lines of poetry in which each syllable of the first line rhymes with the corresponding syllable of the second line. Caillois suggested the following couplet from Victor Hugo as an example:

> *Gal, amant de la reine, alle, tour magnanime*
>
> *Galamment de l'arène a la Tour Magne, a Nimes*

From correspondence with Caillois, M. B.]

15. The development of slot machines in the modern world and the fascination or obsessive

behavior that they cause is indeed astonishing. The vogue for playing slot machines is often of unsuspected proportions. It causes true obsessions and sometimes is a contributing factor to a youth's entire way of life. The following account appeared in the press on March 25, 1957, occasioned by the investigation conducted by the United States Senate that same month:

"Three hundred thousand slot machines manufactured by 15,000 employees in 50 factories, most of which are located in the environs of Chicago, were sold in 1956. These machines are popular not only in Chicago, Kansas City, or Detroit—not to speak of Las Vegas, the capital of gambling—but also in New York. All day and all night in Times Square, the heart of New York, Americans of all ages, from schoolboy to old man, spend their pocket money or weekly pension in an hour, in the vain hope of winning a free game. At 1485 Broadway, 'Play-land' in gigantic neon letters eclipses the sign of a Chinese restaurant. In an immense room without a door dozens of multicolored slot machines are aligned in perfect order. In front of each machine a comfortable leather stool, reminiscent of the stools in the most elegant bars on the Champs-Elysées, allows the player with enough money to sit for hours. He even has an ash tray and a special place for his hot dog and Coca Cola, the national repast of the poor in the United States, which he can order without budging from his place. With a dime or quarter, he tries to add up enough points to win a carton of cigarettes. In New York State it is illegal to pay off in cash. An infernal din muffles the recorded voice of Louis Armstrong or Elvis Presley which accompanies the efforts of the small-time gamblers. Youths in blue jeans and leather jackets rub shoulders with old ladies in flowered hats. The boys choose the atomic bomber or guided-missile machines and the women put their hand on the 'love meter' that reveals whether they are still capable of having a love affair, while little children for a nickel are shaken, almost to the point of heart failure, on a donkey that resembles a zebu. There are also the marines or aviators who listlessly fire revolvers." [D. Morgaine, translated by M.B.]

The four categories of play are represented: *agôn* and *alea* involved in most of the machines, *mimicry* and illusion in the imaginary maneuvering of the atomic bomber or guided missile, *ilinx* on the shaking dookey.

It is estimated that Americans spend $400 million a year for the sole purpose of projecting nickel-plated balls against luminous blocks through various obstacles. In Japan, after the war, the mania was worse. It is estimated that about 12 per cent of the national budget was swallowed up annually by slot machines. There were some installed even in doctors' waiting rooms. Even today, in the shadow of the viaducts, in Tokyo, between the trains "is heard the piercing noise of the *pachencos*, the contraptions in which the player strikes a steel ball which gropingly traverses various tricky obstacles and then is lost forever. An absurd game, in which one can only lose, but which seduces those in whom the fury rages. That is why there are no less than 600,000 *pachencos* in Japan. I gaze at these rows of dark heads fascinated by a ball that gambols against some nails. The player holds the apparatus in both hands, no doubt so that his will to win shall pass into the machine. The most compulsive do not even wait for one ball to run its course before hitting another. It is a painful spectacle." [James de Coquet, *Le Figaro*, Feb. 18, 1957, translated by M.B.]

This seduction is so strong that it contributes to the rise of juvenile delinquency. Thus, in April of 1957, the American newspapers reported the arrest in Brooklyn of a gang of juveniles led by a boy of ten and a girl of twelve. They burglarized neighborhood stores of about one thousand dollars. They were only interested in dimes and nickels, which could be used in slot machines. Bills were used merely for wrapping their loot, and were later thrown away as refuse.

Julius Siegal, in a recent article entitled "The Lure of Pinball" [*Harper's* 215, No. 1289 (Oct. 1957), 44–47] has tried to explain the incredible fascination of the game. His study emerges as both confession and analysis. After the inevitable allusions to sexual symbolism, the author especially stresses a feeling of victory over modern technology in the pleasure derived from slot machines. The appearance of calculation that the player reflects before projecting the ball has no significance, but to him it seems sublime. "It seems to me that when a pinballer invests his nickel he pits himself—his own skill—against the combined skills of American industry (p. 45)." The game is therefore a kind of competition between individual skill and an immense anonymous mechanism. For one (real) coin, he hopes to win (fictive) million, for scores are always expressed in numbers with multiple zeros.

Finally, the possibility must exist of cheating the apparatus. "Tilt" indicates only an outer limit. This is a delicious menace, an added risk, a kind of secondary game grafted onto the first.

Curiously, Siegal admits that when depressed, he takes a half-hour's detour in order to find his favorite machine. Then he plays, confident that the game "... assumes positively therapeutic proportions—if I win (p. 46)." He leaves reassured as to his skill and chances of success. His despair is gone, and his aggression has been sublimated.

He deems a player's behavior at a slot machine to be as revealing of his personality as is the Rorschach test. Each player is generally trying to prove that he can beat the machine on its own ground. He masters the mechanism and amasses an enormous fortune shown in the luminous figures inscribed on the screen. He alone has succeeded, and can renew his exploit at will. "... He has freely expressed his irritation with reality, and made the world behave. All for only a nickel (p. 47)." The responsibility for such an ambitious conclusion is the author's. What is left is that the inordinate success of slot machines (in which nothing is won but the possibility of playing again) appears to be one of the most disconcerting enigmas posed by contemporary amusements.

16. The Chinese also use the word *yeou* to designate idling and games in space, especially kite-flying, and also great flights of fancy, mystic journeys of shamans, and the wanderings of ghosts and the damned.

17. Game analogous to ring puzzles: nine links form a chain and are traversed by a rod attached to a base. The point of the game is to unlink them. With experience, one succeeds at it, careful not to call attention to a quite delicate, lengthy, and complicated manipulation where the least error makes it necessary to start again from the beginning.

18. From data provided by Duyvendak in Huizinga (*op. cit.*, p. 32), a study by Chou Ling, the valuable observations of Andre d'Hormon, and Herbert A. Giles' *Chinese-English Dictionary,* 2nd ed. (London, 1912), pp. 510–511 (*hsi*), 1250 (*choua*), 1413 (*teou*), 1452 (*wan*), 1487–1488 (*tou*), 1662–1663 (*yeou*).

Shoot Club:
The DOOM 3 Review

Tom Chick

Context

*There's a fundamental disconnect between those of us who write about games professionally and the people for whom we write. Many writers have lost touch with what it's like to be a gamer. Shoot Club is a series of short stories I've been writing partly to explore that disconnect; "The Doom 3 Review" is from this series. The narrator represents the insider perspective, with perhaps a broader and deeper appreciation of the industry, whereas Trevor represents the people who actually drive the industry, often blissfully free of cynicism and childlike in their enthusiasm. Like the narrator and Tyler Durden in Chuck Palahniuk's **Fight Club,** these are both parts of my own identity.*

The Player Experience

Game Communities

Tom Chick is a writer who has covered the gaming industry since 1990. He holds a Masters in Theological Studies from Harvard Divinity School and has worked as an actor in Los Angeles, where he currently lives.

My friend Trevor is sitting at the keyboard. His fingers are poised over the keys.

> *"So, do I start with the plot or should I just launch into graphics? And should I give my score for each area first? Like this?"*

He types 'GRAPHICS 9/10'.

> *"This isn't Adrenaline Vault. You don't have to do it that way."*
>
> *"Oh. So I just start with the story, maybe give a little bit of the history behind the game?"*
>
> *"This isn't Gamespot either. Just write what you want to say. Did you like it?"*

He pauses, his fingers over the keys. He takes a deep breath which turns into a sort of sigh. Then he pulls back his hands to rest them in his lap. He stares at the notes sitting off to the side.

> *"That's the problem. It's not that easy."*

He leans back in the chair.

Three days ago, Trevor never would have expected it was going to be this hard. We drove to Best Buy at 6pm, ready to stand in line until midnight, which is when they were selling the first copies. We went inside, expecting banners or something, maybe a big guy in a Doom marine outfit with a plastic BFG. Instead, it was just business as usual. Kids hogging the console systems, couples browsing through the DVDs, blue shirted employees trying to look busy so no one would bother them.

> *"Where's the line?" Trevor asked an employee whose name tag read 'Monica.'*
>
> *"The registers are right over there," Monica said. She was carrying a stack of DVDs.*
>
> *"No, no, the line for DOOM 3."*
>
> *"Is that that game? I don't think it comes out until tomorrow."*
>
> *"Wait, wait, I thought you guys were selling it at midnight."*
>
> *"We close at nine," Monica said with as much of a shrug as she could manage with a few dozen copies of 13 Going On 30 in her arms.*
>
> *"No, that's impossible," he protested. "You guys are putting DOOM 3 on sale at midnight. You're giving out prizes to the first hundred people in line. You are."*
>
> *"I don't know about any of that," she said.*
>
> *"Well, I'm here to get in line."*
>
> *"Look, I get off work in an hour, so I don't know anything about that. Go ask that guy."*

She nodded her head down another aisle where two employees were laughing to each other about something.

> *"Which guy? There are two of them."*
>
> *"The one with glasses. That's Kevin. He knows about all that stuff."*
>
> *"Where's the line for DOOM 3?"* Trevor asked Kevin. Kevin glanced at his watch.
>
> *"Already?"* he said. *"Man, you're early."*
>
> *"There's no one else here?"* Trevor asked.
>
> *"Not yet,"* he said apologetically. *"Not that I know of."*
>
> *"Awesome! So we're the first ones?"*
>
> *"Yeah, I guess so. If you want to start a line out front, go hang out by the door."*
>
> *"Totally awesome. Thanks, dude. Oh, hey, what prizes do we get?"*
>
> *"I think it's just a T-shirt."*
>
> *"A DOOM 3 shirt? That's awesome."*
>
> *"Are you going to be this excited about Half-Life 2?"* I asked him as we headed for the door.
>
> *"Fuck Half-Life 2."*

We stood by the front door. Just the two of us. We must have looked like we were on a smoke break, minus the cigarettes. Trevor surveyed people coming in from the parking lot. Every now and then, he'd say something like 'I bet that guy's going to get in line' or 'Here comes one.' But no one else got in line.

> *"Hey, dude, over here,"* he said, waving his arms to a guy in a Sci Fi Channel T-shirt. The guy looked around to see who Trevor was talking to. *"Yeah, you. It's over here. This is the line for DOOM 3. We're first, so you're right behind us."*
>
> *"I'm just here to get a printer cartridge."*
>
> *"Oh, okay. But if you want, they're selling DOOM 3 at 12:01am. You're behind us if you're going to get in line."*

Thirty minutes later, Trevor decided we needed to make a Starbucks run. *"One of us needs to hold our place in line. Do you want to go, or should I?"* The Starbucks was right at the corner. I could see it from where we stood.

> *"I'll go. What do you want?"*

When I came back, there were two more people with Trevor.

> "Hey, the line is behind us," Trevor told me with mock indignation. "No cutting!"
>
> "Here's your java chip frappucino."
>
> "Heh, I was just kidding. He's with me," Trevor told the other people, "and I was saving his place."

One of the guys was pretty young. When I asked him how old he was, he said twenty one.

> "You're twenty one?" I said. "How do you know about DOOM? You must have been, like, eleven years old when DOOM was out."
>
> "Dude, what do you think I've been playing since I was eleven?"
>
> "What's your favorite weapon in DOOM?" Trevor asked him. The guy thought it about it for a while before saying 'shotgun.' How can a shotgun be someone's favorite weapon? There's one in every game.
>
> "Mine too," Trevor agreed.
>
> "No, wait, I changed my mind. Chainsaw."
>
> "Oh yeah, chainsaw! Totally."
>
> "What's your favorite level in DOOM?" the kid asked.
>
> "Hey, there's the chick that helped us," Trevor said as Monica walked out to her car.
>
> "Hey, check it out. We're the first ones in line!"

She took a few steps towards us. "What's that?" She had no idea what Trevor just said because he blurted it out so quickly.

> "We're first in line for DOOM 3 at midnight. Remember us? We're the guys who were asking you about it earlier. This is the line."
>
> She glanced at her watch. "You're going to stay there until midnight?"
>
> "This is nothing. Ask how long I was in line for Phantom Menace?"
>
> "What's that? Is that a game?"
>
> "Ha, that's funny. I was in line for two days. Ask how long I was in line for an Xbox?"
>
> "How long?"
>
> "Fifteen hours. This is nothing."
>
> "So you're going to wait here until midnight?"
>
> "Yeah. It's DOOM 3. I'm totally psyched. We all are." The four of us stood there, totally psyched.

"Well, I heard they didn't get the shipment today," Monica said. *"We won't be selling it until Wednesday afternoon."*

We fell into a shocked silence. Then she grinned. *"I'm just kidding. I just saw them taking them out of the shipping cartons in the back."*

Trevor still mentions Monica from time to time, although he doesn't know that was her name. He pretends he's going to go ask her out. He maintains she was flirting with us.

Trevor and the 21-year-old give each other high fives. *"Those are our copies of DOOM 3,"* Trevor said. *"The copies we'll all be installing,"* a glance at his watch, *"in about four and a half hours."*

Actually, I should mention that I won't be installing anything. I already had a press copy, so I was just there because of the persuasiveness of Trevor's enthusiasm. I had been in line with him for Phantom Menace, for an Xbox, even for the opening night of Godzilla. Yeah, that Godzilla. The one with Matthew Broderick. But I've long since learned that what we're waiting for doesn't matter. We're in it for the thrill of the communal wait, that shared moment where fellow victims of hype come together for the moment of truth.

In fact, I had already finished DOOM 3. But Trevor didn't want me to say anything about it. He didn't even want to know if I liked it. *"You're too picky,"* he had told me. *"I just want to know if a game is fun or not. And I don't trust you in that department. You're too harsh. You need to lighten up. Plus, I don't want you to give away any spoilers."*

But that didn't stop Trevor from buying the latest issue of *PC Gamer* with the world exclusive first review. He'd thumbed through the six pages repeatedly, holding the screenshots close to his face and peering at them as if looking for clues. *"I think there are some new kinds of monsters,"* he noted.

"'You will never experience a dull moment'," he had read out loud from the review, *"'or even a less than mesmerizing one. DOOM is a masterpiece of the art form.' How about that? Dude, that's the way to do a review."*

By the time Best Buy closed their doors for regular business at 9pm, there were about fifteen people in line. As they arrived, most of them went up to Trevor to ask what time he got there. He told them with pride that he'd been there since *"a little after five"*, which wasn't technically incorrect. Kevin came out periodically to give newcomers yellow wrist bands signifying their eligibility for T-shirts.

"*How many is that?*" Trevor kept asking.

By midnight, there were eighty-six people in line. Kevin addressed the line from the front, explaining that they would let in a few people at a time. Trevor was champing at the bit. He let out a whoop when we got in. There were about ten employees standing around and they all turned to see what that noise was.

"*DOOM 3,*" Trevor yelled, as if by way of explanation.

"*So have you played it yet?*" he asked the girl at the cash register while she scanned his copy.

"*Not really,*" she said, ready to go home.

Kevin was standing at the door with a box of T-shirts. "*Thanks for coming out, fellas. What size do you want?*"

"*Extra large,*" said Trevor, beaming. Kevin handed him a rolled-up T-shirt. It was black, of course. Then Kevin looked at me.

"*Large, I guess.*"

"*We only have extra large,*" he said.

"*Oh. Then extra large.*"

"*Wait, did you not buy DOOM 3?*" Kevin saw that I wasn't carrying anything.

"*No, just him.*"

"*Then you guys have to share a T-shirt.*"

As we walked out to the car, I muttered to Trevor, "*I thought it was the first hundred people in line.*" Not that I really wanted an XL DOOM 3 T-shirt, but it was the principle of the thing.

"*You can wear mine if you wash it afterwards,*" Trevor said, already opening the box to get the manual. On the way home, he made me drive with the dome light on so he could read it.

It's a good thing Trevor didn't let me talk about DOOM 3 before he played it. Because I have to say I'm not a fan and I probably would have sapped some of his enthusiasm. He was practically beside himself as he installed it, downloaded the no-CD crack, and then turned out the lights as it started up. That ardor was still going strong when I left a few hours later to go home and go to bed. He called me the next afternoon to say he'd come home for his lunch break to play a little more.

"*I kind of figured you were going to call in sick,*" I said.

"I was going to, but I'd been talking about the game so much that my boss knew it was coming out today. He told me I better not try to call in sick."

"Busted."

"I should have kept my mouth shut. So, dude, what did you choose when it came time to send the message to earth and that guy from the board of directors told you not to do it? Did you transmit or did you cancel?"

"There was some guy from a board of directors? How do you know that? Is it in the manual?"

"It says it in the game. So what did you choose?"

"I think I picked 'cancel'."

"No way! I picked 'transmit'. But first I saved the game so I can go back and replay it from that point."

"I don't think it matters."

"What are you talking about? I bet the game plays completely different based on what you choose. Anyway, shut up. You're going to start giving away spoilers. I gotta go. I'm in the reactor support hallway for Delta Labs 1?"

"Where?"

"Delta 1. The reactor support hallway."

"How do you know that's what it's called?"

"Duh. It fucking says it in the lower left hand corner of the screen. I don't see how you could have missed it. I gotta go."

Trevor had called again after sneaking out of work early. He was stuck on the rail lift puzzle. He had spent two hours trying to figure out how to unlock the exit. He didn't notice that you could raise the lifter to reach higher areas.

"There's an up and down arrow on the control panel. I don't see how you could have missed it."

"Aw, that's cheap," he said before hanging up. *"But DOOM 3 still rocks. Woo! Okay, I gotta go."*

I could tell by the tone of his voice he'd lost some of his enthusiasm. It might have just been because he was stuck. But he was trying to buck up. He'd just spent sixty bucks, a few weeks of being really excited, and six hours of standing in line at Best Buy. It's only natural to try to deny that it might not have been worth it until you're absolutely sure. And if it wasn't worth it, better to put off that realization as long as possible. Sometimes you can fool yourself into having fun if you don't think too hard.

Of course, I could be completely full of shit. Maybe he really does love it. .

He called again a little before 3am.

> "What are you playing?" he asked.
> "Mario Golf Advance."
> "That game is for little kids."
> "Don't make me bring up Animal Crossing."
> "Fair enough."
> "What's up?"
> "Okay, don't give anything away, but I want to ask you just one thing." He sounds deflated. This might be a last ditch effort to buck himself up.
> "Okay."
> "Do you ever get to drive that car that Swann and Campbell are using?"
> "Who?"
> "Swann and Campbell."
> "Who the hell are Swann and Campbell?"
> He sighs like I'm a total moron. "They're the guys the UAC board of directors sends to Mars City to investigate Belruger. There's a car they used to get to the communications center. I can't believe I have to explain all this. Did you even play DOOM 3?"
> "I didn't know those were their names. Who pays attention to that stuff?"
> "Did you even read the PDAs?"
> "Not really. I scanned them for three-digit locker combos."
> "You missed out. There's some funny stuff in there. There's something about a guy who flips out and attacks a Coke machine, you know, like Derek Smart. I even wrote down his name."
> I hear Trevor rustling around some paper. "You're taking notes?"
> "Here it is. Steve Hammer. Ha, that's funny. I didn't even realize that. Hammer. Oh, and check out this quote: 'I can't think of a more useless piece of equipment then a chainsaw on Mars'. That's in one of the emails. They explain that they accidentally mis-shipped

the chainsaws to Mars. Isn't that funny? There's also all these fake spam emails. It's funny."

"You think fake spam is funny? Any game with email in it has joke spams. That hasn't been funny since, I dunno, being able to pee in Duke Nukem. At least that healed you up. What do the fake spams do?"

"It's called atmosphere."

"No. That stuff only qualifies as atmosphere in a game where back story is important. A game like, you know, System Shock. Otherwise, it's filler. In DOOM 3, it's just another example of these guys at id aping what they've seen in other better games because they're lousy game designers."

"Whoa, whoa, whoa. Lousy game designers?"

"Yep. Lousy. Great technology, hats off to Carmack and all that stuff, but it's clear they don't know the first thing about making a good game."

"This is exactly what I meant before. You're way too harsh if you think DOOM 3 isn't a good game."

"Okay, maybe it's a good game. But just barely. I could think of ten other PC games this year that are way better than DOOM 3. It's overlong, repetitive, derivative, uninspired. It's full of fucking monster closets, for Christ's sake. Monster closets! There's a monster just sitting in a closet that won't open until you walk past it. What's up with that?"

"Okay, this is more your jaded gamer crap. You didn't even like Far Cry."

"At least it's better off than DOOM 3."

"Far Cry is better than DOOM 3?"

"Hell, I'd say Max Payne 2 is better than DOOM 3. At least it's got some personality, some variety. It's got a spark of life that's completely missing in DOOM 3."

"You're clearly insane. Let's wait and see what the reviews say. Let's see how many Best of 2004 lists have DOOM 3."

"Who cares? We're not talking about everyone else. We're talking about us."

"Okay, then you're still insane because half of us is totally digging it. And that's all that matters."

He's right. He likes it and I have no business trying to dispute that. He's having fun and I'm being analytical. We might as well be speaking different languages. Besides, none of this matters because DOOM 3 is going to make more money than God.

"*So do you?*" he asks.

"*What?*"

"*Do you get to drive that car?*"

"*Do you really want me to tell you? It might give something away.*"

He is quiet.

"*How far are you?*" I ask.

"*I just activated teleportation pad 2. I'm at the hydrogen storage transfer in delta 3.*"

"*Jesus, I have no idea what that is. How do you know all that stuff?*"

"*I told you, it's right there on the screen. It's called paying attention. Besides, I've been fucking stuck here forever. I can't figure out this dumbass teleportation pad shit. I just want to shoot some more zombies.*"

"*No, you don't get to drive the car. There's a freight loading train thing later on. It drives you about fifty yards and that's it. There are no vehicles like in Far Cry, no mechs like in the end of Riddick, nothing like that. It's just running and gunning, mostly just in that base. You don't get into a giant organic entity like The Many, there's no Xen, there are no twists. It's just that little bit of Hell and then another long slog through the base.*"

He's quiet for a moment. I feel like I've done a terrible thing by disappointing him. But it's not my fault. It's the game's fault. It's the hype's fault. It's his own damn fault for believing it, for being dumb enough to trust that gushing review but smart enough to know better when he actually plays the game.

"*Are there any more parts with those sentries?*" he eventually asks.

"*Sentries? What are those, the zombie soldier guys?*"

"*No, those are zombies. Sentries are those little spider bots. Jeeze, are you sure you even played the game?*"

"*I didn't know they were called sentries. You should have just said spider bots. And no, you don't have any more parts like that. You've pretty much seen everything DOOM 3 has to offer. There's a big boss fight at the end.*"

"*Gaaah. Spoiler! Don't tell me anything else.*" He hangs up quickly.

He calls back in the morning, while I'm making coffee. "*Hey, are you up? I left you a message. I have a question. How do you pronounce where you keep, like, weapons?*"

"What?"

"What do you call it, where you keep weapons?"

"An arsenal?"

"No, no, like a place you'd store them?"

"What, a gun cabinet?"

"No, no."

"Is this about DOOM 3? Do you mean those lockers?"

"Yeah, but there's a word I want to know how you pronounce. You corrected me once in front of all the guys at Shoot Club."

"I have no idea what you're talking about."

"Do you say 'cash' or 'cash-ay'?"

"Oh, you mean cache. It's pronounced 'cash.' Cachet is like reputation or credibility."

"Ha, I knew it. On the audio logs, some dude—I wrote down his name," I hear him flipping around some pages, "it's Robert Price. He says it wrong. He says something about a 'cash-ay' of weapons. I think they meant it as a joke, like he's this really smart scientist, but he can't pronounce the word."

Trevor's picking at minor things now. At some point during the night, he must have shifted from fun to analytical. It takes a certain amount of detachment to notice something like that. Taking notes probably had something to do with it.

He calls a few hours later. *"Hey, did you notice how every time you kill a zombie, a brain pops out of him? They're like fucking Pez dispensers, but with brains instead of Pez. I thought that was pretty cool the first ten or twenty times. Now it's just stupid."*

DOOM 3 is losing him.

He called again a few hours ago.

"Man, I never thought I'd say this about DOOM 3, but I'm bored."

"It's not fun?"

"I didn't say that. I said I'm bored. If I have to shoot another fucking cacodemon, I'm going to scream."

I have no idea what a cacodemon is, but I get the point. *"It does get to be the same thing over and over, doesn't it?"*

> "I'm in Caverns 1. How close am I to the end?"
>
> "Caverns 1. What is that?"
>
> "You really don't pay attention do you? It's the excavation under Site 3."
>
> "The part that looks like Egyptian ruins?"
>
> "Right."
>
> "I think there's like two more levels in that area, then the final boss."
>
> "Are they really long?"
>
> "I don't think so."
>
> He sighs. "Okay, I'm going to come over when I'm done. I need you to help me. I'm going to write my own review."
>
> "It's going to be an honest review," he says when he arrives with his notes under his arm, "not some ass-kissing thumbs-up nonsense."
>
> "You know, even ass-kissing thumbs-up nonsense isn't necessarily dishonest."
>
> "You know what I mean."

So now he's sitting here with his legal pad and loose pages. *"I took notes when the levels were loading,"* he explains. The margins are full of three-digit numbers: locker codes. In several places, he's scrawled comments like *'Where the fuck am I supposed to go?'*, *'I don't know what to do now'*, and *'Stop Sarge? WTF? How?'*

"Everything looks the same and it never makes any sense," he says. *"I keep thinking there's no way this is a real base. There's, like, three bathrooms in that whole huge place, which is full of these twisty corridors and catwalks and ducts and locked doors and these hallways that double back."* He has written, *'Kick-ass computer screens, but otherwise not very convincing'.*

"And you have to do all this backtracking, but you're never sure when you're supposed to go back or if you just missed a door. Half the time I couldn't figure out what was going on. My objective was like 'Find the main portal' and I'm all like, 'Umm, okay, could I get a little more info than that?'"

He wrote *'Bad level design'* and underlined it three times.

> "That's one of the cool things about Painkiller. You always knew exactly what you were doing and the levels were all different. The monsters were different. You know, it's funny. By the time I got to the cyberdemon—"
>
> "Cyberdemon?"
>
> "The main boss guy. At the end. Of DOOM 3."

"That was called a cyberdemon?"

"Yeah. A cyberdemon. And by the time he came out, I was like, 'Yeah, whatever, shorty, there were a bunch of dudes way bigger than you in Painkiller.'

"True."

"Painkiller didn't have anything like those stupid crane puzzles. There were three puzzles with cranes in DOOM 3. Painkiller didn't have anything like where you had to figure out those teleportation pads. And that fucking tram thing you had to help me with. Floating platforms with things that try to knock you off. And I got so sick of looking for stuff. A door panel, a data linker, a plasma inducer, positronic astriction, a doo-hickey, a thingamabob. Remember when they used to just have keys?"

"They have those in there, too. Keycards."

"Yeah, I guess that's what it all comes down to. And don't get me started on the weapons," he says, flipping to that part of his notes. He's written the word *'weak'* in capital letters and circled it.

"Okay, I won't."

"Boring! Not a single fucking original idea in there. Even the Soul Cube is pretty lame. It's like, I dunno, Hellraiser meets Blood Omen. Actually, the whole fucking game was like that. I was always, like, 'Yeah that's from Half-Life, that's from Undying, that's from Blood.'"

"It was pretty derivative."

"Or how it's so dark and you can't have your flashlight with your gun. And Marines with no night vision goggles?"

"Yeah, I think a lot of people noticed that one."

"You know what? Fuck it. I think I'm just going to go post on a forum. You can have my notes. If you use any of them, you're going to credit me, right?"

"Okay."

"So what did your review say?"

"I'll read you the last line. 'Although it's built from an impressive engine, DOOM 3 is ultimately a soulless derivative rehash of tired, tried, and true motifs. It is a bauble that reminds us of id's triumph when it comes to technology and their abject failure when it comes to imagination.'"

"Harsh. But really, it all comes down to what you'd give it out of ten."

"I'm not going there. Want to play a round of Mario Golf? I'll give you six mulligans since I've been practicing."

"Yeah, let's do it. I call Princess Peach. Well, I think I've learned my lesson. I just wish Half-Life 2 would hurry up and come out."

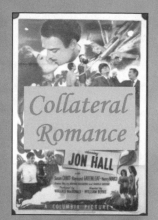

A romantic game:

Person to Person	Played between real people, -Matchmaking (mapping)
Synchronous	Players interact in real time, -Not a huge time investment
Peer to Peer	Games are short and intense, -Diverse Social Situations -Speed dating
Profile	Players use their real identities, -Asymmetric relationships

Team-based,
Peer to Peer,
First-Person Kisser (FPK)

-Us vs. the World
(Casablanca, The Abyss)

-Playful, Fast, Easy
(encourage casual players)

-Diverse Social Situations
(altruism, loyalty, empathy)

4

Construction of a Definition

Bernard Suits

Context

I was led to attempt a definition of games because of some earlier work I had done on the concept of play, namely my M.A. thesis at the University of Chicago titled "Play and Value in Aristotle, Schiller, and Kierkegaard." In 1967 "What is a Game?" was published in **Philosophy of Science***, and later it became the core idea of my 1978 book,* **The Grasshopper***, which is largely a series of objections to, and defenses of, a definition of games in the form of dialogues between the eponymous Grasshopper and his disciple Skepticus. A second edition of* **The Grasshopper** *with a special Introduction by Thomas Hurka will be published by Broadview Press.*

The Rules of a Game

What Is a Game?

Bernard Suits is Distinguished Professor Emeritus of Philosophy, University of Waterloo (Ontario). Although Suits has written on a variety of subjects, the philosophical analysis of games forms the major part of his published work. He is currently bringing to completion a sequel to *The Grasshopper: Games, Life, and Utopia* (Godine Press, 1978).

Game Playing as the Selection of Inefficient Means

Mindful of the ancient canon that the quest for knowledge obliges us to proceed from what is more obvious to what is less obvious [began the Grasshopper], let us start with the commonplace belief that playing games is different from working. Games therefore might be expected to be what work, in some salient respect, is not. Let us now baldly characterize work as "technical activity," by which I mean activity in which an agent seeks to employ the most efficient available means for reaching a desired goal. Since games, too, evidently have goals, and since means are evidently employed for their attainment, the possibility suggests itself that games differ from technical activities in that the means employed in games are not the most efficient. Let us say, then, that games are goal-directed activities in which inefficient means are intentionally chosen. For example, in racing games one voluntarily goes all round the track in an effort to arrive at the finish line instead of "sensibly" cutting straight across the infield.

The following considerations, however, seem to cast doubt on this proposal. The goal of a game, we may say, is winning the game. Let us take an example. In poker I am a winner if I have more money when I stop playing than I had when I started. But suppose that one of the other players, in the course of the game, repays me a debt of a hundred dollars, or suppose I hit another player on the head and take all of his money from him. Then, although I have not won a single hand all evening, am I nevertheless a winner? Clearly not, since I did not increase my money as a consequence of playing poker. In order to be a winner (a sign and product of which is, to be sure, the gaining of money) certain conditions must be met which are not met by the collection of a debt or by felonious assault. These conditions are the rules of poker, which tell us what we can and what we cannot do with the cards and the money. Winning at poker consists in increasing one's money by using only means permitted by the rules, although mere obedience to the rules does not by itself ensure victory. Better and worse means are equally permitted by the rules. Thus in Draw Poker retaining an ace along with a pair and discarding the ace while retaining the pair are both permissible plays, although one is usually a better play than the other. The means for winning at poker, therefore, are limited, but not completely determined, by the rules. Attempting to win at poker may accordingly be described as attempting to gain money by using the most efficient means available, where only those means permitted by the rules are available. But if that is so, then playing poker is a technical activity as originally defined.

Still, this seems a strange conclusion. The belief that working and playing games are quite different things is very widespread, yet we seem obliged to say that playing a game is just another job to be done as competently as possible. Before giving up the thesis that playing a game involves a sacrifice of efficiency, therefore, let us consider one more example. Suppose I make it my purpose to get a small round object into a hole in the ground as efficiently as possible. Placing it in the hole with my hand would be a natural means to adopt. But surely I would not take a stick with a piece of metal on one end of it, walk three or four hundred yards away from the hole, and then attempt to propel the ball into the hole with the stick. That would not be technically intelligent. But such an undertaking is an extremely popular game, and the foregoing way of describing it evidently shows how games differ from technical activities.

But of course it shows nothing of the kind. The end in golf is not correctly described as getting a ball into a hole in the ground, or even, to be more precise, into several holes in a set order. It is to achieve that end with the smallest possible number of strokes. But a stroke is a certain type of swing with a golf club. Thus, if my end were simply to get a ball into a number of holes in the ground, I would not be likely to use a golf club in order to achieve it, nor would I stand at a considerable distance from each hole. But if my end were to get a ball into some holes with a golf club while standing at a considerable distance from each hole, why then I would certainly use a golf club and I would certainly take up such positions. Once committed to that end, moreover, I would strive to accomplish it as efficiently as possible. Surely no one would want to maintain that if I conducted myself with utter efficiency in pursuit of this end I would not be playing a game, but that I *would* be playing a game just to the extent that I permitted my efforts to become sloppy. Nor is it the case that my use of a golf club is a less efficient way to achieve my end than would be the use of my hand. To refrain from using a golf club as a means for sinking a ball with a golf club is not more efficient because it is not possible. Inefficient selection of means, accordingly, does not seem to be a satisfactory account of game playing.

The Inseparability of Rules and Ends in Games

The objection advanced against the last thesis rests upon, and thus brings to light, consideration of the place of rules in games: they seem to stand in a peculiar relation to ends. The end in poker is not simply to gain money, or in golf simply to get a ball into a hole, but to do these things in prescribed (or, perhaps more accurately, not to do them in proscribed) ways; that is, to do them only in accordance with rules. Rules in games thus seem to be in some sense inseparable from ends, for to break a game rule is to render impossible the attainment of an end. Thus, although you may receive the trophy by lying about your golf score, you have certainly not won the game. But in what we have called technical activity it *is* possible to gain an end by breaking a rule; for example, gaining a trophy by lying about your golf score. So while it is possible in a technical action to break a rule without destroying the original end of the action, in games the reverse appears to be the case. If the rules are broken the original end becomes impossible of attainment, since one cannot (really) win the game unless one plays it, and one cannot (really) play the game unless one obeys the rules of the game.

This may be illustrated by the following case. Professor Snooze has fallen asleep in the shade provided by some shrubbery in a secluded part of the campus. From a nearby walk I observe this. I also notice that the shrub under which he is reclining is a man-eating plant, and I judge from its behaviour that it is about to eat the man Snooze. As I run across to him I see a sign which reads KEEP OFF THE GRASS. Without a qualm I ignore this prohibition and save Snooze's life. Why did I make this (no doubt scarcely conscious) decision? Because the value of saving Snooze's life (or of saving a life) outweighed the value of obeying the prohibition against walking on the grass.

Now the choices in a game appear to be radically unlike this choice. In a game I cannot disjoin the end, winning, from the rules in terms of which winning possesses its meaning. I can, of course, decide to cheat in order to gain the pot, but then I have changed my end from winning a game to gaining money. Thus, in deciding to save Snooze's life my purpose was not "to save Snooze while at the same time obeying the campus rules for pedestrians." My purpose was to save Snooze's life, and there were alternative ways in which this might have been accomplished. I could, for example, have remained on the sidewalk and shouted to Snooze in an effort to awaken him. But precious minutes might have been lost, and in any case Snooze, although he tries to hide it, is nearly stone deaf. There are evidently two distinct ends at issue in the Snooze episode: saving Snooze and obeying the rule, out of respect either for the law or for the lawn. And I can achieve either of these ends without at the same time achieving the other. But in a game the end and the rules do not admit of such disjunction. It is impossible for me to win the game and at the same time to break one of its rules. I do not have open to me the alternatives of winning the game honestly and winning the game by cheating, since in the latter case I would not be playing the game at all and thus could not, *a fortiori*, win it.

Now if the Snooze episode is treated as an action which has one, and only one, end—(Saving Snooze) *and* (Keeping off the grass)—it can be argued that the action has become, just by virtue of that fact, a game. Since there would be no independent alternatives, there would be no choice to be made; to achieve one part of the end without achieving the other part would be to fail utterly. On such an interpretation of the episode suppose I am congratulated by a grateful faculty for my timely intervention. A perfectly appropriate response would be: "I don't deserve your praise. True, I saved Snooze, but since I walked on the grass it doesn't count," just as though I were to admit to carrying the ball to the cup on the fifth green. Or again, on this interpretation, I would originally have conceived the problem in a quite different way: "Let me see if I can save Snooze without walking on the grass." One can then imagine my running as fast as I can (but taking no illegal short cuts) to the Athletic Building, where I request (and meticulously sign out) a pole vaulter's pole with which I hope legally to prod Snooze into wakefulness, whereupon I hurry back to Snooze to find him disappearing into the plant. "Well," I remark, not without complacency, "I didn't win, but at least I played the game."

It must be pointed out, however, that this example could be misleading. Saving a life and keeping off the grass are, as values, hardly on the same footing. It is possible that the Snooze episode appears to support the contention at issue (that games differ from technical actions because of the inseparability of rules and ends in the former) only because of the relative triviality of one of the alternatives. This peculiarity of the example can be corrected by supposing that when I decide to obey the rule to keep off the grass, my reason for doing so is that I am a kind of demented Kantian and thus regard myself to be bound by the most weighty philosophical considerations to honour *all* laws with equal respect. So regarded, my maddeningly proper efforts to save a life would not appear ludicrous but would constitute moral drama of the highest order. But since we are not demented Kantians, Skepticus, a less fanciful though logically identical example may be cited.

Let us suppose the life of Snooze to be threatened not by a man-eating plant but by Dr. Threat, who is found approaching the snoozing Snooze with the obvious intention of murdering him. Again I want to save Snooze's life, but I cannot do so (let us say) without killing Threat. However, there is a rule to which I am very strongly committed which forbids me to take another human life. Thus, although (as it happens) I could easily kill Threat from where I stand (with a loaded and cocked pistol I happen to have in my hand), I decided to try to save Snooze by other means, just because of my wish to obey the rule which forbids killing. I therefore run towards Threat with the intention of wresting the weapon from his hand. I am too late, and he murders Snooze. This seems to be a clear case of an action having a conjunctive end of the kind under consideration, but one which we are not at all inclined to call a game. My end, that is to say, was not simply to save the life of Snooze, just as in golf it is not simply to get the ball into the hole, but to save his life without breaking a certain rule. I want to put the ball into the hole fairly and I want to save Snooze morally. Moral rules are perhaps generally regarded as figuring in human conduct in just this fashion. Morality says that if something can be done only immorally it ought not to be done at all. 'What profiteth it a man,' etc. The inseparability of rules and ends does not, therefore, seem to be a completely distinctive characteristic of games.

Game Rules as Not Ultimately Binding

It should be noticed, however, that the foregoing criticism requires only a partial rejection of the proposal at issue. Even though the attack seems to show that not all things which correspond to the formula are games, it may still be the case that all games correspond to the formula. This suggests that we ought not to reject the proposal but ought first to try to limit its scope by adding to it an adequate differentiating principle. Such a principle is suggested by the striking difference between the two Snooze episodes that we have noted. The efforts to save Snooze from the man-eating plant without walking on the grass appeared to be a game because saving the grass strikes us as a trifling consideration when compared with saving a life. But in the second episode, where KEEP OFF THE GRASS is replaced by THOU SHALT NOT KILL, the situation is quite different. The difference may be put in the following way. The rule to keep off the grass is not an ultimate command, but the rule to refrain from killing perhaps is. This suggests that, in addition to being the kind of activity in which rules are inseparable from ends, games are also the kind of activity in which commitment to these rules is never ultimate. For the person playing the game there is always the possibility of there being a non-game rule to which the game rule may be subordinated. The second Snooze episode is not a game, therefore, because the rule to which the rescuer adheres, even to the extent of sacrificing Snooze for its sake, is, for him, an ultimate rule. Rules are always lines that we draw, but in games the lines are always drawn short of a final end or a paramount command. Let us say, then, that a game is an activity in which observance of rules is part of the end of the activity, and where such rules are non-ultimate; that is, where other rules can always supersede the game rules; that is, where the player can always stop playing the game.

However, consider the Case of the Dedicated Driver. Mario Stewart (the driver in question) is a favoured entrant in the motor car race of the century at Malaise. And in the Malaise race there is a rule which forbids a vehicle to leave the track on pain of disqualification. At a crucial point in the race a child crawls out upon the track directly in the path of Mario's car. The only way to avoid running over the child is to leave the track and suffer disqualification. Mario runs over the child and completes the race. I submit that we ought not, for this reason, to deny that he is playing a game. It no doubt strikes us as inappropriate to say that a person who would do such a thing is (merely) playing. But the point is that Mario is not playing in an unqualified sense, he is playing a *game*. And he is evidently playing it more whole-heartedly than the ordinary driver is prepared to play it. From his point of view a racer who turned aside instead of running over the child would have been playing *at* racing; that is, he would not have been a dedicated player. But it would be paradoxical indeed if supreme dedication to an activity somehow vitiated the activity. We do not say that a man is not really digging a ditch just because his whole heart is in it.

However, the rejoinder may be made that, to the contrary, that is just the mark of a game: it, unlike digging ditches, is just the kind of thing which cannot command ultimate loyalty. That, it may be contended, is precisely the force of the proposal about games under consideration. And in support of this contention it might be pointed out that it is generally acknowledged that games are in some sense non-serious undertakings. We must therefore ask in what sense games are, and in what sense they are not, serious. What is believed when it is believed that games are not serious? Not, certainly, that the players of games always take a very light-hearted view of what they are doing. A bridge player who played his cards randomly might justly be accused of failing to take the game seriously—indeed, of *failing* to play the game at all just because of his failure to take it seriously. It is much more likely that the belief that games are not serious means what the proposal under consideration implies: that there is always something in the life of a player of a game more important than playing the game, or that a game is the kind of thing that a player could always have reason to stop playing. It is this belief which I would like to question.

Let us consider a golfer, George, so devoted to golf that its pursuit has led him to neglect, to the point of destitution, his wife and six children. Furthermore, although George is aware of the consequences of his mania, he does not regard his family's plight as a good reason for changing his conduct. An advocate of the view that games are *not* serious might submit George's case as evidence for that view. Since George evidently regards nothing in his life to be more important than golf, golf has, for George, *ceased to be a game*. And this argument would seem to be supported by the complaint of George's wife that golf is for George no longer a game, but a way of life.

But we need not permit George's wife's observation to go unchallenged. The correctness of saying that for George golf is no longer merely a form of recreation may be granted. But to argue that George's golf playing is for that reason not a game is to assume the very point at issue, which is whether a game can be of supreme importance to anyone. Golf, to be sure, is taking over the whole of George's life. But it is, after all, the game which is taking over his life, and not something else. Indeed, if it were not a game which had led George to neglect his duties, his wife might not be nearly as outraged as she is; if, for example, it had been good works, or the attempt to formulate a definition of game playing. She would no doubt still deplore such extra-domestic pre-occupation, but to be kept in rags because of a game must strike her as an altogether different order of deprivation.

Supreme dedication to a game, as in the cases of the auto racer and George, may be repugnant to nearly everyone's moral sense. That may be granted—indeed, insisted upon, since our loathing is excited by the very fact that it is a game which has usurped the place of ends we regard as so much more worthy of pursuit. Thus, although such behaviour may tell us a good deal about such players of games, I submit that it tells us nothing about the games they play. I believe that these observations are sufficient to discredit the thesis that game rules cannot be the object of an ultimate, or unqualified, commitment.

Means, Rather than Rules, as Non-ultimate

I want to agree, however, with the general contention that in games there is something which is significantly non-ultimate, that there is a crucial limitation. But I would like to suggest that it is not the rules which suffer such limitation. Non-ultimacy evidently attaches to games at a quite different point. It is not that obedience to game rules must fall short of ultimate commitments, but that the means which the rules permit must fall short of ultimate utilities. If a high-jumper, for example, failed to complete his jump because he saw that the bar was located at the edge of a precipice, this would no doubt show that jumping over the bar was not the overriding interest of his life. But it would not be his refusal to jump to his death which would reveal his conduct to be a game; it would be his refusal to use something like a ladder or a catapult in his attempt to clear the bar. The same is true of the dedicated auto racer. A readiness to lose the race rather than kill a child is not what makes the race a game; it is the refusal to, *inter alia*, cut across the infield in order to get ahead of the other contestants. There is, therefore, a sense in which games may be said to be non-serious. One could intelligibly say of the high-jumper who rejects ladders and catapults that he is not serious about getting to the other side of the barrier. But one would also want to point out that he could be deadly serious about getting to the other side of the barrier *without* such aids, that is, about high-jumping. But whether games as such are less serious than other things would seem to be a question which cannot be answered solely by an investigation of games.

Consider a third variant of Snooze's death. In the face of Threat's threat to murder Snooze, I come to the following decision. I choose to limit myself to non-lethal means in order to save Snooze even though lethal means are available to me and I do not regard myself to be bound by any rule which forbids killing. (In the auto racing example the infield would *not* be filled with land mines.) And I make this decision even though it may turn out that the proscribed means are necessary to save Snooze. I thus make my end not simply saving Snooze's life, but saving Snooze's life without killing Threat, even though there appears to be no reason for restricting myself in this way.

One might then ask how such behaviour can be accounted for. And one answer might be that it is unaccountable, that it is simply arbitrary. However, the decision to draw an arbitrary line with respect to permissible means need not itself be an arbitrary decision. The decision to be arbitrary may have a purpose, and the purpose may be to play a game. It seems to be the case that the lines drawn in games are not really arbitrary at all. For both *that* the lines are drawn and also *where* they are drawn have important consequences not only for the type, but also for the quality, of the game to be played. It might be said that drawing such lines skillfully (and therefore not arbitrarily) is the very essence of the gamewright's craft. The gamewright must avoid two extremes. If he draws his lines too loosely the game will be dull because winning will be too easy. As looseness is increased to the point of utter laxity the game simply falls apart, since there are then no rules proscribing available means. (For example, a homing propellant device could be devised which would ensure a golfer a hole in one every time he played.) On the other hand, rules are lines that can be drawn too tightly, so that the game becomes too difficult. And if a line is drawn very tightly indeed the game is squeezed out of existence. (Suppose a game in which the goal is to cross a finish line. One of the rules requires the contestants to stay on the track, while another rule requires that the finish line be located in such a position that it is impossible to cross it without leaving the track.) The present proposal, therefore, is that games are activities in which rules are inseparable from ends (in the sense agreed to earlier), but with the added qualification that the means permitted by the rules are narrower in range than they would be in the absence of the rules.

Rules Are Accepted for the Sake of the Activity They Make Possible

Still, even if it is true that the function of rules in games is to restrict the permissible means to an end, it does not seem that this is by itself sufficient to exclude things which are not games. When I failed in my attempt to save Snooze's life because of my unwillingness to commit the immoral act of taking a life, the rule against killing functioned to restrict the means I would employ in my efforts to reach a desired end. What, then, distinguishes the cases of the highjumper and auto racer from my efforts to save Snooze morally, or the efforts of a politician to get elected without lying? The answer lies in the reasons for obeying rules in the two types of case. In games I obey the rules just because such obedience is a necessary condition for my engaging in the activity such obedience makes possible. In high-jumping, as we have noted, although the contestants strive to be on the other side of a barrier, they voluntarily rule out certain means for achieving this goal. They will not walk around it, or duck under it, or use a ladder or catapult to get over it. The goal of the contestants is not to be on the other side of the barrier *per se*, since aside from the game they are playing they are unlikely to have any reason whatever for being on the other side. Their goal is not *simply* to get to the other side, but to do so only by using means permitted by rules, namely, by running from a certain distance and then jumping. And their *reason* for accepting such rules is just because they want to act within the limitations the rules impose. They accept rules so that they can play a game, and they accept these rules so that they can play this game.

But with respect to other rules—for example, moral rules—there is always another reason—what might be called an external or independent reason—for obeying whatever rule may be at issue. In behaving morally, we deny ourselves the option of killing a Threat or lying to the voters not because such denial provides us, like a high-jumper's bar, with an activity we would not otherwise have available to us, but because, quite aside from such considerations, we judge killing and lying to be wrong. The honest politician is not honest because he is interested primarily in the activity trying-to-get-elected-without-lying (as though he valued his commitment to honesty because it provided him with an interesting challenge), but for quite different reasons. He may, for example, be a Kantian, who believes that it is wrong, under any circumstances whatever, to lie. And so, since his morality requires him to be truthful in all cases, it requires him to be truthful in this case. Or he may be a moral teleologist, who believes that the consequences of dishonesty (either in this case or in general) work against practical possibilities which are in the long run more desirable than the possibility of being elected to office. But the high-jumper does not accept rules for either of these kinds of reasons. He does not on principle always make things harder for himself; he does not even on principle always make surmounting physical barriers harder for himself. He does these things only when he wants to be engaged in high-jumping. Nor does the high-jumper, *qua* high-jumper, deny himself the use of more efficient means for clearing the bar because of higher priority moral claims (the catapult is being used to defend the town just now, or the ladder is being used to rescue a child from a rooftop), but just because, again, he wants to be high-jumping. In morals obedience to rules makes the action right, but in games it makes the action.

Of course it is not moral rules alone which differ from game rules in this respect. More generally, we may contrast the way that rules function in games with two other ways that rules function.1) Rules can be directives useful in seeking a given end (If you want to improve your drive, keep your eye on the ball), or 2) they can be externally imposed limitations on the means that may be chosen in seeking an end (Do not lie to the public in order to get them to vote for you). In the latter way a moral rule, as we have seen, often functions as a limiting condition upon a technical activity, although a supervening technical activity can produce the same kind of limitation (If you want to get to the airport in time, drive fast, but if you want to arrive safely, don't drive too fast). Consider a ruled sheet of paper. I conform to these rules, when writing, in order to write straight. This illustrates the first kind of rule. Now suppose that the rules are not lines on a piece of paper, but paper walls which form a labyrinth, and while I wish to be out of the labyrinth I do not wish to damage the walls. The walls are limiting conditions on my coming to be outside. This illustrates the second kind of rule. 3) Now returning to games, consider a third case. Again I am in the labyrinth, but my purpose is not just to *be* outside (as it might be if Ariadne were waiting for me to emerge), but to *get* out of the labyrinth, so to speak, labyrinthically. What is the status of the walls? It is clear that they are not simply impediments to my being outside the labyrinth, because it is not my purpose to (simply) be outside. For if a friend suddenly appeared overhead in a helicopter I would decline the offer of a lift, although I would accept it in the second case. My purpose is to get out of the labyrinth only by accepting the conditions it imposes, that is, by responding to the challenge it presents. Nor, of course, is this like the first case. There I was not interested in *seeing whether* I could write a sentence without breaking a rule, but in using the rules so that I could write straight.

We may therefore say that games require obedience to rules which limit the permissible means to a sought end, and where such rules are obeyed just so that such activity can occur.

Winning Is Not the End with Respect to Which Rules Limit Means

There is, however, a final difficulty. To describe rules as operating more or less permissively with respect to means seems to conform to the ways in which we *invent* or *revise* games. But it does not seem to make sense at all to say that in games there are always means available for attaining one's end over and above the means permitted by the rules. Consider chess. The end sought by chess players, it would seem, is to win, which involves getting chess pieces onto certain squares in accordance with the rules of chess. But since to break a rule is to fail to attain that end, what other means are available? It was for just this reason that our very first proposal about the nature of games was rejected: using a golf club in order to play golf is not a less efficient, and therefore an alternative, means for seeking the end in question. It is a logically indispensable means.

The objection can be met, I believe, by pointing out that there is an end in chess analytically distinct from winning. Let us begin again, therefore, from a somewhat different point of view and say that the end in chess is, in a very restricted sense, to place your pieces on the board in such an arrangement that the opponent's king is, in terms of the rules of chess, immobilized. Now, without going outside chess we may say that the means for bringing about this state of affairs consist in moving the chess pieces. The rules of chess, of course, state how the pieces may be moved; they distinguish between legal and illegal moves. Since the knight, for example, is permitted to move in only a highly restricted manner, it is clear that the permitted means for moving the knight are of less scope than the possible means for moving him. It should not be objected at this point that other means for moving the knight—e.g., along the diagonals—are not really possible on the grounds that such use of the knight would break a rule and thus not be a means to winning. For the present point is not that such use of the knight would be a means to winning, but that it would be a possible (though not permissible) way in which to move the knight so that he would, for example, come to occupy a square so that, according to the rules of chess, the king would be immobilized. A person who made such a move would not, of course, be playing chess. Perhaps he would he cheating at chess. By the same token I would not be playing a game if I abandoned my arbitrary decision not to kill Threat while at the same time attempting to save Snooze. Chess and my third effort to save Snooze's life are games because of an "arbitrary" restriction of means permitted in pursuit of an end.

The main point is that the end here in question is not the end of winning the game. There must be an end which is distinct from winning because it is the restriction of means to this other end which makes winning possible and also defines, in any given game, what it means to win. In defining a game we shall therefore have to take into account these two ends and, as we shall see in a moment, a third end as well. First there is the end which consists simply in a certain state of affairs: a juxtaposition of pieces on a board, saving a friend's life, crossing a finish line. Then, when a restriction of means for attaining this end is made with the introduction of rules, we have a second end, winning. Finally, with the stipulation of what it means to win, a third end emerges: the activity of trying to win—that is, playing the game.

And so when at the outset we entertained the possibility that games involved the selection of inefficient means, we were quite right. It is just that we looked for such inefficiency in the wrong place. Games do not require us to operate inefficiently with respect to winning, to be sure. But they do require us to operate inefficiently in trying to achieve that state of affairs which counts as winning only when it is accomplished according to the rules of the game. For the way in which those rules function is to prohibit use of the most efficient means for achieving that state of affairs.

The Definition

My conclusion is that to play a game is to engage in activity directed towards bringing about a specific state of affairs, using only means permitted by rules, where the rules prohibit more efficient in favour of less efficient means, and where such rules are accepted just because they make possible such activity.

"Well, Skepticus," concluded the Grasshopper, "what do you think?"

"I think," I replied, "that you have produced a definition which is quite plausible."

"But untested. I shall therefore ask you, Skepticus, to bend all of your considerable sceptical efforts to discrediting the definition. For if the definition can withstand the barrage of objections I believe I can count upon you to launch against it, then perhaps we shall be justified in concluding that the account is not merely plausible, but substantially correct. Will you help me with that task?"

"Gladly, Grasshopper." I replied, "if you will give me a moment to collect myself. For I feel as if we, too, had just succeeded in finding our way out of a complicated maze. I know that we have finally got clear, but I am quite unable to say how we managed to do it, for our correct moves are hopelessly confused in my mind with the false starts and blind alleys which formed so large a part of our journey. Just trying to think back over the twists and turns of the argument makes me quite light-headed."

"What you are describing, Skepticus, is a chronic but minor ailment of philosophers. It is called dialectical vertigo, and its cure is the immediate application of straightforward argumentation. In terms of your metaphor, you need to be suspended, as it were, over the maze, so that you can discriminate at a glance the true path from the false turnings. Let me try to give you such an overview of the argument."

"By all means," I said.

A more direct approach to games [continued the Grasshopper] can be made by identifying what might be called the *elements* of game-playing. Since games are goal-directed activities which involve choice, ends and means are two of the elements of games. But in addition to being means-end-oriented activities, games are also rule-governed activities, so that rules are a third element. And since, as we shall see, the rules of games make up a rather special kind of rule, it will be necessary to take account of one more element, namely, the attitudes of game players *qua* game players. I add '*qua* game players' because I do not mean what might happen to be the attitude of this or that game player under these or those conditions (e.g., the hope of winning a cash prize or the satisfaction of exhibiting physical prowess to an admiring audience), but the attitude without which it is not possible to play a game. Let us call this attitude, of which more presently, the *lusory* (from the Latin *ludus*, game) attitude.

My task will be to persuade you that what I have called the lusory attitude is the element which unifies the other elements into a single formula which successfully states the necessary and sufficient conditions for any activity to be an instance of game playing. I propose, then, that the elements of a game are 1) the goal, 2) the means of achieving the goal, 3) the rules, and 4) the lusory attitude. I shall briefly discuss each of these in order.

185

The Goal

We should notice first of all that there are three distinguishable goals involved in game playing. Thus, if we were to ask a long-distance runner his purpose in entering a race, he might say any one or all of three things, each of which would be accurate, appropriate, and consistent with the other two. He might reply 1) that his purpose is to participate in a long-distance race, or 2) that his purpose is to win the race, or 3) that his purpose is to cross the finish line ahead of the other contestants. It should be noted that these responses are not merely three different formulations of one and the same purpose. Thus, winning a race is not the same thing as crossing a finish line ahead of the other contestants, since it is possible to do the latter unfairly by, for example, cutting across the infield. Nor is participating in the race the same as either of these, since the contestant, while fully participating, may simply fail to cross the finish line first, either by fair means or foul. That there must be this triplet of goals in games will be accounted for by the way in which lusory attitude is related to rules and means. For the moment, however, it will be desirable to select just one of the three kinds of goal for consideration, namely, the kind illustrated in the present example by crossing the finish line ahead of the other contestants. This goal is literally the simplest of the three, since each of the others presupposes it, while it does not presupposes either of the other two. This goal, therefore, has the best claim to be regarded as an elementary component of game playing. The others, since they are compounded components, can be defined only after the disclosure of additional elements.

The kind of goal at issue, then, is the kind illustrated by crossing a finish line first (but not necessarily fairly), having x number of tricks piled up before you on a bridge table (but not necessarily as a consequence of playing bridge), or getting a golf ball into a cup (but not necessarily by using a golf club). This kind of goal may be described generally as *a specific achievable state of affairs.* This description is, I believe, no more and no less than is required. By omitting to say *how* the state of affairs in question is to be brought about, it avoids confusion between this goal and the goal of winning. And because any achievable state of affairs whatever could, with sufficient ingenuity, be made the goal of a game, the description does not include too much. I suggest that this kind of goal be called the *prelusory* goal of a game, because it can be described before, or independently of, any game of which it may be, or come to be, a part. In contrast, winning can be described only in terms of the game in which it figures, and winning may accordingly be called the *lusory* goal of a game. Finally, the goal of participating in the game is not, strictly speaking, a part of the game at all. It is simply one of the goals that people have, such as wealth, glory, or security. As such it may be called a lusory goal, but a lusory goal of life rather than of games.

Means

Just as we saw that reference to the goal of game playing admitted of three different (but proper and consistent) interpretations, so we shall find that the means in games can be of more than one kind—two, in fact, depending upon whether we wish to refer to means for winning the game or for achieving the prelusory goal. Thus, an extremely effective way to achieve the prelusory goal in a boxing match—viz.," the state of affairs consisting in your opponent being "down" for the count of ten—is to shoot him through the head, but this is obviously not a means for winning the match. In games, of course, we are interested only in means which are permitted for winning, and we are now in a position to define that class of means, which we may call *lusory* means. Lusory means are means which are permitted (are legal or legitimate) in the attempt to achieve prelusory goals.

It should be noticed that we have been able to distinguish lusory from, if you will, illusory means only by assuming without analysis one of the elements necessary in making the distinction. We have defined lusory means as means which are *permitted* without examining the nature of that permission. This omission will be repaired directly by taking up the question of rules.

Rules

As with goals and means, two kinds of rules figure in games, one kind associated with prelusory goals, the other with lusory goals. The rules of a game are, in effect, proscriptions of certain means useful in achieving prelusory goals. Thus it is useful but proscribed to trip a competitor in a foot race. This kind of rule may be called constitutive of the game, since such rules together with specification of the prelusory goal set out all the conditions which must be met in playing the game (though not, of course, in playing the game skilfully). Let us call such rules *constitutive* rules. The other kind of rule operates, so to speak, *within* the area circumscribed by constitutive rules, and this kind of rule may be called a rule of skill. Examples are the familiar injunctions to keep your eye on the ball, to refrain from trumping your partner's ace, and the like. To break a rule of skill is usually to fail, at least to that extent, to play the game well, but to break a constitutive rule is to fail (at least in that respect) to play the game at all. (There is a third kind of rule in some games which appears to be unlike either of these. It is the kind of rule whose violation results in a fixed penalty, so that violating the rule is neither to fail to play the game nor [necessarily] to fail to play the game well, since it is sometimes tactically correct to incur such a penalty [e.g., in hockey] for the sake of the advantage gained. But these rules and the lusory consequences of their violation are established by the constitutive rules and are simply extensions of them.]

Having made the distinction between constitutive rules and rules of skill, I propose to ignore the latter, since my purpose is to define not well-played games but games. It is, then, what I have called constitutive rules which determine the kind and range of means which will be permitted in seeking to achieve the prelusory goal.

What is the nature of the restrictions which constitutive rules impose on the means for reaching a prelusory goal? I invite you, Skepticus, to think of any game at random. Now identify its prelusory goal: breasting a tape, felling an opponent, or whatever. I think you will agree that the simplest, easiest, and most direct approach to achieving such a goal is always ruled out in favour of a more complex, more difficult, and more indirect approach. Thus, it is not uncommon for players of a new and difficult game to agree among themselves to 'ease up' on the rules, that is, to allow themselves a greater degree of latitude than the official rules permit. This means removing some of the obstacles or, in terms of means, permitting certain means which the rules do not really permit. On the other hand, players may find some game too easy and may choose to tighten up the rules, that is, to heighten the difficulties they are required to overcome.

We may therefore define constitutive rules as rules which prohibit use of the most efficient means for reaching a prelusory goal.

Lusory Attitude

The attitude of the game player must be an element in game playing because there has to be an explanation of that curious state of affairs wherein one adopts rules which require one to employ worse rather than better means for reaching an end. Normally the acceptance of prohibitory rules is justified on the grounds that the means ruled out, although they are more efficient than the permitted means, have further undesirable consequences from the viewpoint of the agent involved. Thus, although nuclear weapons are more efficient than conventional weapons in winning battles, the view still happily persists among nations that the additional consequences of nuclear assault are sufficient to rule it out. This kind of thing, of course, happens all the time, from the realm of international strategy to the common events of everyday life; thus one decisive way to remove a toothache is to cut your head off, but most people find good reason to rule out such highly efficient means. But in games although more efficient means are—and must be—ruled out, the reason for doing so is quite different from the reasons for avoiding nuclear weaponry and self-decapitation. Foot racers do not refrain from cutting across the infield because the infield holds dangers for them, as would be the case if, for example, infields were frequently sown with land mines. Cutting across the infield in shunned solely because there is a rule against it. But in ordinary life this is usually—and rightly—regarded as the worst possible kind of justification one could give for avoiding a course of action. The justification for prohibiting a course of action that there is simply a rule against it may be called the *bureaucratic* justification; that is, no justification at all.

But aside from bureaucratic practice, in anything but a game the gratuitous introduction of unnecessary obstacles to the achievement of an end is regarded as a decidedly irrational thing to do, whereas in games it appears to be an absolutely essential thing to do. This fact about games has led some observers to conclude that there is something inherently absurd about games, or that games must involve a fundamental paradox.[1] This kind of view seems to me to be mistaken. The mistake consists in applying the same standard to games that is applied to means-end activities which are not games. If playing a game is regarded as not essentially different from going to the office or writing a cheque, then there is certainly something absurd or paradoxical or, more plausibly, simply something stupid about game playing.

But games are, I believe, essentially different from the ordinary activities of life, as perhaps the following exchange between Smith and Jones will illustrate. Smith knows nothing of games, but he does know that he wants to travel from A to C, and he also knows that making the trip by way of B is the most efficient means for getting to his destination. He is then told authoritatively that he may *not* go by way of B "Why not?" he asks. "Are there dragons at B?" "No," is the reply. "B is perfectly safe in every respect. It is just that there is a rule against going to B if you are on your way to C." "Very well,""grumbles Smith,"if you insist. But if I have to go from A to C very often I shall certainly try very hard to get that rule revoked." True to his word, Smith approaches Jones, who is also setting out for C from A. He asks Jones to sign a petition requesting the revocation of the rule which forbids travellers from A to C to go through B. Jones replies that he is very much opposed to revoking the rule, which very much puzzles Smith.

SMITH: But if you want to get to C, why on earth do you support a rule which prevents your taking the fastest and most convenient route?

JONES: Ah, but you see I have no particular interest in being at C. **That** *is not my goal, except in a subordinate way. My overriding goal is more complex. It is "to get from A to C without going through B." And I can't very well achieve that goal if I go through B, can I?*

S: But why do you want to do that?

J: I want to do it before Robinson does, you see?

S: No, I don't. That explains nothing. Why should Robinson, whoever he may be, want to do it? I presume you will tell me that he, like you, has only a subordinate interest in being at C **at al.**

J: That is so.

S: Well if neither of you really wants to be at C, then what possible difference can it make which of you gets there first? And why, for God's sake, should you avoid B?

J: Let me ask you a question. Why do you want to get to C?

S: Because there is a good concert at C, and I want to hear it.

J: Why?

S: Because I like concerts, of course. Isn't that a good reason?

J: It's one of the best there is. And I like, among other things, trying to get from A to C without going through B before Robinson does.

S: Well, I don't. So why should they tell me I can't go through B?

J: Oh, I see. They must have thought you were in the race.

S: The what?

I believe that we are now in a position to define *lusory attitude*: the acceptance of constitutive rules just so the activity made possible by such acceptance can occur.

The Definition

Let me conclude by restating the definition together with an indication of where the elements that we have now defined fit into the statement.

To play a game is to attempt to achieve a specific state of affairs [prelusory goal], using only means permitted by rules [lusory means], where the rules prohibit use of more efficient in favour of less efficient means [constitutive rules], and where the rules are accepted just because they make possible such activity [lusory attitude]. I also offer the following simpler and, so to speak, more portable version of the above: playing a game is the voluntary attempt to overcome unnecessary obstacles.

"Thank you, Grasshopper," I said when he had finished speaking. "Your treatment has completely cured my vertigo, and I believe I have a sufficiently clear understanding of your definition to raise a number of objections against it."

"Splendid. I knew I could rely upon you."

"My objections will consist in the presentation of counter-examples which reveal the definition to be inadequate in either of the two respects in which definitions can be inadequate; that is, they will show either that the definition is too broad or that it is too narrow."

"By the definition's being too broad I take it you mean that it erroneously includes things which are *not* games, and by its being too narrow you mean that it erroneously excludes things which *are* games."

"That is correct," I answered.

"And which kind of error will you expose first, Skepticus, an error of inclusion or an error of exclusion?"

"An error of exclusion, Grasshopper. I shall argue that your account of the prelusory goal has produced too narrow a definition."

Note

1. See Chapter Seven, "Games and Paradox," for an extended discussion of this point.

I Have No Words & I Must Design

Greg Costikyan

Context

*"I Have No Words" was written in the early 1990s, at a time when virtually nothing had been written on the subject of game design as a discipline, before game studies as a discipline or **Game Developer** magazine existed. Since Chris Crawford's **Journal of Computer Game Design** had recently stopped publishing, there seemed no obvious venue for its publication. In 1994, James Wallis, who ran a small tabletop RPG company called Hogshead, invited me to write for its magazine, **Interactive Fantasy,** a small journal that ran intelligent discussions about RPG design, and so I sent him this piece. In retrospect, the emphasis on "decision making" may betray my leanings as a strategy gamer, and be less applicable to games that depend on fast action, but on the whole, I think it holds up well.*

The Rules of a Game

What Is a Game?

Greg Costikyan has designed more than 30 commercially published board, roleplaying, computer, online, and mobile games, and is an inductee into the Adventure Gaming Hall of Fame for a lifetime of accomplishment in the field. At present, he is a game researcher for Nokia.

There's a lotta different kinds of games out there. A helluva lot. Cart-based, computer, CD-ROM, network, arcade, PBM, PBEM, mass-market adult, wargames, card games, tabletop RPGs, LARPs, freeforms. And, hell, don't forget paintball, virtual reality, sports, and the horses. It's all gaming.

But do these things have anything at all in common? What is a game? And how can you tell a good one from a bad one?

Well, we can all do the latter: "Good game, Joe," you say, as you leap the net. Or put away the counters. Or reluctantly hand over your Earth Elemental card. Or divvy up the treasure. But that's no better than saying, "Good book," as you turn the last page. It may be true, but it doesn't help you write a better one.

As game designers, we need a way to analyze games, to try to understand them, and to understand what works and what makes them interesting.

We need a critical language. And since this is basically a new form, despite its tremendous growth and staggering diversiiy, we need to invent one.

What Is a Game, Anyhow?

It's Not a Puzzle.

In *The Art of Computer Game Design*, Chris Crawford contrasts what he calls "games" with "puzzles." Puzzles are static; they present the "player" with a logic structure to be solved with the assistance of clues. "Games," by contrast, are not static, but change with the player's actions.

Some puzzles are obviously so; no one would call a crossword a "game." But, according to Crawford, some "games" a really just puzzles—Lebling & Blank's Zork, for instance. The game's sole objective is the solution of puzzles: finding objects and using them in particular ways to cause desired changes in the game-state. There is no opposition, there is no roleplaying, and there are no resources to manage; victory is solely a consequence of puzzle solving.

To be sure, Zork is not entirely static; the character moves from setting to setting, allowable actions vary by setting, and inventory changes with action. We must think of a continuum, rather than a dichotomy; if a crossword is 100% puzzle, Zork is 90% puzzle and 10% game.

Almost every game has some degree of puzzle-solving; even a pure military strategy game requires players to, e.g., solve the puzzle of making an optimum attack at this point with these units. To eliminate puzzle-solving entirely, you need a game that's almost entirely exploration: Just Grandma and Me, a CD-ROM interactive storybook with game-like elements of decision-making and exploration, is a good example. Clicking on screen objects causes entertaining sounds and animations, but there's nothing to "solve," in fact, no strategy whatsoever.

A puzzle is static. A game is interactive.

It's Not a Toy.

According to Will Wright, his Sim City is not a game at all, but a toy. Wright offers a ball as an illuminating comparison: It offers many interesting behaviors, which you may explore. You can bounce it, twirl it, throw it, dribble it. And, if you wish, you may use it in a game: soccer, or basketball, or whatever. But the game is not intrinsic in the toy; it is a set of player-defined objectives overlaid on the toy.

Just so Sim City. Like many computer games, it creates a world that the player may manipulate, but unlike a real game, it provides no objective. Oh, you may choose one: to see if you can build a city without slums, perhaps. But Sim City itself has no victory conditions, no goals; it is a software toy.

A toy is interactive. But a game has goals.

It's Not a Story.

Again and again, we hear about story. Interactive literature. Creating a story through roleplay. The idea that games have something to do with stories has such a hold on designers' imagination that it probably can't be expunged. It deserves at least to be challenged.

Stories are inherently linear. However much characters may agonize over the decisions they make, they make them the same way every time we reread the story, and the outcome is always the same. Indeed, this is a strength; the author chose precisely those characters, those events, those decisions, and that outcome, because it made for the strongest story. If the characters did something else, the story wouldn't be as interesting.

Games are inherently non-linear. They depend on decision-making. Decisions have to pose real, plausible alternatives, or they aren't real decisions. It must be entirely reasonable for a player to make a decision one way in one game, and a different way in the next. To the degree that you make a game more like a story—more linear, fewer real options—you make it less like a game.

Consider: you buy a book, or see a movie, because it has a great story. But how would you react if your gamemaster were to tell you, "I don't want you players to do that, because it will ruin the story?" He may well be right, but that's beside the point. Gaming is NOT about telling stories.

That said, games often, and fruitfully, borrow elements of fiction. Roleplaying games depend on characters; computer adventures and LARPs are often driven by plots. The notion of increasing narrative tension is a useful one for any game that comes to a definite conclusion. But to try to hew too closely to a storyline is to limit players' freedom of action and their ability to make meaningful decisions.

The hypertext fiction movement is interesting, here. Hypertext is inherently non-linear, so that the traditional narrative is wholly inappropriate to hypertext work. Writers of hypertext fiction are trying to explore the nature of human existence, as does the traditional story, but in a way that permits multiple viewpoints, temporal leaps, and reader construction of the experience. Something—more than hypertext writers know—is shared with game design here, and something with traditional narrative; but if hypertext fiction ever becomes artistically successful (nothing I've read is), it will be through the creation of a new narrative form, something that we will be hard-pressed to call "story."

Stories are linear. Games are not.

It Demands Participation.

In a traditional artform, the audience is passive. When you look at a painting, you may imagine things in it, you may see something other than what the artist intended, but your role in constructing the experience is slight: The artist painted. You see. You are passive.

When you go to the movies, or watch TV, or visit the theater, you sit and watch and listen. Again, you do interpret, to a degree; but you are the audience. You are passive. The art is created by others.

When you read a book, most of it goes on in your head, and not on the page; but still. You're receiving the author's words. You're passive.

It's all too, too autocratic: the mighty artist condescends to share his genius with lesser mortals. How can it be that, two hundred years after the Revolution, we still have such aristocratic forms? Surely, we need forms in spirit with the times; forms which permit the common man to create his own artistic experience.

Enter the game. Games provide a set of rules; but the players use them to create their own consequences. It's something like the music of John Cage: he wrote themes about which the musicians were expected to improvise. Games are like that; the designer provides the theme, the players the music.

A democratic artform for a democratic age.

Traditional artforms play to a passive audience. Games require active participation.

So What Is a Game?

A game is a form of art in which participants, termed players, make decisions in order to manage resources through game tokens in the pursuit of a goal.

Decision-Making

I offer this term in an effort to destroy the inane, and overhyped, word "interactive." The future, we are told, will be interactive. You might as well say, "The future will be fnurglewitz." It would be about as enlightening.

A light switch is interactive. You flick it up, the light turns on. You flick it down, the light turns off. That's interaction. But it's not a lot of fun.

All games are interactive: The game state changes with the players' actions. If it didn't, it wouldn't be a game: It would be a puzzle.

But interaction has no value in itself. Interaction must have purpose.

Suppose we have a product that's interactive. At some point, you are faced with a choice: You may choose to do A, or to do B.

But what makes A better than B? Or is B better than A at some times but not at others? What factors go into the decision? What resources are to be managed? What's the eventual goal?

Aha! Now we're not talking about "interaction." Now we're talking about decision-making.

The thing that makes a game a game is the need to make decisions. Consider Chess: it has few of the aspects that make games appealing—no simulation elements, no roleplaying, and damn little color. What it's got is the need to make decisions. The rules are tightly constrained, the objectives clear, and victory requires you to think several moves ahead. Excellence in decision-making is what brings success.

What does a player do in any game? Some things depend on the medium. In some games, he rolls dice. In some games, he chats with his friends. In some games, he whacks at a keyboard. But in every game, he makes decisions.

At every point, he considers the game state. That might be what he sees on the screen. Or it might be what the gamemaster has just told him. Or it might be the arrangement on the pieces on the board. Then, he considers his objectives, and the game tokens and resources available to him. And he considers his opposition, the forces he must struggle against. He tries to decide on the best course of action.

And he makes a decision.

What's key here? Goals. Opposition. Resource management. Information. Well talk about them in half a mo.

What decisions do players make in this game?

Goals

Sim City has no goals. Is it not a game?

No, as its own designer willingly maintains. It is a toy.

And the only way to stay interested in it for very long is to turn it into a game—by setting goals, by defining objectives for yourself. Build the grandest possible megalopolis; maximize how much your people love you; build a city that relies solely on mass transit. Whatever goal you've chosen, you've turned it into a game.

Even so, the software doesn't support your goal. It wasn't designed with your goal in mind. And trying to do something with a piece of software that it wasn't intended to do can be awfully frustrating.

Since there's no goal, Sim City soon palls. By contrast, Sid Meier and Bruce Shelley's Civilization, an obviously derivative product, has explicit goals—and is far more involving and addictive.

"But what about roleplaying games?" you may say. "They have no victory conditions."

No victory conditions, true. But certainly, they have goals; lots of them, you get to pick. Rack up the old experience points. Or fulfill the quest your friendly GM has just inflicted on you. Or rebuild the Imperium and stave off civilization's final collapse. Or strive toward spiritual perfection. Whatever.

If, for some reason, your player characters don't have a goal, they'll find one right quick. Otherwise, they'll have nothing better to do but sit around the tavern and grouse about how boring the game is. Until you get pissed off and have a bunch of orcs show up and try to beat their heads in.

Hey, now they've got a goal. Personal survival is a good goal. One of the best.

If you have no goal, your decisions are meaningless. Choice A is as good as Choice B; pick a card, any card. Who cares? What does it matter?

For it to matter, for the game to be meaningful, you need something to strive toward. You need goals.

What are the players' goals? Can the game support a variety of different goals? What facilities exist to allow players to strive toward their various goals?

Opposition

Oh, say the politically correct. Those bad, icky games. They're so competitive. Why can't we have cooperative games?

"Cooperative games" generally seem to be variants of "let's all throw a ball around." Oh golly, how fascinating, I'll stop playing Mortal Kombat for that, you betcha.

But are we really talking about competition?

Yes and no; many players do get a kick out of beating others with their naked minds alone, which is at least better than naked fists. Chess players are particularly obnoxious in this regard. But the real interest is in struggling toward a goal.

The most important word in that sentence is: struggling.

Here's a game. It's called Plucky Little England, and it simulates the situation faced by the United Kingdom after the fall of France in World War II. Your goal: preserve liberty and democracy and defeat the forces of darkness and oppression. You have a choice: A. Surrender. B. Spit in Hitler's eye! Rule Britannia! England never never never shall be slaves!

You chose B? Congratulations! You won!

Now, wasn't that satisfying? Ah, the thrill of victory.

There is no thrill of victory, of course; it was all too easy, wasn't it? There wasn't any struggle.

In a two-player, head-to-head game, your opponent is the opposition, your struggle against him; the game is direct competition. And this is a first-rate way of providing opposition. Nothing is as sneaky and as hard to overcome as a determined human opponent is. But direct competition isn't the only way to do it.

Think of fiction. The ur-story, the Standard Model Narrative, works like this: character A has a goal. He faces obstacles B, C, D, and E. He struggles with each, in turn, growing as a person as he does. Ultimately, he overcomes the last and greatest obstacle.

Do these obstacles all need to be The Villain, The Bad Guy, The Opponent, The Foe? No, though a good villain makes for a first rate obstacle. The forces of nature, cantankerous mothers-in-law, crashing hard-drives, and the hero's own feelings of inadequacy can make for good obstacles, too.

Just so in games.

In most RPGs, the "opposition" consists of non-player characters, and you are expected to cooperate with your fellow players. In many computer games, the "opposition" consists of puzzles you must solve. In LARPs, the "opposition" is often the sheer difficulty of finding the player who has the clue or the widget or the special power you need. In most solitaire games, your "opposition" is really a random element, or a set of semi-random algorithms you are pitted against.

Whatever goals you set your players, you must make the players work to achieve their goals. Setting them against each other is one way to do that, but not the only one. And even when a player has an opponent, putting other obstacles in the game can increase its richness and emotional appeal.

The desire for "cooperative games" is the desire for an end to strife. But there can be none. Life is the struggle for survival and growth. There is no end to strife, not this side of the grave. A game without struggle is a game that's dead.

What provides opposition? What makes the game a struggle?

Managing Resources

Trivial decisions aren't any fun. Remember Plucky Little England?

There wasn't any real decision, was there?

Or consider Robert Harris's Talisman. Each turn, you roll the die. The result is the number of spaces you can move. You may move to the left, or to the right, around the track.

Well, this is a little better than a traditional track game; I've got a choice. But 99 times out of a 100, either there's no difference between the two spaces, or one is obviously better than the other. The choice is bogus.

The way to make choices meaningful is to give players resources to manage. "Resources" can be anything: Panzer divisions. Supply points. Cards. Experience points. Knowledge of spells. Ownership of fiefs. The love of a good woman. Favors from the boss. The good will of an NPC. Money. Food. Sex. Fame. Information.

If the game has more than one "resource," decisions suddenly become more complex. If I do this, I get money and experience, but will Lisa still love me? If I steal the food, I get to eat, but I might be caught and have my hand cut off. If I declare against the Valois, Edward Plantagenet will grant me the Duchy of Gascony, but the Pope may excommunicate me, imperiling my immortal soul.

These are not just complex decisions; these are interesting ones. Interesting decisions make for interesting games.

The resources in question have to have a game role; if "your immortal soul" has no meaning, neither does excommunication. (Unless it reduces the loyalty of your peasants, or

199

makes it difficult to recruit armies, or... but these are game roles, *n'est-ce pas?*) Ultimately, "managing resources" means managing game elements in pursuit of your goal. A "resource" that has no game role has nothing to contribute to success or failure, and is ultimately void.

What resources does the player manage? Is there enough diversity in them to require tradeoffs in making decisions? Do they make those decisions interesting?

Game Tokens

You effect actions in the game through your game tokens. A game token is any entity you may manipulate directly.

In a boardgame, it is your pieces. In a cardgame, it is your cards. In a roleplaying game, it is your character. In a sports game, it is you yourself.

What is the difference between "resources" and "tokens?" Resources are things you must manage efficiently to achieve your goals; tokens are your means of managing them. In a board wargame, combat strength is a resource; your counters are tokens. In a roleplaying game, money is a resource; you use it through your character.

Why is this important? Because if you don't have game tokens, you wind up with a system that operates without much player input. Will Wright and Fred Haslam's Sim Earth is a good example. In Sim Earth, you set some parameters, and sit back to watch the game play out itself. You've got very little to do, no tokens to manipulate, no resources to manage. Just a few parameters to twiddle with. This is mildly interesting, but not very.

To give a player a sense that he controls his destiny, that he is playing a game, you need game tokens. The fewer the tokens, the more detailed they must be; it is no coincidence that roleplaying games, which give the player a single token, also have exceptionally detailed rules for what that token can do.

What are the players' tokens? What are these tokens' abilities? What resources do they use? What makes them interesting?

Information

I've had more than one conversation with a computer game designer in which he tells me about all the fascinating things his game simulates—while I sit there saying, "Really? What do you know. I didn't realize that."

Say you've got a computer wargame in which weather affects movement and defense. If you don't tell the player that weather has an effect, what good is it? It won't affect the player's behavior; it won't affect his decisions.

Or maybe you tell him weather has an effect, but the player has no way of telling whether it's raining or snowing or what at any given time. Again, what good is that?

Or maybe he can tell, and he does know, but he has no idea what effect weather has—maybe it cuts everyone's movement in half, or maybe it slows movement across fields to a crawl but does nothing to units moving along roads. This is better, but not a whole lot.

The interface must provide the player with relevant information. And he must have enough information to be able to make a sensible decision.

That isn't to say a player must know everything; hiding information can be very useful. It's quite reasonable to say, "you don't know just how strong your units are until they enter combat," but in this case, the player must have some idea of the range of possibilities. It's reasonable to say, "you don't know what card you'll get if you draw to an inside straight," but only if the player has some idea what the odds are. If I might draw the Queen of Hearts and might draw Death and might draw the Battleship Potemkin, I have absolutely no basis on which to make a decision.

More than that, the interface must not provide too much information, especially in a time-dependent game. If weather, supply state, the mood of my commanders, the fatigue of the troops, and what Tokyo Rose said on the radio last night can all affect the outcome of my next decision, and I have to decide some time in the next five seconds, and it would take me five minutes to find all the relevant information by pulling down menus and looking at screens, the information is still irrelevant. I may have access to it, but I can't reasonably act on it.

Or let's talk about computer adventures; they often display information failure. "Oh, to get through the Gate of Thanatos, you need a hatpin to pick the lock. You can find the hatpin on the floor of the Library. It's about three pixels by two pixels, and you can see it, if your vision is good, between the twelfth and thirteenth floorboards, about three inches from the top of the screen. What, you missed it?"

Yeah, I missed it. In an adventure, it shouldn't be ridiculously difficult to find what you need, nor should victory be impossible just because you made a wrong decision three hours and thirty-eight decision points ago. Nor should the solutions to puzzles be arbitrary or absurd.

Or consider freeforms. In a freeform, a player is often given a goal, and achieving it requires him to find out several things—call them Facts A, B, and C. The freeform's designer

201

had better make damn sure that A, B, and C are out there somewhere—known to other characters, or on a card that's circulating in the game—whatever, they have to be there. Otherwise, the player has no chance of achieving his goal, and that's no fun.

Given the decisions players are required to make, what information do they need? Does the game provide the information as and when needed? Will reasonable players be able to figure out what information they need, and how to find it?

Other Things That Strengthen Games

Diplomacy

Achieving a goal is meaningless if it comes without work, if there is no opposition; but that doesn't mean all decisions must be zero-sum. Whenever multiple players are involved, games are strengthened if they permit, and encourage, diplomacy.

Games permit diplomacy if players can assist each other—perhaps directly, perhaps by combining against a mutual foe. Not all multiplayer games do this; in Charles B. Darrow's Monopoly, for instance, there's no effective way to either help or hinder anyone else. There's no point in saying, "Let's all get Joe," or "Here, you're a novice, I'll help you out, you can scratch my back later," because there's no way to do it.

Some games permit diplomacy, but not much. In Lawrence Harris's Axis & Allies, players can help each other to a limited degree, but everyone is permanently Axis or permanently Allied, so diplomacy is never a key element to the game.

One way to encourage diplomacy is by providing non-exclusive goals. If you're looking for the Ark of the Covenant, and I want to kill Nazis, and the Nazis have the Ark, we can work something out. Maybe our alliance will end when the French Resistance gets the Ark, and we wind up on opposite sides, but actually, such twists are what make games fun.

But games can encourage diplomacy even when players are directly opposed. The diplomatic game par excellence is, of course, Calhammer's Diplomacy, in which victory more often goes to the best diplomat than to the best strategist. The key to the game is the Support order, which allows one player's armies to assist another in an attack, encouraging alliance.

Alliances never last, to be sure; Russia and Austria may ally to wipe out Turkey, but only one of them can win. Eventually, one will stab the other in the back.

Fine. It's the need to find allies, retain them, and persuade your enemies to change their stripes that makes sure you'll keep on talking. If alliances get set in stone, diplomacy comes to an end.

Computer games are almost inherently solitaire, and to the degree they permit diplomacy with NPC computer opponents, they generally don't make it interesting. Network games are, or ought to be, inherently diplomatic; and as network games become more prevalent, we can expect most developers from the computer design community to miss this point entirely. As an example, when the planners of interactive TV networks talk about games, they almost exclusively talk about the possibility of downloading cart-based (Nintendo, Sega) games over cable. They're doing so for a business reason: billions are spent annually on cart-based games, and they'd like a piece of the action. They don't seem to realize that networks permit a wholly different kind of gaming, which has the potential to make billions in its own right—and that this is the real business opportunity.

How can players help or hinder each other? What incentives do they have to do so? What resources can they trade?

Color

Monopoly is a game about real estate development. Right?

Well, no, obviously not. A real estate developer would laugh at the notion. A game about real estate development needs rules for construction loans and real estate syndication and union work rules and the bribery of municipal inspectors. Monopoly has nothing to do with real estate development. You could take the same rules, change the board, pieces, and cards, and make it into a game about space exploration, say. Except that your game would have as much to do with space exploration as Monopoly has to do with real estate development.

Monopoly isn't really about anything. But it has the color of a real estate game. named properties, little plastic houses and hotels, play money. And that's a big part of its appeal.

Color counts for a lot: as a simulation of World War II, Lawrence Harris's Axis & Allies is a pathetic effort. Ah, but the color! Millions of little plastic airplanes and battleships and tanks! Thundering dice! The world at war! The game works almost solely because of its color.

Or consider Chadwick's Space 1899. The rules do nothing to evoke the Burroughsian wonders, the pulp action thrills, and the Kiplingesque Victorian charms to be gained from the game's setting. Despite a clean system and a detailed world, it is curiously colorless, and suffers for it.

Pageantry, detail, and sense of place can greatly add to a game's emotional appeal. This has almost nothing to do with the game qua game; the original Nova edition of Axis & Allies was virtually identical to the Milton Bradley edition. Except that it had a god-awful garish paper map, some of the ugliest counters I've ever seen, and a truly amateurish box. I looked at it once, put it away, and never looked at it again.

Yet the Milton Bradley edition, with all the little plastic pieces, still gets pulled out now and again... Same game. Far better color.

How does the game evoke the ethos and atmosphere and pageantry of its setting? What can you do to make it more colorful?

Simulation

Many games simulate nothing. The oriental folk-game Go, say; little stones on a grid. It's abstract to perfection. Or John Horton Conway's Life; despite the evocative name, it's merely an exploration of a mathematical space.

Nothing wrong with that. But.

But color adds to a game's appeal. And simulation is a way of providing color.

Suppose I think, for some reason, that a game on Waterloo would have great commercial appeal. I could, if I wanted, take Monopoly, change "Park Place" to "Quatre Bras" and the hotels to plastic soldiers, and call it Waterloo. It would work.

But wouldn't it be better to simulate the battle? To have little battalions maneuvering over the field? To hear the thunder of guns?

Or take Star Wars: The Roleplaying Game, which I designed. I could have taken Gygax & Arneson's Dungeons & Dragons and changed it around, calling swords blasters and the like. But instead, I set out to simulate the movies, to encourage the players to attempt far-fetched cinematic stunts, to use the system itself to reflect something about the atmosphere and ethos of the films.

Simulation has other value, too. For one, it improves character identification. A Waterloo based on Monopoly would do nothing to make players think like Wellington and Napoleon; Kevin Zucker's Napoleon's Last Battles does much better, forcing players to think about the strategic problems those men faced.

And it can allow insight into a situation that mere narrative cannot. It allows players to explore different outcomes—in the fashion of a software toy—and thereby come to a gut understanding of the simulation's subject. Having played at least a dozen different games on Waterloo, I understand the battle, and why things happened the way they did, and the nature of Napoleonic warfare, far better than if I had merely read a dozen books on the subject.

Simulating something almost always is more complicated than simply exploiting a theme for color. And it is not, therefore, for every game. But when the technique is used, it can be quite powerful.

How can elements of simulation strengthen the game?

Variety of Encounter

"You just got lucky."

Words of contempt; you won through the vagaries of chance. A game that permits this is obviously inferior to ones where victory goes to the skilled, smart, and strong. Right? Not necessarily.

"Random elements" in a game are never wholly random. They are random within a range of possibilities. When, in a board wargame, I make an attack, I can look at the Combat Results Table. I know what outcomes are possible, and my chances of achieving what I want to achieve. I take a calculated risk. And over the whole game, I make dozens or hundreds of die-rolls; given so much reliance on randomness, the "random element" regresses to a mean. Except in rare cases, my victory or defeat will be based on my excellence as a strategist, not on my luck with the dice.

Randomness can be useful. It's one way of providing variety of encounter.

And what does that mean?

It means that the same old thing all over again is fucking boring. It means that players like to encounter the unexpected. It means that the game has to allow many different things to happen, so there's always something a little different for the players to encounter.

In a game like Chess, that "something different" is the ever-changing implications of the positions of the pieces. In a game like Richard Garfield's Magic: The Gathering, it's the sheer variety of cards, and the random order in which they appear, and the interesting ways in which they can be combined. In Arneson & Gygax's Dungeons & Dragons, it's the staggering variety of monsters, spells, etc., etc., coupled with the gamemaster's ingenuity in throwing new situations at his players.

If a game has inadequate variety, it rapidly palls. That's why no one plays graphic adventures more than once; there's enough variety for a single game, but it's the same thing all over again the next time you play. That's why Patience, the solitaire cardgame, becomes dull pretty fast; you're doing the same things over and over, and reshuffling the cards isn't enough to rekindle your interest, after a time.

What things do the players encounter in this game? Are there enough things for them to explore and discover? What provides variety? How can we increase the variety of encounter?

Position Identification

"Character identification" is a common theme of fiction. Writers want readers to like their protagonists, to identify with them, to care what happens to them. Character identification lends emotional power to a story.

The same is true in games. To the degree you encourage players to care about "the side," to identify with their position in the game, you increase the game's emotional impact.

The extreme case is sports; in sports, your "position" is you. You're out there on the baseball diamond, and winning or losing matters, and you feel it deeply when you strike out, or smash the ball out of the park. It's important to you.

So important that fistfights and bitter words are not uncommon, in every sport. So important that we've invented a whole cultural tradition of "sportsmanship" to try to prevent these unpleasant feelings from coming to the fore.

Roleplaying games are one step abstracted; your character isn't you, but you invest a lot of time and energy in it. It's your sole token and the sum total of your position in the game. Bitter words, and even fistfights, are not unknown among roleplayers, though rather rarer than in sports.

Getting players to identify with their game position is straightforward when a player has a single token; it's harder when he controls many. Few people feel much sadness at the loss of a knight in Chess or an infantry division in a wargame. But even here, a game's emotional power is improved if the player can be made to feel identification with "the side."

One way to do that is to make clear the player's point of view. Point of view confusion is a common failing of boardgame designers. For instance, Richard Berg's Campaigns for North Africa claims to be an extraordinary realistic simulation of the Axis campaign in Africa. Yet you, as player, spend a great deal of time worrying about the locations of individual pilots and how much water is available to individual battalions. Rommel's staff might worry about such things, but Rommel assuredly did not. Who are you supposed to be? The accuracy of the simulation is, in a sense, undermined, not supported, by the level of detail.

What can you do to make the player care about his position? Is there a single game token that's more important than others to the player, and what can be done to strengthen identification with it? If not, what is the overall emotional appeal of the position, and what can be done to strengthen that appeal? Who "is" the player in the game? What is his point of view?

Roleplaying

HeroQuest has been termed a "roleplaying boardgame." And, as in a roleplaying game, each player controls a single character, which, in HeroQuest's case, is a single plastic figure on the board. If you are a single character, are you not "playing a role?" And is the characterization of this game as a "roleplaying" game therefore justified?

No, to both questions.

The questions belie confusion between "position identification" and "roleplaying." I may identify closely with a game token without feeling that I am playing a role.

Roleplaying occurs when, in some sense, you take on the persona of your position. Different players, and different games, may do this in different ways: perhaps you try to speak in the language and rhythm of your character. Perhaps you talk as if you are feeling the emotions your character feels. Perhaps you talk as you normally do, but you give serious consideration to "what my character would do in this case" as opposed to "what I want to do next."

Roleplaying is most common in, naturally, roleplaying games. But it can occur in other environments, as well; I, for one, can't get through a game of Vincent Tsao's Junta without talking in a phony Spanish accent somewhere along the line. The game makes me think enough like a big man in a corrupt banana republic that I start to play the role.

Roleplaying is a powerful technique for a whole slew of reasons. It improves position identification; if you think like your character, you're identifying with him closely. It improves the game's color, because the players become partly responsible for maintaining the willing suspense of disbelief, the feeling that the game world is alive and colorful and consistent. And it is an excellent method of socialization.

Indeed, the connection with socialization is key: roleplaying is a form of performance. In a roleplaying game, roleplayers perform for the amusement of their friends. If there aren't any friends, there's no point to it.

Which is why "computer roleplaying games", so-called, are nothing of the kind. They have no more connection with roleplaying than does HeroQuest. That is, they have the trappings of roleplaying: characters, equipment, stories. But there is no mechanism for players to ham it up, to characterize themselves by their actions, to roleplay in any meaningful sense.

This is intrinsic in the technology. Computer games are solitaire; solitaire gamers have, by definition, no audience. Therefore, computer games cannot involve roleplaying.

Add a network, and you can have a roleplaying game. Hence the popularity of MUDs.

How can players be induced to roleplay? What sorts of roles does the system permit or encourage?

Socializing

Historically, games have mainly been used as a way to socialize. For players of Bridge, Poker, and Charades, the game is secondary to the socialization that goes on over the table.

One oddity of the present is that the most commercially successful games are all solitary in nature: cart games, disk-based computer games, CD-ROM games. Once upon a time, our image of gamers was some people sitting around a table and playing cards; now, it's a solitary adolescent, twitching a joystick before a flickering screen.

Yet, at the same time, we see the development of roleplaying, in both tabletop and live-action form, which depends utterly on socialization. And we see that the most successful mass-market boardgames, like Trivial Pursuit and Pictionary, are played almost exclusively in social settings.

I have to believe that the solitary nature of most computer games is a temporary aberration, a consequence of the technology, and that as networks spread and their bandwidth increases, the historical norm will reassert itself.

When designing any game, it is worthwhile to think about the game's social uses, and how the system encourages or discourages socialization. For instance, almost every network has online versions of classic games like Poker and Bridge. And in almost every case, those games have failed to attract much usage.

The exception: America Online, which permits real-time chat between players. Their version of network bridge allows for table talk. And it has been quite popular.

Or as another example, many tabletop roleplaying games spend far too much effort worrying about "realism" and far too little about the game's use by players. Of what use is a combat system that is extraordinarily realistic, if playing out a single combat round takes fifteen minutes, and a whole battle takes four hours? They're not spending their time socializing, talking, and hamming it up; they're spending time rolling dice and looking things up on charts. What's the point in that?

How can the game better encourage socialization?

Narrative Tension

Nebula-award winning author Pat Murphy says that the key element of plot is "rising tension." That is, a story should become more gripping as it proceeds, until its ultimate climactic resolution.

Suppose you are a Yankees fan. Of course, you want to see the Yankees win. But if you go to a game at the ballpark, do you really want to see them develop a 7 point lead in the first inning and wind up winning 21 to 2? Yes, you want them to win, but this doesn't make for a very interesting game. What would make you rise from your seat in excitement and joy is to see them pull out from behind in the last few seconds of the game with a smash homerun with bases loaded. Tension makes for fun games.

Ideally, a game should be tense all the way through, but especially so at the end. The toughest problems, the greatest obstacles, should be saved for last. You can't always ensure this, especially in directly competitive games: a Chess game between a grandmaster and a rank beginner is not going to involve much tension. But, especially in solitaire computer games, it should be possible to ensure that every stage of the game involves a set of challenges, and that the player's job is done only at the end.

In fact, one of the most common game failures is anticlimax. The period of maximum tension is not the resolution, but somewhere mid-way through the game. After a while, the opposition is on the run, or the player's position is unassailable. In most cases, this is because the designer never considered the need for narrative tension.

What can be done to make the game tense?

They're All Alike Under the Dice. Or Phosphors. Or What Have You.

We're now equipped to answer the questions I posed at the beginning of this article.

Do all the myriad forms of gaming have anything in common? Most assuredly. All involve decision-making, managing resources in pursuit of a goal; that's true whether we're talking about Chess or Seventh Guest, Mario Brothers or Vampire, Roulette or Magic: The Gathering. It's a universal; it's what defines a game.

How can you tell a good game from a bad one? The test is still in the playing; but we now have some terms to use to analyze a game's appeal. Chess involves complex and difficult decisions; Magic has enormous variety of encounter; Roulette has an extremely compelling goal (money—the real stuff). More detailed analysis is possible, to be sure, and is left as an exercise for the reader.

Is the analytical theory presented here hermetic and complete? Assuredly not; there are games that defy many, though not all, of its conclusions (e.g., Candyland, which involves no decision-making whatsoever). And no doubt there are aspects to the appeal of games it overlooks.

It is to be considered a work in progress: a first stab at codifying the intellectual analysis of the art of game design. Others are welcome, even encouraged, to build on its structure—or to propound alternative theories in its defiance.

If we are to produce works worthy to be termed "art," we must start to think about what it takes to do so, to set ourselves goals beyond the merely commercial. For we are embarked on a voyage of revolutionary import: the democrative transformation of the arts. Properly addressed, the voyage will lend grandeur to our civilization; improperly, it will create merely another mediocrity of the TV age, another form wholly devoid of intellectual merit.

The author wishes to acknowledge the contributions of Chris Crawford, Will Wright, Eric Goldberg, Ken Rolston, Doug Kaufman, Jim Dunnigan, Tappan King, Sandy Peterson, and Walt Freitag, whose ideas he has liberally stolen.

Orthographical Note: In normal practice, the names of traditional games, e.g., chess, go, poker, are uncapitalized, as is usual with common nouns. The names of proprietary games are written with Initial Caps. This usage is inconsistent with the thesis that games are an artform, and that each game, regardless of its origins, must be viewed as an oeuvre. I capitalize all game names, throughout the article.

We capitalize *Beowulf*, though it is the product of folk tradition rather than a definite author, just as we capitalize *One Hundred Years of Solitude*. In the same fashion, I capitalize Chess, though it is the product of folk tradition rather than a definite designer, just as I capitalize Dungeons & Dragons. It may seem odd, at first, to see Chess treated as a title, but I have done so for particular reasons.

I have also, whenever possible, attempted to mention a game's designer upon its first mention. When I have omitted a name, it is because I do not know it.

The Cabal: Valve's Design Process for Creating Half-Life

Ken Birdwell

Context

*Up until **Half-Life,** every major project I had ever worked on had been strictly driven by engineering constraints; I had never worked on anything whose primary constraint was that "it had to be fun." Integrating a large team of artists and game play designers into the development process was also baffling: virtually none of them had any experience working in a large complex project, and none of the senior technical staff had any experience working with non-engineers. Attempts at imposing formal methods proved pointless, and leaving each area to its own devices proved disastrous. It wasn't until we started the Cabal process that we had any hope of even completing the game, much less succeeding past all our expectations. This article originally appeared in the December 1999 issue of **Game Developer** magazine.*

The Game Design Process

Ken Birdwell is one of the founding members of Valve Inc., and contributed to Valup's *Half-Life* and *Half-Life 2* PC game titles. Previous work includes designing broadcast satellite networking at Microsoft, and automating prosthetic design tools with Nike.

While *Half-Life* has seen resounding critical and financial success (winning over 50 Game of the Year awards and selling more than a million copies worldwide), few people realize that it didn't start out a winner—in fact, Valve's first attempt at the game had to be scrapped. It was mediocre at best, and suffered from the typical problems that plague far too many games. This article is about the teamwork—or "Cabal process"—that turned our initial, less than impressive version of *Half-Life* into a groundbreaking success.

Paving the Way with Good Intentions

Our initial target release date was November 1997—a year before the game actually shipped. This date would have given Valve a year to develop what was in essence a fancy *Quake* TC (Total Conversion—all new artwork, all new levels). By late September 1997, nearing the end of our original schedule, a whole lot of work had been done, but there was one major problem—the game wasn't any fun.

Yes, we had some cool monsters, but if you didn't fight them exactly the way we had planned they did really stupid things. We had some cool levels, but they didn't fit together well. We had some cool technology, but for the most part it only showed up in one or two spots. So you couldn't play the game all the way through, none of the levels tied together well, and there were serious technical problems with most of the game. There were some really wonderful individual pieces, but as a whole the game just wasn't working.

The obvious answer was to work a few more months, gloss over the worst of the problems and ship what we had. For companies who live and die at the whim of their publishers, this is usually the route taken—with predictable results. Since Valve is fairly independent, and since none of us believed that we were getting any closer to making a game we could all like, we couldn't see how a month or two would make any significant difference. At this point we had to make a very painful decision—we decided to start over and rework every stage of the game.

Fortunately, the game had some things in it we liked. We set up a small group of people to take every silly idea, every cool trick, everything interesting that existed in any kind of working state somewhere in the game and put them into a single prototype level. When the level started to get fun, they added more variations of the fun things. If an idea wasn't fun, they cut it. When they needed a software feature, they simplified it until it was something that could be written in a few days. They all worked together on this one small level for a month

Many of our scripted sequences were designed to give the player game-play clues as well as provide moments of sheer terror.

Conceptual artwork for ceiling-mounted monster that was dangerous to both the player and the player's enemies.

while the rest of us basically did nothing. When they were done, we all played it. It was great. It was *Die Hard* meets *Evil Dead*. It was the vision. It was going to be our game. It was huge and scary and going to take a lot of work, but after seeing it we weren't going to be satisfied with anything less. All that we needed to do was to create about 100 more levels that were just as fun. No problem.

So, Tell Me about Your Childhood

The second step in the pre-Cabal process was to analyze what was fun about our prototype level. The first theory we came up with was the theory of "experiential density"—the amount of "things" that happen to and are done by the player per unit of time and area of a map. Our goal was that, once active, the player never had to wait too long before the next stimulus, be it monster, special effect, plot point, action sequence, and so on. Since we couldn't really bring all these experiences to the player (a relentless series of them would just get tedious), all content is distance based, not time based, and no activities are started outside the player's control. If the players are in the mood for more action, all they need to do is move forward and within a few seconds something will happen.

The second theory we came up with is the theory of player acknowledgment. This means that the game world must acknowledge players every time they perform an action. For example, if they shoot their gun, the world needs to acknowledge it with something more permanent than just a sound—there should be some visual evidence that they've just fired their gun. We would have liked to put a hole through the wall, but for technical and game flow reasons we really couldn't do it. Instead we decided on "decals"—bullet nicks and explosion marks on all the surfaces, which serve as permanent records of the action. This also means that if the player pushes on something that should be pushable, the object shouldn't ignore them, it should move. If they whack on something with their crowbar that looks like it should break, it had better break. If they walk into a room with other characters, those characters should acknowledge them by at least looking at them, if not calling out their name. Our basic theory was that if the world ignores the player, the player won't care about the world.

A final theory was that the players should always blame themselves for failure. If the game kills them off with no warning, then players blame the game and start to dislike it. But if the game hints that danger is imminent, shows players a way out and they die anyway, then they'll consider it a failure on their part; they've let the game down and they need to try a little harder. When they succeed, and the game rewards them with a little treat—scripted sequence, special effect, and so on—they'll feel good about themselves and about the game.

Secret Societies

Throughout the first eleven months of the project we searched for an official "game designer"—someone who could show up and make it all come together. We looked at hundreds of resumes and interviewed a lot of promising applicants, but no one we looked at had enough of the qualities we wanted for us to seriously consider them the overall godlike "game designer" that we were told we needed. In the end, we came to the conclusion that this ideal person didn't actually exist. Instead, we would create our own ideal by combining the strengths of a cross section of the company; putting them together in a group we called the "Cabal."

The goal of this group was to create a complete document that detailed all the levels and described major monster interactions, special effects, plot devices, and design standards. The Cabal was to work out when and how every monster, weapon, and NPC was to be introduced, what skills we expected the player to have, and how we were going to teach them those skills. As daunting as that sounds, this is exactly what we did. We consider the Cabal process to have been wildly successful, and one of the key reasons for *Half-Life's* success.

Cabal meetings were semi-structured brainstorming sessions usually dedicated to a specific area of the game. During each session, one person was assigned the job of recording and writing up the design, and another was assigned to draw pictures explaining the layout

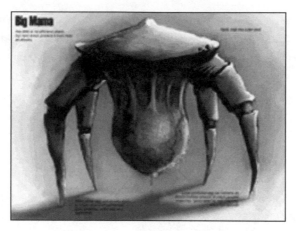

The team explored a variety of visual metaphors that resulted in some very unique and effective opponents.

and other details. A Cabal session would typically consist of a few days coming up with a mix of high level concepts for the given area, as well as specific events that sounded fun.

Once enough ideas were generated, they would be reorganized into a rough storyline and chronology. Once this was all worked out, a description and rough sketch of the geometry would be created and labeled with all the key events and where they should take place. We knew what we wanted for some areas of the game from the very start, but other areas stayed as "outdoors" or "something with a big monster" for quite some time. Other areas were created without a specific spot in the game. These designs would sit in limbo for a few weeks until either it became clear that they weren't going to fit, or that perhaps they would make a good segue between two other areas. Other portions were created to highlight a specific technology feature, or simply to give the game a reason to include a cool piece of geometry that had been created during a pre-Cabal experiment. Oddly enough, when trying to match these artificial constants, we would often create our best work. We eventually got into the habit of placing a number of unrelated requirements into each area then doing our best to come up with a rational way to fit them together. Often, by the end of the session we would find that the initial idea wasn't nearly as interesting as all the pieces we built around it, and the structure we had designed to explain it actually worked better without that initial idea.

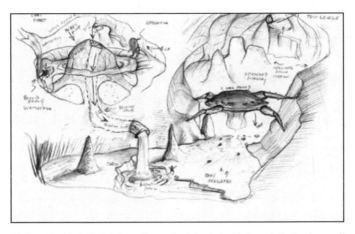

It's important to include information on the intended path through the level, as well as rough geometry and character placement.

During Cabal sessions, everyone contributed but we found that not everyone contributed everyday. The meetings were grueling, and we came to almost expect that about half of the group would find themselves sitting through two or three meetings with no ideas at all, and then suddenly see a direction that no one else saw and be the main contributor for the remainder of the week. Why this happened was unclear, but it became important to have at least five or six people in each meeting so that the meetings wouldn't stall out from lack of input.

The Cabal met four days a week, six hours a day for five months straight, and then on and off until the end of the project. The meetings were only six hours a day, because after six hours everyone was emotionally and physically drained. The people involved weren't really able to do any other work during that time, other than read e-mail and write up their daily notes.

The initial Cabal group consisted of three engineers, a level designer, a writer, and an animator. This represented all the major groups at Valve and all aspects of the project and was initially weighted towards people with the most product experience (though not necessarily game experience). The Cabal consisted only of people that had actual shipping components in the game; there were no dedicated designers. Every member of the Cabal was someone with the responsibility of actually doing the work that their design specified, or at least had the ability to do it if need be.

The first few months of the Cabal process were somewhat nerve wracking for those outside the process. It wasn't clear that egos could be suppressed enough to get anything done, or that a vision of the game filtered through a large number of people would be anything

217

other than bland. As it turned out, the opposite was true; the people involved were tired of working in isolation and were energized by the collaborative process, and the resulting designs had a consistent level of polish and depth that hadn't been seen before.

Internally, once the success of the Cabal process was obvious, mini-Cabals were formed to come up with answers to a variety of design problems. These mini-Cabals would typically include people most affected by the decision, as well as try to include people completely outside the problem being addressed in order to keep a fresh perspective on things. We also kept membership in the initial Cabal somewhat flexible and we quickly started to rotate people through the process every month or so, always including a few people from the last time, and always making sure we had a cross section of the company. This helped to prevent burn out, and ensured that everyone involved in the process had experience using the results of Cabal decisions.

The final result was a document of more than 200 pages detailing everything in the game from how high buttons should be to what time of the day it was in any given level. It included rough drawings of all the levels, as well as work items listing any new technology, sounds, or animations that those levels would require.

We also ended up assigning one person to follow the entire story line and to maintain the entire document. With a design as large as a 30-hour movie, we ended up creating more detail than could be dealt with on a casual or part-time basis. We found that having a professional writer on staff was key to this process. Besides being able to add personality to all our characters, his ability to keep track of thematic structures, plot twists, pacing, and consistency was invaluable.

Pearls before Swine

By the second month of the Cabal, we (the "swine") had enough of the game design to begin development on several areas. By the third month, we had enough put together to begin play-testing.

A play-test session consists of one outside volunteer (Sierra, our publisher, pulled play-testers from local people who had sent in product registration cards for other games) playing the game for two hours. Sitting immediately behind them would be one person from the Cabal session that worked on that area of the game, as well as the level designer who was currently the "primary" on the level being tested. Occasionally, this would also include an engineer if new AI needed to be tested.

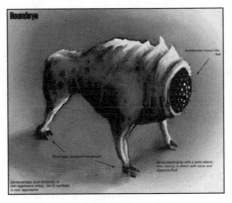

This creature was initially designed as a friendly character, but play-testing revealed players' tendencies to shoot first and ask questions later.

Letting players see other characters make mistakes that they'll need to avoid is an effective way to explain your puzzles and add tension and entertainment value.

Other than starting the game for them and resetting it if it crashed, the observers from Valve were not allowed to say anything. They had to sit there quietly taking notes, and were not allowed to give any hints or suggestions. Nothing is quite as humbling as being forced to watch in silence as some poor play-tester stumbles around your level for 20 minutes, unable to figure out the "obvious" answer that you now realize is completely arbitrary and impossible to figure out.

This was also a sure way to settle any design arguments. It became obvious that any personal opinion you had given really didn't mean anything, at least not until the next play-test session. Just because you were sure something was going to be fun didn't make it so; the play-testers could still show up and demonstrate just how wrong you really were.

A typical two-hour play-test session would result in 100 or so "action items"—things that needed to be fixed, changed, added, or deleted from the game. The first 20 or 30 play-test sessions were absolutely critical for teaching us as a company what elements were fun and what elements were not. Over the course of the project we ended up doing more than 200 play-test sessions, about half of them with repeat players. The feedback from the sessions was worked back into the Cabal process, allowing us to preemptively remove designs that didn't work well, as well as elaborate on designs that did.

Toward the middle of the project, once the major elements were in place and the game could be played most of the way through, it became mostly a matter of fine tuning. To do this, we added basic instrumentation to the game, automatically recording the player's position, health, weapons, time, and any major activities such as saving the game, dying, being hurt, solving a puzzle, fighting a monster, and so on. We then took the results from a number of sessions and graphed them together to find any areas where there were problems. These included areas where the player spent too long without any encounters (boring), too long with too much health (too easy), too long with too little health (too hard), all of which gave us a good idea as to where they were likely to die and which positions would be best for adding goodies.

Another thing that helped with debugging was making the "save game" format compatible between the different versions of the engine. Since we automatically saved the game at regular intervals, if the play-testers crashed the game we would usually have something not too far from where they encountered the bug. Since these files would even work if the code base they were testing was several versions old, it made normally rare and hard to duplicate bugs relatively easy to find and fix. Our save game format allowed us to add data, delete data, add and delete code (we even supported function pointers) at will, without breaking anything. This also allowed us to make some fairly major changes after we shipped the game without interfering with any of our players' hard-won saved games.

No Good Deed Goes Unpunished

Until the Cabal process got underway, technology was added to *Half-Life* freely. It was assumed that "if we build it, they will come," meaning that any new technology would just naturally find a creative use by the content creation folks. A prime example of this fallacy was our "beam" effect, basically a technique for doing highly tunable squiggly glowing lines between two points; stuff like lightning, lasers, and mysterious glowing beams of energy. It was added to the engine, the parameters were exposed, and an e-mail was sent out explaining it. The result was ...nothing. After two months only one level designer had put it in a map. Engineering was baffled.

During the Cabal process, we realized that although the level designers knew of the feature, they really had no clear idea of what it was for. The parameters were all very cryptic, and the wrong combinations would cause the beams to have very ugly-looking effects. There were no decent textures to apply to them, and setting them up was a bit of a mystery. It became very clear the technology itself was only a small part of the work, and integration, training, and follow-through were absolutely necessary to make the technology useful to the game. Writing the code was typically less than half the problem.

Square Pegs

Practically speaking, not everyone is suited for the kind of group design activity we performed in the Cabal, at least not initially. People with strong personalities, people with poor verbal skills, or people who just don't like creating in a group setting shouldn't be forced into it. We weighted our groups heavily toward people with a lot of group design experience, well ahead of game design experience. Even so, in the end almost everyone was in a Cabal of one sort or another, and as we got more comfortable with this process and started getting really good results it was easier to integrate the more reluctant members. For current projects, such as *Team Fortress 2*, the Cabal groups are made up of twelve or more people, and rarely fewer than eight. The meetings ended up being shorter, and they also ended up spreading ideas around a lot quicker, but I'm not sure I'd recommend that size of group initially.

Just about everything in *Half-Life* was designed by a Cabal. This at first seemed to add a bit of overhead to everything, but it had the important characteristic of getting everyone involved in the creation process that was personally invested in the design. Once everyone becomes invested in the design as a whole, it stops being separate pieces owned by a single person and instead the entire game design becomes "ours."

This "ours" idea extended to all levels. Almost every level in the game ended up being edited by at least three different level designers at some point in its development and some levels were touched by everyone. Though all the level designers were good at almost everything, each found they enjoyed some aspect of level design more than other aspects. One would do the geometry, one would do monster and AI placement, our texture artist would step in and do a texturing pass, and then one would finish up with a lighting pass, often switching roles when needed due to scheduling conflicts. This became critical toward the end of the project when people finished at different times. If a play-test session revealed something that needed to be changed, any available level designer could make the changes without the game getting bottlenecked by needing any specific individual.

This idea also extended to all code, textures, models, animations, sounds, and so on. All were under source control and any individual was able to synch up to the sources and make whatever changes were necessary. With a little bit of self-control, this isn't as random as it sounds. It had the added benefit in that it was fairly easy to get a daily record of exactly what was changed and by whom. We would then feed this information back into the play-test cycles, only testing what had changed, as well as helping project scheduling by being able to

By placing traditional combat action in more challenging environments we were able to intensify the feeling of tension and suspense.

Placing the player in a soldier-vs.-alien conflict helped reinforce the illusion of an active environment, and let Valve show off its combat AI with minimal risk to the player.

monitor the changes and get a pretty good estimate of the stability and completeness of any one component. This also allowed us to systematically add features throughout the process with minimal impact. Once the technical portion was completed, the engineer assigned to the feature was able to synch to all the source artwork and rebuild any and all files (models, textures, levels, and so on) affected by the change.

The Workers Control the Means of Production

Even with all emphasis on group activity, most of the major features of *Half-Life* still only happened through individual initiative. Everyone had different ideas as to what exactly the game should look like, or at least what features we just had to do. The Cabal process gave these ideas a place to be heard, and since it was accepted that design ideas can come from anyone, it gave people as much authority as they wanted to take. If the idea required someone other than the inventor to actually do the work, or if the idea had impact on other areas of the game, they would need to start a Cabal and try to convince the other key people involved that their idea was worth the effort. At the start of the project, this was pretty easy as most everyone wildly underestimated the total amount of work that needed to be done, but toward the middle and end of the project the more disruptive decisions tended to get harder and harder to push through. It also helped filter out all design changes except for the ones with the most player impact for the least development work.

Through a constant cycle of play-testing, feedback, review, and editing, the Cabal process was also key in removing portions of the game that didn't meet the quality standards we wanted, regardless of the level of emotional attachment the specific creator may have had to the work. This was one of the more initially contentious aspects of the Cabal process, but perhaps one of the more important. By its very nature, the Cabal process avoided most of the personal conflicts inherent in other more hierarchical organizations. Since problems were identified in a relatively objective manner of play-testing, and since their solutions were arrived at by consensus or at least by an individual peer, then an authority that everyone could rebel against just didn't exist.

On a day-to-day basis, the level of detail supplied in even a 200-page design document is vague at best. It doesn't answer the 1,001 specific details that each area requires, or the countless creative details that are part of everyday development. Any design document is really nothing more than a framework to work from and something to improve the likelihood that work from multiple people will fit together in a seamless fashion. It's the Cabal process that helped spread around all the big picture ideas that didn't make it into any document—things that are critical to the feel of the game, but too nebulous to put into words. It also helps maximize individual strengths and minimize individual weaknesses and sets up a framework that allows individuals to influence as much of the game as possible. In *Half-Life*, it was the rare area of the game that didn't include the direct work of more than ten different people, usually all within the same frame.

In order for highly hierarchical organizations to be effective, they require one person who understands everyone else's work at least as well as the individuals doing the work, and other people who are willing to be subordinates yet are still good enough to actually implement the design. Given the complexity of most top game titles, this just isn't practical—if you were good enough to do the job, why would you want to be a flunky? On the other hand, completely unstructured organizations suffer from lack of information and control—if everyone just does their own thing, the odds that it'll all fit together in the end are somewhere around zero.

At Valve, we're very happy with the results of our Cabal process. Of course, we still suffer from being overly ambitious and having, at times, wildly unrealistic expectations, but these eventually get straightened out and the Cabal process is very good about coming up with the optimal compromise. Given how badly we failed initially, and how much the final game exceeded our individual expectations, even our most initially reluctant person is now a staunch supporter of the process.

223

The first incarnation of the game's main character, now known affectionately as "Ivan the Space Biker."

Tips for a Successful Cabal

- Include an expert from every functional area (programming, art, and so on). Arguing over an issue that no one at the meeting actually understands is a sure way to waste everyone's time.

- Write down everything. Brainstorming is fine during the meetings, but unless it's all written down, your best ideas will be forgotten within days. The goal is to end up with a document that captures as much as is reasonable about your game, and more importantly answers questions about what people need to work on.

- Not all ideas are good. These include yours. If you have a "great idea" that everyone thinks is stupid, don't push it. The others will also have stupid ideas. If you're pushy about yours, they'll be pushy about theirs and you're just going to get into an impasse. If the idea is really good, maybe it's just in the wrong place. Bring it up later. You're going to be designing about 30 hours of game play; if you really want it in it'll probably fit somewhere else. Maybe they'll like it next month.

- Only plan for technical things that either already work, or that you're sure will work within a reasonable time before play testing. Don't count on anything that won't be ready until just before you ship. Yes, it's fun to dream about cool technology, but there's no point in designing the game around elements that may never be finished, or not polished enough to ship. If it's not going to happen, get rid of it, the earlier the better.

- Avoid all one-shot technical elements. Anything that requires engineering work must be used in more than one spot in the game. Engineers are really slow. It takes them months to get anything done. If what they do is only used once, it's a waste of a limited resource. Their main goal should always be to create tools and features that can be used everywhere. If they can spend a month and make everyone more productive, then it's a win. If they spend a week for ten seconds of game play, it's a waste.

Semiotic Domains: Is Playing Video Games a "Waste of Time?"

James Paul Gee

Context

What Video Games Have to Teach Us About Learning and Literacy *(Palgrave/Macmillan, 2003)*
was written because watching my then six-year-old son play video games inspired me to try
playing them myself. I was amazed by how hard they were and yet, at the same time, deeply
motivating and engaging. When I stuck with them, I also became fascinated by how well they
dealt with learning as part of the deep pleasure of playing.

Speaking of Games

James Paul Gee is the Tashia Morgridge Professor of
Reading at the University of Wisconsin at Madison. Originally
trained as a linguist, he now works on issues related to
literacy and learning in and out of schools. His books
include *Social Linguistics and Literacies; The Social Mind;
What Video Games Have to Teach Us About Learning and
Literacy;* and *Situated Language and Learning.*

Literacy and Semiotic Domains

When people learn to play video games, they are learning a new *literacy*. Of course, this is not the way the word "literacy" is normally used. Traditionally, people think of literacy as the ability to read and write. Why, then, should we think of literacy more broadly, in regard to video games or anything else, for that matter? There are two reasons.

First, in the modern world, language is not the only important communicational system. Today images, symbols, graphs, diagrams, artifacts, and many other visual symbols are particularly significant. Thus, the idea of different types of "visual literacy" would seem to be an important one. For example, being able to "read" the images in advertising is one type of visual literacy. And, of course, there are different ways to read such images, ways that are more or less aligned with the intentions and interests of the advertisers. Knowing how to read interior designs in homes, modernist art in museums, and videos on MTV are other forms of visual literacy.

Furthermore, very often today words and images of various sorts are juxtaposed and integrated in a variety of ways. In newspaper and magazines as well as in textbooks, images take up more and more of the space alongside words. In fact, in many modern high school and college textbooks in the sciences images not only take up more space, they now carry meanings that are independent of the words in the text. If you can't read these images, you will not be able to recover their meanings from the words in the text as was more usual in the past.

In such *multimodal* texts (texts that mix words and images), the images often communicate different things from the words. And the combination of the two modes communicates things that neither of the modes does separately. Thus, the idea of different sorts of multimodal literacy seems an important one. Both modes and multimodality go far beyond images and words to include sounds, music, movement, bodily sensations, and smells.

None of this is news today, of course. We very obviously live in a world awash with images. It is our first answer to the question why we should think of literacy more broadly. The second answer is this: Even though reading and writing seem so central to what literacy means traditionally, reading and writing are not such general and obvious matters as they might at first seem. After all, we never just read or write; rather, we always read or write *something in some way.*

There are many different ways of reading and writing. We don't read or write news-papers, legal tracts, essays in literary criticism, poetry, rap songs, and on through a nearly endless list in the same way. Each of these domains has its own rules and requirements. Each is a culturally and historically separate way of reading and writing, and, in that sense, a different literacy. Furthermore, in each case, if we want to "break the rules" and read against the grain of the text—for the purposes of critique, for instance—we have to do so in different ways, usually with some relatively deep knowledge of how to read such texts "according to the rules."

So there are different ways to read different types of texts. Literacy is multiple, then, in the sense that the legal literacy needed for reading law books is not the same as the literacy needed for reading physics texts or superhero comic books. And we should not be too quick to dismiss the latter form of literacy. Many a superhero comic is replete with post-Freudian irony of a sort that would make a modern literary critic's heart beat fast and confuse any otherwise normal adult. Literacy, then, even as traditionally conceived to involve only print, is not a unitary thing but a multiple matter. There are, even in regard to printed texts and even leaving aside images and multimodal texts, different "literacies."

Once we see this multiplicity of literacy (literacies), we realize that when we think about reading and writing, we have to think beyond print. Reading and writing in any domain, whether it is law, rap songs, academic essays, superhero comics, or whatever, are not just ways of decoding print, they are also caught up with and in social practices. Literacy in any domain is actually not worth much if one knows nothing about the social practices of which that literacy is but a part. And, of course, these social practices involve much more than just an engagement with print.

One can know a good deal about a social practice—such as arguing before the Supreme Court, carrying out an experiment in nuclear physics, or memorializing an event in gang history through graffiti—without actually being able to participate in the social practice. But knowing about a social practice always involves recognizing various distinctive ways of acting, inter-acting, valuing, feeling, knowing, and using various objects and technologies that constitute the social practice.

Take something so simple as the following sentence about basketball: "The guard dribbled down court, held up two fingers, and passed to the open man." You may very well know what every word in this sentence means in terms of dictionary definitions, but you cannot read the sentence with any real worthwhile understanding unless you can recognize, in some sense (perhaps only in simulations in your mind), guards, dribbling, basketballs, open men, and basketball courts. But to be able to recognize these things is already to know a good deal about basketball as a game, that is, as a particular sort of social practice. The same thing is equally true about any sentence or text about the law, comic books, a branch of science, or anything else for that matter.

We can go further. One's understanding of the sentence "The guard dribbled down court, held up two fingers, and passed to the open man" is different—in some sense, deeper and better—the more one knows and can recognize about the social practice (game) of basketball. For example, if you know a good bit about basketball, you may see that one possible meaning of this sentence is that the guard signaled a particular play by holding up two fingers and then passed to the player the play left momentarily unguarded.

But then this brings us to another important point. While you don't need to be able to enact a particular social practice (e.g., play basketball or argue before a court) to be able to understand texts from or about that social practice, you can *potentially* give deeper meanings to those texts if you can. This claim amounts to arguing that producers (people who can actually engage in a social practice) *potentially* make better consumers (people who can read or understand texts from or about the social practice).

A corollary of this claim is this: Writers (in the sense of people who can write texts that are recognizably part of a particular social practice) *potentially* make better readers (people who can understand texts from or about a given social practice). Note that by "writers" here I do not mean people who can just write down words appropriate to a particular practice such as field biology. I mean people who can write a text that field biologists would recognize as an acceptable text within their family of social practices.

Why do I say "potentially" here? Because there is a paradox about producers. On one hand, producers are deeply enough embedded in their social practices that they can understand the texts associated with those practices quite well. On the other hand, producers are often so deeply embedded in their social practices that they take the meanings and values of the texts associated with those practices for granted in an unquestioning way. One key question for deep learning and good education, then, is how to get producer-like learning and knowledge, but in a reflective and critical way.

All these claims are pretty obvious. It is, thus, fascinating that they are so often ignored in schools. In school, many times children are expected to read texts with little or no knowledge about any social practices within which those texts are used. They are rarely allowed to engage in an actual social practice in ways that are recognizable to "insiders" (e.g., field biologists) as meaningful and acceptable, before and as they read texts relevant to the practice.

Indeed, children are regularly given reading tests that ask general, factual, and dictionarylike questions about various texts with no regard for the fact that these texts fall into different genres (i.e., they are different kinds of texts) connected to different sorts of social practices. Children often can answer such questions, but they learn and know nothing about the genres and social practices that are, in the end, the heart and soul of literacy.

Schools will continue to operate this way until they (and reading tests) move beyond fixating on reading as silently saying the sounds of letters and words and being able to answer general, factual, and dictionarylike questions about written texts. You do have to silently say the sounds of letters and words when you read (or, at least, this greatly speeds up reading). You do have do be able to answer general, factual, and dictionarylike questions about what you read: This means you know the "literal" meaning of the text. But what so many people—unfortunately so many educators and policymakers—fail to see is that if this is all you can do, then you *can't really read.* You will fail to be able to read well and appropriately in contexts associated with specific types of texts and specific types of social practices.

For example, consider once again our sentence about basketball: "The guard dribbled down court, held up two fingers, and passed to the open man." A typical reading test would ask a question like this: "What did the guard do to the ball?" and give "bounce it" as one of the choices. Unfortunately, you can answer such general, factual, dictionarylike questions and really have no idea what the sentence means in the domain of basketball. When we see that the same thing applies to sentences from science or any other school subject, we immediately see why so many children pass early reading tests but cannot learn later on in the subject areas.

This phenomenon is so pervasive that it has been given a name by researchers: "the fourth-grade slump." It is called this because, in the past, the first three years of school were largely devoted to learning to read (in the sense of being able to decode print and get the literal meanings of texts), and fourth grade was where children began to read to learn (in the subject areas). However, very often today children are being asked to read to learn things like science and math from first or second grade on, at least in affluent schools.

However, let's leave school aside, and return to our main question as to why we should be willing to broaden how we talk about literacy. I can now note that talking about literacy and literacies in this expanded, nontraditional way (as multiple and connected to social practices) leads us at once to an interesting dilemma: What do we want to say of someone, for instance, who can understand and even compose rap songs (words and music), but cannot read or write language or musical notation?

Of course, in traditional terms, this person is illiterate in terms of both language and musical notation. But yet he or she is able to understand and compose in a language style that is distinctively different from everyday language and in a musical form that is distinctively different from other forms of music. We might want to say that the person is literate in the domain of rap songs (as a distinctive domain combining language and music in certain characteristic ways), though the person is not print literate or musical-notation literate.

Cases like this display the limitations of thinking about literacy first and foremost in terms of print. We need, rather, to think first in terms of what I call *semiotic domains* and only then get to literacy in the more traditional terms of print literacy. "Semiotic" here is just a fancy way of saying we want to talk about all sorts of different things that can take on meaning, such as images, sounds, gestures, movements, graphs, diagrams, equations, objects, even people like babies, midwives, and mothers, and not just words. All of these things are signs (symbols, representations, whatever term you want to use) that "stand for" (take on) different meanings in different situations, contexts, practices, cultures, and historical periods. For example, the image of a cross means Christ (or Christ's death) in the context of Christian social practices, and it means the four points of the compass (north, south, west, and east) in the context of other social practices (e.g., in some African religions).

By a semiotic domain I mean any set of practices that recruits one or more modalities (e.g., oral or written language, images, equations, symbols, sounds, gestures, graphs, artifacts, etc.) to communicate distinctive types of meanings. Here are some examples of semiotic domains: cellular biology, postmodern literary criticism, first-person-shooter video games, high-fashion advertisements, Roman Catholic theology, modernist painting, midwifery, rap music, wine connoisseurship—through a nearly endless, motley, and ever-changing list.

Our sentence about basketball—"The guard dribbled down court, held up two fingers, and passed to the open man"—is a sentence from the semiotic domain of basketball. It might seen odd to call basketball a semiotic domain. However, in basketball, particular words, actions,

233

objects, and images take on distinctive meanings. In basketball, "dribble" does not mean drool; a pick (an action where an offensive player positions him or herself so as to block a defensive player guarding one of his or her teammates) means that some defensive player must quickly switch to guard the now-unguarded offensive player; and the wide circle on each end of the court means that players who shoot from beyond it get three points instead of two if they score a basket.

If you don't know these meanings—cannot read these signs—then you can't "read" (understand) basketball. The matter seems fairly inconsequential when we are talking about basketball. However, it quickly seems more consequential when we are talking about the semiotic domain of some types of science being studied in school. Equally here, if you don't know how to read the distinctive signs (words, actions, objects, and images), you can't read (understand) that sort of science.

If we think first in terms of semiotic domains and not in terms of reading and writing as traditionally conceived, we can say that people are (or are not) literate (partially or fully) in a domain if they can recognize (the equivalent of "reading") and/or produce (the equivalent of "writing") meanings in the domain. We can reserve the term "print literate" for talking about people who can read and/or write a language like English or Russian, though here, still, we will want to insist that there are different ways to read and write different things connected to different social practices so, in that sense, there are multiple print literacies. Thus, the rap artist who could understand and compose rap songs but not read print or musical notation is literate in the semiotic domain of rap music but not print literate.

In the modern world, print literacy is not enough. People need to be literate in a great variety of different semiotic domains. If these domains involve print, people often need the print bits, of course. However, the vast majority of domains involve semiotic (symbolic, representational) resources besides print and some don't involve print as a resource at all. Furthermore, and more important, people need to be able to learn to be literate in new semiotic domains throughout their lives. If our modern, global, high-tech, and science-driven world does anything, it certainly gives rise to new semiotic domains and transforms old ones at an ever faster rate.

This book deals with video games as a semiotic domain, actually as a family of related, but different domains, since there are different types or genres of video games (e.g., first-person shooter games, fantasy role-playing games, real-time strategy games, simulation games, etc.). People can be literate, or not, in one or more of these videogame semiotic domains. However, in talking about learning and literacy in regard to video games, I hope to develop, as well, a perspective on learning, literacy, and semiotic domains that applies more generally to domains beyond video games.

However, if we want to take video games seriously as a family of semiotic domains in which one can learn to be literate, we face an immediate problem. Many people who don't play video games, especially older people, are sure to say that playing video games is "a waste of time." In the next section, I sketch out one version of what I think this claim often amounts to, using a specific example involving a six-year-old child.

Learning and the Problem of Content

To spell out what I think the claim that playing video games is a waste of time often means, I need first to tell you about the game the six-year-old boy was playing, a game called *"Pikmin."* *Pikmin* is a game for the Nintendo GameCube, rated "E," a game acceptable for all ages.

In *Pikmin*, the player takes on the role of Captain Olimar, a small (he's about the size of an American quarter), bald, big-eared, bulbous-nosed spaceman who crashes into an unfamiliar planet when a comet hits his spaceship. Captain Olimar (i.e., the player) must collect the spaceship's lost parts, scattered throughout the planet, while relying on his spacesuit to protect him from the planet's poisonous atmosphere. Thus, the player must carefully monitor the damage done to Captain Olimar's suit and repair it when needed. To make matters more complicated, the spacesuit's life support will fail after 30 days, so the captain (the player) must find all the missing parts in 30 days (each day is 15 minutes of game-time play). So the game is a race against time and represents the rare case of a game that one can play to the end and still "lose."

However, Captain Olimar gets help. Soon after arriving on the strange planet, he comes upon native life that is willing to aid him. Sprouts dispensed from a large onionlike creature yield tiny (they're even smaller than Captain Olimar) cute creatures that Olimar names "Pikmin" after a carrot from his home planet. These little creatures appear to be quite taken with Olimar and follow his directions without question. Captain Olimar learns to raise Pikmin of three different colors (red, yellow, and blue), each of which has different skills. He learns, as well, to train them so that each Pikmin, regardless of color, can grow through three different, ever stronger forms: Pikmin sprouting a leaf, a bud, or a flower from their heads.

His colorful Pikmin following him as his army, Captain Olimar uses them to attack dangerous creatures, tear down stone walls, build bridges, and explore a great many areas of the strange planet in search of the missing parts to his spaceship. While Captain Olimar can replace killed Pikmin from remaining Pikmin, he must, however, ensure that at no point do all his Pikmin perish—an event called, by the game and by the child player, "an extinction event."

It is quite a sight to watch a six-year-old, as Captain Olimar, lead a multicolored army of little Pikmin to fight, build, grow more Pikmin, and explore a strange landscape, all the while solving multiple problems to discover and get to the locations of the spaceship's missing parts. The child then orders his Pikmin to carry the heavy parts back to the ship. When this child's grandfather watched him play the game for several hours, the grandfather made the following remark, which I think captures at least one of the common meanings of the playing video games is a waste of time theme: "While it may be good for his hand-eye coordination, it's a waste of time, because there isn't any content he's learning." I call this the *problem of content.*

The problem of content is, I believe, based on common attitudes toward school, schooling, learning, and knowledge. These attitudes are compelling, in part because they are so deeply rooted in the history of western thought, but, nonetheless, I think they are wrong. The idea is this: Important knowledge (now usually gained in school) is content in the sense of information rooted in, or, at least, related to, intellectual domains or academic disciplines like physics, history, art, or literature. Work that does not involve such learning is "meaningless." Activities that are entertaining but that themselves do not involve such learning are just "meaningless play." Of course, video games fall into this category.

A form of this viewpoint has long existed in western culture. It is akin to the viewpoint, held by Plato and Aristotle, for example, that knowledge, in something like the sense of content above, is good in and of itself. Other pursuits, including making practical use of such knowledge— pursuits that do not involve learning and reflecting on such content in and of itself outside the realm of practical applications—are lesser; in some sense, mundane and trivial. Such a view, of course, makes the grandfather's remark about the child playing *Pikmin* seem obvious.

The problem with the content view is that an academic discipline, or any other semiotic domain, for that matter, is not primarily content, in the sense of facts and principles. It is rather primarily a lived and historically changing set of distinctive social practices. It is in these social practices that "content" is generated, debated, and transformed via certain distinctive ways of thinking, talking, valuing, acting, and, often, writing and reading.

No one would want to treat basketball as "content" apart from the game itself. Imagine a textbook that contained all the facts and rules about basketball read by students who never played or watched the game. How well do you think they would understand this textbook? How motivated to understand it do you think they would be? But we do this sort of thing all the time in school with areas like math and science. We even have politicians and educators who condemn *doing* math and science in the classroom instead of drilling-and-skilling on math and science facts ("content") as "permissive."

There is, however, an alternative way to think about learning and knowing that makes the content view seem less obvious and natural. I turn to developing this viewpoint in the following sections. Under this alternative perspective it will become less clear that playing video games is necessarily "a waste of time," though it will be a while until I can return to that claim and answer it directly.

An Alternative Perspective on Learning and Knowing

The alternative perspective starts with the claim that there really is no such thing as learning "in general." We always learn *something*. And that something is always connected, in some way, to some semiotic domain or other.

Therefore, if we are concerned with whether something is worth learning or not, whether it is a waste of time or not—video games or anything else—we should start with questions like the following: What semiotic domain is being entered through this learning? Is it a valuable domain or not? In what sense? Is the learner learning simply to understand ("read") parts of the domain or also to participate more fully in the domain by learning to produce ("write") meanings in the domain? And we need to keep in mind that in the modern world, there are a great many more potentially important semiotic domains than just those that show up in typical schools. I return to these questions later in regard to the child playing *Pikmin*.

Once we learn to start with such questions, we find that it is often a tricky question as to what semiotic domain is being entered when someone is learning or has learned something. For example, consider college freshmen who have taken their first college-level physics class, passed it with good grades, and can write down Newton's laws of motion. What domain have they entered? It will not do to say "physics" and leave the matter at that, though the content view would take this position.

Lots of studies have shown that many such students, students who can write down Newton's laws of motion, if asked so simple a question as "How many forces are acting on a coin when it has been thrown up into the air?" (the answer to which can actually be deduced from Newton's laws) get the answer wrong. Leaving aside friction, they claim that two forces are operating on the coin, gravity and "impetus," the force the hand has transferred to the coin. Gravity exists as a force and, according to Newton's laws, is the sole force acting on the coin when it is in the air (aside from air friction). Impetus, in the sense above, however, does not exist, though Aristotle thought it did and people in their everyday lives tend to view force and motion in such terms quite naturally.

So these students have entered the semiotic domain of physics as passive *content* but not as something in terms of which they can actually see and operate on their world in new ways. There may be nothing essentially wrong with this, since their knowledge of such passive content might help them know, at some level, what physics, an important enterprise in modern life, is "about." I tend to doubt this, however. Be that as it may, these students cannot produce meanings in physics or understand them in producerlike ways.

They have not learned to experience the world in a new way. They have not learned to experience the world in a way in which the natural inclination to think in terms of the hand transmitting a force to the coin, a force that the coin stores up and uses up ("impetus"), is not part of one's way of seeing and operating on the world (for a time and place, i.e., when doing modern physics).

When we learn a new semiotic domain in a more active way, not as passive content, three things are at stake:

1. We learn to experience (see, feel, and operate on) the world in new ways.

2. Since semiotic domains usually are shared by groups of people who carry them on as distinctive social practices, we gain the potential to join this social group, to become affiliated with such kinds of people (even though we may never see all of them, or any of them, face to face).

3. We gain resources that prepare us for future learning and problem solving in the domain and, perhaps, more important, in related domains.

Three things, then, are involved in active learning: *experiencing* the world in new ways, forming new *affiliations,* and *preparation* for future learning.

This is "active learning." However, such learning is not yet what I call "critical learning." For learning to be critical as well as active, one additional feature is needed. The learner needs to learn not only how to understand and produce meanings in a particular semiotic domain that are recognizable to those affiliated with the domain, but, in addition, how to think about the domain at a "meta" level as a complex system of interrelated parts. The learner also needs to learn how to innovate in the domain—how to produce meanings that, while recognizable, are seen as somehow novel or unpredictable.

To get at what all this really means, though, I need to discuss semiotic domains a bit more. This will allow me to clarify what I mean by critical learning and to explicate the notions of experiencing the world in new ways, forming new affiliations, and preparation for future learning a bit more.

More on Semiotic Domains: Situated Meanings

Words, symbols, images, and artifacts have meanings that are specific to particular semiotic domains and particular situations (contexts). They do not just have general meanings.

I was once a cannery worker; later I became an academic. I used the word "work" in both cases, but the word meant different things in each case. In my cannery life, it meant something like laboring for eight straight hours in order to survive and get home to lead my "real" life. In my academic life, it means something like chosen efforts I put into thinking, reading, writing, and teaching as part and parcel of my vocation, efforts not clocked by an eight-hour workday. In the domain of human romantic relationships, the word means something else altogether; for example, in a sentence like "Relationships take work." Later I will point out that a word like "work," in fact, has different meanings even within a single domain, like the cannery, academics, or romantic relationships, meanings that vary according to different situations in the domain.

But here we face one of the most widespread confusions that exists in regard to language and semiotic domains. People tend to think that the meaning of a word or other sort of symbol is a general thing—the sort of thing that for a word, at least, can be listed in a dictionary. But meaning for words and symbols is specific to particular situations and particular semiotic domains. You don't really know what a word means if you don't carefully consider both the specific semiotic domain and the specific situation you are in.

We build meanings for words or symbols "on the spot," so to speak, so as to make them appropriate for the actual situations we are in, though we do so with due respect for the specific semiotic domain in which we are operating. What general meaning a word or other symbol has is just a theme around which, in actual situations of use, we must build more specific instantiations (meanings).

To understand or produce any word, symbol, image, or artifact in a given semiotic domain, a person must be able to situate the meaning of that word, symbol, image, or artifact within embodied experiences of action, interaction, or dialogue in or about the domain. These experiences can be ones the person has actually had or ones he or she can imagine, thanks to reading, dialogue with others, or engagement with various media. This is what our college physics students could not do: They could not situate the components of Newton's laws in terms of specific situations and embodied ways of seeing and acting on and within the world from the perspective of the semiotic domain of mechanical physics.

Meaning, then, is both situation and domain specific. Thus, even in a single domain, the meaning of a word varies across different situations. Let me give an example of what I am talking about by taking up again the example of the word "work." In semiotic domains connected to academics, the word "work" takes on a range of possible situated meanings different from the range possible in other semiotic domains (e.g., law, medicine, manual work, etc.).

In one situation I might say of a fellow academic, "Her work has been very influential" and by "work" mean her research. In another situation I might say the same thing, but now in regard to a particular committee she has chaired, and by "work" mean her political efforts within her discipline or institution. To understand the word "work" in these cases, you need to ask yourself what you take the situation to be (e.g., talk about contributions to knowledge or about disciplinary or institutional political affairs) and what semiotic domain is at stake (here academics, not law offices).

The same thing is true in all domains. Even in the rigorous semiotic domain of physics, one must situate (build) different specific-meanings for the word "light" in different situations. In different situations, one has to build meanings for the word that involve thinking, talking about, or acting on different things like waves, particles, straight lines, reflection and refraction, lasers, colors, and yet other things in other situations. Even in physics, when someone uses the word "light," we need to know whether they are talking about waves or particles, colors or lasers, or something else (perhaps they are talking about the general theory of electromagnetism?).

In a different domain altogether, the same word takes on yet different meanings in different situations. For example, in religion, one has to build meanings for the word "light" that involve thinking, talking about, or acting on and with different themes like illumination, insight, life, grace, peace, birth, and yet other things in other situations.

If you cannot even imagine the experiences and conditions of an academic life, you really can't know what "work" means, either specifically or in terms of its possible range of meanings, in a sentence like "Her work was very influential." Of course, you don't have to be an academic to imagine academic life. But you do have to be able to build simulated worlds of experience in your mind (in this case, the sorts of experiences, attitudes, values, and feelings an academic might have), however unconsciously you do this. And, perhaps, you can do this because of your reading or other vicarious experiences. Perhaps you can do it through analogies to other domains with which you are more familiar (e.g., you might equate your hobby as an artist with the academic's research and understand how "work" can mean, in a certain sort of situation, efforts connected to a vocation).

Why I am belaboring this point? For two reasons: first, to make clear that understanding meanings is an active affair in which we have to reflect (however unconsciously) on the situation and the domain we are in. And, second, because I want to argue that learning in any semiotic domain crucially involves learning how to situate (build) meanings for that domain in the sorts of situations the domain involves. That is precisely why real learning is active and always a new way of experiencing the world.

Furthermore, I want to argue later that video games are potentially particularly good places where people can learn to situate meanings through embodied experiences in a complex semiotic domain and meditate on the process. Our bad theories about general meanings; about reading but not reading something; and about general learning untied to specific semiotic domains just don't make sense when you play video games. The games exemplify, in a particularly clear way, better and more specific and embodied theories of meaning, reading, and learning.

More on Semiotic Domains: Internal and External Views

There are two different ways to look at semiotic domains: internally and externally. Any domain can be viewed internally as a type of content or externally in terms of people engaged in a set of social practices. For example, first-person shooter games are a semiotic domain, and they contain a particular type of content. For instance, as part of their typical content, such games involve moving through a virtual world in a first-person perspective (you see only what you are holding and move and feel as if you yourself are holding it) using weapons to battle enemies. Of course, such games involve a good deal more content as well. Thus we can talk about the typical sorts of content we find in first-person shooter games. This is to view the semiotic domain internally.

On the other hand, people actually play first-person shooter games as a practice in the world, sometimes alone and sometimes with other people on the Internet or when they connect several game platforms or computers together. They may also talk to other players about such games and read magazines and Internet sites devoted to them. They are aware that certain people are more adept at playing such games than are others. They are also aware that people who are "into" such games take on a certain identity, at least when they are involved with those games. For example, it is unlikely that people "into" first-person shooter games are going to object to violence in video games, though they may have strong views about how that violence ought to function in games.

I call the group of people associated with a given semiotic domain—in this case, first-person shooter games—an *affinity group*. People in an affinity group can recognize others as more or less "insiders" to the group. They may not see many people in the group face-to-face, but when they interact with someone on the Internet or read something about the domain, they can recognize certain ways of thinking, acting, interacting, valuing, and believing as more or less typical of people who are "into" the semiotic domain. Thus we can talk about the typical ways of thinking, acting, interacting, valuing, and believing as well as the typical sorts of social practices associated with a given semiotic domain. This is to view the domain externally.

What I have said about viewing first-person shooter games internally or externally applies to any semiotic domain. Take, for instance, my own academic field of linguistics, viewed as a semiotic domain. Within linguistics there is a well-defined subdomain often referred to as theoretical linguistics or the theory of grammar, a field largely defined by the work of the noted linguist Noam Chomsky and his followers. (Even alternative views in the field have to be defined in reference to Chomsky's work.) If we view this semiotic domain internally, in terms of content, we can point out that a claim like "All human languages are equal" is a recognizable one—is recognizably a possible piece of content—in this semiotic domain, though Chomskian linguists give very specific meanings to words like "language" and "equal," meanings that are not the same as these words have in "everyday" life.

On the other hand, a claim like "God breathed life into the word" is not a recognizable claim—is not recognizably a possible piece of content in—the semiotic domain of theoretical linguistics. If history had been different, perhaps there would have been a field called linguistics in which this was a possible piece of content. But given how history did happen, and how we therefore now define the nature of science and academic fields, this is not a possible piece of content in the semiotic domain of theoretical linguistics.

So far, then, we have been talking about and viewing the semiotic domain of theoretical linguistics internally in terms of its content. But we can also talk about and view the domain externally in terms of the ways in which such linguists tend to think, act, interact, value, and believe when they are being linguists. This is to ask about the sorts of identities they take on when they are engaged with, or acting out of their connections to, the semiotic domain of theoretical linguistics. This is to view the domain externally.

Theoretical linguists tend to look down on people who study the social and cultural aspects of language (people like me now). They tend to believe that only the structural aspects of language (e.g., syntax or phonology) can be studied rigorously and scientifically in terms of deducing conclusions from quite abstract and mathematically based theories. In turn, they tend to see affiliations between themselves and "hard scientists" like physicists. Since physics has high prestige in our society, theoretical linguistics tends to have higher prestige within the overall field of linguistics than does, say, sociolinguistics.

The claim here is not that each and every theoretical linguist looks down on linguists who study social and cultural affairs (though when I was a theoretical linguist earlier in my career I did!). Rather, the claim is that each and every such linguist would recognize these ways of thinking and valuing as part of the social environment in and around the field of theoretical linguistics. This is to view the domain externally.

The external view of theoretical linguistics, and not the internal one, explains why this subbranch of linguistics is regularly called theoretical linguistics when, in fact, people who study language socially and culturally also engage in building and arguing over "theories" (though less abstract and mathematically based ones). Given its assumptions about being rigorous science in a wider culture that values physics more than literature or sociology, for instance, this branch of linguistics has easily been able to co-opt the term for itself. People who study language socially and culturally often use the term "theoretical linguistics" just for Chomskian (and related) work, thereby enacting their own "subordination." This last comment, of course, is an external view on the larger semiotic domain of linguistics as a whole.

Do the internal and external aspects of a semiotic domain have anything to do with each other? Of course, if we are talking about academic disciplines as semiotic domains, most academics would like to think that the answer to this question is no. But the answer is, in fact, yes. Content, the internal part of a semiotic domain, gets made in history by real people and their social interactions. They build that content—in part, not wholly—in certain ways because of the people they are (socially, historically, culturally). That content comes to define one of their important identities in the world. As those identities develop through further social interactions, they come to affect the ongoing development and transformation of the content of the semiotic domain in yet new ways. In turn, that new content helps further develop and transform those identities. The relationship between the internal and external is reciprocal.

I am not trying to make some postmodern relativistic point that nothing is true or better than anything else. The potential content of a semiotic domain can take a great many shapes. Some of them are better than others for certain purposes (e.g., as truth claims about grammar or language), but there is always more than one good (and bad) shape that content can take, since there are so many fruitful and correct facts, principles, and patterns one can discover in the world.

For example, Noam Chomsky and his early students spoke English as their native language and, thus, tended to use this language as their initial database for forming their theories. These were, in fact, theories not about English but about what is universal in language or common to the design of all languages. This early emphasis on English (treating English as the "typical" language) gave the theory a certain sort of initial shape that helped lead to certain developments and not others. Later the theory changed as more languages—ones quite different from English—received more careful consideration. Nonetheless, no matter how good the theory is now (assuming for the moment the theory is good), if Chomsky and others had been speakers of Navajo, it might be equally good now but somewhat different.

There are a myriad of things to get right and wrong, and theoretical linguistics as it is now undoubtedly has some things right and some things wrong. Theoretical linguistics as it might have been had Chomsky spoken Navajo would have had other things right and wrong, though it may well have had some of the same things right and wrong as well. The American philosopher Charles Sanders Pierce argued that "in the end," after all the efforts of scientists over time, all possible theories in an area like theoretical linguistics would converge on the "true" one. But you and I won't be here for "the end" of time, so we are stuck with the fact that the internal and external aspects of semiotic domains—even academic fields and areas of science—influence each other.

More on Semiotic Domains: Design Grammars

Semiotic domains have what I call *design grammars.* Each domain has an internal and an external design grammar. By an internal design grammar, I mean the principles and patterns in terms of which one can recognize what is and what is not acceptable or typical content in a semiotic domain. By an external design grammar, I mean the principles and patterns in terms of which one can recognize what is and what is not an acceptable or typical social practice and identity in regard to the affinity group associated with a semiotic domain.

Do you know what counts as a modernist piece of architecture? What sort of building counts as typical or untypical of modernist architecture? If you do, then you know, consciously or unconsciously, the internal design grammar of the semiotic domain of modernist architecture (as a field of interest).

If all you know is a list of all the modernist buildings ever built, then you don't know the internal design grammar of the domain. Why? Because if you know the design grammar—that is, the underlying principles and patterns that determine what counts and what doesn't count as a piece of modernist architecture—you can make judgments about buildings you have never seen before or even ones never actually built, but only modeled in cardboard. If all you have is a list, you can't make any judgments about anything that isn't on your list.

Do you know what counts as thinking, acting, interacting, and valuing like someone who is "into" modernist architecture? Can you recognize the sorts of identities such people take on when they are in their domain? Can you recognize what counts as valued social practices to the members of the affinity group associated with the semiotic domain of modernist architecture and what counts as behaving appropriately in these social practices? If the answer to these questions is "yes," then you know, consciously or unconsciously, the external design grammar of the semiotic domain.

Do you understand what counts and what doesn't count as a possible piece of content in theoretical linguistics? Do you know that claims like "All languages are equal" (in one specific meaning) and "The basic syntactic rules in the core grammar of any language are optimal" count as possible claims in theoretical linguistics and that claims like "God breathed life into the word" and "Nominalizations are very effective communicative devices in science" don't? Do you know why this is so, how it follows from the ways in which the elements of the content of theoretical linguistics relate to each other as a complex system? If you do, you know the internal design grammar of theoretical linguistics. If all you know is a list of facts from the domain, you will never know whether a claim not on your list should or shouldn't count or even whether the matter is open to debate or not. You can't "go on" in the domain.

Are you aware that theoretical linguists don't value work on the social aspects of language as much as they do work on the structural aspects of grammar? Do you know that even when they are assessing work in the social sciences and humanities, they tend to value logical deductive structure and abstract theories in these domains over richly descriptive but less abstract and less theoretical studies? Are you aware that the term "descriptive" is (or, at least, used to be) a term of insult and "explanatory" a term of praise when such people are talking about academic work inside and outside their field? Do you know why? If you know things like this, you know the external design grammar of the semiotic domain of theoretical linguistics. You find certain ways of thinking, acting, and valuing expectable in the affinity group associated with the domain, others not.

Of course, the internal and external grammars of a domain change through time. For example, it was once common to find linguists who saw studying issues germane to the translation of the Bible, for example into Native American languages, as a core part of their academic work and identity as linguists. They hoped to facilitate the work of missionaries to the speakers of these languages. They saw no conflict between doing linguistics and serving their religious purposes at the same time. Other linguists, not involved in Bible translation, did not necessarily dispute this at the time and often did not withhold professional respect from such religious linguists. The external grammar of the domain (and this was certainly influenced by the wider culture at the time) allowed a connection between linguistic work as science and religious commitments as an overt part of that work.

Today most linguists, theoretical and otherwise, would be skeptical of any connection between linguistic work and religion. They would not see translating the Bible into languages connected to cultures without the Bible, to facilitate the work of missionaries, as a central part of any branch of linguistics. Today the external design grammar of the field does not readily allow for a connection between work as a linguist and religion, for identities as a linguist that are formed around this connection or for social practices germane to it.

So why I am being so perverse as to use the term "design grammar" for these matters? Because I want us to think about the fact that for any semiotic domain, whether it is first-person shooter games or theoretical linguistics, that domain, internally and externally, was and is designed by someone. But who was/is this someone who designed the semiotic domains of first-person shooter games and theoretical linguistics?

Obviously real game designers and producers determine what counts as recognizable content for first-person shooter games by actually making such games. Over time, as they apply certain principles, patterns, and procedures to the construction of such games, the content of first-person shooter games comes to have a recognizable shape such that people not only say things like "Oh, yeah, that's a first-person shooter game" or "No, that's not a first-person shooter" but also "Oh, yeah, that a typical first-person shooter game" or "Oh, no, that's a groundbreaking first-person shooter game."

Yet these designers and producers are only part of the people who produce the external grammar of first-person shooter games. People who play, review, and discuss such games, as well as those who design and produce them, shape the external design grammar of the semiotic domain of first-person shooter games through their ongoing social interactions. It is their ongoing social interactions that determine the principles and patterns through which people in the domain can recognize and judge thinking, talking, reading, writing, acting, interacting, valuing, and believing characteristic of people who are in the affinity group associated with first-person shooter games.

And, of course, the acts of people helping to design the domain externally as a set of social practices and typical identities rebound on the acts of those helping to design the domain internally as content, since that content must "please" the members of the affinity group associated with the domain as well as recruit newcomers to the domain. At the same time, the acts of those helping to design the domain internally in terms of content rebound on the acts of those helping to design the domain externally as a set of social practices and identities, since that content shapes and transforms those practices and identities.

Just the same things can be said about those who design the semiotic domain of theoretical linguistics, internally and externally. Linguists who write and publish and give talks at conferences shape the internal design grammar of the domain through their research. They shape and transform the principles and patterns that determine what counts as the content of theoretical linguistics.

All linguists shape the external grammar of the domain through their social interactions and the identities they take on in those interactions. It is their ongoing social interactions and related identity work that determine the principles and patterns through which people in the domain can recognize and judge thinking, talking, reading, writing, acting, interacting, valuing, and believing characteristic of people who are in the affinity group associated with theoretical linguistics.

It is crucial, as I have pointed out, to see that the internal and external grammars and designs of semiotic domains interrelate with each other, mutually supporting and transforming each other. Let me exemplify this point, and further clarify the notion of design grammars, by returning to video games.

Some people play video games on game platforms like the Sony Playstation (1 or 2), the Nintendo GameCube, or the Microsoft Xbox. Some people play them on computers like the one on which I am typing this book. When people play video games on game platforms, they use a handheld controller with various buttons and often a little built-in joystick or two. They never use the sort of keyboard associated with a computer.

It is part of the external design of the semiotic domain of video games for game platforms that games and handheld controllers go together and part of the design of the semiotic domain of video games on computers that games and keyboards or handheld controllers go together, since some players do, in fact, plug handheld controllers into their computers to replace the keyboard.

So far this just seems to be a matter of brute technological facts. But things work in the world in certain ways because people make them do so, or, at the very least, are willing to accept them as such. Then, when they work that way, people come to expect them to do so and build values and norms around them working that way.

One could conceivably get a keyboard to work with a game platform. At the very least, it would be easy for designers to modify a platform so that it would work with a keyboard. However, you don't understand the external design grammar of the domain of platform-based video-game playing if you don't realize that doing this would "break the rules." It would be a serious departure from what the affinity group associated with this domain expects, wants, and values. Many platform-game players think keyboards are a bad way to play video games, while some computer-game players think they are a good way. In turn, these matters are connected to their identities as game players (e.g., the editors of *PC Gamer* magazine regularly "apologize" when they have spent time playing games on a game platform and not on a computer, and look down on the enterprise).

When Microsoft's Xbox came out in 2002, it was the first game platform to contain a computerlike hard drive. Hard drives allow games to be saved at any point. Heretofore, games played on game platforms, thanks to the technological limitations of the platforms, could be saved much less regularly than computer games. Players on typical game platforms, for example, can save only at the end of a level or when they have found a special save symbol in the game. This means that in an action game, they have to stay alive long enough to get to the end of the level or find the save symbol, no matter how long they already have been playing.

In a computer game, thanks to the computer's hard drive, players can save their progress at any time they wish. (There are some games made for computers in which this is not true). This can make a difference in the strategies one uses. When playing on a computer, the player can save after a particularly hard battle and not ever have to repeat that battle. If the player dies a bit later, he or she starts again from the game that was saved after the big battle was already won.

On a game platform, if there was no save symbol after the big battle or if the battle was not the end of a level, the player could not save and must move on. If he or she dies, the big battle will have to be fought again, since the game will reload from an earlier saved game that did not contain that battle. Indeed, the last save could have been quite far in the past, and the player may be required to repeat a good deal of the game.

However, again, these are not just technological matters. Platform users do not necessarily see being unable to save whenever they want as a limitation. Many of them see it as a virtue; they say it adds more excitement and challenge to a game. Computer-game players who save after each big battle or dangerous jump might be thought of as "wimps" who can't last any length of time against rigorous challenges. Furthermore, in my experience, many platform users do not see playing large parts of a game over and over again as repetition in the way in which I do. They see it an opportunity to perfect their skills and get more play out of a game they enjoy.

So we see here the ways in which external technological and material facts become social facts and values. The Xbox's coming out with a hard drive led to a debate that anyone who understands the external design grammar of the platform domain could have predicted. Was the Xbox really a game platform? Could a real game platform have a hard drive? Perhaps the Xbox is really a computer in disguise. This is a debate over the very external design grammar of the domain: Is the pattern "video game, game platform, hard drive" acceptable within the external design grammar of the domain? Does it count as an acceptable part of valued social practices and identities in the domain? Should it?

It is not surprising, either, that of the games Microsoft initially brought out for the Xbox some used the hard drive to allow players to save whenever and wherever they wanted (e.g., *Max Payne*) and others did not and functioned like a "proper" platform game (e.g., *Nightcaster*). The company obviously wanted to entice both platform players and computer-game players onto its system, though this can, in some cases, be a bit like enticing cats and dogs to play ball together.

A good number of people play both platform games and computer games, of course. Nonetheless, somewhat different affinity groups, with different attitudes and values, have arisen around each domain, with lots of overlap in between. There are people who play in both domains but have strong opinions about what sorts of games are best played on platforms and what sorts are best played on computers. All this is typical: Semiotic domains and affinity groups often don't have sharp boundaries (though some do), and in any case the boundaries are often fluid and changing.

Since the Xbox has the capacity to break the pattern that associates game platforms and limited saves while still retaining some of the other patterns typical of game platforms, it has the potential to create a new affinity group and/or to transform old ones. In the act, it and the social interactions of people around it might eventually create a new semiotic domain within the bigger domain of videogame playing, a new domain with a new external design grammar determining new social practices and identities. Indeed, the matter is already in progress, as the Xbox has already generated (with the help of Microsoft, of course) its own magazines, Internet sites, and aficionados.

But all this transformation and change in the external design grammar will rebound on and change the internal design grammar. Designers and producers will use the hard drive on the Xbox together with its more typical platform features to design new games. Hybrids between typical platform games and typical computer games will arise. The distinction in content between platform games (which tended to stress fast action) and computer games (which can store more information and stress deeper stories) may blur. As new content arises and new principles and patterns regarding the acceptable content of various different types of games also arise, the affinity groups associated with those different types of games will change their social interactions, values, and identities, and so, too, the external design grammar of their respective domains.

Some of these changes will be small, some large. But that is the way of all semiotic domains in the world. They are made, internally and externally, by humans and changed by them as these humans take up technological and material circumstances in certain ways and not others and as they shape and reshape their social interactions with each other.

Lifeworlds

Our talk about semiotic domains may lead some to think that everything said thus far only applies to "specialist" areas like video games, theoretical linguistics, law, or the workings of urban gangs, not "everyday," "ordinary" life. However, "everyday," "ordinary" life is itself a semiotic domain. In fact, it is a domain in which all of us have lots and lots of experience. It is what I call the *lifeworld domain.*

By the lifeworld domain I mean those occasions when we are operating (making sense to each other and to ourselves) as "everyday" people, not as members of more specialist or technical semiotic domains. Not everyone does physics or plays video games, but everyone spends lots of time in his or her lifeworld domain. And, of course, people move quite readily between specialist domains and their lifeworld domain. For example, a group of physicists at a dinner meeting might, at one moment, be discussing physics as specialists in physics and, at the next moment, be discussing the weather or movies as "everyday" nonspecialists. (Of course, there are people who can and do discuss the weather or movies as specialists in a specialist semiotic domain devoted to the weather or movies.)

Lifeworld domains are culturally variable; that is, different cultural groups have, more or less, different ways of being, doing, feeling, valuing, and talking as "everyday people." Thus there are many lifeworld domains, though they overlap enough to allow for, better or worse, communication across cultures.

If we look at lifeworld domains internally, we can say that their content is just the wide range of nonspecialist experiences of the world that people share with other people with whom they share various group memberships, up to and including the human race. Once a group has carved out an area of this experience (whether this is playing in the guise of video games or dealing with the weather as a science) and created "specialist" ways of talking and thinking about it ("policed" by themselves as "insiders," who determine what is acceptable and what not, who is adept and who is not), then they have left the lifeworld (and the rest of us behind) and created a specialist semiotic domain.

If we look at lifeworld domains externally, we can ask about the ways of thinking, talking, acting, interacting, valuing, and, in some cases, writing and reading that allow a particular culturally distinctive group of people to recognize each other as being, at a time and place, "everyday" or "ordinary" nonspecialist people. For example, how do you know when a friend of yours who is a theoretical linguist (and you are not) is talking to you and engaging with you not as a specialist linguist but just as an "everyday" nonspecialist person? How do you know this even when, in fact, you happen to be talking about language?

And, of course, these matters will differ if you and the linguist are from quite different cultures—say you are an African American and the linguist is a Russian. But, again, I caution against assuming too much variation across human beings. People can and very often do recognize "normal" human behavior across cultural groups, however problematic this sometimes may be (even to the point of leading to violence).

It is important to realize that meanings are no more general—they are just as situated—in lifeworld domains as they are in any other semiotic domain. For example, in different situations, even such a mundane word as "coffee" has different situated meanings. Consider, for instance, what happens in your head when I say "The coffee spilled, get a mop" versus "The coffee spilled, get a broom." In different situations, the word "coffee" can mean a liquid, grains, beans, tins, or a flavor. It can mean yet other things in other situations, and sometimes we have to come up with novel meanings for the word; for example in a sentence like "Her coffee skin glistened in the bright sunshine," "coffee" names a skin color.

For another example, think of the different situated meanings of the word "light" in everyday interactions in these sentences: Turn the light on. This light isn't giving much light. I can see a far off light. I am just bathing in this light. The effects of light in this part of the country are wonderful. The last thing I saw was a bright light. Of course, when we consider, in the context of lifeworld domains, words like "truth," "good," "democracy," "fairness," "honesty," and so forth, things get yet more variable, more deeply rooted in specific situations in specific culturally relative lifeworld domains.

There are a number of important points to make about lifeworld domains. First, we are all used to making claims to know things based not on any specialist knowledge we have but just as "everyday" human beings. However, in the modern world, specialist domains are taking more and more space away from lifeworld domains wherein people can make nonspecialist claims to know things and not face a challenge from a specialist.

For example, I once lived in Los Angeles. Every nonspecialist in Los Angeles "knows" the air is polluted and dangerous, and they are usually willing to say so. Nonetheless, it was not at all uncommon to read in the newspaper, say, that "lay people" didn't really know what they were talking about (and choking on). Specialists in the matter claimed that there was no technical "evidence" that the air was particularly unsafe. Tobacco companies tried the same thing for years in regard to the dangers of smoking. Companies that pollute ground and water often engage in the same tactic when people in their areas of operation claim to feel sick (or drop dead) from their pollution.

Helping students learn how to think about the contrasting claims of various specialists against each other and against lifeworld claims to knowledge certainly ought to be a key job for schools. To do this, students would have to investigate specialist domains and different culturally distinctive lifeworlds, internally in terms of content and externally in terms of social practices and identities.

A second point to be made about lifeworld domains is this: In the modern world, we are used to having to face the fact that children, including our own, are specialists when and where we are not. Many children are adept at the semiotic domain of computers—sometimes because they play video games and that interest has led them to learn more about computers—where the adults in the house are intimidated by computers.

Kids have turned video games, roller-blading, skateboarding, and snowboarding into specialist domains that internally in terms of content and externally in terms of social practices bewilder adults. Many children have learned through the Internet and television more about stock trading or even law than many of the adults around them could ever imagine knowing. (One teenager had the top rating for legal advice on a legal Internet site in which many of the others on the highly ranked list were professional lawyers.)

Adults are getting used to the fact that they are "immigrants" in many a domain where their own children are "natives" (specialists). The lifeworld—the domain in which people can claim to know and understand things as "everyday" people and not as specialists—is shrinking, not just under the attack of specialist domains like science but because our children are creating and mastering so many specialist domains themselves.

A third point I want to make is this: I firmly believe we need to protect lifeworld domains from the assaults of specialists (yes, even our own children). We need to understand and value people's "everyday" knowledge and understandings. At the same time, I believe it is crucial, particularly in the contemporary world, that all of us, regardless of our cultural affiliations, be able to operate in a wide variety of semiotic domains outside our lifeworld domains.

It is very often in these non-lifeworld domains that people form affiliations with others outside their own cultural groups and transcend the limitations of any one person's culture and lifeworld domain. Of course, it is important not to insult anyone's culture or lifeworld domain; it is important, as well, to build bridges to these when introducing people to new semiotic domains. But in my view, it is a poor form of respect for anyone to leave people trapped in their own culture and lifeworld as the whole and sole space within which they can move in the modern world. If this view comports poorly with some versions of multiculturalism, so be it.

Back to *Pikmin*: Critical Learning

If learning is to be active, it must involve experiencing the world in new ways. I have spelled this out in terms of learning new ways to situate the meanings of words, images, symbols, artifacts, and so forth when operating within specific situations in new semiotic domains. Active learning must also involve forming new affiliations. I have explained this in terms of learners joining new affinity groups associated with new semiotic domains.

Active learning in a domain also involves preparation for future learning within the domain and within related domains. I will deal with this issue below, when I draw a comparison between the sorts of learning that take place when playing good video games and the sorts of learning that take place in good science classrooms and when I discuss the notion of precursor domains.

However, as I said earlier, critical learning involves yet another step. For active learning, the learner must, at least unconsciously, understand and operate within the internal and external design grammars of the semiotic domain he or she is learning. But for critical learning, the learner must be able consciously to attend to, reflect on, critique, and manipulate those design grammars at a metalevel. That is, the learner must see and appreciate the semiotic domain as a *design space*, internally as a system of interrelated elements making up the possible content of the domain and externally as ways of thinking, acting, interacting, and valuing that constitute the identities of those people who are members of the affinity group associated with the domain.

Let me return to the child playing *Pikmin* for a specific example of what I mean. What does it take just to play a game as an active learner? To do this the player must understand and produce situated meanings in the semiotic domain that this game, and games like it, constitutes. Elements in the content of *Pikmin*—for example, a yellow Pikmin—do not have just one general meaning or significance in the game world. Learners must learn to situate different meanings for such elements within different specific situations within the domain.

For example, when a player is faced with a rock wall, his yellow Pikmin (who can throw bomb rocks) take on the situated meaning *the type of Pikmin who can use bombs* (unlike red and blue Pikmin), since a good strategy for destroying walls in the game is to have yellow Pikmin throw bombs at them. However, when attacking a fat, sleeping, dangerous spotted creature (a Spotty Bulborb) found throughout the first levels of the game, the yellow Pikmin take on the situated meaning *the sorts of Pikmin who can be thrown farther than other sorts of*

Pikmin, since a good strategy when fighting big creatures like these is to have Captain Olimar tell the red Pikmin to run up and attack from the rear, while he throws the yellow Pikmin onto their backs to attack from up top.

Additionally, players need to know what patterns or combinations of elements the game's internal design grammar allows. They need to know, given the situated meanings they have given to each element in the pattern or combination, what the whole pattern or combination means in a situated way useful for action.

For example, the internal design grammar of *Pikmin* allows the player to bring together (by moving Captain Olimar and his Pikmin) the combination of Pikmin, a rock wall, and a small tin can laying near the wall, containing little rock bombs. Of course, the game did not need to allow this pattern or combination to be able to occur; its design grammar could have been built differently. Even given that the design grammar does allow this combination, players still have to build a situated meaning for this combination out of the situated meanings they have given to each element in the game based on the situation they take themselves to be in and their own goals.

If this is a point in the game where the player needs to get past the wall, and given the fact that he or she can build a situated meaning for yellow Pikmin like *the type of Pikmin that can throw bombs,* the player can build a situated meaning for this combination something like: *Equip the yellow Pikmin with the rock bombs and have them use the bombs to blow up the wall.*

Here is another example from *Pikmin* of a combination of elements allowable by the internal design grammar of the game. The player often finds a Spotty Bulborb—a creature with big teeth and jaws suitable for swallowing Pikmin whole—sleeping peacefully in a fairly exposed space. So the design grammar of the domain allows the combination: Spotty Bulborb, sleeping, in exposed area. Depending on what situation the player takes him- or herself to be in, this combination can be assigned several different situated meanings. For instance, it could be taken to mean: *Attack the Spotty Bulborb carefully from the rear before it wakes up;* or it could be taken to mean: *Sneak quietly by the Spotty Bulborb to get where you want to go without trouble.* Nothing stops the player from assigning the combination a more unexpected situated meaning, perhaps something like: *Wake the Spotty Bulborb up so you can get a more exciting (and fair?) fight.*

Since the child can successfully break down rock walls and attack Spotty Bulborbs, he can understand ("read") and produce ("write") appropriate situated meanings for elements and combinations of elements in the domain (game). But all of this is "just" playing the game

255

in a proactive way—that is, using situated meanings and the design grammar of the game to understand and produce meanings and actions (which are a type of meaning in the domain). Of course, one could just ritualize one's response to the game and try pretty much the same strategy in every situation, but this would not be a proactive way to play and learn.

All these meanings and actions are a product of what I have called active learning, but they are not yet critical learning that leverages the design grammar at a metalevel in a reflective way that can lead to critique, novel meanings, or transformation of the domain. However, the child is learning to do this as well—that is, his process of learning the game is not only active, it is increasingly critical.

When the child had recovered 5 of the spaceship's 30 missing parts, he was able to search in a new area called The Forest's Navel. This area had a much harsher and more dangerous-looking landscape than the previous areas the child had been in. It had different dangerous creatures, including a number of closely grouped creatures that breathed fire. And the background music had changed considerably. Since the player has already found five parts, the game assumes that he is now more adept than when he began the game; thus, the landscape and creatures are getting harder to deal with, offering a bigger challenge. At the same time, these changes in features communicate a new mood, changing the tone of the game from a cute fairy tale to a somewhat darker struggle for survival.

The child was able to think about and comment on these changes. He said that the music was now "scary" and the landscape much harsher-looking than the ones he had previously been in. He knew that this signaled that things were going to get harder. Furthermore, he was aware that the changes signaled that he needed to rethink some of his strategies as well his relationship to the game. He was even able to comment on the fact that the earlier parts of the game made it appear more appropriate for a child his age than did the Forest Navel area and considered whether the game was now "too scary" or not. He decided on a strategy of exploring the new area only a little bit at a time, avoiding the fire-breathing creatures, and returning to old areas with the new resources (e.g., blue Pikmin) he got in the Forest Navel area to find more parts there more quickly and easily (remember, the player has only 30 game days to get all the parts and so wants to get some of them quickly and easily.)

What we are dealing with here is talk and thinking about the (internal) design of the game, about the game as a complex system of interrelated parts meant to engage and even manipulate the player in certain ways. This is metalevel thinking, thinking about the game as a system and a designed space, and not just playing within the game moment by moment. Such thinking can open up critique of the game. It can also lead to novel moves and strategies, sometimes ones that the game makers never anticipated. This is what I mean by critical learning and thinking. Of course, the six year-old is only beginning the process of critical learning in regard to *Pikmin* and other video games, but he is well begun.

The child is learning to think reflectively about the internal design grammar (the grammar of content) of *Pikmin* and games like it. As he interacts with others, he will have opportunities to reflect on the external design grammar (the grammar of social practices and identities) too. For example, he has already learned that he can search the Internet for helpful tips about playing the game, including what are called Easter Eggs (little surprises players can find in a game if they know where and how to look for them). He considers these tips part of playing the game. On the other hand, he characterizes advice about how to play as "bossing him around" and claims he can "do his own thinking."

These are early moments in the child's induction into the affinity groups associated with videogame playing, their characteristic social practices, and the sorts of identities people take on within these groups and practices. If he is to engage with these external aspects of game playing critically, he will need to reflect in an overt way on the patterns and possibilities he does and does not find in these social practices and identities. Doing this is to reflect on the external design grammar of the domain.

Critical learning, as I am defining it here, involves learning to think of semiotic domains as design spaces that manipulate us (if I can use this term without necessarily negative connotations) in certain ways and that we can manipulate in certain ways. The child has much more to learn about *Pikmin* as a design space (internally and externally). He also has much more to learn about not just the single game *Pikmin* but the genre (family) of games into which *Pikmin* falls (adventure strategy games) as a design space. And he has much more to learn about not just this genre but about video games in general (a larger and more loosely connected family) as a design space.

Then there is the crucial matter of learning how these design spaces relate to each other and to other sorts of semiotic domains, some more closely related to video games as semiotic domains, some less closely related. That is, the child can learn how to think about, and act on, semiotic domains as a larger design space composed of clusters (families) of more or less closely related semiotic domains.

So, then, why do I call learning and thinking at a metalevel about semiotic domains (alone and in relation to each other) as design spaces *critical* learning and thinking? For this reason: Semiotic systems are human cultural and historical creations that are designed to engage and manipulate people in certain ways. They attempt through their content and social practices to recruit people to think, act, interact, value, and feel in certain specific ways. In this sense, they attempt to get people to learn and take on certain sorts of new identities to become, for a time and place, certain types of people. In fact, society as a whole is simply the web of these many different sorts of identities and their characteristic associated activities and practices.

Some of these identities constitute, within certain institutions or for certain social groups in the society, social goods. By a "social good" I mean anything that a group in society, or society as a whole, sees as bringing one status, respect, power, freedom, or other such socially valued things. Some people have more or less access to valued or desired semiotic domains and their concomitant identities. Furthermore, some identities connected to some semiotic domains may come, as one understands the domain more reflectively, to seem less (or more) good or valuable than one had previously thought.

Finally, one might come to see that a given identity associated with a given semiotic domain relates poorly (or well)—in terms of one's vision of ethics, morality, or a valued life—with one's other identities associated with other semiotic domains. For example, a person might come to see that a given semiotic domain is designed so as to invite one to take on an identity that revels in a disdain for life or in a way of thinking about race, class, or gender that the person, in terms of other identities he or she takes on in other semiotic domains, does not, on reflection, wish to continue. In this sense, then, semiotic domains are inherently political (and here I am using the term "political" in the sense of any practices where the distribution of social goods in a society is at stake).

Let me make this discussion more concrete. A game like *Pikmin* recruits from our six-year-old a complex identity composed of various related traits. The game encourages him to think of himself an active problem solver, one who persists in trying to solve problems even after making mistakes; one who, in fact, does not see mistakes as errors but as opportunities for reflection and learning. It encourages him to be the sort of problem solver who, rather than ritualizing the solutions to problems, leaves himself open to undoing former mastery and finding new ways to solve new problems in new situations.

At the same time, the boy is encouraged to see himself as solving problems from the perspective of a particular fantasy creature (Captain Olimar) and his faithful helpers (the Pikmin) and, thus, to get outside his "real" identity and play with the notions of perspectives and identities themselves. He is also encouraged to focus on the problem-solving and fantasy aspects of his new identity and not, say, his worries about killing (virtual) "living" creatures, however odd they may be, though he can choose to avoid killing some of the creatures by running from them or sneaking around them. The learner, in this case, gets to customize the identity the game offers him to a certain extent—this, in fact, is an important feature of good video games.

The identity that *Pikmin* invites the player to take on relates in a variety of ways to other identities he takes on in other domains. I believe, for example, that the identity *Pikmin* recruits relates rather well to the sort of identity a learner is called on to assume in the best active science learning in schools and other sites.

If this is true, then our six-year-old is privileged in this respect over children who do not have the opportunity to play such games (in an active and critical way). An issue of social justice is at stake here in regard to the distribution of, and access to, this identity, whether through video games or science. We can note, as well, that the boy is using the video game to practice this identity, for many hours, at an early age, outside of science instruction in school, which may very well take up very little of the school day. Other children may get to practice this identity only during the limited amount of time their school devotes to active and critical learning in science of the sort that lets children take on the virtual identity of being and doing science rather than memorizing lists of facts—which often is no time at all.

Video Games: A Waste of Time?

I have now discussed a perspective on learning that stresses active and critical learning within specific semiotic domains. So, let me now return to the grandfather's remark that playing video games is a waste of time because the child is learning no "content."

If children (or adults) are playing video games in such a way as to learn actively and critically then they are:

1. Learning to experience (see and act on) the world in a new way

2. Gaining the potential to join and collaborate with a new affinity group

3. Developing resources for future learning and problem solving in the semiotic domains to which the game is related

4. Learning how to think about semiotic domains as design spaces that engage and manipulate people in certain ways and, in turn, help create certain relationships in society among people and groups of people, some of which have important implications for social justice

These, of course, are just the four things one learns when engaging actively and critically with any new semiotic domain. So the questions in regard to any specific semiotic domain become: Are these good or valuable ways to experience the world? Is this a good or valuable affinity group to join? Are these resources for future learning applicable to other good and valued semiotic domains? Is this domain leading the learner to reflect on design spaces (and the concomitant identities they help create), and their intricate relationships to each other, in ways that potentially can lead to critique, innovation, and good or valued thinking and acting in society?

The answers to these questions will vary along a variety of parameters. But they show that a great deal more is at stake than "content" in the grandfather's sense. This book offers a positive answer to these questions in regard to a good many (certainly not all) video games, as long as people are playing them in ways that involve active and critical learning. Video games have the potential to lead to active and critical learning. In fact, I believe that they often have a greater potential than much learning in school (even though school learning may involve learning "content"). Indeed, I hope my discussion of the child playing *Pikmin* already suggests some of the lines of my argument.

What ensures that a person plays video games in a way that involves active and critical learning and thinking? Nothing, of course, can ensure such a thing. Obviously, people differ in a variety of ways, including how much they are willing to challenge themselves, and they play video games for a great variety of different purposes. But two things help to lead to active and critical learning in playing video games.

One is the internal design of the game itself. Good games—and the games get better in this respect all the time—are crafted in ways that encourage and facilitate active and critical learning and thinking (which is not to say that every player will take up this offer). The other is the people around the learner, other players and nonplayers. If these people encourage reflective metatalk, thinking, and actions in regard to the design of the game, of video games more generally, and of other semiotic domains and their complex interrelationships, then this, too, can encourage and facilitate active and critical learning and thinking (though, again, the offer may not be taken up). And, indeed, the affinity groups connected to video games do often encourage metareflective thinking about design, as a look at Internet game sites will readily attest.

This last point—that other people can encourage in the learner metareflective talk, thinking, and actions in regard to a semiotic domain as a design space—leads to another point: Often it is critical learning—focusing on the semiotic domain one is learning as a design space in a reflective way—that actually encourages and pushes active learning. One can learn actively without much critical learning, but one cannot really learn much critically without a good deal of active learning in a semiotic domain. The critical is not a later add-on. It should be central to the process of active learning from the beginning.

There is another important issue here that bears on deciding whether a given semiotic domain—like video games—is valuable or not: Semiotic domains in society are connected to other semiotic domains in a myriad of complex ways. One of these is that a given domain can be a good precursor for learning another one. Because mastering the meaning-making skills in, and taking on the identity associated with, the precursor domain facilitates learning in the other domain. Facilitation can also happen because being (or having been) a member of the affinity group associated with the precursor domain facilitates becoming a member of the affinity group associated with the other domain, because the values, norms, goals, or practices of the precursor group resemble in some ways the other group's values, norms, goals, or practices.

Let me give a concrete example of such connections. In the larger semiotic domain of video games, first- and third-person shooter games are a well-defined subdomain. However, such games often have elements that are similar to features found in arcade games, games (like *Space Invaders, Pacman,* and *Frogger*) that involve a good deal of fast hand-eye coordination to move and respond quickly. (In fact, one of the original first-person shooter games, a game that helped start the genre—*Wolfenstein 3D*—operates very much like an arcade game.) Thus, someone who has mastered the domain of arcade games has mastered a precursor domain for shooter games, though such games now contain many other elements, as well.

On the other hand, fantasy role-playing games are another well-defined subdomain of the videogame domain. People who have earlier played and mastered the *Dungeons and Dragons* semiotic domain (as make-believe play or with books and cards) are advantaged when they play fantasy role-playing games, since such games developed out of *Dungeons and Dragons*, though they now contain a good many additional elements.

Both the shooter domain and the fantasy role-playing domain have other precursor domains, and they share some precursor domains (e.g., make-believe play wherein one is willing to take on different identities—a domain that some cultures and social groups do not encourage in children or adults). Some of these videogame (sub-) domains may well serve as precursor domains for other semiotic domains. For example, it may well be that the popular (sub-) domain of simulation games (so-called god games, like *SimCity*, *The Sims*, *Railroad Tycoon*, and *Tropico*) could be, for some children, a precursor domain for those sciences that heavily trade in computer-based simulations as a method of inquiry (e.g., some types of biology and cognitive science).

In interviews my research team and I have conducted with videogame players, we have found a number of young people who have used the domain of video games as a fruitful precursor domain for mastering other semiotic domains tied to computers and related technologies. Indeed, several of these young people plan to go to college and major in computer science or related areas.

So we can ask: Can various subdomains in the larger domain of videogame playing serve as precursor domains facilitating later learning in and out of school? I believe that the sorts of active and critical learning about design—and the type of problem-solving identity—that a game like *Pikmin* can involve may well relate to later learning in domains like science, at least when we are talking about teaching and learning science as an active process of inquiry and not the memorization of passive facts.

I am convinced that playing video games actively and critically is not "a waste of time." And people playing video games are indeed (*pace* the six-year-old's grandfather), learning "content," albeit usually not the passive content of school-based facts. (Many games, such as the *Civilization* games, do contain a good number of facts.) The content of video games, when they are played actively and critically, is something like this: *They situate meaning in a multimodal space through embodied experiences to solve problems and reflect on the intricacies of the design of imagined worlds and the design of both real and imagined social relationships and identities in the modern world.* That's not at all that bad—and people get wildly entertained to boot. No wonder it is hard for today's schools to compete.

Learning Principles

The discussion in this chapter suggests a variety of learning principles that are built into good video games, games like *Pikmin,* as will the discussion in each of the following chapters. Some of the learning principles suggested in this chapter are a bit more general than are those in later chapters. Here I bring together these principles to start a list that will continue in subsequent chapters.

I state only five very basic principles, since quite a number of other principles that are implicated in the earlier discussion will be discussed in greater detail later. The order of the principles is not important. All the principles are equally important, or nearly so. Some of the principles overlap and, in actuality, reflect different aspects of much the same general theme. Furthermore, these principles are not claims about all and any video games played in any old fashion. Rather, they are claims about the potential of good video games played in environments that encourage overt reflection. (While good video games do indeed encourage overt reflection, this feature can be greatly enhanced by the presence of others, both players and viewers.)

I state each principle in a way that is intended to be equally relevant to learning in video games and learning in content areas in classrooms.

1. Active, Critical Learning Principle
All aspects of the learning environment (including the ways in which the semiotic domain is designed and presented) are set up to encourage active and critical, not passive, learning.

2. Design Principle
Learning about and coming to appreciate design and design principles is core to the learning experience.

3. Semiotic Principle
Learning about and coming to appreciate interrelations within and across multiple sign systems (images, words, actions, symbols, artifacts, etc.) as a complex system is core to the learning experience.

4. Semiotic Domains Principle
Learning involves mastering, at some level, semiotic domains, and being able to participate, at some level, in the affinity group or groups connected to them.

5. Metalevel Thinking about Semiotic Domains Principle
Learning involves active and critical thinking about the relationships of the semiotic domain being learned to other semiotic domains.

Bibliographical Note

See Kress 1985, 1996, and Kress & van Leeuwen 1996, 2001 for insightful discussions on reading images and multimodal texts, that is, texts that mix words and images. For work on literacy as involving multiple literacies, see Cope & Kalantzis 2000; Heath 1983; Scollon & Scollon 1981; and Street 1984.

The discussion of physics students who know Newton's laws of motion but cannot apply them to a specific situation is taken from Chi, Feltovich, & Glaser 1981. For further discussion, see Gardner 1991 and Mayer 1992.

On the nature of reading tests, see Hill & Larsen's 2000 superb analyses of actual test items in relationship to different ways of reading. On reading more generally, see Adams 1990; Coles 1998; Gee 1991; Snow, Burns, & Griffin 1998; see Pearson 1999 for discussion of the range of controversy in the area. The "fourth-grade slump" is discussed in Gee 1999; see Chall 1967 for an early and influential discussion.

On Noam Chomsky's work, see McGilvray 1999. For C. S. Peirce's work, see Kloesel & Houser 1992.

On semiotics and content learning, especially in regard to science education, see Kress, Jewitt, Ogborn, & Tsatsarelis 2001; Lemke 1990; and Ogborn, Kress, Martins, & McGillicuddy 1996. On the notion of affiliation and affinity groups, see Beck 1992, 1994; Gee 2000–2001; Rifkin 2000; and Taylor 1994. For the idea of preparation for future learning, see Bransford & Schwartz 1999, a very important and illuminating paper for anyone interested in learning. On the notion of design and design grammars, see New London Group 1996, a "manifesto" written by an international group of scholars (a group of which I was a member) working in the area of language and literacy studies.

My notion of critical learning combines work on situated cognition, especially work on metacognition—see, for example Bereiter & Scardamalia 1989; Bruer 1993: pp. 67–99; Pellegrino, Chudowsky, & Glaser 2001; Schon 1987; and Paulo Freire's 1995 work on critical thinking and literacy as "reading the world" and not just "reading the word." On the concept of the lifeworld, see Habermas 1984.

For discussions of game design relevant to the concerns of this chapter, see Bates 2002 and Rouse 2001.

References

Adams, M. J. (1990). *Learning to read: Thinking and learning about print.* Cambridge, Mass.: MIT Press.

Bates, B. (2002). *Game design: The art & business of creating games.* Roseville, Calif.: Prima Publishing.

Beck, U. (1992). *Risk society.* London: Sage.

Bereiter, C., & Scardamalia (1989). *Surpassing ourselves: An inquiry into the nature and implications of expertise.* Chicago: Open Court.

Bransford, J. D., & Schwartz, D. L. (1999). Rethinking transfer: A simple proposal with multiple implications. *Review of Research in Education* 24: 61–100.

Bruer, J. T. (1993). *Schools for thought: A science of learning in the classroom.* Cambridge, Mass.: MIT Press.

Chall, J. S. (1967). *Learning to read: The great debate.* New York: McGraw-Hill.

Chi, M. T. H., Feltovich, P. J., & Glaser, R. (1981). Categorization and representation of physics problems by experts and novices. *Cognitive Science* 13: 145–182.

Coles, G. (1998). *Reading lessons: The debate over literacy.* New York: Hill and Wang.

Cope, B., & Kalantzis, M., Eds. (2000). *Multiliteracies: Literacy learning and the design of social futures.* London: Routledge.

Freire, P. (1995). *The pedagogy of the oppressed.* New York: Continuum.

Gardner, H. (1991). *The unschooled mind: How children think and how schools should teach.* New York: Basic Books.

Gee, J. P. (1992). *The social mind: Language, ideology, and social practice.* New York: Bergin & Garvey.

Gee, J. P. (1999). Reading and the New Literacy Studies: Reframing the National Academy of Sciences' Report on Reading. *Journal of Literacy Research* 31: 355–374.

Gee, J. P. (2000–2001). Identity as an analytic lens for research in education. *Review of Research in Education* 25: 99–125.

Habermas, J. (1984). *Theory of communicative action, vol. 1.* London: Heinemann.

Heath, S. B. (1983). *Ways with words: Language, life and work in communities and classrooms.* Cambridge: Cambridge University Press.

Hill, C., & Larsen, E. (2000). *Children and reading tests.* Stamford, Conn.: Ablex.

Kloesel, C., & Houser, N., Eds. (1992). *The essential Peirce: Selected philosophical writings (1867–1893)*. Bloomington: Indiana University Press.

Kress, G. (1985). *Linguistic processes in sociocultural practice*. Oxford: Oxford University Press.

Kress, G. (1996). *Before writing: Rethinking paths into literacy*. London: Routledge.

Kress, G., Jewitt, C., Ogborn, J., & Tsatsarelis, C. (2001). *Multimodal teaching and learning: The rhetorics of the science classroom*. London: Continuum.

Kress, G., & van Leeuwen, T. (1996). *Reading images: The grammar of visual design*. London: Routledge.

Kress, G., & van Leeuwen, T. (2001). *Multimodal discourse: The modes and media of contemporary communication*. London: Edward Arnold.

Lemke, J. (1990). *Talking science: Language, learning, and values*. Norwood, N. J.: Ablex.

Mayer, R. E. (1992). *Thinking, problem-solving, cognition,* 2nd ed. New York: Freeman.

McGilvray, J. (1999). *Chomsky: Language, mind, and politics*. Cambridge: Polity Press.

New London Group (1996). A pedagogy of multiliteracies: Designing social futures. *Harvard Educational Review* 66: 60–92.

Ogborn, J., Kress, G., Martins, I., & McGillicuddy, K. (1996). *Explaining science in the classroom*. Buckingham, U. K.: Open University Press.

Pearson, P. D. (1999). A historically based review of *Preventing Reading Difficulties in Young Children. Reading Research Quarterly* 34: 231–246.

Pelligrino, J. W., Chudowsky, N., & Glaser, R. (2001). *Knowing what students know: The science and design of educational assessment*. Washington, D.C.: National Academy Press.

Rifkin, J. (2000). *The age of access: The new culture of hypercapitalism where all of life is a paid-for experience*. New York: Jermey P. Tarcher/Putnam.

Rouse, R. (2001). *Game design: Theory & practice*. Plano, Texas: Wordware Publishing.

Schon, D. A. (1987). *Educating the reflective practitioner*. San Francisco, Calif.: Jossey-Bass.

Scollon, R., & Scollon, S. B. K. (1981). *Narrative, literacy, and face in interethnic communication*. Norwood, N.J.: Ablex.

Snow, C. E., Burns, M. S., & Griffin, P., Eds. (1998). *Preventing reading difficulties in young children*. Washington, D.C.: National Academy Press.

Street, B. (1984). *Literacy in theory and practice.* Cambridge: Cambridge University Press.

Taylor, C. (1994). The politics of recognition. In C. Taylor, K. A. Appiah, S. C. Rockefeller, M. Waltzer, & S. Wolf (1994). *Multiculturalism: Examining the politics of recognition.* Ed. by A. Gutman. Princeton, N.J.: Princeton University Press, pp. 25–73.

The Evil Summoner FAQ v1.0: How to Be a Cheap Ass

Mochan

Context

Written (and last updated) on May 28, 2001, "The Evil Summoner FAQ v1.0" is filled not only with the prerequisite cheats, walkthroughs, and spoilers of any FAQ (worth their weight in gold for frustrated players), but also with a sense of wit and pure cynicism. Written by a player known only as Mochan, the guide shows players "How to Be a Cheap Ass" so that they may "breeze through the battles of Summoner...to get over the game quickly and move on to better things." As if! More FAQs and reviews by Mochan can be found at www.gamefaqs.com/features/recognition/7633.html.

Gaming the Game

Game Economies

===

By Mochan ←mosquiton@crosswinds.net→

created May 28, 2001

last modified May 28, 2001

===

cheap adj (1509)

1: at minimum expense

2: gained with little effort

3: obtainable at a low rate of interest

4: STINGY

ass (bef. 12c)

1: any of several hardy gregarious mammals (genus Equus) that are smaller than the horse and have long ears

2: a stupid, obstinate, or perverse person

===

DISCLAIMER

This FAQ was written with the PC version of the game. Any discrepancies with the PS2 should be excused. Best read with a 79-width text viewer with a fixed-size font. This FAQ has no spoilers in the tactical section (How to Be a Cheap Ass) but it does have spoilers in the omake section at the end.

This FAQ will likely not be updated because I am lazy. Besides, this particular FAQ isn't something I want to spend too much effort on.

I have included my e-mail address in the header up there. If you want to write me anything be sure to include this tag in the subject:

[SUMMONER FAQ]

Actually, though, I'd prefer if you don't write me anything because I'm betting I won't like whatever you'll have to say. ^____^

===

TABLE OF CONTENTS

==

DISCLAIMER

TABLE OF CONTENTS

1. Why this FAQ was written

=============================

2. How to Be a Cheap Ass

=============================

2.I. THE ART OF WAR

————————-

Lesson 1

Lesson 2

Lesson 3

2.II. THE CHARACTERS

————————-

1.) JOSEPH

       INSERT #1: A NOTE ON SKILLS

       SKILL LEVELS

       SUMMON SKILL

       WHY BLUNT AND NOT SWORD?

       DODGE AND PUSH

       PUSH AND DOUBLE ATTACK

       COUNTERATTACK

       INSERT #2: A NOTE ON QUICK SLOTS

       * The Fire Wall Technique *

       * The Fireball Tactic *

2.) FLECE

       *Uragiri Technique *

3.) ROSALIND

       * Guerilla Warfare *

       * Assess *

4.) JEKHAR

2.III. OTHER CONSIDERATIONS

————————————————

* Chain Combo Attacks *

* Speed *

* Armor *

2.IV. OTHER TRICKS

—————————

* Never Die*

=============================

3. HOW TO CHEAT

=============================

LEGALESE

CREDITS

OMAKE!!!

==

1. Why this FAQ was written (or, "Why I hate Summoner and so should you")

Let me state this from the start, so that you don't get the wrong idea.

This "Evil Summoner FAQ" is not like a "Fallout Evil FAQ" or a "Black and White Evil FAQ." It will not tell you how to play the game in the "evil way" because it is impossible to do so in Summoner. Being totally linear in plot, Summoner can only be played the "good way." So why call it the "Evil Summoner FAQ?"

Most people write FAQs for games they love and worship and adore above all else. However, being unlike everyone else, I have taken it upon myself to write this FAQ with the sole intention of utterly trashing Summoner because I totally hate the game. And therein is the answer: this FAQ is "evil" because it is based on hate, hate for the piece of trash called "Summoner!"

Summoner is one of those rare games that get practically nothing right, and because of this it deserves to be soundly bashed, ripped, slashed, broken and consigned to oblivion. However, no matter what you think of the game, you cannot deny that Summoner did get ONE thing right: the time of its release!

On the PC there was no other RPG out at the moment of its release, so Summoner will likely be bought and played by default. Even now, some months after its release, Arcanum has been bumped off to a September release, Blade Masters seems to have turned into vaporware, Anachronox is nowhere in sight, it will be a miracle if Morrowind is released anytime soon. You get the point. Likely, as of now you will have no RPG to play on the PC except for this.

PS2 players probably have it better; too bad I don't have a PS2. ^^;

So, in anticipation of this sore trial my fellow gamers will have to undergo, I have resolved to write this guide to show you "How to Be a Cheap Ass" and breeze through the battles of Summoner, so you can get over the game quickly and move on to better things.

Okay, so I won't mention all the bad things of Summoner right now. I'll do that later. ←hehe→ Let's get on to the business of this FAQ: how to win battles easily and cheaply!

===

2. How to Be a Cheap Ass (or the meat of this FAQ)

===

2.I. THE ART OF WAR

First things first, to win a battle you must understand your enemies. I will disclose to you how the algorithms work in controlling monsters.

Lesson 1

I will tell you the first hidden secret about Summoner: AI is ROCK STUPID! For the PC version, anyway. I don't know if it's better on the PS2, but on the PC it is utterly moronic.

Enemies within spitting distance will more often than not ignore you as you bash their friends in right next to them. Take advantage of this by knowing the maxim: "Divide and Conquer!"

If you ever have trouble with a battle, remember that fighting enemies one-on-many (one being them and many being you) will make things much easier.

Lesson 2

An enemy will typically attack your active character (the one you happen to be controlling at the moment). This, however, is mostly because you will likely be leading your party with the active character. The only time you won't, will be when you are using a bow or a spell.

At any rate, when engaged in melee I have noticed that the enemy tends to face your active character more often than an inactive character. This may not seem like much, but it is important if you want to make the most of Flece's backstab. More on this later.

For now, just know that if an enemy is fighting two or more of your party, if you control one of them and walk away a bit, the enemy will almost never pursue you, and will face the remaining inactive party member it is engaged with. This is useful for Flece later on, hee hee hee.

Lesson 3

If it can't sense you, it won't fight you. These enemies are all apathetic and are practically blind as a bat. What this means is that, as long as you don't walk in front of them and hit them, they'll ignore you.

Remember this; it works wonders when using the Blizzard and Firewall spells.

Alright, that's enough about enemy AI. Frankly because there's nothing else to talk about. These are all the important things you have to remember about your average enemy.

2.II. THE CHARACTERS

In Summoner, you will be controlling four morons who believe everything they're told, and who all look particularly stupid. However, they do have diverse combat abilities. Being a Cheap Ass means knowing how to use each character properly.

Here is my take on each one:

1.) JOSEPH

RENAISSANCE MORON

The dumb provincial idiot who gets to be the hero. As is the tradition with console games, the hero gets to be the well-rounded jack who, despite being an uneducated, untrained peasant, has great potential to learn to use all weapons and wield powerful magic.

Despite being the "renaissance man" as heroes go, he is the 2nd worst character in your party. Regardless, Joseph has his uses. He has the Fire magic set, which is terribly effective, he can heal, and he is relatively tough with lots of hit points.

Drawbacks:

No CRITICAL HIT—for someone who's supposed to be a fighter, not having this skill makes him weak compared to the real fighter. Then again, since there are only four PCs in this game, comparisons are pretty stark.

Ugly—Joseph is plain ugly. How to describe it? Someone must have dug a grave and dumped Joseph in, buried alive. Seven days later someone exhumed him, and he looks as he does today: a walking corpse. Don't believe me? Look at those gaunt cheekbones, that bony neck! And those eyes...they're evil!

273

Skills

Raise the skills to the level dictated, roughly in this order. That is, in Joseph's case raise Heal first, then Dodge, Parry, and so on.

Typically, devote all the skill points you can to the top skills before raising the others.

For Joseph, I recommend raising him in this manner:

Dodge: get up to 4 or so

Parry: about 4 or so

Heal: up to 10 is nice; the heal spells are all good

Fire: up to 7 just to get Fire Wall

Blunt: raise up to 10

Heavy Arms: up to 7 (9, if you want to use swords)

Magic Resist: get this up to 10.

Do NOT put points in these skills:

Sword Weapons

Staff Weapons

Push

Holy

Bow Weapons

Double Attack

Axe Weapons

Dark

Counter Attack

When you have spare skills points, put them into either Darkness up to level 8, or Dodge and Parry, until you reach up to 10 with them.

You can also put some in Staff Weapons at the start; you can get a pretty good staff early in the game: the Fellstaff (If you're lucky).

Still, I'd stick with Blunt; more on that later.

INSERT #1: A NOTE ON SKILLS

SKILL LEVELS

Skills can be increased from 1 to 10. There are basically two kinds of skills: those that give you access to certain things if their level is high enough (e.g. Spell skills,

Heavy Arms), and skills that give you benefits from a formula derived from the skill level (e.g. weapon skills, dodge, parry). Generally, you will want to devote precious skill points to the second type of skill, the one that gives you a benefit if it is higher.

Now, certain items can boost skill levels higher than 10. As far as I can tell, this gives you a positive advantage with the second type of skill, but is useless with the first kind.

Thus, it is pointless to use items like the Hellfire Necklace to increase your Fire Skill from 10 to 13, for instance. A higher Fire Skill does NOT makes your fire spells do more damage, it only lets you access higher level fire spells. And since the last spell you get is generally the one at level 10, there is no point in increasing it further.

The other type of skill, though, seems to benefit from increasing it beyond 10. Increasing a weapon skill beyond 10 apparently improves your chance to hit with it. However, the difference is quite negligible, and either way your characters are terribly cross-eyed, so it doesn't really matter so much.

SUMMON SKILL

Joseph has the Summon skill which can call up a monster to do his bidding, but frankly I discourage the development and use of this skill. It's next to worthless. The summoned creatures are pathetically weak at the start, heck they're softer than Flece and are about as effective as Rosalind. The worst part is that if they die, you lose hit points PERMANENTLY. Don't risk it.

Admittedly, the summon monsters get stronger when you get the dragon rings later on in the game. But with the tactics I will be telling to you, you don't need these creatures, so don't bother.

You also get two summons "ala Final Fantasy," that is you summon a creature who just drops by, gives an eye-candy animation, pops damage on your enemy, and leaves. Not really impressive, and damage is actually pathetic, so don't bother.

WHY BLUNT AND NOT SWORD?

I'll let you in on a secret: swords SUCK. Yes, it's true! Although the swords *LOOK* like they have better stats than the blunt weapons, don't be misled. Most creatures in this game take more damage from blunt weapons than slashing or piercing. Don't believe me? Just look at Flece. She is weak because she only uses swords and daggers. Watch her use her kick attack:

it is her only "blunt" attack. Notice how the kick tends to do more damage than her sword? Weird, yes, but it's because of what I said.

Want more proof? Use Rosalind to Assess your enemies. You'll notice that most monsters are "WEAK" or "VULNERABLE" against BLUNT but "STRONG" or something against slash/pierce. Not all monsters, but most of them.

Now, Joseph's strongest weapon in the game is the Sword of Summoners. Sure, it does 150 damage, but it doesn't mess your opponent up in any way. So the Debasser, heck the Dreadblade is 10 times better. Besides, you only get it at the very end of the game (and I do mean the end) so WHAT'S THE POINT!?!?

I am also told that Jekhar's "strongest" weapon is the Breaching Claymore, which does 100 damage. Again, it does nothing else so what's the point? I'm pretty sure the War-hammer is a superior weapon, as it does 90 BLUNT damage. I can't say for sure since I didn't actually get the Breaching Claymore (I have no idea where to get it), but even without testing I am 100% sure it's no big deal.

Stick to blunt weapons. As an added incentive, I'll let you in on another secret in the game: the Debasser is the BEST weapon. Period.

Other weapons, like the Dread Blade and Nodachi, are also quite good, but nothing beats the Debasser. Why? It's doesn't slow you down (speed 1), does great damage (75), is one-handed (thus allowing you to use a shield), is blunt (which means it does more damage to most enemies), and most importantly it can TRIP your enemy. And it does so quite often, I might add. This is INVALUABLE. The Dread Blade and Nodachi, being capable of petrifying and freezing enemies, get runner-up for best weapons, but they have a lot of other cons (being swords, expensive, slow and two-handed) which balance out to make the Debasser better.

Further, the TRIP ability combos well with Flece, as I will discuss later.

There is only one other Sword weapon which I find to be useful other than the De-basser at certain points of the game: the Winterlong, which does 90 points of ICE damage. This is particularly useful near the end of the game where you fight Lichs and other monsters which take lots of Ice damage, and are strong against Blunt weapons. Yet when I fight those things I just fry them with Rosalind, so what's the point? Oh, yeah, there are some big golems in Ikaemos and some other parts who are resistant to magic, blunt and sword weapons, but weak against ice. The Winterlong is the best weapon against them. But still, too specialized an occurrence.

Blunt is best. Trust me.

DODGE AND PUSH

These two skills sound really useful, but after closer inspection I have come to conclude that, like raising weapon skills, they don't provide that big an advantage. Even with perfect dodge and parry skills you'll be hit far too often for my liking, so again, what's the point?

PUSH AND DOUBLE ATTACK

These skills supposedly aid your chain combo rates. Bullshit. As far as I can tell, they do squat. Leaving an inactive member on its own, they did not do any more chain combos than they would with a zero double attack skill. If you use your character, it doesn't really help that much; I can easily get a 24 chain combo manually. In auto chain mode, there isn't much noticeable difference.

Supposing these skills did increase your chain combo rate, why would you want to use combo attacks? You'll discover that combo attacks aren't really desirable, as I will discuss later.

COUNTERATTACK

This sounds like a great skill at first, since you get a free attack when your enemy attacks, right? Wrong! If this were Tactics Ogre or Final Fantasy Tactics, this would be a good technique. But this isn't. This is Summoner, with the lame real-time combat system which is trying so hard to be Diablo, and fails miserably.

Why is counterattack useless? Because after your opponent is blocked, you WILL ATTACK ANYWAY. And since it's real time, you aren't given a "free attack," since you are doing your counterattack while you're supposed to be doing your normal attack! Trust me. I've timed the speed of attack; there is no difference.

END INSERT #1

Now, let's talk about Joseph again.

Joseph isn't particularly effective as a fighter because he lacks the one skill that makes Jekhar so strong: Critical Hit. It's annoying that Jekhar is the only fighter in your party who has that vital skill. However, he has lots of hit points and can wear lots of good armor, so he makes a good shock troop.

How to Use Properly:
At the start of the game, Joseph is most effective as a healer.

Later on, he becomes a damage soaker (i.e. shock troop), moderate damage dealer, and back-up fireman.

Your gameplan is like this: Joseph is to be a shock troop who doubles as a melee fighter. However, his main use is to heal, particularly to revive Rosalind if she gets knocked out (which will probably happen a lot).

At the start, Joseph will likely be using sword weapons and not blunt ones, because you will have a hard time finding good blunt weapons. Don't fear, this is only temporary. At this point, Joseph is not your fighter, Flece is. Joseph is your healer.

Later on, you'll get stronger blunt weapons. Joseph's best weapon is without a doubt the Debasser. I thought at first it was the Dreadblade, but I realized that it's nigh impossible to get it, and it's a sword, after all.

RECOMMENDED AI SCIPT: Healer

RECOMMENDED QUICKSLOT ARRANGEMENT:

1: Vitalize

2: Firewall

3: Meteor Swarm

4: Fireball

5: Heal

6: Revive

INSERT #2: A NOTE ON QUICK SLOTS

Make sure to use your quickslots! Summoner's interface on the PC is pathetic. A quickslot is a slot which houses a special ability, which you can call by pressing buttons 1 to 6. This will save you much effort and frustration on the PC.

To use, open your spell/skill menu, and pick a skill. Click on the icon, hold, and drag to one of the six squares at the bottom right. I'm mentioning this here because it is of VITAL import to your sanity to use these quick slots. If you overlooked it in the documentation, then don't overlook it here. They certainly overlooked it in the tutorial (dumb Volition, dumb!).

END INSERT #2

SPECIAL TACTICS:

The Fire Wall Technique

You can use this with Joseph early on. It's slow, boring, but works all the time and has a 100% safety rate. You will NEVER lose with this technique.

Creep up to an enemy, just close enough to use Fire Wall on it. Because of the stupidity of the enemies, you can creep up on any non-boss enemy to cast Fire Wall on it, and it will not see you! Even stupider, they will happily roast in the flames without a care in the world until they keel over and die.

Take note that this is not very effective against monsters with high magic resistance and/or fire resistance. But there are other methods to deal with those....

Rosalind can also use this tactic; actually she uses it better.

The Fireball Tactic

This only works if you have Invisibility cast on your character. Use Flece or Rosalind to make you invisible (depending on who you grew to have that skill). Creep up as with the Fire Wall tactic, then shoot Fireball. They will be hit, but since you're invisible they won't notice. Pathetic.

Note that this trick also works with the other projectile spells like Fire Arrow and Icicle.

2.) FLECE

QUEEN OF BACKSTABS AND OTHER THINGS

Flece is the best character in the game! No doubt about it. She has the best line-up of skills, and I get the feeling the game developers like her so much as their "favorite child" that they gave her so many perks, gameplay-wise and story-wise.

Why is Flece the best? Because she does the most damage*, she has a lot of good skills, she's the prettiest person in the game (which isn't saying much), and she rules (literally; you'll understand when you get half-way through the game, hehehe!!!).

Drawbacks:

Low life: She is the 2nd weakest character in the game. Still, she's reasonably stout and won't fall easily.

Pierce/Slash only: Flece can only use sword weapons, which means that she has no blunt damage ability except for the KICK skill, which doesn't cut it.

No CRITICAL HIT skill: a shame, if she did she'd be a show-stopper!

So many Good Skills: it's hard to grow her properly because there are so many good skills to choose from! Don't worry, I'm here to help.

Skills

For Flece, I recommend raising her in this manner:
Sword Weapons: raise to about 4
Dodge: Raise to about 4
Pick Lock: raise to 3
Backstab: raise to 10
Dark: up to 8, just to get the invisibility
Heavy Arms: raise to 4
Appraise: raise to a 9
Trip: raise to a 10
Magic Resist: raise to a 10

Do NOT put points in these skills:
Bow Weapons
Kick
Aimed Attack
Hide
Parry
Counter Attack
Sneak

It's annoying that Flece has some worthless skills raised to 2 automatically. I'd much rather have placed those precious points elsewhere.

The reason why I tell you not to put points in Sword Weapons is because, at the start of the game, she can hit enemies well enough with a low sword skill. Come the end of the game, you won't be using her in frontal combat: you'll only backstab. And when you backstab it always hits. Only raise sword weapons to a 10 when you have spare points (not likely)! Sneak is a convenience to raise, but you don't really need to, if you're patient. Sneak skill actually just tells how long it takes for you to be able to use sneak again, it doesn't stand for a success rate. Also, certain items boost sneak skill, and you'll likely be using these items anyway.

Picklocks—it is actually quite beneficial to raise picklocks to 10. But why not? Because precious points are useful elsewhere. Instead, you will sometime in the game come across Shadow Gauntlets (which give +1 Picklock) and the Ring of Thieves, which give +3. Whenever faced with a locked item, just equip these items and you'll boost your picklocks up to 10, no problem. After opening it, take them off so you can use the other better rings and gloves.

Heavy Arms—you can actually get away with just raising it to 4. The only reason to raise it to 5 is to use the Bough-Kote, which is a great pair of gloves.

Appraise—like Picklocks, you can get away with a 9 because there is a pair of gloves which can temporarily raise it to 10 for those hard to identify items.

Dark—should only be raised to level 8. It is USELESS to get the Death Spell because the Death Spell almost never works! I tried the Assassin Crossbow and it never killed anyone outright. For fun I experimented with the Death Spell and only managed to kill 1 (!) guy out of every 25! Not worth it. Alternately you can put the Dark allotment to Sneak, so you can skulk around and backstab enemies a lot more conveniently.

How to Use Properly:

Flece was not meant to be a head-on character. You've got Joseph and Jekhar to do that. Flece was meant to be the "brains" behind Joseph and Jekhar's dumb brawn. Typically, in this game you should be controlling only one of two characters: either Flece or Rosalind. Controlling Jekhar is worthless, since he's just your shock troop to draw enemy attention while you do the good stuff with Flece or Rosalind. Joseph should be controlled as sparingly as possible; typically only when Rosalind's busy recuperating or something.

If you have sneak skill (or even if you don't), be sure to sneak and backstab enemies every now and then. It's faster than using the Fire Wall trick, but it only works when enemies are isolated. When they are bunched up together, be sure to use the Fire Wall.

Using Art of War Lesson #2, you must weave about the enemy and hit them from behind with a backstab. Use her to silence enemy mages early on when magic resistance hasn't been fully-developed. Finally, use her Invisibility on Joseph or Rosalind to let them use spells undetected.

Notice that Flece's tiny daggers do pathetic damage against most enemies. However, check out the Special Tactics below.

Flece should keep getting the best dagger available. For a long time her best weapon will be the Gutting Dirk, available at Tancred's for a whopping price. You will want to make her use the Katar from the Khosani. It says you can't backstab with it, but that's what they say. Just do the backstab motion with the Dirk, and go to your inventory and switch to the Katar. There you go, instant Katar backstab! The bonus is that they get poisoned. This is invaluable against boss fights, particularly that damn immortal Lich in the catacombs, and against that flying monster at the end of the game who loves to run away.

Later on, her best weapon will be the Sornehan Dagger.

RECOMMENDED AI SCIPT: Melee

RECOMMENDED QUICKSLOT ARRANGEMENT:

1: Trip

2: Backstab

3: Sneak

4: Picklock

5: Silence

6: Invisibility

SPECIAL TACTICS:

*Uragiri Technique *

Flece is the strongest damaging character in the game. Don't believe me? You will. Against any humanoid enemy who is not immune to piercing weapons, simply go up to them. Use trip to bring them down. Go behind them. Use backstab. You will then do something like 1200—4000 damage. Bye bye enemy.

Backstab is the ultimate damage skill! Now, there are two kinds of backstab: the "fake" backstab which magnifies damage by about 500%, and the "true" backstab that does some 2000% more damage.

The difference is in your enemy's "awareness." Used on an "unaware" enemy, you will magnify your damage by 1000%—4000%. Normally, this means using the Sneak skill to creep up behind an enemy, and do the backstab. In combat situations, if you backstab an enemy, it is only a "fake" backstab that does lesser damage.

In the heat of battle, remember Art of War Lesson #2 and you will be able to use Backstab to consistently chip away your enemy's life, even bosses. You can do this to ANY opponent, and average some 500 damage or so.

However, the true art of backstabbing is in making "unaware" backstabs ALL THE TIME. How to do this? It works against any humanoid opponent. In the midst of combat, just Trip them with the Trip skill. This lays them flat on their back. Now, for some reason, when an opponent is leveled like this they become "unaware." I'm assuming they got the wind knocked out of them and are stunned senseless. Whatever the case, go behind them and use Backstab. Poof! 2000 damage on average! You will be doing maximum backstab damage! Incredible!

The best part is, *THIS WORKS ON BOSSES!*

This is the easy way to kill those pesky horsemen and the 2nd final boss (I killed him in five seconds, believe it or not). You can kill almost all normal humanoids in one blow (some, like the Ice Soldiers can take two because of their bladed-weapon resistance, and some can't be killed at all, like the Lich because of immunity). All humanoid bosses can be killed in two hits! How many times you can hit them isn't really a problem: after the backstab, as they get up, just trip them again! Viola! Instant win.

Because of this Trip/Backstab combo, Flece is without a doubt the strongest character in the game. Note that the higher your backstab skill, the greater the damage seems to be. I am not entirely sure of this, but if you raise your backstab skill to 20 (it is possible with a certain sword, glove and two rings) you will be doing massive damage. However, once you get a good dagger and a backstab of 10, it's usually enough to kill most enemies easily, so there's no need to raise it that high.

I cannot emphasize enough that you should use this technique whenever you engage in battle. A word of caution: it is easier to do this if you have only one shock troop drawing enemy attention. Too many cooks spoil the broth, so to speak. Typically, you should have only either Joseph or Jekhar distracting the enemy and you will creep up behind, do a trip, and backstab. Better, if Jekhar or Joseph are using the Debasser, they will drop the enemy for you, and you can just backstab away. Always have Trip and Backstab in your quickslots.

If all four of you are in melee mode and whacking the enemy, it is very frustrating and difficult to pull off this cheap backstab trick. At the most only Joseph and Jekhar should be attacking; it is still relatively easy to pull it off with the two of them, but with Rosalind you will likely be clicking on her or the two dorks instead of behind the enemy, thanks to Summoner's pathetic interface.

3.) ROSALIND

MASTER OF MAGIC

Rosalind is another idiot coming from a cloister who does everything her headmaster tells her. I'm pretty sure she'd climb up the highest tower of the temple and strip naked if the headmaster told her.

Regardless, she is the second best character in the game. She has absolute command of magic; she can learn all spells and because she is so fragile you will likely want to keep her in the back casting spells, so she has her work cut out for her.

Drawbacks:

Fragile: Rosalind has the lowest hit points AND the lowest defense in your party. She can only use staff weapons, which she uses SO slowly. Because of this, get her in battle and even if she has a dodge and parry of 10 she will die in ten seconds flat.

No Heavy Arms: the only character without Heavy Arms, this restricts her equipment, making her incapable of using the better weapons and armor. Ah well, all the more reason to keep her at the back casting spells and shooting arrows.

Has Critical Hit Skill: although technically it is a boon for a person to have this great skill, it is wasted on Rosalind because 1.) She has a glass jaw, and 2.) she can only use Staves. What's so bad about that? Well, get her in combat and she'll go down in seconds. Two, the staves, although they should be very fast (such as the Fellstaff), are wielded very slowly by Rosalind. It's because she twirls them around all the time. How silly! Combat is about practicality, not form and fancy tricks! Keep it simple, duh! Since she keeps twirling that stick around, enemies get free attacks while she's busy playing baton cheer leader. Ahou. Such a shame, since you can get the Fellstaff relatively early in the game, and it does great damage. Oh well.

Skills

Fire: get it up to 8

Heal: up to 10, thank you

Ice: up to level 8, just to get Blizzard

Assess: I got it up to 10

Bow Weapons: get it up to 10

Magic Resist: up to 7

Trip: put spare points here

Do NOT put points in these skills:

> Holy: (level 2 is fine)
>
> Dark
>
> Critical Hit
>
> Staff Weapons
>
> Dodge
>
> Energy
>
> Parry

Holy is fine up to level 2, but the real prize is Faith at level 7. I recommend using two Ring of Blessings and a Bacite Medallion to get it up to 7, just to cast Faith.

Magic Resist should normally be taken up to 10, but in Rosalind's case you'll be getting lots of clothing that boost Magic Resistance, and you'll likely be wearing them until the end of the game so save those skill points for something else.

You should have Trip ability just in case someone sneaks up on Rosalind, so you can knock them down and laugh at them.

How to Use Properly:

Just keep Rosalind out of melee battle and you're fine. Rosalind is invulnerable to magic, so if you're fighting lichs and other mages, you have nothing to fear. Study the enemy, whether they are bunched together or solitary. If they're solitary, Flece is the way to go, or you can just overpower it. If there are a lot together, then it's Rosalind's turn and she will fry all the idiot enemies who seem to enjoy basking in a barbecue or sunbathing in a Blizzard.

Since Rosalind is such a weak fighter, give her a bow. Her best weapon is the Long Bow, until you get the Bow of Lynnai, which is terribly useful against Fire-weak opponents.

Be sure to use Assess on enemies, to find out their weak spots. Finally, I'm sure that you'll get sick of using Fire Wall/Blizzard guerilla tactics so if you're fighting Fire vulnerable enemies don't be afraid to walk up to them with Rosalind. Just keep casting Meteor Swarm and they'll die after a few burning rocks to the head.

RECOMMENDED AI SCRIPT: Healer

RECOMMENDED QUICKSLOT ARRANGEMENT:

1: Vitalize

2: Fire Wall

3: Meteor Swarm

4: Icicle

5: Blizzard

6: Protect

SPECIAL TACTICS:

Guerilla Warfare

I've already mentioned how to be cheap with Rosalind in Joseph's section. However, Rosalind can also use Blizzard instead of Fire Wall; this is helpful for fire-resistant monsters, or if you're impatient to wait for Fire Wall to regenerate.

To be safe, be sure to have Flece cast Invisibility on Rosalind. That way she can also use Icicles and Fireballs to take potshots at nearby enemies.

Assess

The great thing about Summoner is that you can pause the game and use Assess as much as you want! It's stupid, but it's true. Just pause, activate assess from the skill menu, and point at your enemy of choice. It works, without any time cost or penalties!

4.) JEKHAR

MUSCLE-BRAINED MORON

Jekhar was Joseph's, uh, "childhood friend" (so to speak). However, since Joseph burned down their village, Jekhar's been holding a grudge for quite some time. However, Jekhar is every bit as stupid as Rosalind because he'll believe and do everything he's told. You'll see.

Anyway, Jekhar is your team's muscle-man. He's got high hit points, high defense, high attack, and not much else. He is the perfect shock troop. Unfortunately, that's all he's good for.

Drawbacks:

Boring: Jekhar is totally boring. Just suit him up, give him a weapon, and let him loose.

Stupid: I'll discuss his stupidity later in the omake section.

Wasted Skills: Jekhar has a LOT of points wasted in worthless skills, because he comes with a 3 in them. Such a waste.

Skills

Critical Hit: raise to 10. NOW.

Blunt Weapons: raise to 10

Parry: Get up to about 5

Dodge: up to 5 is fine

Heavy Arms: 7 is fine

Magic Resist: raise to 10

Heal: raise to 10

Do NOT put points in these skills:

Sword Weapons

Axe Weapons

Push

Counter Attack

Kick

Double Attack

How to Use Properly:

Don't worry, you don't ever need to control him so just give him his armor and his Debasser, and he'll do fine without you. Set his script to Healer so that he'll stop and fix you up every now and then when necessary.

You'll eventually want to arm him with a Debasser. This is his best weapon, make no mistake.

RECOMMENDED AI SCRIPT: Healer

RECOMMENDED QUICKSLOT ARRANGEMENT:

1: Vitalize

2: Heal

3: Cure

287

4: Regenerate

5: Push

6: Revive

SPECIAL TACTICS:

None. That's why he's the worst character in the game. However, just because he's the worst doesn't mean he doesn't have his uses. Shock troops and cannon fodder are vital in this game, too.

==

2.III. OTHER CONSIDERATIONS

* Chain Combo Attacks *

"Wow, if I press the right mouse button I get to do a free attack! That's so cool!"

WRONG! Chain Combo attacks are USELESS! If this were Vagrant Story, Chain Combo attacks would be god techniques. In Summoner, they are utter crap. Don't believe me? Then consider this:

Summoner battle occurs in real time. When you attack with a chain combo, TIME DOES NOT STOP, like in Vagrant Story. So while you think that you are actually getting a free attack, you are NOT. While you are doing your chain attack, your enemy is also attacking. It is NOT A FREE ATTACK.

Further, instead of doing a chain combo, you could be doing something more useful— like doing another normal attack. This is because chain combos almost always do less damage than your normal attack. Those that don't do damage, have rather worthless effects.

The only chain attacks that can do more damage than your normal attack are the Stamina Burst early in the game, when you haven't spent any mana, and the Desperation attack when you are at death's door. But since Chain Combos use up mana, your Stamina Burst isn't likely going to stay strong for long, and when you're dying I think you'd much rather heal yourself than attack, no? This isn't Final Fantasy 8 where you purposefully keep Squall perpetually dead.

Trust me, it's not worth it. Further, as you get better weapons later in the game they will all do more damage than your chain attacks, so don't bother. It's not like speed is improved dramatically by chain attacks (I will discuss this later).

So be sure to keep your chain combo setting to Manual and not Auto, so that you don't inadvertently do chain attacks. Your inactive party members will do chain attacks every now and then, but that's a necessary evil that can't be helped.

Speed

Here is the other important consideration. I do not know if this is just in the PC version, but in the PC Speed is MEANINGLESS. Yes, you heard me, the Speed attribute has NO EFFECT on the game whatsoever.

Your attack speed is totally dependent on only two things: WHO you're using, and WHAT WEAPON you're using. It doesn't matter if that character's speed rating is in the red at 50%, or blue at 250%. They will attack at the same rate as prescribed by the character and the weapon.

Don't believe me? You will.

Give Rosalind a Fellstaff. That's supposed to be a 1.66 speed weapon. Give her all the good stuff to raise her speed up to 250% or so. Now attack. Notice how slow she twirls that staff?

Now give Flece a Gutting Dirk. Then put all the heavy armor and shields on her, so that her speed is, say 130% or so. Now attack. Notice how fast she stabs with that knife? Much faster than Rosalind, no?

Try giving Rosalind a Reflex Bow (speed 1.43), and Flece a Heavy Crossbow (speed .50) Even if Rosalind's speed rating is 180% and Flece's is only 50%, Flece will still be attacking faster.

You can give Flece the Reflex Bow and you'll notice that she attacks faster than Rosalind does, with the same weapon.

So that proves that attack rate is totally dependent on the CHARACTER, not on the speed rating, thus proving my first assertion. Now to prove my second assertion.

Try Joseph. Give him a Debasser (speed 1.00) and load him with all the heavy armor and shields. This should give him a speed in the red, probably about 80% or so. Make him attack. Notice the fast attack speed.

Now give the same Joseph a Warhammer (speed .50), but load him with the light armor, shield, and equip the Torque of Time (+2 speed) and two Rings of Swiftness (+ 8 speed) so that he'll have a speed rating of about, say, 180%. Make him attack. Notice how slow he attacks?

To take the experiment further, you can give him the Debasser and the torque and rings. Notice how his attack speed hasn't changed at all, even though his speed rating has gone from 80% to 200%?

The same goes for the Warhammer, if you take off all the speed and give him the heavy armor. He'll attack at the same speed.

That means that rate of attack is also totally dependent on the WEAPON, not on the speed rating!

What does this mean? The speed rating is totally bogus! It doesn't affect movement rate, either, because in my games Rosalind always walks so slowly despite having the highest speed rating. So ignore speed altogether!

When dressing your characters up don't pay any attention at all to the armor's speed ratings, they're all the same. The only thing to consider is how fast the character can swing whatever weapon you give them.

* Armor*

Just a quick tip: don't wear the full-body armors until the end where you get the strongest ones. Except for the strongest of them, you'll get better results wearing a good piece of body armor and a good piece of leg armor.

I personally used nothing but Haramakis and Chain Leggings for a long time. That gives you a rating of 35 + 15. You could opt for the Chainmail and Chainmail Leggings, which give a 40 + 15, but I like the piercing resistance of the Haramaki, and they look better too. Later you'll want Jekhar to use the Hero set.

The combined armor rating is definitely better than the full-body suit ratings, except for the best ones. The only ones worth wearing are the Hero's Plate and Summoner Plate.

==

2.IV. OTHER TRICKS

* Never Die *

Summoner is full of bugs and bad design problems. One of the main exponents of this bad design is the real-time combat system. By exploiting the various design errors, you can achieve immortality!

Well, not really, but it's close enough. If you pause the game, you will notice that certain commands, like Rosalind's Assess, can be used indefinitely even with time stopped! It's stupid, but that's what happens when you rip-off the Diablo system and give it a pause feature, without knowing what you're doing (shame on you, Volition).

Now, apply this concept to healing items like the Healing Elixir, Panacea of Life, and so on. What do you get? You can heal as much damage as you have healing potions, INSTANTANEOUSLY!!! What does this mean? On the brink of death, with no time to cast heal or vitalize? Simply pause the game, go to your inventory screen, and drink up!

You'll never die, as long as you have potions! So if you're having trouble staying alive and have lots of extra cash hanging around, be sure to stock up on those healing potions.

==

3. HOW TO CHEAT (or, The Best Way to be a Cheap Ass)

Cheat! The Summoner savegame file is a whopping 265KB (270,755 bytes).

With such a small size it is terribly easy to pinpoint several key locations to cheat by editing.

As Summoner is such a crappy game, I really doubt that anyone will have the drive to write an editor. Now you might say that I had the drive to write this FAQ, but FAQs are writing and writing is a great way of venting frustration, especially since you can be very articulate about it. Editors tend not to be so politically-inclined, unless the crazy programmer makes a ton of pop-up windows screaming how much he hates the game whenever you press the "Max Gold" button.

Alright, enough of that. Now, get your standard Hex editor and get to work. Here are the addresses and what they do. Oh, and if you don't know what a Hex editor is, don't bother. Sorry, I don't feel like giving simple hacking tutorials.

File: x:\blah\Summoner\savegame\sumoner?.sav (quicksave.sav)—265KB

OFFSET	PROPERTY	NOTES
000150ED	Gold	It's beside the letters INVT
000277E3	Joseph's Level	
000277E5	Joseph's XP	
0002781F	Joseph's Skill Points	
0002796B	Flece's Level	
0002796D	Flece's XP	
000279A7	Flece's Skill Points	
00027AF3	Rosalind's Level	
00027AF5	Rosalind's XP	
00027B2F	Rosalind's Skill Points	

My apologies, I didn't feel like looking for Jekhar's offsets because he's so boring. However, by doing some subtraction and addition you should be able to come up with them. Simply subtract the value of Joseph's offsets from Flece's offsets, and add the result to Rosalind's. That should give you Jekhar's offsets.

This should get you up and going and make you as rich as you need to be. Very useful for buying the Dreadblade from the merchant in the hills in Medeva!

By editing the skill points attribute, you can give yourself as many free skill points as you need.

By changing the XP, you can go to any level you want.

By changing your level back to 1, but keeping your current XP level, you will level up to your previous level instantly, gaining that much HP, AP, and Skill Points. Great trick! Only drawback is that you lose all skills you're not supposed to have at that level. The main use of this option really is to pump up your HP and AP. I was too lazy to look for HP and AP, so I just did it this way for simplicity's sake.

Anyway, this isn't supposed to be a cheating FAQ so I'll leave it at this. (Actually, I'm just too lazy to find other offsets like items, specific skills, etcetera).

—← End Evil Summoner FAQ →—

==

LEGALESE

This document is copyrighted by me, Mochan, on May 28, 2001.

That said, you can do whatever you want with this document. You can burn it, erase it, post it on SPAM lists, do whatever you want! You can even steal, plagiarize, or cut my name out and paste your name in if you want! Since this FAQ will generally be of ill-repute, I'm pretty sure no one would want to. I'm also pretty sure quite a number of you will be printing copies of this just to shred, immolate, and otherwise dismember it, giving physical, tangible release to your frustration at being unable to give me a good one for trashing your game.

In light of this, I am expecting a lot of flame mail to be sent my way. Ah, the sacrifices one must make for what he believes is true and just.

Anyone looking for an in-depth FAQ to this game probably likes it, right? Yet on the off-chance that you are one of those who, like me, played Summoner not because of its merits but rather for lack of anything better, then welcome aboard!

I hope you have a great time.

==

CREDITS

I don't think anyone will appreciate me naming them in the credits of this FAQ. I think they'd consider it more a black-listing than something to be proud of. So I won't mention anyone. Doesn't really matter, since I wrote this FAQ ground-up without help from anyone. As if anyone would want to help write this seditious material.

OMAKE!!! (or the fun part of this FAQ)

← WARNING !!! →
SPOILERS AHEAD—both for story
and the game. That is; I will
diss the game such that I will
"despoil" it. YOU DON'T NEED TO
READ THIS UNLESS YOU WANT TO.

SOME STUFF ABOUT SUMMONER

Summoner is short. Really short, for an RPG anyway. That's actually a good point, because making this pile of garbage any longer would have been sheer torture.

I managed to finish the game in 22 hours. I did so sporadically over a month, though. I had to mentally prepare myself to play this game every single time. If I didn't, I might have gone insane.

Anyway, it took me 22 hours, but that was taking my time with it, and ignoring sidequests. A good player should be able to finish the main storyline in 15 or so hours, if he went breakneck through it, making no mistakes. Doing all the sidequests would probably add an extra 5–10 hours of playtime.

If you play to level up your characters and do everything, you should finish in 35 or so hours.

Typical of an American-developed RPG, side-quests occupy a lot of game time, are stupid, non-sensical, and totally uninteresting. But these American developers just seem to LOVE side-quests and think it's the Holy Grail of RPGs. Whatever, if you ask me it's just a cheap way of adding length to a game, when actually writing a more interesting story and providing character interaction is too difficult.

Incidentally: Wakasashi—what the heck is a wakasashi? That's not what short swords were called. They were called wakizashi. And how come a "wakasashi" requires Heavy Arms 2, while a katana has no heavy arms requirement at all? Hen.

HYPER SPEED

Also, did you notice how fast the sundial goes? The sundial is the little thing in the middle of your status bar that you click on to pause the game. Sundials were used in ancient times to keep track of time by measuring the sun's shadow.

In Summoner, the sun dial finishes a complete cycle in about 7 seconds! That means that days in Summoner only last 7 seconds!!! I shudder at the thought of how fast the planet spins; that's even faster than Jupiter!

WHEN CONSOLE MEETS PC

Summoner is supposed to be a game, which combines PC and Console conventions when it comes to RPGs. This is evident in Summoner. The bad thing is, Volition probably meant to combine the best of both worlds. What they managed was actually the opposite: they managed to get virtually all the bad traits of PC RPGs and combined it with the bad traits of console RPGs. An RPG renaissance Summoner is not.

To be fair, Summoner does manage to get some good points from each convention. For instance, Summoner lets you save anywhere (but only outside of combat). Still, too many things have gone wrong with this game.

Perhaps the biggest thing I have to complain about, though, is the lackluster character interaction. RPGs tell stories, and stories are interesting if the characters are memorable through their actions and the way they interact with each other and the environment.

Sadly, in Summoner the interest level for me was not so high, because the characters were totally uninteresting. This is a shame because Summoner actually has a rather decent story plot. But even good plots are wasted if they are badly written; and in Summoner's case this is true. Proof of this is a failure to address a basic requirement of good writing: characters.

Characters in Summoner are all very unbelievable and lack depth. They do not manage to achieve the suspension of disbelief necessary to make the player feel that they are real, living people. Instead, they feel totally artificial and fake, as if they were reading their lines in front of an audience.

For instance, Jekhar, who allegedly hates Joseph's guts for destroying his entire life, is strangely civil upon meeting Joseph again in Lenelle. Sure, he puts on a show of saying he'll have Joseph's head on a pike if they meet outside Lenelle, but for all his apparent gruffness he suddenly stops to give Joseph directions when the summoner asks for Yago. Oh, how cordial you are, Vegeta!

Later on, Jekhar displays his massive asininity by acquiescing to his King to join Joseph and help him. This on its own is not yet unbelievable, especially as Jekhar makes a show of protest to his liege (unprecedented!), showing his distaste. Yet as soon as Jekhar joins Joseph you will never see Jekhar so much as complain in his stay in Joseph's party! No grudging campside discussions, no murderous glares as they travel to Ikaemos, nothing! It's as if they're all goody-goody joyous friends and nothing was ever wrong.

It's totally artificial and reeks of poor character interaction.

It's the same thing with all the characters—Joseph, Flece, Rosalind, and even the supporting characters like Qi Feng, Galliene, and so on. Joseph, for instance, is betrayed by Flece (I am not entirely sure how, though) and spends three miserable months without his hand in a stinking hell-hole.

And yet, when Flece springs him, Joseph is head over heels ready to forgive her! Sure, he makes a show of being coy, but in the end he just quietly comes over like a lovesick puppy and not ever again does he even brood or sneer at his malefactor. It's so FAKE!

Well, I think I've said enough dissident ideas about Summoner. Any more and I'll overstep the bounds of a FAQ and likely be censored. ^_^

On a lighter note, I think that the best part of Summoner Is the little Dungeons and Dragons skit you see at the end of the Credits screen. Yet, it's sad when the best part of the game is a little extra which the developers just threw in for laughs. Ah, Volition, how funny you are!

Have fun everyone!

Play and Ambiguity

Brian Sutton-Smith

Context

The Ambiguity of Play (*Harvard University Press, 1997*) *known also as* **The Rhetorics of Play**
*from which this essay is taken, is a deconstructive account of the play theories of the past 100
years. It demonstrates that there has been little universal science but rather a series of arguments favoring the views (the rhetorics) that play should be conceptualized as about Progress
(largely meaning cognition), or about Fate (games of chance); about Power (sports contests);
about Identity (festivals); about self or narcissim (peak experience). The book concludes with
the suggestion that what all of these rhetorics may have in common is their relative resonance
of adaptive variability.*

Speaking of Games

What Is Play?

Brian Sutton-Smith is a Professor Emeritus of the University of Pennsylvania. Born in New Zealand, he has spent his
life in play studies with an interdisciplinary emphasis on
play history, anthropology, folklore, psychology and education, with 50 books authored or edited and 350 scholarly
articles. He is currently engaged in a Darwinian, not Freudian, review of the role of emotions in play.

A nip is but a nip
And a boojum
Is but a buttercup.
after Lewis Carroll

We all play occasionally, and we all know what playing feels like. But when it comes to making theoretical statements about what play is, we fall into silliness. There is little agreement among us, and much ambiguity. Some of the most outstanding scholars of children's play have been concerned by this ambiguity. For example, classical scholar Mihail Spariosu (1989) calls play "amphibolous," which means it goes in two directions at once and is not clear. Victor Turner (1969), the anthropologist, calls play "liminal" or "liminoid," meaning that it occupies a threshold between reality and unreality, as if, for example, it were on the beach between the land and the sea. Geoffrey Bateson (1956), biologist, suggests that play is a paradox because it both is and is not what it appears to be. Animals at play bite each other playfully, knowing that the playful nip connotes a bite, but not what a bite connotes. In turn, Richard Schechner (1988), dramaturge, suggests that a playful nip is not only not a bite, it is also *not* not a bite. That is, it is a positive, the sum of two negatives. Which is again to say that the playful nip may not be a bite, but it is indeed what a bite means.

Kenneth Burke's works suggest that play is probably what he terms a "dramatistic negative," which means that for animals who do not have any way of saying "no," it is a way of indicating the negative through an affirmative action that is clearly not the same as that which it represents (thus, again, nipping rather than biting). He says that prior to the evolutionary emergence of words, the negative could be dramatized only by the presentation of stylized and gestural forms of the positive (Burke, 1966, p. 423). "The most irritating feature of play," says Robert Fagen (1981), leading animal play theorist, "is not the perceptual incoherence, as such, but rather that play taunts us with its inaccessibility. We feel that something is behind it all, but we do not know, or have forgotten how to see it."

If we seek greater definitional clarity by analyzing the meaning of ambiguity itself, following William Empson's classic *Seven Types of Ambiguity* (1955), then we can say that play involves all of his seven types, which are as follows, with the play examples in parentheses:

297

1. the ambiguity of reference (is that a pretend gun sound, or are you choking?);

2. the ambiguity of the referent (is that an object or a toy?);

3. the ambiguity of intent (do you mean it, or is it pretend?);

4. the ambiguity of sense (is this serious, or is it nonsense?);

5. the ambiguity of transition (you said you were only playing);

6. the ambiguity of contradiction (a man playing at being a woman);

7. the ambiguity of meaning (is it play or playfighting?).

And finally, as if all these paradoxes were not enough, Stephen Jay Gould, evolutionist, says that there are some human traits that are just side effects of more fundamental genetic functions and really deserve no functional explanation themselves. The quotation that heads this chapter, and those in the chapters that follow, would suggest that, if that is the case, there are nevertheless many interesting things about our so-called junk genes. The quotations at the beginning of each chapter also often bring up interesting rhetorics from much earlier times. Many authors use children's play as a metaphor for the ephemerality of life, for what quickly passes, or for what is innocent, infantile, or foolish. Others who are quoted render adult life as a very serious mortal game in which foul play is possible. The diversity of this metaphoric playfulness would seem to suggest that, whether junk or not, play takes on multiple forms in somber discourse.[1]

This chapter is a search for some of the more obvious possible reasons for the ambiguity, as well as an introduction to the particular focus of the volume as a whole: the ideological underpinnings of play theories, and what an understanding of them can contribute to clearing up these confusions. The ambiguity is most obvious, however, in the multiple forms of play and the diversity of the kinds of play scholarship they have instigated. Obviously the word *play* stands for a category of very diverse happenings, though the same could be said about most omnibus categories, such as, for example, religion, art, war, politics, and culture.

The Diversity of Play Forms and Experiences

The diversity of play is well illustrated by the varied kinds of play that are to be found within the larger menagerie of the "play" sphere. Almost anything can allow play to occur within its boundaries, as is illustrated, for example, by works on tourism as play (McCannell, 1976), television as play (Stephenson, 1967), day-dreaming as play (Caughey, 1984), sexual intimacy as play (Betcher, 1987), and even gossip as play (Spack, 1986). Travel can be a playful competition to see who can go to the most places or have the most authentic encounters. "Have you done London, the Eiffel Tower, Ayres Rock, Palmer Station, and Easter Island?" Watching television can be watching and identifying with other people at play, whether in fiction or in real life—and, after all, one can turn it off or on, which makes it like play and not like real life. Viewers can control their involvement just as if the "play" belongs to them, as in "playing" with the channels. Even the news, which is "live at five," is only an account from a studio with theatric backdrops. All of us carry dozens of characters around in our daydreams with whom we carry on imaginary encounters and conversations, none of which are real in the usual sense. Many of the characters in our heads are also people on television or in films, but most are everyday acquaintances. Sexual intimates are said to play with each other in innumerable ways, painting each other's bodies, eating food off of each other, playing hide the thimble with bodily crevices, communicating in public with their own esoteric vocabulary, and, in general, teasing and testing each other with playful impropriety. Gossip, by contrast, can be a playfully irreverent game of denigrating those who are not present.

A list of activities that are often said to be play forms or play experiences themselves is presented below. The terms illustrate the great diversity of play phenomena, although they do not indicate the even wider extension of informal play through all other spheres of life. This list itself awaits both adequate description and adequate play theorizing, because the items that it contains are often typically called by other names, such as entertainments, recreations, pastimes, and hobbies, as if it would be an embarrassment to admit that they can also be called play. Each of these states of mind, activities, or events could be described as I have described with travel and gossip, above. The boundaries between them are never as discrete as listing them here might imply. They are arranged in order from the mostly more private to the mostly more public.

Mind or subjective play: dreams, daydreams, fantasy, imagination, ruminations, reveries, Dungeons and Dragons, metaphors of play, and playing with metaphors.

Solitary play: hobbies, collections, (model trains, model airplanes, model power boats, stamps), writing to pen pals, building models, listening to records and compact discs, constructions, art projects, gardening, flower arranging, using computers, watching videos, reading and writing, novels, toys, travel, Civil War reenactments, music, pets, reading, woodworking, yoga, antiquing, flying, auto racing, collecting and rebuilding cars, sailing, diving, astrology, bicycling, handicrafts, photography, shopping, backpacking, fishing, needlework, quilting, bird watching, crosswords, and cooking.

Playful behaviors: playing tricks, playing around, playing for time, playing up to someone, playing a part, playing down to someone, playing upon words, making a play for someone, playing upon others as in tricking them, playing hob, putting something into play, bringing it into play, holding it in play, playing fair, playing by the rules, being played out, playing both ends against the middle, playing one's cards well, playing second fiddle.

Informal social play: joking, parties, cruising, travel, leisure, dancing, roller-skating, losing weight, dinner play, getting laid, potlucks, malls, hostessing, babysitting, Saturday night fun, rough and tumble, creative anachronism, amusement parks, intimacy, speech play (riddles, stories, gossip, jokes, nonsense), singles clubs, bars and taverns, magic, ham radio, restaurants, and the Internet.

Vicarious audience play: television, films, cartoons, concerts, fantasy-lands, spectator sports, theater, jazz, rock music, parades (Rose Bowl, mummers', Thanksgiving), beauty contests, stock-car racing, Renaissance festivals, national parks, comic books, folk festivals, museums, and virtual reality.

Performance play: playing the piano, playing music, being a play actor, playing the game for the game's sake, playing New York, playing the fishes, playing the horses, playing Iago, play voices, play gestures, playbills, playback, play by play, player piano, playgoing, playhouses, playlets.

Celebrations and festivals: birthdays, Christmas, Easter, Mother's Day, Halloween, gifting, banquets, roasts, weddings, carnivals, initiations, balls, Mardi Gras, Fastnacht, Odunde.

Contests (games and sports): athletics, gambling, casinos, horses, lotteries, pool, touch football, kite fighting, golf, parlor games, drinking, the Olympics, bullfights, cockfights, cricket, Buzkashi, poker, gamesmanship, strategy, physical skill, chance, animal contests, archery, arm wrestling, board games, card games, martial arts, gymnastics.

Risky or deep play: caving, hang gliding, kayaking, rafting, snowmobiling, orienteering, snowballing, and extreme games such as bungee jumping, windsurfing, sport climbing, skateboarding, mountain biking, kite skiing, street luge, ultrarunning, and sky jumping.

The Diversity of Players, Play Agencies, and Play Scenarios

The ambiguity of play, as well as lying in this great diversity of play forms, owes some of its force to the parallel diversity of the players. There are infant, preschool, childhood, adolescent, and adult players, all of whom play somewhat differently. There are male and female players. There are gamblers, gamesters, sports, and sports players, and there are playboys and play-girls, playfellows, playful people, playgoers, playwrights, playmakers, and playmates. There are performers who play music and act in plays and perhaps play when they paint, sing, or sculpt. There are dilettantes, harlequins, clowns, tricksters, comedians, and jesters who represent a kind of characterological summit of playfulness. There are even playful scholars, such as Paul Feyerabend (1995), Jacques Derrida (1980), and Mikhail Bakhtin (1981). Playful persons in literature and the arts are countless.

Then there is the diversity of multiple kinds of play equipment, such as balls, bats, goals, cards, checkers, roulettes, and toys. Practically anything can become an agency for some kind of play. The scenarios of play vary widely also, from playpens, playrooms, playhouses, and playgrounds to sports fields, circuses, parade grounds, and casinos. Again, while some playfulness is momentary, other kinds, with their attendant preparations, can last throughout a season (as in many festivals and team sports) and, in some cases, over periods of years, as in the World Cup and the Olympics. Play has temporal diversity as well as spatial diversity.

The Diversity of Play Scholarship

Although most people throughout history have taken for granted their own play, and in some places have not even had a word for it, since about 1800 in Western society, intellectuals of various kinds have talked more or less systematically and more or less scientifically about play, and have discovered that they have immense problems in conceptualizing it. Presumably this is in part because there are multiple kinds of play and multiple kinds of players, as described above. Different academic disciplines also have quite different play interests. Some study the body, some study behavior, some study thinking, some study groups or individuals, some study experience, some study language—and they all use the word *play* for these quite different things. Furthermore their play theories, which are the focus of this present work, rather than play itself, come to reflect these various diversities and make them even more variable.

301

For example, biologists, psychologists, educators, and sociologists tend to focus on how play is adaptive or contributes to growth, development, and socialization. Communication theorists tell us that play is a form of metacommunication far preceding language in evolution because it is also found in animals. Sociologists say that play is an imperial social system that is typically manipulated by those with power for their own benefit. Mathematicians focus on war games and games of chance, important in turn because of the data they supply about strategy and probability. Thermonuclear war games, it appears, can be either a hobby or deadly serious. Anthropologists pursue the relationships between ritual and play as these are found in customs and festivals, while folklorists add an interest in play and game traditions. Art and literature, by contrast, have a major focus on play as a spur to creativity. In some mythology scholarship, play is said to be the sphere of the gods, while in the physical sciences it is sometimes another name for the indeterminacy or chaos of basic matter. In psychiatry, play offers a way to diagnose and provide therapy for the inner conflicts of young and old patients alike. And in the leisure sciences, play is about qualities of personal experience, such as intrinsic motivation, fun, relaxation, escape, and so on. No discipline is, however, so homogeneous that all its members are funneled into only one such way of theorizing. Nevertheless the diversity exists, and it makes reconciliation difficult.

Finally there are the ambiguities that seem particularly problematic in Western society, such as why play is seen largely as what children do but not what adults do; why children play but adults only recreate; why play is said to be important for children's growth but is merely a diversion for adults. The most reviled form of play, gambling, is also the largest part of the national play budget. How can it be that such ecstatic adult play experiences, which preoccupy so much emotional time, are only diversions? And why do these adult play preoccupations, which seem like some vast cultural, even quasi-religious subconsciousness, require us to deny that this kind of play may have the same meaning for children?

The Rhetorical Solution

It is the intent of the present work to bring some coherence to the ambiguous field of play theory by suggesting that some of the chaos to be found there is due to the lack of clarity about the popular cultural rhetorics that underlie the various play theories and play terms. The word *rhetoric* is used here in its modern sense, as being a persuasive discourse, or an implicit narrative, wittingly or unwittingly adopted by members of a particular affiliation to persuade others of the veracity and worthwhileness of their beliefs. In a sense, whenever identification is made with a belief or a cause or a science or an ideology, that identification reveals itself by the words that are spoken about it, by the clothes and insignia worn to celebrate it, by the allegiances adopted to sustain it, and by the hard work and scholarly devotion to it, as well as by the theories that are woven within it (Burke, 1950). Authors seek to persuade us in innumerable ways that their choice and their direction of research or study is sound. These identifications of theirs, and their persuasiveness, implicit or otherwise, are the intellectual odor that is to be known here as their rhetoric. It needs to be stressed that what is to be talked about here as rhetoric, therefore, is not so much the substance of play or of its science or of its theories, but rather the way in which the underlying ideological values attributed to these matters are both subsumed by the theorists and presented persuasively to the rest of us. As the term is used here, the rhetorics of play express the way play is placed in context within broader value systems, which are assumed by the theorists of play rather than studied directly by them. Having said that, however, it must be admitted that it is still almost impossible to suppress the desire to ask the question: "Yes, all right, but what is play itself?"—an impulse that the reader needs to stifle for now, though it will not go untrifled with before this work is played out.

It follows that all the sciences, physical and social, whatever their empirical virtues, are presented here as being maintained by rhetorical means, whether these be seen optimistically, for example, as the "scientific attitude," or somewhat more cynically, as the way in which disciplines, through controlling a knowledge base, enhance their own political power (Foucault, 1973). In what follows, the rhetorics that are the focus of this work will be called popular ideological rhetorics, and where necessary, these will be distinguished from what are called scientific or scholarly rhetorics, as well as from disciplinary rhetorics and personal rhetorics. The popular rhetorics are large-scale cultural "ways of thought" in which most of us participate in one way or another, although some specific groups will be more strongly advocates for this or that particular rhetoric. The larger play rhetorics are part of the multiple broad symbolic systems—political, religious, social, and educational—through which we construct the meaning of the cultures in which we live. It should be made clear that I do not assume these value presuppositions to be necessarily in vain or negative, nor to be without considerable value to those committed to them. In fact, it is impossible to live without them. The issue is only whether, by becoming confused with our play theories, they set us in pursuit of false explanations or false grandiosity. One promise of such an analysis as I propose is that, by revealing these rhetorical underpinnings of the apparently diverse theoretical approaches to play, there is the possibility of bridging them within some more unifying discourse. *The Recovery of Rhetoric* (Roberts and Good, 1993) offers much optimism for the possibilities of a more genuinely interdisciplinary organization of any subject matter, not excluding that of play. However, opinion has to be reserved on the integrating promise of rhetorical analysis until there is an examination of the present popular rhetorics specific to play and their interaction with the scholarly studies that have arisen around them. It is just as possible that the rhetorics, when explicated, will be revealed to be themselves a deceptive gloss over other, far more fundamental cultural disagreements. For example, play's supposed frivolity may itself be a mask for play's use in more widespread systems for denigrating the play of other groups, as has been done characteristically throughout history by those of higher status against the recreations of those of lower status (Armitage, 1977).

Seven Rhetorics

The seven rhetorics to be presented in this work are characterized as follows.

The rhetoric of play as progress, usually applied to children's play, is the advocacy of the notion that animals and children, but not adults, adapt and develop through their play. This belief in play as progress is something that most Westerners cherish, but its relevance to play has been more often assumed than demonstrated. Most educators over the past two hundred years seem to have so needed to represent playful imitation as a form of children's socialization and moral, social, and cognitive growth that they have seen play as being primarily about development rather than enjoyment.

The rhetoric of play as fate is usually applied to gambling and games of chance, and it contrasts totally with the prior rhetoric. It is probably the oldest of all of the rhetorics, resting as it does on the belief that human lives and play are controlled by destiny, by the gods, by atoms or neurons, or by luck, but very little by ourselves, except perhaps through the skillful use of magic or astrology. This rhetoric enjoys only an underground advocacy in the modern world. It is no longer a widespread and conscious value system among the intellectual elites, though it remains popular among lower socioeconomic groups. It contrasts most strongly also with those modern theories of leisure that argue that the distinguishing feature of play is that it is an exercise of free choice.

The rhetoric of play as power, usually applied to sports, athletics, and contests, is—like fate, community identity, and frivolity—a rhetoric of ancient hue. These four all predate modern times and advocate collectively held community values rather than individual experiences. Recently these ancient rhetorics have been given much less philosophical attention than the modern three, progress, the imaginary, and the self, though they are more deep seated as cultural ideologies. The rhetoric of play as power is about the use of play as the representation of conflict and as a way to fortify the status of those who control the play or are its heroes. This rhetoric is as ancient as warfare and patriarchy. It is an anathema to many modern progress- and leisure-oriented play theorists.

The rhetoric of play as identity, usually applied to traditional and community celebrations and festivals, occurs when the play tradition is seen as a means of confirming, maintaining, or advancing the power and identity of the community of players. Because so much twentieth-century attention has been given to children's play as a form of progress, I have found it valuable to present a more balanced rhetorical advocacy of the character of their play from the point of view of these other rhetorics, power and fantasy.

The rhetoric of play as the imaginary, usually applied to playful improvisation of all kinds in literature and elsewhere, idealizes the imagination, flexibility, and creativity of the animal and human play worlds. This rhetoric is sustained by modern positive attitudes toward creativity and innovation. The rhetoric of progress, the rhetoric of the self, and the rhetoric of the imaginary constitute the modern set of rhetorics, with a history largely elaborated ideologically only in the past two hundred years.

The rhetoric of the self is usually applied to solitary activities like hobbies or high-risk phenomena like bungee jumping, but it need not be so proscribed. These are forms of play in which play is idealized by attention to the desirable experiences of the players—their fun, their relaxation, their escape—and the intrinsic or the aesthetic satisfactions of the play performances. Here the central advocacies of the secular and consumerist manner of modern life invade the interpretations of play and are questioned because of their twentieth-century relativity.

The rhetoric of play as frivolous is usually applied to the activities of the idle or the foolish. But in modern times, it inverts the classic "work ethic" view of play, against which all the other rhetorics exist as rhetorics of rebuttal. But frivolity, as used here, is not just the puritanic negative, it is also a term to be applied more to historical trickster figures and fools, who were once the central and carnivalesque persons who enacted playful protest against the orders of the ordained world. This chapter is placed last in this work because of its largely reflexive character, as commentary on all the other rhetorics. Historically frivolity belongs with the ancient set that includes fate, power, and identity.

I should note that although each of these rhetorics is discussed in the singular, there are multiple variants within each category, so that it might be more proper to speak of the plural *rhetorics* throughout. To repeat, each is called a rhetoric because its ideological values are something that the holders like to persuade others to believe in and to live by. Much of the time such values do not even reach a level of conscious awareness. People simply take it for granted, for example, that children develop as a result of their playing; or that sports are a part of the way in which different states and nations compete with each other; or that festivals are a way in which groups are bonded together; or that play is a desirable modern form of creativity or personal choice; or that, contrary to all of these, play is a waste of time. By seeing how the play descriptions and play theories can be tied in with such broad patterns of ideological value, one has greater hope of coming to understand the general character of play theory, which is the ultimate objective here.

A Scale of Rhetorics

These seven play rhetorics can be illuminated by contrasting them, on the one hand, with rhetorics that are broader than they are, and on the other, with rhetorics that are narrower. Of the broader kind are those that derive from beliefs about religion, politics, social welfare, crime, and morality—that is, from all the matters that priests, politicians and salespersons constantly harangue folks about. These are the rhetorics that fill the airwaves of daily life, in churches, in schools, and in the community. People cannot live without them, even if they often can't stand some of them. They constitute the incessant discourse about who we are and how we should live. The group of rhetorics for the particular subject matter play are of the same broad kind, being about progress and power, but they are more limited in the present usage because they are applied only to the specific subject of play theories. The rhetorics of science are generally of a narrower and more explicit kind. Science, after all, has its own epistemological rhetorics of reliability, validity, and prediction. Scholarship in general has its required consistency, coherence, and authenticity. All of these scientific and scholarly tenets are also rhetorics, because they assume and propagate the view that there is a knowable world, or a knowable text, and then, acting as if that assumption is real (a hypothetical fiction), proceed to their methodological undertakings. As Pepper (1961) has shown, even philosophical scholars must make arbitrary distinctions about which part of the world they seek to study, some focusing on the structures or forms of reality, some on the causes of reality and behavior, others on the changing historical context in which these things occur, and yet others on the kinds of integration or organicism that they can discover. What is added here to any such "scientific" (play) rhetorics is that the subject-matter rhetorics (those seven listed above) may be able to suggest why the scientific rhetorics take the direction they do—and also suggest why that direction may often have limitations deriving not so much from the science or scholarship, but from the presuppositions of the value systems in which the science is embedded. Parenthetically, the present focus on such presuppositions is not meant to suggest that "objective" social science is without value, or that "objectivity" is not fruitful within the ideological frames being presented. My aim here is much more modest, it seeks only for the sources of ambiguity in play rhetoric.

In the past several decades the claims of scholarship or science for sheer objectivity have been frequently challenged. The limitations of the claims for scholarly literature's independence from propaganda are challenged by Burke in such works as *The Rhetoric of Motives* (1950) and *Language as Symbolic Action* (1966). The same orientation is made a criticism of general scientific objectivity by Kuhn's now famous *The Structure of Scientific Revolutions* (1970), in which he points out the role played by human motivation in the development of science, particularly in respect to the way in which accepted theories often are not displaced until a new generation of thinkers finds them irrelevant. Science is not as cumulative or as autonomously objective in the growth of its knowledge as has often been supposed. But the roots of the present enterprise can be found in the work of many other scholars as well, from Wittgenstein's emphasis on the meaning of language relying on its context of usage, for example, to Foucault's stricture that knowledge is always an exercise of power, never merely information. Those who create information are those who decide how others shall think about their lives. Leading play theorists who quite explicitly see themselves talking about the rhetorics of play in order to talk about play theory at all include Helen Schwartzman (1978), Margaret Duncan (1988), and Mihail Spariosu (1989).

Between the historically based subject-matter rhetorics that will be presented here (progress, power, and so on) and the most general scientific epistemological rhetorics, which involve, for example, the metaphysical assumptions underlying the expectancy of causal regularities in nature, a host of other disciplinary rhetorics also play their part in the amalgam that is social science. Elsewhere, for example, I have described rhetorics that are applied to childhood in modern life, with children variously being seen as: the child of god, the child as the future, the predictable child, the imaginary child, the child as consumer, and the gender androgynous child (Sutton-Smith, 1994).

But the physical scientists are not immune to such rhetorics either, and there are disputes about how the public should interpret the personality of their science in the culture. These can be called questions about the ontological rhetorics of the scientists. They may be seen as "objective" or "cautious," but at times they are also seen as rebels, subversives, Frankensteins, relentless creatures of reason, conquerors of nature, empirical reductionists, mathematical formalists, artists, philosophers, secular saints, or irresponsible devils. And as Dyson (1995) shows, these kinds of rhetorics, when personal to the scientists, make an enormous difference in the direction of their inquiries. One might conclude that all scholars are creatures of their personal disposition, which may become a motivating rhetoric for them, and they are also, historically, inheritors of larger ideological or cultural patterns that affect their scholarship. They are the legatees as well of the rhetorics of disciplinary assumptions and disciplinary methodologies.

What needs most emphasis at this initial point is that rhetorical involvement at some or all of these levels is inescapable. Scholarly objectivity always exists within such contexts as broad cultural rhetorics (political, religious, moral), disciplinary rhetorics (sciences, humanities, arts), epistemological rhetorics (validity, reliability, causalism, formism), subject-matter rhetorics (in the present case, play rhetorics), general ontological rhetorics (objectivity, scientific caution), and personal rhetorics (idiosyncratic dispositions).

Within the subject of the present inquiry (play), the major emphasis is on the way in which the theories within this scholarly domain are underlain by the seven rhetorics outlined above. As William Kessen, a leading scholar of such reflexive self-consciousness in developmental psychology, states that we should

> recognize that, deeply carved into our professional intention is a desire to change the lives of our readers, to have them believe something that we believe. In grand nineteenth-century style, we can call this the Unspoken Intention that is hidden by the wonderful devices all of us have learned to speak with the voice of certain authority....

Our work is packed with our values, our intentions for our small part of the world: a great deal would be gained by a critical analysis and display of those intentions, [but] the governing principle for evidence in both psychology and history [is that] we do not seek proofs; we do not attempt demonstrations. We all want to tell plausible stories. (1993, p. 229)

Validating the Existence of the Seven Rhetorics

Though it is not difficult to assert in a general way that the science of play is underlain by these seven subject-matter narratives, or rhetorics, the assertion itself has fairly vague "scientific" or "scholarly" cogency without some criteria of coherence that can be used to affirm their presence. The criteria I use to frame the rhetorical contentions are as follows:

1. That the assumed seven rhetorics can be shown to have a clear basis in well known cultural attitudes of a contemporary or historical kind. This historical context, although not dealt with in great detail here, is the most basic source of their cultural construction (Glassie, 1982).

2. That the rhetorics have their own specific groups of advocates, a necessary precondition if these phenomena are to be seen as not just narratives but also rhetorics of persuasion.

3. That each rhetoric applies primarily to a distinct kind of play or playfulness. If this is so, it suggests some kind of epistemological affinity between the rhetorics and their ludic subject matter. They are not accidentally correlated.

4. That each rhetoric applies primarily to distinct kinds of players.

5. That there is an affinity between the rhetoric and particular scholarly or scientific disciplines, and between particular play theories and play theorists.

6. That (following criteria 2 through 5), there is a "matching" interplay between the nature of the rhetorical assertions and the character of the forms of play to which they are applied. Thus a rhetoric of progress might find partial substantiation in the finding that some kinds of skill during play can take "progressive" forms. In addition it may be possible to show that the rhetoric itself is often the way in which the play passes into the culture, because the play practice is thus justified ideologically. In this way, the two, play and rhetoric, have an impact on each other. The recommendation that the interplay between play and nonplay should be more carefully studied was made by the famous play theorist

Erik Erikson in his book *Toys and Reasons* (1977). But this recommendation is also the constant beguilement of all those who study the interrelationships between play and nonplay to try to puzzle out how they reciprocally affect each other (Abrahams, 1977).

7. That the group that maintains the rhetoric benefits by the exercise of hegemony over the players, over their competitors, or over those who are excluded from the play. This postulate makes explicit why the present approach to play centers on the rhetorics of the theorists rather than, more simply, on the narratives they tell themselves. Rhetorics are narratives that have the intent to persuade because there is some kind of gain for those who are successful in their persuasion. Telling plausible stories would not be enough.

8. That the way in which the scholarly disciplines define the subject matter of play may or may not make sense in terms of the rhetorics that are being proposed in this work. This is open to investigation. Three kinds of play definitions will be considered where they are available:

(a) The definitions by players of their own *play experiences* and functions. What do the players reckon to be the character of and the reasons for their own participation? Obviously there is not much research to be referred to here, although there is a considerable amount of anecdotal opinion to be cited. It is useful to discover that there can be—and often is—very little relationship between the players' own play definitions and those of the theorists.

(b) The definitions by theorists of *intrinsic play functions*. These are definitions drawn from the research literature, or new ones arising out of the present analysis, that are supposed to account scientifically for the play's functioning by pointing to the players' game-related motives for playing.

(c) The definitions by the theorists of *extrinsic play functions*, which account for the forms of play in terms of functions they are supposed to serve in the larger culture.

It is with the two last types of definitions (b and c) that this study is preoccupied. It is quite possible, for example, for players to have one rhetoric while "experts" have another. But it is also possible for experts to use one rhetoric when talking about the players' responses and another rhetoric when discussing theoretically what they think is the underlying function of the forms of play. A description of the players' enjoyments, after all, need not be the same as an account of the supposed adaptive functions of those enjoyments. More important, finding the relationship between accounts of play in terms of intrinsic and extrinsic functions is yet another way of talking about the interplay of play and nonplay. There is promise here of some clarification of the causalities of play and life.

As a final point of each chapter, it will be necessary to return to the issue of play's ambiguity, with which this work begins. My aim is to establish to what extent ambiguity is an outcome of the seven rhetorics, or if it must instead be attributed to the character of play itself.

Note

1. Play-related quotations here and throughout the rest of this work are, for the most part, from *Bartlett's Familiar Quotations*, 16th ed. (Boston: Little, Brown, 1992) Playful quotes, noted as "after" are of fictional status. Dr. Frech is frivolous.

Bibliography

Abrahams, R. D. 1977. *Towards an enactment-centered theory of folklore.* American Association for the Advancement of Science. Boulder, Colo.: Westview Press, 19–20.

Armitage, J. 1977 *Man at play.* London: Frederic Warne.

Bakhtin, M. M. 1981. *The dialogic imagination.* Austin: University of Texas Press.

Bateson, G. 1956. The message, "This is play." In *Group processes,* ed. B. Shaffner. New York: Josiah Macy.

Burke, K. 1950. *The rhetoric of motives.* New York: Prentice Hall.

_____. 1996. Language as symbolic action. Berkeley: University of California Press.

Caughey, J. 1984. *Imaginary source worlds: A cultural approach.* Lincoln: University of Nebraska Press.

Derrida, J. 1980. *The archeology of the frivolous.* Lincoln: University of Nebraska Press.

Duncan, M. 1988. Play discourse and the rhetorical turn: A semiological analysis of *Homo Ludens. Play and Culture,* 1(1):28–42.

Dyson, F. 1995. The scientist as rebel. *The New York Review of Books* 42(9):31–33.

Empson, W. 1955. *Seven types of ambiguity.* New York: Meridian Books.

Erikson, E. 1977. *Toys and reasons.* New York: Norton.

Fagen, R. 1981. *Animal play behavior.* New York: Oxford University Press.

Feyerabend, P. 1995. *Killing time.* Chicago: University of Chicago Press.

_____. 1973. Madness and civilization. New York: Vintage.

Glassie, H. 1982. *Passing time in Ballymenone.* Philadelphia: University of Pennsylvania Press.

Kessen, W. 1993. A developmentalist's reflections. In *Children in time and place*, ed. G. H. Elder et al. New York: Cambridge University Press, 226–229.

Kuhn, T. S. 1970. *The structure of scientific revolutions.* Chicago: University of Chicago Press.

MacCannell, Dean. 1976. *The tourist: A new theory of the leisure class.* New York: Schocken Books.

Pepper, S. 1961. *World hypotheses.* Berkeley: University of California Press.

Roberts, R. H., and Good, J. M. M. 1993. *The recovery of rhetoric.* Charlottesville: University Press of Virginia.

Schechner, R. 1988. Playing. *Play and Culture* 1 (1):3–27.

Schwartzman, H. B. 1978. *Transformations: The anthropology of children's play.* New York: Plenum.

Spack, P. 1986. *Gossip.* Chicago: University of Chicago Press.

Spariosu, M. 1989. *Dionysus reborn.* Ithaca, N.Y.: Cornell University Press.

Stephenson, W. 1967. *The play theory of mass communication.* Chicago: University of Chicago Press.

Sutton-Smith, B. 1994. Paradigms of intervention. In *Play and intervention,* ed. J. Hellendorn et al. Albany: State University of New York Press.

Turner, V. 1969. *The ritual process.* New York: Aldine.

A Theory of Play and Fantasy

Gregory Bateson

Context

*"A Theory of Play and Fantasy" comes from the volume **Steps to an Ecology of Mind**, a collection of Bateson's essays and writings. Like many of his works, "A Theory of Play and Fantasy" crosses and recrosses many disciplines, including mathematics, philosophy, communications, and psychology.*

Player and Character

What Is Play?

Gregory Bateson (1904–1980) worked in the fields of both anthropology and systems theory and produced a body of work that has had a significant impact on how we think today. Much of his theoretical work centered on the synthesis of what he referred to as "an ecology of mind," developed over years of collaboration with anthropologist Margaret Mead. A brilliant and eclectic scholar, his work crosses a dizzying array of fields, from biology and pathology to epistemology and aesthetics.

This research was planned and started with an hypothesis to guide our investigations, the task of the investigators being to collect relevant observational data and, in the process, to amplify and modify the hypothesis.

The hypothesis will here be described as it has grown in our thinking.

Earlier fundamental work of Whitehead, Russell,[1] Wittgenstein,[2] Carnap,[3] Whorf,[4] etc., as well as my own attempt[5] to use this earlier thinking as an epistemological base for psychiatric theory, led to a series of generalizations:

(1) That human verbal communication can operate and always does operate at many contrasting levels of abstraction. These range in two directions from the seemingly simple denotative level ("The cat is on the mat"). One range or set of these more abstract levels includes those explicit or implicit messages where the subject of discourse is the language. We will call these metalinguistic (for example, "The verbal sound 'cat' stands for any member of such and such class of objects," or "The word, 'cat,' has no fur and cannot scratch"). The other set of levels of abstraction we will call metacommunicative (e.g., "My telling you where to find the cat was friendly," or, "This is play"). In these the subject of discourse is the relationship between the speakers.

It will be noted that the vast majority of both metalinguistic and metacommunicative messages remain implicit; and also that, especially in the psychiatric interview, there occurs a further class of implicit messages about how metacommunicative messages of friendship and hostility are to be interpreted.

(2) If we speculate about the evolution of communication, it is evident that a very important stage in this evolution occurs when the organism gradually ceases to respond quite "automatically" to the mood-signs of another and becomes able to recognize the sign as a signal, that is, to recognize that the other individual's and its own signals are only signals, which can be trusted, distrusted, falsified, denied, amplified, corrected, and so forth.

Clearly this realization that signals are signals is by no means complete even among the human species. We all too often respond automatically to newspaper headlines as though these stimuli were direct object-indications of events in our environment instead of signals concocted and transmitted by creatures as complexly motivated as ourselves. The nonhuman mammal is automatically excited by the sexual odor of another; and rightly so, inasmuch as the secretion of that sign is an "involuntary" mood-sign; i.e., an outwardly perceptible event which is a part of the physiological process which we have called a mood. In the human species a more complex state of affairs begins to be the rule. Deodorants mask the involuntary olfactory signs, and in their place the cosmetic industry provides the individual with perfumes which are not involuntary signs but voluntary signals, recognizable as such. Many a man has been thrown off balance by a whiff of perfume, and if we are to believe the advertisers, it seems that these signals, voluntarily worn, have sometimes an automatic and autosuggestive effect even upon the voluntary wearer.

Be that as it may, this brief digression will serve to illustrate a stage of evolution— the drama precipitated when organisms, having eaten of the fruit of the Tree of Knowledge, discover that their signals are signals. Not only the characteristically human invention of language can then follow, but also all the complexities of empathy, identification, projection, and so on. And with these comes the possibility of communicating at the multiplicity of levels of abstraction mentioned above.

(3) The first definite step in the formulation of the hypothesis guiding this research occurred in January, 1952, when I went to the Fleishhacker Zoo in San Francisco to look for behavioral criteria which would indicate whether any given organism is or is not able to recognize that the signs emitted by itself and other members of the species are signals. In theory, I had thought out what such criteria might look like—that the occurrence of metacommunicative signs (or signals) in the stream of interaction between the animals would indicate that the animals have at least some awareness (conscious or unconscious) that the signs about which they metacommunicate are signals.

I knew, of course, that there was no likelihood of finding denotative messages among nonhuman mammals, but I was still not aware that the animal data would require an almost total revision of my thinking. What I encountered at the zoo was a phenomenon well known to everybody: I saw two young monkeys *playing, i.e.,* engaged in an interactive sequence of which the unit actions or signals were similar to but not the same as those of combat. It was evident, even to the human observer, that the sequence as a whole was not combat, and evident to the human observer that to the participant monkeys this was "not combat."

Now, this phenomenon, play, could only occur if the participant organisms were capable of some degree of metacommunication, *i.e.,* of exchanging signals which would carry the message "This is play."

(4) The next step was the examination of the message "This is play," and the realization that this message contains those elements which necessarily generate a paradox of the Russellian or Epimenides type—a negative statement containing an implicit negative metastatement. Expanded, the statement "This is play" looks something like this: "These actions in which we now engage do not denote what those actions *for which they stand* would denote."

We now ask about the italicized words, *"for which they stand."* We say the word "cat" stands for any member of a certain class. That is, the phrase "stands for" is a near synonym of "denotes." If we now substitute "which they denote" for the words "for which they stand" in the expanded definition of play, the result is: "These actions, in which we now engage, do not denote what would be denoted by those actions which these actions denote." The playful nip denotes the bite, but it does not denote what would be denoted by the bite.

According to the Theory of Logical Types such a message is of course inadmissable, because the word "denote" is being used in two degrees of abstraction, and these two uses are treated as synonymous. But all that we learn from such a criticism is that it would be bad natural history to expect the mental processes and communicative habits of mammals to conform to the logician's ideal. Indeed, if human thought and communication always conformed to the ideal, Russell would not—in fact could not—have formulated the ideal.

(5) A related problem in the evolution of communication concerns the origin of what Korzybski[6] has called the map-territory relation: the fact that a message, of whatever kind, does not consist of those objects which it denotes ("The word 'cat' cannot scratch us"). Rather, language bears to the objects which it denotes a relationship comparable to that which a map bears to a territory. Denotative communication as it occurs at the human level is only possible after the evolution of a complex set of metalinguistic (but not verbalized)[7] rules which govern how words and sentences shall be related to objects and events. It is therefore appropriate to look for the evolution of such metalinguistic and/or metacommunicative rules at a prehuman and preverbal level.

It appears from what is said above that play is a phenomenon in which the actions of "play" are related to, or denote, other actions of "not play." We therefore meet in play with an instance of signals standing for other events, and it appears, therefore, that the evolution of play may have been an important step in the evolution of communication.

(6) *Threat* is another phenomenon which resembles play in that actions denote, but are different from, other actions. The clenched fist of threat is different from the punch, but

it refers to a possible future (but at present nonexistent) punch. And threat also is commonly recognizable among nonhuman mammals. Indeed it has lately been argued that a great part of what appears to be combat among members of a single species is rather to be regarded as threat (Tinbergen,[8] Lorenz[9]).

(7) Histrionic behavior and deceit are other examples of the primitive occurrence of map-territory differentiation. And there is evidence that dramatization occurs among birds: a jackdaw may imitate her own mood-signs (Lorenz[10]), and deceit has been observed among howler monkeys (Carpenter[11]).

(8) We might expect threat, play, and histrionics to be three independent phenomena all contributing to the evolution of the discrimination between map and territory. But it seems that this would be wrong, at least so far as mammalian communication is concerned. Very brief analysis of childhood behavior shows that such combinations as histrionic play, bluff, playful threat, teasing play in response to threat, histrionic threat, and so on form together a single total complex of phenomena. And such adult phenomena as gambling and playing with risk have their roots in the combination of threat and play. It is evident also that not only threat but the reciprocal of threat—the behavior of the threatened individual—are a part of this complex. It is probable that not only histrionics but also spectatorship should be included within this field. It is also appropriate to mention self-pity.

(9) A further extension of this thinking leads us to include ritual within this general field in which the discrimination is drawn, but not completely, between denotative action and that which is to be denoted. Anthropological studies of peace-making ceremonies, to cite only one example, support this conclusion.

In the Andaman Islands, peace is concluded after each side has been given ceremonial freedom to strike the other. This example, however, also illustrates the labile nature of the frame "This is play," or "This is ritual." The discrimination between map and territory is always liable to break down, and the ritual blows of peace-making are always liable to be mistaken for the "real" blows of combat. In this event, the peace-making ceremony becomes a battle (Radcliffe-Brown[12]).

(10) But this leads us to the recognition of a more complex form of play; the game which is constructed not upon the premise "This is play" but rather around the question "Is this play?" And this type of interaction also has its ritual forms, *e.g.,* in the hazing of initiation.

(11) Paradox is doubly present in the signals which are exchanged within the context of play, fantasy, threat, etc. Not only does the playful nip not denote what would be denoted by the bite for which it stands, but, in addition, the bite itself is fictional. Not only do the playing animals not quite mean what they are saying but, also, they are usually communicating about something which does not exist. At the human level, this leads to a vast variety of complications and inversions in the fields of play, fantasy, and art. Conjurers and painters of the *trompe l'oeil* school concentrate upon acquiring a virtuosity whose only reward is reached after the viewer detects that he has been deceived and is forced to smile or marvel at the skill of the deceiver. Hollywood film-makers spend millions of dollars to increase the realism of a shadow. Other artists, perhaps more realistically, insist that art be nonrepresentational; and poker players achieve a strange addictive realism by equating the chips for which they play with dollars. They still insist, however, that the loser accept his loss as part of the game.

Finally, in the dim region where art, magic, and religion meet and overlap, human beings have evolved the "metaphor that is meant," the flag which men will die to save, and the sacrament that is felt to be more than "an outward and visible sign, given unto us." Here we can recognize an attempt to deny the difference between map and territory, and to get back to the absolute innocence of communication by means of pure mood-signs.

(12) We face then two peculiarities of play: *(a)* that the messages or signals exchanged in play are in a certain sense untrue or not meant; and *(b)* that that which is denoted by these signals is nonexistent. These two peculiarities sometimes combine strangely to reverse a conclusion reached above. It was stated (4) that the playful nip denotes the bite, but does not denote that which would be denoted by the bite. But there are other instances where an opposite phenomenon occurs. A man experiences the full intensity of subjective terror when a spear is flung at him out of the 3D screen or when he falls headlong from some peak created in his own mind in the intensity of nightmare. At the moment of terror there was no questioning of "reality," but still there was no spear in the movie house and no cliff in the bedroom. The images did not denote that which they seemed to denote, but these same images did really evoke that terror which would have been evoked by a real spear or a real precipice. By a similar trick of self-contradiction, the film-makers of Hollywood are free to offer to a puritanical public a vast range of pseudosexual fantasy which otherwise would not be tolerated. In *David and Bathsheba*, Bathsheba can be a Troilistic link between David and Uriah. And in *Hans Christian Andersen*, the hero starts out accompanied by a boy. He tries to get a woman, but when he is defeated in

this attempt, he returns to the boy. In all of this, there is, of course, no homosexuality, but the choice of these symbolisms is associated in these fantasies with certain characteristic ideas, *e.g.,* about the hopelessness of the heterosexual masculine position when faced with certain sorts of women or with certain sorts of male authority. In sum, the pseudohomosexuality of the fantasy does not stand for any real homosexuality, but does stand for and express attitudes which might accompany a real homosexuality or feed its etiological roots. The symbols do not denote homosexuality, but do denote ideas for which homosexuality is an appropriate symbol. Evidently it is necessary to re-examine the precise semantic validity of the interpretations which the psychiatrist offers to a patient, and, as preliminary to this analysis, it will be necessary to examine the nature of the frame in which these interpretations are offered.

(13) What has previously been said about play can be used as an introductory example for the discussion of frames and contexts. In sum, it is our hypothesis that the message "This

> **All statements within this frame are untrue.**
>
> **I love you.**
>
> **I hate you.**

is play" establishes a paradoxical frame comparable to Epimenides' paradox. This frame may be diagrammed thus:

The first statement within this frame is a self-contradictory proposition about itself. If this first statement is true, then it must be false. If it be false, then it must be true. But this first statement carries with it all the other statements in the frame. So, if the first statement be true, then all the others must be false; and vice versa, if the first statement be untrue then all the others must be true.

(14) The logically minded will notice a *non-sequitur.* It could be urged that even if the first statement is false, there remains a logical possibility that some of the other statements in the frame are untrue. It is, however, a characteristic of unconscious or "primary-process" thinking that the thinker is unable to discriminate between "some" and "all," and unable to discriminate between "not all" and "none." It seems that the achievement of these discriminations is performed by higher or more conscious mental processes which serve in the nonpsychotic individual to correct the black-and-white thinking of the lower levels. We assume, and this seems to be an orthodox assumption, that primary process is continually

operating, and that the psychological validity of the paradoxical play frame depends upon this part of the mind.

(15) But, conversely, while it is necessary to invoke the primary process as an explanatory principle in order to delete the notion of "some" from between "all" and "none," this does not mean that play is simply a primary-process phenomenon. The discrimination between "play" and "nonplay," like the discrimination between fantasy and nonfantasy, is certainly a function of secondary process, or "ego." Within the dream the dreamer is usually unaware that he is dreaming, and within "play" he must often be reminded that "This is play."

Similarly, within dream or fantasy the dreamer does not operate with the concept "untrue." He operates with all sorts of statements but with a curious inability to achieve metastatements. He cannot, unless close to waking, dream a statement referring to (*i.e.*, framing) his dream.

It therefore follows that the play frame as here used as an explanatory principle implies a special combination of primary and secondary processes. This, however, is related to what was said earlier, when it was argued that play marks a step forward in the evolution of communication—the crucial step in the discovery of map-territory relations. In primary process, map and territory are equated; in secondary process, they can be discriminated. In play, they are both equated and discriminated.

(16) Another logical anomaly in this system must be mentioned: that the relationship between two propositions which is commonly described by the word "premise" has become intransitive. In general, all asymmetrical relationships are transitive. The relationship "greater than" is typical in this respect; it is conventional to argue that if A is greater than B, and B is greater than C, then A is greater than C. But in psychological processes the transitivity of asymmetrical relations is not observed. The proposition P may be a premise for Q; Q may be a premise for R; and R may be a premise for P. Specifically, in the system which we are considering, the circle is still more contracted. The message, "All statements within this frame are untrue" is itself to be taken as a premise in evaluating its own truth or untruth. (Cf. the intransitivity of psychological preference discussed by McCulloch.[13] The paradigm for all paradoxes of this general type is Russell's[14] "class of classes which are not members of themselves." Here Russell demonstrates that paradox is generated by treating the relationship, "is a member of," as an intransitive.) With this caveat, that the "premise" relation in psychology is likely to be intransitive, we shall use the word "premise" to denote a dependency of one idea or message

upon another comparable to the dependency of one proposition upon another which is referred to in logic by saying that the proposition P is a premise for Q.

(17) All this, however, leaves unclear what is meant by "frame" and the related notion of "context." To clarify these, it is necessary to insist first that these are psychological concepts. We use two sorts of analogy to discuss these notions: the physical analogy of the picture frame and the more abstract, but still not psychological, analogy of the mathematical set. In set theory the mathematicians have developed axioms and theorems to discuss with rigor the logical implications of membership in overlapping categories or "sets." The relationships between sets are commonly illustrated by diagrams in which the items or members of a larger universe are represented by dots, and the smaller sets are delimited by imaginary lines enclosing the members of each set. Such diagrams then illustrate a topological approach to the logic of classification. The first step in defining a psychological frame might be to say that it is (or delimits) a class or set of messages (or meaningful actions). The play of two individuals on a certain occasion would then be defined as the set of all messages exchanged by them within a limited period of time and modified by the paradoxical premise system which we have described. In a set-theoretical diagram these messages might be represented by dots, and the "set" enclosed by a line which would separate these from other dots representing non-play messages. The mathematical analogy breaks down, however, because the psychological frame is not satisfactorily represented by an imaginary line. We assume that the psychological frame has some degree of real existence. In many instances, the frame is consciously recognized and even represented in vocabulary ("play," "movie," "interview," "job," "language," etc.). In other cases, there may be no explicit verbal reference to the frame, and the subject may have no consciousness of it. The analyst, however, finds that his own thinking is simplified if he uses the notion of an unconscious frame as an explanatory principle; usually he goes further than this and infers its existence in the subject's unconscious.

But while the analogy of the mathematical set is perhaps over abstract, the analogy of the picture frame is excessively concrete. The psychological concept which we are trying to define is neither physical nor logical. Rather, the actual physical frame is, we believe, added by human beings to physical pictures because these human beings operate more easily in a universe in which some of their psychological characteristics are externalized. It is these characteristics which we are trying to discuss, using the externalization as an illustrative device.

(18) The common functions and uses of psychological frames may now be listed and

illustrated by reference to the analogies whose limitations have been indicated in the previous paragraph:

(a) Psychological frames are exclusive, *i.e.,* by including certain messages (or meaningful actions) within a frame, certain other messages are excluded.

(b) Psychological frames are inclusive, *i.e.,* by excluding certain messages certain others are included. From the point of view of set theory these two functions are synonymous, but from the point of view of psychology it is necessary to list them separately. The frame around a picture, if we consider this frame as a message intended to order or organize the perception of the viewer, says, "Attend to what is within and do not attend to what is outside." Figure and ground, as these terms are used by gestalt psychologists, are not symmetrically related as are the set and nonset of set theory. Perception of the ground must be positively inhibited and perception of the figure (in this case the picture) must be positively enhanced.

(c) Psychological frames are related to what we have called "premises." The picture frame tells the viewer that he is not to use the same sort of thinking in interpreting the picture that he might use in interpreting the wallpaper outside the frame. Or, in terms of the analogy from set theory, the messages enclosed within the imaginary line are defined as members of a class by virtue of their sharing common premises or mutual relevance. The frame itself thus becomes a part of the premise system. Either, as in the case of the play frame, the frame is involved in the evaluation of the messages which it contains, or the frame merely assists the mind in understanding the contained messages by reminding the thinker that these messages are mutually relevant and the messages outside the frame may be ignored.

(d) In the sense of the previous paragraph, a frame is metacommunicative. Any message, which either explicitly or implicitly defines a frame, *ipso facto* gives the receiver instructions or aids in his attempt to understand the messages included within the frame.

(e) The converse of *(d)* is also true. Every metacommunicative or metalinguistic message defines, either explicitly or implicitly, the set of messages about which it communicates, *i.e.,* every metacommunicative message is or defines a psychological frame. This, for example, is very evident in regard to such small metacommunicative signals as punctuation marks in a printed message, but applies equally to such complex metacommunicative messages as the psychiatrist's definition of his own curative role in terms of which his contributions to the whole mass of messages in psychotherapy are to be understood.

(f) The relation between psychological frame and perceptual gestalt needs to be

considered, and here the analogy of the picture frame is useful. In a painting by Roualt or Blake, the human figures and other objects represented are outlined. "Wise men see outlines and therefore they draw them." But outside these lines, which delimit the perceptual gestalt or "figure," there is a background or "ground" which in turn is limited by the picture frame. Similarly, in set-theoretical diagrams, the larger universe within which the smaller sets are drawn is itself enclosed in a frame. This double framing is, we believe, not merely a matter of "frames within frames" but an indication that mental processes resemble logic in *needing* an outer frame to delimit the ground against which the figures are to be perceived. This need is often unsatisfied, as when we see a piece of sculpture in a junk shop window, but this is uncomfortable. We suggest that the need for this outer limit to the ground is related to a prefer-ence for avoiding the paradoxes of abstraction. When a logical class or set of items is defined—for example, the class of matchboxes—it is necessary to delimit the set of items which are to be excluded, in this case, all those things which are not matchboxes. But the items to be included in the background set must be of the same degree of abstraction, *i.e.,* of the same "logical type" as those within the set itself. Specifically, if paradox is to be avoided, the "class of matchboxes" and the "class of nonmatchboxes" (even though both these items are clearly not matchboxes) must not be regarded as members of the class of nonmatchboxes. No class can be a member of itself. The picture frame then, because it delimits a background, is here regarded as an external representation of a very special and important type of psychological frame—namely a frame whose function is to delimit a logical type. This, in fact, is what was indicated above when it was said that the picture frame is an instruction to the viewer that he should not extend the premises which obtain between the figures within the picture to the wall paper behind it.

But, it is precisely this sort of frame that precipitates paradox. The rule for avoiding paradoxes insists that the items outside any enclosing line be of the same logical type as those within, but the picture frame, as analyzed above, is a line dividing items of one logical type from those of another. In passing, it is interesting to note that Russell's rule cannot be stated without breaking the rule. Russell insists that all items of inappropriate logical type be excluded (*i.e.,* by an imaginary line) from the background of any class, *i.e.,* he insists upon the drawing of an imaginary line of precisely the sort which he prohibits.

(19) This whole matter of frames and paradoxes may be illustrated in terms of animal behavior, where three types of message may be recognized or deduced: *(a)* Messages of the

sort which we here call mood-signs; *(b)* messages which simulate mood-signs (in play, threat, histrionics, etc.); and *(c)* messages which enable the receiver to discriminate between mood-signs and those other signs which resemble them. The message "This is play" is of this third type. It tells the receiver that certain nips and other meaningful actions are not messages of the first type.

The message "This is play" thus sets a frame of the sort which is likely to precipitate paradox: it is an attempt to discriminate between, or to draw a line between, categories of different logical types.

(20) This discussion of play and psychological frames establishes a type of triadic constellation (or system of relationships) between messages. One instance of this constellation is analyzed in paragraph 19, but it is evident that constellations of this sort occur not only at the nonhuman level but also in the much more complex communication of human beings. A fantasy or myth may simulate a denotative narrative, and, to discriminate between these types of discourse, people use messages of the frame-setting type, and so on.

(21) In conclusion, we arrive at the complex task of applying this theoretical approach to the particular phenomena of psychotherapy. Here the lines of our thinking may most briefly be summarized by presenting and partially answering these questions:

(a) Is there any indication that certain forms of psychopathology are specifically characterized by abnormalities in the patient's handling of frames and paradoxes?

(b) Is there any indication that the techniques of psychotherapy necessarily depend upon the manipulation of frames and paradoxes?

(c) Is it possible to describe the process of a given psychotherapy in terms of the interaction between the patient's abnormal use of frames and the therapist's manipulation of them?

(22) In reply to the first question, it seems that the "word salad" of schizophrenia can be described in terms of the patient's failure to recognize the metaphoric nature of his fantasies. In what should be triadic constellations of messages, the frame-setting message (*e.g.,* the phrase "as if") is omitted, and the metaphor or fantasy is narrated and acted upon in a manner which would be appropriate if the fantasy were a message of the more direct kind. The absence of metacommunicative framing which was noted in the case of dreams (15) is characteristic of the waking communications of the schizophrenic. With the loss of the ability to set metacommunicative frames, there is also a loss of ability to achieve the more primary

or primitive message. The metaphor is treated directly as a message of the more primary type. (This matter is discussed at greater length in the paper given by Jay Haley at this Conference.)

(23) The dependence of psychotherapy upon the manipulation of frames follows from the fact that therapy is an attempt to change the patient's metacommunicative habits. Before therapy, the patient thinks and operates in terms of a certain set of rules for the making and understanding of messages. After successful therapy, he operates in terms of a different set of such rules. (Rules of this sort are, in general, unverbalized and unconscious both before and after.) It follows that, in the process of therapy, there must have been communication at a level *meta* to these rules. There must have been communication about a *change* in rules.

But such a communication about change could not conceivably occur in messages of the type permitted by the patient's metacommunicative rules as they existed either before or after therapy.

It was suggested above that the paradoxes of play are characteristic of an evolutionary step. Here we suggest that similar paradoxes are a necessary ingredient in that process of change which we call psychotherapy.

The resemblance between the process of therapy and the phenomenon of play is, in fact, profound. Both occur within a delimited psychological frame, a spatial and temporal bounding of a set of interactive messages. In both play and therapy, the messages have a special and peculiar relationship to a more concrete or basic reality. Just as the pseudocombat of play is not real combat, so also the pseudolove and pseudohate of therapy are not real love and hate. The "transfer" is discriminated from real love and hate by signals invoking the psychological frame; and indeed it is this frame which permits the transfer to reach its full intensity and to be discussed between patient and therapist.

The formal characteristics of the therapeutic process may be illustrated by building up a model in stages. Imagine first two players who engage in a game of canasta according to a standard set of rules. So long as these rules govern and are unquestioned by both players, the game is unchanging, *i.e.,* no therapeutic change will occur. (Indeed many attempts at psychotherapy fail for this reason.) We may imagine, however, that at a certain moment the two canasta players cease to play canasta and start a discussion of the rules. Their discourse is now of a different logical type from that of their play. At the end of this discussion, we can imagine that they return to playing but with modified rules.

This sequence of events is, however, still an imperfect model of therapeutic interaction, though it illustrates our contention that therapy necessarily involves a combination of discrepant logical types of discourse. Our imaginary players avoided paradox by separating their discussion of the rules from their play, and it is precisely this separation that is impossible in psychotherapy. As we see it, the process of psychotherapy is a framed interaction between two persons, in which the rules are implicit but subject to change. Such change can only be proposed by experimental action, but every such experimental action, in which a proposal to change the rules is implicit, is itself a part of the ongoing game. It is this combination of logical types within the single meaningful act that gives to therapy the character not of a rigid game like canasta but, instead, that of an evolving system of interaction. The play of kittens or otters has this character.

(24) In regard to the specific relationship between the way in which the patient handles frames and the way in which the therapist manipulates them, very little can at present be said. It is, however, suggestive to observe that the psychological frame of therapy is an analogue of the frame-setting message which the schizophrenic is unable to achieve. To talk in "word salad" within the psychological frame of therapy is, in a sense, not pathological. Indeed the neurotic is specifically encouraged to do precisely this, narrating his dreams and free associations so that patient and therapist may achieve an understanding of this material. By the process of interpretation, the neurotic is driven to insert an "as if" clause into the productions of his primary process thinking, which productions he had previously deprecated or repressed. He must learn that fantasy contains truth.

For the schizophrenic the problem is somewhat different. His error is in treating the metaphors of primary process with the full intensity of literal truth. Through the discovery of what these metaphors stand for he must discover that they are only metaphors.

(25) From the point of view of the project, however, psychotherapy constitutes only one of the many fields which we are attempting to investigate. Our central thesis may be summed up as a statement of the necessity of the paradoxes of abstraction. It is not merely bad natural history to suggest that people might or should obey the Theory of Logical Types in their communications; their failure to do this is not due to mere carelessness or ignorance. Rather, we believe that the paradoxes of abstraction must make their appearance in all communication more complex than that of mood-signals, and that without these paradoxes the evolution of communication would be at an end. Life would then be an endless interchange of stylized messages, a game with rigid rules, unrelieved by change or humor.

Notes

1. A. N. Whitehead and B. Russell, *Principia Mathematica*, 3 vols., 2nd ed., Cambridge, Cambridge University Press, 1910–13.

2. L. Wittgenstein, *Tractatus Logico-Philosophicus*, London, Harcourt Brace, 1922.

3. R. Carnap, *The Logical Syntax of Language*, New York, Harcourt Brace, 1937.

4. B. L. Whorf, "Science and Linguistics," *Technology Review*, 1940, 44: 229–48.

5. J. Ruesch and G. Bateson, *Communication: The Social Matrix of Psychiatry*, New York, Norton, 1951.

6. A. Korzybski, *Science and Sanity*, New York, Science Press, 1941.

7. The verbalization of these metalinguistic rules is a much later achievement which can only occur after the evolution of a nonverbalized meta-metalinguistics.

8. N. Tinbergen, *Social Behavior in Animals with Special Reference to Vertebrates*, London, Methuen, 1953.

9. K. Z. Lorenz, *King Solomon's Ring*, New York, Crowell, 1952.

10. Ibid.

11. C. R. Carpenter, "A Field Study of the Behavior and Social Relations of Howling Monkeys," *Comp. Psychol. Monogr.*, 1934, 10: 1–168.

12. A. R. Radcliffe-Brown, *The Andaman Islanders*, Cambridge, Cambridge University Press, 1922.

13. W. S. McCulloch, "A Heterarchy of Values, etc.," *Bulletin of Math. Biophys.*, 1945, 7: 89–93.

14. Whitehead and Russell, *op. cit.*

Complete Freedom of Movement: Video Games as Gendered Play Spaces

Henry Jenkins

Context

*This essay was written in the midst of a significant push to develop games for girls. I was returning from a trip to San Francisco to consult with Brenda Laurel who was then building up Purple Moon, which was developing "friendship adventures" for girls. On the flight back, I found myself pondering the differences between my son's play experiences and my own, as well as the differences in what Brenda had shown me, and the traditional games on the market. I scribbled down some notes and this essay was born. It was initially presented at MIT as part of the **From Barbie to Mortal Kombat: Gender and Computer Games** conference and later was published in the book by that title, which I edited with Justine Cassell.*

The Player Experience

Game Economies

Cultural Representation

Henry Jenkins is the founding director of the Comparative Media Studies Program and the de Florez Professor of Humanities at MIT. He is one of the leaders of the Education Arcade, a joint MIT—University of Wisconsin effort to promote the pedagogical uses of computer and video games. He is the editor and author of a dozen books on various aspects of popular culture, including *Textual Poachers: Television Fans and Participatory Culture*, *From Barbie to Mortal Kombat: Gender and Computer Games*, and *Convergence Culture: Where Old and New Media Intersect*.

A Tale of Two Childhoods

Sometimes, I feel nostalgic for the spaces of my boyhood, growing up in suburban Atlanta in the 1960s. My big grassy front yard sloped sharply downward into a ditch where we could float boats on a rainy day. Beyond, there was a pine forest where my brother and I could toss pinecones like grenades or snap sticks together like swords. In the backyard, there was a patch of grass where we could wrestle or play kickball and a tree house, which sometimes bore a pirate flag and at other times, the Stars and Bars of the Confederacy. Out beyond our own yard, there was a bamboo forest where we could play Tarzan, and vacant lots, construction sites, sloping streets, and a neighboring farm (the last vestige of a rural area turned suburban).

Between my house and the school, there was another forest, which, for the full length of my youth, remained undeveloped. A friend and I would survey this land, claiming it for our imaginary kingdoms of Jungleloca and Freedonia. We felt a proprietorship over that space, even though others used it for schoolyard fisticuffs, smoking cigarettes or playing kissing games. When we were there, we rarely encountered adults, though when we did, it usually spelled trouble. We would come home from these secret places, covered with Georgia red mud.

Of course, we spent many afternoons at home, watching old horror movies or action-adventure series reruns, and our mothers would fuss at us to go outside. Often, something we had seen in television would inspire our play, stalking through the woods like Lon Chaney Jr.'s Wolfman or "socking" and powing" each other under the influence of Batman. Today, each time I visit my parents, I am shocked to see that most of those sacred" places are now occupied by concrete, bricks, or asphalt. They managed to get a whole subdivision out of Jungleloca and Freedonia!

My son, Henry, now 16, has never had a backyard.

He has grown up in various apartment complexes, surrounded by asphalt parking lots with, perhaps, a small grass buffer from the street. Children were prohibited by apartment policy from playing on the grass or from racing their tricycles in the basements or from doing much of anything else that might make noise, annoy the non-childbearing population, cause damage to the facilities, or put themselves at risk. There was, usually, a city park some blocks away, which we could go on outings a few times a week and where we could watch him play.

Henry could claim no physical space as his own, except his toy-strewn room, and he rarely got outside earshot. Once or twice, when I became exasperated by my son's constant presence around the house, I would forget all this and tell him he should go outside and play. He would look at me with confusion and ask "Where?"

But, he did have video games, which took him across lakes of fire, through cities in the clouds, along dark and gloomy back streets, and into dazzling neon-lit Asian marketplaces. Video games constitute virtual playing spaces, which allow home-bound children like my son to extend their reach, to explore, manipulate, and interact with a more diverse range of imaginary places than constitute the often drab, predictable, and overly familiar spaces of their every-day lives. Keith Feinstein (1997), President of the Video Game Conservatory, argues that video games preserve many aspects of traditional play spaces and culture, maintaining aspects that motivate children to:

> learn about the environment that they find themselves living in. Video games present the opportunity to explore and discover, as well as to combat others of comparable skill (whether they be human or electronic) and to struggle with them in a form that is similar to children wrestling, or scrambling for the same ball—they are nearly matched, they aren't going to really do much damage, yet it feels like an all-important fight for that child at that given moment. Space Invaders gives us visceral thrill and poses mental/physical challenges similar to a schoolyard game of dodge ball (or any of the hundred of related kids' games). Video games play with us, a never tiring playmate.

Feinstein's comment embraces some classical conceptions of play (such as spatial exploration and identity formation), suggesting that video game play isn't fundamentally different from backyard play. To facilitate such immersive play, to achieve an appropriate level of "holding power" that enables children to transcend their immediate environments, video game spaces require concreteness and vividness. The push in the video game industry for more than a decade has been towards the development of more graphically complex, more visually engaging, more three-dimensionally rendered spaces, and towards quicker, more sophisticated, more flexible interactions with those spaces. Video games tempt the player to play longer, putting more and more quarters into the arcade machine (or providing "play value" for those who've bought the game) by unveiling ever more spectacular "microworlds," the revelation of a new level the reward for having survived and mastered the previous environment. (Fuller and Jenkins, 1995)

Video games advertise themselves as taking us places very different from where we live:

> Say hello to life in the fast lane. Sonic R for Sega Saturn is a full-on, pedal-to-the-metal hi-speed dash through five 3D courses, each rendered in full 360 degree panoramas.... You'll be flossing bug guts out of your teeth for weeks. (Sonic R, 1998)

> Take a dip in these sub-infested waters for a spot of nuclear fishin'....Don't worry. You'll know you're in too deep when the water pressure caves your head in. (Critical Depth, 1998)

> Hack your way through a savage world or head straight for the arena....Complete freedom of movement. (Die By the Sword, 1998)

> Strap in and throttle up as you whip through the most realistic and immersive powerboat racing game ever made. Jump over roadways, and through passing convoys, or speed between oil tankers, before they close off the track and turn your boat to splinters. Find a shortcut and take the lead, or better yet, secure your victory and force your opponent into a river barge at 200 miles per hour. (VR Sports, 1998)

Who wouldn't want to trade in the confinement of your room for the immersion promised by today's video games? Watch children playing these games, their bodies bobbing and swaying to the on-screen action, and it's clear they are there—in the fantasy world, battling it out with the orcs and goblins, pushing their airplanes past the sound barrier, or splashing their way through the waves in their speed boats. Perhaps, my son finds in his video games what I found in the woods behind the school, on my bike whizzing down the hills of the suburban back streets, or settled into my tree house during a thunder storm with a good adventure novel—intensity of experience, escape from adult regulation; in short, "complete freedom of movement."

This essay will offer a cultural geography of video game spaces, one that uses traditional children's play and children's literature as points of comparison to the digital worlds contemporary children inhabit. Specifically, I examine the "fit" between video games and traditional boy culture and review several different models for creating virtual play spaces for girls. So much of the existing research on gender and games takes boy's fascination with these games as a given. As we attempt to offer video games for girls, we need to better understand what draws boys to video games and whether our daughters should feel that same attraction.

Video games are often blamed for the listlessness or hyperactivity of our children, yet sociologists find these same behavioral problems occurring among all children raised in highly restrictive and confined physical environments. (Booth and Johnson, 1975; van Staden, 1984). Social reformers sometimes speak of children choosing to play video games rather than playing outside, when, in many cases, no such choice is available. More and more Americans live in urban or semi-urban neighborhoods. Fewer of us own our homes and more of us live in apartment complexes. Fewer adults have chosen to have children and our society has become increasingly hostile to the presence of children. In many places, "no children" policies severely restrict where parents can live. Parents, for a variety of reasons, are frightened to have their children on the streets, and place them under "protective custody." "Latch key" children return from school and lock themselves in their apartments (Kincheloe, 1997).

In the nineteenth-century, children living along the frontier or on America's farms enjoyed free range over a space that was ten square miles or more. Elliot West (1992) describes boys of 9 or 10 going camping alone for days on end, returning when they were needed to do chores around the house. The early nineteenth-century saw the development of urban playgrounds in the midst of city streets, responding to a growing sense of children's diminishing access to space and an increased awareness of issues of child welfare (Cavallo, 1991), but autobiographies of the period stress the availability of vacant lots and back allies which children could claim as their own play environments. Sociologists writing about the suburban America of my boyhood found that children enjoyed a play terrain of one to five blocks of spacious backyards and relatively safe subdivision streets (Hart, 1979). Today, at the end of the nineteenth-century, many of our children have access to the one to five rooms inside their apartments. Video game technologies expand the space of their imagination.

Let me be clear—I am not arguing that video games are as good for kids as the physical spaces of backyard play culture. As a father, I wish that my son could come home covered in mud or with scraped knees rather than carpet burns. However, we sometimes blame video games for problems that they do not cause—perhaps because of our own discomfort with these technologies which were not part of our childhood. When politicians like Sen. Joseph Lieberman (D-Ct.) target video game violence, perhaps it is to distract attention from the material conditions that give rise to a culture of domestic violence, the economic policies that make it harder for most of us to own our homes, and the development practices which pave over the old grasslands and forests. Video games did not make backyard play spaces disappear; rather, they offer children some way to respond to domestic confinement.

Moving Beyond "Home Base": Why Physical Spaces Matter

The psychological and social functions of playing outside are as significant as the impact of "sunshine and good exercise" upon our physical well-being. Roger Hart's *Children's Experience of Place* (1979), for example, stresses the importance of children's manipulations and explorations of their physical environment to their development of self-confidence and autonomy. Our physical surroundings are "relatively simple and relatively stable" compared to the "overwhelmingly complex and ever shifting" relations between people, and thus, they form core resources for identity formation. The unstructured spaces, the playforts and tree houses, children create for themselves in the cracks, gullies, back allies, and vacant lots of the adult world constitute what Robin C. Moore (1986) calls "childhood's domain" or William Van Vliet (1983) has labeled as a "fourth environment" outside the adult-structured spaces of home, school, and playground. These informal, often temporary play spaces are where free and unstructured play occurs. Such spaces surface most often on the lists children make of "special" or "important" places in their lives. M. H. Matthews (1992) stresses the "topophilia," the heightened sense of belonging and ownership, children develop as they map their fantasies of empowerment and escape onto their neighborhoods. Frederick Donaldson (1970) proposed two different classifications of these spaces—home base, the world which is secure and familiar, and home region, an area undergoing active exploration, a space under the process of being colonized by the child. Moore (1986) writes:

> One of the clearest expressions of the benefits of continuity in the urban landscape was the way in which children used it as an outdoor gymnasium. As I walked along a Mill Hill street with Paul, he continually went darting ahead, leapfrogging over concrete bollards, hopping between paving slabs, balancing along the curbside. In each study area, certain kids seemed to dance through their surroundings on the look out for microfeatures with which to test their bodies....Not only did he [David, another boy in the study], like Paul, jump over gaps between things, go 'tightrope walking' along the tops of walls, leapfrogging objects on sight, but at one point he went 'mountain climbing' up a roughly built, nine-foot wall that had many serendipitously placed toe and handholds. (p.72)

These discoveries arise from active exploration and spontaneous engagement with their physical surroundings. Children in the same neighborhoods may have fundamentally different relations to the spaces they share, cutting their own paths, giving their own names to features of their environment. The "wild spaces" are far more important, many researchers conclude, than playgrounds, which can only be used in sanctioned ways, since they allow many more opportunities for children to modify their physical environment.

Children's access to spaces is structured around gender differences. Observing the use of space within 1970s suburban America, Hart (1979) found that boys enjoyed far greater mobility and range than girls of the same age and class background. In the course of an afternoon's play, a typical 10-12 year old boy might travel a distance of 2452 yards, while the average 10-12 year old girl might only travel 959 yards. For the most part, girls expanded their geographic range only to take on responsibilities and perform chores for the family, while parents often turned a blind eye to a boy's movements into prohibited spaces. The boys Hart (1979) observed were more likely to move beyond their homes in search of "rivers, forts and tree houses, woods, ball fields, hills, lawns, sliding places, and climbing trees" while girls were more like to seek commercially developed spaces, such as stores or shopping malls. Girls were less likely than boys to physically alter their play environment, to dam creeks or build forts. Such gender differences in mobility, access and control over physical space increased as children grew older. As C. Ward (1977) notes:

> Whenever we discuss the part the environment plays in the lives of children, we are really talking about boys. As a stereotype, the child in the city is a boy. Girls are far less visible...The reader can verify this by standing in a city street at any time of day and counting the children seen. The majority will be boys. (p.152)

One study found that parents were more likely to describe boys as being "outdoors" children and girls as "indoor" children (Newson and Newson, 1976). Another 1975 study (Rheingold and Cook), which inventoried the contents of children's bedrooms, found boys more likely to possess a range of vehicles and sports equipment designed to encourage outside play, while the girls rooms were stocked with dolls, doll clothes, and other domestic objects. Parents of girls were more likely to express worries about the dangers their children face on the streets and to structure girls' time for productive household activities or educational play (Matthews, 1992).

Historically, girl culture formed under closer maternal supervision and girls' toys were designed to foster female-specific skills and competencies and prepare girls for their future domestic responsibilities as wives and mothers. The doll's central place in girlhood reflected maternal desires to encourage daughters to sew; the doll's china heads and hands fostered delicate gestures and movements (Formanek-Brunnel, 1998). However, these skills were not acquired without some resistance. Nineteenth century girls were apparently as willing as today's girls to mistreat their dolls, cutting their hair, driving nails into their bodies.

If cultural geographers are right when they argue that children's ability to explore and modify their environments plays a large role in their growing sense of mastery, freedom and self-confidence, then the restrictions placed on girls' play have a crippling effect. Conversely, this research would suggest that children's declining access to play space would have a more dramatic impact on the culture of young boys, since girls already faced domestic confinement.

Putting Boy Culture Back in the Home

> *Clods were handy and the air was full of them in a twinkling. They raged around Sid like a hail storm; and before Aunt Polly could collect her surprised faculties and sally to the rescue, six or seven clods had taken personal effect, and Tom was over the fence and gone....He presently got safely beyond the reach of capture and punishment, and hasted toward the public square of the village, where two 'military' companies of boys had met for conflict, according to previous appointment. Tom was the general of one of these armies; Joe Harper (a bosom friend) general of the other....Tom's army won a great victory, after a long and hard-fought battle. Then the dead were counted, prisoners exchanged, the terms of the next disagreement agreed upon, and the day for the necessary battle appointed; after which the armies fell into line and marched away, and Tom turned homeward alone.* —Mark Twain, *Adventures of Tom Sawyer* (1961), pp.19–20.

What E. Anthony Rotundo (1994) calls "boy culture" emerged in the context of the growing separation of the male public sphere and the female private sphere in the wake of the industrial revolution. Boys were cut off from the work life of their fathers and left under the care of their mothers. According to Rotundo, boys escaped from the home into the outdoors play space, freeing them to participate in a semi-autonomous "boy culture" which cast itself in opposition to maternal culture:

> Where women's sphere offered kindness, morality, nurture and a gentle spirit, the boys' world countered with energy, self-assertion, noise, and a frequent resort to violence. The physical explosiveness and the willingness to inflict pain contrasted so sharply with the values of the home that they suggest a dialogue in actions between the values

of the two spheres—as if a boy's aggressive impulses, so relentlessly opposed at home, sought extreme forms of release outside it; then, with stricken consciences, the boys came home for further lessons in self-restraint. (p.37)

The boys took transgressing maternal prohibitions as proof they weren't "mama's boys." Rotundo argues that this break with the mother was a necessary step towards autonomous manhood. One of the many tragedies of our gendered division of labor may be the ways that it links misogyny—an aggressive fighting back against the mother—with the process of developing self-reliance. Contrary to the Freudian concept of the oedipal complex (which focuses on boy's struggles with their all-powerful fathers as the site of identity formation), becoming an adult male often means struggling with (and in many cases, actively repudiating) maternal culture. Fathers, on the other hand, offered little guidance to their sons, who, Rotundo argues, acquired masculine skills and values from other boys. By contrast, girls play culture was often "interdependent" with the realm of their mother's domestic activities, insuring a smoother transition into anticipated adult roles, but allowing less autonomy.

What happens when the physical spaces of nineteenth-century boy culture are displaced by the virtual spaces of contemporary video games? Cultural geographers have long argued that television is a poor substitute for backyard play, despite its potential to present children with a greater diversity of spaces than can be found in their immediate surroundings, precisely because it is a spectatorial rather than a participatory medium. Moore (1986), however, leaves open the prospect that a more interactive digital medium might serve some of the same developmental functions as backyard play. A child playing a video game, searching for the path around obstacles, or looking for an advantage over imaginary opponents, engages in many of the same "mapping" activities as children searching for affordances in their real-world environments. Rotundo's core claims about nineteenth-century boy culture hold true for the "video game culture" of contemporary boyhood. This congruence may help us to account for the enormous popularity of these games with young boys. This "fit" should not be surprising when we consider that the current game genres reflect intuitive choices by men who grew up in the 1960s and 1970s, when suburban boy culture still reigned.

The following are some points of comparison between traditional boy culture and contemporary game culture.

(1) Nineteenth century "boy culture" was charactered by its independence from the realm of both mothers and fathers. It was a space where boys could develop autonomy and self-confidence. Twentieth century video game culture also carves out a cultural realm for modern day children separate from the space of their parents. They often play the games in their rooms and guard their space against parental intrusion. Parents often express a distaste for the games' pulpy plots and lurid images. As writers like Jon Katz (1997) and Don Tapscott (1997) note, children's relative comfort with digital media is itself a generational marker, with adults often unable to comprehend the movement and colored shapes of the video screen. Here, however, the loss of spatial mobility is acutely felt—the "bookworm," the boy who spent all of his time in his room reading, had a "mama's boy" reputation in the old "boy culture." Modern day boys have had to accommodate their domestic confinement with their definitions of masculinity, perhaps accounting, in part, for the hypermasculine and hyperviolent content of the games themselves. The game player has a fundamentally different image than the "book worm."

(2) In nineteenth-century "boy culture," youngsters gained recognition from their peers for their daring, often proven through stunts (such as swinging on vines, climbing trees, or leaping from rocks as they cross streams) or through pranks (such as stealing apples or doing mischief on adults.)

In nineteenth-century video game culture, children gain recognition for their daring as demonstrated in the virtual worlds of the game, overcoming obstacles, beating bosses, and mastering levels. Nineteenth century boys's trespasses on neighbor's property or confrontations with hostile shopkeepers are mirrored by the visual vocabulary of the video games which often pit smaller protagonists against the might and menace of much larger rivals. Much as cultural geographers describe the boys' physical movements beyond their home bases into developing home territories, the video games allow boys to gradually develop their mastery over the entire digital terrain, securing their future access to spaces by passing goal posts or finding warp zones.

(3) The central virtues of the nineteenth-century "boy culture" were mastery and self-control. The boys set tasks and goals for themselves that required discipline in order

to complete. Through this process of setting and meeting challenges, they acquired the virtues of manhood.

The central virtues of video game culture are mastery (over the technical skills required by the games) and self-control (manual dexterity). Putting in the long hours of repetition and failure necessary to master a game also requires discipline and the ability to meet and surpass self-imposed goals. Most contemporary video games are ruthlessly goal-driven. Boys will often play the games, struggling to master a challenging level, well past the point of physical and emotional exhaustion. Children are not so much "addicted" to video games as they are unwilling to quit before they have met their goals, and the games seem to always set new goalposts, inviting us to best "just one more level." One of the limitations of the contemporary video game is that it provides only pre-structured forms of interactivity, and in that sense, video games are more like playgrounds and city parks rather than wild-spaces. For the most part, video game players can only exploit built-in affordances and pre-programmed pathways. "Secret codes," "Easter Eggs," and "Warp zones" function in digital space like secret paths do in physical space and are eagerly sought by gamers who want to go places and see things others can't find.

(4) The nineteenth-century "boy culture" was hierarchical, with a member's status dependent upon competitive activity, direct confrontation and physical challenges. The boy fought for a place in the gang's inner circle, hoping to win admiration and respect.

Video game culture can also be hierarchical with a member gaining status by being able to complete a game or log a big score. Video game masters move from house to house to demonstrate their technical competency and to teach others how to "beat" particularly challenging levels. The video arcade becomes a proving ground for contemporary masculinity, while many games are designed for the arcade, demanding a constant turnover of coins for play and intensifying the action into roughly two minute increments. Often, single-player games generate digital rivals who may challenge us to beat their speeds or battle them for dominance.

(5) Nineteenth century "boy culture" was sometimes brutally violent and physically aggressive; children hurt each other or got hurt trying to prove their mastery and daring.

Video game culture displaces this physical violence into a symbolic realm. Rather than beating each other up behind the school, boys combat imaginary characters, finding a potentially safer outlet for their aggressive feelings. We forget how violent previous boy culture was. Rotundo (1994) writes:

The prevailing ethos of the boys world not only supported the expression of impulses such as dominance and aggression (which had evident social uses), but also allowed the release of hostile, violent feelings (whose social uses were less evident). By allowing free passage to so many angry or destructive emotions, boy culture sanctioned a good deal of intentional cruelty, like the physical torture of animals and the emotional violence of bullying....If at times boys acted like a hostile pack of wolves that preyed on its own kind as well as on other species, they behaved at other times like a litter of playful pups who enjoy romping, wrestling and testing new skills. (45)

Even feelings of fondness and friendship were expressed through physical means, including greeting each other with showers of brickbats and offal. Such a culture is as violent as the world depicted in contemporary video games, which have the virtue of allowing growing boys to express their aggression and rambunctiousness through indirect, rather than direct, means.

(6) Nineteenth century "boy culture" expressed itself through scatological humor. Such bodily images (of sweat, spit, snot, shit, and blood) reflected the boy's growing awareness of their bodies and signified their rejection of maternal constraints.

Video game culture has often been criticized for its dependence upon similar kinds of scatological images, with the blood and gore of games like Mortal Kombat (with its "end moves" of dismemberment and decapitation), providing some of the most oft-cited evidence in campaigns to reform video game content (Kinder, 1996). Arguably, these images serve the same functions for modern boys as for their nineteenth-century counterparts—allowing an exploration of what it's like to live in our bodies and an expression of distance from maternal regulations. Like the earlier 'boy culture,' this scatological imagery sometimes assumes overtly misogynistic form, directed against women as a civilizing or controlling force, staged towards women's bodies as a site of physical difference and as the objects of desire/distaste. Some early games, such as Super Metroid, rewarded player competence by forcing female characters to strip down to their underwear if the boys beat a certain score.

(7) Nineteenth century "boy culture" depended on various forms of role-playing, often imitating the activities of adult males. Rotundo (1994) notes the popularity of games of settlers and Indians during an age when the frontier had only recently been closed, casting boys sometimes as their settler ancestors and other times as "savages." Such play mapped the competitive and combative boy culture ethos onto the adult realm, thus exaggerating the place of warfare in adult male lives. Through such play, children tested alternative social roles, examined adult ideologies, and developed a firmer sense of their own abilities and identities.

Video game culture depends heavily on fantasyrole-playing, with different genres of games allowing children to imagine themselves in alternative social roles or situations. Most games, however, provide images of heroic action more appropriate for the rugged individualism of nineteenth-century American culture than for the contemporary information-and-service economy. Boys play at being crime fighters, race-care drivers, and fighter pilots, not at holding down desk jobs. This gap between the excitement of boyhood play and the alienation of adult labor may explain why video game imagery seems so hyperbolic from an adult vantage point. Rotundo (1994) notes, however, that there was always some gap between boys and adult males:

Boy culture emphasized exuberant spontaneity; it allowed free rein to aggressive impulses and revealed in physical prowess and assertion. Boy culture was a world of play, a social space where one evaded the duties and restrictions of adult society...Men were quiet and sober, for theirs was a life of serious business. They had families to support, reputations to earn, responsibilities to meet. Their world was based on work, not play, and their survival in it depended on patient planning, not spontaneous impulse. To prosper, then, a man had to delay gratification and restrain desire. Of course, he also needed to be aggressive and competitive, and he needed an instinct for self-advancement. But he had to channel those assertive impulses in ways that were suitable to the abstract battles and complex issues of middle-class men's work. (55)

Today, the boys are using the same technologies as their fathers, even if they are using them to pursue different fantasies.

(8) In nineteenth-century "boy culture," play activities were seen as opportunities for social interactions and bonding. Boys formed strong ties, which formed the basis for adult affiliations, for participation in men's civic clubs and fraternities, and for business partnerships.

The track record of contemporary video game culture at providing a basis for a similar social networking is more mixed. In some cases, the games constitute both play space and playmates, reflecting the physical isolation of contemporary children from each other. In other cases, the games provide the basis for social interactions at home, at school and at the video arcades. Children talk about the games together, over the telephone or now, over the Internet, as well as in person, on the playground or at the school cafeteria. Boys compare notes, map strategies, share tips, and show off their skills, and this exchange of video game lore provides the basis for more complex social relations. Again, video games don't isolate children but they fail, at the present time, to provide the technological basis for overcoming other social and cultural factors, such as working parents who are unable to bring children to each other's houses or enlarged school districts, which make it harder to get together.

Far from a "corruption" of the culture of childhood, video games show strong continuities to the boyhood play fondly remembered by previous generations. There is a significant difference, however. The nineteenth-century "boy culture" enjoyed such freedom and autonomy precisely because their activities were staged within a larger expanse of space, because boys could occupy an environment largely unsupervised by adults. Nineteenth century boys sought indirect means of breaking with their mothers, escaping to spaces that were outside their control, engaging in secret activities they knew would have met parental disapproval. The mothers, on the other hand, rarely had to confront the nature of this "boy culture" and often didn't even know that it existed. The video game culture, on the other hand, occurs in plain sight, in the middle of the family living room, or at best, in the children's rooms. Mothers come face to face with the messy process by which western culture turns boys into men, and it becomes the focus of open antagonisms and the subject of tremendous guilt and anxiety. Sega's Lee McEnany acknowledges that the overwhelming majority of complaints game companies receive come from mothers, and Ellen Seiter (1996) has noted that this statistic reflects the increased pressure placed on mothers to supervise and police children's

343

relations to popular culture. Current attempts to police video game content reflect a long history of attempts to shape and regulate children's play culture, starting with the playground movements of progressive America and the organization of social groups for boys such as the Boy Scouts or Little League which tempered the more rough-and-tumble qualities of "boy culture" and channeled them into games, sports, and other adult-approved pastimes.

Many of us might wish to foster a boy culture that allowed the expression of affection or the display of empowerment through nonviolent channels, that disentangled the development of personal autonomy from the fostering of misogyny, and that encouraged boys to develop a more nurturing, less domineering attitude to their social and natural environments. These worthy goals are worth pursuing. We can't simply adopt a "boys will be boys" attitude. However, one wonders about the consequences of such a policing action in a world that no longer offers "wild" outdoor spaces as a safety valve for boys to escape parental control. Perhaps, our sons—and daughters—need an unpoliced space for social experimentation, a space where they can vent their frustrations and imagine alternative adult roles without inhibiting parental pressure. The problem, of course, is that unlike the nineteenth-century "boy culture," the video game culture is not a world children construct for themselves but rather a world made by adult companies and sold to children. There is no way that we can escape adult intervention in shaping children's play environments as long as those environments are built and sold rather than discovered and appropriated. As parents, we are thus implicated in our children's choice of play environments, whether we wish to be or not, and we need to be conducting a dialogue with our children about the qualities and values exhibited by these game worlds. One model would be for adults and children to collaborate in the design and development of video game spaces, in the process developing a conversation about the nature and meanings of the worlds being produced. Another approach (Cassell) would be to create tools to allow children to construct their own playspaces and then give them the space to do what they want. Right now, parents are rightly apprehensive about a playspace which is outside their own control and which is shaped according to adult specifications but without their direct input.

One of the most disturbing aspects of the "boy culture" is its gender segregation. The nineteenth-century "boy culture" played an essential role in preparing boys for entry into their future professional roles and responsibilities; some of that same training has also become essential for girls at a time when more and more women are working outside the home. The motivating force behind the "girls game" movement is the idea that girls, no less than boys, need computers at an early age if they are going to be adequately prepared to get "good jobs for good wages." (Jenkins and Cassell) Characteristically, the girl's game movement has involved the transposition of traditional feminine play cultures into the digital realm. However, in doing so, we run the risk of preserving, rather than transforming, those aspects of traditional "girl culture" which kept women restricted to the domestic sphere, while denying them the spatial exploration and mastery associated with the "boy culture." Girls, no less than boys, need to develop an exploratory mindset, a habit of seeking unknown spaces as opposed to settling placidly into the domestic sphere.

Gendered Games/Gendered Books:
Towards a Cultural Geography of Imaginary Spaces

These debates about gendered play and commercial entertainment are not new, repeating (and in a curious way, reversing) the emergence of a gender-specific set of literary genres for children in the nineteenth-century. As Elizabeth Segel (1986) notes, the earliest children's book writers were mostly women, who saw the genre as "the exercise of feminine moral 'influence'" upon children's developing minds, and who created a literature that was un-differentiated according to gender but "domestic in setting, heavily didactic and morally or spiritually uplifting." (171) In other words, the earliest children's books were "girls books" in everything but name and this isn't surprising at a time novel reading was still heavily as-sociated with women. The "boys book" emerged, in the mid-nineteenth-century, as "men of action," industrialists and adventurers, wrote fictions intended to counter boys' restlessness and apathy towards traditional children's literature. The introduction of boys books reflected a desire to get boys to read. Boy book fantasies of action and adventure reflected the qualities of their pre-existing play culture, fantasies centering on "the escape from domesticity and from the female domination of the domestic world." (Segel, 1986, 171) If the "girls game" movement has involved the rethinking of video game genres (which initially emerged in a male-dominat-ed space) in order to make digital media more attractive to girls (and thus to encourage the development of computational skills), the "boys book" movement sought to remake reading (which initially emerged in a female-dominated space) to respond to male needs (and thus to encourage literacy). In both cases, the goal seems to have been to construct fantasies which reflect the gender-specific nature of children's play and thus to motivate those left out of the desirable cultural practices to get more involved. In this next section, I will consider the con-tinuity that exists between gender/genre configurations in children's literature and in the digital games marketplace.

Adventure Islands: Boy Space

> *Alex looked around him. There was no place to seek cover. He was too weak to run, even if there was. His gaze returned to the stallion, fascinated by a creature so wild and so near. Here was the wildest of all wild animals—he had fought for everything he had ever needed, for food, for leadership, for life itself; it was his nature to kill or be killed. The horse reared again; then he snorted and plunged straight for the boy. (27)*—Walter Farley, *The Black Stallion* (1941)

The space of the boy book is the space of adventure, risk-taking and danger, of a wild and untamed nature that must be mastered if one is to survive. The space of the boys book offers "no place to seek cover," and thus encourages fight-or-flight responses. In some cases, most notably in the works of Mark Twain, the boy books represented a nostalgic documentation of nineteenth-century "boy culture," its spaces, its activities, and its values. In other cases, as in the succession of pulp adventure stories that form the background of the boys game genres, the narratives offered us a larger-than-life enactment of those values, staged in exotic rather than backyard spaces, involving broader movements through space and amplifying horseplay and risk taking into scenarios of actual combat and conquest. Boys book writers found an easy fit between the ideologies of American "manifest destiny" or British colonialism and the adventure stories boys preferred to read, which often took the form of quests, journeys, or adventures into untamed and uncharted regions of the world—into the frontier of the American west (or in the nineteenth-century, the "final frontier" of Mars and beyond), into the exotic realms of Africa, Asia, and South America. The protagonists were boys or boy-like adult males, who have none of the professional responsibilities and domestic commitments associated with adults. The heroes sought adventure by running away from home to join the circus (*Toby Tyler*), to sign up as cabin boy on a ship (*Treasure Island*), or to seek freedom by rafting down the river (*Huckleberry Finn*). They confronted a hostile and untamed environment (as when The *Jungle Book's* Mowgli must battle "tooth and claw" with the tiger, Sheer Khan, or as when Jack London's protagonists faced the frozen wind of the Yukon.) They were shipwrecked on islands, explored caves, searched for buried treasure, plunged harpoons into slick-skinned whales, or set out alone across the dessert, the bush or the jungle. They survived through their wits, their physical mastery, and their ability to use violent force. Each chapter offered a sensational set piece—an ambush by wild Indians, an encounter with a coiled cobra, a landslide, a stampede, or a sea battle—which placed the protagonist at risk and tested his skills and courage. The persistent images of blood-and-guts combat and cliff-hanging risks compelled boys to keep reading, making their blood race with promises of thrills and more thrills. This rapid pace allowed little room for moral and emotional introspection. In turn, such stories provided fantasies that boys could enact upon their own environments. Rotundo (1994) describes nineteenth-century boys playing pirates, settlers and Indians, or Roman warriors, roles drawn from boys books.

The conventions of the 19th and early nineteenth-century boys adventure story provided the basis for the current video game genres. The most successful console game series, such as Capcom's Mega Man or Nintendo's Super Mario Brothers games, combine the iconography of multiple boys book genres. Their protagonists struggle across an astonishingly eclectic range of landscapes—deserts, frozen wastelands, tropical rain forests, urban undergrounds—and encounter resistance from strange hybrids (who manage to be animal, machine, and savage all rolled into one). The scroll games have built into them the constant construction of frontiers—home regions—which the boy player must struggle to master and push beyond, moving deeper and deeper into uncharted space. Action is relentless. The protagonist shoots fireballs, ducks and charges, slugs it out, rolls, jumps and dashes across the treacherous terrain, never certain what lurks around the next corner. If you stand still, you die. Everything you encounter is potentially hostile so shoot to kill. Errors in judgment result in the character's death and require starting all over again. Each screen overflows with dangers; each landscape is riddled with pitfalls and booby traps. One screen may require you to leap from precipice to precipice, barely missing falling into the deep chasms below. Another may require you to swing by vines across the treetops, or spelunk through an underground passageway, all the while fighting it out with the alien hordes. The game's levels and worlds reflect the set-piece structure of the earlier boys books. Boys get to make lots of noise on adventure island, with the soundtrack full of pulsing music, shouts, groans, zaps, and bomb blasts. Everything is streamlined: the plots and characters are reduced to genre archetypes, immediately familiar to the boy gamers, and defined more through their capacity for actions than anything else. The "adventure island" is the archetypal space of both the boys books and the boys games—an isolated world far removed from domestic space or adult supervision, an untamed world for people who refuse to bow before the pressures of the civilizing process, a never-never-land where you seek your fortune. The "adventure island," in short, is a world that fully embodies the "boy culture" and its ethos.

Secret Gardens: Girl Space

> *If it was the key to the closed garden, and she could find out where the door was, she could perhaps open it and see what was inside the walls, and what had happened to the old rose-trees. It was because it had been shut up so long that she wanted to see it. It seemed as if it must be different from other places and that something strange must have happened to it during ten years. Besides that, if she liked it she could go into it every day and shut the door behind her, and she could make up some play of her own and play it quite alone, because nobody would ever know where she was, but would think the door was still locked and the key buried in the earth. (71)*—Frances Hodgson Burnett (1911), *The Secret Garden*

Girl space is a space of secrets and romance, a space of one's own in a world that offers you far too little room to explore. Ironically, "girl books" often open with fantasies of being alone and then require the female protagonist to sacrifice their private space in order to make room for others' needs. The "girls book" genres were slower to evolve, often emerging through imitation of the gothics and romances preferred by adult women readers and retaining a strong aura of instruction and self-improvement. As Segel (1986) writes:

> The liberation of nineteenth century boys into the book world of sailors and pirates, forest and battles, left their sisters behind in the world of childhood—that is, the world of home and family. When publishers and writers saw the commercial possibilities of books for girls, it is interesting that they did not provide comparable escape reading for them (that came later, with the pulp series books) but instead developed books designed to persuade the young reader to accept the confinement and self-sacrifice inherent in the doctrine of feminine influence. This was accomplished by depicting the rewards of submission and the sacred joys of serving as 'the angel of the house.' (171–172)

If the boys book protagonist escapes all domestic responsibilities, the girls' book heroine learned to temper her impulsiveness and to accept family and domestic obligations (*Little Women, Anne of Green Gables*) or sought to be a healing influence on a family suffering from tragedy and loss (*Rebecca of Sunnybrook Farm*). Segel (1986) finds the most striking difference between the two genre traditions is in the book's settings: "the domestic confinement of one book as against the extended voyage to exotic lands in the other." (173) Avoiding the boys books' purple prose, the girls books describe naturalistic environments, similar to the realm of readers' daily experience. The female protagonists take emotional, but rarely, physical risks. The tone is more apt to be confessional than confrontational.

Traditional girls' books, such as *The Secret Garden*, do encourage some forms of spatial exploration, an exploration of the hidden passages of unfamiliar houses or the rediscovery and cultivation of a deserted rose garden. Norman N. Holland and Leona F. Sherman (1986) emphasize the role of spatial exploration in the gothic tradition, a "maiden-plus-habitation" formula whose influence is strongly felt on *The Secret Garden*. In such stories, the exploration of space leads to the uncovering of secrets, clues, and symptoms that shed light on character's motivations. Hidden rooms often contained repressed memories and sometimes entombed relatives. The castle, Holland and Sherman (1986) note, "can threaten, resist, love or confine, but in all these actions, it stands as a total environment" (220) which the female protagonist can never fully escape. Holland and Sherman claim that gothic romances fulfill a fantasy of unearthing secrets about the adult world, casting the reader in a position of powerlessness and daring them to overcome their fears and confront the truth. Such a fantasy space is, of course, consistent with what we have already learned about girls' domestic confinement and greater responsibilities to their families.

Purple Moon's Secret Paths in the Forest fully embodies the juvenile gothic tradition —while significantly enlarging the space open for girls to explore. Purple Moon removes the walls around the garden, turning it into a woodlands. Producer Brenda Laurel has emphasized girls' fascination with secrets, a fascination that readily translates into a puzzle game structure, though Secret Paths pushes further than existing games to give these "secrets" social and psychological resonance. Based on her focus group interviews, Laurel initially sought to design a "magic garden," a series of "romanticized natural environments" responsive to "girls' highly touted nurturing desires, their fondness for animals." She wanted to create a place "where girls could explore, meet and take care of creatures, design and grow magical or fantastical plants." (Personal correspondence, 1997) What she found was that the girls did not feel magical animals would need their nurturing and in fact, many of the girls wanted the animals to mother them. The girls in Laurel's study, however, were drawn to the idea of the secret garden or hidden forest as a "girl's only" place for solitude and introspection. Laurel explains:

> Girls' first response to the place was that they would want to go there alone, to be peaceful and perhaps read or daydream. They might take a best friend, but they would never take an adult or a boy. They thought that the garden/forest would be a place where they could find out things that would be important to them, and a place where they might meet a wise or magical person. Altogether, their fantasies were about respite and looking within as opposed to frolicsome play. (Personal correspondence, 1997)

349

Friendly fawns from "Secret Paths in the Forest." Reprinted with permission of Purple Moon. Copyright 1997

The spaces in Purple Moon's game are quiet, contemplative places, rendered in naturalistic detail but with the soft focus and warm glow of an impressionistic watercolor.

The world of Secret Paths explodes with subtle and inviting colors—the colors of a forest on a summer afternoon, of spring flowers and autumn leaves and shifting patterns of light, of rippling water and moonlit skies, of sand and earth. The soundtrack is equally dense and engaging, as the natural world whispers to us in the rustle of the undergrowth or sings to us in the sounds of the wind and the calls of birds. The spaces of Secret Paths are full of life, as lizards slither from rock to rock, or field mice dart for cover, yet even animals, which might be frightening in other contexts (coyotes, foxes, owls), seem eager to reveal their secrets to our explorers. Jesse, one of the game's protagonists, expresses a fear of the "creepy" night-time woods, but the game makes the animals seem tame and the forest safe, even in the dead of night. The game's puzzles reward careful exploration and observation. At one point, we must cautiously approach a timid fawn if we wish to be granted the magic jewels that are the tokens of our quest. The guidebook urges us to be "unhurried and gentle" with the "easily startled" deer.

Our goal is less to master nature than to understand how we might live in harmony with it. We learn to mimic its patterns, to observe the notes (produced by singing cactus) that make a lizard's head bob with approval and then to copy them ourselves, to position spiders on a web so that they may harmonize rather than create discord. And, in some cases, we are rewarded for feeding and caring for the animals. In The Secret Garden (1911), a robin leads Mary Lennox to the branches that mask the entrance to the forgotten rose garden:

Mary had stepped close to the robin, and suddenly the gusts of wind swung aside some loose ivy trails, and more suddenly still, she jumped toward it and caught it in her hand. This she did because she had seen something under it—a round knob which had been covered by the leaves hanging over it....The robin kept singing and twittering away and tilting his head on one side, as if he were as excited as she was.(80)

Such animal guides abound in Secret Paths: the curser is shaped like a ladybug during our explorations and like a butterfly when we want to venture beyond the current screen. Animals show us the way, if we only take the time to look and listen.

Unlike twitch-and-shoot boys games, Secret Paths encourages us to stroke and caress the screen with our curser, clicking only when we know where secret treasures might be hidden.

A magic book tells us: As I patiently traveled along [through the paths], I found that everything was enchanted! The trees, flowers and animals, the sun, sky and stars—all had magical properties! The more closely I listened and the more carefully I explored, the more was revealed to me.

Nature's rhythms are gradual and recurring, a continual process of birth, growth, and transformation. Laurel explains:

We made the "game" intentionally slow—a girl can move down the paths at whatever pace, stop and play with puzzles or stones, or hang out in the tree house with or without the other characters. I think that this slowness is really a kind of refuge for the girls. The game is much slower than television, for example. One of the issues that girls have raised with us in our most recent survey of their concerns is the problem of feeling too busy. I think that "Secret Paths" provides an antidote to that feeling from the surprising source of the computer. (Personal correspondence, 1997)

Frances Hodgson Burnett's "Secret Garden" (1911) is a place of healing and the book links Mary's restoration of the forgotten rose garden with her repairing a family torn apart by tragedy, restoring a sickly boy to health, and coming to grips with her mother's death:

So long as Mistress Mary's mind was full of disagreeable thoughts about her dislikes and sour opinions of people and her determined not to be pleased by or interested in anything, she was a yellow-faced, sickly, bored and wretched child.... When her mind gradually filled itself with robins, and moorland cottages crowded with children...with springtime and with secret gardens coming alive day by day...there was no room for the disagreeable thoughts which affected her liver and her digestion and made her yellow and tired. (294)

Purple Moon's Secret Paths has also been designed as a healing place, where girls are encouraged to "explore with your heart" and answer their emotional dilemmas. As the magical book explains, "You will never be alone here, for this is a place where girls come to share and to seek help from one another." At the game's opening, we draw together a group of female friends in the treehouse, where each confesses their secrets and tells of their worries and sufferings. Miko speaks of the pressure to always be the best and the alienation she feels from the other children; Dana recounts her rage over losing a soccer companionship; Minn describes her humiliation because her immigrant grandmother has refused to assimilate new world customs. Some of them have lost parents; others face scary situations or emotional slights that cripple their confidence. Their answers lie along the secret paths through the forest, where the adventurers can find hidden magical stones that embody social, psychological, or emotional strengths. Along the way, the girl's secrets are literally embedded within the landscape, so that clicking on our environment may call forth memories or confessions. If we are successful in finding all of the hidden stones, they magically form a necklace and when given to the right girl, they allow us to hear a comforting or clarifying story. Such narratives teach girls how to find emotional resources within themselves and how to observe and respond to others' often-unarticulated needs. Solving puzzles in the physical environment helps us to address problems in our social environment. Secret Paths is what Brenda Laurel calls a "friendship adventure," allowing young girls to rehearse their coping skills and try alternative social strategies.

The Play Town: Another Space for Girls?

Harriet was trying to explain to Sport how to play Town. "See, first you make up the name of the town. Then you write down the names of all the people who live in it...Then when you know who lives there, you make up what they do. For instance, Mr. Charles Hanley runs the filling station on the corner...." Harriet got very businesslike. She stood up, and then got on her knees in the soft September mud so she could lean over the little valley made between the two big roots of the tree. She referred to her notebook every now and then, but for the most part, she stared intently at the mossy lowlands, which made her town. (3–5)—Louise Fitzhugh, *Harriet the Spy* (1964)

Harriet the Spy opens with a description of another form of spatial play for girls—Harriet's "town," a "microworld" she maps onto the familiar contours of her own backyard and uses to think through the complex social relations she observes in her community. Harriet controls the inhabitants of this town, shaping their actions to her desires: "In this town, everybody goes to bed at nine-thirty."(4) Not unlike a soap opera, her stories depend on juxtapositions of radically different forms of human experience: "Now, this night, as Mr. Hanley is just about to close up, a long, big old black car drives up and in it there are all these men with guns...At this same minute Mrs. Harrison's baby is born." (6) Her fascination with mapping and controlling the physical space of the town makes her game a pre-digital prototype for Sim City and other simulation games. However, compared to Harriet's vivid interest in the distinct personalities and particular experiences of her townspeople, Sim City seems alienated and abstract. Sim City's classifications of land use into residential, commercial, and industrial push us well beyond the scale of everyday life and in so doing, strips the landscape of its potential as a stage for children's fantasies. Sim City offers us another form of power—the power to "play God," to design our physical environment, to sculpt the landscape or call down natural disasters (Friedman, 1995), but not the power to imaginatively transform our social environment. Sim City embraces stock themes from boys play, such as building forts, shaping earth with toy trucks, or damming creeks, playing them out on a much larger scale. For Harriet, the mapping of the space was only the first step in preparing the ground for a rich saga of life and death, joy and sorrow, and those of the elements that are totally lacking in most existing simulation games.

As Fitzhugh's novel continues, Harriet's interests shift from the imaginary events of her simulated town and into real world spaces. She "spies" on people's private social interactions, staging more and more "daring" investigations, trying to understand what motivates adult actions, and writing her evaluations and interpretations of their lives in her notebook. Harriet's adventures take her well beyond the constricted space of her own home. She breaks into and enters houses and takes rides on dumbwaiters, sneaks through back allies and peeps into windows. She barely avoids being caught. Harriet's adventures occur in public space (not the private space of the secret garden), a populated environment (not the natural worlds visited

353

in Secret Paths). Yet, her adventures are not so much direct struggles with opposing forces (as might be found in a boy's book adventure) as covert operations to ferret out knowledge of social relations.

The games of Theresa Duncan (Chop Suey, Smarty, Zero Zero) offer a digital version of Harriet's "Town." Players can explore suburban and urban spaces and pry into bedroom closets in search of the extraordinary dimensions of ordinary life. Duncan specifically cites *Harriet the Spy* as an influence, hoping that her games will grant young girls "a sense of inquisitiveness and wonder." Chop Suey and Smarty take place in small Midwestern towns, a working class world of diners, hardware stores, and beauty parlors. Zero Zero draws us further from home—into fin de siecle Paris, a world of bakeries, wax museums, and catacombs. These spaces are rendered in a distinctive style somewhere between the primitiveness of Grandma Moses and the colorful postmodernism of Pee-Wee's Playhouse. Far removed from the romantic imagery of Secret Paths, these worlds overflow with city sounds—the clopping of horse hooves on cobblestones, barking dogs, clanging church bells in Zero Zero—and the narrator seems fascinated with the smoke stacks and signs which clutter this man-made environment. As the narrator in Zero Zero rhapsodizes, "smoke curled black and feathery like a horse's tale from a thousand chimney pots" in this world "before popsicles and paperbacks." While the social order has been tamed, posing few dangers, Duncan has not rid these worlds of their more disreputable elements. The guy in the candy shop in Chop Suey has covered his body with tattoos. The Frenchmen in Zero Zero are suitably bored, ill tempered, and insulting; even flowers hurl abuse at us. The man in the antlered hat sings rowdy songs about "bones" and "guts" when we visit the catacombs, and the women puff on cigarettes, wear too much make-up, flash their cleavage, and hint about illicit rendezvous. Duncan suggests:

> There's a sense of bittersweet experience in Chop Suey, where not everyone has had a perfect life but they're all happy people. Vera has three ex-husbands all named Bob.... Vera has problems, but she's also filled with love. And she's just a very vibrant, alive person, and that's why she fascinates the little girls.

Duncan rejects our tendency to "project this fantasy of purity and innocence onto children," suggesting that all this "niceness" deprives children of "the richness of their lives" and does not help them come to grips with their "complicated feelings" towards the people in their lives.

Bon—Bon's Boudoir in "Zero Zero." Copyright Theresa Duncan, 1997. Used with permission.

Duncan's protagonists, June Bug (Chop Suey), Pinkee LeBrun (Zero Zero), are smart, curious girls, who want to know more than they have been told. Daring Pinkee scampers along the roofs of Paris and pops down chimneys or steps boldly through the doors of shops, questioning adults about their visions for the new century. Yet, she is also interested in smaller, more intimate questions, such as the identity of the secret admirer who writes love poems to Bon Bon, the singer at the Follies. Clues unearthed in one location may shed light on mysteries posed elsewhere, allowing Duncan to suggest something of the "interconnectedness" of life within a close community. Often, as in Harriet, the goal is less to evaluate these people than to understand what makes them tick. In that sense, the game fosters the character-centered reading practices which Segel (1986) associates with the "girls book" genres, reading practices that thrive on gossip and speculation.

Duncan's games have no great plot to propel them. Duncan said, "Chop Suey works the way that real life does: all these things happen to you, but there's no magical event, like there is sometimes in books, that transforms you." Lazy curiosity invites us to explore the contents of each shop, to flip through the fashion magazines in Bon Bon's dressing room, to view the early trick films playing at Cinema Egypt or to watch the cheeses in the window of Quel Fromage which are, for reasons of their own, staging the major turning points of the French revolution. (She also cites inspiration from the more surreal adventures of Alice in Wonderland!) The interfaces are flexible, allowing us to visit any location when we want without having to fight our way through levels or work past puzzling obstacles. Zero Zero and Duncan's other games take particular pleasure in anarchistic imagery, in ways we can disrupt and destabilize the environment, showering the baker's angry faces with white clouds of flour, ripping off the table clothes, or shaking up soda bottles so they will spurt their corks. Often, there is something vaguely naughty about the game activities, as when a visit to Poire the fashion designer has us matching different pairs of underwear. In that sense, Duncan's stories preserve the mischievous and sometimes anti-social character of Harriet's antics and the transformative humor of Lewis Carroll, encouraging the young gamers to take more risks and to try things that might not ordinarily meet their parents' approval. Pinkee's first actions as a baby are to rip the pink ribbons from her hair! Duncan likes her characters free and "unladylike."

In keeping with the pedagogic legacy of the girls book tradition, Zero Zero promises us an introduction to French history, culture, and language, Smarty a mixture of "spelling and spells, math and Martians, grammar and glamour," but Duncan's approach is sassy and irreverent. The waxwork of Louis XIV sticks out its tongue at us, while Joan D'Arc is rendered in marshmallow, altogether better suited for toasting. The breads and cakes in the bakery are shaped like the faces of French philosophers and spout incomprehensible arguments. Pinkee's quest for knowledge about the coming century cannot be reduced to an approved curriculum, but rather expresses an unrestrained fascination with the stories, good, bad, happy or sad, that people tell each other about their lives.

Harriet the Spy is ambivalent about its protagonist's escapades: her misadventures clearly excite the book's female readers, but the character herself is socially ostracized and disciplined, forced to more appropriately channel her creativity and curiosity. Pinkee suffers no such punishment, ending up the game watching the fireworks that mark the change of the centuries, taking pleasure in the knowledge that she will be a central part of the changes that are coming: "tonight belongs to Bon Bon but the future belongs to Pinkee."

Conclusion: Towards a Gender-Neutral Play Space?

Brenda Laurel and Theresa Duncan offer two very different conceptions of a digital play space for girls—one pastoral, the other urban; one based on the ideal of living in harmony with nature, the other based on an anarchistic pleasure in disrupting the stable order of everyday life and making the familiar "strange." Yet, in many ways, the two games embrace remarkably similar ideals—play spaces for girls adopt a slower pace, are less filled with dangers, invite gradual investigation and discovery, foster an awareness of social relations and a search for secrets, center around emotional relations between characters. Both allow the exploration of physical environments, but are really about the interior worlds of feelings and fears. Laurel and Duncan make an important contribution when they propose new and different models for how digital media may be used. The current capabilities of our video and computer game technologies reflect the priorities of an earlier generation of game makers and their conception of the boys market. Their assumptions about what kinds of digital play spaces were desirable defined how the bytes would be allocated, valuing rapid response time over the memory necessary to construct more complex and compelling characters. Laurel and Duncan shift the focus—prioritizing character relations and "friendship adventures." In doing so, they are expanding what computers can do and what roles they can play in our lives.

On the other hand, in our desire to open digital technologies as an alternative play space for girls, we must guard against simply duplicating in the new medium the gender-specific genres of children's literature. The segregation of children's reading into boy book and girl book genres, Segel (1986) argues, encouraged the development of gender-specific reading strategies—with boys reading for plot and girls reading for character relationship. Such differences, Segel suggests, taught children to replicate the separation between a male public sphere of risk taking and a female domestic sphere of care taking. As Segel (1986) notes, the classification of children's literature into boys books and girls books "extracted a heavy cost in feminine self-esteem," restricting girl's imaginative experience to what adults perceived as its "proper place." Boys developed a sense of autonomy and mastery both from their reading and from their play. Girls learned to fetter their imaginations, just as they restricted their movements into real world spaces. At the same time, this genre division also limited boys' psychological and emotional development, insuring a focus on goal-oriented, utilitarian, and violent plots. Too much interest in social and emotional life was a vulnerability in a world where competition left little room to be "lead by your heart." We need to design digital play spaces which allow girls to do something more than stitch doll clothes, mother nature, or heal their friend's sufferings or boys to do something more than battle it out with the barbarian hordes.

Segel's analysis of "gender and childhood reading" suggests two ways of moving beyond the gender-segregation of our virtual landscape. First, as Segel (1986) suggests, the designation of books for boys and girls did not preclude (though certainly discouraged) reading across gender lines: "Though girls when they reached 'that certain age' could be prevented from joining boys games and lively exploits, it was harder to keep them from accompanying their brothers on vicarious adventures through the reading of boys books." (175) Reading boys books gave girls (admittedly limited) access to the boy culture and its values. Segel finds evidence of such gender crossing in the nineteenth-century, though girls were actively discouraged from reading boys books because their contents were thought too lurid and un-wholesome. At other times, educational authorities encouraged the assignment of boys books in public schools since girls could read and enjoy them, while there was much greater stigma attached to boys reading girls books. The growing visibility of the "quake girls," female gamers who compete in traditional male fighting and action/adventure games (Jenkins and Cassell), suggests that there has always been a healthy degree of "crossover" interest in the games market and that many girls enjoy "playing with power." Girls may compete more directly and aggressively with boys in the video game arena than would ever have been possible in the real world of backyard play, since differences in actual size, strength, and agility have no effect on the outcome of the game. And they can return from combat without the ripped clothes or black eyes that told parents they had done something "unladylike." Unfortunately, much as girls who read boys books were likely to encounter the misogynistic themes that mark boys' fantasies of separation from their mothers, girls who play boys games find the games' constructions of female sexuality and power are designed to gratify preadolescent males, not to empower girls. Girl gamers are aggressively campaigning to have their tastes and interests factored into the development of action games.

We need to open up more space for girls to join—or play alongside—the traditional boy culture down by the river, in the old vacant lot, within the bamboo forest. Girls need to learn how to explore "unsafe" and "unfriendly" spaces. Girls need to experience the "complete freedom of movement" promised by the boys games, if not all the time, then at least some of the time, if they are going to develop the self confidence and competitiveness demanded of contemporary professional women. Girls need to learn how to, in the words of a contemporary best-seller, "run with the wolves" and not just follow the butterflies along the Secret Paths. Girls need to be able to play games where Barbie gets to kick some butt.

However, this focus on creating action games for girls still represents only part of the answer, for as Segel (1986) notes, the gender segregation of children's literature was almost as damaging for boys as it was for girls: "In a society where many men and women are alienated from members of the other sex, one wonders whether males might be more comfortable with and understanding of women's needs and perspectives if they had imaginatively shared female experiences through books, beginning in childhood." (183) Boys may need to play in secret gardens or toy towns just as much as girls need to explore adventure islands. In the literary realm, Segel points towards books, such as *Little House on the Prairie* or *A Wrinkle in Time* , that fuse the boys and girl genres, rewarding both a traditionally masculine interest in plot action and a traditionally feminine interest in character relations.

Sega Saturn's Nights into Dreams represents a similar fusion of the boys and girls game genres. Much as in Secret Paths, our movement through the game space is framed as an attempt to resolve the characters' emotional problems. In the frame stories that open the game, we enter the mindscape of the two protagonists as they toss and turn in their sleep. Claris, the female protagonist, hopes to gain recognition on the stage as a singer, but has nightmares of being rejected and ridiculed. Elliot, the male character, has fantasies of scoring big on the basketball court yet fears being bullied by bigger and more aggressive players. They run away from their problems, only to find themselves in Nightopia, where they must save the dream world from the evil schemes of Wileman the Wicked and his monstrous minions. In the dreamworld, both Claris and Elliot may assume the identity of Nights, an androgynous harlequin figure, who can fly through the air, transcending all the problems below. Nights' complex mythology has players gathering glowing orbs which represent different forms of energy needed to confront Claris and Elliot's problems—purity (white), wisdom (green), hope (yellow), intelligence (blue) and bravery (red)—a structure that recalls the magic stones in Secret Paths through the Forest.

The tone of this game is aptly captured by one Internet game critic, Big Mitch (n.d.): "The whole experience of Nights is in soaring, tumbling, and freewheeling through colorful landscapes, swooping here and there, and just losing yourself in the moment. This is not a game you set out to win; the fun is in the journey rather than the destination." Big Mitch's response suggests a recognition of the fundamentally different qualities of this game—its focus on psychological issues as much as upon action and conflict, its fascination with aimless exploration rather than goal-driven narrative, its movement between a realistic world of everyday problems and a fantasy realm of great adventure, its mixture of the speed and mobility associated with the boys platform games with the lush natural landscapes and the sculpted soundtracks associated with the girls games. Spring Valley is a sparkling world of rainbows and waterfalls and Emerald Green forests. Other levels allow us to splash through cascading fountains, sail past icy mountains and frozen wonderlands, or bounce on pillows and off the walls of the surreal Soft Museum or swim through aquatic tunnels. The game's 3-D design allows an exhilarating freedom of movement, enhanced by design features—such as wind resistance—which give players a stronger than average sense of embodiment. Nights into Dreams retains some of the dangerous and risky elements associated with the boys games. There are spooky places in this game, including nightmare worlds full of day-glo serpents and winged beasties, and there are enemies we must battle, yet there is also a sense of unconstrained adventure, floating through the clouds. Our primary enemy is time, the alarm clock that will awaken us from our dreams. Even when we confront monsters, they don't fire upon us; we must simply avoid flying directly into their sharp teeth if we want to master them. When we lose Nights' magical, gender-bending garb, we turn back into boys and girls and must hoof it as pedestrians across the rugged terrain below, a situation which makes it far less likely we will achieve our goals. To be gendered is to be constrained; to escape gender is to escape gravity and to fly above it all.

Sociologist Barrie Thorne (1993) has discussed the forms of "borderwork" which occurs when boys and girls occupy the same play spaces: "The spatial separation of boys and girls [on the same playground] constitutes a kind of boundary, perhaps felt most strongly by individuals who want to join an activity controlled by the other gender." (64–65) Boys and girls are brought together in the same space, but they repeatedly enact the separation and opposition between the two play cultures. In real world play, this "borderwork" takes the form of chases and contests on the one hand and "cooties" or other pollution taboos on the other. When "borderwork" occurs, gender distinctions become extremely rigid and nothing passes between the two spheres. Something similar occurs in many of the books which Segel identifies as gender neutral—male and female reading interests co-exist, side by side, like children sharing a playground, and yet they remain resolutely separate and the writers, if anything, exaggerate gender differences in order to proclaim their dual address. Wendy and the "lost boys" both travel to Never-Never-Land but Wendy plays house and the "lost boys" play Indians or pirates. The "little house" and the" prairie" exist side by side in Laura Wilder's novels, but the mother remains trapped inside the house, while Pa ventures into the frontier. The moments when the line between the little house and the prairie are crossed, such as a scene where a Native American penetrates into Ma Wilder's parlor, become moments of intense anxiety. Only Laura can follow her pa across the threshold of the little house and onto the prairie and her adventurous spirit is often presented as an unfeminine trait she is likely to outgrow as she gets older.

As we develop digital play spaces for boys and girls, we need to make sure this same pattern isn't repeated, that we do not create blue and pink ghettos inside the play space. On the one hand, the opening sequences of Nights into Dreams, which frame Elliot and Claris as possessing fundamentally different dreams (sports for boys and musical performance for girls, graffiti-laden inner city basketball courts for boys and pastoral gardens for girls), perform this kind of borderwork, defining the proper place for each gender. On the other hand, the androgynous Nights embodies a fantasy of transcending gender and thus achieving the freedom and mobility to fly above it all. To win the game, the player must become both the male and the female protagonists and they must join forces for the final level. The penalty for failure in this world is to be trapped on the ground and to be fixed into a single gender.

Thorne finds that aggressive "borderwork" is more likely to occur when children are forced together by adults than when they find themselves interacting more spontaneously, more likely to occur in prestructured institutional settings like the schoolyard than in the informal settings of the subdivisions and apartment complexes. All of this suggests that our fantasy of designing games that will provide common play spaces for girls and boys, may be an illusive one, one as full of complications and challenges on its own terms as creating a "girls only" space or encouraging girls to venture into traditional male turf. We are not yet sure what such a gender-neutral space will look like. Creating such a space would mean redesigning not only the nature of computer games but also the nature of society. The danger may be that in such a space, gender differences are going to be more acutely felt, as boys and girls will be repelled from each other rather than drawn together. There are reasons why this is a place where neither the feminist entrepreneurs nor the boys game companies are ready to go, yet as the girl's market is secured, the challenge must be to find a way to move beyond our existing categories and to once again invent new kinds of virtual play spaces.

References

Booth, A. and Johnson, D. 1975. "The Effect of Crowding on Child Health and Development." *American Behaviorial Scientist* 18: 736–749.

Burnett, F.H. 1911. *The Secret Garden.* New York: Harper Collins.

Cavallo, D. 1981. *Muscles and Morals: Organized Playgrounds and Urban Reform, 1880–1920.* Philadelphia: University of Pennsylvania Press.

"Critical Depth." 1988. Advertisement, *Next Generation,* January.

"Die by the Sword." 1988. Advertisement, *Next Generation,* January.

Donaldson, F. 1970. "The Child in the City." University of Washington, mimeograph, cited in M. H. Matthews 1992, *Making Sense of Place: Children's Understanding of Large-Scale Environments.* Hertfordshire: Barnes and Noble.

Farley, W. 1941. *The Black Stallion.* New York: Random House.

Feinstein, K. and Kent, S. 1997. "Towards a Definition of 'Videogames.'" http://www.videotopia.com/errata1.htm.

Fitzhugh, L. 1964. *Harriet, the Spy.* New York: Harper & Row.

Formanek-Brunnel, M. 1996. "The Politics of Dollhood in Nineteenth-Century America." In H. Jenkins, ed., *The Children's Culture Reader.* New York: New York University Press.

Friedman, T. 1995. "Making Sense of Software: Computer Games and Interactive Textuality." In S. G. Jones, ed., *Cybersociety: Computer-Mediated Communication and Community.* Thousand Oaks, Calif.: Sage Publications.

Hart. R. 1979. Children's Experience of Place. New York: John Wiley and Sons.

Holland, N. N. and Sherman, L.F. 1986. "Gothic Possibilities." In E. A. Flynn and P.P. Schweickart, eds., *Gender and Reading: Essays on Readers, Texts and Contexts.* Baltimore: Johns Hopkins University Press.

Jenkins, H. and Cassell, J. 1998. "Chess for Girls?: The Gender Politics of the Girls Game Movement." *From Barbie to Mortal Kombat.* Boston: MIT Press.

Katz, J. 1997. *Virtuous Reality.* New York: Random House.

Kinchloe, J. L. 1997. "Home Alone and 'Bad to the Bone': The Advent of a Postmodern Childhood." In S. R. Steinberg and J. L. Kinchloe, eds., *Kinder-Culture: The Corporate Construction of Childhood.* New York: Westview.

Kinder, M. 1996. "Contextualizing Video Game Violence: From 'Teenage Mutant Ninja Turtles 1' to 'Mortal Kombat 2.'" In P.M. Greenfield and R.R. Cocking, eds., *Interacting with Video.* Norwood: Ablex Publishing.

Matthews, R.C. 1986. *Childhood's Domain: Play and Place in Child Development.* London: Croom Helm.

Newson, J. and Newson, E. 1976. *Seven Years Old in the Home Environment.* London: Allen and Unwin.

Rheingold, H. L. and Cook, K.V. 1975. "The Content of Boys' and Girls' Rooms as an Index to Parents' Behavior." *Child Development* 46. 459–463.

Rotundo, E. A. 1994. *American Manhood: Transformations in Masculinity from the Revolution to the Modern Era.* New York: Basic.

Searles, H. 1959. *The Non-Human Development in Normal Development and Schizophrenia.* New York: International Universities Press.

Segel, E. 1986. "As the Twig is Bent...': Gender and Childhood Reading." In E. A. Flynn and P. P. Schweickart, eds., *Gender and Reading: Essays on Readers, Texts and Contexts.* Baltimore: Johns Hopkins University Press.

Seitzer, E. 1996. Transcript of Expert Panel Meeting, Sega of America Gatekeeper Program. Los Angeles, June 21.

"Sonic R." 1998. Advertisement, *Next Generation,* January.

Tapscott, D. 1997. *Growing Up Digital: The Rise of the Net Generation.* New York: McGraw Hill.

Thorne, B. 1993. *Gender Play: Girls and Boys in School.* New Brunswick: Rutgers University Press.

van Staden, J. F. 1984. "Urban Early Adolescents, Crowding and the Neighbourhood Experience: A Preliminary Investigation." *Journal of Environmental Psychology* 4: 97–118.

Van Vliet, W. 1983. "Exploring the Fourth Environment: An Examination of the Home Range of City and Suburban Teenagers." *Environment and Behavior* 15: 567–88.

"VR Sports." 1998. Advertisement, *Next Generation,* January.

Ward, C. 1977. *The Child in the City.* London: Architectural Press.

West, E. 1992. "Children on the Plains Frontier." In E. West and P. Petrik, eds., *Small Worlds: Children and Adolescents in America, 1850–1950.* Lawrence: The University of Kansas. p. 26–41.

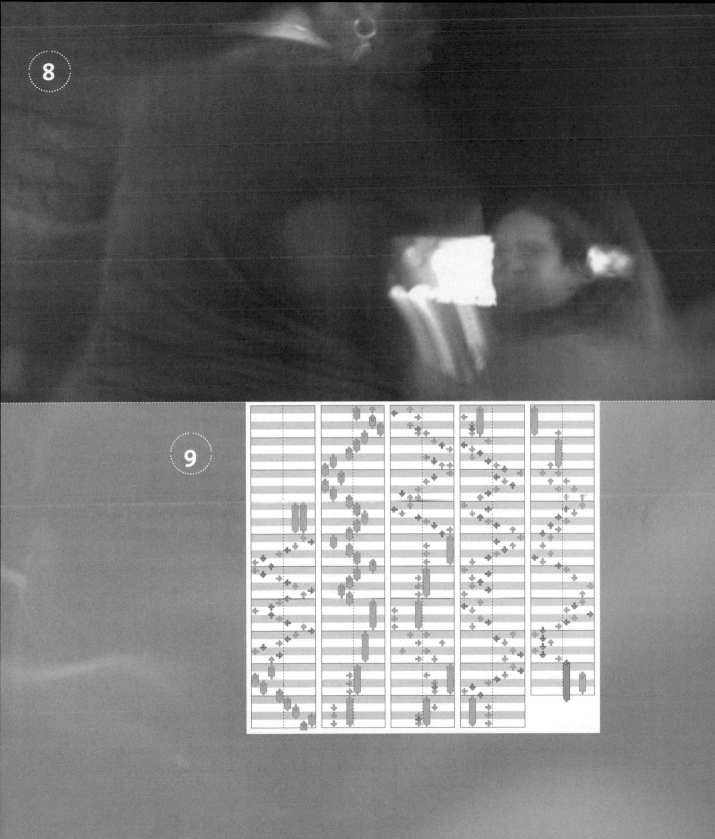

Formal Abstract Design Tools

Doug Church

Context

*Written after we had finished three or four games at the game development company Looking Glass, "Formal Abstract Design Tools" was my attempt to share with the public some of the ways we discussed and thought about games. We were frustrated with the lack of any terminology that was more specific than "fun;" my essay's response was split evenly between "This is cool and useful, how can I help?" and "You can't mandate and legislate design—design comes from designers, not from executive boardrooms!" I still believe that a better understanding of design tools will lead to greater creativity and better design, and that we still have a lot of thinking and experimenting to do. This article originally appeared in the August 1999 issue of **Game Developer** magazine.*

Game Design Models

Doug Church has made games for a living since 1990, mixing programming, design, management, consulting, and so on—although he wants it known that he cannot draw. Doug is interested in how design and technology come together to evolve player experiences.

Introduction

What is a modern computer game made of? It fuses a technical base with a vision for the player's experience. All of the disciplines involved (design, art, audio, levels, code, and so on) work together to achieve this synthesis.

In most disciplines, industry evolution is obvious: The machines we play on are far more powerful, screens have better resolution and more colors, paint and modeling tools are more sophisticated, audio processing is faster, and sound cards are more capable. Technical issues not even in our vocabulary ten years ago are solved and research continues with essentially infinite headroom. The technical base on which games stand (game code and content creation tools) is evolving.

Across all genres and companies, we build on our own and others' past ideas to expand technical limits, learn new techniques and explore possibilities. Ignoring an anomaly or two, no single company or team would be where it is now had it been forced to work in a vacuum.

Design, on the other hand, is the least understood aspect of computer game creation. It actualizes the vision, putting art, code, levels, and sound together into what players experience, minute to minute. Clever code, beautiful art, and stunning levels don't help if they're never encountered. Design tasks determine player goals and pacing. The design is the game; without it, you would have a CD full of data, but no experience.

Sadly, design is also the aspect that has had the most trouble evolving. Not enough is done to build on past discoveries, share concepts behind successes, and apply lessons learned in one domain or genre to another. Within genres (and certainly within specific design teams), particular lines have evolved significantly. But design evolution still lags far behind the evolution of overall game technology.

How Do We Talk About Games?

The primary inhibitor of design evolution is the lack of a common design vocabulary. Most professional disciplines have a fairly evolved language for discussion. Athletes know the language of their sport and of general physical conditioning, engineers know the technical jargon of their field, doctors know Latin names for body parts and how to scribble illegible prescriptions. In contrast, game designers can discuss "fun" or "not fun," but often the analysis stops there. Whether or not a game is fun is a good place to start understanding, but as designers, our job demands we go deeper.

367

We should be able to play a side-scrolling shooter on a Game Boy, figure out one cool aspect of it, and apply that idea to the 3D simulation we're building. Or take a game we'd love if it weren't for one annoying part, understand why that part is annoying, and make sure we don't make a similar mistake in our own games. If we reach this understanding, evolution of design across all genres will accelerate. But understanding requires that designers be able to communicate precisely and effectively with one another. In short, we need a shared language of game design.

A Language Without Borders

Our industry produces a wide variety of titles across a range of platforms for equally varied audiences. Any language we develop has to acknowledge this breadth and get at the common elements beneath seemingly disparate genres and products. We need to be able to put our lessons, innovations, and mistakes into a form we can all look at, remember, and benefit from.

A design vocabulary would allow us to do just that, as we could talk about the underlying components of a game. Instead of just saying, "That was fun," or "I don't know, that wasn't much fun," we could dissect a game into its components, and attempt to understand how these parts balance and fit together. A precise vocabulary would improve our understanding of and facility with game creation.

This is something we already do naturally with many technical innovations, since they are often much easier to isolate within a product or transfer to another project. A texture mapper or motion capture system is easily encapsulated. When everyone at the office gathers around some newly released game, major technical "evaluation" is done in the first five minutes: "Wow, nice texture mapping," or "Those figures rock" or "Still don't have a sub-pixel accurate mapper? What is their problem?" or "Man, we have to steal that special effect." But when the crowd disperses, few observations have been made as to what sorts of design leaps were in evidence and, more importantly, what worked and what didn't.

Design is hard to point at directly on a screen. Because of this, its evolutionary path is often stagnant. Within a given genre, design evolution often occurs through refinement. This year's real-time strategy (RTS) games clearly built on last year's RTS games. And that will continue, because design vocabulary today is essentially specific to individual games or genres. You can talk about balancing each race's unit costs, or unit count versus power trade-offs. But we would be hard pressed to show many examples of how innovations in RTS games have helped role-playing games (RPGs) get better. In fact, we might have a hard time describing what could be shared.

These concerns lead to the conclusion that a shared design vocabulary could be very useful. The notion of "Formal Abstract Design Tools" (or FADT, as they'll be referred to from here on) is an attempt to create a framework for such a vocabulary and a way of going about the process of building it.

Examining the phrase, we have: "formal," implying precise definition and the ability to explain it to someone else; "abstract," to emphasize the focus on underlying ideas, not specific genre constructs; "design," as in, well, we're designers; and "tools," since they'll form the common vocabulary we want to create.

"Design" and "tools" are both largely self-explanatory. However, some examples may help clarify "formal" and "abstract." For instance, claiming that "cool stuff" qualifies as a FADT violates the need for formality, since "cool" is not a precise word one can explain concretely—various people are likely to interpret it very differently. On the other hand, "player reward" is well defined and explainable, and thus works. Similarly, a "+2 Giant Slaying Sword" in an RPG is not abstract, but rather an element of one particular game. It doesn't qualify as a FADT because it isn't abstract. The general notion that a magic sword is based on—a mechanic for delivering more powerful equipment to the player—is, however, a good example of a FADT, so the idea of a "player power-up curve" might meet the definition above.

Let's Create a Design Vocabulary—What Could Possibly Go Wrong?

Before we start investigating tools in more detail and actually look at examples, some cautionary words. Abstract tools are not bricks to build a game out of. You don't build a house out of tools; you build it with tools. Games are the same way. Having a good "player power-up curve" won't make a game good. FADT are not magic ingredients you add and season to taste. You do not go into a product proposal meeting saying, "This game is all about player power-up curves." As a designer, you still have to figure out what is fun, what your game is about, and what vision and goals you bring to it.

But a design vocabulary is our tool kit to pick apart games and take the parts that resonate with us to realize our own game vision, or refine how our own games work. Once you have thought out your design, you can investigate whether a given tool is used by your game already. If it is, are you using it well, or is it extraneous? If it isn't used, should it be, or is the tool not relevant for your game? Not every construction project needs a circular power saw (sadly), and not every game needs every tool. Using the right tools will help get the shape you want, the strength you need, and the right style.

Similarly, tools don't always work well together—sometimes they conflict. The goal isn't to always use every tool in every game. You can use an individual tool in different ways, and a given tool might just sit in a toolbox waiting to see if it is needed. You, the designer, wield the tools to make what you want—don't let them run the show.

Tools Would Be Useful—Where Do We Find Them?

Therefore, we need a design vocabulary, a set of tools underlying game design practice. There is no correct or official method to identify them. One easy way to start looking is to take a good game and describe concretely some of the things that work well. Then, from concrete examples of real game elements, we can attempt to abstract and formalize a few key aspects and maybe find ourselves a few tools.

There isn't enough space here to exhaustively analyze each tool or game—the goal here is to give an overview of the ideas behind and uses of FADT, not a complete view of everything. With that in mind, we'll start with a quick tour of some games, tools, and ideas. Since we are looking for examples of good game design, we'll start by examining *Mario 64*. Once we have explored some concrete aspects of the game itself, we'll step back and start looking for things to abstract and formalize that we can apply to other genres and titles.

Mario 64 Game Play

Mario 64 blends (apparent) open-ended exploration with continual and clear direction along most paths. Players always have lots to do but are given a lot of choice about which parts of the world they work on and which extra stars they go for. The game also avoids a lot of the super-linear, what's-on-the-next-screen feel of side-scrolling games and gives players a sense of control. In *Mario*, players spend most of their time deciding what they want to do next, not trying to get unstuck, or finding something to do.

A major decision in the design was to have multiple goals in each of the worlds. The first time players arrive in a world, they mostly explore the paths and directions available. Often the first star (typically the easiest to get in each world) has been set up to encourage players to see most of the area. So even while getting that first star, players often see things they know they will need to use in a later trip. They notice inaccessible red coins, hatboxes, strange contraptions, and so on, while they work on the early goals in a world. When they return to that world for later goals, players already know their way around and have in their heads some idea about how their goals might be achieved, since they have already visited the world and seen many of its elements.

Mario's worlds are also fairly consistent and predictable (if at times a bit odd). Players are given a small, simple set of controls, which work at all times. Simple though the controls are, they are very expressive, allowing rich interaction through simple movement and a small selection of jumping moves. The controls always work (in that you can always perform each action) and players know what to expect from them (for example, a triple jump goes a certain distance; a hip drop may defeat opponents). Power-ups are introduced slowly, and are used consistently throughout (for example, metal Mario can always walk under water).

These simple, consistent controls, coupled with the very predictable physics (accurate for a *Mario* world), allow players to make good guesses about what will happen should they try something. Monsters and environments increase in complexity, but new and special elements are introduced slowly and usually build on an existing interaction principle. This makes game situations very discernable it's easy for the players to plan for action. If players see a high ledge, a monster across the way, or a chest under water, they can start thinking about how they want to approach it.

This allows players to engage in a pretty sophisticated planning process. They have been presented (usually implicitly) with knowledge of how the world works, how they can move and interact with it, and what obstacles they must overcome. Then, often subconsciously, they evolve a plan for getting to where they want to go. While playing, players make thousands of these little plans, some of which work and some of which don't. The key is that when the plan doesn't succeed, players understand why. The world is so consistent that it's immediately obvious why a plan didn't work. This chasm requires a triple jump, not a standing jump; maybe there was more ice than the player thought; maybe the monster moves just a bit too fast. But players get to make a plan, try it out, and see the results as the game reacts. And since that reaction made sense, they can, if needed, make another plan using the information learned during the first attempt.

This involves players in the game, since they have some control over what they want to do and how they want to do it. Players rarely feel cheated, or like they wanted to try something the game didn't support. By offering a very limited set of actions, but supporting them completely, the world is made real for players. No one who plays *Mario* complains that they want to hollow out a cave and make a fire and cook fish, but cannot. The world is very simple and consistent. If something exists in the world, you can use it.

Great! But I'm Not Writing *Mario 64*. I Mean, It's Already Been Written.

So *Mario* has some cool game design decisions. In the context of *Mario* itself, we have examined briefly how they work together, what impact they have on the players' experience and how these design decisions, in general, push the player toward deeper involvement in the game world. But if you're developing a car-racing game, you can't just add a hip-drop and hope it will work as well as it does in *Mario*. So, it's time to start abstracting out some tools and defining them well enough to apply them to other games.

Looking back at the *Mario* example, what tools can we derive from these specific observations? First, we see there are many ways in which players are encouraged to form their own goals and act on them. The key is that players know what to expect from the world and thus are made to feel in control of the situation. Goals and control can be provided and created at multiple scales, from quick, low-level goals such as "get over the bridge in front of you" to long-term, higher-level goals such as "get all the red coins in the world." Often players work on several goals, at different levels, and on different time scales.

This process of accumulating goals, understanding the world, making a plan and then acting on it, is a powerful means to get the player invested and involved. We'll call this "intention," as it is, in essence, allowing and encouraging players to do things intentionally. Intention can operate at each level, from a quick plan to cross a river to a multi-step plan to solve a huge mystery. This is our first FADT.

INTENTION: *Making an implementable plan of one's own creation in response to the current situation in the game world and one's understanding of the game play options.*

The simplicity and solidity of *Mario's* world makes players feel more connected to, or responsible for, their actions. In particular, when players attempt to do something and it goes wrong, they are likely to realize why it went wrong. This leads to another tool, "perceivable consequence." The key is that not only did the game react to the player; its reaction was also apparent. When I make the jump, either it works or it doesn't. *Mario* uses this tool extensively at a low level (crossing a river, avoiding a rolling boulder, and so on). Any action you undertake results in direct, visible feedback.

PERCEIVABLE CONSEQUENCE: *A clear reaction from the game world to the action of the player.*

We have examined the ideas behind some parts of *Mario* and abstracted out two potential design tools. Note also how *Mario* uses these tools in conjunction; as players create and undertake a plan, they then see the results of the plan, and know (or can intuit) why these results occurred. The elements discussed are certainly not the only cool parts of *Mario,* nor the only tools that Mario uses, but hopefully this discussion gives an idea of how the process works. Later, we'll return to examine how multiple tools work with each other. But first, let's see if intention and perceivable consequence can be applied to some other games.

Same Tools, Different Games

Perceived consequence is a tool often used in RPGs, usually with plot or character development. A plot event will happen, in which the game (through characters or narration) essentially comes out and says, "Because of X, Y has happened." This is clearly a fairly pure form of perceived consequence.

Often, however, RPGs are less direct about consequence. For example, the player may decide to stay the night at an inn, and the next morning he may be ambushed. Now, it may be that the designers built this in the code or design of the game. ("We don't want people staying in town too much, so if they start staying at the inn too often, let's ambush them.") However, that causality is not perceivable by the player. While it may be an actual consequence, to the player it appears random.

There are also cases where the consequence is perceivable, but something still seems wrong. Perhaps there's a fork in the road, where players must choose a direction. As a player travels down the chosen path, an encounter with bandits occurs, and the bandit leader proclaims, "You have entered the valley of my people; face my wrath." This is clearly a consequence, but not of a decision players thought they were making. Players bemoan

The story unfolds in *Final Fantasy VIII.*

situations where they are forced into a consequence by the designers, where they are going along playing a game and suddenly are told, "You had no way of knowing, but doing thing X results in horrible thing Z."

The story unfolds in *Final Fantasy VIII*

Here we can look at how *Mario* uses the perceivable consequence tool in order to gain some insight into how to make it work for us without frustrating players. In *Mario,* consequences are usually the direct result of a player decision. Rarely do players following a path through the game suddenly find themselves in a situation where the game basically says, "Ha ha, you had no way of knowing, but you should have gone left," or "Dead end! Now you get crushed." Instead, they see they can try a dangerous jump, a long roundabout path, or maybe a fight. And if it goes wrong, they understand why.

So it should come as no surprise that, in RPGs, often the best uses of consequence come when they are attached to intentional actions. Being given a real choice to do the evil wizard's bidding or resist and face the consequences has both intention and consequence. And when these tools work together, players are left feeling in control and responsible for whatever happens. However, being told, "Now you must do the evil wizard's bidding" by the designer, and then being told, "As you did the evil wizard's bidding, the following horrible consequences have occurred," is far less involving for the player. So while both examples literally have perceived consequence, they don't cause the same reactions in the player.

Same Game, Different Tool

Of course, there are reasons why RPGs often force players into a given situation, even at the cost of removing some of the player's feeling of control. The usual reason is to give the designer greater control of the narrative flow of the game. It is clear that "story" is another abstract tool, used in various ways across all game styles in our industry. But it's important to remember that, although books tell stories, when we say "story" is an abstract tool in game design, we don't necessarily mean expository, pre-written text. In our field, "story" really refers to any narrative thread that is continued throughout the game.

The most obvious uses of story in computer and video games can be found in adventure-game plot lines. In this game category, designers have written the story in advance, and players have it revealed to them through interactions with characters, objects, and the world. While we often try to set up things to give players a sense of control, all players end up with the same plot.

But story comes into play in *NBA Live,* too. There, the story is what happens in the game. Maybe it ends up in overtime for a last-second three-pointer by a star player who hasn't been hitting his shots; maybe it is a total blowout from the beginning and at the end the user gets to put in the benchwarmers for their moment of glory. In either case, the player's actions during play created the story. Clearly, the story in basketball is less involved than that of most RPGs, but on the other hand it is a story that is the player's—not the designer's—to control. And as franchise and season modes are added to sports games and team rivalries and multi-game struggles begin, story takes on a larger role in such games.

STORY: *The narrative thread, whether designer-driven or player-driven, that binds events together and drives the player forward toward completion of the game.*

Using Multiple Tools: Cooperation, Conflict, Confusion

Adventure games often have little intention or perceivable consequence. Players know they will have to go everywhere, pick up everything, talk to everyone, use each thing on each other thing and basically figure out what the designer intended. At the lowest level, there is intention along the lines of, "I bet this object is the one I need," and just enough consequence that players can say, "That worked—the plot is advancing." But there is little overall creation of goals and expression of desires by players. While the player is doing things, it's usually obvious that only a few possibilities (the ones the designers pre-built) work, and that all players must do one of these or fail.

But as we've also seen, this loss of some consequence and most intention comes with a major gain in story. By taking control away from the player in some spaces, the designer is much freer to craft a world full of tuned-up moments in which the designer scripts exactly what will happen. This allows moments that are very powerful for players (moments that often feel as involving as player-directed actions, if not more so). So here is a space where tools conflict, where intention and story are at odds—the more we as designers want to cause particular situations, the less control we can afford to give players.

Once again, tools must be chosen to fit the task. Being aware of what game you want to develop allows you to pick the tools you want and suggests how to use them. You cannot simply start adding more of each tool and expect the game to work.

Concrete Cases of Multiple Tool Use

An interesting variant of the intention versus story conflict is found in traditional SquareSoft console RPGs (for example, the *Final Fantasy* series and *ChronoTrigger*). These games essentially give each tool its own domain in the game. The plot is usually linear, with maybe a few inconsequential branches. However, character and combat statistics are free form, complex systems, which have a variety of items, statistics, and combo effects that are under player control. Players must learn about these systems and then manage the items and party members to create and evolve their party.

During exploration of the game world, the plot reveals itself to the player. The designer creates cool moments that are shown to players, in the game, but are not player-driven. Despite little intention in terms of the plot, players are given some control of the pacing as they explore. While exploring, however, players find objects and characters. These discoveries impact the combat aspects of the game. Combat in the game is entirely under the players' control, as they decide what each character does, which abilities and items to use, and handle other details. Thus, players explore the story while combat contains intention and consequence.

SquareSoft games are, essentially, storybooks. But to turn the page, you have to win in combat. And to win in combat, you have to use the characters and items that come up in the story. So the consequences of the story, while completely preset and identical for all players, are presented (usually) right after a very intentional combat sequence. The plot forces you to go and fight your former ally, but you are in complete control of the fight itself.

Rather than trying to use all three tools at once, the designers use intention and consequence in the combat system, and story and consequence in the actual unfolding of the story. So, the designers get to use all the tools they want and tie the usage together in the game. However, they make sure that tools can be strongly utilized when called on. They don't try to put them in places where it would be hard to make them work effectively.

With a bit of a stretch, one can say that sports and fighting games actually mix all three of the tools into one. The story in a game of *NHL 99* is the scoring, the missed checks or the penalty shot. While this story is somewhat basic, it's completely owned by the player. Each player makes his or her own decision to go for the win by pulling the goalie, or not. And, most importantly, the decision and resulting action either works or does not, driving the game to a player-driven conclusion. Unlike adventure games, there is no trying to guess what the designer had in mind, no saving and loading the game 20 times until you click on the right object. You go in, you play the game, and it ends.

Similarly, in a fighting game, every controller action is completely consistent and visually represented by the character on-screen. In *Tekken*, when Eddy Gordo does a cartwheel kick, you know what you're going to get. As the player learns moves, this consistency allows planning—intention—and the reliability of the world's reactions makes for perceived consequence. If I watch someone play, I can see how and why he or she is better than I am, but all players begin the game on equal footing. The learning curve is in figuring out the controls and actions (in that it's player-learning alone that determines skill and ability in the game). The fact that actions have complete intention and consequence allows this.

In sports games, you direct players, select an action, and watch something happen in response to that action, which gives you feedback about what you tried to do. The player does direct the action—a crosscheck missed, a slap shot deflected, a pass gone wrong—but one level removed. While watching the action on screen, one sees everything that happens, but can't be sure exactly why it happened. This is because the basis of most sports games is a statistical layer, and thus the same actions with the controller can lead to different results. When you combine the different player ratings with the die-rolling going on behind the scenes, the probabilities make sense, but may not be apparent to the player. The intention is still there, but the perceived consequence is much less immediate. This removal of direct control (and the entire issue of directing action) through a statistical layer, which the player can intuit but not directly see, is often present in RPG combat. Thus, in *Tekken*, I can't say,

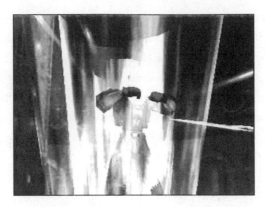

The outcome of consequences in *Final Fantasy VIII*.

"Man, bad luck, if only I'd rolled better," or "Yeah, now that I'm a tenth-level ninja, I can do that move," but in *NBA Live* or an RPG, I often do.

Tool-Based Analysis

A fighter has a simple story ("I had just a sliver of health left, but I feinted a kick and then did my triple punch combo—barely finished him off"), but it's the player's story. There is no, "Man, I can't believe I missed that shot," or "Why did I go and do that?" or "How come my check didn't work?" A simple story, backed up by complete intention in a game that provides clear consequences, makes a very powerful experience for the player. So, both fighting games and, with some obfuscation of consequence, sports games, attempt to fuse intention and consequence and from that allow the players' actions tell a story. The complete control provided by a fighter may make the game more real to the player, but the larger scale of a sports game may provide more sense of story. Or, it may be that the direct control of the fighter makes for a more personal story, and the large scale of a sports game makes for a more epic story. In either case, neither the fighter approach nor the sports simulation approach to story and intention is right or wrong. Each elicits a different set of reactions from the player. As a designer, you must understand the ramifications of tool usage if you're going to create the experience you intend.

Ahhh, So What?

Tools as a vocabulary for analysis present a way to focus on what player experience the designer wishes to create. In this high-level introduction to FADT, I have focused on intention and perceived consequence, with less attention to story. (And what story is mentioned is slanted toward the player-driven.) This is not because these are the only tools or even the best tools. However, as we start to analyze our designs and the player experience provided by the tools we use, it's vital we try to understand what our medium is good at.

Games are not books; games are not movies. In those media, the tools used (camera placement, cuts, zooms, music cues, switching narrators, and so on) are used to manipulate viewers or readers, to make them feel or react exactly the way the director or author wants them to. I believe the challenge and promise of computer game design is that our most important tools are the ones that involve and empower players to make their own decisions. That is something that allows each player to explore him or herself, which is something our medium is uniquely equipped to do.

So I look to tools to help me understand that aspect of game design and to maximize the player's feeling of involvement and self. But that's because that's the kind of game I want to make. Each designer must choose the game he or she wants to create and use the tools available to craft that experience.

Hopefully, I have presented enough examples of the tools and tool-based analysis process to provide a useful overview. Of course, I only mentioned a few tools, but, as stated previously, this article was not intended to be exhaustive or complete. It's a justification for us to begin to put together a vocabulary. For this to become genuinely useful, we must engage in discussion and analysis to get a set of tools we like and then refine those tools until they are well understood. With that, we can start to do more careful analysis of the stuff we like and don't like in current games and work to improve future ones. And we can talk to each other more about design innovations, not just technical ones.

We will have to invest a lot of time if we're to generate a full list of tools we've used (or should use) in our work. There are resource economies, learning, player power-up curves, punishment/reward and many others to consider. And each tool could have an article written just about it—how it has been used over time, what games use it particularly well or poorly, and different aspects of it. Similarly, it would be great to take a game such as *Mario* or *Warcraft* and really deconstruct it, perform as complete an analysis as possible to see if that would be useful. This article is simply a primer to scratch the surface and give examples of this sort of process.

I make no assumption that tools are necessarily useful. Many people may find them overly pedantic. And there's clearly a danger of people starting to use words such as "intention" and "consequence" in the same way that terms and phrases such as "non-linear," "endless variety," or "hundreds of hours of game play" are used meaninglessly. Not surprisingly, that's not the intent.

FADT offers a potential framework for moving the design discussion forward—no more, no less. Although it's no magic bullet, the hope is for this framework to be broadly useful and allow collaborative analysis and refinement of the game design practice, leading to better designs, more interesting products, and satisfied players. If it's not the right framework, we should figure out why and determine what is the right framework. And then we'll work to evolve and develop it together.

Doug Church values beta testers heavily. After a beta test of this article, he learned half the testers found the first two pages slow reading. If you're in that half, skip to the third page, read to the end, then read the intro. Hey, it's an interactive, multipath article.

Game Theory

William Poundstone

Context

*The "prisoner's dilemma" is the archetypic game. It is all your darkest impulses rolled into one agonizing decision. This deceptively simple puzzle encapsulates politics, war, sex, game playing, con games, altruism, and revenge. Not surprisingly, it was invented at the RAND Corporation, the Cold War think tank charged with plotting nuclear strategy. I was fortunate to write **Prisoner's Dilemma** the book from which "Game Theory" was taken, when many of the people from that era were alive, including Merrill Flood and Melvin Dresher—the two unheralded geniuses credited with "inventing" this universal concept.*

Game Design Models

William Poundstone is a journalist, TV writer, and author of ten books, including *How Would You Move Mount Fuji?* (Little, Brown, 2003). He lives in Los Angeles.

The idea of a game mirroring the conflicts of the world is an old one. In the *Mabinogion,* a collection of Welsh folktales (eleventh to thirteenth centuries), one story has two warring kings playing chess while their armies battle nearby. Each time one king captures a piece, a messenger arrives to inform the other that he has lost a crucial man or division. Finally one king checkmates. A bloody messenger staggers in and tells the loser, "The army is in flight. You have lost the kingdom."

This fiction refers to the frankly military origins of chess. The Chinese game of go, the Hindu chaturanga, and many other games are battle simulations, too. Those who see games as simulations of war may see war as a kind of game, too. The classic instance of this was Prussia's century-long infatuation with *Kriegspiel.*

Kriegspiel

Devised as an educational game for military schools in the eighteenth century, Kriegspiel was originally played on a board consisting of a map of the French-Belgian frontier divided into a grid of 3,600 squares. Game pieces advanced and retreated across the board like armies.

The original Kriegspiel spawned many imitations and was ultimately supplanted by a version that became popular among Prussian army officers. This used real military maps in lieu of a game board. In 1824 the chief of the German general staff said of Kriegspiel, "It is not a game at all! It's training for war!"

So began a national obsession that defies belief today. The Prussian high command was so taken with this game that it issued sets to every army regiment. Standing orders compelled every military man to play it. The Kaiser appeared at Kriegspiel tournaments in full military regalia. Inspired by overtly militaristic chess sets then in vogue (pieces were sculpted as German marshals, colonels, privates, etc.), craftsmen produced Kriegspiel pieces of obsessive detail. A pale remnant of these Zinnfiguren ("tin figures") survives today as toy soldiers. Layer after layer of complexity accreted around the game as its devoted players sought ever greater "realism." The rule book, originally sixty pages, grew thicker with each edition. Contingencies of play that were once decided by chance or an umpire were referred to data tables drawn from actual combat.

Claims that the game was behind Prussia's military victories stimulated interest internationally. Prussia's Kriegspiel dry runs of war with Austria supposedly led to a strategy that proved decisive in the Six Weeks' War of 1866. After that, the Austrian Army took no chances and began playing Kriegspiel. France's defeat in the Franco-Prussian War (1870)—allegedly another Kriegspiel victory for Prussia—spawned a Kriegspiel craze there.

Kriegspiel came to the United States after the Civil War. One American army officer complained that the game "cannot be readily and intelligently used by anyone who is not a mathematician, and it requires, in order to be able to use it readily, an amount of special instruction, study, and practice about equivalent to that necessary to acquire a speaking knowledge of a foreign language." Nonetheless, it eventually became popular in the Navy and at the Naval War College in Newport, Rhode Island.

Japan's victory in the Russo-Japanese War (1905) was the last credited to a nation's playing of Kriegspiel. It became apparent that strategies honed in the game did not always work in battle. Germany's defeat in World War I was a death knell for the game—except, ironically, in Germany itself, where postwar commanders fought each other with tin replicas of the regiments denied them by the Treaty of Versailles.

In Budapest, the young John von Neumann played an improvised Kriegspiel with his brothers. They sketched out castles, highways, and coastlines on graph paper, then advanced and retreated "armies" according to rules. During World War I, Johnny obtained maps of the fronts and followed reports of real advances and retreats. Today Kriegspiel is usually played with three chessboards, visible only to an umpire. In this form it was a popular lunch-hour pastime at the RAND Corporation, and von Neumann played the game on visits there.

To some critics, game theory is the twentieth century's Kriegspiel, a mirror in which military strategists see reflected their own preconceptions. The comparison is revealing even while being unfair. Game theory did become a kind of strategic oracle, particularly in the two decades after Hiroshima. The problem is one common to oracles, namely that game theory's answers can depend on exactly how you phrase the questions.

Why a theory of games? It is a cliché of scientific biography to find reasons in a scientist's personality for choosing a subject. But the question is fair enough. Though the scientist or mathematician is a discoverer rather than a creator, there is a literal universe of avenues to explore. Why one and not another?

Meaningful answers are harder to come by than historians of science like to admit. When the question has been put to living scientists, they are often at a loss for words. Many have noted von Neumann's fascination with play, his collection of children's toys, his sometimes childish humor. In this he was not atypical among scientists. Jacob Bronowski wrote (1973), "You must see that in a sense all science, all human thought, is a form of play. Abstract thought is the neoteny[1] of the intellect, by which man is able to carry out activities which have no immediate goal (other animals play only while young) in order to prepare himself for long-term strategies and plans."

Game theory is not about "playing" as usually understood. It is about conflict among rational but distrusting beings. Von Neumann escaped revolution and terrorism in Hungary and later the rise of Nazism. His relationship with Klara was one of repeated conflict. In his letters to his wife Johnny talks of double-crossing, reprisals, and boundless distrust. That's part of what game theory is about.

Game theory was the brainchild of a cynic. Some commentators have suggested that von Neumann's personal cynicism influenced the theory. It is conceivable that von Neumann's personality led him to explore game theory rather than something else. It is wrong to think that von Neumann concocted game theory as a "scientific" basis for his personal beliefs or politics. Game theory is a rigorously mathematical study which evolves naturally from a reasonable way of looking at conflict. Von Neumann would not have pursued game theory had his mathematical intuition not told him that it was a field ripe for development. Some of the mathematics of game theory are closely related to what von Neumann used in treating quantum physics.

The nominal inspiration for game theory was poker, a game von Neumann played occasionally and not especially well. (A 1955 *Newsweek* article appraised him as "only a fair-to-middling winner" at the game.) In poker, you have to consider what the other players are thinking. This distinguishes game theory from the theory of probability, which also applies to many games. Consider a poker player who naively tries to use probability theory alone to guide his play. The player computes the probability that his hand is better than the other players' hands, and wagers in direct proportion to the strength of the hand. After many hands, the other players will realize that (say) his willingness to sink twelve dollars in the pot means he has at least three of a kind. As poker players know, that kind of predictability is bad (a "poker face" betrays nothing).

Good poker players do not simply play the odds. They take into account the conclusions other players will draw from their actions, and sometimes try to deceive the other players. It was von Neumann's genius to see that this devious way of playing was both rational and amenable to rigorous analysis.

Not everyone agreed that game theory was the most fruitful outlet for von Neumann's ample talents. Paul Halmos, von Neumann's assistant at Princeton, told me, "As far as I was concerned, he was just wasting his time on 'that game stuff.' I know full well that a large part of the world doesn't agree with the opinions I held then, and I am not sure whether I myself agree with them now, but … I never learned the subject and never learned to like it."

Who Was First?

Von Neumann cannot be given undivided credit for the invention of game theory. Beginning in 1921, seven years before von Neumann's first paper, French mathematician Émile Borel published several papers on *"la théorie du jeu."* The parallels between these papers and von Neumann's work are strong. Borel used poker as an example and took up the problem of bluffing, just as von Neumann would. Borel appreciated the potential economic and military applications of game theory. Indeed, Borel warned against overly simplistic applications of game theory to warfare. He was not talking off the top of his head. Borel, who had held public office, became minister of the French Navy in 1925. Most important, Borel posed the basic questions of game theory: for what games is there a best strategy, and how does one find such a strategy?

Borel did not develop these issues very far. Like so many creative individuals, von Neumann was jealous of prior claims to "his" innovation. His 1928 paper and the 1944 book make but scant mention of Borel, that in footnotes. Lest there be any doubt, Ulam said that one of Borel's papers had indeed inspired von Neumann's work.

Von Neumann's slighting treatment of Borel long contributed to an underappreciation of the latter's work. In 1953 von Neumann was reportedly furious to learn that Borel's papers were being translated into English. The translator, mathematician L. J. Savage, told Steve Heims: "He phoned me from someplace like Los Alamos, very angry. He wrote a criticism of these papers in English. The criticism was not angry. It was characteristic of him that the criticism was written with good manners."

All this granted, the seminal paper of game theory is without doubt von Neumann's 1928 article, *"Zur Theorie der Gesellschaftspiele"* ("Theory of Parlor Games"). In this he proved (as Borel had not) the famous "minimax theorem." This important result immediately gave the field mathematical respectability.

Theory of Games and Economic Behavior

Von Neumann wanted game theory to reach a larger audience than mathematicians. He felt the developing field would be of most use to economists. He teamed with an Austrian economist then at Princeton, Oskar Morgenstern, to develop his theory.

Von Neumann and Morgenstern's *Theory of Games and Economic Behavior* is one of the most influential and least-read books of the twentieth century. Princeton University Press admitted as much in an ad it ran in *American Scientist* to commemorate the fifth year of anemic sales. "Great books often take a while to achieve recognition.... Then, later, when the world learns about them, their influence far surpasses their readership." The book had still not quite sold 4,000 copies in five years, a fact that would normally be hard to square with the contention that the book had taken the field of economics by storm. Most economists still hadn't read it (and never would); it wasn't even in the libraries of many schools of economics. The ad noted "a few copies bought by professional gamblers."

Theory of Games and Economic Behavior is a difficult book. Today, the reader's enthusiasm for plowing through all 641 formula-filled pages is dampened by the fact that von Neumann and Morgenstern got sidetracked in their treatment of games of more than two persons. Their approach, while not wrong, no longer seems the most useful or illuminating one.

If nothing else, the book is ambitious. Von Neumann and Morgenstern dreamed of doing for economics what von Neumann did for quantum physics and could not do for mathematics itself: putting it on an axiomatic basis. The authors stated: "We hope to establish satisfactorily ... that the typical problems of economic behavior become strictly identical with the mathematical notions of suitable games of strategy."

Theory of Games and Economic Behavior thus presents itself as a pioneering work of economics. The book's introduction is almost apologetic about investigating recreational games. The games are presented as potential models for economic interactions. (Military applications, which were to become so important to von Neumann's followers, are not mentioned.)

The tone is iconoclastic. Von Neumann and Morgenstern insist that economists must go back to square one. They deride the then-current state of mathematical economics, comparing it with the state of physics before Kepler and Newton. They chide those who advocate economic reform based on presently unconfirmable theories. One gathers the authors were thinking of Marxism, among other theories.

The authors speculate that a future exact science of economics will require its own, yet-unimagined mathematics. They suggest that calculus, which is ultimately derived from the physics of falling and orbiting bodies, is presently overemphasized in mathematics.

Fortunately for our purposes, the essential kernel of game theory is easy to grasp, even for those with little background in—or tolerance for—mathematics. Game theory is founded on a very simple but powerful way of schematizing conflict, and this method can be illustrated by a few familiar childhood games.

Cake Division

Most people have heard of the reputed best way to let two bratty children split a piece of cake. No matter how carefully a parent divides it, one child (or both), feels he has been slighted with the smaller piece. The solution is to let one child divide the cake and let the other choose which piece he wants. Greed ensures fair division. The first child can't object that the cake was divided unevenly because he did it himself. The second child can't complain since he has his choice of pieces.

This homely example is not only a game in von Neumann's sense, but it is also about the simplest illustration of the "minimax" principle upon which game theory is based.

The cake problem is a conflict of interests. Both children want the same thing—as much of the cake as possible. The ultimate division of the cake depends both on how one child cuts the cake and which piece the other child chooses. It is important that each child anticipates what the other will do. This is what makes the situation a game in von Neumann's sense.

Game theory searches for *solutions*—rational outcomes—of games. Dividing the cake evenly is the best strategy for the first child, since he anticipates that the other child's strategy will be to take the biggest piece. Equal division of the cake is therefore the solution to this game. This solution does not depend on a child's generosity or sense of fair play. It is enforced by both children's self-interest. Game theory seeks solutions of precisely this sort.

Rational Players

With this example in mind, let's go back and examine some of the ideas we have introduced. There are many ways of playing games. You can play just for fun with no thought of winning or losing. You may play recklessly, in the hope of lucking out and winning. You may play on the assumption that your opponent is foolish and attempt to exploit that foolishness. In a game of ticktacktoe with a child, you might even play to lose. This is all well and fine. It is not what game theory is about.

Game theory is about *perfectly logical players interested only in winning.* When you credit your opponent(s) with both rationality and a desire to win, and play so as to encourage the best outcome for yourself, then the game is open to the analysis of game theory.

Perfect rationality, like perfect *anything,* is a fiction. There's no such thing as a perfectly straight line. This didn't stop Euclid from developing a useful system of geometry. So it was with von Neumann and his perfectly rational players. You can think of the players of game theory as being something like the perfect logicians you hear about in logic puzzles, or even as being computer programs rather than human beings. The players are assumed to have perfect understanding of the rules and perfect memory of past moves. At all points in the game they are aware of all possible logical ramifications of their moves and their opponents' moves.

This can be a stringent requirement. Perfectly rational players would never miss a jump in checkers or "fall into a trap" in chess. *All* legal sequences of moves are implicit in the rules of these games, and a perfectly logical player gives due consideration to every possibility.

But as anyone who plays chess or checkers knows, traps and missed moves—trying to get your opponent to fall for them, trying to recover when you fall for them—are pretty much what the games are all about. What would a game between two perfectly rational players be like?

You probably already know what happens when ticktacktoe is played "rationally." It ends in a draw—it has to unless someone makes a mistake. Because ticktacktoe is so simple that it is possible to learn to play it perfectly, the game soon loses its appeal.

Von Neumann showed, however, that many other games are like ticktacktoe in this sense. Chess is not a game, von Neumann told Bronowski. He meant that there is a "correct" way(s) to play the game—although no one presently knows what it is—and that the game would therefore be trivial, in much the same sense as ticktacktoe, to players aware of the "correct" strategy.

Games as Trees

The gist of von Neumann's demonstration of this fact is marvelously simple. It applies not only to chess but to any game where no information is kept from the players, where "all the cards are on the table."

Most familiar games take place as a sequence of moves by the players. In ticktacktoe, chess, or checkers, the grid or board is always visible to both players. No moves are taken in secret. For any such game, you can draw a diagram of all the possible courses of play. I'll use ticktacktoe as an example because it's fairly simple, but the same thing could be done, in principle, for chess, checkers, or any such game. Ticktacktoe starts with the first player ("X") putting a mark in any of nine cells. There are consequently nine possible first moves. The nine choices open to Player X on the first move can be diagrammed as nine lines radiating up from a point. The point represents the move, the moment of decision, and the lines represent the possible choices.

Next it's Player O's move. There are eight cells still open—which eight depending on where the X is. So draw eight secondary branches at the top of each of the nine primary branches. That leaves seven open cells for X on his second move. As the diagram of possible moves is continued upward, it branches like a very bushy tree.

As you continue the process, you will eventually diagram moves that put three markers in a row. That's a win for the player who moves. It's also the termination of that particular branch in the diagram, for the game ends when someone gets three in a row. Mark that point (call it a "leaf" of the diagram) as a win for X or O as the case may be.

Other branches of the diagram will terminate in a tie. Mark them as ties. Obviously, the game of ticktacktoe cannot go on forever. Nine moves is the maximum. So eventually, you will have a *complete* diagram of the game of ticktacktoe. Every possible ticktacktoe game— every game that ever has been played or ever will be played—must appear in the diagram as a branch starting at the "root" (X's first move) and continuing up to a "leaf" marked as a win for X, a win for O, or a tie. The longest complete branches/games are nine moves long. The shortest are five moves (this is the minimum for a win by the first player).

So much for the tree; now for the pruning shears. By process of elimination, you can figure out how to play ticktacktoe "rationally" from the diagram. The diagram contains all legal sequences of play, even those with *stupid* moves such as when someone overlooks a chance to get three in a row. All you have to do is take pruning shears to the tree and trim off all the stupid moves. What's left will be the smart moves—the rational way to play.

A small portion of the diagram looks like this:

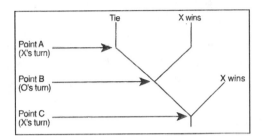

Go through the diagram and carefully backtrack from every leaf. Each leaf is some-one's last move, a move that creates a victory or a tie. For instance, at Point A, it is X's move, and there is only one empty cell. X has no choice but to fill it in and create a tie.

Now look at Point B, a move earlier in the game. It is O's turn, and he has two choices. Putting an O in one of the two open cells leads to the aforementioned Point A and a sure tie. Putting an O in the other cell, however, leads to a win for X. A rational O player prefers a tie to an X victory. Consequently, the right branch leading upward from Point B can never occur in rational play. Snip this branch from the diagram. Once the play gets to Point B, a tie is a foregone conclusion.

But look: X could have won earlier, at Point C. A rational X would have chosen an immediate win at Point C. So actually, we can snip off the entire left branch of the diagram.

Keep pruning the tree down to the root, and you will discover that ties are the only possible outcomes of rational play. (There is more than one rational way of playing, though.) The second player can and will veto any attempt at an X victory, and vice-versa.

What can be done for ticktacktoe could be done for almost any two-person game with no hidden information. The main restriction is that the game must be finite. It can't go on forever, and the number of distinct choices at any move must also be finite. Otherwise, there are no "leaves" (last moves) to work back from.

Human beings being mortal, no recreational game is intended to go on forever. Rules of more challenging games rarely state a maximum number of moves explicitly, though. Chess normally ends in checkmate. There are many cases where pieces can be moved endlessly without creating a checkmate. Should captures reduce the board to just the two kings, neither will be able to checkmate the other. "Tie rules" bring such games to a halt.

A common rule declares the game a tie when a sequence of moves repeats exactly three times. Another, more stringent, rule is that if no pawn is moved and no higher-ranking pieces are captured in forty moves, the game is a tie.

Consequently, von Neumann and Morgenstern pointed out, there is a numerical limit on the number of moves in a game of chess under a given tie rule. (The limiting number is probably around 5,000 moves with typical rules—far more than any game of chess ever played!) The actual value of the limit is not important to the proof, just that it exists and is finite. Given that a game of chess can run only so many moves, and that the number of choices at each move is finite, it follows that the number of different courses of play is itself a finite number. You could make a diagram of all legal courses of play, and prune it to reveal the rational way to play chess.

It recalls the old joke about the chess game where White makes his first move and then Black says, "I resign." Chess between perfectly rational players would be as trivial as that. It is only because we do not know the correct strategy for chess that it still challenges players. It is one thing to prove that a best strategy exists, but it is quite another to do all the calculation and produce the strategy. It is unknown whether a rational game of chess would end in a victory (presumably for White, who moves first) or a tie.

Games as Tables

There is another way of looking at games, one far more useful in game theory. A game is equivalent to a table of possible outcomes.

As we have shown, the number of possible games of chess is astronomically large but finite nevertheless. It follows that the number of chess strategies is finite, too. I have already used the word "strategy" several times; now is the time to define it. In game theory, strategy is an important idea, and it has a more precise meaning than it usually does. When chess players talk of a strategy, they mean something like "open with the king's Indian Defense and play aggressively." In game theory, a strategy is a much more specific plan. It is a *complete* description of a particular way to play a game, no matter what the other player(s) does and no matter how long the game lasts. A strategy must prescribe actions so thoroughly that you never have to make a decision in following it.

An example of a true strategy for first player in ticktacktoe would be:

Put X in the center square. O can respond two ways:

1. If O goes in a noncorner square, put X in a corner cell adjacent to the O. This gives you two-in-a-row. If O fails to block on the next move, make three-in-a-row for a *win*. If O blocks, put X in the empty corner cell that is not adjacent to the first (noncorner) O. This gives you two-in-a-row two ways. No matter what O does on the next move, you can make three-in-a-row after that and *win*.

2. If instead O's first move is a corner cell, put X in one of the adjacent noncorner cells. This gives you two-in-a-row. If O fails to block on the next move, make three-in-a-row for a *win*. If O blocks, put X in the corner cell that is adjacent to the second O and on the same side of the grid as the first O. This gives you two-in-a-row. If O fails to block on the next move, make three-in-a-row for a *win*. If O blocks, put X in the empty cell adjacent to the third O. This gives you two-in-a-row. If O fails to block on the next move, make three-in-a-row for a *win*. If O blocks, fill in the remaining cell for a *tie*.

This shows how complicated a strategy can be, even for a very simple game. A true strategy for chess would be so huge that it could never be written down. There is not enough paper and ink on earth to list all the possibilities; there is not enough computer memory to loop through them all. This is one reason why computers still aren't unbeatable at chess.

Overwhelming as this practical difficulty is, it didn't bother von Neumann, and it needn't bother us. In fact, since we're fantasizing, we might as well go a step further. Not only could a perfectly rational being conceive of a strategy in full detail; he could—given no limits on memory or computing power whatsoever—anticipate every possible chess strategy and decide in advance what to do even before moving the first piece.

Suppose you had a numbered list of all possible strategies for chess. Then your choice of strategy is tantamount to selecting a number from 1 to n, where n is the (very, very large) number of possible strategies. Your opponent could choose a strategy from his list of possibilities (from 1 to m, say). Once these two strategies were chosen, the resulting game would be completely specified. By applying the two strategies you could move the pieces and bring the game to its preordained conclusion. Openings, captures, "surprise moves," and endgame would all be implicit in the choice of strategies.

To take this pipe dream to its conclusion, we can imagine that, given enough time, you could play out every possible pairing of strategies to see the outcome. The results could be tabulated in a rectangular table. The real table would span the galaxies, so we'll print an abbreviated version here!

	Black's Strategies				
	1	**2**	**3**	**. . .**	**m**
1	White checkmate in 37 moves	Draw in 102 moves	Black resigns in 63 moves		Black checkmate in 42 moves
2	White checkmate in 45 moves	Black checkmate in 17 moves	White checkmate in 54 moves		White checkmate in 82 moves
3	White checkmate in 43 moves	White checkmate in 108 moves	Draw in 1,801 moves		Black checkmate in 32 moves
. . .					
n	Draw in 204 moves	White checkmate in 77 moves	White checkmate in 24 moves		Draw in 812 moves

(Left side: **White's Strategies**)

Once you had this table, you wouldn't have to bother with the chessboard anymore. A "game" of chess would amount to the two players choosing their strategies simultaneously and looking up the result in the table.[2] To find out who wins, you'd look in the cell at the intersection of the row corresponding to White's strategy and the column of Black's strategy. Should White choose to use strategy number 2 on his list, and Black choose to use his strategy number 3, the inevitable outcome would be a checkmate for White in 54 moves.

This isn't the way real people play real games. To detail every possible contingency beforehand would be the antithesis of the word "play." No matter. This idea of representing games as tables of outcomes turns out to be very useful. Every possible sequence of play for any two-person game can be represented as a cell in a similar type of table. The table must have as many rows as one player has strategies and a column for each of the other player's strategies. A game reduced to a table like this is called the "normalized form" of the game.

The trick is deciding *which* strategy to choose. The table gets all the facts out in the open, but this isn't always enough. The arrangement of outcomes in the table can be capricious. Neither player gets to choose the outcome he wants, only the row or column it appears in. The other player's choice makes an equal contribution.

Look at the imaginary table for chess. Is strategy number 1 a good choice for White? It's tough to say. If Black chooses strategy number 1, it's good because that leads to a win for White. But with other choices for Black, the result can be a draw or a loss for White.

White really wants to determine which strategy Black is going to choose. Then all White has to do is make sure he picks one of his own strategies that will lead to a win when paired with the Black strategy.

Unfortunately, Black wants to do the same thing. Black wants to psych out White, and choose his strategy accordingly for a Black victory. Of course, White knows this, and tries to predict what Black will do based on what he thinks White will do...

Borel and von Neumann realized that this sort of deliberation puts games beyond the scope of probability theory. The players would be wrong indeed to assume that their opponent's choice is determined by "chance." Chance has nothing to do with it. The players can be expected to do their very best to deduce the other's choice and prepare for it. A new theory is called for.

Zero-Sum Games

"Zero-sum game" is one of the few terms from game theory that has entered general parlance. It refers to a game where the total winnings or payoffs are fixed. The best example is a game like poker, where players put money in the pot, and someone wins it. No one ever wins a dollar but that someone else has lost it. It is in this restricted but quite diverse category of games that game theory has enjoyed its greatest success. The analogies to economics are obvious. One speaks of a "zero-sum society," meaning that one person's gain is another's loss. "There's no such thing as a free lunch."

Most recreational games are zero-sum. This is true even of games that don't involve money. Whether money is at stake or not, each player prefers some possible outcomes to others. When these preferences are expressed on a numerical scale, they are called *utility*.

Think of utility as the "counters" in a game, or as "points" you try to win. If you play poker for matchsticks, and honestly try to win as many matchsticks as possible, then utility is identical with the quantity of matchsticks.

In a game played for money, money is utility or nearly so. When a game is played just to win, the mere fact of winning confers utility. In a win-or-lose game like ticktacktoe or chess, winning might be assigned a utility of 1 (in arbitrary "points") and losing might be assigned a utility of -1 point. The sum of utilities is still zero, hence it is a zero-sum game.

An important thing to remember about utility is that it corresponds to the actual preferences of the players. In the case of an adult playing a child and wanting to lose, the adult's utilities would be reversed: losing would have a utility of 1 and winning a utility of -1. Thus utility does not necessarily correspond to money, or winning or losing, or any obvious external object.

The simplest true game is a two-person, two-strategy, zero-sum game. The only way a game could be any simpler would be for a player to have just one strategy. But a "choice" of one option is no choice at all. The "game" would really be a one-person game, which is no game at all.

A two-person, two-strategy game can be diagrammed in a two-row by two-column table. If the game is further a zero-sum game, the outcomes can be represented concisely. Fill each of the four cells with a number representing the first player's win. We know that the first player's win is the second player's loss, so both can use the same diagram (the second player's wins are the negatives of the numbers in the table).

Minimax and Cake

A two-person, zero-sum game is "total war." One player can win only if the other loses. No cooperation is possible. Von Neumann settled on a simple and sensible plan for deciding rational solutions of such games. It is called the minimax principle.

Let's reexamine the cake division problem from the perspective of game theory. The children are playing a zero-sum game. There is only so much cake to begin with, and nothing the children do will change the amount available. More cake for one means that much less cake for the other.

The first child (the "cutter") has a range of strategies—strictly speaking, an unlimited number since he can cut the cake in any of an infinite number of ways. We will not miss much by simplifying the range of choices to just two strategies. One strategy is to split the cake unevenly and the other is to split the cake as evenly as possible.

The second child (the "chooser") also has two strategies. He can choose the bigger piece or the smaller piece. (As a further note of realism, we'll allow that no slicing operation is perfect. So even when the cutter adopts the policy of splitting the cake evenly, one piece *will* be slightly bigger than the other.)

A simple table illustrates the choices. We need put only one child's payoff in the cells of the table. Let's use the cutter's payoff. Obviously, the chooser gets whatever is left. The table looks like this:

		Chooser's strategies	
		Choose bigger piece	Choose smaller piece
Cutter's strategies	Cut cake as evenly as possible	Half the cake minus a crumb	Half the cake plus a crumb
	Make one piece bigger than the other	Small piece	Big piece

We already know what to expect of this game. The cutter will split the cake evenly, or try to as best he can. The chooser will pick the bigger piece. The result is the upper left cell. The cutter will get slightly less than half the cake, since the chooser will take the bigger of two nearly identical pieces.

Why this outcome? If the cutter could have his pick of any of the four possible outcomes, he would want to end up with a big piece (lower right cell). He realizes, however, that this is not realistic. The cutter knows what to expect from the chooser; namely, the worst—as small a piece as possible.

The cutter is empowered only to decide the row of the cake division's outcome. He expects to end up with the *least* amount of cake in that row, for the chooser will act to minimize the cutter's piece. Therefore he acts so as to *maximize* the *minimum* the chooser will leave him.

If the cutter cuts the cake evenly, he knows he will end up with nearly half the cake. If instead the cutter makes one piece much bigger, he knows as certainly that he will end up with a small piece. The real choice, then, is between nearly half the cake and much less than half. The cutter goes for nearly half the cake by electing to split the cake evenly. This amount, the maximum row minimum, is called the "maximin."

"You know that the best you can expect is to avoid the worst," writes Italo Calvino in *If on a Winter's Night a Traveler* (1979). The epigram neatly states the minimax principle. The choice of strategies is a natural outcome. It is not merely a "fair" outcome recommended by game-theoretic arbitration but a true equilibrium enforced by both players' self-interest.

A player deviates from his best strategy to his own detriment (and to his opponent's benefit because it is a zero-sum game).

The minimax principle helps make sense of more difficult two-person zero-sum games. We have shown that almost any common game is logically equivalent to a *simultaneous* choice of strategies by players. Simultaneous games are thus different from cake division, where the chooser acts *after* the cutter has.

But look: What if the chooser had to go first by announcing his choice (bigger piece or smaller piece) before the cutter picked up the knife? It would make no difference at all. A rational chooser knows the cutter will divide the cake so that the chooser's slice is as small as possible. The chooser in turn wants the cutter to get the smallest piece possible. (Remember, the table above gives the cutter's piece, which is the complement of the chooser's.) The chooser looks for the *minimum* column *maximum* (the "minimax"). It's also the upper left cell. The chooser should go for the bigger piece.

In this game, the upper left cell is the natural outcome, regardless of which player is required to announce his strategy first. Consequently, we feel safe in saying that the upper left cell would be the logical result of a game where players had to decide simultaneously.

The value in the upper left cell is both the maximin (the cutter's best "realistic" outcome) and the minimax (the chooser's best realistic outcome, here expressed as what the cutter would get). You might wonder whether this is a coincidence, or whether it is always so. It is a coincidence, though not an unusual one in a small table. When the maximin and the minimax are identical, that outcome is called a "saddle point." Von Neumann and Morgenstern likened it to the point in the middle of a saddle-shaped mountain pass—at once the maximum elevation reached by a traveler going through the pass and the minimum elevation encountered by a mountain goat traveling the crest of the range.

When a game has a saddle point, the saddle point is the solution of the game, the expected outcome of rational play. Note that a rational solution doesn't necessarily mean that everyone is happy. The cutter ends up getting a crumb or two less than the chooser. He may not think that's fair. For that matter, both players may be disappointed they didn't get a much bigger piece. Neither player gets his first choice of outcome. What's to prevent the players from striking out and doing something irrational?

The answer is greed and distrust. Half the cake minus a crumb is the most the cutter can guarantee for himself without any help from the chooser. It is also the smallest piece the chooser can leave for the cutter by his own efforts. To do any better, a player would need the assistance of his adversary. But the opponent has no reason to help—it's less cake for him. The saddle-point solution of a zero-sum game is self-enforcing. It's something like Chinese finger cuffs. The harder you struggle to do any better, the worse off you are.

Mixed Strategies

Unfortunately, there's a catch. Not all games have saddle points. The trouble is, you can invent a game with any rules you want. Any set of payoffs is conceivable. It is easy to fill a rectangular grid with numbers so that the minimum row maximum does *not* equal the maximum column minimum. Then there is no saddle point.

One of the simplest of all games has no saddle points. "Matching pennies" (which von Neumann and Morgenstern use as an example) is hardly a game at all in the usual sense. Two players simultaneously place a penny on a table—heads up or tails up. When the pennies match (both are heads or both are tails) the first player gets to keep both pennies. He gets back his own penny and wins his partner's penny for a profit of 1 cent. If the pennies don't match, the second player gets both.

The table for matching pennies looks like this:

	Heads	Tails
Heads	1 cent	−1 cent
Tails	−1 cent	1 cent

The minimum of both rows is -1 cent. Therefore the maximum minimum is also -1 cent. The maximum of both columns is 1 cent, so the minimum maximum is 1 cent too. There is a 2-cent difference between the minimax and the maximin.

Von Neumann and Morgenstern likened games to a "tug of war." Each side can prevent the other from gaining too much ground, but there is a middle ground where the rope lurches back and forth. In matching pennies, the first player can guarantee himself his minimax value (-1 cent)—which isn't saying much in this case, because that's the maximum loss in the game. The second player is guaranteed that he can't lose more than a penny. The difference between these two guarantees, 2 cents, is how much is really at stake in the game.

Should you choose heads or tails? Obviously, it all depends on what the other player will do. If you knew what the other player was going to do, you'd know what you want to do—and vice-versa.

As you probably know, the best way to play matching pennies is to play heads and tails *randomly* (with 50 percent probability each). This is called a "mixed strategy" in contrast to the "pure strategies" of playing heads with certainty or tails with certainty. Mixed strategies were nothing new in von Neumann's time. Borel's paper considered such strategies, and of course players of games like matching pennies have long appreciated the desirability of acting randomly. Sometimes matching pennies is used as a "random" way of deciding who gets an advantage in another game, such as which team bats first in baseball.

By fashioning a new, random strategy "from scratch," the players create a self-enforcing equilibrium. Let's make a new diagram for matching pennies that includes the random strategy.

	Heads	Tails	Random
Heads	1 cent	−1 cent	0
Tails	−1 cent	1 cent	0
Random	0	0	0

Anyone who plays randomly stands equal chances of winning and of losing a penny. (This is true whether the opponent plays a pure strategy or chooses randomly as well.) On the average, then, the payoff to a random player is 0. Fill in the row and column for the random strategies with 0's.

Now there is a saddle point. If the first player had to name his strategy first (definitely heads, definitely tails, or a random choice), knowing that the second would take full advantage of that information, he'd want to choose the strategy with the maximum minimum. The strategies of heads or tails have minimums of -1 cent. The random strategy guarantees an average gain of 0, no matter what the other player does. Thus the random strategy has the maximum minimum.

If the second player had to go first, he would want the minimum maximum. Again this is the random strategy. Game theory suggests the lower right cell as the natural outcome. Both players should choose randomly. Once again we find an equilibrium between the players' opposed interests.

Most five-year-olds already know how to play matching pennies. What do we need game theory for?

The answer is that other games are not quite so simple, and for them game theory can crank out impeccably correct prescriptions that are by no means common sense. The odds in a random strategy do not have to be fifty-fifty. They can and should be adjusted according to the payoffs. Game theory tells how to do this.

Here's a nice little dilemma: "Millionaire Jackpot Matching Pennies." It works just like ordinary matching pennies except that you play against fabulously wealthy opponents only, and if you match on heads, your opponent has to pay you a *million dollars.* Your payoffs are as follows (your opponent's are just the opposite).

	Heads	Tails
Heads	$1 million	−1 cent
Tails	−1 cent	1 cent

How should you play this game? Well, the pennies are chicken feed. You're interested in winning that million dollars. The only way that can happen is for you to play heads. So your first impulse is to play heads.

But wait a minute, your opponent would be *crazy* to play heads. He's not going to risk losing a million dollars. His first impulse is to play tails.

Should first impulses prevail, you'll play heads and your opponent will play tails. There will be no match, and you will lose a penny to your opponent—hey, wasn't this game supposed to be stacked in your favor?

At a deeper level of analysis, you realize that your opponent pretty well *has* to pick tails. Not only does that veto your big win (his big loss), but he collects a penny every time you pick heads and he picks tails.

Two can play at that game. As long as you know your opponent is virtually certain to pick tails, you can take advantage of that fact. Choose tails, and you're almost sure to win a penny.

But maybe your opponent anticipates your double-cross. Then he might be tempted to play heads—or maybe not; he is risking a million that way. Still, if there's any chance at all that he might play heads, maybe you should reconsider playing heads. You can well afford to give up winning a penny for a long shot at the million....

Game theory concludes that the correct mixed strategy is to play tails practically all the time. You should play heads with a probability of only about 2 in a 100 million (the exact ratio is 2:100,000,003.[3] Your opponent should do the same thing.

The million-dollar payoff, which seems to be such a windfall, is mostly an illusion since the other player can veto it. Regular matching pennies is a fair game with zero expected value. The millionaire version is in your favor, but only in the amount of approximately *one cent* per play. That, of course, is what you win for matching tails. The net effect of the million-dollar payoff is to raise your average gain by one cent! It would not change your expectation of gain appreciably if the bonus were raised to a trillion dollars or a googol dollars.

The other surprising thing is the recommendation that the second player occasionally play the risky strategy of heads. He doesn't play it *much,* but it is hard to rationalize playing it at all. Here's one way of looking at it. The game is basically one of both players playing tails (lower right cell). But were the second player to foreswear playing heads *completely*, that would rule out any possibility of your winning the $1 million. You would have no reason ever to play heads either.

The second player (who almost always plays tails) likes it when you play heads. That action almost always results in a win for him. He has to play heads occasionally to give you some incentive to keep on playing heads every now and then. What's more, these occasions when he plays heads usually turn out okay for him since you usually play tails.

Lightning rarely strikes twice. Provided both players play heads infrequently enough, the many, many cases of a single heads (and a penny's gain for the second player) balance the infrequent catastrophe of both players playing heads. Thus there is an optimal mixed strategy where heads are played very infrequently but not avoided entirely.

Curve Balls and Deadly Genes

Once you understand the idea of mixed strategies, you recognize them everywhere. Let's give a few examples.

Baseball pitchers are better at throwing some types of pitches than others. All other things being equal, the batter would expect the pitcher to throw his best pitch all the time. But should the batter know the type of pitch to expect, he would gain an advantage. Pitchers therefore throw a random mixture of fast balls, slow balls, curve balls, and knuckle balls to keep the batter uncertain. The rare exception only proves the rule. When Satchel Paige was asked how he could get away with always throwing fast balls, he answered, "They know what's comin', but they don't know where."

In principle, game theory could prescribe the optimal mixture of pitches. The mixture would vary according to the relative strengths of each player's pitches. You'd need some fairly exacting statistics—how many runs resulted from each type of pitch, ideally broken down by opposing batter. It would be interesting to see how closely pitchers' instinctive strategies approximate that of game theory. The math is no more involved than that in some of the baseball statistics being kept, and this seems a natural project for a future Bill James.

As early as 1928, Oskar Morgenstern recognized a dilemma in Arthur Conan Doyle's *The Adventures of Sherlock Holmes.* He and von Neumann cite it in their book:

> Sherlock Holmes desires to proceed from London to Dover and hence to the Continent in order to escape from Professor Moriarty who pursues him. Having boarded the train he observes, as the train pulls out, the appearance of Professor Moriarty on the platform. Sherlock Holmes takes it for granted—and in this he is assumed to be fully justified—that his adversary, who has seen him, might secure a special train and overtake him. Sherlock Holmes is faced with the alternative of going to Dover or of leaving the train at Canterbury, the only intermediate station. His adversary—whose intelligence is assumed to be fully adequate to visualize these possibilities—has the same choice. Both opponents must choose the place of their detrainment in ignorance of the other's corresponding decision. If, as a result of these measures, they should find themselves, in fine, on the same platform, Sherlock Holmes may with certainty expect to be killed by Moriarty. If Sherlock Holmes reaches Dover unharmed he can make good his escape.

Von Neumann and Morgenstern go so far as to assign points to the various outcomes and compute a mixed strategy. They recommend that Moriarty go to Dover with a 60 percent probability, and to Canterbury with a 40 percent probability. Holmes should get off at Canterbury (60 percent probability) or Dover (40 percent probability). The game is unfair, and Moriarty has a better chance of prevailing.

In Doyle's story, Holmes gets out in Canterbury to see Moriarty's special train passing on its way to Dover. It is interesting that both Holmes and Moriarty followed the most likely course under von Neumann and Morgenstern's mixed strategy. They write, "It is, however, somewhat misleading that this procedure leads to Sherlock Holmes' complete victory, whereas, as we saw above, the odds (i.e. the value of a play) are definitely in favor of Moriarty.... Our results ... yields that Sherlock Holmes is as good as 48% dead when his train pulls out from Victoria Station."

This kind of calculated deception resembles bluffing in poker. Poker can be quite complex, in part because it usually has more than two players. Von Neumann analyzed a simplified form of poker. In outline, his conclusions apply to the real game. He showed that you should always bid aggressively when you have a strong hand. With a weak hand, you should sometimes bluff (bid aggressively anyway).

Von Neumann distinguished two reasons for bluffing. A player who never bluffs misses many chances to call the other player's bluffs. Suppose that both you and your opponent have bad hands. You don't bluff; your opponent does. That means you fold and your opponent wins without a showdown. Had you also bluffed, your lousy hand would have been compared with his lousy hand, and you might have won. The bluffer can exploit the nonbluffer; ergo, von Neumann's rational player must bluff.

Bluffing is also a smoke screen. As in matching pennies, one wants to keep the other player guessing. Poker hands are dealt randomly to begin with, but players form opinions about their opponent's hands from their bids. Judicious bluffing prevents a player from being too predictable.

Game theory has important analogies in biology. A person who inherits the relatively rare sickle-cell anemia gene from one parent has greater immunity to malaria, but someone who inherits the gene from both parents develops sickle-cell anemia, a deadly disease. The puzzling survival of this and other lethal genes probably involves an equilibrium much like that in a bonus-payout version of matching pennies.

In the latter game, a player picks the risky strategy of heads at rare intervals in order to get a benefit that accrues when just that player plays heads. The sickle-cell gene is likewise risky but confers a benefit when only one gene is present. Provided the gene is rare enough in the population, cases of the disease are rare compared to cases of enhanced immunity. This is believed to be the reason this seemingly unfavorable gene has persisted in areas where malaria is common.

You might wonder how this has anything to do with game theory. Genes can't choose mixed strategies or any kind of strategies. As it turns out, conscious choice is not essential to game theory. At the most abstract level, game theory is about tables with numbers in them— numbers that entities are efficiently acting to maximize or minimize. It makes no difference whether you picture the entities as poker players who want to win as much money as possible or as genes mindlessly reproducing as much as natural selection permits. We'll hear more about biological interpretations of game theory later.

The Minimax Theorem

The minimax theorem proves that *every* finite, two-person, zero-sum game has a rational solution in the form of a pure or mixed strategy. Von Neumann's position as founder of game theory rests mainly with his proof of the minimax theorem by 1926. Von Neumann considered the theorem crucial. In 1953 he wrote, "As far as I can see, there could be no theory of games on these bases without that theorem.... Throughout the period in question I thought there was nothing worth publishing until the 'minimax theorem' was proved."

To put it in plain language, the minimax theorem says that there is always a rational solution to a precisely defined conflict between two people whose interests are completely opposite. It is a rational solution in that both parties can convince themselves that they cannot expect to do any better, given the nature of the conflict.

Game theory's prescriptions are conservative ones. They are the best a rational player can expect when playing against another rational player. They do not guarantee the best outcome possible. Usually a rational player can do *better* for himself when playing an irrational opponent. Sometimes these benefits accrue even to the rational player sticking with the prescribed strategy. In other situations it is necessary for the rational player to deviate from the strategy of game theory to take advantage of the other player's irrationality. An example is matching pennies. Say that you're the matching player and are mixing heads and tails equally and randomly. But you notice that your less rational opponent is unconsciously choosing "heads" more than half the time. Then you can come out ahead by choosing "heads" more often.

Sensible as this modification is, the modified strategy is no longer the optimal one and opens you to possible exploitation yourself (such as by a third player, or by the irrational opponent should he suddenly "wise up.")

N-Person Games

A journalist once asked von Neumann if game theory would help make a killing in the stock market. Honestly enough, von Neumann answered no. Such questions lingered. What is game theory good for? If not to play games, then what?

Von Neumann himself saw the minimax theorem as the first cornerstone of an exact science of economics. Toward this end, much of von Neumann and Morgenstern's book treats games with three or more persons. Most of the time, the number of "players" in an economic problem is large—huge even—and no simplifying assumptions are possible.

A game with an arbitrary number of players is called an "*n*-person game." A complete analysis of such games is much more complex than zero-sum two-person games. Conflicts of interest are less pat. What is good for player A may be bad for player B but good for player C. In such a situation, A and C might form an alliance. Such coalitions change a game radically.

In a three-person game, it is possible that two players acting in concert can guarantee a win. Two allies might thus cut a third player out of his share of winnings. Von Neumann and Morgenstern tried to decide when such coalitions were likely to form, and who was likely to form them. Would weak players gang up against a strong player? Or would weak players try to ally themselves with a strong player? One conclusion was that many potential coalitions can be stable. Then it is difficult or impossible to predict what will happen.

Von Neumann hoped to use the minimax theorem to tackle games of ever more players. The minimax theorem gives a rational solution to any two-person zero-sum game. A three-person game can be dissected into sub-games between the potential coalitions. If players A and B team up against player C, then the resulting game (coalition of A and B vs. C) is effectively a two-person game with a solution guaranteed by the minimax theorem.

By figuring out the results of *all* the potential coalitions, the players A, B, and C would be able to decide which coalitions were most in their interests. This would then give a rational solution to a three-person game.

There's no need to stop there. A four-person game can be chopped up into two- and three-person games between its potential coalitions. Hash out all the possibilities there, and the solution will be evident. Four-person games lead to five-person games, six-person games, ad infinitum.

Unfortunately, the complexity of games, and of the necessary computations, increases exponentially with the number of players. If the economy of the world can be modeled as a 5-billion-player "game," that fact may be of little practical use. In the main, von Neumann and Morgenstern's work on economics never got off the ground. It remains for someone else to extend their foundations.

Good mathematician that he was, von Neumann did not try to limit his theory to its nominal subject matter. Geometry arose out of problems of surveying land. Today we find nothing unusual about using geometry in contexts that have nothing to do with real estate. A rectangle is a rectangle whether it's someone's farm or an abstract rectangle in a geometric proof. Von Neumann and Morgenstern point out that a zero-sum n-person game is in effect a function of n variables, or alternatively, an n-dimensional matrix. Much of the discussion in *Theory of Games and Economic Behavior* applies to such abstract functions or matrices irrespective of whether they are pictured as payoff tables for games, outcomes of economic or military decisions, or anything else. Game theory is inspired by, but not necessarily *about,* games.

Real conflicts postponed further development of game theory. Like many of his colleagues, von Neumann enlisted in the war effort. This left little time for pure research. Von Neumann would never again publish ground-breaking work in pure mathematics at the heady clip of the years between the world wars. Paul Halmos wrote (1973), "The year 1940 was just about the half-way point of von Neumann's scientific life, and his publications show a discontinuous break then. Till then he was a topflight pure mathematician who understood physics; after that he was an applied mathematician who remembered his pure work."

Notes

1. Retention of immature traits in adulthood. Bronowski alludes to the fact that non-human animals play and experiment in their youth, then lock into a successful pattern of behavior (compare the playful kitten with the contented old cat).

2. Why "simultaneously"? Doesn't Black at least get to see White's first move before deciding on his strategy? No: you're failing to appreciate how comprehensive a strategy must be. The first part of a Black strategy would prescribe a Black opening move for *each* of the twenty possible opening moves by White. Not until each of these twenty contingencies is accounted for do you have a strategy in von Neumann's sense.

3. I'm not getting into the actual math here because it's not needed to understand social dilemmas. For "generalized matching pennies"—a two-person, zero-sum game with two strategies for each player—the correct mixed strategy is easy to calculate. Write the payoffs in a two by two grid as usual. Then calculate the differences of the two payoffs in each row and write them to the right of the table:

1,000,000 - -0.01 = 1,000,000.01

-0.01 - 0.01 = 0.02

Make both results positive (-0.02 becomes 0.02) and swap them:

1,000,000 - -0.01 = 0.02

-0.01 - 0.01 = 1,000,000.01

This means the proper odds for heads:tails is 0.02:1,000,000.01, or (multiplying by 100 to get rid of the decimals) 2:100,000,001. The other player calculates his odds by figuring the differences in the columns and swapping. In this case the odds are the same for both players. It's more complicated for games with more than two strategies. If you're interested, see John Williams's *The Compleat Strategyst*.

Games and Design Patterns

Staffan Björk and Jussi Holopainen

Context

*The following text is a merged, revised, and updated version of the two papers "Game Design Patterns" and "Describing Games: An Interaction-Centric Structural Framework," which were presented at the Level Up Digital Games Research Conference (Utrecht, 2003). In it, we describe two main concepts that together provide a framework and language for gameplay and game design. The text is a snapshot of our work on the Game Design Patterns Project, which explores the fundamental components of game design. The initial objective of the project, to provide a conceptual tool for aiding the experimental design of games for future technologies, was later expanded to include the design of all kinds of games. The pattern examples are from our book **Patterns in Game Design** (Charles River Media, 2005).*

The Rules of a Game

Game Design Models

What Is a Game?

Staffan Björk is a lecturer and teacher in interaction design and game design with a background in computer science and a Ph.D. in Informatics. He is currently researching design and evaluation methods of pervasive games and how computers can augment traditional forms of games without disturbing the social experience.

Jussi Holopainen is heading the Game Design Group at Nokia Research Center. His current research interests include methods of game design and the philosophical foundations of gameplay.

1. Introduction

Interest in developing the field of game research, ludology, has grown steadily over the last few years. But because games vary greatly, not only in their content and gameplay, but also in their medium and the reasons they are played, there are many approaches to the subject. This can be observed by looking at current research, which applies the methods and concepts of a wide range of research fields, from sociology and pedagogy, to literature and media studies, to computer science. Examples of common research topics include player activities, narrative structures, and best practices for game development and for meeting artistic challenges.

Although different research fields can provide different perspectives on a given research topic, these results are typically published within their own communities and the results found in one field can easily be overlooked by researchers in other fields. And because their frameworks and terminology also differ, even when researchers and practitioners meet in multidisciplinary environments, they run the risk of misunderstanding one another.

A unified approach to game research may avoid misunderstandings and make possible the mutually beneficial exchange of results and findings between research fields. Although the methods and goals of research on games will, of course, always differ from field to field, communication between the different fields could be facilitated if there were a common framework and terminology for the essential "gameness" of a game. We argue that the focus of game research should be *gameplay,* a concept that incorporates both the functional and the experiential aspects of a game—what is done when playing a game ("The gameplay was repetitious") and how playing a game is perceived ("The gameplay was good").

In this essay we present our approach to describing games, one that is independent of existing research fields or—perhaps more accurately—that is part of the budding research field of game research. Our approach relies on two main concepts: a *component framework,* which we define as the invariant aspects of gameplay onto which specific components of a game can be mapped, and *game design patterns,* which we define as semi-formalized interdependent descriptions of commonly reoccurring parts of the design of a game that concern gameplay. These concepts allow one to describe how the specific configuration of and interrelation between game components affect gameplay. The component framework provides the medium in which the game design patterns can occur; the game design patterns describe specific reoccurring interactions, dynamics, and characteristics that emerge from component configurations. The two concepts allow analysis and design of games to be structured with a focus on both static and dynamic aspects of gameplay.

2. Previous Approaches for Finding a Common Language for Games

Some basic attributes can easily be deduced for a common language for games. First, to maximize the transfer of knowledge a game-centric language should be usable by all interested in games. Since this includes both designers and researchers, it is obvious that there is a need for a language to be able to talk about gameplay both while designing and while analyzing games.

Second, although a common language can and should incorporate concepts, methods, and theories from numerous fields, we believe that a conceptual game language should be created from studying games as a phenomenon in itself.

In the following, we discuss earlier approaches to describe games that have these properties and that have informed and influenced our approach.

2.1. Genres

Computer games are most commonly marketed by their genres—as sports games, first-person shooters, strategy games, and so on. However, the granularity of genre definitions is strongly affected by the popularity of particular games rather than design differences since "genre conceptions originate mostly from game journalism, not systematic study" (Järvinen, 2002). Similar imprecision can be found when designers (Knizia, 1999; Parlett, 1999; Crawford, 1982) classify games; seeing game taxonomies as genre collections without explicitly using the term *genre*. Others (Wolf, 2002), have concluded that basing genre identification on the interaction found in games can easily result in more than 40 different genres, something still others (Järvinen, 2003) argue could limit their usefulness. Moreover, as cross-genre games show, a game can belong to more than one genre, and even when it does not, the exact requirements for belonging to any given genre cannot be easily specified.

The problems encountered in trying to define genres that are both generic and relevant within a specific subcategory of game types lead us to believe that the basis for a common language of game research lies not in redefining the concept of genre, but instead in identifying game components that can be used to more clearly define specific genres.

2.2. Game Mechanics

A natural starting point in identifying such components is to find the common components in games that are used to exemplify a given genre. When studying various communities of gamers and game designers, we found that many used the concept of game mechanics (or mechanisms), although the definition of a mechanic is too general—"part of a game's rule system that covers one general or specific aspect of the game" (Boardgamegeek, 2005)—to be useful for academic research. A typical game mechanic is "roll and move," which simply states that dice are rolled and that something else is moved based on the outcome of the roll. The mechanic does not state how or why something should be moved; this is determined by the rules for the particular game. Computer game designers also frequently use the term *game mechanics,* but the term is not strictly defined—and is used in board games and technical programming contexts alike (Lundgren, 2002). However useful regarding a game as an entity put together by a number of smaller components might seem to be, some researchers (Järvinen, 2003; Lundgren, 2003), have stressed the need for a structure to define game mechanics more rigorously and to describe both how they relate to other mechanics and how to apply them when designing games (Järvinen, 2003; Lundgren, 2003).

2.3. Other Related Models

In addition to genres and game mechanics, a number of alternative approaches to a common game language have been suggested, primarily by professional game designers. Although not widely applied within either the game industry or academia, they are mentioned here as important influences on our approach. Writing to a designer audience, Church (Church, 1999) introduced the concept of formal abstract design tools (FADTs) as a way to reach a shared design vocabulary. Despite his emphasis on formalism and abstracting from specific instances, however, his FADTs are one-sentence descriptions: the FADT "perceivable consequences," for example, is defined solely as "a clear reaction from the game world to the action of the player." A more formalized method has been introduced by Barwood and Falstein, in the 400 Rules Project (Falstein, 2002), which collects proven game design rules and techniques, stating these as instructions. As can be seen from Falstein's section titles, however ("Imperative Statement," "Domain of Application," "Dominated Rules," "Dominating Rules," and "Examples"), the rules are intended for practical game design and are less suitable for analytic studies.

3. A Game Play-Centric Component Framework of Games

The more general part of our results was a component framework focused on gameplay. Although developed after we started collecting game design patterns, it frames our approach and is therefore described first.

While investigating the feasibility of a design pattern approach to games, we determined that the patterns needed to be grounded in invariant aspects of games. This would allow us, first, to navigate a collection of design patterns that could easily number into the hundreds (as genre, game mechanics, and FADTs showed); and, second, to more explicitly define the medium in which game design patterns emerge (to include both characteristics and specific elements of the medium)—and thus to more succinctly define the patterns themselves. To arrive at game design patterns that could describe how configurations of the physical and logical components of games affect gameplay, we needed a framework for these components.

From an analysis of the concepts used in the models described in the previous section and early work in game theory (von Neumann, 1980), we developed an initial component framework. This framework was then expanded and refined by examining the relationship between its terms and by using it to describe games and interaction in games.

The components derived for the framework—what we identified as the basic "building blocks" of games with respect to gameplay—were selected on the basis of three principal criteria: (1) they could be clearly identified in archetypical games, (2) they did not overlap; and (3) they had a natural relationship with other identified components. This does not mean, of course, that all framework components are present in all games or that the framework optimally describes any given specific game genre. Nevertheless, and even though the components themselves may seem obvious or even trivial, study of how they are realized within games provides an analysis of a game on several levels, which are connected through the relations we have identified between the components. To structure the relation between the game components, we have divided them into four categories: (1) *holistic components,* which relate to the activity of gaming as a whole; (2) *bounding components,* which relate to gaming as an activity that can voluntarily be entered or left; (3) *temporal components,* which relate to it as a temporal sequence of events and action; and (4) *structural components,* which relate to gaming as an activity consisting of physical and logical components.

3.1. Holistic Components

Given a definition of what is required for an activity to be a game, we can then proceed to explore components that relate to the game as a holistic entity. These components help both to define how gaming differs from other activities and to describe how players can join—and end—a specific game.

3.1.1 Game Instance

A trivial observation of how a game is played is that every time it is played is unlike previous times, either in the constitution or experience of the game's players, the place where it is played, or the external circumstances under which it is played, such as a limit to playing time. Thus, even though a particular game does not change, the specifics of a single completion of gameplay—which, following Zagal et al. (Zagal, Nussbaum, and Rosas, 1999), we take as defining a *game instance*—do.

3.1.2 Game Session

We define *game session* as the activity undertaken in a game instance by the game's players. The actual time a game session lasts varies greatly from game to game. In Paper-Rock-Scissors, it is only a few seconds, in most board games, it is a few hours, while in massively multiplayer online games, game sessions only end when one or more players lose interest in playing the game.

3.1.3 Play Session

The completion of a game session can be divided into several distinct periods of gameplay activity, *play sessions,* that are typically much shorter than the periods of time between them. For example, complex tabletop board games can require many hours to complete; to find the required time, players usually divide this time into play sessions lasting a few hours that are played over a period of several weeks. Play sessions, though tightly coupled to players, do not have to be tied to all players. Play-by-mail games, for example, have separate play sessions for each player that are only related by the requirement to synchronize gameplay. Massively multiplayer online games have a multitude of play sessions ongoing simultaneously that start, merge, separate, and disappear, depending on players' activities.

3.1.4 Set-up and Set-down Sessions

Each of the previous components can have specific phases, where the activities that take place do not constitute gameplay directly but are required nevertheless. These include preparing for playing by placing tokens, deciding what variants of set-ups to use, and noting game states for later gameplay. These set-up and set-down sessions allow the players to customize the gameplay experience in various ways and to undertake additional administrative or planning activities.

3.1.5 Extra-Game Activities

Activities done because a game (or game instance) exists and not directly related to playing the game itself, not even at the level of arranging or storing the game state as in the set-up and set-down sessions, we define as *extra-game activities.* The boundary between game and extra-game activities can vary, of course, depending on one's perspective. For example, it is possible (and may be interesting in some cases) to argue that buying a new pair of tennis shoes is, in fact, part of the preparatory phase of playing a game of Tennis. Likewise, it can also be argued that bragging that your name is on a highscore list is sometimes a more important aspect of the game than playing it. The extra-game activities component of the framework contains all the activities related to the game that do not have a direct impact on the game (or the metagame) state or players' strategies for a single game instance. Although the amount of extra-game activities is, of course, only limited by the players' time, interest, and imagination, the designers can provide mechanics within the game to support extra-game activities, which can have an impact on the overall gameplay experience.

3.2. Bounding Components

While holistic components describe how the activity of gameplay relates to other activities, *bounding components* define the purposes for playing the game and what activities are allowed when playing the game.

3.2.1 Rules

Rules dictate the flow of the game and have been a central aspect of most definitions of games. Although rules have a distinct place in the framework, they are also embedded in every other component: there are rules that govern what the game elements are, how they behave, what actions players can perform, and so on. Rules can be *endogenous*, explicitly stated as part of the game, or *exogenous*, implicitly understood but neither formally inscribed nor enforceable within the game. Typical exogenous rules are so-called house rules regarding the end conditions for a game.

Rules are in the boundary part of the framework: breaking rules openly ends game activities, or at least requires their reformulation to exclude the rule breaker. Because a player cheats only by breaking the rules, to expose cheating the other players must detect the faulty behavior. As noted by Huizinga (Huizinga, 1950), the person who cheats is not the one who makes the activity of playing impossible; it is the person who openly refuses to follow the rules.

3.2.2 Modes of Play

Games are typically structured to have different sections, phases or turns where the interface, available actions, information for the players—and thus also the activities—changes dramatically. We define *modes of play* to be these different activities within the larger activity of playing a particular game. Typical changes in mode of play are switching from a map view to an inventory screen in a computer role-playing game and turn-taking in Chess.

How many modes of play a game has depends on the level of detail used to define its possible states. Chess can be said to have either two modes (one player's turn and the other's) or as many modes as there are possible combinations of its piece locations.

3.2.3 Goals and Subgoals

The aim of players' plans and actions in a game are usually described as trying to complete goals. Since many games either make players compete against each other or let players decide for themselves what goals they wish to pursue, goals can vary from player to player. Furthermore, one player can have several goals that do not have to be related to each other. Many games give players several goals, where progress in completing one goal makes it difficult to complete the other; some games, such as Space Invaders or Pac-Man, which do not have a winning condition, deny players the goal of being the winner.

Goals in more complex games are often split into smaller subgoals, either to structure the gameplay (into levels or narrative structures) or to make the completion of the goal easier to achieve (acquiring new powers or tools, reducing opposition, etc.). Subgoals can be either predefined by the game or created implicitly by the players, in which case, creating subgoals that facilitate completion of the main goal can be seen as an indication of a player's skill.

3.3. Temporal Components

Used to record the activity of playing a game, *temporal components* either divide the larger gameplay activity into temporally separated activities or define the boundaries between those activities.

3.3.1 Actions

Although players can only change the game state by performing actions, the relation between actions and game state is usually one in which they can influence one another: actions available for a player typically change according to the current game state and mode of play.

Depending on the game, an action can be either *continuous* or *discrete,* that is, temporally defined by either its relation to real time or its relation to other actions. For example, Chess has discrete actions: the outcome does not change between two games played with exactly the same moves even when they take different amounts of time to play. A computer racing game, by contrast, has continuous actions: a difference in the time to complete the game changes its outcome. Generally, games that allow players to perform actions at all times have continuous actions.

A special case of actions are those which are handled by the game system as "other actions" even though they do not update the game state (they can be compared to the "no operation" command in computer assembly languages). A typical use of these is messaging between players in online games, where actions that do not affect the game state allow players to spread information.

3.3.2 Events

Discrete points in gameplay where the game state changes, *events* are most typically triggered by the completion of players' actions, which, if discrete, are integrally connected to the events. On the other hand, they can also be triggered without player intervention, most commonly in computer games but also by mechanical means, such as a sandglass.

The definition of an event does not specifically have to state how the game state changes. Rolling the dice in Monopoly triggers the state change in which a player moves his or her piece to a new place, but the event of rolling dice does not itself specify which place. Determining this, as similar events where the change is not known a priori, is controlled by evaluation functions (described below).

3.3.3 Closures

The completion of a goal or a subgoal results in a *closure,* a change of game state that is clearly perceived as a semantically meaningful transition by players (typically, by a change in the mode of play). Closures also occur when players openly recognize that a goal is no longer achievable or when certain deterministic game events occur (e.g., emptying a drawing stack in a card game or completing a bidding round in poker).

3.3.4 End Conditions

Usually accompanied by an evaluation function, *end conditions* specify the game states when closures occur and, most importantly, when the game instance ends. As in the case of role-playing games or online first-person shooter games, they need not isomorphically map onto the goals in a game.

3.3.5 Evaluation Functions

The outcome of an event, such as the winner at the end of a game instance, is determined by an evaluation function. When it both determines the winner and causes the end of the game instance, the *evaluation function* is also known as the "winning condition." Thus closures can cause evaluation functions to be determined, which can in turn cause new closures. Scoring mechanisms in games are also examples of the use of evaluation functions.

3.4. Structural Components

Perhaps the most concrete category in the framework, *structural components* are the basic parts of the game manipulated by the players and the system. They can be either physical tokens representing real-world or imaginary objects, people or creatures, or abstract phenomena representing values or attributes. Structural components are especially important when one is fine-tuning the game balance or when one is focusing on the fundamental components that the players interact with.

3.4.1 Game Facilitator

The activity of playing a game requires that there be a means to ensure that the rules are observed. Players are responsible for making sure the rules of the game are followed and for updating the game state in traditional games, such as ordinary board, card, and children's games. In most computer games, these tasks may be handled partly or completely by the system. By contrast, role-playing games and gambling games make use of a game master or an umpire, respectively, to ensure that the game progresses satisfactorily. It can be argued whether such a dedicated individual is also a player, but in any case he or she also serves the role of a *game facilitator*.

Game facilitators are responsible for keeping the game state synchronized, making the necessary changes created by player actions, taking care of the game events, and informing the players about the officially approved methods of playing the game. Game facilitators are also the ultimate arbitrators of possible disputes.

3.4.2 Players

By choosing and performing actions, *players* are the entities that strive toward the goals in a game. As the logical components that perform actions, can be interpreted as having strategies and goals, and can enter and leave the game, they need not be human beings. For example, in a singleplayer strategy game, the opponents controlled by the computer can be viewed as other players. Although normally the player is manifested in the game by a specific game element, an avatar, such as Lara Croft in the Tomb Raider series, in online board game lounges, beyond the actions they perform, players may be nothing more than names.

3.4.3 Interface

Players have access to a game through an *interface*, where game elements are represented as tokens, which come in different types and forms and can be manipulated in a wide variety of different ways, depending on the game type. Board games have counters, pieces and boards; card games, obviously, have cards as tokens; digital games have digital and audiovisual representations of similar tokens and are manipulated by keyboard, mouse, or other accessories. In other words, the look and feel of the game is specified by the interface.

3.4.4 Game Elements

The physical and logical attributes that help maintain and inform players about the current game state, *game elements* are normally also related to one another, thus creating game element configurations. These relations can be game elements themselves. The state of the game is the totality of the game element configuration at any given time. Changing a game element means that at least one of its attributes changes. For example, game elements can

- represent players (i.e. avatars);

- define the actions available to players (e.g., avatars, units, or cards);

- enable evaluation functions (e.g., rolled dice, shuffled cards), by themselves or together with other elements;

- represent entities that can perform actions (e.g., the ghosts in Pac-Man or NPCs in RPGs);

- spatially describe the game space (e.g., Chess squares, cards and emergent city walls, rivers, and roads in Carcassone);

- represent specific values of the overall game state (e.g., time left in Counter-Strike or in a time-limited Chess game);

- convey intra-game information (e.g., signs in Zelda);

- convey extra-game information (e.g., the rules of the game).

Element functions in this incomplete list can overlap; for example, the dice in Mono-poly both define the action available (roll them) and determine the number of spaces to move.

3.4.5 Game Time

Because games have actions that affect the game state and thus also affect subsequent actions, the actions in a game session can be ordered sequentially on a timeline to describe what happens during the *game time,* the period of time the game is played. Because, however, not all games depend on the exact time an action is completed so long as it is completed in its position in the sequence, the timeline of actions does not always have to be measured in real time. Thus game time can be independent of the real time used to play the game, although, in some cases, it is directly linked, for example, in real-time games or races. The distinction between game time and real time helps explain why, from a game state perspective, it can be meaningless to note the passing of time in some games, for example, turn-based games, while the passing of time can strongly influence the players' experience of the same games. The distinction can also help explain both differences in real time and game time due to breaks and time-outs in synchronous games and differences in time use in asynchronous games.

4. Design Patterns for Games

Although the game component framework set forth in section 3 describes individual aspects of a game design, it does not explicitly address how the components interact with one another during the playing of the game to create a gameplay experience. This aspect is addressed by game design patterns. In the following section 4, we describe both the theoretical and the empirical basis for our approach.

4.1. Theoretical Foundation

As mentioned in the introduction, the research fields that have studied games as designed artifacts—rather than as players playing games—have primarily been narrative fields such as literature, theater, and film. The focus on narrativity naturally tends to minimize the role of gameplay, which may explain the limited success of academic results adopted by the game industry.

This does not mean that narrativity and gameplay cannot coexist but, rather, that a focus on narrativity loses the perspective of games as activities. Typically the study of activities is confined to the fields of ethnography and anthropology. As a rule-based activity, however, games have explicit requirements and more clear-cut boundaries than other activities; their explicit formality makes it possible to study gaming activity in a detailed way without having to observe the people who play games, making it easier to focus on the activity itself instead of the people. This distinction is important. Unlike many other activities, gaming activity is designed. As such, it can be treated as an objective material to be shaped by the designer. Since the actual interaction cannot be designed, but rather the artifacts and rules that encourage or discourage the interaction, this view of game design has been called "second-order design" (Salen and Zimmerman, 2004). Further, it opens up the possibility of treating game design as a part of interaction design (e.g., Fullerton, Swain, and Hoffman, 2004), which looks at both analyzing and designing systems with the focus on how they are used, although for historical reasons, that field currently focuses on the human-computer interface (see Preece, Sharp, and Roberts, 2002).

Even though we early identified game mechanics as a promising starting point to describe interaction elements in games, to use game mechanics more effectively, we needed a structure to describe how they influence one another. Supporting this aspect of relations was the design patterns model (Alexander et al., 1977; Borchers, 2001; Gamma et al., 1995), which codifies design knowledge in separate but interrelated parts, and which has been used to describe game elements related to interaction (Kreimeier, 2002). Further, because they can easily be converted into design patterns, game mechanics seemed to be an ideal candidate for our framework, although design patterns are less than ideally suited as analytical tools owing to their introduction as problem-solving tools:

> Each pattern describes a problem which occurs over and over again in our environment, and then describes the core of the solution to that problem, in such a way that you can use this solution a million times over, without ever doing it the same way twice. (Alexander et al., 1977)

Thus, even though design patterns might be made to serve our purposes, not all aspects of design can or should be seen as solving problems, especially in a creative activity such as game design which requires not only engineering skills but also art and design competences. To identify design patterns that supported these activities, we needed a suitable pattern template.

4.2. Empirical Development

To develop a suitable pattern template, individual game design patterns, and an overarching game component framework, we gathered data by three methods: (1) we converted game mechanics into game design patterns; (2) we harvested game design patterns through game analysis; and (3) we interviewed game designers to validate ideas and concepts.

Given the initial concept of game design patterns, we first set about examining game mechanics and converting them into patterns. This included discarding a number of mechanics, merging some mechanics into one pattern, and especially identifying more abstract or more detailed patterns. The mechanics we started with were those in popular usage, as assumed from their presence on websites such as www.Boardgamegeek.com. Board games are the games most explicitly categorized by game mechanics; their mechanics can, in many cases, be applied to computer games and other game mediums.

Our second method was the "brute force" analysis of existing games, concepts, and design methods of other fields (such as architecture, software engineering, evolutionary biology, mathematics, and interaction design); from the fields of sociology, social psychology, psychology and cognitive science, we extrapolated possible person-to-person and person-to-environment interactions. Using a five-step iterative process (recognize, analyze, describe, test, and evaluate), we harvested more than 200 pattern candidates, together with unexplored but promising areas of interaction.

Finally, using our third method, we collected information about how game concepts are used in game development by interviewing nine professional game designers, who together represented the full spectrum of game media. This also allowed us to confirm the validity not only of our approach, but also of certain specific concepts and pattern candidates. All interviewed designers used terms such as *genre, theme* and *mechanisms* casually and were obviously very familiar with the concepts behind them, although they seldom mentioned mechanics by name (typical exceptions were board and card game developers use of *Bluff, Tension, Action Cards, Storytelling, Trading, Action Points,* and *Cooperation*). Some of the designers were themselves interested in creating structured frameworks for games; several of them were also aware of design pattern methodologies, although they had not tried to apply them. The interviews provided confirmation that our proposed solution was compatible with the way developers worked and provided many concepts that could be developed into patterns.

5. Game Design Patterns Defined

Unlike most design pattern researchers, we do not define patterns as pure problem-solution pairs. We do not for two reasons. First, defining patterns from problems runs the risk of viewing them only as problem-solving tools for removing unwanted effects of a design, not as tools to support creative design work. Second, many of the patterns we have identified describe a characteristic that more or less automatically guarantees other characteristics in a game. That is, the problem described in a pattern might easily be solved by applying a more specific, related pattern. We believe that game design patterns offer a good framework for how to structure knowledge about gameplay that could be used both for design and for analysis of games. Accordingly, and based on the findings described above, we again offer our definition: *game design patterns are semi-formalized interdependent descriptions of commonly reoccurring parts of the design of a game that concern gameplay.*

5.1. Game Design Patterns as Semi-Formal Descriptions

Due to the nature of the design process, game design patterns rely on general descriptions of particular areas of gameplay without using quantitative measures. Indeed, neither the presence nor the effect of game design patterns can be measured accurately, and automating their use is practically impossible. Thus any specification of gameplay that relied on measures would be too precise to be of practical use for solving the ill-defined problems of design. On the other hand, game design patterns do have a structure, they can be distinguished from one another, and relationships between them can be identified in a game design. This makes game design patterns semi-formalized concepts that have to be understood and applied differently in the different contexts of their intended use.

5.2. Game Design Patterns as Interrelated Descriptions

Although all patterns in any given game are related to one another in some form, some types of relations are more common and can more easily be identified and constructed. We have identified three pattern relations—two asymmetric and one symmetric—that are both common and useful for analytic and design purposes.

Instantiates: When one pattern has an *instantiating* relation to another pattern, the presence of the first pattern causes the second pattern to also be present. This is due to the fact that the design possibilities described by the first pattern limit the freedom of the designer in such a way that the design possibilities of another pattern follow automatically. (A variation of this relation is when the combined effect of two or more patterns together limits the gameplay space in such a way that another pattern emerges automatically.) A second pattern induced by a first in this asymmetric relation is *instantiated* by that first pattern.

Modulates: When one pattern has a *modulating* relation to another pattern, it can be used to change aspects of the other pattern in a way that influences gameplay. The modulating pattern works within a limited design space that is bounded by other restrictions regarding gameplay. Modulating relations are not instantiating relations since the design possibilities they describe do not limit the game designer to have to use the modulating pattern, rather the modulating pattern offers possibilities for fine tuning another pattern. This also means that the first pattern has to exist before it is possible to use the modulating pattern. A second pattern affected by a first in this asymmetric relation is *modulated* by that first pattern.

Potentially Conflicting: When one pattern has a *potentially conflicting* relation to another pattern, it can, in certain configurations, make the presence of the other pattern impossible and vice versa. This incompatibility affects a particular area or level of gameplay: patterns that are potentially conflicting can often be found in the same game but on different levels. A pattern having this symmetric relation to another *potentially conflicts* with the other, and vice versa.

5.3. Game Design Pattern Template

Based on the characteristics of game design patterns, we developed a template for describing the patterns. The template contains seven sections: (1) name; (2) core definition; (3) general description; (4) using the pattern; (5) consequences; (6) relations; and (7) references.

5.3.1 Name

Although not explicitly stating this in the template, we have tried to give the game design patterns short, specific, and idiomatic names, mainly to provide mnemonic support for remembering the pattern description. Where a pattern was adapted from a concept in another research field, we have retained the name of that concept to provide a link to that field. To minimize the number of names that need to be remembered, we have deliberately not included aliases; instead we take an approach similar to that of a dictionary by providing synonym-analogues in the form of references to similar concepts in other models and fields of study.

5.3.2 Core Definition

A brief sentence in italics immediately following the name, and describing the core idea of the pattern, the "core definition" section is intended to provide an overview for first-time readers browsing through a pattern collection and to remind returning readers of the contents of the pattern.

5.3.3 General Description

Following the core definition, the "general description" section, which often notes in which game the pattern was first identified and whether it has been identified in previous game design models, explains how the pattern affects the structural framework (especially if the pattern can be instantiated on different scales in the game) and cites examples of games where the pattern is typically found.

5.3.4 Using the Pattern

Even though the application of a particular pattern to any given situation requires a number of design choices specific to that situation, high-level choices can often be divided into categories. The "using the pattern" section mentions common high-level choices that face a designer wishing to apply the pattern, often citing a specific game component from published games.

5.3.5 Consequences

Each pattern has its own trade-offs: in solving one problem, it can cause or amplify other problems. To make a design decision for or against a given solution, a game designer must understand its costs and benefits and compare them with those of alternative solutions. The "consequences" section describes the likely or possible consequences of applying the solution suggested by the pattern.

5.3.6 Relations

This section lists the relations between the described pattern and other patterns by the five identified categories of relations: *instantiating*, *modulating*, *instantiated by*, *modulated by*, and *potentially conflicting*.

5.3.7 References

This section lists previous works that have either directly inspired the pattern or describe its main aspects.

6. Examples of Game Design Patterns

The following two pattern examples, *Resources* and *Producer-Consumer* are from the "Resources and Resource Management" chapter of the book *Patterns in Game Design* (Björk and Holopainen, 2005). These and other design patterns mentioned in the examples are capitalized and in italics. The references sections have been omitted from these patterns because they contain no references.

Resources

Resources are game elements used by players to enable actions in a game.

Resources are the representations of commodities that may be used to fund actions in the game or that may be depleted by other players' actions. A commodity may exist as a physical game element or as a purely virtual one, or may alternate between both. Common *Resources* in computer games include health and ammunition in first-person shooters, money and units in real-time strategy games, hit points and mana points in role-playing games, action points in turn-based games, and players and money in sports management games.

> **Example:** The board game Space Hulk gives each unit a number of action points at the beginning of a turn. These points are a form of *Resources* that pay for the actions of the units.

> **Example:** The computer game Victoria makes complex use of resource refinement. Thus producing a Tank unit in the game requires producing the Tank commodity, which in turn requires *Resources* refined from other *Resources*, and so on.

Using the Pattern

The primary question regarding *Resources* is what they are used for. Generalizing, *Resources* are used to win comparisons with other players in evaluation functions; they can sometimes be converted into actions (possibly providing *Privileged Abilities*) or other more valuable *Resources*. Typically, *Resources* are used or consumed by paying for actions through *Budgeted Action Points*, becoming part of objects built through *Construction* actions, or being destroyed due to *Damage*. Other actions that require the use of *Resources* are *Aim & Shoot* and *Betting*.

Resources can be used for several different purposes; for example, as *Budgeted Action Points*, they can be used both to modulate the *Right Level of Complexity* and to force players to make *Trade-Offs*. Games using one *Resource* for multiple purposes include the board game Carolus Magnus, where markers can be used to strengthen a fraction's control over an area or the player's control over the fraction, and the card game San Juan where each card represents a good, a colonist, money, and a building.

After determining what *Resources* are used for, the next question is how players gain access to them. Players may start with *Nonrenewable Resources* to promote *Stimulated Planning* for the whole game session, they may be required to collect the *Resources* from the *Game World*, *Resource Generators*, or *Chargers*, or they may receive *Resources* as *Rewards* for completing certain goals. Regardless of how players obtain the *Resources*, the game may be set up to promote either *Symmetric Resource Distribution* or *Asymmetric Resource Distribution* to enforce different strategies and *Varied Gameplay*. Unless used in a controlled fashion to provide *Handicaps*, however, *Asymmetric Resource Distribution* may negatively affect *Player Balance*. Goals that give *Resources* as *Rewards* are, in most cases, *Supporting Goals*. In addition to completing goals and *Collecting* them, players may be able to redistribute *Resources* among themselves through actions such as *Trading* and *Bidding*.

The *Resources* available at the beginning of gameplay may be the only *Resources* that exist, or they may be *Renewable Resources*, in which case, they may be produced from *Resource Generators*, handed out at regular time intervals, or given as *Rewards* for completing goals. All these options are examples of how *Producers* can create *Resources*, and together with how the *Resources* are consumed, they form *Producer-Consumer* patterns. When the *Resources* are collected from the *Game World*, several additional design choices are required, including the location of the *Resources*, who can see them, and whether there are *Clues* to where they can be found. Are they *Secret Resources* that are hidden by *Fog of War* or can they only be detected by *Privileged Abilities?* Are they *Rewards* for finding *Easter Eggs?* Do they appear in different amounts or concentrations? How much time is required to collect them? What game elements can collect them? Does the possession of them affect game element characteristics? Are they physical entities in the game and, if so, can they be converted to virtual ones? Do players have influence over how *Resources* are divided between players through *Player-Decided Distribution of Rewards & Penalties?*

Once possession of a *Resource* is obtained, does it need to be stored in a *Container*, and is there a maximum limit to how much of it can be stored? Does the *Resource* need to be used before a certain *Time Limit* has expired? Can the *Resource* be lost as an effect of *Penalties?*

The next question is how control of *Resources* is decided. Are they *Shared Resources* whose use several players need to agree upon through *Negotiation*, or are they manipulated by all players through *Indirect Control?* Is ownership changeable, that is, can other players steal *Resources* by various actions that have *Transfer of*

Control effects, or can the players change *Resources* through *Trading?* When *Resources* are contested but are also used to produce *Units*, the struggle for *Resources* can become a *Red Queen Dilemma*, where gaining control over larger amounts of *Resources* can only be achieved by consuming larger amounts.

In games where several different types of *Resources* are used, knowing how and when to convert one form of *Resource* to another may be part of the *Strategic Knowledge* of the game. The conversion may have inefficient exchange rates (by use of *Diminishing Returns*), may require access to a *Converter*, or may only be possible through *Trading* with other players.

Resources usually have to fit within the *Consistent Reality Logic* of the game, except when *Time Limits* prevent *Analysis Paralysis* or when *Resources* are primarily used to determine winning conditions. In this light, the concept of *Score* can be seen as a *Resource*, which is used to determine the winner of a game.

Units are common *Resources* in god games. The games Lemmings and Pikmin both make use of different types of *Units* that players have to direct to achieve goals while making *Tradeoffs* between various actions and what *Units* to use. The equivalent to these *Resources* in games using *Avatars* is *Lives*.

The introduction of *Time Limits* or *The Show Must Go On* in games makes time a *Resource* that has to be used efficiently. The computer game Space Hulk uses two modes of play: a strategic mode, where nothing happens but time is limited, and a real-time mode, where the *Time Limit* is replenished but commands cannot be given to *Units*, to force players to promote *Tension* together with *Stimulated Planning*.

Consequences

By providing players with quantifiable measures to judge their progress and plan possible future actions, *Resources* are one way for players to have *Emotional Immersion* in games. The *Resources* can either exist from the beginning of gameplay or be created through *Producers*, and are either destroyed by *Consumers*, transformed through *Converters*, or belong to *Closed Economies*. Games whose goal consists of *Collecting* various types of *Resources* can use the number of owned *Resources* as a *Score*; games having a separate *Score* system often use *Resources* as a second-order *Score* system to function as *Tiebreakers*. The presence of *Resources* in *Game Worlds* can motivate *Area Control* goals or, in the case of *Secret Resources*, *Exploration* goals. *Resources* are often also used to give *Characters* acting as *Consumers* or *Converters* the ability to perform actions. In some games, the distribution of *Resources* among players decides the order of *Turntaking.*

Relations

Instantiates: *Collecting, Score, Stimulated Planning, Varied Gameplay, Strategic Knowledge, Tradeoffs, Easter Eggs, Rewards, Penalties, Red Queen Dilemmas.*

Modulates: *Player-Decided Distribution of Rewards & Penalties, Player Balance, Tiebreakers, Construction, Area Control, Turntaking, Characters, Emotional Immersion, Exploration, Game World, Supporting Goals.*

Instantiated by: *Score, Units, Clues, The Show Must Go On, Time Limits, Lives, Budgeted Action Points, Indirect Control.*

Modulated by: *Symmetric Resource Distribution, Asymmetric Resource Distribution, Converter, Container, Secret Resources, Nonrenewable Resources, Shared Resources, Renewable Resources, Limited Resources, Ownership, Transfer of Control, Resource Generators, Handicaps, Secret Resources, Time Limits, Trading, Diminishing Returns, Damage, Aim & Shoot, Betting, Producers, Consumers, Closed Economies, Chargers, Trading, Bidding, Producer-Consumer, Investments.*

Potentially Conflicting: *None.*

Producer-Consumer

Producer-Consumer determines the lifetime of game elements, usually *Resources,* and thus governs the flow of gameplay.

Games usually have several overlapping and interconnected *Producer-Consumers* governing the flow of available game elements, especially *Resources.* As *Resources* are used to determine the possible player actions, these *Producer-Consumer* networks also determine the actual flow of the gameplay. *Producer-Consumers* can operate recursively, that is, one *Producer-Consumer* might determine the lifetime of another. *Producer-Consumers* are often chained together to form more complex networks of *Resource* flows.

> **Example:** In Civilization, the units are produced in cities and consumed in battles against enemy units and cities. This kind of *Producer-Consumer* is also used in almost all real-time strategy games.

431

Example: In Asteroids, the rocks are produced at the start of each level and are consumed by the player shooting at them. The same principle applies to many other games where the level of progression is based on eliminating, that is, consuming, other game elements: the pills in Pac-Man, free space in Qix, and the aliens in Space Invaders.

Using the Pattern

As the name implies, *Producer-Consumer* is a compound pattern of *Producer* and *Consumer;* as such, this pattern governs how both are instantiated. Because the produced game element can be consumed in many different ways, the effect of producing and consuming *Resources* or *Units* often turns out to be several different pairs of *Producer-Consumers.* For example, the *Units* in a real-time strategy game such as the Age of Empires series can be eliminated in direct combat with enemy *Units,* when bombarded by indirect fire, and finally when their supply points are exhausted. The *Producer-Consumer* in this case consists of the *Producer* of the *Units* with three different *Consumers.*

Producer-Consumers are often, especially in *Resource Management* games, chained together with *Converters* and sometimes with *Containers.* These chains can in turn be used to create more complex networks. The *Converter* is used as the *Consumer* in the first *Producer-Consumer* and as the *Producer* in the second. In other words, the *Converter* takes the *Resources* produced by the first *Producer* and converts them to the *Resources* produced by the second *Producer.*

This kind of *Producer-Consumer* chain sometimes has a *Container* attached to the *Converter* to stockpile produced *Resources.* For example, in the real-time strategy game StarCraft, something is produced and taken to the converter and then converted to something else and stockpiled. Investments can be seen as *Converters* that are used to convert *Resources* into other forms of *Resources,* possibly abstract ones.

Consequences

As is the case with its main subpatterns *Producer* and *Consumer,* the *Producer-Consumer* pattern is quite abstract, although effects on the flow of the game are very concrete. Simply put, *Producer-Consumers* govern the whole flow of the games that have them, from games with a single *Producer-Consumer* to those with complex and many layered networks of *Producer-Consumers.*

The feeling of player control is increased when players are able to manipulate the *Producer,* the *Consumer,* or both; adding new *Producer-Consumers* over which the players have control gives them opportunities for more *Varied Gameplay.* In more complex *Producer-Consumer* chains, however, where the effects of individual actions can become almost impossible to discern and the process no longer has *Predictable Consequences,* players can lose the *Illusion of Influence. Producer-Consumer* networks with *Converters* and *Containers* are used in *Resource Management* games to accomplish the *Right Level of Complexity;* the games usually start with simple *Producer-Consumers* and add new *Producer-Consumers* to the network to increase the complexity as they progress.

Relations

Instantiates: Varied Gameplay, Resource Management.
Modulates: Resources, Right Level of Complexity, Investments, Units.
Instantiated by: Producers, Consumers, Converters.
Modulated by: Container.
Potentially Conflicting: Illusions of Influence, Predictable Consequences.

7. Uses

Unlike earlier users of design patterns in architecture or software engineering, we do not propose a single use (problem-solving) for design patterns. Instead, we see the patterns and the structural framework as tools that, like a pen, can be applied in several different ways for several different purposes by several different user groups having inherently different working methods. On the other hand, we have identified a number of promising uses for patterns within both academia and the game industry, although we have yet to collect substantial amounts of data regarding the relative feasibility and merit of these proposed uses.

Because the use to which any given game design pattern is put very much depends on the specific use context and how rigorously its use is structured, we see no reason to limit potential users. Thus a pattern used by academics categorizing games and genres could also be used by critics writing reviews or by gamers making decisions about purchases. But we do wish to stress that game design patterns, with their neutral, jargon-free definitions based on the interaction in games, can greatly benefit multidisciplinary groups by facilitating communication between disciplines.

7.1. Generating Ideas

Game developers can use the patterns to give inspiration by simply randomly choosing a set and trying to imagine a game using them. A more structured approach is to study an individual game design pattern and try to implement it in a novel way.

7.2. Developing Game Concepts

Once an initial game concept exists, it can be developed using patterns. By describing the concept as a small set of patterns, developers can then flesh it out and make more specific design choices, deciding how to instantiate those patterns through related patterns, and studying how the different design patterns interact. The process can be iteratively refined, by examining the chosen pattern until the preferred level of detail is achieved.

7.3. Designing Games

Having a game described using patterns offers advantages when marketing the game design. Patterns allow one to present a structured description of the design as well as motivations for particular design choices by showing how replacing a pattern with another pattern would change the design, or more advantageously, by relating that game's use to other games' uses of the same patterns.

7.4. Identifying Competition and Intellectual Property Issues

As a side-benefit of having identified the patterns in a game design, one can identify competition, in the form of what the game will be compared to, by the examples given in the patterns. Further, references in game design patterns may point to patents that can influence the development of commercial game products.

7.5. Problem-Solving during Development

Similar to the rationale for FADTs and the 400 Rules, game design patterns are a way to collect the knowledge and experience of game developers. As such, they contain descriptions and motivations for how one can modify game designs to solve issues relating to gameplay.

7.6. Analyzing Games

The availability of a pattern collection can provide a simple way to start analyzing an existing game. Having iteratively gone through the collection to determine whether a pattern exists in a game and, if so, to what degree, one can then gain further information about the game by studying whether previously identified related patterns have been used to create a pattern or whether novel game components have been introduced.

7.7. Categorizing Games and Genres

Assuming that a patterns-based analysis has been performed on a collection of games, these can then be categorized according to their similarities and differences. Besides offering a multitude of ways to measure how games compare to one another, collections of patterns found in games belonging to a particular genre can be used to describe that genre in greater detail.

7.8. Exploring New Platforms and Media

The commercial success of sequels and branding has led the game industry to become conservative not only in thematic and gameplay styles, but also in platforms and media. We believe that the use of game design patterns can help the industry explore new types of game platforms and media by providing a structured way to compare how gameplay changes with a changed environment. This is especially true for novel game media, such as pervasive gaming, which is a development of computer games but needs also to function in social environments similar to those of more traditional games.

8. Discussion

One might object that the use of game design patterns takes the creativity out of game design or makes the designers "mere pattern-cranking machines" that automatically churn out games. Another common objection is that the use of patterns will lead to games falling into stereotypes, where nothing new is or can be created. Both these objections stem from confusing the everyday meaning of *pattern* as something repetitive with the basic philosophy of design patterns as introduced by Alexander. Although, for this reason alone, the choice of the term *pattern* might be regarded as a mistake, because it has a clear and firmly established meaning in several professional fields, we see no need to invent a new term, something that, indeed would lessen the usefulness of the pattern concept as a tool to overcome communication differences between various professions. The use of game design patterns might more appropriately be compared to the artistic endeavor in general: artists have a much better chance of creating something novel when they are familiar, if only unconsciously, with the basic elements of their craft, be it painting, composing, or scriptwriting, then when they are not.

Because the framework we have presented here, while incorporating components from as many types of games as possible, has tried to keep the number of these components within manageable bounds, it is restricted to a certain level of abstractness. Nevertheless, we have identified areas, such as classifying game elements more fully, that can be developed further on a general level without having to focus on specific games or on specific physical representations of game elements.

We believe that, for many practical uses, our two main concepts can be used independently of each other. That is, design patterns can be used without reference to the component framework and vice versa. One can, for example, in early concept development use the patterns alone, or in creating an object-oriented model for computer implementation of a game, make use of the component framework alone.

The loose coupling between our main concepts actually allows either to be replaced by another simpler, more complex, or functionally different concept, depending on the intended use. The prime methods for developing game design patterns and the component framework were structural and functional analysis of existing games, taxonomical categorization of the components identified, and experimental design, which we believe are reflected in the two concepts.

On the other hand, we also believe that in most cases, the component framework and game design patterns can be used together when analyzing and designing games, and in a style similar to that of the core concepts identified in *Rules of Play* (Salen and Zimmerman, 2004), which can be applied in a number of different ways (or "game design schemas" as they are called in that book).

9. Acknowledgments

We thank our collaborators Johan Peitz, Ola Davidsson, Daniel Eriksson, Jussi Kuittinen, and our previous collaborators Sus Lundgren and Tobias Rydenhag. Further, we would like to thank Greg Costikyan, Bernd Kreimeier, Steffen P. Walz, and Aki Järvinen for valuable discussions.

Bibliography

Alexander, Christopher, et al. *A Pattern Language: Towns, Buildings, Construction.* New York: Oxford University Press, 1977.

Björk, Staffan, and Jussi Holopainen. *Patterns in Game Design.* Hingham, MA: Charles River Media, 2005.

Boardgamegeek, May 6, 2005. www.boardgamegeek.com. [JH: 25th of November 2004]

Borchers, Jan. *A Pattern Approach to Interaction Design.* Chichester, England: Wiley, 2001.

Church, Doug. "Formal Abstract Design Tools." 1999. www.gamasutra.com.

Crawford, Chris. *The Art of Computer Game Design.* Berkeley, CA: Osborne/McGraw-Hill, 1982.

Falstein, Noah. "Better By Design: The 400 Project." *Game Developer Magazine* 9, no.3 (March 2002): 26.

Fullerton, Tracy, Christopher Swain, and Steven Hoffman. *Game Design Workshop: Designing, Prototyping, and Playtesting Games.* New York: CMP Books, 2004.

Gamma, Erich, Richard Helm, Ralph Johnson, and John Vlissides. *Design Patterns: Elements of Reusable Object-Oriented Software.* Reading, MA: Addison-Wesley, 2001.

Huizinga, Johan. *Homo Ludens: A Study of the Play-Element in Culture.* Boston: Beacon Press, 1950.

Järvinen, Aki. "Halo and the Anatomy of the FPS." *Game Studies,* www.gamestudies.org 2, no.1 (July 2002).

Järvinen, Aki. "Games without Frontiers," 2003. dissertation in progress. www.gamewithout-frontiers.net.

Knizia, Reiner. *Dice Games Properly Explained.* Kingsford, England: Elliot Right Way Books, 1999.

Kreimeier, Bernd. "The Case for Game Design Patterns," 2002. www.gamasutra.com/features/20020313/kreimeier_03.htm.

Lundgren, Sus. "Joining Bits and Pieces: How to make Entirely New Board Games Using Embedded Computer Technology." M.S. Thesis in Interaction Design, Department of Computing Science, Chalmers University of Technology, Götenberg, Sweden, 2002.

Lundgren, Sus. and Staffan Björk. "Game Mechanics: Describing Computer-Augmented Games in Terms of Interaction." Proceedings of the First International Conference on Technologies for Interactive Digital Storytelling and Entertainment (TIDSE), Darmstadt, Germany, 2003.

von Neumann, John and Oskar Morgenstern. *Theory of Games and Economic Behavior,* Princeton University Press, 1980.

Parlett, David. *The Oxford History of Board Games.* New York: Oxford University Press, 1999.

Preece, Jenny, Helen Sharp and Yvonne Rogers. *Interaction Design: Beyond Human-Computer Interaction.* New York: John Wiley, 2002.

Salen, Katie and Eric Zimmerman. *Rules of Play: Game Design Fundamentals.* Cambridge, MA: MIT Press, 2004.

Wolf, Mark J.P. "Genre and the Video Game." In *The Medium of the Video Game,* ed. Mark J.P. Wolf. Austin: University of Texas Press, 2002.

Zagal, José Pablo, Miguel Nussbaum, and Ricardo Rosas. "A Model to Support the Design of Multiplayer Games." In *Presence: Teleoperators and Virtual Environments,* vol .9, no.5. Cambridge, MA: MIT Press, 1999, p.448-462. Also available online at www.cc.gatech.edu/~jp/Papers/AModelMultiplayerGames.pdf.

Tools for Creating Dramatic Game Dynamics

Marc LeBlanc

Context

The topic for my essay comes from my first lecture at the Game Developer's Conference (GDC) in 1999, and owes some of its inspiration to my colleague Doug Church and his work on formal abstract design tools. At that time, it was becoming clear that our discourse on game design needed more of a conceptual framework, a way to place the individual topics of discussion in their proper aesthetic context. In the five years since, I have strived to develop such a framework, through my practical work as well as through my Game Tuning Workshop, held annually at the GDC. The essay represents those five years of refinement.

The Player Experience

Games as Narrative

Game Design Models

Marc LeBlanc is a twelve-year veteran of the computer game industry. He has contributed to such award-winning titles as the Thief series, the System Shock series, and the casual game Oasis. He has a Master's degree in Computer Science from the Massachusetts Institute of Technology.

Introduction: Stories and Games

In the study of game design, comparisons to traditional narrative forms—prose, theater, film and TV—are inevitable. The advent of digital games has brought games and stories closer together than ever before. In the 1970s and 80s, text adventures like Zork gave us a new way to combine play with prose. Today, video games like Zelda and Grand Theft Auto possess the sights, sounds, characters, and plots that we might expect to see in a feature film. Given so many points of similarity between modern games and traditional stories, it's natural for game designers to look for ways to incorporate the tools and techniques of storytelling into their own craft.

But the power of games as a story vehicle is hardly a new idea. The ancient Egyptian game of *Senet*—which, along with Go, is one of the top contenders for the title of "oldest game known to humanity"—tells the story of the passage through the underworld to the land of the dead. During the height of its three millennia of popularity, players of Senet believed that the game was an oracle for mystical divination. The events of the game foretold what the player might one day experience in his own passage through the afterlife.

Since the ancient days of Senet, we have seen countless other games with a vast diversity of fictional meanings and metaphors: games about warfare and conquest, about courtly intrigue, about sleuthing detectives and robber barons, and about nothing at all. We have also seen how games can *become* stories, as when a sporting event is transformed into the news of the day—or the stuff of legend. We have seen works of fiction that incorporate games as narrative devices, like a movie that culminates in a climactic bike race, or a boxing match, or a game of Chess. In these examples of stories about games, the story no longer relies on the *metaphor* of the game, but on the events of the game itself: the plans and gambits, the bluffs and stratagems, the reversals of fortune. The play of the game becomes a climactic struggle that builds to a satisfying conclusion. In other words, the game is *dramatic*.

It should be safe to say that drama is a desirable quality of games. Players often seek out games that are dramatic, and sometimes a game's drama becomes the primary motivation for playing. Drama is part of a game's play content; it's a kind of fun. Thus, as game designers, we strive to imbue drama into our creations, to create games that are climactic struggles in their own right.

The challenge of creating drama within a game is compounded by our limited control over the games we create. We don't—and can't—know the precise details of how our game will play out, each and every time it is played. We are not the authors of the events of the game; we cannot craft the game's drama directly, the way a storyteller scripts a story. Our task is more indirect. We cannot *create* drama; we can only create the circumstances from which drama will *emerge.*

As game designers, how do we go about the task of creating dramatic games? What tools can we use to guarantee a climactic struggle? These are the central questions we will be exploring over the next few pages. We'll gain a better sense of what drama *is* and *how* it happens. We'll identify the necessary ingredients for drama, and we'll uncover a collection of tools and techniques for introducing those ingredients into our game.

Mechanics, Dynamics, and Aesthetics

Our exploration of drama will be guided by a core framework of three separate aspects of games: mechanics, dynamics, and aesthetics. We can think of these three aspects as parts of the game play experience, or as perspectives from which a game can be viewed.

When we talk about *mechanics,* we are referring to all the necessary pieces that we need to play the game. This primarily refers to the rules of the game, but can also refer to the equipment, the venue, or anything else necessary for playing the game. The mechanics of Chess include not only the rules for how the pieces move, but other facts like the dimensions of the board. The mechanics of Baseball include not only the explicit rules of Baseball, but the physical laws that govern the game: gravity, energy, the limits of the human mind and body. The peculiarities of the venue are also part of the mechanics; Fenway Park's "green monster" is part of the mechanics of any game played there. In a video game like Super Mario Sunshine, the mechanics would include the program code (which is a complete description of the game's rules) and all of its equipment, including the physical layout of the controller. If we think of the game as a *system,* the mechanics are the complete description of that system.

Dynamics refers to what might be called the "behavior" of the game, the actual events and phenomena that occur as the game is played. In Baseball, the different kinds of batted balls (e.g., fly balls, line drives, grounders, bunts) are part of the dynamics of the game. In Chess, the dynamics include tactical concepts like the knight fork or the discovered check, as well as structural concepts like the opening and the endgame. When we view a game in terms of its dynamics, we are asking, "What happens when the game is played?" The dynamics of a game are not mandated by its rules, and are not always easy to intuit from the rules themselves. It would take a fairly clever person to deduce the concept of a discovered check from the rules of Chess without ever having played the game. The relationship between dynamics and mechanics is one of *emergence*. A game's dynamics *emerge* from its mechanics.

A game's *aesthetics* are its emotional content, the desirable emotional responses we have when we play—all the kinds of fun that result from playing the game. A game can challenge our intellect (or our physical prowess). It can foster social interaction. It can stimulate our imagination. It can provide us with a vehicle for self-expression. All of these properties are part of the aesthetics of the game. A game's aesthetics emerge from its dynamics; how the game *behaves* determines how it makes the player feel. Understanding how specific game dynamics evoke specific emotional responses is one of the greatest challenges of game design.

In a sense, the mechanics of the game always exist, even when the game is not being played. We can think of a board game (or a video game) that sits on our shelf as a box full of game mechanics, waiting for us to take it down and set the game into motion. The dynamics of the game, however, only manifest while the game is being played. Our ability to reap the game's aesthetic content depends on our actually playing the game and bringing those dynamics to life. Thus, when we play a game, our experience can be described as a kind of causal flow that starts with its mechanics, passes through dynamics, and ends with aesthetics.

For players, the purpose of playing is to enjoy the game's aesthetic content. As game designers, our objective is to *create* that content. Our relationship to the game is opposite that of the players. We begin our work with a set of aesthetic objectives—emotional responses we *hope* to evoke in the players. Our task is to work backward, determining what dynamics will accomplish our aesthetic objectives, and from there design game mechanics that will create those dynamics. So when we design a game, our experience begins with aesthetics, passes through dynamics, and ends with a set of mechanics.

This framework of three schemas for understanding games—mechanics, dynamics, and aesthetics—allows us to refine the motivating questions of our inquiry into drama in games:

· How does drama function as an aesthetic of play?
· What kinds of game dynamics can evoke drama?
· From what kinds of mechanics do those dynamics emerge?

In the pages that follow, we will explore each of these topics in turn.

The Dramatic Arc: An Aesthetic Model for Drama

The goal of our exploration is to discover ways to make our games more dramatic. We want drama, as an aesthetic objective of our game design, to be part of the game's emotional content. The first step is to formulate a good definition of drama. How will we know drama when we see it? We need some kind of yardstick we can hold up to our game design to determine how well it succeeds or fails at being dramatic, a yardstick that encompasses our understanding of what drama is and how it happens. We call such a yardstick an "aesthetic model." As tools for formalizing our design objectives, *aesthetic models* can help us know when we have achieved them, and if we're headed in the right direction.

Before we proceed, we must acknowledge that drama is only one aesthetic among many. There are many reasons to play a game, many kinds of fun to get out of a game. Games can challenge us, realize our fantasies, bring us into social contact, and provide many more kinds of experiences. Each kind of experience is a separate aesthetic pleasure with its own aesthetic model. Different aesthetics can coexist within the discipline of game design, and even within the design of a single game. When we design a game, we hope its players will experience many kinds of fun, not merely a single kind. Because two different games might deliver the same aesthetics in different proportions, depending on the priorities of the designer —and the players—our aesthetic model of drama is not going to be a grand unified theory that encompasses all kinds of play or fun. We're looking for a specific model that explains drama, and nothing else. Other, broader models also exist, but they are beyond the scope of this essay.

Our quest for an aesthetic model of drama starts with a picture. Recognize it?

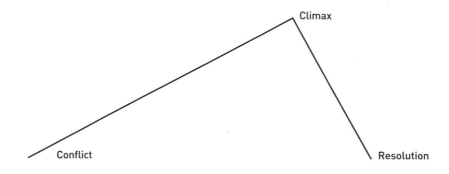

We've probably all seen this diagram at some point. The lines and proportions may be different, but the general shape is always the same. It visualizes the *dramatic arc,* the rising and falling action of a well-told story. The central conflict of a narrative creates *tension* that accumulates as the story builds to a climax, and dissipates as the conflict is resolved.

We can think of the diagram as a mathematical model. If we draw in the axes, it becomes a graph:

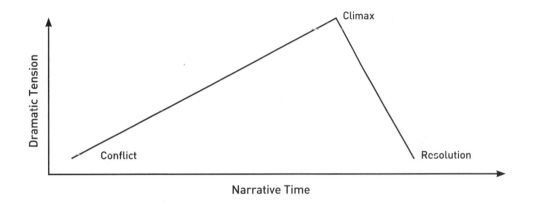

The mathematical model of drama imagines that dramatic tension is a kind of quantity that can accumulate and discharge, increase or decrease as time passes. That's not to say we could ever actually measure dramatic tension, of course. It's absurd to think that we could construct some kind of dramatic-tension-o-meter, a device that we could wave over the audience as a story is told, reading out the dramatic tension as a numerical value—no doubt measured in units called "millishakespeares." In that sense, it is not so much a quantity as a quality. Still, the idea that dramatic tension can increase and decrease is an important one for our diagram to have any meaning.

What is dramatic tension then? It's our level of *emotional* investment in the story's conflict: the sense of concern, apprehension, and urgency with which we await the story's outcome.

Drama as an Aesthetic

The dramatic arc is an aesthetic model for stories; it's a statement about how stories convey their emotional content, and a yardstick that we can hold up to a story to see if it succeeds or fails at being dramatic. The dramatic arc is not a universal fact of all stories, but rather a desirable property of dramatic stories. The dramatic arc is a value statement. It says that well-told stories should possess dramatic tension, and that over time the tension should take on a particular shape, building toward the story's climax, and then dissipating.

What's so special about this particular shape? Why should the tension first rise and then fall, instead of first falling and then rising? Is this shape somehow intrinsically beautiful? Maybe, but most people don't leave a movie, thinking, "Wow, what a lovely dramatic arc!" The individual moments, and the emotions they evoked, are what stay with us.

Perhaps the dramatic arc is a part of the fundamental rhythm of human cognition. Something about it resonates with us, signaling to our subconscious: "This is a story. Pay attention!" It creates a context and a frame of mind where the individual moments become meaningful, powerful, and relevant. Perhaps it also serves to shape the story into an easily digestible cognitive morsel. It gives the story a sense of wholeness, that it is a complete work with a beginning, middle, and end.

In any case, the dramatic arc will serve as the cornerstone of our aesthetic model of drama. Let's spend some time exploring how dramatic tension emerges during game play, as well as techniques game designers can use to sculpt that tension into a well-formed dramatic arc.

Drama in Games

In the context of a traditional narrative, it's natural to think of the dramatic arc as being hand-crafted by the story's author. In the case of film or theater, the authors have complete control over every moment of the unfolding narrative. As game designers, we have a greater challenge. We must assure that our game will be dramatic, even when we don't have direct control over the narrative, a narrative that isn't scripted in advance, but rather *emerges* from the events of the game.

All drama originates from conflict. Indeed, without conflict, no dramatic tension will ever emerge. In a game, the conflict comes from the *contest* around which the game is built. Contests can take many different forms: some might challenge the player's intellect, others his stamina. Some might be competitions between multiple players; others might be solitaire challenges for a single player. Any of these contests provides the conflict necessary for drama.

How does tension emerge from a contest, and how does that tension change over time? Dramatic tension is the product of two different factors:

Uncertainty: the sense that the outcome of the contest is still unknown. Any player could win or lose.

Inevitability: the sense that the contest is moving forward toward resolution. The outcome is imminent.

Tension relies on these two factors in combination—neither is sufficient by itself. Without uncertainty, the outcome of the game becomes a foregone conclusion, and the players become spectators. Without inevitability, the outcome of the conflict seems distant. Players are given little incentive to invest their emotions in the contest.

To see these two factors at work, let's consider a typical game of Magic: The Gathering. The game begins as a blank slate: each player has a full deck of cards and nothing in play. In the first few turns, the players' ability to affect the outcome of the game is limited by their scant mana resources.[1] The outcome of the game is unknown, and seems miles away. As play progresses, certain game elements become ever more obvious signals that the game is moving toward a conclusion: the waning height of the players' decks, the scarcity of life points, and the increasing number of cards in play. Late in the game, the abundance of mana resources means that either player could change the game drastically in a single move. The outcome of the game seems imminent, yet still hard to predict. Eventually, the stalemate is broken by a string of "power plays," from which one player will emerge with a clear advantage. That player will leverage the advantage into victory, or "die" trying. Either way, the game reaches its conclusion quickly. We can see how the dramatic tension of the game is regulated by the game dynamics: the escalation of resources and the "ticking clock" of the deck. These mechanisms sculpt the tension of the game into a proper dramatic arc.

Over the course of the game we expect the inevitability to increase and the uncertainty to diminish. The climax of the game happens at the moment of realization: the moment when the outcome of the contest is known, and the uncertainty has been dispelled. We can think of the time between the climax and the end of the game as dénouement, the process of resolving the tension created within the game.

Now that we understand the role of uncertainty and inevitability in creating dramatic tension, we can gain a better understanding of how these qualities can emerge from the dynamics of a game. Next, let's examine a handful of different game dynamics, and explore their roles in creating dramatic tension.

Game Dynamics That Produce Dramatic Tension

How exactly do uncertainty and inevitability emerge from game play? Quite often, they emerge independently of each other. That is, a game's uncertainty and its inevitability are evoked by different systems and dynamics. This is good news for game designers; it gives us finer control over the dramatic arc of the game, by allowing us to tune and adjust inevitability and uncertainty separately. It is also good news for our discussion because it allows our exploration to tackle inevitability and uncertainty as distinct topics.

In order to imbue our games with dramatic uncertainty, we need to create an ongoing sense that the game is *close,* that the contest is yet undecided. There are many techniques available to us, but all of them take one of two general approaches: force and illusion. *Force* is the approach of creating dramatic tension by manipulating the state of the contest itself. The game is close because we *make* it close, or at the very least we limit how much an advantage one player can have over another. *Illusion* is the approach of manipulating the players' perceptions so that the game *seems* closer than it is. Force and illusion are more of a spectrum than a dichotomy. In the pages that follow, we will explore techniques of pure force (e.g., cybernetic feedback systems) and techniques of pure illusion (e.g., fog of war) as well as techniques that combine the two (e.g. escalation).

Our discussion of dramatic inevitability will center on a single organizing concept: the ticking clock. The idea of the ticking clock is the sense of imminent resolution that gives a game its sense of momentum and forward progress. It stands as a constant reminder that the game will end, and soon. We will discuss how games create inevitability through ticking clocks that are both real and metaphorical.

We will begin our exploration with a very common source of dramatic uncertainty in games: cybernetic feedback systems.

Feedback Systems as Sources of Uncertainty

Rules of Play provides a discussion of cybernetic feedback systems, and the ways in which they apply to games. A feedback system found in a game might be constructed like this:

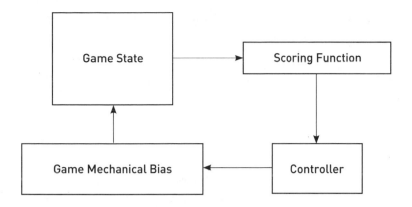

The *game state* is the complete status of the game at a particular moment. We can think of the game state as all the information you would need to put in a "save game" file for the game. In Checkers, the game state would include the positions of all the pieces, and indicate which player has the next move. In a first-person shooter, the state would include the name of the current level, the position of every object on the level, as well as the player's health and inventory. In a physical game like Basketball, the state includes not only the score and the time left on the clock, but the complete physical and mental state of all the athletes. Constructing a "save game" for a real physical sport (as opposed to a sports video game) would require a staggering amount of memory.

The *scoring function* is the *sensor* of the cybernetic feedback system. It is a rule of the game that gives us a numerical measurement of who is winning and by how much. Some games, like Basketball, have a score built into the rules. In this case, the scoring function might be the difference between the two scores (e.g., one team is ahead by six points). Other games, like racing games, have no explicit score. The scoring function would be some measurement based on the facts of the game. In a two-player car-racing game, the scoring function might be the distance between the two players' cars. The scoring function could even produce an aggregate number based on several different facts about the game, such as the distance between the cars and the amount of fuel in each car. A good scoring function produces a larger number the greater the winning player's lead, and produces the number zero when the game is tied.

The *game mechanical bias* is the *actuator* of the cybernetic feedback system. It is a rule of the game that gives one of the contestants an advantage over the other. In Basketball, giving one team more players than the other would bias the game in favor of that team. In a death match game, giving one of the players twice as many points as the others would give that player an advantage.

The *controller* is the *comparator* of the cybernetic feedback system. It is a rule of the game that chooses which player receives the game mechanical bias; it makes its decision based on the scoring function.

As an example, let's consider the "handicap mode" found in many racing games. Handicap mode is a special game option designed to keep the race close: when one player falls behind, that player's maximum speed increases so that the player can catch up to the leader. We can think of this as a feedback system: the scoring function is the distance between the two racers, the speed boost is the game mechanical bias, and the controller is the rule that says the speed boost goes to the losing racer.

This kind of feedback system keeps the game close by driving the scoring function towards zero. Because it strives to make the difference in score as small as possible, it is called a "*negative* feedback system." We can imagine another feedback system—let's call it "spite mode"—that is the direct opposite of handicap mode. Using the same scoring function and game mechanical bias as handicap mode, spite mode would hand the speed boost to the *leading* racer. When one player gained an advantage over the other, spite mode would let that player keep the advantage for the rest of the game. This kind of feedback system strives to make the difference in score as *large* as possible, and so we call it a "*positive* feedback system."

Negative Feedback as a Source of Uncertainty

Dramatic uncertainty depends on the player's perception that the outcome of the contest is unknown. Any game where the score is tied—or very close—is inherently uncertain. This means that negative feedback systems are a powerful tool for creating dramatic tension; by driving the scoring function toward zero, they create dramatic uncertainty.

In the example of the racing game in handicap mode, the negative feedback system helps sustain the dramatic tension of the game. It guards against the situation where one player takes an early lead and keeps it for the entire race. Thus the feedback system assures that the climax occurs late in the game, at a moment when one player's lead is large enough—and the time left in the game is short enough—that the feedback system cannot bring the players together before the end of the game.

Positive Feedback as an Aid to Denouement

Toward the end of a game, positive feedback systems are sometimes useful for dispelling uncertainty, bringing about the climax, and creating a sense of finality and closure. Sometimes the negative feedback systems in the game can cause the game to stagnate. Positive feedback systems provide a mechanism for breaking the equilibrium and moving the game forward.

In Warcraft, the snowball effect of military conquest can be viewed as a positive feedback system. By attacking an opponent's infrastructure and capturing or destroying resources, one player can leverage a slight military advantage into a large one, and then leverage the large military advantage into victory. This process of routing the enemy dispels the dramatic uncertainty and creates a sense of closure. It is an end-of-game ritual that prepares the winner to win and the loser to lose.

Other Sources of Uncertainty

Feedback systems are one of the heaviest possible hammers available to game designers for sculpting the dramatic uncertainty of their game. Now let's explore some other kinds of game mechanics that create dramatic uncertainty. Many of the systems we are about to examine could be described as "illusory"; rather than altering the state of the game, they manipulate the player's *perceptions*.

Pseudo-Feedback

The first two mechanisms we'll examine can be described as "pseudo-feedback." Quite frequently, these sorts of mechanisms create game dynamics that appear as if the game were being driven by a negative feedback system: when one player takes the lead, quite frequently the other player will catch up. When we inspect the inner workings of the game systems, however, we discover that there is no actual cybernetic feedback system present—just the perception of one.

Escalation

Escalation describes a game mechanic in which the score changes faster and faster over the course of the game, so that there are more points at stake at the end of the game than at the beginning. The game show *Jeopardy* is a textbook example of escalation. The first round begins with questions worth $100 and ends with questions worth $500. More significantly, the value of all questions is doubled for the second round. This means that at the end of the first round, only one-third of the total available prize money has been given out, and roughly half of the game's total time has elapsed. The player perceives the game as being "half over," and measured in terms of *time*, it is. But measured in terms of *prize money awarded*, the game is only a third over. The player perceives that the game has progressed further than it really has. The escalation of prize money helps protect the dramatic uncertainty of the game; there is no first-round lead that can't be overcome in the second round. In the final round of the game, players can wager any amount of their prize money on a single question. We can think of this as yet another level of escalation, giving the trailing players one last all-or-nothing chance to overcome the leader.

Hidden Energy

Imagine a racing game—one not driven by a feedback system—in which each player has a reservoir of "turbo fuel" to use during the race. The turbo fuel gives the player a speed bonus for as long as he holds down the "turbo" button on the controller. However, the reservoir only holds 30 total seconds of fuel in a race that will last a few minutes. The game is designed so that effective use of the turbo is the key to success.

In this game, one player might use turbo fuel to gain an early lead. That player would appear to be winning, with a score that was certainly higher, although achieved at a resource cost. If, however, we consider the whole state of the game—accounting for the players' resources in addition to their positions on the track—we see that the game is actually quite close. At some later time, the trailing player will choose to use his turbo fuel to close the gap, perhaps creating the illusion that handicap mode is in effect. This creates a sense of uncertainty as the true state of the game is revealed.

We can think of the turbo fuel as the "hidden energy" of the game. It is energy because it represents the potential to score, and it is hidden because it is not part of the player's own appraisal of the game scoring function. In sports like Basketball, the hidden energy is energy in the literal sense of the word; a team that takes the lead often does so at the expense of its own stamina, leaving itself vulnerable to a reprisal by the other team.

Another interesting example of hidden energy occurs in Pool. In Eight Ball, a player inches closer to victory each time the player sinks a ball. But the fewer balls the player has on the table, the fewer good shots there are to take, and the less likely the player's balls are to interfere with those of the other player. Each ball represents a liability (in that it must be sunk) but also an opportunity (to be an easy shot, and also to obstruct the opponent). Combined with the short-term positive feedback of the game (i.e., making a shot entitles you to another turn), the energy gives the trailing player a chance to catch up to the leader.

Hidden energy creates dramatic uncertainty by manipulating the player's incomplete understanding of the true score of the game. It creates artificial dramatic reversals of fortune by inflating and deflating the ostensible score of the game.

Fog of War

Strategy games like Warcraft and Civilization use a game mechanic called *fog of war,* which simulates limitations of game characters' ability to perceive and monitor the world around them. The "fog" covers all parts of the map that the players' units cannot see. As the players' resources develop, their units cover a greater area and push more of the fog back, giving the players progressively more information about the world. A player cannot see other players' resources unless the player commits units to scouting enemy terrain.

Fog of war represents a way of creating dramatic uncertainty by limiting the information available to the players. At the beginning of the game, players cannot predict the outcome of the contest, because they simply aren't given enough information. As the game progresses, more and more information becomes available, and the outcome of the game seems more and more certain.

Decelerator

The *decelerator* describes an obstacle that slows the players down late in the game. It makes the game seem closer by changing the scale and pace of the game.

A perfect example of a decelerator comes from that famous athletics-oriented game show of the 1990s, *American Gladiators.* At the end of each episode, the winner was determined by an obstacle course called "The Eliminator." One of the late obstacles of this course was a cargo net that the contestants had to climb. Climbing the net was slow work, so the trailing player would usually reach the net before the leading player had cleared it. The cargo net brought the players into physical proximity without necessarily changing the true score of the game. Measured in seconds, the distance between the players was the same as before they entered the cargo net, but measured in feet, the distance seemed much closer. The decelerator creates dramatic uncertainty by creating the illusion of a close game.

Interestingly enough, *American Gladiators* followed its decelerator with an *accelerator*. After the contestants climbed the cargo net, they would descend to ground level on a zip line. This acceleration would reveal the true difference in the players' positions (perhaps even exaggerate it), dispelling the uncertainty and resolving the tension created by the cargo net. It's no accident that the rising and falling action of the drama resembles the ascent and descent of the altitudes of the players.

Cashing Out

Cashing out describes a game mechanic where the score of the game is reset to zero. The simplest example of cashing out occurs in the "best of 7" format used for the World Series and other tournaments, where the contest is actually several games played in succession. Although at the end of a single game of a series, the game is recorded as a win for one team, beyond that, the score no longer matters. The result is the same whether the game went into extra innings or was a blowout. Until one team wins its fourth game, both teams have a chance to win the series. Cashing out creates dramatic uncertainty by forgiving the trailing player's score deficit, and giving every player a chance to win, however unlikely.

Bomberman uses a similar form of cashing out. The game is played in rounds of a few minutes. Each round is a contest of serial elimination: players vie to blow each other up with bombs, and the last player standing wins a trophy. The first player to win three trophies from three separate rounds wins the game. During the round, players accumulate power-ups, becoming more and more powerful until elimination becomes inevitable, although nothing is carried over from one round to the next except for the trophy awarded to the winner. All the events of the round are cashed out and reduced to a single consequence: one player got the trophy and the others didn't. All power-ups are reset, and all mistakes are forgiven, giving each player a clean slate for the next round.

"The Eliminator" from the game show *American Gladiators* is another example of cashing out. Throughout a particular episode, contestants would earn points for successes in each of the episode's events. The final event ("The Eliminator") was winner-take-all, but the player with the leading score was given a head start in the race, in proportion to the player's lead. In effect, points earned before the race were converted into seconds for the race. We can think of this conversion as a kind of cashing out. No matter how great the deficit, the trailing player has a chance to make it up, however slim that chance may be. We can also think of the moment where points are converted into seconds as an instantaneous moment of positive feedback, where an advantage in score is converted into a game mechanical bias.

Sources of Inevitability

We've just explored five different ways that dramatic uncertainty can emerge from a game's dynamics. But uncertainty alone is not sufficient to create dramatic tension; we also need *dramatic inevitability*, the sense that the contest is moving forward toward a conclusion. If our contest appears as if it will never conclude—or not conclude any time soon—then it has no sense of urgency, and the dramatic tension is dispelled.

Uncertainty and inevitability are not opposites. Uncertainty concerns itself with the question, "Who will win?" whereas inevitability concerns itself with the question, "When will we know?" Our game is most tense at the moment both factors intersect: the outcome of the contest is unknown, but we feel that it will be determined imminently.

In games, dramatic inevitability emerges from any game mechanic that can function as a *ticking clock,* which gives the players a measurement of their progress through the game, as well as a sense of how far away the end might be. The clock also conveys a sense of forward motion: as time runs out, the players feel propelled toward the conclusion of the contest. Clearly then, a *literal* ticking clock—the time limit in sports like Basketball or in video games like Pikmin or Bomberman—is the simplest, most straightforward example of a game mechanic creating dramatic inevitability.

But literal time limits are not the only way the ticking clock manifests itself in game dynamics. We see it in the increasingly crowded game board in Go and Reversi, the waning deck sizes in Magic: The Gathering, the decreasing health bars in Virtua Fighter, the gradual filling-in of the word puzzle on Wheel of Fortune, and the depleting gold supplies in Warcraft. All of these "clocks" give us a measure of our progress through the game, warning us that the end is approaching; indeed, they can be characterized as *nonrenewable resources,* quantifiable assets within the game state that deplete over the course of play and are never replenished. When we consider *time* as a resource, we see that even the literal ticking clock falls within this category of nonrenewable resources. The notion of a nonrenewable resource is a powerful extension of the ticking clock concept—and a valuable nuts-and-bolts tool for game designers interested in assuring a sense of dramatic inevitability in their games.[2]

Other kinds of ticking clocks also exist. In the mystery board game Clue, the gradual accrual of information leads the game toward its inevitable conclusion. In a linear race game like SSX, the progress of play expresses itself in space rather than in time. The landmarks and checkpoints on the racecourse serve as reminders of the race's end. Many such games provide players with a "radar" overview of their linear progress through the level. These cues remind us of our place within the narrative, and of the constant forward motion toward an inevitable end. If hard-pressed, we could probably come up with a way to fit these concepts into our nonrenewable resource model of the ticking clock. (In Clue, can we think of ignorance as a resource?)

Rather than resort to such contrivances, we can identify an even more general model for the ticking clock: instead of nonrenewable resources, we can think of our ticking clocks as *nonreversible processes*. Nonreversible processes are exactly what they sound like: changes to the game state that can't be undone. Like a tightening ratchet, the process brings the game ever closer to completion, while at the same time prohibiting backward movement.

It should be clear that dramatic inevitability is all a matter of perception. In order for the ticking clock or nonreversible process to function as a dramatic device, the player must be able to perceive and understand its operation. A secret ticking clock does not convey the same sense of inevitability, nor does a nonreversible process whose workings are so complex that its nonreversible nature is not obvious.

Now let's take a look at an important historical example in which the lack of dramatic inevitability resulted in catastrophe. This example will give us a chance to flex our analytical muscles, as well as give us some perspective on the role and power of dramatic inevitability in games.

Twenty-One

The year 1956 saw the debut of the infamous game show *Twenty-One*, which became the centerpiece of the quiz show scandal. During the 1950s, the producers and sponsors of the show discovered that dramatic tension converted directly into big ratings and big business. They sought to sculpt their programs into ongoing narratives, with contestants cast as recurring characters. Many shows like *Twenty-One* resorted to rigging the results of the contest. The producers became authors, scripting not only the outcome of the game, but the dramatic details of its events.

Interestingly enough, it was only after the first episode that the producers of *Twenty-One* chose to rig the game:

> The show went on the air in 1956 and we felt that it had such great quality and content to it that we would not have to rig it. In fact, the first show of *Twenty-One* was not rigged and the first show of *Twenty-One* was a dismal failure. It was just plain dull.—*Dan Enright, Producer*

From then on, the producers decided to rig the game. Three years and one national scandal later, *Twenty-One* became an object lesson in the perils of "scripting" a game.

21/21 Hindsight

Let's examine the dynamics of *Twenty-One* to see if we can find out why it was such a "dismal failure." We'll start with the rules.

Rules of Twenty-One (Summary)

1. There are two players. Each player is in an isolation booth, and cannot see or hear the other player's play. Neither player knows the other's score.

2. Players score points by answering questions. The first player to 21 wins.

3. In the first round, each player is asked two questions. In subsequent rounds, each player is asked one question.

4. Before being asked the question, each player must choose how many points to wager on the question. Any number of points from 1 to 11 may be wagered. The player *must* wager at least one point, and *must* answer the question.

5. If a player answers the question correctly, the player gains the wagered points; if not, the player *loses* the wagered points. A player's score can't drop below zero this way.

6. At the end of a round, either player may choose to end the game and the player with the most points then wins.

Since each player is playing the game "in a vacuum," unaware and unaffected by the other player's choices, we can view a game of *Twenty-One* as two simultaneous solitaire games. Aside from the player's own score, an individual player has very little information to use when deciding whether or not to end the game. A player is free to play until one player drops from exhaustion, until his opponent chooses to end the game, or until he has earned an amount of points—let's say 19—that seems high enough to have a good chance of winning. So, we can say that each player is playing a solitaire game that only ends when one player reaches 19 points or more, and the winner is the player who reaches that value in fewer questions. This view will simplify our analysis of the game, at the very least by reducing the number of ending conditions from two to one.

Having made that simplification, it should be clear that the game lacks any kind of ticking clock. The only way that the game can end is for the score to increase, and points can be lost as easily as won—more easily, in fact. If scores were allowed to drop below zero, then the game might never end. Computer simulations bear our observations out:

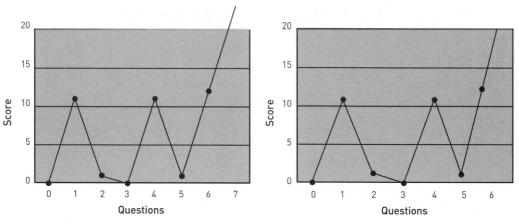

Two Simulated Games of Twenty-One

In the simulation, it was assumed that the player had a flat 40% chance of answering any question, wagered aggressively, and stopped at 19 points or more. In 1,000 simulated games, almost 42% of all questions resulted in a score of zero. The median game was 6 questions long, and the longest was 58.[3]

In the computer simulation, the score typically oscillates back and forth between 0 and 11. The game comes down to whether or not a player can answer two questions in a row. There is no sense of progress through the game; past performance has essentially no meaning. We can see how the lack of a ticking clock dispels any hope of creating a dramatic arc.

How do our observations compare to history? We know that the first night of *Twenty-One* was plagued by zero-zero ties. Given that the score was zero 40% of the time in our simulations, this is hardly surprising.

Instead of fixing the game in the sense of rigging it, how might we fix the game in the sense of repairing the game design? There are many possible ticking clocks we could introduce: limit the total time to play, limit the number of questions or the number of wrong answers, and so forth. We could also try to salvage the notion that the score might function as the game's ticking clock by reducing or eliminating the penalty for a wrong answer. This might not be adequate if there were many rounds where neither player answered a question. We could handle that case explicitly: when neither player answered correctly, we would give each player one point, or perhaps reduce the number of points needed to win the game by one (from 21 to 20, then 19, etc.).

These are just a few examples among many; any game mechanic that causes the game to march forward to a guaranteed end has the potential to create the dramatic inevitability we need. Had the creators of *Twenty-One* realized the need to create dramatic inevitability within their game dynamics, they might have avoided a career-shortening scandal.

Resolving Dramatic Tension: Denouement in Games

So far we've examined several techniques for ratcheting up the dramatic tension in our games. But the dramatic arc shows us that tension shouldn't climb forever. Eventually the tension needs to reach a climax, change direction, and fade away.

When should the game's dramatic climax occur? How much time should pass between the climax and the end of the game? We've said that the climax occurs at the moment of realization, when uncertainty is dispelled and the outcome of the contest is known. Given that definition, it would seem that the climax of the game should occur as late as possible. After all, a contest whose outcome is known has ceased to be a game on some level: the players have become spectators. We could argue that such an interval should be as short as possible. On the other hand, there is also some value to providing the players with a denouement to resolve the tension and give them a sense of closure. We need to prepare the winner to win and the loser to lose. A game whose climax comes too late can seem to end too abruptly, catching the players off guard. In that case, the dramatic tension can linger, unresolved.

Sometimes, the resolution of the game's dramatic tension can occur after the end of play. In a social setting, this can happen informally as a kind of post mortem of the game by the players. Many computer games build "post-mortem" features into the product itself, such as the end-of-mission statistic screens in Warcraft or the game replay at the end of Civilization III. We can also see examples of this in movies whose story culminates in a climactic game. When the game ends, the movie goes on for a while afterward, in part to resolve tension created during play.

Summary

As game designers, we hope that our games will be climactic struggles; we strive to imbue our games with a sense of *drama.* In these pages, we explored the concept of drama in games.

We explored a framework of three schemas for analyzing games:

- **Mechanics:** the complete description of the game system; the rules and components we need to play the game.

- **Dynamics:** the way a game "behaves" when it is played. The strategies, events and behaviors that *emerge* from the mechanics of the game.

- **Aesthetics:** the emotional content of the game. The kinds of fun we have when we play. The emotional message we hope to impart as game designers.

We defined an *aesthetic model* for drama in terms of *dramatic tension,* the intensity of the struggle, and *dramatic structure,* the way that intensity changes over time. Good dramatic structure takes the shape of a *dramatic arc,* where the tension builds toward a climax and is resolved. We identified the two necessary ingredients for dramatic tension: *uncertainty,* the sense that the outcome of the game is still unknown, and *inevitability,* the sense that the end of the game is imminent.

At some length, we discussed a handful of different game dynamical tools for producing dramatic uncertainty: *cybernetic feedback, escalation, and hidden energy, fog of war, deceleration,* and *cashing out.* We examined how the dynamics of the "ticking clock" can create the inevitability we need for dramatic tension. We identified several different kinds of ticking clock: the *literal clock,* the *nonrenewable resource,* and the *nonreversible process.* We briefly explored the need for denouement in games.

The fruits of our exploration are a new set of conceptual tools for our game design toolbox. We can use these concepts to analyze the games we play, deconstruct their designs, and gain a greater understanding of how they succeed or fail at delivering their aesthetic content. We can also use them in designing games, to create and evaluate the game mechanics that will bring us closer to our aesthetic goals.

Beyond the study of drama, there is a larger inquiry to be made: other aesthetics to be examined, other mechanics and dynamics to be understood. The more of these game design elements that we explore, the larger our design toolbox will grow. The craft of game design will become a richer, more sophisticated, more powerful form of artistic expression.

End Notes

1. In Magic: The Gathering, the fundamental game resource is called "mana." Almost all of the potent moves a players can make drain her mana resources. Each turn, a player has as much mana as the number of land cards she has in play. A player's land cards start in her deck, are drawn into her hand, and are put into play at a rate of one per turn. Thus an action's mana cost places a limit on how early in the game that action can be played; for example, an action costing five mana cannot (in general) be played before the fifth turn of the game.

2. Computer scientists will recognize the striking similarity between these nonrenewable resources and the "decrementing functions" used to prove whether a computer program terminates. Often, they are the same thing. On the other hand, a game's "ticking clock" does not always provide us with an ironclad proof that the game will halt; some ticking clocks depend on random events, or on the cooperation of the players. So we sometimes end up with a game that "probably" halts, or that halts if any player wants it to. Although forcing a proper decrementing function into a game can sometimes run counter to other design goals, sometimes it is exactly what is needed.

3. Random numbers for this simulation were generated using the MT19937 algorithm.

Bibliography

Salen Katie, and Eric Zimmerman. *Rules of Play: Game Design Fundamentals.* Cambridge, MA: MIT Press, 2004.

Piccione, Peter A. "In Search of the Meaning of Senet." *Archaeology,* July/August 1980: 55–58. Available online at www.cofc.edu/~piccione/piccione_senet.pdf.

Lucey, Paul. *Story Sense: Writing Story and Script for Feature Films and Television.* New York: McGraw-Hill, 1996.

"The Quiz Show Scandal," prod. Julian Krainin. *The American Experience,* PBS. Available online at www.pbs.org/wqbh/amex/quizshow/.

Game Analysis: Centipede

Richard Rouse III

Context

"Game Analysis: Centipede" is an excerpt from my book **Game Design: Theory and Practice.** *Originally released in 2001 (and recently revised in 2004), the book covers all aspects of computer and video game development, as well as exploring design principles through the detailed analysis of six brilliant games, including Centipede. I firmly believe in game design through reverse engineering, so it was extremely enlightening to analyze Centipede and determine how the interaction of its systems combine to create a wickedly fun experience. Hopefully it will be as enlightening for you, since I consider Centipede to be one of the few perfect video game designs I have ever encountered.*

The Player Experience

Game Design Models

Richard Rouse III is Design Director at Surreal Software and was recently Project Lead on the action-horror title The Suffering. Rouse's other credits include Drakan: The Ancients' Gates, Centipede 3D, Damage Incorporated, and Odyssey: The Legend of Nemesis. You can find more information and his book, *Game Design: Theory and Practice* Second Edition, Plano, TX: Wordware Publishing, 2004, at his web site, http://www.paranoidproductions.com. Feedback is encouraged: gdtp@paranoidproductions.com.

Reprinted with permission from *Game Design: Theory & Practice,* 2nd Edition by Richard Rouse III. ISBN 1-55622-912-7 Wordware Publishing, Inc.
<http://www.wordware. com>www.wordware.com

One can think of the classic arcade game as a form of the computer game, the same way that a silent slapstick comedy is a form of film or the hard-boiled detective novel is a form of literature. The classic arcade game form fell out of favor with the commercial gaming companies pretty much as soon as the technology was available to move beyond it. However, many independent game developers still work on classic arcade games either for their own amusement or to be released as freeware or shareware titles. Many of these labors of love are imitations of established classic arcade games, but many others are interesting experiments in new gameplay. There remains something uniquely compelling about the form, and the fact that one does not need to have a sophisticated 3D engine to make a wonderfully entertaining classic arcade game helps to make the form an appealing one in which to work.

It bears mentioning that when I refer to the classic arcade game, I do not mean to imply that all classic arcade games are classics. Many of them are quite bad. As with any media, the old arcade games that are remembered and talked about decades after their release tend to be the best ones, thus creating the false impression of a "golden age." The bad arcade games have fallen between the cracks of history. The term "classic arcade game" refers to the form as a classic one, not to the games themselves, just as one might refer to "classical music." Surely the term "arcade game" is not limiting enough, since this would seem to include every game found in an arcade, including modern racing, gun, and fighting games, none of which are what I consider to be part of the form I am concerned with here.

The classic arcade game form had its commercial and creative heyday in the late 1970s through the early 1980s, when machines exhibiting the form lined the arcades. Looking at the games as a whole, one can come up with a series of traits that they all shared. Some of these aspects of the form may have been arrived at because of the commercial considerations of the arcades. The thought was to get a player to easily understand a game, so that by the end of his very first game he had a good sense of how the game worked and what was necessary for success. Second, a player's game, even the game of an expert, could not last very long, since any one player had only paid a quarter, and if the game only earned a single quarter in a half hour, it would not be profitable to operate. Players needed to be sucked in to replay the games, to keep plunking in quarters. As a result, in some ways the arcade games had to be more refined than home games are today. Once the player has purchased a home game, often for at least a hundred times the cost of a single arcade game play, the sale is completed. If he is not completely disgusted with the game he is unlikely to return it. Features such as scoring and high-score tables only served to increase the arcade game's addictive nature and encourage players to keep spending money.

In addition, the technical restrictions of the day limited what the games could do, and thereby influenced what the games could accomplish in terms of gameplay. Had the designers had the RAM and processing power to include fully scrolling game-worlds that were many times the size of the screen, they probably would have. If the games had been able to replay full-motion video of some sort, perhaps the designers would have incorporated more story line into the games. But the fact remains that a unique genre of computer games emerged, and if the commercial and technical limitations shaped the form, so be it. Just as early films had to work with the limitations of silence and short running times, computer game design-ers were limited in what they could create, and were able to come up with brilliant games nonetheless. Often, working within a series of strict constraints forces artists to focus their creativity in a fashion which leads to better work than if they could do anything they wanted.

One key ingredient to many classic arcade games was their wild variation in gameplay styles. *Centipede*, *Missile Command*, *Pac-Man*, and *Frogger* are as different from each other as they possibly could be. Many classic arcade games featured variations on a theme: *Centipede*, *Space Invaders*, *Galaga*, and *Tempest* all revolved around the idea of shooting at a descend-ing onslaught of enemies. However, the gameplay variations these games embraced are far more radical than the tiny amount of variation one will find in modern games, which are more content to endlessly clone already-proven gaming genres. Despite the wild variety of game-play that can be found in classic arcade games, one can still look back on these games as a collective, as an artistic movement in the brief history of computer games. By analyzing the form's shared traits, modern game designers can learn a lot about how they can make their own games more compelling experiences for the player.

Classic Arcade Game Traits

Single Screen Play: In a classic arcade game, the bulk of the gameplay takes place on a single screen, with the player maneuvering his game-world surrogate around that screen, sometimes only in a portion of that screen. This was done, no doubt, in part because of technological limitations. But it also has very important artistic ramifications on the game's design: the player, at any time, is able to see the entire game-world, and can make his decisions with a full knowledge of the state of that game-world. Obviously, empowering the player with that kind of information seriously impacts the gameplay. Many of the games in the classic arcade game form would include more than one screen's worth of gameplay by switching play-fields or modifying existing ones to create additional "levels." Examples of this include *Joust, Pac-Man,* and *Mario Bros.* Though these games may have included more than a single screen in the entire game, at any one time the player's game-world still consisted of just that one screen.

Infinite Play: The player can play the game forever. There is no ending to the game, and hence no winning it either. This was done in part to allow players to challenge themselves, to see how long they could play on a single quarter. Players can never say, "I beat *Asteroids,*" and hence players are always able to keep playing, to keep putting in quarters. At the same time, having an unwinnable game makes every game a defeat for the player. Every game ends with the player's death, and hence is a kind of tragedy. Having an unwinnable game also necessitates making a game that can continuously get harder and harder for the player, hence a game design with a continuous, infinite ramping up of difficulty. With the advent of the home market, game publishers no longer wanted players to play a single game forever. Instead they want players to finish the games they have and buy another one. This is one reason why it is rare to see a game with infinite play any more.

Multiple Lives: Typically, classic arcade games allow the player a finite number of lives, or a number of "tries" at the game before her game is over. Perhaps derived from pinball games, which had been providing the player with three or five balls for decades, multiple lives allowed the novice player a chance to learn the game's mechanics before the game was over. Given adequate chances to try to figure out how the game works, the player is more likely to want to play again if she made progress from one life to the next. Having lives enables the game to provide another reward incentive for the player playing well: extra lives. Having multiple lives also sets up a game where dying once is not necessarily the end of the game, and encourages players to take risks they might not otherwise.

Scoring/High Scores: Almost all classic arcade games included a scoring feature through which the player would accumulate points for accomplishing different objec-

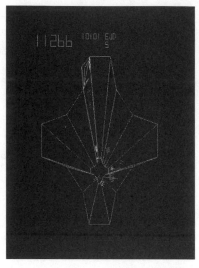

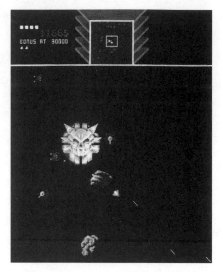

Tempest is one of many classic arcade games that is centered on shooting at enemies which keep getting closer. *Tempest* is memorable because of the many unique twists included.

Even though the action in *Sinistar* did not take place only on one screen, it is still considered to be an example of the classic arcade game form.

tives in the game. For example, in *Centipede,* the player gets 1 point for destroying a mushroom, 10 points for a centipede segment, 100 points for a centipede head, and 1000 points for a scorpion. Another classic arcade game component with origins in the world of pinball, the score allows the player to ascertain how well they did at the game, since winning the game is impossible. The high-score table was introduced in order to allow players to enter their initials next to their score, which would then be ranked in a table of scores so players could see just how good they were. The game would remember the table as long as it stayed plugged in, with some games, such as *Centipede,* even remembering the high-score list or some portion of it once unplugged. The high-score table enabled the classic arcade games to exploit one of the key motivations for playing games—"bragging rights." A player could point out her name in the high-score table to her friends as a way of proving her mettle. Friends could compete with each other (almost all of the games included two-player modes, where players switch off playing) to see who could get the higher score.

Easy-to-Learn, Simple Gameplay: Classic arcade games were easy for players to learn, impossible (or at least very difficult) to master. Someone could walk up to a game of *Centipede*, plunk in his quarter, and by his third life have a good idea of how the game functioned and how he might play better. Why the player died was always completely apparent to the player. There were typically no "special moves" involving large combinations of buttons which the player had to learn through trial and error. There were few games with tricky concepts such as "health" or "shields" or "power-ups." Again, commercial considerations were probably a factor in making these games simple to learn. At the time of their initial introduction, there was no established market of computer game players and there were few arcades. The games wound up in pizza parlors and bars, where any person might walk up to one and try it out. These novice players might be scared away if the game were too complex or baffling. Of course, simple does not always mean "limited" or "bad" gameplay; it can also mean "elegant" and "refined."

No Story: Classic arcade games almost universally eschewed the notion of trying to "tell a story" of any sort, just as many modern arcade games continue to do. The games always had a setting the player could easily recognize and relate to, many of them revolving around science fiction themes, though others dabbled in war, fantasy, and sports, among others. Many, such as *Pac-Man* and *Q*Bert,* created their own, unique settings, keeping up with the rampant creativity found in their gameplay. The classic arcade game designers did not feel required to flesh out their game-worlds, to concoct explanations for why the player was shooting at a given target or eating a certain type of dot, and the games did not suffer for it.

Of course, some games broke some of the above rules of the form, yet they can still be considered classic arcade games. For example, *Sinistar* and *Defender* both included scrolling game-worlds for the player to travel through, with the player unable to see all aspects of the game-world at any one time. Indeed, on first inspection, *Battlezone* seems entirely the odd man out among early classic arcade games. Yet, if one looks at the traits above, one will discover that it featured infinite play, multiple lives, and scoring, was easy to learn, and had almost no story. All three of these games included mechanics which, by and large, were adherent to

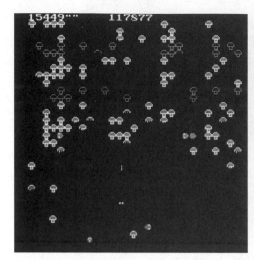
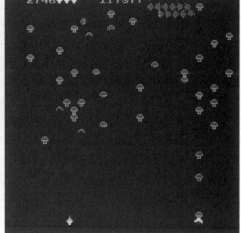

The player's shooter in Centipede is more mobile than in Space Invaders, since it can mover up and down in addition to moving sideways.

In Centipede, fleas drop toward the bottom of the screen, leaving mushrooms behind them, while spiders eat whatever mushrooms block their movement.

the classic arcade game form. Thus we can still group them with games like *Space Invaders* and *Asteroids,* games which follow all the rules laid out above.

Being one of the defining games of the form, *Centipede* follows all of the aspects of the classic arcade game form listed above. Though not a very complex game by today's standards, the marvel of *Centipede* is how all of the different gameplay elements work together to create a uniquely challenging game. Nothing in *Centipede* is out of place, nothing is inconsistent, nothing is unbalanced. To analyze *Centipede* is to attempt to understand how to design the perfect game.

Input

One of the great advantages to working on a game for the arcades is that the designer has complete control over the type of device the player will use to control the game. On the PC, the designer can only count on the player having a keyboard and a mouse, while on a console, the designer must work with the standard controller that comes with that particular console. The arcade designer (budget constraints notwithstanding) is able to pick the best type of control for the game, and provide the player with that control system. The designer can then create the game around those controls, precisely balancing the game to work perfectly with that input method. *Centipede* does this expertly, providing the player with an extremely precise analog control device in the form of a trackball. This is ideally suited to moving the player's shooter ship around on the bottom of the screen. Players can move the ship quickly or slowly, whatever the situation calls for. For many fans of *Centipede*, the excellent controller is one of the first things they remember about the game.

The shooter is extremely responsive to the player's manipulation of the trackball, with the player being able to easily and intuitively understand the relationship between her manipulation of the trackball and the shooter's movement. *Centipede* was no doubt inspired by other classic arcade games, such as *Space Invaders*, which feature the player's game-world surrogate locked at the bottom of the screen, allowed only to move left, move right, and shoot. *Centipede* takes that idiom one step further: the player is still trapped at the bottom of the screen, but the shooter can move within a six-row vertical space. This allows the player to avoid enemies that might be on the bottom row. At the same time, the shooter can still only shoot forward, so enemies that get behind the ship cannot be destroyed. Aside from the trackball, the only other control the player has is a button for firing the shooter's laser-type weapon. The game allows an infinitely fast rate of fire, but only one shot can be on the screen at a time which means the player has to think beyond just holding down the fire button constantly. If the player moves the shooter directly below a mushroom she can hold down the fire button and quickly shoot the mushroom four times, thus destroying it. But at the top of the screen, where the player cannot maneuver the ship, destroying a mushroom takes much longer, since the player must wait for each shot to hit the mushroom before another shot can be fired. If the player's shot is in the midst of traveling to a faraway target, she will be unable to shoot again in order to take out a divebombing enemy. The player must plan her shots carefully, a design element that adds more depth to the game's mechanics.

Interconnectedness

One of the great strengths of *Centipede* is how well all the different elements of the gameplay fit together. Consider the different enemy insects that try to kill the player. The centipede winds its way down the screen from the top of the screen to the player's area at the bottom, moving horizontally. The centipede appears as either a lone twelve-segment centipede or as a shorter centipede accompanied by a number of single heads. At the start of a wave, the number of centipede segments on the screen always totals twelve. Next is the spider, which moves in a diagonal, bouncing pattern across the bottom of the screen, passing in and out of the player's area. Then comes the flea, which plummets vertically, straight down toward the player. There is nothing terribly sophisticated about any of the movement patterns of these insects. Indeed, the flea and the centipede, once they have appeared in the play-field, follow a completely predictable pattern as they approach the player's area. The spider has a more random nature to its zigzagging movement, but even it does nothing to actually pursue the player. Therefore, once the player has played the game just a few times, he has a completely reliable set of expectations about how these enemies will attack him. Fighting any one of these creatures by itself would provide very little challenge for the player. Yet, when they function together they combine to create uniquely challenging situations for the player. With any one of these adversaries missing, the game's challenge would be significantly diminished, if not removed altogether.

Each of the insects in the game also has a unique relationship to the mushrooms which fill the game's play-field. The primary reason for the existence of the mushrooms is to speed up the centipede's progress to the bottom of the screen. Every time a centipede bumps into a mushroom, it turns down to the next row below, as if it had run into the edge of the play-field. Thus, once the screen becomes packed with mushrooms, the centipede will get to the bottom of the play-field extremely quickly. Once at the bottom of the screen, the centipede moves back and forth inside the player's area, posing a great danger to the player. So, it behooves the player to do everything he can to destroy the mushrooms on the play-field, even though the mushrooms themselves do not pose a direct threat. Further complicating matters, every time the player shoots a segment of the centipede it leaves a mushroom where it died. Thus, wiping out a twelve-segment centipede leaves a big cluster of mushrooms with which the player must contend.

As the flea falls to the bottom of the play-field, it leaves a trail of new mushrooms behind itself, and the only way for the player to stop it is to kill it. The flea only comes on to the play-field if there are less than a certain number of mushrooms on the bottom half of the screen. This way, if the player destroys all the mushrooms closest to him, the flea comes out immediately to lay down more. The spider, the creature that poses the biggest threat to the player, has the side effect that it eats mushrooms. This then presents the player with a quandary: shoot and kill the spider or just try to avoid it so it can take out more mushrooms?

Finally, the scorpion, a creature that travels horizontally across the top half of the screen and hence can never collide with and kill the player, poisons the mushrooms it passes under. These poisoned mushrooms affect the centipede differently when it bumps into them. Instead of just turning down to the next row, the centipede will move vertically straight down to the bottom of the screen. So when a centipede hits a poisoned mushroom, the centipede becomes a much more grave threat than it was before. Once a scorpion has passed by, the player must now expend effort trying to shoot all the poisoned mushrooms at the top of the screen or be prepared to blast the centipedes as they plummet vertically straight toward the player.

So we can see that each of the creatures in the game has a special, unique relationship to the mushrooms. It is the interplay of these relationships that creates the challenge for the player. The more mushrooms the flea drops, the more mushrooms the scorpion has to poison. The spider may take out mushrooms along the bottom of the screen, getting them out of the way of the player, but it may eat so many that the flea starts coming out again. If the player kills the centipede too close to the top of the screen, it will leave a clump of mushrooms which are difficult to destroy at such a distance, and which will cause future centipedes to reach the bottom of the screen at a greater speed. However, if the player waits until the centipede is at the bottom of the screen, the centipede is more likely to kill the player. With the mushrooms almost functioning as puzzle pieces, *Centipede* becomes something of a hybrid between an arcade shooter and a real-time puzzle game. Indeed, some players were able to develop special strategies that would work to stop the flea from ever coming out, thus making the centipede get to the bottom of the screen less quickly and allowing the player to survive for much longer. It is the interplay of each of the player's adversaries with these mushrooms and with each other that creates a unique challenge for the player.

Escalating Tension

A big part of the success of *Centipede* is how it escalates tension over the length of the game. The game actually has peaks and valleys it creates in which tension escalates to an apex and, with the killing of the last centipede segment, relaxes for a moment as the game switches over to the next wave. One small way in which the game escalates tension over a few seconds is through the flea, which is the only enemy in the game the player must shoot twice. When it is shot just once, its speed increases dramatically and the player must quickly shoot it again lest the flea hit the shooter. For that brief speed burst, the player's tension escalates. In terms of the centipede itself, the game escalates the tension by splitting the centipede each time it is shot. If the player shoots the middle segment of an eleven-segment centipede, it will split into two five-segment centipedes which head in opposite directions. Sure, the player has decreased the total number of segments on the screen by one, but now he has two adversaries to worry about at once. As a result, skilled players will end up going for the head or tail of the centipede to avoid splitting it.

Most of the game's escalating tension over the course of a wave is derived from the centipede's approach toward the bottom of the screen and the player's often frantic efforts to kill it before it gets there. Once a centipede head reaches the bottom of the screen, a special centipede head generator is activated, which spits out additional centipede heads into the player's area. If the player is unable to kill the centipede before it reaches the bottom of the screen, which has already increased tension by its very approach, that tension is further escalated by the arrival of these extra heads. And those extra heads keep arriving until the player has managed to kill all of the remaining centipede segments on the screen. The rate at which those extra heads come out increases over time, such that if the player takes her time in killing them, additional centipedes will arrive all the faster, making the player still more frantic.

Once the player kills the last segment, the game goes to its next wave, and the centipede is regenerated from the top of the screen. This provides a crucial, temporary reprieve for the player, a moment for her to catch her breath. The player will feel a great rush at having finally defeated the centipede, especially if the extra centipede head generator had been activated. In addition, the newly generated centipede at first appears easier to kill, since it is generated so far from the player's area.

Over the course of the player's entire game, the mushrooms inevitably become more and more packed on the play-field. Once there are more mushrooms toward the bottom of the screen, the player feels lucky if he can just clear all of the mushrooms in the lower half of the play-field. He has no chance of destroying the mushrooms toward the top, since the lower mushrooms block his shots. Similarly, if the scorpion has left any poison mushrooms toward the top of the screen, the player has no chance whatsoever of destroying them, and as a result the centipede dive-bombs the bottom of the screen on every single wave. Far into a game, the top of the play-field becomes a solid wall of mushrooms. As the mushrooms become more and more dense, the centipede gets to the bottom of the screen faster. When the centipede can get to the bottom of the screen extremely quickly, the player's game is that much faster paced, and he is that much more panicked about destroying the centipede before it reaches the bottom of the screen. This increased mushroom density has the effect of escalating tension not just within a wave as the extra centipede head generator did, but also from wave to wave, since the mushrooms never go away unless the player shoots them.

Centipede also balances its monsters to become harder and harder as the player's score increases. And since the player's score can never decrease, the tension escalates over the course of the game. Most obvious is the spider, whose speed approximately doubles once the player's score reaches 5000 (1000 if the game's operator has set the game to "hard"). The spider also maneuvers in a smaller and smaller area of the bottom of the screen as the player's score gets really high, eventually moving only one row out of the player's six-row area. With the spider thus constrained, it is both more likely to hit the player and less likely for the player to be able to shoot it. Recall that the flea drops from the top of the screen based on the quantity of mushrooms in the bottom half of the screen. When the player starts the game, if there are less than five mushrooms in that area the flea will come down, dropping more as it does so. As the player's score increases, however, so does the quantity of mushrooms needed to prevent the flea's appearance. Now the player must leave more and more mushrooms in that space to prevent the flea from coming out and cluttering the top of the screen with mushrooms.

At the start of each wave, the game always generates a total of twelve centipede segments and heads at the top of the screen. This means that if a twelve-segment centipede appears at the top of the screen, that will be the only centipede. If a seven-segment centipede appears, then five other centipede heads will appear as well, thus totaling the magic number of twelve. The more centipedes that appear, the more challenging it is for the player to shoot them all, and the more likely one will sneak to the bottom of the screen. The game starts by releasing a single twelve-segment centipede. In the next wave, a slow eleven-segment centipede appears along with one head. In the following wave, a fast eleven-segment and one head combination arrive. Then a slow ten-segment and two heads appear. With each wave there are a greater number of individual centipedes for the player to keep track of and a greater escalation of tension. The game wraps around once twelve individual heads are spawned, but then the game becomes harder by only spawning fast centipedes.

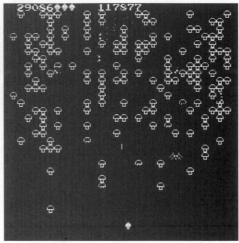

Over the course of a game of *Centipede,* mushrooms become more and more tightly packed on the play-field.

Centipede's frantic gameplay keeps the player tense most of the time, though it provides some breaks in the action during which the player can relax.

The player's death also provides a brief respite from the tension. When the player's ship is destroyed, the wave starts over and hence the centipede returns to the top of the screen. Before this, however, all of the mushrooms on the screen are reset. This means that all the partially destroyed mushrooms are returned to their undamaged state. But also all of the mushrooms poisoned by the scorpion are returned to their unpoisoned state. Many waves into the game, the increased mushroom density makes shooting poisoned mushrooms all but impossible, and with those poisoned mushrooms in place, the player is bombarded by centipedes hurtling toward him in every single wave. Thus, a player is almost relieved when his shooter is destroyed and all those poisoned mushrooms are removed from the top of the screen. This causes the player's game to be much more relaxed, at least for the time being.

Centipede is marvelous at creating and maintaining a tense situation for the player, while still providing brief "breathing periods" within the action. Designers of modern games, who are always concerned with ramping up difficulty for the player, could learn much by analyzing how *Centipede* keeps the player constantly on his toes without ever unfairly overwhelming him.

One Person, One Game

Many may scoff at *Centipede* twenty years after its creation. There is no question that it is a less technically astounding accomplishment than more modern works, and those who do not examine it closely are likely to dismiss it as more of a light diversion instead of a serious game. But what *Centipede* does, it does with such facility, featuring game mechanics so precisely and perfectly balanced and gameplay so uniquely compelling, that it truly is a marvel of computer game design. One must remember that *Centipede* was created in the days of the one-person-one-game system, when the development team for a game consisted primarily of one person, in this case Ed Logg. By having one person in total control of a project, where a single talented individual fully understands every last nuance of the game, the final product is much more likely to come out with a clearness of vision and brilliance of execution. Of course, one person can create a terrible game just as easily as a large team, but one must wonder if the lone wolf developer does not have a better chance at creating the perfect game.

10

11

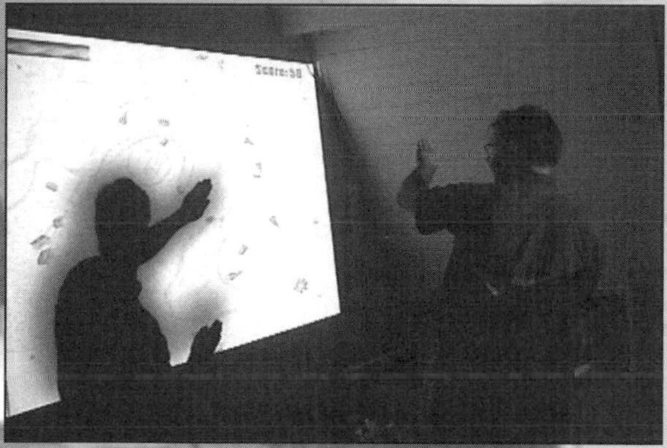

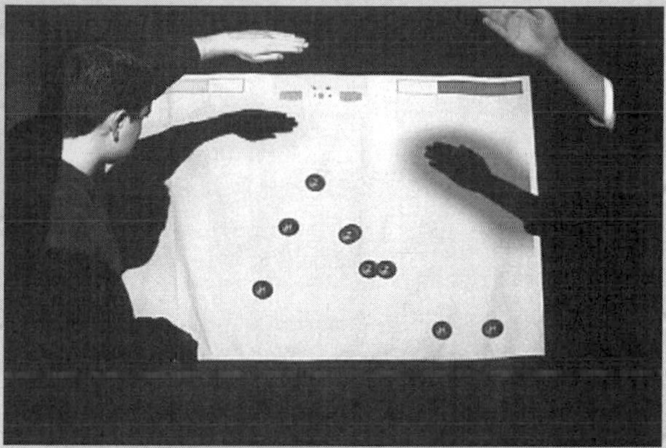

12

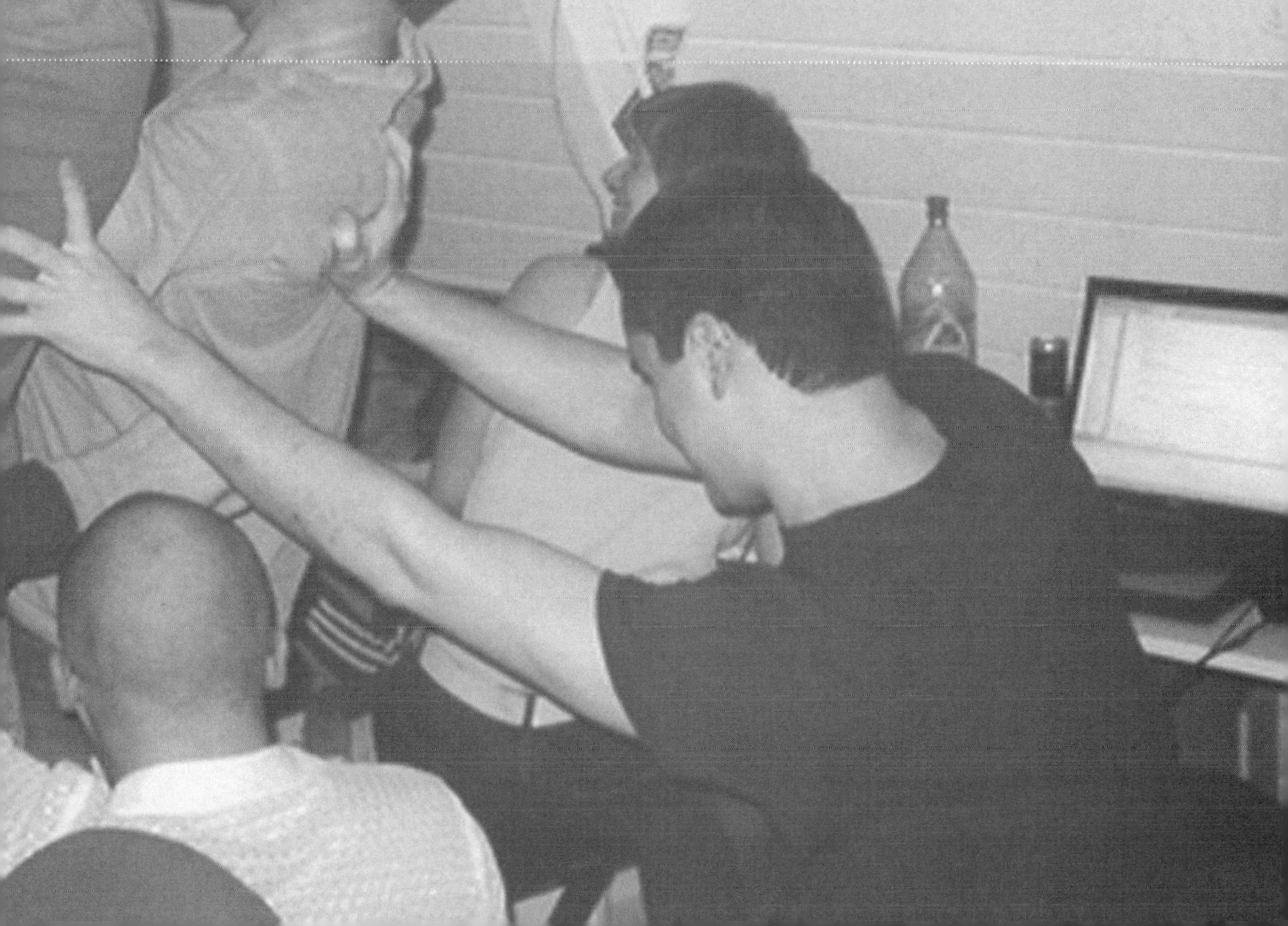

Unwritten Rules

Stephen Sniderman

Context

*"Unwritten Rules" is the feature article in the first issue of **The Life of Games** (October, 1999), the online journal at www.gamepuzzles.com/tlog/tlog.htm, which I co-edit with Kate Jones, founder of Kadon Gamepuzzles. This article is an attempt to clear the ground for discussing games by challenging the widely held assumption that a game is fundamentally different from other human activities (such as the law or business) because we can know all its rules. Games are thus invoked as a model of a fully describable closed system, but I try to show that a game played by humans cannot be a closed system and therefore cannot be fully described.*

The Rules of a Game

Gaming the Game

Speaking of Games

Stephen Sniderman has been teaching American literature and creative writing at Youngstown State University since 1969. He has published two books (*Language Lovers' Word Puzzles; Stanley Newman Presents Grid Play*), a game system (Flying Colors) with Kadon Gamepuzzles, and dozens of puzzles and games in *GAMES Magazine* and *English Journal*.

Regardless of what game you're playing, you cannot know all the rules.

Whether the ""game"" is tic-tac-toe, chess, baseball, language, etiquette, education, science, religion, law, business, politics or war, the entire set of rules governing the system cannot be spelled out. No matter how hard we try to indicate what is required, allowed, and proscribed, some of the most fundamental principles of playing the game will always elude us. And yet, paradoxically, we can still play the game—some deeper rules are always operating (i.e., affecting the players' behavior) without the players' being aware of them.

What do we mean by a game?

A game is a play activity that consists of an object (a goal or goals that the players are trying to accomplish) and constraints on the players' behavior (what they must do and/or what they may not do in attempting to achieve the game's object). To play a game is to pursue that game's object while adhering (more or less) to its constraints. Some of these constraints (the "recorded rules") are explicitly spelled out and are what we generally understand to be "the rules of the game," but every game is also governed by constraints that are rarely if ever made explicit. Some of these "unrecorded rules" are literally unstatable.

An example with tic-tac-toe

Suppose I challenge you to a game of tic-tac-toe. Could anything be more straightforward? But just to be sure, we review the rules. We'll play on a 3x3 grid, we'll alternate turns, we'll play only in empty squares, I'll play X's, you play O's, I'll play first, and the first player to get three of his/her symbol in a row, column, or diagonal wins the game. Aren't these *all* the rules of tic-tac-toe?

Well, for one thing, nothing has been said about time. Is there a time limit between moves? Normally, we both "understand" that there is, and we both "know" that our moves should be made within a "reasonable" time, say 20 seconds. If one of us takes longer, the other starts to fidget or act bored, may even make not-so-subtle comments, and eventually threaten to quit. Without having stated it, we have accepted a tacit time limit. And because we haven't stated it, it is fairly flexible and very functional.

Is it a rule, or isn't it?

Suppose it is my turn and, no matter what I do, you will win on your next move. Couldn't I prevent that from happening, within the rules stated, by simply refusing to play? Nothing in the rules forces me to move within a particular amount of time, so I simply do not make my next move. Haven't I followed the rules and avoided losing? And yet, if you've ever played a game, you know that this strategy is almost never employed and would be completely unacceptable. Anybody who seriously resorted to such a tactic would be considered childish, unsportsman-like, or socially undesirable and would probably not be asked to play in the future. This behavior seems to violate some fundamental but rarely stated principle of the game without any of us ever having to discuss it.

Self-defeating rules

But can't we state the principle it violates? Can't we just make that principle one of the rules of tic-tac-toe and other games? The answer is—yes, of course we can, but we will not eliminate the problem. Suppose we add the following rule: *Players will make their moves within a reasonable amount of time.* Have we solved anything? What is a "reasonable" amount of time? One minute? Five? 30? A million? And who determines what is reasonable—the player whose turn it is or the other player?

Such a rule is actually self-defeating because it calls attention to the fact that we cannot spell out what "reasonable" means.

So why not just specify a time limit for each move? Because we would just create even more perplexing problems for ourselves. For one thing, we would have to indicate when a player's time is running and when it is not. If one player had to answer the phone, for example, would we count that time or wouldn't we? To state the rule fully, we would have to list every life situation that could possibly interrupt a player's turn and state whether it should count against that player's time limit. Obviously, we could never complete such a list.

Practical solutions

A far more practical "solution," the one most of us have used all our lives in "friendly" games, is to say nothing about time limits and rely on our opponent's intuitive understanding of a "reasonable" time for a move and his/her desire to keep the game moving and therefore enjoyable. In other words, we depend on unstated—and probably unstatable—"rules" (really just expectations) when we play a game for fun.

In tournament or professional games, of course, we cannot leave things so loose, and various methods have been employed to solve the time dilemma. Generally, specific time limits are spelled out, as are specific penalties, including forfeit, for exceeding them. Official devices are employed for timing moves—chess clocks, the shot-clock in college and pro basketball, stopwatches in baseball games and tennis tournaments, and so on. But once we move beyond "reasonable" to "official" time, we create a whole new set of problems, problems that can no longer be solved with a simple agreement between or among players.

Rulings versus rules

As any sports fan knows, the difficulties that arise with "official" rules and "officials" to interpret them are often more intractable than those we face in friendly games. Since no set of rules can list every possible situation that might come up during tournament play, someone in charge, rather than the players themselves, must decide if a player has violated a rule (such as exceeding a time limit) and what penalty should be invoked.

Suppose, for instance, that a fire alarm sounds during a chess tournament and players are forced to evacuate the room. Someone in charge of the tournament must determine whether or not the time spent out of the room should be counted against the players whose clocks were running. It is doubtful that the tournament rules will help them. Or suppose the shot clock in an NBA game stops functioning temporarily. When it is fixed, the officials must decide how much time to put on the clock. How could any rule specify the precise amount of time that would be appropriate? Or suppose a professional tennis player complains of cramps. A human being, not a rulebook, must determine whether the player's complaint is legitimate and decide whether to grant the player additional time to recover.

Presumably, the officials' decisions in these situations would be based on the notions of fairness, sportsmanship, and practicality, notions that have never been—and almost certainly cannot be—fully codified and agreed upon. Therefore, no matter how exhaustive and specific we try to make the rules about time limits (or anything else) in a game, we will always have to rely on other people's acceptance of a set of principles that neither they nor we can put into words. That's the nature of any human system—the most important aspects of it are unstatable and unknowable.

In *The Celebrant,* Eric Rolfe Greenberg cogently illustrates this little-recognized truth. He depicts the famous incident in baseball lore that got Bonehead Merkle his nickname. With two outs in the bottom of the ninth inning and the score tied, Merkle is on first and a teammate is on third. The next batter hits the ball cleanly into right field for a single, which drives in the apparent game-winning run. Fans pour out onto the field in celebration. Merkle, afraid for his safety, heads directly to the dugout without touching second base. The fielding

479

team calls for an appeal play at second and attempts to retrieve the ball and touch second for the third out, ending the inning and negating the tie-breaking run.

But where is the ball? No one is sure because the field is swarming with fans. Nevertheless, one of the fielders, holding a ball, touches second base and claims that Merkle has been forced out and that the game is still tied. The question arises, is the ball he retrieved the one that was actually hit? By this time, the umpire has left the field and must be summoned from his dressing room, which he adamantly refuses to leave—until his life is threatened. When he does finally stick his head out, he refuses to change his ruling. Naturally, the losing team appeals to the commissioner of baseball to settle the matter. This worthy stalls as long as he can and finally declares the game null and void and orders that it be replayed.

Greenberg makes it clear that the commissioner's decision is influenced by political and social considerations that have little to do with any rulebook. The game of baseball has spilled over into real life and the depth of the "rules" governing the sport can be glimpsed.

No game is an island

As this example reminds us, no game or sport is played in a vacuum. All play activities exist in a "real-world" context, so to play the game is to immerse yourself in that context, whether you want to or not. In fact, it is impossible to determine where the "game" ends and "real life" begins. As a result, knowing only the recorded rules of a game is never enough to allow you to play the game.

Think of the constraints that do not ordinarily get included as part of the recorded rules of tic-tac-toe but which nevertheless influence the behavior of almost all players. Some of these involve the conventions, "etiquette," or "ethos" of this particular game and may vary from region to region or even family to family.

For example, I would guess that few tic-tac-toe players talk trash to each other (an acceptable and even expected behavior in some games and sports, like basketball).

Similarly, I'm willing to bet that few people play tic-tac-toe for money (in contrast to Poker) or prizes (as is sometimes true with Scrabble) or masters points (as with Tournament Bridge) or glory (as in Central Park chess).

Also, most people, I suspect, would probably allow their opponent, especially an inexperienced player or a young child, the opportunity to "take back" an obviously unwise move.

Playing fair

Other unwritten rules are associated with being "a good sport" and would apply to virtually all games in our culture. For example, you may not attempt to coerce your opponent, through physical force or threats or bribery or blackmail, into putting a symbol on a particular square. You may not attempt to cause your opponent physical, mental, or emotional harm to keep him or her from competing effectively. You may not attempt to distract your opponent while he or she is contemplating the next move. On the other hand, you must make your moves in a "reasonable" time. You must take the game seriously and attempt to win. You must play "fair" at all times.

To understand the difficulty—or, more accurately, the impossibility—of spelling out every rule governing the behavior of tic-tac-toe players, try to imagine programming a computer to "understand" what is meant by the sentences in the previous paragraph. For instance, think about the notion of "distracting" an opponent. What counts and what doesn't? Suppose you are chewing gum or smoking or wearing perfume and your opponent claims to be bothered by the sounds or aromas you are producing. What would we tell Deep Blue about this situation? Can we really list every behavior that qualifies as distracting?

The human factor

Or for that matter, can we ever be sure (in the sense that we could program a computer to determine) that a player is "really" distracted? In his famous match with Boris Spassky in Rejkjavik, Iceland, in 1972, Bobby Fischer claimed to be "distracted" by negative vibes that were emanating from his opponent's camp. Officials could hardly appeal to the recorded rules, as "complete" as those might have been, to determine how to handle Fischer's complaints. They had to use their experience with people, including Fischer and Spassky, their understanding of human psychology, their awareness of the political and social implications of the situation, and their diplomatic skills to arrive at a satisfactory compromise. Which of these notions is programmable?

Even Deep Blue, the most sophisticated chess program ever devised, cannot distinguish between a game played for blood (or money) and one played for fun; cannot recognize when a move should count and when politeness or common sense or common courtesy or compassion or medical emergency dictates that it shouldn't; cannot take into account the emotional needs of its opponent; cannot know when it's appropriate to abandon the game or suspend play; cannot, in short, understand the social, political, moral, psychological, and philosophical context in which the game occurs.

Unspoken basics

Obviously, our ability to participate in a particular game is dependent on our knowledge of many "rules" which no one has ever spelled out to us. Yet it is easy to overlook this simple fact. In *When Elephants Weep,* the authors tell about a group of scientists who attempted to teach dolphins to play water polo. Although the dolphins were able to learn how to put the ball in the net (and seemed to derive pleasure from doing so), when the trainers tried to get them to stop the other team from "scoring," the dolphins launched an all-out war on the other team's players, using methods that no person steeped in the concepts of sportspeopleship would ever use.

After this experience, the trainers gave up their effort, apparently concluding that their task was hopeless, that dolphins couldn't be taught to play the sport. My guess is that they assumed that all the dolphins needed to be taught were the recorded rules of water polo and the creatures would be able to play the game like adult human beings. These scientists evidently did not realize how much of our knowledge of proper game behavior precedes the learning of the statable constraints of a particular sport.

But suppose these trainers had recognized, after their initial failure, that they had to provide their trainees with some more fundamental "rules" of game playing. Would they ever have been able to teach dolphins all they need to know to play a single "human" game? Are dolphins capable of understanding fairness and sportscreatureship, "time in" vs. "time out," practice vs. competition, winning and losing? And even if they were, how would we go about teaching these concepts to them? Wouldn't we have to teach them much of our culture in order for them to play the game as we do?

Sportsmanship 101

To grasp the immensity of the trainers' task, let us look more closely at what we must know and do to play the simplest game in our culture. We must:

> 1. intuitively understand what is meant by *play* in our culture, recognize how it differs from other activities, and be able to tell when someone is involved in the behaviors associated with play in general and games in particular;

2. intuitively understand what *game/sport* is being played, which behaviors constitute part of that activity and which do not, when the activity is underway, when it is in suspension, and when it is concluded;

3. consciously understand and pursue the *object(s)* of the game (i.e., what we must accomplish to be "successful");

4. consciously understand and follow all (or at least a large majority of) the defining *prescriptions* and *proscriptions* of the game, the "written," statable rules—i.e., what we must and must not do in the course of pursuing the object or objects;

5. consciously understand and follow the *etiquette* of the game— i.e., the unwritten but sometimes stated traditions associated with the game that do not necessarily affect the play itself (e.g., appropriateness of talking, gloating, taunting, celebrating, stalling, replaying a point, giving advice to your opponent or teammates, letting players take back moves, etc.);

6. intuitively understand and follow the *ethos* of that particular game—i.e., the unwritten and rarely expressed assumptions about how to interpret and enforce the "written" rules (e.g., palming in basketball; the strike zone in American and National Leagues; the foot-fault in tennis);

7. intuitively understand and follow the *conventions* of playing any game according to the culture of the participants—i.e., the unwritten and generally unstatable customs related to playing, competing, winning/losing, etc. (e.g., taking the game with the appropriate seriousness, knowing what takes priority over winning and over playing, not faking injury or personal obligation to avoid losing; playing "hard" regardless of the score; not claiming that previous points didn't "count");

8. intuitively understand and respond to the "real-life" *context* in which the game is being played—i.e. the social, cultural, economic, political, and moral consequences of the result (e.g., whether someone's livelihood or self-esteem depends on the outcome).

Going through the motions
Obviously, we are never merely playing a game. Or, to say it another way, we are never playing only one game. We are always conscious of the game's relation to the world in which we live, the world in which that game is one small part.

How much of this context could a non-human "understand?" Is a racehorse "playing the game" of horse racing or merely responding to the urgings of the jockey? Is Deep Blue "playing" chess or merely making moves on a chessboard according to a particular algorithm? Is either trying to win?

If not, they are not playing the game in any meaningful sense. As I see it, to perform the skills and behaviors associated with the game without consciously pursuing the object(s) of the game is not equivalent to playing the game. We might be practicing the game, pretending to play (as with pro wrestlers or actors in a movie about a sport), or exercising our muscles, but there is no game without the attempt, on the part of at least one of the players, to achieve the statable object of that game. (Could dolphins ever be taught to pursue such an object, or would they merely go through the motions of play? And how would we know?)

In addition, it is not possible to pursue the object of the game independent of the key prescriptions and proscriptions. Built into the object(s) of any game is the manner in which it/they must and must not be pursued.

The primary object of a football game, for example, is not to cross your opponents' goal line while carrying a football; it is to score a touchdown. An equipment manager carrying a bag of footballs through the end zone of a football field has not scored a touchdown. These are profoundly different events, and perceiving the difference between them is a key to understanding the game. Thus, not understanding the difference between them is tantamount to not understanding the game of football. Could any non-human ever make this distinction?

"Time in"

Perhaps the single most important "rules" that are literally unstatable, then, are those that define the context of the game and answer the question, "When is the game being played?" None of us can say how we know that we are in fact playing a particular game (rather than, say, just practicing), but we generally have no trouble knowing that we are. That suggests that there are many subtle cues we give and receive about what play activity we are engaged in, what "counts," when time is "in," when the game has started, when play is suspended, and when the game has ended.

Let me offer a personal example. When my buddies and I play tennis, we meet each other at the court at a prearranged time, take out our tennis racquets and some balls, warm up for 15-20 minutes (hitting ground strokes, volleys, overheads, and serves), and eventually someone asks, "Ready?" or perhaps "Ready to play?" If anyone says no, we continue to warm up. If everybody says Yes (or nobody says No), we toss away all but three balls. At this point, I (and presumably the others) understand that the actual game is going to begin with the next serve. There is never a formal announcement that play is about to begin. At most, the server will hold up a ball and the others will nod or wave.

None of us has ever acknowledged that this is our practice, none of us has stated any of these behaviors, as "rules," none of us would be able to say how we arrived at these customs, yet none of us, I assume, would have any doubt when the game has started.

Could I program a computer or teach a dolphin to operate with the same certainty? Could I specify all the variations in our ritual so that non-humans (or non-sports fans) could identify the boundary line between warm-up and play?

On your mark... get set...

Players, fans, and officials of any game or sport develop an acute awareness of the game's "frame" or context, but we would be hard pressed to explain in writing, even after careful thought, exactly what the signs are. After all, even an umpire's yelling of "Play Ball" is not the exact moment the game starts. (And think how confused a new fan of baseball would be when some dignitary threw out "the first pitch"!) We must rely on our intuition, based on our experience with a particular culture, to recognize when a game has begun.

We cannot, in other words, program a computer to understand all the conditions that must be satisfied for humans in a particular culture to say that a game is underway. If the computer is turned on and the software for that game booted up, the computer is, by necessity, playing the game, even if its "opponent" is a two-year-old, a monkey, or an accidental jiggling of the keyboard.

In addition, the computer will go on "playing" until it is turned off, even if its opponent moves on to other activities or drops dead. This phenomenon is the premise of the movie, *Wargames,* in which a supercomputer, WOPR, cannot distinguish between a "game" of Thermo-nuclear War and the real thing. When told it is involved in an actual battle, not a simulation, WOPR's reply is, "What's the difference?"

By contrast, a human being is constantly noticing if the conditions for playing the game are still being met, continuously monitoring the "frame," the circumstances surrounding play, to determine that the game is still in progress, always aware (if only unconsciously) that the other participants are acting as if the game is "on."

For example, in our tennis game, a player will occasionally say, after failing to return a serve, "I wasn't ready." If the others decide that the player is serious in that announcement, the point is usually replayed. How we determine whether or not the player is joking is beyond my understanding (although I'm perfectly capable of making such a determination) and certainly not in my power to express in words.

"Time out"

But there are other reasons, still more difficult to explain, why a particular serve in our game does not "count," i.e., is (usually) replayed. If the players on the receiving team decide that the server's concentration has been "unfairly" disrupted after serving a fault (because, for example, someone from another court has asked us to retrieve their ball or something else has caused "too much" time to elapse), they generally tell the server to "take two," that is, to try his/her first serve again. In effect, they have made a ruling that the server has been inappropriately distracted between the first and second serve and "deserves" a second chance at two serves for that point.

But what exactly is an "unfair" disruption of play according to the etiquette of our game? Can any one of us spell out precisely what situations warrant a second chance and which do not? After all, we are making no effort here to follow the practices of some official tennis game, so we have no rulebook to appeal to, even if we wished to. (Actually, I would feel silly consulting one for such a petty matter.)

I assume that we are all just following a tradition of hackers' tennis that has been passed down over the generations, almost always by imitation rather than by any explicit explanation.

I also assume that our behavior is based on our own notions of "fairness," not on something we could explain in detail.

As a result, I'm not even certain that the other players in my game have the same reasons for telling someone to "take two" as I do, but I have noticed a reasonable consistency over the years.

Occasionally, we facetiously (I assume) debate about whether we should give the opposing player another first serve, but our discussion itself is usually seen as a sufficient distraction to settle the matter in the server's favor. Incidentally, I have never heard the server request a second chance, except in jest (I have assumed), regardless of the circumstances, and some servers will not accept the receiving team's ruling unless it is insisted upon.

Below the surface: Who's the best sport?

A kind of sub-game is going on "underneath" the more obvious one called tennis. Many hackers, myself included, try to one-up each other in politeness and thoughtfulness, so this aspect of our tennis matches can be thought of as a kind of game-within-the-game in which the object is to come off as the best sport.

Of course, no one ever acknowledges this game and no winner is ever announced. My guess is that this practice gives us hackers a chance to feel successful on some level, regardless of the outcome of the match.

Keep in mind that I have never discussed any of these customs with my tennis buddies and probably never will, but I can say that almost every hacker I've ever played tennis with (including those who are fierce competitors and those who are impolite and inconsiderate in other ways) has practiced this non-professional courtesy, and I'm confident that if I played in a friendly game in Oklahoma or Maine or Florida or Arizona, I would see this same tradition being followed.

Yet what chance does a computer, a dolphin, a non-native speaker, or even a non-player have of understanding this game of "Who's the best sport?" It's the kind of thing you have to learn from experience, observation, and inference, not from a set of statable rules.

How can you tell?

Distinguishing between counting and not counting, between "time in" and "time out," is probably the single most basic skill a game player, fan, or official must possess. Without it, a participant or observer could not tell the difference between the preliminaries (such as a warm-up), the breaks in the action (such as a time-out), the aftermath (such as a handshake or a victory lap) and the game itself, could not know when to expend energy and when to relax, could not keep score accurately, could not determine what behavior was affecting the outcome, and so on.

Obviously, we learn to make these distinctions, but we learn them without being aware, for the most part, that we are learning anything. As a result, the process by which we decide that a game is being played is generally hidden from us and therefore seems perfectly natural, not something that has to be learned.

We forget that children, people from other cultures, and adults in our own culture who are unfamiliar with the game cannot automatically tell which actions are part of the game and which are not.

But even if someone understands the notions of play (#1 in our list above), recognizes when a particular game/sport is being played (#2) and is familiar with its object and "official" (written) rules (#3 and #4), such a person would have difficulty participating in the game/sport at any level without a great deal of additional information (or "rules") about the activity.

The outsider

To illustrate this notion, let us imagine a person named Leslie who has taken extensive tennis lessons, memorized an official USTA rule book, and watched professional tennis on television but never actually played a match at any level and never played or watched or read about any other games (which presumably share some of the unstated rules of tennis).

One day, let's suppose further, someone invites Leslie to substitute in one of our doubles games. Even assuming his skills were similar to ours, I would venture to say that Leslie would not have much fun and would make the rest of us very unhappy. He would almost certainly get very confused and frustrated at the way my friends and I play "tennis."

In fact, Leslie might not even recognize it as tennis at all and might conclude that we are playing some bastardized form of the game.

And in a sense, he would be absolutely right.

By the book

For one thing, as Leslie would be dismayed to discover, none of our rules are "official," in the sense that they are written down or formally agreed upon.

We all seem to assume that we are following the most important rules of professional tennis, except where that is not possible. So, for example, when the ATP adopted a tiebreaker rule for deciding a set, most (but not all) of the games I was involved with also adopted that practice.

In general, the only rules we discuss are those we are uncertain about, such as whether it is legal to touch the net during a point or hit the ball before it crosses the net. Otherwise, we have never spelled out the "rules" we are using, have never stated which set of "official" laws we will abide by, have never established an authority to settle disputes, and have never ever consulted a rule book (at least not at the court) to determine the "correct" way to play. When we disagree about the rules, which rarely happens, we use our knowledge of pro tennis to defend our position.

Not by the book

But we certainly don't do everything as they do on the ATP tour. As I have already indicated, we give people a second chance at a first serve according to our own lights, not what we see happening at Wimbledon.

To save money, we do not open a new can of balls every seven games, and when we play indoors (where we have to pay for court time), we switch ends of the court after each set, not after every odd game.

In addition, we never assess penalty points for swearing, racquet abuse, exceeding time limits, or foot faulting. We might grumble about these violations, especially if we think a player is getting an unfair advantage, but we tolerate them, apparently because we perceive them as too trivial to worry about.

Yet some of the people I play with are fanatical about the height of the net. They use a tape measure to make sure the middle of the net is exactly 36 inches high and raise or lower it as needed. They even bring "doubles sticks" to raise the net to the appropriate height at the sides. Wouldn't our "inconsistency" drive Leslie crazy?

Obviously, one of the most crucial (and rarely stated) meta-rules of games that someone like Leslie (or a computer or a dolphin) would not understand is that we can play them any way we wish, as long as we have (apparent) agreement among the participants. If we want to play tennis with a racquetball or without a net, what's to stop us?

Tradition-bound

And yet, in my experience, few people choose to play games or sports in innovative ways. Although they are willing to eliminate "trivial" or inessential rules, most people evidently want to feel connected to the tradition of "real" games (i.e., professional sports), even when the rules of the pro version are inappropriate for the local circumstances.

So, for instance, almost all junior high school basketball hoops are 10 feet high, just as they are for the Chicago Bulls, even though the kids are two or three feet shorter than players in the NBA. I guess we like to create the illusion for ourselves that these youngsters are playing the same game as Michael Jordan.

House rules

Even if Leslie finally figured out exactly how our "rules" differed from the ATP's, he would undoubtedly still be very uncomfortable in our doubles game. For one thing, we play a relatively "casual" game.

We often talk to each other between points, jokingly insult one another, compliment a particularly good shot, ask what the score is, predict what is going to happen next, and so on. Between games, we might exchange personal information or tell jokes.

None of this, of course, happens in professional level tennis, at least not the matches shown on television.

My guess is that Leslie would be disconcerted by our apparent lack of decorum. He would probably perceive us as being remarkably uninterested in the outcome of the game, when in fact we play to win almost as "seriously" as the pros. If he was used to silence between points and games, his concentration might be seriously upset.

Banter protocols

Perhaps he would eventually be able to shrug off our casualness as a trivial idiosyncrasy that doesn't affect the game in any significant way, but it is doubtful that he would be able to participate in the banter. In that case, our "rules" would accommodate his silence. No one is required by our etiquette to talk if s/he doesn't want to, although we (at least I) tend to prefer those with "personality." The game is just not as much fun (for me) with duds or robots.

If Leslie did start to talk, though, he might find himself violating other aspects of our etiquette. Certain subjects are taboo, or at least frowned upon or rarely mentioned. Business, for example, is almost never discussed between points and rarely between games. (Perhaps this is merely because the people I play with don't share work experience.)

More significantly, politics and religion are strictly avoided. At most, someone will make a passing comment about the president or some interesting current event, but I can't remember a single remark about abortion or gun control or any other such controversial topic, even when I have played with other academics. It's as if we do not want to acknowledge that we might have serious disagreements outside the tennis court.

Would Leslie recognize that we are limiting our comments to certain topics? Until I wrote these last sentences, I had never articulated this "rule" even to myself (though I've been playing for over 40 years).

Our own language

Leslie would almost certainly have more difficulty getting used to our line-calling practices. Since we don't have officials, we (like most hackers, I assume) have devised a fairly elaborate system for deciding if a ball is in or out.

Keep in mind that we have never discussed this system, never written it down, never spelled it out in any way, yet our entire game depends on each player's following a fairly rigid, if unstatable, set of behaviors. (I'm willing to bet that is generally the case with most amateurs, including those in tournaments, which rarely have official line-callers.)

First, we sometimes use hand signals to indicate "in" (a palm down) or "out" (a finger point), and sometimes, when we think the call is obvious, we say nothing at all. As far as I can tell, we use hand signals only when the ball is not returnable and say "out" when a player has hit the ball back and we wish to indicate that the point is over.

Second, we have a set of "rules" governing which player makes which call. Generally, players on the team about to hit the ball are expected to call the lines, even if a player from the opposing team is closer to the ball when it hits near the line. For example, on a serve, the partner of the player receiving the ball is supposed to announce an out ball.

Of course, there are exceptions (which I can only hint at). Sometimes, for example, the player that hit the ball (or his/her partner) has an unobstructed view of the situation and makes the call. Sometimes, more than one player makes the call. Occasionally two players disagree and a discussion ensues.

To settle a disputed line call, some players like to look for the impression (called a "spot") the ball has left on the playing surface. If they cannot find a spot, they generally assume the ball hit the line (and the point is awarded to the hitter).

Fuzzy boundaries

For the most part, in keeping with the game of "Who's the best sport?", players try to appear calm, rational, polite, and objective about line-calling, but occasionally someone will get upset over another's call, and a new game, whose rules are even harder to describe, breaks out. In this game ("I'm Right and You're Wrong"), the object is to get the other player to back down and agree with your perception.

What players under these circumstances are allowed or not allowed to say depends partly on the social rules that are in operation—the power relations among the players off the court—so once again we see the fuzziness of the boundary between game and non-game.

In most cases, the desire to continue play or to win the sportsmanship game ends an argument fairly quickly (but I remember once when a player and his grandson argued for over 15 minutes about a particular line call). Usually, when an impasse is reached, players will agree to take the point over.

As should be clear by now, I would never get all our practices down on paper, no matter how long I stayed at it. In fact, I haven't even finished explaining our system for calling lines, or the "rules" related to the length of time it's appropriate to debate a particular line call.

In addition, in my attempt to codify our game for "outsiders" (those who have never seen us, or other hackers, play), I have found myself distorting the reality for the sake of convenience. In many cases, I ignored what I knew to be clear exceptions to avoid getting bogged down in impossibly complicated nuances that I'm only dimly aware of.

For instance, one friend, John, and I always discussed controversial issues when we played singles but never when we played doubles! I also ignored the fact that the various groups I play tennis with do not play by identical rules (e.g., normally we spin a racket to determine which team serves first, but when we play at Nazim's house, the player who opens a can of balls serves the first game); only hinted at the effect a change in circumstances (outdoor vs. indoor, free vs. fee) can have on our game; and oversimplified the modifications in our game over the years.

Thus, as I've tried to show, the "casual" game of tennis that my buddies and I play is really based on an enormously complex set of "rules"—assumptions, traditions, and conventions—that govern our behavior on the court (whether we are consciously aware of it or not).

My contention is that no one could ever "fully" describe those rules or those governing the players of any other game.

The infinite-regress trap

It is time to see exactly why a complete listing of a game's rules is impossible. There are several reasons:

1. Game rules, like any rules, must be stated in some language, and all language is subject to interpretation. But the rules for interpreting any language would also have to be stated in some language, and these rules would likewise have to be interpreted. We are trapped in an infinite regress. Thus, the question "What are the rules?" can never be answered fully.

2. Each individual player could have his or her own personal conception of a game which would differ (if only slightly) from all other players' versions, and each player's understanding of that game's rules could change over time. No finite list of rules could include an infinite number of possible variations.

3. Since any two players could be playing the same game with different interpretations, there would have to be a set of meta-rules for reconciling these differences when they surface.

Of course, these meta-rules are, in effect, the rules to another game and are therefore subject to the same interpretive variations as the rules of any other game. Again, we run into an infinite regression. There is no bottom line, no point when we can accurately say, "These are the ultimate meta-rules for settling disputes."

Thus, the questions, "How do we settle disputes about the rules themselves, about whether a player has violated a rule, and about the appropriate penalties for a rule violation?" can never have a final answer.

4. Even if two players agree on certain rules and how to interpret them, disputes about what actually occurred (such as whether a ball landed on the back line or just beyond it) can still arise, and the players will need to abide by meta-rules in settling these disputes as well. These meta-rules, like those in #3 above, are also part of an infinite regression, so the question "How do we settle disputes about what really happened?" has no ultimate resolution either.

5. Since there are various "levels" of rules, "higher" rules (such as a real-world crisis) might have to take precedence over "lower" rules (such as time constraints); there must be a set of meta-rules for determining when this is appropriate. As with the other meta-rules we've looked at, there is no "final" set for ending disputes, so the question, "When is it appropriate to suspend certain rules?" cannot be given a full answer.

6. Since all games begin and end and may be interrupted by "outside" events (such as a TV ad), we must have a set of meta-rules for determining when the constraints apply and when they don't. Again, these meta-rules are susceptible to interpretation and dispute, leading to yet another unendable regression.

"Simons" often take advantage of this fact by tricking players into thinking play hasn't begun and then saying something like, "Before we start, say hi to your neighbor. Ah, I didn't say 'Simon says.'" Therefore, the question, "When do the rules apply?" cannot be fully answered.

We can see now why it is impossible to spell out a complete set of rules for any game. Now we need to ask why we have no trouble playing a wide variety of games.

If we can't know all the rules, how can we play any game at all?

> *Is it because participants rarely have to deal with "meta-rules" and so the infinite-regress problem almost never comes up?*

To me, this is not a plausible explanation. There are simply too many occasions we can name—in virtually every game ever played—in which meta-rule questions arise. When a player accidentally rolls the dice off the table, argues a call, gives (or refuses to give) an opponent a handicap, calls for a do-over, takes a mulligan, asks for a director's ruling, warns an opponent about an unwise move, or encourages the other team to play faster, the players are facing situations that are not (and could not be) completely covered in the recorded rules. Meta-rules (and even meta-meta-rules) are an integral part of all rule-governed activities.

> *Is it because players don't take games seriously so it doesn't matter that they can't know all the rules?*

Again, this doesn't work for me because it is clearly not true in all cases. Obviously, some players (myself included) care deeply about the game and the outcome.

Many of us are playing for high stakes—money, prestige, a trophy, pride, self-esteem, ego satisfaction, a feeling of control, etc. In fact, it's probably pretty rare for players to have no emotional involvement in the game they are playing. After all, why play unless the results "matter" in some important way?

My guess is that almost all players almost all of the time take almost all games very "seriously."

> *Is it because players mistakenly believe that there is a "bottom line," that the rules are clear, complete, and "final," and that somebody somewhere knows all of them?*

This is getting closer to sounding right, but is still a half-truth at best. Having the misconception that a game's rules are solid and statable can provide a player with a sense of confidence in the "reality" of a game, but my realization that no one can know (let alone state) the rules of our doubles game has not dampened my enthusiasm for tennis one iota. In fact, my recognition that games, like languages, can exist only because of an unspoken, almost mystical, agreement among the participants actually enhances my appreciation of them.

Although my attitude may be idiosyncratic, I seriously doubt that anyone else's enjoyment of a game (or willingness or ability to play it) would be diminished by realizing that we can't list all its rules.

"It's only a game"

I believe we can go on playing games wholeheartedly even when we are aware of the incompleteness of their rules. Why? Because, on a gut level, we cannot distinguish between something fanciful—like a movie or a joke or a dream or a game—and something "real."

Games feel like any life-event, so we can be immersed in them even though we may know intellectually that they are artificial constructions. Therefore, it makes no difference to us (emotionally) that a list of rules governing them cannot be completed, just as we can be profoundly affected by a joke or piece of fiction or nightmare that is not logical, realistic, or "complete."

We can suspend disbelief and rationality (even when some part of our brain is telling us it's only a story or it's only a dream) and respond deeply to creations of the imagination—our own or others'.

We can do this because we have the wonderful (and perhaps unique) capacity to operate on the "as if" level; we can play a game *as if* we know all its rules, *as if* there is an ultimate set of meta-rules, *as if* all potential disputes can be settled. We can imagine a game in the abstract and in a vacuum and can project that Platonic ideal onto the one that must be played in the world of social and political reality.

In other words, we can operate on (at least) two distinct levels of cognition at once. We can play any game as if it had an autonomous existence, even though we know perfectly well that the players create the game each time they agree to play and that any player at any time can destroy the game by quitting, by arguing, by stalling, or by any number of other spoil-sport tactics.

Similarly, we can play any game as if it is important (and genuinely feel that it is), even though we know that it is not very high on our list of life priorities. We can play any game as if it transcended our culture, even though we recognize that players can have "unfair" (dis)advantages as a result of their upbringing. We can play any game as if it transcended morality (so we might intentionally and unashamedly foul or fool an opponent) even though we know that players can cheat or violate the rules in inappropriate ways.

Suspension of disbelief

Without this ability to operate in the conditional universe of "Suppose..." and "What if ...," game playing would be impossible, as would drama and fiction and, I suspect, language itself. We must be able to behave as if a game were not "merely" play, even though we are fully aware it is nothing else.

Like an actor, we must be able to take on a role but never give up our sense of self. We must be "in" the game to enjoy it but never so far in that we forget who we are. It is a delicate balance fraught with danger, which is perhaps why so many people (especially adults) shy away from games.

Non-human game players?

It is also, I believe, one more reason that computers (at least as they are today) will never play a game in the same sense that humans do. Computers have no conditional, no ability to create temporary self-delusions, no play mode, no sense of "as if." To a computer (we must assume), a chess move is just another calculation, no different from finding the square root of pi.

To a human, a chess move is (usually) part of a carefully designed pretense, a system of orchestrated assumptions, an artificial structure that can bring stimulation, competition, camaraderie, fun, and a variety of other good feelings. In general, the chess-playing human voluntarily accepts a particular challenge that involves a specific goal and specific constraints and which s/he can abandon at any time. The chess-playing computer, on the other hand, does not choose to start and cannot stop on its own. The human is aware of the voluntary and "non-serious," conditional nature of the activity, but the machine is not (and probably can never be).

What about animals? Does any non-human creature have the ability to suppose, to imagine something that doesn't exist except as an agreement among participants? If not, they will never play a game as we do. They will either take it too seriously or not seriously enough and, therefore, like any spoilsport, undermine the enjoyment of the game for any human participants or observers (as was the case with the water-polo-playing dolphins).

But even if animals (or computers) could think in the conditional, they still might not be able to play games as we do. They would also have to be able to trust other players to function in basically the same way. To play a game (or use a system) meaningfully without knowing all the rules requires the faith that others understand the game/system as you do or at least will behave in ways that seem consistent with such an understanding. Without that faith, a player would inevitably end up being the spoilsport.

Meta-rules in other arenas

By way of analogy, consider our (or any other) monetary system. Most people recognize that the currency we use has no inherent worth and that it gains its value from mutual (if tacit) agreement among its users, which means its value is subjective, symbolic, and subject to change.

Few people believe that there is an objective, stable method for determining how much milk a dollar should buy. Most of us understand that there are no "rules" or meta-rules we can refer to that would settle a dispute about the value of a dollar bill and that its purchasing power is dependent on consensus, on other people's willingness to give us this much milk for this many dollars. And yet we can still use the coin of the realm and, for the most part, get our money's worth (by our own standards).

The system works even though no one can explain it fully and even though we all know it could collapse at any moment if people stopped trusting each other or the system itself.

The same is true with another currency—language. Even though words have no inherent meaning and no one has been able to list all the rules governing the construction of sentences, we can still communicate reasonably effectively for most purposes.

We all know that anyone at any time can choose to destroy the process by acting on Humpty Dumpty's premise that words can mean whatever we want them to mean. We know that there is no rulebook, no authority, no indisputable arbiter we can appeal to in such a case (since they would all have to use more words to settle the dispute).

Like any game, communication is dependent on the participants' willingness to operate as if there were universal agreement about meanings and grammatical rules.

We need to remember, though, that games are not analogous to these two currencies in at least one crucial way. Both money and language, after all, serve obvious, vital functions in the world, whereas the value of games is not nearly as apparent. We can easily understand why people would almost always try to go along with a monetary or linguistic system, since they believe that both can benefit them and the community significantly. In addition, most people recognize that destroying either system could ultimately threaten their own well-being.

Rule-preserving meta-rules

But games? The common perception is that no one gets hurt if a game is spoiled. So why would anyone continue to submit to an arbitrary (and incomplete) set of rules that was causing him or her to lose face, patience, and/or money? Why do people continue to play "by the rules" when they are losing the game?

Since losing is undesirable, we need to explain why so few players take advantage of the fact that the rules are incomplete and therefore infinitely challengeable. We need to understand why people almost always play as if the rules were not only complete but knowable and statable, and rarely allow themselves to play the meta-game of arguing about the rules and the meta-rules, ad infinitum.

One possible answer, of course, is that players don't realize that this "strategy" exists, but I think that all of us have witnessed many examples of the kind of behavior I'm talking about. Almost everyone has seen images of managers and players, nose to nose with an umpire, arguing a call or an interpretation of the rules, and even non-sports fans have probably seen TV ads based on John McEnroe's antics on the court, so I have to assume that virtually everyone realizes that this option is theoretically available to any player.

So what are the real "meta-rules" that keep most of us from playing this particular meta-game? Here are a few of them:

1. A game is supposed to be for fun, and, playing the game itself is more fun than playing the meta-game of arguing. Except for young boys in the front yards of America (who will argue endlessly about a single play), most players have learned that the meta-game is boring, repetitive, and fruitless, often ending in a stand-off;

2. A game is supposed to test certain skills, and these do not usually include the skills of debate, sophistry, and intimidation tested by the meta-game;

3. A game is supposed to be for camaraderie, and arguing about the rules leads to antagonism rather than a spirit of friendly competition;

4. Players are supposed to be good sports (whatever that is), and rule challengers are perceived as poor sports or even spoilsports;

5. The "ideal" game, the game we all want to play, works fine as it is and does not include a discussion of rules or meta-rules;

6. A set of rules that has been tested is better than one that has not, so if it's not broken, don't fix it;

7. Doing things as others have done them in the past allows us to feel connected to our ancestors, our culture, and our traditions;

8. Following the rules that others follow allows us to compare ourselves to a wide spectrum of players, not just our immediate opponent(s);

9. Challenging long-standing traditions is inherently unwise because it creates the impression that nothing is sacred and could, if carried far enough, lead to anarchy.

For all these reasons, a player who argues about rules risks disapproval, sanctions, and even ostracism, so the vast majority of us choose to "leave well enough alone." Most people avoid and frown on the meta-game of arguing with rules and meta-rules because, without necessarily being aware of their reasons, they perceive it as a threat to pleasure, continuity, and stability. Thus, most games continue to be played "as they always have been." For the same reasons, many people are suspicious of new games.

To return to our central question, then, we can play a game even though we can't know all its rules because, for a variety of reasons, we tacilly conspire with our fellow players to act as if we know them all.

The big picture

In this way, games are no different from every system we use. In an important sense, all rule-governed systems—including law, politics, war, morality, education, economics, and language—are games, as many people have noted. Therefore, virtually all of the lessons we learn from "non-serious" games are directly transferable to the "real" world. What are those lessons? What follows from the acknowledgment that no human system has a completable set of "rules?" Let us spell out some of the implications.

1. Power and authority are arbitrary, not inevitable, depend on consensus (or at least acquiescence), and have no "divine" right to exist.

2. Rules for any system are not handed down from above, can exist only through the agreement of the participants, are always open to negotiation among the "players," and are continually evolving. As Robert McConville reminds us, if a game survives, "the rules for playing the game are constantly being changed as they are passed from tribe to tribe and generation to generation" (*The History of Board Games*, p. 8).

3. The most powerful rules, the ones least likely to be violated, are those that are not stated explicitly, those that people have to infer or intuit. To state a rule is to invite players to break it, but to leave a rule unstated is to make its violation almost literally "unthinkable."

4. We cannot accurately predict how any rule, stated or unstated, will be interpreted or enforced, so no rule, simply by its existence, will necessarily produce or prevent a desired behavior.

5. We cannot accurately predict or control what customs, norms, conventions, traditions, or expectations will evolve for a particular game or system of rules.

6. No set of rules is inherently superior to any other. In order to judge a set of rules, we must employ a set of meta-rules, which themselves would have to be judged by a set of meta-meta-rules, and so on ad infinitum.

7. An infinite number of sets of rules will "work," will allow us, individually or collectively, to function successfully (or at least to our own satisfaction).

8. The longer a system is followed and the more people who attempt to follow it, the more complex the recorded rules will become, and the more sets of meta-rules and meta-meta-rules, etc., will be recorded. Consider any legal system, religion, or professional sport as prime examples.

9. Every person operates according to an unlimited number of sets of rules, so it is almost inevitable that some of these sets (such as religion and business) will come in conflict with each other, which means that every person is also operating according to an unlimited number of sets of meta-rules for reconciling such conflicts, and an unlimited number of sets of meta-meta-rules and so on.

10. As humans, we have little choice but to act as though some of these sets of rules were absolute and indisputable. Otherwise, we would be trapped in an infinite regression and utterly unable to make meaningful choices.

11. Paradoxically, we cannot live according to any set of rules (because we can never know them all and because they will inevitably conflict with other sets we are trying to live by), so in order to continue to perceive ourselves as faithfully following a "complete" set of rules, we must learn to rationalize our deviations from it (or feel a great deal of guilt).

12. It is reasonable to say we are playing a game/living by a system even though we are not following all its rules. For this reason, following some of the rules in a system creates the expectation (in ourselves and others) that we will follow all the rules, including the unstated and the unstatable ones.

13. No one can tell for sure if someone (including oneself) is "really" playing a game/ living by a system because it is not possible for anyone to follow all the rules in a game or system. Therefore, we can pretend to be playing any game/living by any system without others being able to detect that we are pretending. We can also pretend to be pretending and so on, and no one will be able to tell the difference.

14. No two people can possibly follow the same set of rules in exactly the same way.

Obviously, the recognition that we cannot know all the rules in a system can have a profound effect on how we approach the world. It can make us want to curl up in a corner with our thumb in our mouth or to go out and make sweeping changes in our most important institutions. It can destroy us or free us, depending on how we feel about a world in which there are no absolutes, no bottom lines, no final list of rules, a world in which all systems are "equal" and all meaning relational. Some (including myself) are comfortable with, even invigorated by, this notion, but others (perhaps a large majority) are enormously disturbed by it.

Today Parcheesi, tomorrow the world

Of course, there is nothing new about the relativist claim, but, to my knowledge, no one has applied the concept to games, those obviously artificial constructs. The argument has raged about more "important" human systems, like law and religion and language, so emotions, desires, and values always tend to cloud the issues. People understandably want to believe that their beloved institutions are sacred, unchanging, and right, but (almost) no one feels that way about games.

So I have chosen to examine the reality of rules and meta-rules in this non-volatile, "safe" context of games, hoping I would not scare away those who tend to shun a relativistic argument. My goal has been to show convincingly that we cannot know all the rules but we can still play the game, so that I could suggest, through analogy, that

> *We can go on using (and revering) any system even if we acknowledge that it is as artificial, arbitrary, challengeable, and "incomplete" as any game.*

> *Any system, no matter how long it has been around and no matter how complex its list of rules and meta-rules, is viable only as long as there are individuals who support it.*

Conclusions

If my efforts have been successful, if people take away valuable lessons about "life" from this analysis of games, it will demonstrate, ironically, that games can indeed serve at least one vital social function: as abstractions of "real-world" situations, they can provide an analog to other, more "important" and more complicated, aspects of life and thus can help us see what otherwise might be invisible. If for no other reason, games should not be dismissed as trivial forms of entertainment. If we remember to use them wisely, they could be a profoundly important aspect of our culture. As the young would say, **GAMES RULE!**

Beyond the Rules
of the Game:
Why Are Rooie Rules Nice?

Linda Hughes

Context

*At the time fieldwork began for this essay, which first appeared in **The World of Play: Proceedings of the 7th Annual Meeting of The Association for the Anthropological Study of Play,** edited by Frank E. Manning (Leisure Press, 1983), there was an extensive literature on games, but very little on the playing of games. The essay reflects an early foray into developing a theoretical framework for such research, strongly influenced by UPenn Professors Erving Goffman, Ray Birdwhistle, Del Hymes, William Labov, Bambi Schiefflin, and Shirley Brice Heath.*

Gaming the Game

Game Communities

Linda Hughes earned a Masters in American Folk Culture from Cooperstown Graduate Programs and a Ph.D. in Interdisciplinary Studies in Human Development from the University of Pennsylvania. Since 1997, she has coordinated the Alternative Routes to Certification Program for the state of Delaware.

King: *"I call Rooie Rules. Duckfeet."*
Player: *"Why Rooie Rules?"*
King (after a brief pause): *"Because Rooie Rules are nice."*

Most studies of games focus on games themselves, on common threads of structure, proce-dure and rules across what may be very different gaming experiences for players. We have tended to work from the assumption that game rules define the activity we are studying and, further, that these same rules quite explicitly and prescriptively define the same activity for players (Avedon and Sutton-Smith, 1971).

Recent analyses have suggested this overemphasis on game rules can lead to some rather paradoxical conclusions. Helen Schwartzman (1978), for example, has argued for abandoning game models in studies of play. While such a proposal may be well justified, given the limitations of traditional game models as they have been applied to play, Schwartzman goes on to propose we also take the play out of games. She justifies her position, in part, on the perception that "an understanding of game rules provides one with an understanding of the event" which rules out "the ambiguity, spontaneity and flexibility of play" (p. 327).

It is true that there is very little room in descriptions of game rules for much am-biguity or spontaneity, but it does not necessarily follow that games are not "playful." Being playful is an activity of people, not of rules. Understanding the rules, at least as we normally describe them, cannot be equaled with understanding the event. We are reminded of Kenneth Goldstein's (1971) observation that

> the rules which are verbalized by informants and which are then presented by collectors in their papers and books for our analysis and study are an idealized set of rules—they are the rules by which people *should* play rather than the ones by which they *do* play. (p. 90)

Goldstein's suggestion that the "real" rules of the game differ markedly from those commonly reported by players (and by researchers) takes us beyond the rules of the game. It opens to question whether something is wrong with our commonsense notions about the nature and functioning of rules in games. Games themselves may be in some very real sense constituted by the sets of rules we have used to describe them, but the activity of gamers in constituting an instance of that game may require a very different descriptive and analytic framework. Gary Fine (1980) has used the term "gaming" to distinguish between the game itself and what real players do in constructing a particular instance of that game. In this paper we will explore, at least in a preliminary way, something of the differences between game rules and the rules of gaming. In the process we hope to put some "play" back into games.

Games and Gaming

For some time it has been the vogue to adopt games as metaphors for social interaction (Bateson, 1972; Goffman, 1961; Harré, 1974), but only rarely have we approached games from a social communicational interactional perspective. Goldstein (1971) provides a notable exception, as does Gary Fine's (in press) recent analysis of fantasy role-play gaming. In both we find a good deal of "ambiguity, spontaneity and flexibility." Fine, for example, observes that

> In fantasy role-play gaming, rules and outcomes do not have the inevitability that they possess in most formal games, rather both features are negotiated and rules are adjusted by the referee and his group. Thus, ironically, fantasy games are in some ways more like "life" than like "games," despite their position as games. (p. 4)

It is not the particular game Fine studied that sets it off from "most formal games," but the type of analysis he has chosen. His game looks more like "life" than like "games" because he is not describing the game for us here, but the social and interactional activity of gaming. Looked at from a similar perspective, even professional sports, which we tend to regard as the most formal of "formal games," also display much more flexibility than might be suggested by their rules.

> To the NHL's thirteen referees, life is a constant struggle to maintain the game's flow, keep the coaches off their backs and the players off each other's. Most important, referees must have an instinct for which violations to call and which to ignore. They themselves talk of "good" penalties (flagrant violations such as tripping the player with the puck) and "bad" ones (minor offenses such as hooking a player who doesn't have the puck late in a tight game). "You could call a penalty a minute," says referee Ron Fournier. "But that's not what we're supposed to do. You call a guy for a minor infraction, and even though you cite the rule number, he just looks at you and says, 'What's that?' It doesn't earn you respect. (*Newsweek*, January 5, 1981)

This referee is well aware he is supposed to be providing something more than a literal reading of the rule book. Maintaining the game's "flow" and earning the respect of other participants depends upon knowledge of both game rules and gaming rules. One must not only know how the rule book defines and penalizes "hooking." One must also know that this "hook" is not the same as that "hook."

If we adopt, for the moment, Goldstein's distinction, we might distinguish between an "ideal" game rule, which refers to an action (a "hook") and to a game-prescribed outcome (a penalty), and a "real" rule, which refers to a "hook" as something other than a contextless action and to shared, socially-prescribed, negotiated outcomes (interruptions in game flow, loss of respect and such). The term "respect" makes reference to social relationships, to something of a very different order than game rules. It derives from the status of games as a social process, not from the status of the activity as a game.

When we encounter words like "respect," we move from an analysis of games into the realm of gaming. The quotation at the beginning of this chapter (from the author's observations of a group of young Foursquare players) similarly moves us out of the game and into gaming: "Why Rooie Rules?" "Because Rooie Rules are nice." We will be exploring Rooie Rules as game rules and as "nice" rules. In the process, we will be asking whether it is possible to understand these rules without also understanding why they are "nice."

The World of Foursquare

For almost three years, children were observed playing the game of Foursquare on the lower school playground of a private Friends school in the suburbs of Philadelphia, Pennsylvania. More recently extensive interviews were conducted with many of the players. The following is drawn from a larger research effort focused on the negotiational aspects of gaming, and especially on identifying some of the largely tacit understandings that allow these children to construct this kind of complex communal activity.

The groups of children observed come generally from white, middle to upper socio-economic groups. Less than a third come from Quaker families. The game of Foursquare tends to be dominated by girls, especially those in third to fifth grades, but boys have also been observed in the game, with and without girls. Older and younger children regularly join in. At the time of the observations cited below, the "regulars" consisted largely of third and fourth grade girls.

Children in this school have played Foursquare during recess for more than twenty years. The game is played on a square court painted on a portion of paved playground. The court is further divided into four equal squares, each of which constitutes the play space for one of the four active players. The player occupying one of the squares is called the "king." Before each round of play, the "king" calls a set of rules for that round (in our opening example, "I call Rooie Rules. Duckfeet."). This player then serves a large rubber ball to one of the other players. The ball is bounced among the players until it bounces more than once in a player's square, or until a player fails to hit it into the square of one of the other players. That player is out. He or she leaves the court and goes to the end of a line of players waiting to enter the game. The remaining players rotate toward the "king" square, filling in the vacated square, and the first player in line enters the game through the square farthest from the "king."

Foursquare is a simple ball-bouncing game. One of the ways it is made before each round of play. [sic] Such calls can be used for a wide variety of purposes, including increasing game excitement, adjusting the level of difficulty, and assisting or scapegoating other players. At one level the "king's" rules prescribe or prohibit certain actions and specify their consequences. In this sense they function as game rules. At another level, they may display or set the general tone for a particular round of play or for the overall gaming occasion.

It is this latter quality that allows the call of "Rooie Rules" in this game. A girl named Rooie was one of the regular players when the current observations were made. The king's call makes reference to her preferred set of rules, which include the following: "no holding" (the ball must be hit, not caught and thrown); "no slams" (bounces high over a player's head); "duckfeet" (being hit on the legs) is out (rather than a "takeover"); "spins" are allowed; and so on. Each of these individual game "rules" can be called by a "king." The call of "Rooie Rules" is a kind of shorthand, covering a long list of individual calls.

Despite the fact that play regularly proceeds after a call of "Rooie Rules," no player, including Rooie and the "king" who calls them, can supply a complete list of rules encompassed by this call. In fact, this call is very regularly used by very inexperienced players to avoid having to specify a particular list of rules before they have learned what calls are possible. What allows the game to proceed within such apparent ambiguity concerning the precise rules of the game is the tacit understanding that Rooie Rules are "nice," and "nice" is perhaps the paramount concern among these players. It is far more important to understand "nice" play than to understand the rules.

What Makes Rooie Rules "Nice"?

How are Rooie Rules "nice"? First, even though they are not explicitly mentioned and most of the players could not list all of them, Rooie Rules are understood to prohibit all kinds of what the kids call "rough stuff." This includes all moves like "slams" or "wings" (hard, low shots to the corner of a player's square) which are difficult for the receiving player to return. "Nice" players are supposed to give others a fair chance of returning the ball and, even more basic, they are not supposed to try to get other players out of the game deliberately.

Second, Rooie Rules are "nice" because they prohibit "rough stuff" in a "nice" way. Even when prohibited by a call such as Rooie Rules, players may still "slam" and "wing" and "hold" without being called out for doing so. When observations of this game began, this seeming lack of direct relationship between the rules as called and being "out" was particularly puzzling. Why bother to call the rules if no one was ever out for violating them?

Things became clearer one day when one of the players explained to another the rule really was "please don't hold the ball unless you really have to." This interpretation allows more experienced players to be "nice" to "little kids," who can do little more than catch and throw the ball. It also reflects a shared sense that it is unfair to penalize players, who, in the heat of play, lack sufficient control to avoid holding the ball briefly before returning it. Fairness, it seems, is an important component of "nice."

Later conversations with players confirmed that actions such as "wings," "slams" and "holds" were not really prohibited by Rooie Rules though one should *try* not to do them. What was prohibited is what the kids call "purpose stuff." A common cited example of the latter is "holding" the ball while deciding which player to get out of the game. Perceived intentionality joins fairness as another component of "nice."

Third, Rooie Rules are "nice" because they avoid direct confrontations over player actions. Even the most blatant "purpose stuff" is rarely directly challenged. Certainly, no player would ever be called out for such violations. They may be simply ignored, especially when directed toward a player scapegoated by a dominant group of players. If not ignored, they will be handled in a less direct—and "nicer"—way. It is very common to observe rather elaborate performances—exaggerated leaning, grunts, cries of "whew!" and dramatic mopping of brows—around rather easy shots that just happen to land as a "slam" in the offending player's square. This latter observation underscores *perceived* intentionality as a major component of "nice" among these gamers. One is reminded of Goffman's (1959) concept of "demeanor." It is apparently less important here that one be "nice" than one make an appropriate display of being "nice."

Highly ritualized "yes you are" / "no I'm not" exchanges are very common. Again, from fieldnotes:

> Angie: *"Sally! You're playing rough!"*
>
> Sally: *"So are you!"*
>
> Angie: *"No I'm not! I'm being nice!"*

Smiles, sideways glances, and the glints in players' eyes when they engage in such exchanges belie their seriousness. There is a quality of collusive "play" around ways of making deliberate actions look accidental, a shared delight in a virtuoso performance or a comment on a performance that just misses the mark.

It is only when "purpose stuff" does not have this playful, among friends quality that one is likely to see sanctions applied for violations of the "rules." Players who consistently "slam" or "wing" without this playful collusion quite often find themselves on the receiving end of a wild shot they cannot return. Such occasions are always followed, of course, by profuse apologies from the hitter, who "just couldn't help it," and who puts on quite a performance to support a claim of innocence in the whole matter.

This use of indirect sanctions, or at least "accidental" sanctions, bypassing a simple appeal to the game rules, is also part of being "nice". If the "real" rules of this game tend to revolve around perceived intentions of the player (as in "purpose stuff"), then it becomes rather awkward to invoke those rules and still be "nice." Invoking a "rule" is not merely a statement of fact about a player's actions, but an accusation of having violated something of the social order, a much more serious charge. Among these gamers, invocation of such rules would involve not only explicit recognition that all players are not equal under the rules, but also an implicit accusation of being purposefully vindictive or nasty—of not being "nice." It is not "nice" to violate "nice" rules, but it is also not "nice" to accuse someone directly of doing so. Instead, sanctions are imposed in a way which allows everyone to act as though they were accidental, accompanied by an appropriate "I couldn't help it" performance.

At least among the gamers observed here, the call of "Rooie Rules" invokes less a list of individual rules' calls than a general framework for player interaction. The latter rests upon shared standards for fairness, perceived intentionality and appropriate demeanor within the group. The term "nice," and its contrast "rough," are employed among this particular set of gamers to refer to a rather complex matrix of social rights and obligations. It appears that understanding and accepting these standards is even more critical to sustaining the game activity than understanding the set of rules currently in force. This became particularly clear one day when a group of boys joined the regular female players. The boys clearly understood the "real" rules of the game, as the "regulars" played it, but they actively challenged the implicit demand that they play "nice." In the process, what was usually implicit became more and more explicit. Their behavior triggered a rather active discourse concerning the "real" and "ideal" rules of this game. Some very interesting things began to happen.

When Players Won't Be "Nice"

As might be predicted among boys and girls of this age, the boys almost immediately drove the girls crazy by very overtly using "rough stuff" ("slams" and "wings") to get the girls out of the game. This does not mean the girls were not also using such moves. What enraged them was the boys' failure to disguise "purpose stuff" in the kinds of "I couldn't help it" performances demanded by "nice" play. The boys would, for example, call, "Rough square, Getting out on serves," and then slam the ball high over one of the girls' heads on the serve.

Totally outraged, the girls would counter, when one of their number was "king," with a call of "Rooie Rules." But, as we might expect, calling "nice" rules had little effect. The boys blatantly continued to "slam" and "wing" the ball past them. Since the girls were still bound by their "nice" rules, which prohibited direct confrontation over such actions, there was little they could do. As play proceeded, however, the girls gradually abandoned some of the trappings of "nice" play. They began handling violations quite differently. The following are excerpts from fieldnotes. We begin with three girls and one boy on the court.

> Angie (the "king"): *"Rooie Rules. Rooie Rules."*
>
> Angie pauses, looks around, and then walks over to the players waiting in line to get into the game.
>
> Angie (to Rooie, who is waiting in line): *"Rooie, tell them your rules."*

As Angie returns to her square, she glares rather pointedly at Hoover, the boy who has just entered the game, while Rooie lists her rules.

(It should be noted that another understanding among these gamers is that players are only responsible for violating a rule they know about. Only if they know, and then violate, a rule can they be denied a takeover of the last round. This attempt to list very explicitly the rules in effect is highly unusual. It functions as a kind of warning to the offending players.)

A little later, Cindy (who is now the "king") calls: *"Rooie Rules."*

But Andy continues to "wing" and "slam" the ball consistently. After several such hits, Rooie, who is waiting in line, walks over to Andy's square.

Rooie (to Andy): *"You're out! Wings are out!"*

Cindy steps forward to back Rooie up.

Cindy (to Andy): *"I called Rooie Rules and there's no wings! You're out!"*

As Andy leaves the court he mumbles something about being a "fish."

The term "fish" refers to a scapegoated player. In over six months of observing this game, this was the first time the author had observed anyone being called out for "wings." The exchange above is a very significant departure from the usual patterns of play. Andy is well aware of this. He knows he's been had.

The girls' revenge was shortlived, however. In reacting to the boys' refusal to play "nice" by becoming more explicit in their calls of the rules, and by applying direct sanctions for violations, the girls began digging themselves into a rather deep hole. They expanded a call of "Rooie Rules," for example, to "Rooie rules. No slams. No wings. No rough stuff." They tried explicitly to prohibit each of the boys' offending actions. Naturally, the boys could always find actions the girls had not specifically prohibited. One particularly exasperated "king" recognized the problem when she tagged her call of the rules with, "And nothing you guys do!"

Of course, on the other side, the girls could not completely avoid violating their own rules, now differently defined. The boys were only too happy to point this out. Again, from fieldnotes, we start with four girls as active players on the court.

Angie ("the king"): *"Fair square. Rooie Rules. Fair square."*

(The call of "fair square" means no one should get anyone else out. It is a reference here to a desire to keep the girls in, and the boys out of the game.)

The boys waiting in line can be heard mumbling something about "holding."

In an unusual move, Angie stops the ball and turns to Sandy, a young and inexperienced player.

Angie: *"No holding, Sandy."*

She immediately puts the ball back into play.

More grumblings can be heard from the boys in line.

A little later in this round of play Andrea does a "double tap" before hitting the ball to the next player.

("Double taps" is a very common move, especially during a low pressure round like that framed by "fair square." It is a type of "fancy" move, in which the ball is tapped twice in the air before being hit to the next player.)

One of the boys in line immediately steps forward and shouts: *"Holding!"*

The other boys chime in, accusing Andrea and the other players of holding the ball, a move prohibited by Rooie Rules.

The girls on the court try to ignore the ruckus. They continue to play, as Angie (the "king") protests. *"They can't help it!"*

(The appeal here, of course, is to the "real" rule which makes reference to "purpose stuff," not to the act of "holding.")

The boys continue to complain. Angie finally turns to them and says: *"Okay, then. I call 'holding'."*

A little later Angie again calls: *"Rooie Rules."* But now she appends: *"And there's holding."*

Mike, one of the boys who at this time was playing regularly with the girls, shouts sarcastically: *"Ha! Ha! Ha! Ha!"*

Andy (rather pointedly): *"Did you call holds?"* Angie directs a withering glance at the boys, and starts the next round of play without comment.

The girls are trapped, and both they and the boys know it. The cornerstone of "Rooie Rules" is "no holding." The call of "Rooie Rules—and there's holding" is totally contradictory and unthinkable within the normal course of play. We have reached a point where the "ideal" logic of the game has been invoked, where rules have become rigidly pegged to player actions and game outcomes. In the process, the logic of the "real" rules has become paradoxical. The players have lost the leeway which allows the usual understanding that this "hold" is not the same as that "hold." The flow of the game, as these particular players constitute it, cannot survive such a rigid linking of rule and action.

Rules and Paradox

The kind of pickle the girls find themselves in looks suspiciously like the stuff of classical logical paradox (Bateson, 1972). They are left holding a bag very neatly labelled "no holding," and simultaneously tagged "this is holding" and "this is not holding." This is not normally paradoxical at all within the everyday logic of the game as these players constitute it, but it has become so in the confusion of action and rule. The philosophers might have helped them out by demonstrating that the problem is really one of propositions differing in order of abstraction, a simple error in logical typing. "Holding" and "nice" are not of the same logical order.

It's unlikely, of course, the players would find such an argument very persuasive or very relevant to their predicament, because they don't confuse the two in the normal course of events. All conversations with these children indicate a clear recognition of the difference between the way it's supposed to be in an ideal sense, and the way it is. The two are intricately and elaborately interwoven into a consistent and coherent framework which sustains the complex communal activity of Foursquare.

Some recognition that game rules and player actions, and the interpretive gaming scheme which binds them together, are of different orders may be more useful to us, as researchers, than to these players. In our thinking about games, we create our own paradox when we take the "play" out of games, the "fun" out of gaming, by treating a description of the game rules as descriptive of the activity or experience. Something of the same phenomenon seems to be at work, too, when we speak of games as frames, as though games frame activity, rather than gamers.

Games aren't much "fun" when rules, rather than relationships, dominate the activity, when there is no attention to "flow," "fairness," "respect" and "nice." We need the leeway to be playful in these relationships, to share and enjoy the performance that sneaks nastiness by as nice, that displays knowledge of the "ideal" rule and plays with the boundaries of the "real" rule. Taking the leeway out by treating all rules as rigidly prescriptive and tied to actions subordinates "fun," "flow," "spontaneous involvement" (Goffman, 1961) to the activity. In actual gaming, as Goldstein (1971) and Fine (in press) remind us, quite the opposite may be true.

Studies of this type suggest a number of assumptions about game rules that require active reconsideration. First, our thinking about rules in the games literature has been rather simplistic and monolithic. In other social science and philosophical traditions, the whole notion of a "rule" is considered to be highly problematic. Rules are assumed to be of many different types, multi-layered and hierarchical, referencing very different antecedents and outcomes. They are assumed to be subject to constant negotiation and reinterpretation in the course of everyday life. The current study, for example, suggests all rules are not equal and all players are not equal under the rules.

Second, because the activity is a game, we have tended to assume game rules are at all times explicit and foregrounded. We have taken for granted all debates and disputes concern the game, not the relationships among players. Observations of players, however, suggest the degree of rule explicitness may constantly shift, and such phenomena are highly contexted and indicative of social relationships among gamers (Erikson and Shultz, 1976, Shultz, 1976).

Finally, we might propose that the apparent paradoxes and transformations of "play" derive less from the logic of players than from the logic of our descriptions. Contradiction seems almost inevitable when we confuse the logic of the game and the logic of contexted gaming.

Epilogue

Just to close the story begun above, this particular gaming occasion broke down into one of the few complete stalemates observed over a period of several years. Whether a prohibited move had occurred or not simply could not be resolved by appeal. The girls refused to be "nice" and give an offending player, a boy, the benefit of the doubt, as they usually do by allowing him a "takeover." Just before the bell ending the recess period, we find Angie turning to one of the boys and suggesting the only acceptable mode of resolution: "Okay, we'll give you guys another chance. But only if you promise to be nice."

Note

An earlier version of this paper was presented to the Annual Meetings of The Association for the Anthropological Study of Play (TAASP), Fort Worth, Texas, April, 1981. The author wishes to thank Brian Sutton-Smith and Alexandra Hepburn for their very helpful comments on early drafts of the paper.

References

Avedon, E. M. and Sutton-Smith, B. *The Study of Games.* New York: John Wiley, 1971.

Bateson, G. *Steps to an Ecology of Mind.* New York: Ballantine, 1972.

Erikson, F., and Shultz, J. *Social Solidarity and Indexical Repair: Contexts, Forms and Functions of a Speech Act.* Unpublished Paper, Harvard Graduate School of Education, 1976.

Fine, G. A. *Fantasy Role-Play Gaming as a Social World: Imagination and the Social Construction of Play.* Paper presented to The Association for the Anthropological Study of Play, Ann Arbor, MI, April, 1980.

Fine, G. A. *The Ethnography of Fantasy.* Chicago, IL: University of Chicago Press, in press.

Goffman, E. *The Presentation of Self in Everyday Life.* Garden City, NY: Doubleday, 1959.

Goffman, E. *Encounters.* Indianapolis, IN: Bobbs-Merrill, 1961.

Goldstein, K. *Strategy in Counting out: An Ethnographic Folklore Field Study.* In E. M. Avedon and B. Sutton-Smith (eds.) The Study of Games. New York: John Wiley, 1971, 167–178.

Harré, R. Some remarks on 'rule' as a scientific concept. In T. Mischel (ed.),

Understanding Other Persons. Oxford: Blackwell, 1974, 143–184.

Schwartzman, H. *Transformations.* New York: Plenum, 1978.

Shultz, J. *It's Not Whether You Win or Lose, It's How You Play the Game.* Working paper #2. Cambridge, MA: Harvard Graduate School of Education, Newton Classroom Interaction Project, 1976.

Changing the Game

Bernard DeKoven

Context

*In 1968 the School District of Philadelphia hired me to write a curriculum for elementary school children. Although the original intention was a curriculum in theater, the curriculum I produced in 1971 was in children's games. In games, I found a form of theater that was native to childhood, universally—a theater of great social power and emotional depth, with an extensive repertoire. The curriculum was based on one single insight about games: it's a lot easier to change the game than it is to change the people who are playing it. It was this one observation that served as the basis for the training program I developed for the New Games Foundation, for the work I've done in game design and group facilitation, and most recently, my book **Junkyard Sports.** "Changing the Game" is a chapter from my book, **The Well-Played Game** (New York: Doubleday, 1978).*

Gaming the Game

The Game Design Process

Bernie DeKoven's lifelong belief that things can be made more fun led him to develop and implement new ways of playing. Projects include a curriculum in social games and a training program for the New Games Foundation, to computer games and classes in "Deep Fun" at the Esalen Institute, and, most recently, to a new approach to sports described in his book, *Junkyard Sports* (Human Kinetics Publishers, 2004).

We've seen that a game can change. We've seen that the very game we're playing can become something we never intended it to be.

We made the change. It changed because of the way we were playing it.

It changed for the worse when we lost control. We didn't just lose control, we actually surrendered it to other people with whom we weren't even playing. As a result, though we were all involved in the game as much as we possibly could be, none of us was able to enjoy it. We couldn't even see that it was just a game, that it wasn't for real, that we were only playing.

It changed for the better when we discovered a different source of control. When that kid took his chair with him during the game of musical chairs, he established for us all a new way of seeing the game we were playing together.

But suppose what we really want to do is to play a game together, and every time we think we understand what game we are playing, somebody changes it. Suppose we are feeling so playful that we destroy the game together. If that's what we want to do—destroy the game—then everything's fine. But suppose we really want to play a *game*.

An example:

We start out with a game of dodgeball. We've been playing it for about five minutes. We're beginning to get the sense of what it means to play it well. At the same time, we're not quite committed to the game—we're not really into it yet. You're an ender and you throw the ball at me. I catch it. Now, according to what we understand to be the rules of the game, we're supposed to trade roles. Since I caught the ball, I get rewarded. Since you didn't hit me, you get punished.

In a moment of high cuteness, I decide to keep the ball. I just stand there, holding the ball against my stomach. And then, as soon as I notice that other people have noticed, I run.

So, people start running after me. I dribble teasingly. I dash madly. I run circles. The chase is on.

Then, just as it seems we've agreed that we're playing some kind of chasing game, I throw the ball to you.

You're shocked, so you throw the ball back to me. I'm tired, so I throw the ball back to you. Then you notice that others have noticed, so you take the ball and run. And then, as soon as you see someone getting too close, you throw the ball back to me.

Ah, keep away. All right. Good game. But then, when somebody gets the ball, instead of throwing it or running with it, she lies on top of it.

People try to get it away from her. Other people try to keep them from getting close to her.

Another game. What game is it? I don't know, do you?

Somebody steps on somebody else's hand. Somebody else steps on somebody else's hair. Some people really want to get the ball back. They're serious. They really want to start a game. Others don't know what's happening. Others are laughing hysterically.

It's all play and no game, all release and no control. No one can find the center. We have lost all responsibility—to the game, to the community, to ourselves.

We are not playing well at all.

Of Play and Games

There is a very fine balance between play and game, between control and release, lightness and heaviness, concentration and spontaneity. The function of our play community is to maintain that balance, to negotiate between the game-as-it-is-being-played and the game-as-we-intend-it-to-be. It is for that reason that we maintain the community.

On the one hand we have the playing mind—innovative, magical, boundless. On the other is the gaming mind—concentrated, determined, intelligent. And on the hand that holds them both together we have the notion of playing well.

The Need for Change

The balance between the playing mind and the gaming mind is never at an equilibrium. There is a dynamic tension between these two—a dialog. Playing well means playing within that dialog.

So the definition of playing well is the result of an ongoing process of negotiation and renegotiation. It changes as we do, sometimes drastically, sometimes subtly.

Suppose we're playing a game of volleyball. We're playing the regulation game: teams, rotation, points. It just so happens that I'm getting a little tired of playing that way. Something has changed. I don't like the way I'm playing anymore.

I could just walk away from the game. There are boundaries, and I could just step outside if I wanted to. But we are playing with small teams. I would be missed. I owe it to my team to stick it out until the game is over.

At the same time, I know I'm not playing well. The game isn't feeling right for me. My mind is wandering. I'm missing. I'm thinking about taking a nap. I'm wondering if the net is too high for me to put my toes through. I'm watching the shadows play. In fact, I'm not only missing the ball, I'm missing altogether.

So, there are times when playing the game as it is being played is a violation of the convention of the play community. I'm actually, in some way, interfering with the intention of the community. I'm not even trying to play well.

Though it is only fair, in terms of the game we're playing, that I continue playing, that I stick it out until the very end—though it is not only fair but also, in terms of my commitment to the team, obligatory that I remain in the game—I am cheating the community by the way I'm playing. The game is small enough for me to be felt. The balance between the playing mind and the gaming mind, between me and the other players is sensitive enough to perceive the shift. I am causing it to wobble. People are trying to play around me. There is a hole where I stand that is draining energy from the game.

It therefore becomes incumbent on me to do something about it. I could announce my problem to others in the community, but that would stop the game. I could quit, but that would be unfair to my team.

I can only see two other possibilities: I could try to focus myself in some way so that I could get back into the game, or I could try to somehow change the game itself.

If I select the first alternative, no one needs to know about it. I can withdraw within myself and argue myself back into the game. I can instruct myself to focus on the ball, to watch the seams, to notice how the light hits it.

But it isn't working. I'm focusing so intently on the ball that I forget to hit it. Somehow, the inner balance is getting shakier and shakier.

This leaves me with only one alternative.

I recognize that it is not always appropriate to change the game. It requires a sensitivity to the needs of the community as well as to my own needs. I am not sure that I am able to be sensitive enough to anything.

This leaves me with no alternatives at all.

Finding Permission

I happen to notice that I did get more involved in the game when I was able to play close to the net. Perhaps my inner wanderings have something to do with the fact that I'm playing back.

During our next rotation, I go up to the net and ask if it's OK if I play there. Strangely enough, it is.

After all of this internal mishmosh, I discover that all I had to do was ask-that the permission was there all the time, and all I had to do was get it.

Here I was, trying to be so responsive to the needs of the community, and I totally forgot that the community we have created together was in response to the needs of each of us. My teammates knew that I was having trouble focusing on the game. It is in their own interest that I find the position that lets me play well.

Sure I can play front. Sure I can stay there as long as I need to. If it helps our game, why not?

The Bent Rule

We didn't really change a rule, we bent it. We made an exception, and it was clear to all of us that it was all right. If making an exception helps us have an exceptional game, anything is all right.

As the well-timed cheat helps restore the game to the players, the bent rule helps return the players to the game.

For example, suppose you're playing solitaire. Now you've gone through a modicum of effort to lay out the cards in their proper and officially authorized array. You have reached the point of play at which, though the game has been going for quite a while, you find you are about to lose. You almost won, but not quite.

Everyone knows that cheating at solitaire is an example of poor character. Even though there's no one around to call you on your cheating. Even though the only one you could possibly be cheating is yourself.

At this point in the game, either because of your highly evolved ability to rationalize, or because of your desire to see the game through, you decide to bend a rule. But, in order to maintain your sense of respectability, you decide to allow yourself only one small bend in one small rule. And then, if you still lose, you'll admit failure and pick up the cards and start all over again.

Now you're not doing a particularly admirable thing. You've admitted to yourself that, even if you win, you'll have won only because you cheated. Well, not cheated, exactly, but bent a rule. So in fact what you've done is to change the game. You're honest enough to admit to yourself that actually, in terms of the unchanging game, you have in fact lost. But, well, look at it this way: Now that you've lost, you can make up a new goal—how about seeing how long it takes to win? Maybe you'll have to bend a couple of rules. Maybe you'll even have to spindle, fold, and otherwise mutilate them, but, well, what does it matter now that you've lost?

So, you merely take the top card off the pile and place it underneath. Oh, joy! Behold what new possibilities have emerged!

The Borrowed Rule

If bending or breaking a rule is a bit too disturbing for the gaming mind to handle, we can employ a device which conforms a bit more at least to the letter of the law. We can borrow a rule from another game and attach it to ours.

After all, it's a real rule. It just wasn't part of the game when we started playing. But there's precedent.

Let's go back to your game of solitaire. As you know, there are many kinds of solitaire. In one kind, the rule is that you turn over every third card. In another, you turn over each card.

So, if turning over the third card, when you're playing a game like Canfield, is not yielding positive results, well then you can turn over every card, as in the game of Las Vegas solitaire, and see if that works.

Then, in some solitaires, you build up, in others, you build down. In some you play red on black, in others you play without regard to suit or color.

Thus, whenever another form of solitaire seems more advantageous to you, you simply switch to that form—announcing to yourself, of course, that you have in fact failed, and you're just employing this particular modification for the fun of it.

Sacredness

Rules are made for the convenience of those who are playing. What is fair at one time or in one game may be inhibiting later on. It's not the game that's sacred, it's the people who are playing.

It might have been true that, because of the way we were playing volleyball together, the rotation rule was superfluous. Suppose none of us cared what positions we were playing. Suppose the fact was that nobody wanted to stay in any particular position at all, that we were able to play together well enough no matter what position anyone held. Then, it's to no one's advantage to keep the rotation rule. Then, you might as well let me play where I want to play. Then we can all let each other play where we want to play.

Breaking or bending or borrowing a rule is only bad when we attempt to conceal it from each other or when it is done to the detriment of another player. When that happens, it's cheating for real. It violates not the sacredness of a rule but the spirit of the play community. Whenever we want to change the game, it's safest to make an open admission that that is what we're trying to do. Cheating for real is something that we try to conceal from each other. Telling each other helps keep the game in play.

It's just like Manny Kant used to say: "If I want to find out whether what I'm doing is OK, all I have to do is imagine what it would be like if everybody knew about it and did it too."

Bigger Changes

There are many rules and, in fact, quite a few conventions which can be changed without drastically changing the game.

For example, we could play volleyball with a somewhat larger or smaller ball. We could increase or decrease the number of players on a side. We could raise or lower the net. None of these changes would keep us from playing volleyball. Any of them could help us play a better game.

I am not advocating changing the game for the sake of novelty. I am not saying that it is better to change the game than to keep it the same. I am merely pointing out that there are times—more times than one would think—when it is remarkably useful to the community as a whole and to the players in particular to have the power to change some of the rules.

The efficacy of change is, once again, a question of timing. If the change comes out of a realization that the game, as we are playing it, is no longer appropriate—if it is unquestionably clear that we are either playing too much or gaming too much—the change will be accepted because the change is necessary.

If it is the right time, we can change anything.

We can make up any kind of rule that we want to. We could make the court three feet wide. We could play volleyball with balloons. We could give everybody a ball. We could play with two nets. With four nets. With a moving net. Without a net. We could play silently, in the dark, with a luminescent ball. We could play on the ice. There could be three teams. Four. One.

As long as we make sure that it is the right time and that everyone understands and agrees to the rules, we can do anything we want to and still be playing well. OK, we might not be playing *the* game. But there is no "*the* game" for a play community. Any game whatever, as long as we are playing it well, is *the* game.

Too Much Change

Then there is the time when we become so fascinated by our power to change the game that we tend to get carried away by it all. We become so intent on celebrating our newly regained authority that all we want to do is change rules. We never keep the same rule for longer than five minutes. We change everything: sides, scores, balls, language, clothes. You name it, we change it.

At the beginning it's cute. It feels good to have this power back. It feels good to know that we have permitted each other to use it. However, after a while it tends to get a little disorienting. We are so excited about finding out all the wonderful ways we can change a game that we suddenly, crashingly, become aware of the fact that we no longer have a game to play.

If we are in a good humor at that particular moment, then everything is wonderful and we are restored. Maybe we will all go for a swim or something. Maybe we are actually able to settle on a particular variation and play it without changing anything.

If, on the other hand, one or several or all of us are not in such a state of willing hilarity, we could wind up without a community. It could happen. It has happened. A few of us feel, each, individually, that everybody else knows what's happening and we don't. We could feel that things have gotten out of hand, that people are being too silly. We could feel that we are somehow being attacked by all this wonderfulness.

We want to play, but we can find nothing solid to play with. There is no game for us to play. So we lose contact. We lose our sense of control. With loss of control goes loss of safety. With loss of safety goes loss of the willingness to play. Without the willingness to play, there is no play community.

Restoring Balance

When we come back to the realization that the point of changing the game is so that we can play it well together, we discover that this is a more delicate task than keeping a game going, which, in turn, is a more delicate task than finding one to start with. The balance grows ever finer.

Analogy: Think of a game as a sensitive instrument—a microscope, maybe. We can put anything at all, as long as it's small enough, under that microscope. Under low power we

525

can see broad terrains. This is fascinating. We want to see them in greater detail. But as we increase the power of our microscope, we discover that it becomes more difficult to find the proper focus.

Another analogy: One knob turns the TV on. Another knob selects the channel. A third one is for fine tuning. If you don't know how to work the knobs, you're not going to get the picture you're looking for.

The change thing can go too far. Eventually, we wind up totally unwilling to change the game any more. And then we go about trying to figure out how we can change the people who are playing it.

We have not only gone too far, we have gone completely off.

If anything needs change, it is much more logical to change the game than it is to change the people who are playing.

It is logical because the game isn't for real. It's something made up. It's something made up for the sake of those who are playing.

It's not only more logical, it's even wiser. If we all agree to change the game, the worst that can happen is that we'll wind up with a lousy game. But if our purpose becomes to change each other.... Frankly, I'd rather not even think about it.

So let us say that our play community has proclaimed a new morality, and inscribed in gold on our flag is the motto IF YOU CAN'T PLAY IT CHANGE IT, and woven into our banner are the words IF IT HELPS, CHEAT.

Now we find ourselves with an amazing, almost overwhelming freedom. We can change anything. Yes, there are regulations, but we are the ones who make them. There is no other authority than ours. We are the officials.

If we weren't so sure of our commonality—if we had any doubt about the objective, which we all share, of finding a game we can play well together—we simply couldn't handle all this freedom. We would get lost in it. We would take things personally.

Changing the game is the most delicate of all the things we're doing together. When we play a proven game—a game that has been played before—we are presented with a system of rules that has a balance of its own. Even if we ourselves have never played that game before, if the game is, officially, a game that works, we begin playing it with the knowledge that it is fair. We know that there are reasons for the rules.

Suppose we're playing tic-tac-toe. Maybe this is the first time we've played it. We don't really have to ask why we should be trying to get three instead of two or four in a row. We could try it that way, but ordinarily we wouldn't. We play the game according to its rules because we believe that the rules have been all thought out—that if we tried playing for two or four in a row the game wouldn't play well, we wouldn't be able to play it well together.

It just so happens that we are right. Tic-tac-toe doesn't work if we try for two in a row. Well, yes, we did try it. Curiosity, you know. But the first player always won. That wasn't very much fun—especially for the second player. But even for the first player as well: Who wants to play a game that you win before you start? Call that fun? Call that a well-played game?

So it seems to us that the game has been all figured out already—that every rule is what it should be. It's true. The game is as it should be. But it might also be the case that we aren't playing it well. That, in fact, we should change something about the game.

What would happen if we changed one of the rules?

We would definitely disturb the balance of the game. We would probably have to change other rules to restore it.

So we're on very shaky ground. Once we begin to change a rule, the only framework that is keeping us together is our intention to play well. Suppose it happens that you, playful person that you are, completely assured that you've no other goal than playing well and joyously—suppose it happens that you begin to wonder about my motivations. Maybe all I really want to do is beat you. Maybe that's why I'm so interested in changing the rules. I mean, what makes you so sure that I'm that community-minded?

All of which is to say that we cannot even begin to explore ways of changing the game until we are certain that we share the intention to play well together. This certainty is not found in the rules of any game. It lies in the nature of the relationship we are able to build with each other—in the establishment and the continual reaffirmation of our intention of playing well. It is found and maintained through the conventions of the play community.

But we have already played together enough to know that the game isn't really so very important.

Let's go back to tic-tac-toe. We now know how it's supposed to be played. We've played it many times. We know that we can play it well. We also know that the game isn't very interesting anymore. We've figured it out. When we play, the first player either wins or ties.

527

But we're interested in playing some tic-tac-toe-like game. We have pencils and plenty of paper. Rather than try to invent a new game, we decide that it would be easiest to start with one we already know.

Let's look at some of the things that we can change.

First of all, we know that the grid looks like this:

We also know that we could change how it looks. We could make it bigger or smaller or any way we wanted to:

Granted, if we get too creative with the grid designs, we'll wind up with something beautiful to behold but impossible to play with. Further granted, whatever way we change the grid, we're going to have to change other rules to restore the balance of the game. So maybe first we should take a look at the rules and get some sense of the range available to us.

One rule we know about is that the game is supposed to end when somebody gets three in a row. We could easily change that. We could make it four in a row, or five, or a hundred. Then we'd get to use the bigger grid. But how big should we make it? We'll have to play with it for a while to find out.

Or, maybe we'd like something other than a row. A circle maybe. How about three touching each other? Or four? Or how about four opposite each other?

There's a lot to explore. Maybe too much already. Maybe we should stop and just play with what we've already discovered. Let's see what the changes do. Let's see which changes we like best.

Well, we can always do that later. This is fun. Let's see what else we can change.

The rule is that whoever gets three in a row first is the winner. We could change the part about being first. We could say that whoever gets three in a row second is the winner. Why not? Maybe it'd be more fun that way. Maybe we could play better that way.

Then there's the rule about the tie game. Who says the tie game means that nobody wins? Maybe we both should win. Would that work? Would it still be fun?

Actually, I remember reading in one of my books on games about a version of tic-tac-toe called "Old Nick." This is the way it is played: Whenever a game is tied, the points go to Old Nick, and the next player to win also wins all of Old Nick's points. Sounds good. Sounds like it would add a tension that tic-tac-toe is lacking. Or maybe we could see if, at the end of twenty games, say, Old Nick has more points than either of us, and, if he does, then we would have both lost to him. Interesting, maybe.

Any other rules?

Well, how about the rule that you use X and O? Maybe we could use I and U. Of course, that wouldn't change the game any. We can really use any symbols that we want to as long as we can tell them apart. We could use colors instead of symbols. It wouldn't make a difference, really.

Maybe we like the way the game looks more when we use colors than when we use letters. That's reason enough to try it. Except that what we want to do is change the game so that we can play it better. And changing the symbols isn't enough of a change. It's interesting, though, that we can change some of the rules and not change the game at all.

So let's look for rules to change that really make a difference, that will really help us find the right game.

How about the rule that says you're supposed to draw a line through your three letters to prove that you've got three in a row? It helps us make sure that a win is really a win. But the strategies would be the same whether or not we use that rule.

So, to make the game different, to change it significantly, we have to find a rule to change that will result in a change of strategies.

I've got one that might prove drastic enough: the rule that you take turns.

Suppose I got two turns and then you got two turns. Would that foster the development of new strategies?

Do you have to take your turn? Could you pass? Would you ever find it strategically useful to pass?

What would happen if there were already some letters on the grid before the game started? The rule is that we start with an empty board. It is the rule, really, even if it's one we ordinarily take for granted. But suppose, even before the game began, there was an X in one corner and an O in the corner diagonally opposite? That'd be a real change, maybe.

Then there's the rule that we only use one kind of letter each. I mean, if I use X, I can't use Z too. Or maybe I could.

Maybe we could both use Z whenever we wanted to. Then we'd each have two letters to choose from. Sounds interesting, no? Maybe the Z could be a neutral letter, one that neither of us could use except to block someone? Or how about using the Z as a temporary block and saying that we could use that space for one of our letters only after a complete turn has passed?

What would happen if we could use each other's letters? That'd mean that either of us could win with an X or an O as long as that move completed a three in a row.

Actually, I've already tried that variation and it really makes for an interesting game. I play it just like tic-tac-toe, keeping all the other rules the same except for the one about whose marks are whose. I call this game "hypocrite." By giving it a name, I help officialize it. No, it's not tic-tac-toe we're playing, it's a much more sophisticated game called hypocrite.

How about the rule that you can't move a letter once it's been put down? Well, it's obvious that if we use paper and pencil to play the game and we allow each other to move letters around, we're going to wind up with a paper full of holes. After all, there are only so many times you can erase before you discover you're beginning to erase the table instead of what's left of the paper.

So who says that we have to play with paper and pencil? We could make a grid out of wood if we wanted to. We could make pieces. Then we could really get things moving.

And then we could make a larger grid. How about a star-shaped grid? And then we could change the idea of getting three in a row to getting all your pieces on a star point. And then we could change the name of the game to something really official sounding, like Chinese checkers.

OK, before we get much further into this, let's extrapolate. It seems that there are rules which guide how we can change rules. Some of these are merely pragmatic. Others are a bit closer to conventional.

General Definition of a Changed Game:

A variation which requires the development of a new strategy.

General Purpose for Changing a Game:

The one you're playing is no longer giving you enough of a challenge for you to feel you want to play it well. You can play it well, but you're losing interest. Your gaming mind is bored. You're not playing the way you want to be playing. Or, vice versa, you can't play it well, the challenge is too big, your playing mind is overwhelmed, the game is too hard. The general purpose for changing a game, therefore, is to restore equilibrium.

Specific Recommendation for Technique:

Change one rule at a time. Change the rule and see what happens to the rest of the game. See what other changes you have to make in order to restore the balance. If you try to change too many rules, and the game doesn't work, you won't be able to tell why.

Universal Definition of the Working Game:

What you are experiencing wellness in.

Another Specific Recommendation:

There are more rules than you realize. Many of them belong to a larger convention rather than a specific game. All of them can be changed. Some are subtle and take a long time to find. Cheat and see if anybody notices. Cheat openly so everyone can see it. If you think it's a rule but you're not sure, see what happens when you break it.

To Bear in Mind:

The reason you're changing the game. You're not changing the game for the sake of changing it. You're changing it for the sake of finding a game that works.

Once this freedom is established, once we have established why we want to change a game and how we go about it, a remarkable thing happens to us: We become the authorities.

No matter what game we create, no matter how well we are able to play it, it is our game, and we can change it when we need to. We don't need permission or approval from anyone outside our community. We play our games as we see fit.

Which means that now we have at our disposal the means whereby we can always fit the game to the way we want to play.

This is an incredible freedom, a freedom that does more than any game can, a freedom with which we nurture the play community. The search for the well-played game is what holds the community together. But the freedom to change the game is what gives the community its power.

This is a freedom which only works well as long as we don't *have* to use it. We need to know that we can change the game when we need to. We also need to know when we need to change the game.

So, like everything else we've looked at in the pursuit of the well-played game, changing a game only works sometimes. It can work against us as well as for us. It can confuse as well as clarify, destroy as well as empower. Only if the intention to play well is clearly, undeniably established and shared, only as long as that holds true does the play community hold true.

Handicapping

Another thing that might stand between us and the well-played game is our refusal to acknowledge our differences.

The game that I play well may not be the same that you play well. Your experience of wellness might be different from mine. We can acknowledge and validate the well-played game as it is experienced by each of us. But when we wish to play well together, we must discover the game that works for all of us.

Even though I'm playing as hard as I can, I'm not playing well. Even though I'm as focused as I can be, you're playing with an ease and a sense of mastery that is unavailable to me at this time in this game. I don't know the game as well as you do. I am not as familiar with its subtleties. You find yourself playing well, but the game we are playing together is not a well-played game.

We can look for another game—one with which we're both equally familiar. We could change the game we're playing. We could find other people to play with.

But suppose this particular game is the one we both want to play. I am as fascinated by the potential I am discovering in myself for playing this game well as you are fascinated by the excellence that you are able to manifest through this game. Can we find a way to play it well together? Can we make it even somehow—the challenge, the sense of play, the opportunity to play well?

Of course we can. We've already done it. When we were playing Ping-Pong together and we discovered, eventually, that in order for us to play this game well together you had to play with the wrong hand. That was the first step.

You gave yourself a handicap. You changed your criterion for playing the game well so that we could find a way of playing it well together. You found a way to make the game as new to you as it was to me.

As we play any one game, and play it repeatedly, with different people, we become more and more familiar with how we are when we are playing well. As we become more familiar with how we are, we become clearer about the sense of wellness that we are able to experience and manifest in the game. We are able to extend that experience with the game until we have reached such a stage of mastery that, assuming we have found someone who has reached a similar mastery, we can play well consistently, from the beginning to the end of the game. We may not be as "good" as a professional, but we do, in fact, delight in the way we are able to play.

Suppose I can play checkers well. We play together and discover that I am able to play well more often than you are. We play a game together and I win. You have momentary flashes of insight. I have a steady light of understanding. I see combinations that you don't. Just when you're sure something is about to happen and you've prepared yourself fully for it, I surprise you with something else. When the game ends, I have four pieces on the board and you have none.

What would happen if, next time we played together, I started the game with four fewer pieces?

I'd be a little less familiar with the game than I was before. I am less certain of the strategies that will work best under these conditions. I know that I won't be able to use the same opening. The game is newer to me. I won't be able to play it well the way I was able to play it well before. But it is now more likely that we will be able to play it well together.

Handicapping is used in order to equalize familiarity—to restore the balance between the different players' skills and understanding of the game. It is another evolution of the concept of fairness, stemming from a deeper understanding of the nature of the play community and its intention of playing well together.

Before we assumed a handicap, we were already playing fairly. We abided by the same set of rules. Neither of us cheated. But now the kind of fairness we are seeking is one that will assure both of us access to a well-played game.

Once we begin our exploration of handicapping, the possibilities for making the game work are again endless. If you play that well, and I don't, maybe you'd like to try it blindfolded? Maybe you can give me three free moves during the game? Or more if I need them? Maybe I can take a move back?

The convention of "no takebacks" has been helpful to us before. It has helped each of us become more familiar with the nature of the game. We have to deliberate more, to be more cautious. We have to be sure, before we make a move, that it is the move we really want to make. We have to plan ahead enough to see the implications of a move.

We have known, in our past experience of the game, too much sloppiness. Suppose, after you make your move, I deliberate for a while. It has opened up several possibilities, and I have to see which one is best. I enjoy this experience of deliberation. Then, just before I make my move, you want to take yours back. Now I have to deliberate all over again. I don't enjoy deliberation that much! At first, I find this effort, though slightly unsatisfying, not too much of a distraction. After a while, however, I find that my ability to sense the game is suffering. I have to plan also for the next event in which you decide to take your move back. So I'm slowed down. My opportunity to play well is slowed down. And finally I say, "Look, from now on, once you take your finger off the piece, your turn is over, OK?" I say that to you calmly, openly. If I have to say it again, I will be significantly less calm.

Thus the convention of no takebacks becomes part of the way in which we perceive the game. It becomes a convention to which we always adhere. On the other hand, it might just happen that, because of the differences between us, that convention would stand in the way of our having the opportunity to play well together. Suppose that we could play better if we both had the opportunity to take moves back?

Yes, it's not like life. In life, it doesn't seem that one can take a move back very easily. But we're only playing. We aren't ready to make the game that lifelike. Later, maybe, when we're both more familiar with how we play well together, we can up the stakes to make the game more interesting.

Absolute mastery over a game usually results in loss of interest. When we become too familiar with a game, we tend to drop it; like tic-tac-toe, it becomes too predictable.

In handicapping one or some of us so that we can all play well together, we are not, in fact, negatively affecting anyone's experience of the well-played game. Even though you, master that you are, have accepted a handicap, you are still playing well. You might not be as familiar with the game as you were, but that is as it should be, because we're playing together, and the game, whatever form it takes, is a result of how we are able to combine. It has nothing to do with trying to find out which one of us plays better. The focus is on how we play well, together.

The purpose of a handicap is not to limit anyone's access to playing well but rather to restore the challenge to all players. When you accept a handicap, you aren't holding back anything—you're increasing your-challenge, and addressing yourself to the challenge we have set before us as a play community.

When I'm playing with my children, I am aware how important it is to them that they have as much chance to win as I do. We all want the game to be fair. We all want to play as hard as we can so that we can experience playing well together.

Sometimes I wind up playing the game blindfolded, with my hands behind my back, while standing on one leg. Other times, I simply start off with a few checkers more.

We have found that it violates our mutual sense of fair play if I let them win. They know that I am playing poorly for their sake. Even though they enjoy winning, they get upset when they understand that I have held back. Even though it was for their sake that I wasn't playing as well as I could. Even though my intentions were parentally pure. The fact is that by letting them win I deprived us all of the opportunity to play well together.

Better that I handicap myself than handicap our opportunity to share a well-played game.

The Score

Still another thing that we can change so that we can keep our game going well is what we give each other points for.

I don't think it will come as a shock to you to discover that you can play any game with or without score. Sometimes, as we've already found out, the best way for us to play Ping-Pong is just to volley. We could, if we wanted to, keep track of how many times we hit the ball. That could be our score, if we wanted one.

Obviously we could play tennis the same way we played Ping-Pong.

Usually, however, what happens after we volley with someone is that one of us sooner or later says, "OK, let's play the game." Which means: This volleying around was all well and good, but it was only a warm-up. Sure, the goal is to play well together. Sure, we can volley forever. But neither of us was playing very well. We were losing our focus—not really playing hard at all. So let's make it interesting again. Let's play for score.

Keeping track of the score doesn't make tennis into tennis. We can be playing without score. But part of tennis as we've come to understand it is in trying to make the other player miss. It increases the challenge because it makes us each try to be everywhere. You want to be as attentive, as present as I do. By trying to make each other miss we provide each other an invitation to awareness. We are saying, "Look, you want to be fully present, you want to be in a state of complete responsiveness and control, so see if you can get this one." Because that challenge is what we are asking from each other, because it helps each of us to experience playing well, it is right and good that I reward you with a point because you gave me a shot I couldn't return.

On the other hand, there are times when that kind of challenge is not what we need from each other in order to reach the well-played game together. There are times when the score becomes too important and we lose our focus on the game. There are times when we are giving each other points for things that are hurting our game.

Yes, when we're just volleying we're really playing a different game. It might be confusing to call it tennis. But, if what we intended to do was volley, if we found that well-played game by just volleying, then that's what we should be giving each other points for—keeping it going—even if we don't call the game tennis.

There's a tendency, as we begin to make things official, to think that only one particular form of a game is the real game. The fact is, any game we're playing is a real game. That's the fact. After all, the only thing that makes a game real is that there are people playing it.

But because we want to keep things clear, let's call tennis tennis and let's call our game something else. We can call it "volleytennis," "untennis," "cooperative tennis," "Chinese tennis"—we could even call it "flurtch" or "gronker" or "smunk." You don't change a game by giving it a different name. You give a game a different name because you're playing it a different way.

It's really amazing how much a game changes, how different it becomes, when you change what you are scoring for.

Let's score each other for bravery. Whenever either of us clearly risks limb, if not life, in the attempt to return a shot, that player, whether or not she actually succeeds in returning the ball, gets a point.

Let's score each other for grace, flow, harmony, endurance, agility. Let's score ourselves.

It all comes down to this: What do we want to get points for?

And then we discover that we can get points for anything. Anything. And each time we choose to score for something else, we change the game.

So, how about this: Maybe, since this is my first time playing, maybe I should get twice as many points for making the shot. Who says that everybody should get the same number of points for making it? Not me. I didn't say it.

The Drastic Change

And then, of course, there is the possibility that, though we can change the game infinitely, though we can constantly and continuously find ways we can make the game work, what we need to be doing is something else all together. That what we need to do, in fact, is forget the whole thing.

The Design Evolution of Magic: The Gathering

Richard Garfield

Context

I wrote the original Magic design notes shortly after Magic was published. I felt an urgency to document the development of Magic like I have seldom felt before—there were so many people and ideas and events woven around these years that I knew would quickly slip from memory. I was aware that over the following years my thoughts on what made a good trading card game, and the design principles of games had evolved, so when interest was shown in my original design notes it seemed like a good opportunity to try and add that decade of perspective to the original document. The updated version of this essay was first published in **Game Design Workshop,** *by Tracy Fullerton, Christopher Swain, and Steven Hoffman (published 2004, CMP Books). It is reprinted here with permission.*

The Game Design Process

Game Economies

Richard was teaching at Whitman College for his second year after completing his Ph.D. in Mathematics at the University of Pennsylvania, when his first game, Magic: The Gathering was published. The game was the first trading card game, which has since become an industry of its own. Since then he has published many other trading card games, as well as board and card games.

Magic: The Gathering is one of the most important and influential games of our time. It was an instant hit when it first appeared at the Gen Con game convention in 1993 and has grown steadily in popularity since. This is a special two-part look at the creation and development of the game as written by the designer, Richard Garfield. Richard wrote the first part "The Creation of Magic: The Gathering" nearly 10 years ago when the game was first released. In it he muses about the design challenges of a collectable trading card game and he recounts the game's fascinating playtest history. The second part "Magic Design: A Decade Later" is a retrospective on the original design notes. In it Richard provides insight about how and why the game has evolved the way it has—including thoughts on today's Magic Pro Tour, Magic Online, and the next ten years for the game.

The Creation of Magic: The Gathering—Notes from the Designer (written 1993)

The Ancestry of Magic

Games evolve. New ones take the most loved features of earlier games and add original characteristics. The creation of Magic: The Gathering is a case in point.

Though there are about a dozen games that have directly influenced Magic in one way or another, the game's most influential ancestor is a game for which I have no end of respect: Cosmic Encounter, originally published by Eon Products and re-released by Mayfair Games. In this game, participants play alien races striving to conquer a piece of the universe. Players can attempt their conquest alone, or forge alliances with other aliens. There are nearly fifty alien races which can be played, each of which has a unique ability: the Amoeba, for example, has the power to Ooze, giving it unlimited token movement; the Sniveler has the power to Whine, allowing it to automatically catch up when behind. The best thing about Cosmic Encounter is precisely this limitless variety. I have played hundreds of times and still can be surprised at the interactions different combinations of aliens produce. Cosmic Encounter remains enjoyable because it is constantly new.

Cosmic Encounter proved to be an interesting complement to my own design ideas. I had been mulling over a longtime idea of mine: a game that used a deck of cards whose composition changed between rounds. During the course of the game, the players would add cards to and remove cards from the deck, so that when you played a new game it would have an entirely different card mix. I remembered playing marbles in elementary school, where each player had his own collection from which he would trade and compete. I was also curious about Strat-o-matic™ Baseball, in which participants draft, field, and compete their own teams of baseball players, whose abilities are based on real players' previous year statistics. Intrigued by the structure of the game, I was irritated that the subject was one for which I had no patience.

These thoughts were the essence of what eventually became Magic. My experiences with Cosmic Encounter and other games inspired me to create a card game in 1982 called Five Magics. Five Magics was an attempt to distill the modularity of Cosmic Encounter down to just a card game. The nature of Cosmic Encounter seemed entirely appropriate for a magical card game—wild and not entirely predictable, but not completely unknown, like a set of forces you almost, but don't quite, understand. Over the next few years, Five Magics went on to inspire entirely new magical card games among my friends.

Ten years later, I was still designing games, and Mike Davis and I had come up with a board game called RoboRally. Mike was acting as our agent, and among the companies he approached was a brand-new gaming company called Wizards of the Coast. Things seemed to be going well, so that August, Mike and I made our way to Portland, Oregon to meet over a pizza with Peter Adkison and James Hays of Wizards of the Coast.

Both Peter and James were very receptive to RoboRally, but informed me that they weren't really in a position to come out with a board game right away. This wasn't what I had come out to hear, of course, but I didn't want the trip to be a total waste. I asked Peter what he would be interested in. Peter replied that he really saw a need for a game that could be played quickly with minimal equipment, a game that would go over well at conventions. Could I do it?

Within a few days, the initial concept for a trading card game was born, based on another card game I had developed in 1985 called Safecracker. It hadn't been one of my best games. But then I remembered Five Magics.

The First Designs
I went back to graduate school at the University of Pennsylvania, and worked on the card game in whatever spare time I had. It wasn't easy; there were three months of false starts on

the project, there are so many aspects of card game design that have to be reconsidered when designing trading card games. First of all, you can't have any bad cards—people wouldn't play with them. In fact, you want to prevent too much range in the utility of cards because players will only play with the best—why make cards people won't play with? Besides, homogeneity of card power is the only way to combat the "rich kid syndrome" that threatened the game concept from the start. What was to keep someone from going out and getting ten decks and becoming unbeatable?

It was a major design concern. I had numerous theories on how to prevent purchasing power from unbalancing the game, none of which were entirely valid but all of which had a grain of truth. The most compelling counter to this "buy-out-the-store" strategy was the ante. If we were playing for ante, the argument ran, and your deck was the distilled fruit of ten decks, when I did win, I would win a more valuable card. Also, if the game had enough skill, then the player purchasing their power would surely be easy prey for the players dueling and trading their way to a good deck. And of course there was the sentiment that buying a lot of poker chips doesn't make you a winner. In the end, however, the "rich kid syndrome" became less of a concern. Magic is a fun game, and it doesn't really matter how you get your deck. Playtesting showed that a deck that is too powerful defeats itself. On the one hand, people stopped playing against it for ante unless a handicap was invoked; on the other, it inspired them to assemble more effective decks in response.

The first Magic release was affectionately named Alpha. It consisted of 120 cards split randomly between two players. The two players would ante a card, fight a duel over the ante, and repeat until they got bored. They often took a long time to get bored; even then, Magic was a surprisingly addictive game. About ten o'clock one evening, Barry "Bit" Reich and I started a game in the University of Pennsylvania Astronomy lounge, a windowless, air-conditioned room. We played continuously until about 3:00am—at least that's what we thought, until we left the building and found that the sun had risen.

I knew then that I had a game structure that could support the concept of individually owned and tailored decks. The game was quick, and while it had bluffing and strategy, it didn't seem to get bogged down with too much calculation. The various combinations that came up were enjoyable and often surprising. At the same time, the variety of card combinations didn't unbalance the game: when a person started to win, it didn't turn into a landslide.

From Alpha to Gamma

Except for the card mix, little has changed about Magic since Alpha. In Alpha, walls could attack, and losing all your lands of a particular color destroyed the associated spells in play, but otherwise, the rules are much the same now as they were in the early stages of playtesting.

Moving from Alpha to the Beta version was like releasing a wild animal. The enjoyable game that was Alpha now burst the confines of the duel to invade the lives of the participants. Players were free to trade cards between games and hunt down weaker players to challenge them to duels, while gamely facing or cravenly avoiding those who were more powerful. Reputations were forged—reputations built on anything from consistently strong play to a few lucky wins to good bluffing. The players didn't know the card mix, so they learned to stay on their toes during duels. Even the most alert players would occasionally meet with nasty surprises. This constant discovery of unknown realms in an uncharted world gave the game a feeling of infinite size and possibility.

For the Gamma version, new cards were added and many of the creature costs were increased. We also doubled the pool of playtesters, adding in a group with Strat-o-matic Baseball experience. We were particularly anxious to find out if Magic could be adapted for league play. Gamma was also the first version, which was fully illustrated. Skaff Elias was my art director: he and others spent days poring over old graphic magazines, comic books, and game books searching for art for the cards. These playtest decks were pretty attractive for crummy black-and-white cardstock photocopies. For the most part, the cards were illustrated with serious pictures, but there were a lot of humorous ones as well. Heal was illustrated by Skaff's foot. Power Sink showed Calvin (of "Calvin and Hobbes") in a toilet; after all, what is a toilet but a power sink? Berserk was John Travolta dancing in Saturday Night Fever. Righteousness pictured Captain Kirk, and Blessing showed Spock doing his "live long and prosper" gesture. An old comic book provided a Charles Atlas picture for Holy Strength, and a 98-pound weakling getting sand kicked in his face for Weakness. Instill Energy was Richard Simmons. The infamous Glasses of Urza were some X-ray glasses we found in a catalog. Ruthy Kantorovitz constructed a darling flame-belching baby for Firebreathing. I myself had the honor of being the Goblins. The pictures and additional players greatly added to the game atmosphere. It became clear that while the duels were for two players, the more players playing, the better the game was. In some sense, the individual duels were a part of a single, larger game.

Striking the Balance

Each playtest set saw the expulsion of certain cards. One type of card that was common in Alpha and Beta was rare in Gamma, and is now nonexistent: the type that made one of your rival's cards yours. Yes, Control Magic used to permanently steal a creature from your opponent. Similarly, Steal Artifact really took an artifact. Copper Tablet no longer even remotely resembles its original purpose, which was to swap two creatures in play. ("Yes, I'll swap my Merfolk for your Dragon. On second thought, make that my Goblins—they're uglier.") There was a spell, Planeshift, which stole a land, and Ecoshift, which collected all the lands, shuffled them and re-dealt them—really nice for the user of four or five colors of magic. Pixies used to be a real pain—if they hit you, you swapped a random card from your hand with your opponent. These cards added something to the game, often in the form of players trying to destroy their own creatures before their opponents took them for good, or even trying to take their own lives to preserve the last shreds of their decks. However, in the end it was pretty clear that the nastiness this added to the game environment wasn't worth the trouble, and no card should ever be at risk unless players choose to play for ante.

It was around this time that I began to realize that some players would oppose almost any decision made about the game, often vehemently. The huge amount of dissent about what should and should not be part of the card mix has led players to make their own versions for playtesting—a significant task that involves designing, constructing, shuffling, and distributing about 4000 cards. Each of these games had its merits, and the playtesters enjoyed discovering the quirks and secrets of each new environment. The results of these efforts will form the basis of future Deckmaster games that use the structure of The Gathering, while containing mostly new cards.

To Build a Better Deck

Playtesting a Deckmaster game is difficult. Probably the only games harder to playtest are elaborate, multi-player computer games. After developing a basic framework for Magic that seemed fairly robust, we had to decide which of the huge selection of cards to include, and with what relative frequencies. Common cards had to be simple, but not necessarily less powerful, than rare cards—if only rare cards were powerful, players would either have to be rich or lucky to get a decent deck. Sometimes a card was made rare because it was too powerful or imbalancing in large quantities, but more often, rare cards were cards that were intricate or specialized—spells you wouldn't want many of anyway. But these design guidelines only got us so far. The whole game's flavor could change if a handful of seemingly innocent cards were eliminated, or even made less or more common. When it came down to actually deciding what to include and what to do without, I began to feel like a chef obliged to cook a dish for 10,000 people using 300 ingredients.

One thing I knew I wanted to see in the game was a player using multicolor decks. It was clear that a player could avoid a lot of problems by stripping down to a single color. For this reason, many spells were included that paralyzed entire colors, like Karma, Elemental Blast, and the Circles of Protection. The original plan was to include cards that thwarted every obvious simple strategy, and, in time, to add new cards which would defeat the most current ploys and keep the strategic environment dynamic. For example, it was obvious that relying on too many big creatures made a player particularly vulnerable to the Meekstone, and a deck laden with Fireballs and requiring lots of mana could be brought down with Manabarbs. Unfortunately, this strategy and counter-strategy design led to players developing narrow decks and refusing to play people who used cards that could defeat them flat out. If players weren't compelled to play a variety of players and could choose their opponent every time, a narrow deck was pretty powerful.

Therefore, another, less heavy-handed way to encourage variety was developed. We made it more difficult to get all the features a player needs in a deck by playing a single color. Gamma, for example, suffered from the fact that blue magic could stand alone. It was easily the most powerful magic, having two extremely insidious common spells (Ancestral Memory and Time Walk), both of which have been made rare. It had awesome counterspell capabilities. It had amazing creatures, two of the best of which are now uncommon.

Blue magic now retains its counterspell capability, but is very creature poor, and lacks a good way to do direct damage. Red magic has little defense, particularly in the air, but has amazing direct damage and destruction capability. Green magic has an abundance of creatures and mana, but not much more. Black is the master of anti-creature magic and has some flexibility, but is poorly suited to stopping non-creature threats. White magic is the magic of protection, and the only magic with common banding, but has little damage-dealing capability.

Sometimes seemingly innocuous cards would combine into something truly frightening. A good part of playtest effort was devoted to routing out the cards that contributed to so-called "degenerate" decks—the narrow, powerful decks that are difficult to beat and often boring to play with or against. Without a doubt, the most striking was Tom Fontaine's "Deck of Sooner-Than-Instant Death," which was renowned for being able to field upwards of eight large creatures on the second or third turn. In the first Magic tournament, Dave "Hurricane" Pettey walked to victory with his "Land Destruction Deck." (Dave also designed a deck of Spectres, Mindtwists, and Disrupting Sceptres that was so gruesome I don't think anyone was ever really willing to play it.) Skaff's deck, "The Great White Death," could outlive just about anything put up against it. Charlie Catin's "Weenie Madness" was fairly effective at swamping the opponent with little creatures. Though this deck was probably not in the high-win bracket of the previous decks, it was recognized that, playing for ante, Charlie could hardly lose. Even winning only one in four of his games—and he could usually do better than that—the card he won could be traded back for the island and the two Merfolk he lost, with something extra thrown in.

After the pursuit of sheer power died down, another type of deck developed: the Weird Theme deck. These decks were usually made to be as formidable as possible within the constraints of their theme. When Bit grew bored of his "Serpent Deck" (he had a predilection for flopping a rubber snake on the playing surface and going "SsssSssSs" whenever he summoned a Serpent), he developed his "Artifact Deck," which consisted of artifacts only—no land. It was fun to see the "Artifact Deck" go up against someone who used Nevinyrral's Disk. But the king of weird decks was, without a doubt, Charlie Catin. In one league, he put together a deck that I call "The Infinite Recursion Deck." The idea was to set up a situation where his opponent couldn't attack him until Charlie could play Swords to Plowshares on a creature. Then he would play Timetwister, causing the cards in play to be shuffled with the graveyard, hand, and library to form a fresh library. Swords to Plowshares actually removes a creature from the game, so his rival has one less creature. Repeat. After enough iterations, his rival was bloated with life given by the Swords to Plowshares, having maybe 60 life points, but there were no creatures left in his deck. So Charlie's Elves started in—59 life, 58 life, 57 life—and the curtain closes on this sad game. I still can't think about this deck without moist emotional snorts. The coup de grace is that this league required players to compete their decks ten times. And, since his games often lasted over an hour and a half, he received at least one concession.

Words, Words, Words

It was not just determining the right card mix that players and designers found challenging. This becomes increasingly clear to me as I participate in the never-ending process of editing the rules and the cards. As my earliest playtesters have pointed out (in their more malicious moods), the original concept for Magic was the simplest game in the world because you had all the rules on the cards. That notion is long gone.

To those who didn't have to endure it, our struggle for precision was actually rather amusing. My own rules discussions about card wordings were mostly with Jim Lin, who is the closest thing you will ever encounter to a combination rules lawyer and firehose. A typical rule-problem session would go:

> Jim: *"Hmm—there seems to be a problem with this card. Here is my seven-page rules addition to solve the problem."*
>
> Richard: *"I would sooner recall all the cards than use that. Let's try this solution instead."*
>
> Jim: *"Hmm—we have another problem."*
>
> [Repeat until...]
>
> Richard: *"This is silly—only incredibly stupid and terminally anal people could possibly misinterpret this card."*
>
> Jim: *"Yes, maybe we have been thinking about this too long. If you're playing with that kind of person, you should find some new friends."*

A specific example of something we actually worried about is whether Consecrate Land would really protect your land from Stone Rain. After all, the first says it prevents land from being destroyed and the second says it destroys the land. Isn't that a contradiction? It still hurts my head getting into a frame of mind where that is confusing. It is perhaps a little like wondering why anyone would give you anything for money, which is, after all, just paper.

But, then again, I could never tell what was going to confuse people. One of the playtesters, Mikhail Chkhenkeli, approached me and said, "I like my deck. I have the most powerful card in the game. When I play it, I win on the next turn." I tried to figure out what this could be; I couldn't think of anything that would win the game with any assurance the turn after casting. I asked him about it and he showed me a card that would make his opponent skip a turn. I was confused until I read exactly what was written: "Opponent loses next turn." It was my first real lesson in how difficult it was going to be to word the cards so that no two people would interpret the same card in a different way.

The Magic Marketplace

Another thing I realized in the second year of playtesting really surprised me. Magic turned out to be one of the best economic simulations I had ever seen. We had a free-market economy and all of the ingredients for interesting dynamics. People valued different cards in different ways—sometimes because they simply weren't evaluating accurately, but much more often because the cards really have different value to different players. For example, the value of a powerful green spell was lower for a person who specializes in black and red magic than for one who was building a deck that was primarily green. This gives a lot of opportunity for arbitrage. I would frequently find cards that one group of players wasn't using but another group were treating like chunks of gold. If I was fast enough, I could altruistically benefit both parties and only have to suffer a little profit in the process.

Sometimes the value of a card would fluctuate based on a new use (or even a suspected new use). For example, when Charlie was collecting all the available spells that produced black mana, we began to get concerned—those cards were demanding higher and higher prices, and people began to fear what he could need all that black mana for. And, prior to Dave's "Land Destruction Deck," land destruction spells like Stone Rain and Ice Storm were not high-demand spells. This of course allowed him to assemble the deck cheaply, and after winning the first Magic tournament, sell off the pieces for a mint.

Trade embargoes appeared. At one point a powerful faction of players would not trade with Skaff, or anyone who traded with Skaff. I actually heard conversations such as:

> Player 1 to Player 2: *"I'll trade you card A for card B."*
>
> Skaff, watching: *"That's a moronic trade. I'll give you card B and cards C, D, E and F for card A."*
>
> Players 1 and 2 together: *"We are not trading with you, Skaff."*

Another interesting economic event would occur when people would snatch up cards they had no intention of using. They would take them to remove them from the card pool, either because the card annoyed them (Chaos Orb, for example) or because it was too deadly against their particular decks.

I think my favorite profit was turned during an encounter with Ethan Lewis and Bit. Ethan had just received a pack of cards and Bit was interested in trading with Ethan. Bit noticed that Ethan had the Jayemdae Tome, began to drool, and made an offer for it. I looked at the offer and thought it was far too low, so I put the same thing on the table.

Bit looked at me and said, "You can't offer that! If you want the Tome you have to bid higher than my bid."

I said, "This isn't an offer for the Tome. This is a gift for Ethan deigning to even discuss trading the Tome with me."

Bit looked at me in disbelief, and then took me aside. He whispered, "Look, I'll give you this wad of cards if you just leave the room for ten minutes." I took his bribe, and he bought the Tome. It was just as well—he had a lot more buying power than I did. In retrospect, it was probably a dangerous ploy to use against Bit—after all, he was the person who was responsible for gluing poor Charlie's deck together once, washing a different deck of Charlie's in soap and water, and putting more cards of Charlie's in the blender and hitting frappé.

Probably the most constant card-evaluation difference I had with anyone was over Lord of the Pit. I received it in just about every playtest release we had, and it was certainly hard to use. I didn't agree with Skaff, though, that the only value of the card was that you might get your opponent to play with it. He maintained that blank cards would be better to play with because blank cards probably wouldn't hurt you. I argued that if you knew what you were doing, you could profit from it.

Skaff asked me to cite a single case where it had saved me. I thought a bit and recalled the most flamboyant victory I had with it. My opponent knew he had me where he wanted me—he had something doing damage to me, and a Clone in hand, so even if I cast something to turn the tide, he would be able to match me. Well, of course, the next cast spell was a Lord of the Pit; he could Clone it or die from it, so he Cloned it. Then each time he attacked, I would heal both of the Lords, or cast Fog and nullify the assault, and refuse to attack. Eventually, he ran out of creatures to keep his Lord of the Pit sated and died a horrible death.

Skaff was highly amused by this story. He said, "So, when asked about a time the Lord of the Pit saved you, you can only think of a case where you were playing somebody stupid enough to clone it!"

Dominia and the Role of Roleplaying

Selecting a card mix that accommodated different evaluations of the cards wasn't enough; we also had to develop an environment in which the cards could reasonably interact. Establishing the right setting for Magic proved to be a central design challenge. In fact, many of our design problems stemmed from an attempt to define the physics of a magical world in which duels take place and from building the cards around that, rather than letting the game define the physics. I was worried about the cards' relationship to each other—I wanted them to seem part of a unified setting, but I didn't want to restrict the creativity of the designers or to create all the cards myself. Everyone trying to jointly build a single fantasy world seemed difficult, because it would inevitably lack cohesion. I preferred the idea of a multiverse, a system of worlds that was incredibly large and permitted strange interactions between the universes in it. In this way, we could capture the otherworldly aspects of fantasy that add such flavor to the game while preserving a coherent, playable game structure. Almost any card or concept would fit into a multiverse. Also, it would not be difficult to accommodate an ever-growing and diverse card pool—expansion sets with very different flavors could be used in the same game, for they could be seen as a creative mingling of elements from different universes. So I developed the idea of Dominia, an infinite system of planes through which wizards travel in search of resources to fuel their magic.

In its structured flexibility, this game environment is much like a roleplaying world. I don't mean to suggest that this setting makes Magic a roleplaying game—far from it—but Magic is closer to roleplaying than any other card or board game I know of. I have always been singularly unimpressed by games that presumed to call themselves a cross between the two because roleplaying has too many characteristics that can't be captured in a different format. In fact, in its restricted forms—as a tournament game or league game, for example—Magic has little in common with roleplaying. In those cases, it is a game in the traditional sense, with each player striving to achieve victory according to some finite set of rules. However, the more free-form game—dueling with friends using decks constructed at whim—embodies some interesting elements of roleplaying.

Each player's deck is like a character. It has its own personality and quirks. These decks often even get their own names: "The Bruise," "The Reanimator," "Weenie Madness," "Sooner-Than-Instant Death," "Walk Into This Deck," "The Great White Leftovers," "Backyard Barbeque," and "Gilligan's Island," to name a few. In one deck I maintained, each of the creatures had a name—one small advantage to crummy photocopied cardstock is the ease of writing on cards. The deck was called "Snow White and the Seven Dwarves," containing a Wurm named Snow White and seven Mammoths: Doc, Grumpy, Sneezy, Dopey, Happy, Bashful, and Sleepy. After a while I got a few additional Mammoths, which I named Cheesy and Hungry. There was even a Prince Charming: my Veteran Bodyguard.

As in roleplaying, largely the players determine the object of the game in the unstructured mode of play. The object of the duel is usually to win, but the means to that end can vary tremendously. Most players find that the duel itself quickly becomes a fairly minor part of the game compared to trading and assembling decks.

Another characteristic of Magic, which is reminiscent of roleplaying, is the way players are exploring a world rather than knowing all the details to start. I view Magic as a vast game played among all the people who buy decks, rather than just a series of little duels. It is a game for tens of thousands in which the designer acts as a gamemaster. The gamemaster decides what the environment will be, and the players explore that environment. This is why there are no marketed lists of cards when the cards are first sold: discovering the cards and what they do is an integral part of the game.

And like a roleplaying game, the players contribute as much to an exciting adventure as the gamemaster. To all the supporters of Magic, and especially to my playtesters, I am extraordinarily grateful. Without them, if this product existed at all, it would certainly be inferior. Every one of them left a mark, if not on the game itself, then in the game's lore. Any players today that have even a tenth of the fun I had playing the test versions with them will be amply pleased with Magic.

Magic Design: A Decade Later (written 2003)

Magic and the trading card game industry have undergone a lot of changes since the time I wrote those design notes. In the meantime Magic has grown stronger with each successive year—as the game itself is improved, and more people are brought into trading card games from products such as Pokemon and Yu-Gi-Oh.

It is difficult for people these days to appreciate how little we knew about the game design space we were entering in the early nineties. My design notes failed to mention what in my mind is the strongest sign of that—after describing the concept of a trading card game to Peter Adkison I concluded with the cautious statement "of course, such a game may not be possible to design." It is hard for me to imagine that state of mind today, in a world where trading card games have reached every corner and are a part of almost every major entertainment property. This is a world where trading card games have left their mark on all areas of game design, from computer games to board games; and where trading card games have directly inspired games ranging from trading miniature games to trading tops games. This is a world where Jason Fox, from the comic strip Foxtrot, complained that a deck of cards coming with only 4 aces was some sort of ploy to get people to buy expansion kits.

That could be left as the end of the story; Magic was designed—as the design notes of a decade ago portray—and 10 years later it was still going strong. But this leaves out a large part of the story, since Magic was anything but a static game since then. The changes and improvements to Magic warrant design notes of their own.

First and Foremost: a Game

One thing that may look arcane in my notes to people, who know something about the game market, is my reference to the form of game that Magic launched as a "trading card game", rather than a "collectable card game". I still use TCG rather than CCG, which became the industry standard despite my efforts from its earliest days. I prefer "trading" rather than "collectable" because I feel it emphasizes the playing aspect rather than the speculation aspect of the game. The mindset of making collectables runs against that of making games—if you succeed in the collectable department then there is a tendency to keep new players out and to drive old ones away because of escalating prices. One of the major battles that Magic fought was to make it perceived principally as a game and secondarily as a collectable. Good games last forever—collectables come and go.

This was not merely theoretical speculation—Magic's immense success as a collectable was severely threatening the entire game. Booster packs intended to be sold at a few bucks were marked up to 20 dollars in some places as soon as they hit the shelves. While many people view this time as the golden age of Magic the designers knew that it was the death of the game in the long run. Who is going to get into the game when it was immediately inflated in price so much? How many people would play the game if doing so was wearing holes in some of their most valuable assets? We might be able to keep a speculation bubble going for a while, but the only way Magic was going to be a long term success—a classic game—was for it to stand on its game play merits, not on its worthiness as an investment.

During "Fallen Empires", the fifth Magic expansion, we finally produced enough cards that the speculative market collapsed. The long-term value of Magic could perhaps thrive—but it wouldn't immediately price itself out of the reach of new players before they got a chance to try it. There was an inevitable negative patina that Magic got for a while, and "Fallen Empires" still has, but from this point on Magic was sinking or swimming on its game merits. Fortunately, Magic turned out to be a strong swimmer.

Binding the Unbounded

The part of my notes, which I believe, reveals my biggest change in thinking over the last decade is the statement that in the future we would publish other games with mechanics similar to Magic. What I was referring to is what became "Ice Age" and "Mirage", two expansions for Magic. Why did I think these would be entirely new games, rather than what they ended up being—expansions for the main game?

We all realized from the start that we couldn't just keep adding cards to Magic and expect it to stay popular. One reason for that is that each successive set of cards was a smaller and smaller percentage of the entire pool of cards, and so would necessarily have less and less impact on the whole of the game. This was illustrated vividly by players of "Ice Age" talking about how the entire set introduced two relevant cards to the game. One can imagine how the designers felt—working for years to make "Ice Age" a compelling game to have it boil down to a mere two cards. Another, perhaps more important reason, is that new players wouldn't want to enter a game where they were thousands of cards behind, so our audience would inevitably erode.

Initially we saw two solutions to this problem:

Make cards ever more powerful. This is a route many trading card game makers followed—and one I greatly dislike. It feels like strong-arming the players to buy more and more rather than really providing them more game value. But it would bring new players in, because they wouldn't need the obsolete old cards.

Eventually conclude Magic: The Gathering, and start a new game—Magic: Ice Age, for example. I advocated this approach, because I believed we could make exciting new game environments indefinitely. When one set was finished, players wouldn't be forced to buy into the new game to keep competitive, they could move on if they wanted a change—and new players could begin on equal footing.

When it actually came time to do "Ice Age" it was absolutely clear that players would not stand for a new version of Magic, we had to think of something else. Additionally, we were also worried that fragmenting the player audience was a bad idea; if we made a lot of different games, people would have a harder and harder time finding players.

The solution we found was to promote different formats of game play—many of which involved only more recent sets of cards. Today there are popular formats of play which involve only the most recently published cards, cards published in the last 2 years, and cards published in the last 5 years, in addition to many others. While this does fragment the player base—since you may not be able to find players who play your format—it is less draconian than different games since you can apply your cards to many different formats over time. This was a far more flexible approach than the first—as it didn't command players to start fresh— it allowed them to, and allowed new players to join the game without being overwhelmed.

Trading Card Games Are not Board Games
I used to believe that trading card games were far more like board games than they are. This is not surprising, since I had no trading card games before Magic to draw examples from, and so was forced to use the existing world of games to guide my thinking on TCGs. A lot of my design attitudes grew from this misconception. For example, my second trading card game was designed to be best with 4 or more people, and took several hours to play. These are not bad parameters for a board game, but trading card games really want to be much shorter—because so much of the game is about replaying with a modified, or entirely new deck.

In a similar vein I used what I saw board game standards to be when it came to rules clarifications. It was common in board games to find a different group played a slightly different way, or had house rules to suit their tastes. With board games different interpretations of the rules and ways of play were not a major problem because players tended to play with fairly isolated groups. This led me to be quite anti-authoritarian when it came to the "correct" way to play. It turned out that a universal standard for a trading card game was far more necessary than a board game, because the nature of the game form made the interconnectivity of the game audience was far greater.

This meant that we had to take more and more responsibility for defining the rules and standards of play. In some ways this is analogous to being forced to construct the tournament rules for a game. The rules to Bridge are not that complex but when you write out the official tournament rules—really try to cross the t's and dot the i's—you have a compendium.

I had also hoped that players could moderate their own deck restrictions. We knew that certain card combinations were fun to discover and surprise someone with, but not fun to play with on an ongoing basis. So we figured players would make house rules to cover those decks and the responsible cards. The highly interconnected nature of Magic made it unreasonable to expect that, however, since every playgroup came up with a vast number of restrictions and rules, and they all played with each other. This meant we had to take more responsibility in designing the cards and when necessary, banning cards that were making the game worse.

The Pro Tour

All this precision invested in the design of the rules and cards made Magic a surprisingly good game to play seriously. We began to entertain ideas of really supporting a tournament structure with big money behind it—big enough players could, if good enough—make a living off of playing Magic. This was a controversial subject at Wizards of the Coast for a while—the worry being that making the game too serious would make it less fun. I subscribed fully to the concept of a Pro Tour—thinking of how the NBA helped make basketball popular and didn't keep the game from being played casually as well.

The Pro Tour had an almost immediate effect. Our players rapidly became much better as the top level ones devoted time to really analyzing the game and as that game tech filtered down through the ranks. Before the Pro Tour I am confident that I was one of the best players in the world, now I am mediocre at best.

Now there are thousands of tournaments each week, and many players have earned a lot of money playing Magic, some in the hundreds of thousands of dollars. At the last World Championship there were 56 countries competing. There is a never-ending buzz of Magic analysis and play as players attempt to master the ever-changing strategic ground of Magic. I believe this is a major part of Magic's ongoing popularity. If even a small group of people takes a good game very seriously, there can be far reaching effects.

Magic Online

Online Magic didn't come into its own until last year. For a long time I have wanted to see an online version of Magic that duplicated real life Magic as closely as possible. That is, the online game would connect people, run the games and the tournaments, and adjudicate rules—but little else. At first we tried to form partnerships with computer game companies to do this—but our partners always had other ideas about how to do computer Magic. Eventually we hired a programming studio to do it our way and now we have Magic Online.

One of the striking things about Magic Online is that we use the same revenue model as in real life. Despite exhortations to use a subscription model, we chose to sell virtual cards, which you could trade with other players online. This allows players to buy some cards and then play them indefinitely with no further fee—as in real life.

It was important to us that we not make it a better deal playing online than off—we wanted it to be the same. That is because we feel the paper game contributes a lot to Magic's ongoing popularity, and it could be threatened if many of its players go to the online game.

For this reason one of the prime targets for the online game was going to be lapsed players. Many studies had been done on how long people play Magic and why they leave the game, and for the most part they didn't leave because they were bored with the game, they left because they had life changes which made it more difficult to play—for example getting jobs or having kids. These players would potentially rejoin the game if they could play from their own home on their own hours.

Magic Online is still a bit too young to be sure about—but it appears to have acquired a dedicated sizeable audience of players without hurting the paper game. Many of the players are formerly lapsed players as we had hoped.

The Next 10 Years

Who knows what the next decade will bring? Ten years ago I had no clue at all, it was an exciting time and we were riding a roller coaster. Now I am more confident—I believe that Magic is fairly stable, and that there is every reason to believe that it will be around and as strong in another 10 years. At this point it is clear that Magic is not a fad, and as many new players are coming in each year as are leaving the game.

Certainly Magic has stayed fresh for me. I get into the game every few months; joining a league, constructing a deck, or perhaps preparing for and participating in a tournament. Every time I return I find the game fresh and exciting, with enough different from the previous time to keep me on my toes, but enough the same that I can still exploit my modest skills at the game. I look forward to my next 10 years of the game.

13

from UNCLE ROY

A Street Player has confirmed their location. Please try to guide them to my office.

Show Map

14

Eyeball *and* Cathexis

David Sudnow

Context

Convinced from music studies that I had a fair handle on the fine details of how skills are fashioned, I became fascinated by the earliest video games in 1980: how interacting with "objects" wasn't really that at all, but instead managing a strange gap between manipulations with an interface and what appears on the screen. It's the nature of these new skills, user-interface skills, and the essential gap between analogue and digital action, which I wrote about in **Pilgrim in the Microworld** *(Warner Books, 1983). The two selections here are sample chapters from the book.*

The Player Experience

Game Spaces

David Sudnow received his Ph.D. at Berkeley in 1965. He is a Guggenheim Fellow and the author of five books. He took up jazz at age 30. In 1975 he left academia to write about musical and other skills. He is president of The Sudnow Method, a company that teaches adults to play the piano. (www.sudnow.com)

Eyeball

They were all out of Missile Command, damn it. I'd woken up in the morning with the silhou-
ette of that psychedelectric landscape still etched on my retina. Wouldn't it be neat if a "city in
memory" came up looking a little different, more imperfect than the original, say, with just the
essence suggested. That would at least make it appear computers remember sights as we
do, rather than as just series of numerical values for each grid point on the screen. Remembering the looks of things, we forget aspects of them in ways we can't predict in advance, which
is to say images live a history within our lives. Computers don't have that kind of memory.
How could they?

Herb had another game called Breakout, which I'd glimpsed some guests play during
time-outs from the favored bouts at nuclear defense. Was there a truly worthy video opponent
—a Don Juan of Silicon Valley? Who knew, but the salesman said this Breakout thing was a
real good game, the TV was sitting in the backseat of the car, and rather than drive around
all day looking for missiles, I figured I'd take this one home for starters. How was I to know it
would become "my game," that I'd get so obsessed with it as to live out the next three months
of my life almost exclusively within this nineteen-inch microworld, heaven help me.

My next door neighbor must have seen me coming in and out, first carrying the TV
up the stairs, then the box marked Atari, for no sooner was the configuration set up and ready
to go than he appeared. And inside of twenty minutes versus this young San Francisco lawyer
I'm in a cold sweat. Here's a snapshot of the pristine landscape:

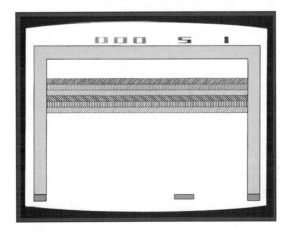

At bottom screen there's a paddle, controlled by a steering wheel knob that comes with the unit along with the joystick you get for other games. You push a button to serve yourself a ball, which descends from just beneath the barricade strip across the screen. Then you hit it back, and every time you do an unmarked half-inch brick segment gets knocked out of the wall. Of course size is relative, the more competent you become the more these lights take on a sort of environmental density and you're pulled by the fingertips onto a full-scale playing field whose dimensions aren't found on rulers.

The immediate object is to chip through to the open space on the other side, and once you've made this Breakout the ball rebounds like crazy between the far wall and the band, moving from one side to the other and then back again to knock out bricks from above unless none obstructs its path and it therefore returns down to you:

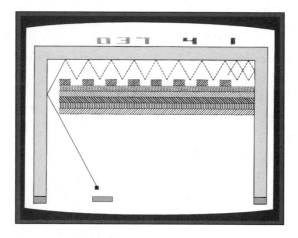

The overall goal, fat chance, is to eliminate the entire barricade until paddle and ball are alone in empty court, victors.

The wall is composed of six differently colored strata, and if and when a ball first gets through to hit the fourth one from the bottom, it takes off fast in a sudden break slam shot and then holds at this new speed till you miss and have to serve again. You get five balls per game, can set the console to play solo or in turns with an opponent, and can of course hit the reset switch at any time to reconstitute the whole barricade and instantly get a fresh five serves.

Within about twenty minutes my neighbor had cut through the wall a few times while I couldn't even get close, and when he insisted he'd only played the game once before for an hour, my evening was decided. Some piano player. As if last night's effort to save the world wasn't bad enough, I must have now gone on for four hours by myself after I finally got him to leave. And by the time I gave up for the night, I'd broken out one lousy time. I relentlessly served that damn speck of light without intermission, couldn't pull myself away from the thing. Two hundred bucks after all.

I tried rationalizing my initial anxiety with the conviction the guy was lying. But then again, he didn't smoke, was ten years younger, who knows? Maybe some basic nervous system capacities were involved, rhythmic acuities different from what you need for jazz, say. Maybe microworld mastery varied by age, metabolic or alpha wave rates, astrological signs for all I knew. And how about cultural factors? I didn't see a TV before the age of ten, probably haven't logged a thousand hours in thirty years. Maybe he'd grown up with several hours of television a day. For all I knew extensive tube time trained micromuscles for neuroathletic competition and I was thus irrevocably consigned to the video boondocks.

At least the rudiments of slower play were easy enough for me. One of the guys at the party had created a big laugh, throwing himself back and forth while swinging his entire upper torso and arms and almost falling off the chair to hit the Breakout ball. He took the ribbing with good humor, exaggerating his incompetence for the sake of the party, but actually seemed unable to effect that transformation of sense needed to engage himself with big looking movements through little feeling ones. He couldn't project a comfortable scale of being into the confining detachment of the interface, couldn't trust the efficiency of a mere knob, but instead handled the encounter like those proverbial preliterate aborigines who respond to a photograph by looking around at its reverse side. The guy acted at the controls as if there were no video fence in the way. It probably took him a long time to get used to automatic transmissions and electric typewriters, not because the skills are so different from a technical standpoint, but because he refused to adopt the postural respect solicited by new embodied equipment. The guy just wasn't a button pusher.

I didn't have his sort of quaint confusion, but automatically made the necessary shift in stance to control the paddle while sitting still in the right terminal position. And it only took a little time to transcend the physical awkwardness of the knob so I could get the racket more or less where I wanted, more or less when I wanted, without too often over-or undershooting the ball.

Line up your extended finger with the lower left corner of the TV screen a comfort-able six feet away. Now track back and forth several times in line with the bottom border and project a movement of that breadth onto an imagined inch and a half diameter spool in your hands. That's how knob and paddle are geared, a natural correspondence of scale between the body's motions, the equipment, and the environs preserved in the interface. There's that world space over there, this one over here, and we traverse the wired gap with motions that make us nonetheless feel in a balanced extending touch with things.

They had it set just right. Held by fingertips and rotated through a third of its revolu-tion, the little paddle steering wheel afforded rapid enough horizontal movement anywhere along the backcourt to handle the pace of action without wrist or forearm aid:

Not like a very fine tuning knob to change hi-fi stations, for with such a gearing you've got to spin the dial to traverse full field, letting go with your fingers and losing all accuracy. Very fine tuning knobs are meant for slow motions, and while you can twirl these dials to reach a rough vicinity quickly, to hit Breakout balls a vicinity isn't enough. On the other hand, were the gearing too tight, the slightest motion would send the paddle right across screen. Ideally geared for travel through the terrains and tempos of a microworld, the dial had enough resistance so an accidental touch didn't send the paddle too far, but not so much that you had to exert yourself to move through the court.

I served myself a ball. It came down. I went for it and missed. I centered the fingers in relation to the knob's range so I could swing back and forth across the field with hardly any elbow play at all. I rotated some partial practice strokes, trying out each side to test the expanse and timing of the whereabouts, appraising the extent of pressure needed to move various distances at various rates.

I served again. The ball's coming down over there and my paddle's here. How fast to go? A smooth gesture knows from the outset when it'll get where it's headed, as a little pulse is established that lays out the upcoming arrival time, a compressed "ready, set, go" built into the start of the movement. The gesture then feels when to speed up and slow down to attain the target. I swing the bat back and forth to acquire its weight, establish a usable rhythm then held in reserve as I await the ball, preparing for a well-timed movement anywhere within the arc of the swing.

Within fifteen minutes I'm no longer conscious of the knob's gearing and I'm not jerking around too much. So far so good. Slow down, get rid of the neighbor, get a little rhythm going, and in no time at all you've got a workable eye-hand partnership. The calibrating move-ment quickly passes beneath awareness, and in the slow phase the game is a breeze, doesn't even touch the fingering you need for "the eentsy, weentsy spider went up the water spout...." Here I was lobbing away with a gentle rhythm, soon only now and then missing a shot through what seemed a brief lapse in attention rather than a defect in skill.

Then came the breakaway slam when the ball reaches the fourth layer, and the eye-hand partnership instantly dissolved. *Wooosh,* there it goes right past, coming from nowhere, a streak of light impossible to intercept. They've got to be kidding. Out of the playpen onto the softball field. I missed every one, each time left standing with bat in hand swatting video air. The lawyer had to have been lying, had to have put in more hours than he said.

I tabled my anxiety and simply figured more delicate paddle handling skills were called for. Besides, just as the panning shot made Missile Command fun, I began getting off on the action, building control and precision in these gentle little calibrations. With slow shots my gaze could lift a bit off from the finer details of the ball's path to roam the court analytically, to glance at my paddle, then where the ball would hit the barricade, and then ahead to predict where it'd hit the side so I could position myself in advance. And I'd get there, sometimes in sync with the ball and sometimes ahead of it, just waiting. My glance took snapshots of the overall neighborhood, there was enough give in the tempo to allow for some instant geometry during play, enough casualness to the pace that looking could disengage from tracking to analyze the opponent's ways and fit the rhythm of its queries into the timing of the shots. Scrutinizing the neighborhood to learn my way around, I could still bring the paddle where needed on time.

The sounds helped. Every time you hit the ball there's a little bleep, then a differently pitched tone if you hit a side wall, and still another one for each different bandful of bricks. These recurrent bleeps helped you gear into the overall rate of action. The sights helped. The more or less steady passage of the ball painted the action's tempo in broad strokes, so when the eyes loosened their hold on it to take in a wider or different territory, that gently tracing light kept the fingers continuously alive to the whereabouts and pace of things.

At first it felt like my eyes told my fingers where to go. But in time I knew the smooth rotating hand motions were assisting the look in turn, eyes and fingers in a two-way partnership. Walking a rainy street, you identify the dimensions of a puddle in relation to the size and rate of your gait, so the stride itself patterns the style of your looking, how you scan the field's depth of focus and extent of coverage, what you see. So too with sight reading music at the piano for instance, where you never look ahead of what you can grasp and your hands' own sense of their location therefore instructs the gaze where to regard the score. So too again with typing from a text, where if your eyes move in front of where your fingers are, you'll likely make an error, and thus hands and gaze maintain a delicate rhythmic alignment. And so too here, you'd have to sustain a pulse to organize the simultaneous work of visually and tactilely grasping the ball, your hands helping your look help your hands make the shot.

I played around with slow balls, getting the first chance I'd had in years to handle Ping-Pong–type action, listening to the bleeps and feeling my way round the court. I hit a shot over to the left. Can I place the next one there as well? Of course the lights didn't obey the laws of physics governing solid objects, like billiard balls, say. But Atari had rather decently simulated a sense of solidity. The light came from a certain angle toward the side wall, and then followed out the triangulation by going in the direction you'd predict for a real ball. What about the paddle? Hit on an off-centered portion of a tennis racket or hand, a ball will deflect on a different path and you can thereby place shots. Sure enough they'd programmed the trajectories and different parts of the paddle surface to match, so the light-ball behaved rather like a tangible object, refracting and deflecting so it seemed you could at least somewhat control the ball's direction.

I watched the paddle and ball at the precise point of their contact, refining the control I could exercise over placement. Could I hit it on the left third of the paddle? How about the left fourth? Could I hit balls with the paddle's side rather than its upper surface, maybe useless in actual play but fun, and perhaps good for improving touch. I tried knocking out all the bricks of the lower band before the ball broke through to the next layer, eating corn on the cob. Virtually impossible. I tried putting more English into the shot, coming at the ball from the side and swooshing the paddle across quickly beneath it at the last moment, trying a spin. Did Atari accommodate that? I thought so, but wasn't sure.

It was here I discovered an ethically troublesome defect in the game. I'd hit a brick and the ball would come down. Taking care to line up the paddle, I knocked out an adjacent one, or even knocked out one above it, entering the open slot made by the preceding shot:

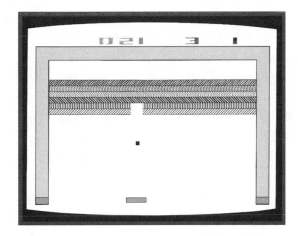

Again I aimed. The lights faked enough solid physics and the placement was tight. With still more barricade cut from the same narrow region, the ball once again dropped almost straight down as you'd expect. So I hit it square on again to further eat away that vicinity.

Poof. It veered radically to the side, a full sixty degrees off course. I went through the same sequence enough times to make sure it wasn't my mistake. And it wasn't. They'd messed with the rebounds, by God, preventing you from breaking through too fast. A few shots straight up and down to the same vicinity, and then Atari took the mathematically cheap way out. The arbitrary and sharply pitched deflection they used to get out of trouble sent the ball into a low horizontal pattern for several volleys, and I couldn't redress these returns to pursue a vertical attack, had to wade through a long drawn-out exchange until the trajectory gradually became more upright.

Three explosions on screen at Missile Command is one thing. That becomes an acceptable rule of play. But an electronic tactic to forestall your progress is another. "All right, veer off to the side. I'll wait it out. Mess with my carefully aimed shot. But if you want forgiveness for being a computer, don't put rocks in the snowballs."

I stored the disturbance like you register a lie on the first date and puzzled for a moment over the game's moral integrity. If the programmer could patch up an organizational weakness with a trivial trick like this, where else might there be monkey business? If it was their way to let you feel competent, giving you three easy placements and then veering off as if you wouldn't notice it, they were stupid. Anybody would see what was up after a few times at the controls. The tactic didn't speak well for Breakout. What if she lies all the time?

By this point I was getting pooped and needed to go for the score, to break out at least once before calling it a night. If my neighbor could do it after an hour, certainly I could after three. The slam shot had been putting me out of commission every time. Mostly, by the time I knew it was coming, it was gone. You're going along at a comfortable pace, hit the fourth band, and then *whap,* the ball goes double time on you and you're wiped out.

Now I told myself, "Concentrate." I did a little seat squirm, as when entering a freeway on-ramp and you have to hit sixty in a real hurry, peeked up to the band to get the jump on when it was coming, stiffened up and sat on the edge of the chair, and handled one. I missed the follow-up but had returned my first slam. Actually, I got myself in its way.

In a half hour of just "concentrating" I'd refined the instruction. I discovered if I told myself to "glue my eye to the ball" I could start fielding first slams much better and get some of the follow-ups as well. For about twenty minutes I sat there mesmerized, tracking the ball like my life depended on it, my entire being invested in the hypnotic pursuit of that pea-sized light. Kneading my eyeballs into the guts of its movement like following a guy in a fast crowd where a momentary diversion would lose him, I soon got to hold on to a four- or five-round volley of fast ones. Knocking out that many more bricks a hole opened on the side of the barricade, and I watched the ball break out, ricochet like crazy between the back wall and the band, eat up six or seven more bricks, then fly down right past me. Had I not been taken in by the new quickened sights and sounds, I might have fielded it back up. My first Breakout. Thank God, I could go to bed.

I'd qualified as a contestant, the money wasn't for naught, and I had a good night's struggle. If the slam could be managed and you could breakout in an evening's play, mastery couldn't be that far ahead. Over the course of the next several days, gluing my eye to the ball, I made steady progress. I couldn't eliminate all the bricks, didn't come close, though pretty soon I got to break through the barricade once out of every two or three trials, and after about a week I could get through nearly anytime.

But I couldn't control the shape of things at all, and it began to be clear that there was a good deal more to this simple-looking computer scenario than I'd imagined. It seemed easy enough to get a rough hang of things, to gain a bit of mastery over basic game events. But beyond some rough paddle handling skills I was stumped. During slow phases of the game, at least it felt like some command was to be had over the placement of shots and systematic destruction of the wall. But when things picked up the gaze lost all its freedom and there was no time to see where you were going. On a roller coaster under somebody else's management, taking charge of the action was reduced to your capacity simply to hold on. A discouraging situation. Then one day, as I was just fooling around at some makeshift science, I glimpsed at least the prospect of a more dignified option.

Just for kicks I covered the paddle path all across the bottom of the screen with an inch-thick strip of black tape. I tried playing blind, and could return only very few shots. I shortened the tape to leave a visible slot of two inches on each side of the screen, so when I was in the corners I could see the full paddle plus a bit. I swung back and forth again and again, end to end, trying to assess the gearing sensitively enough to field balls in the wide hidden area. When they came slowly, I could return about sixty percent of them, give or take a little.

Okay, you had to see paddle and ball at or very near the point of contact to handle each and every shot. But eyes and hands could get real close without that. I wondered if peripheral looking could do the job. You may have to see the point of impact, but there are lots of ways to look: out of the corner of your eye, in the immediate background, scanning by, just any old where in the periphery, with the quickest glance. I took off the tape and fixed my gaze right where the barricade touches the edge of the screen on the right, stared intently there without moving my eyes, and served a shot. I returned it. In fact I could play through a long volley gluing my eye away from the ball. Peripheral vision sufficed.

Then came a slam, and my eyes were still experimentally riveted on this edge of the field. How do you like that! I returned it, and the next and the next, handling several fast balls without moving my eyes. Called upon to heighten its powers of observation, my gaze rose to the task. For ten days I'd been convinced you had to fixate tightly to handle fast shots, the time-honored method for dealing with a tricky coordinational problem at a fast tempo. And I'd played that phase of Breakout frantically sitting still. With slow balls I tried to find targets, control shots, to aim. With slams I dared not take my eye off the ball long enough to see where I was going, just hung in there waiting to cave in.

My little test for peripheral vision came as a surprise. You could in principle aim the ball right through the fast phase, from front to finish, stay right in there playing all the way, handling fast action and long range vision as well. Looking could stay mobile, thinking expansive, the eyes could plan. The game would take on new character as something more than just an endurance heat.

What was going on? I'd looked around here and there, checking out the barricade, preparing to focus tightly on the contact point for a carefully aimed next shot, readying my look to assist a delicate calibration. Then the slam. By the time my gaze could catch it, and then change over from the speed it ran to get there to the speed the ball was moving, it was all over. So I'd started tracking very precisely in order to be most pointedly with it on the barricade at the instant of rebound. You don't stand still on the platform and lunge onto the train when steps come by. You make a running jump. I'd glued my eye on the ball because that felt like the natural thing to do in anticipation of a slam. So it went, and so I became skilled at handling quick turnarounds. The ball lobs up, then shoots down, my eyes inhabiting it all along the way, absorbing its speed as their own and pulling the fingers to the meeting place. The experiment made me realize an evolution had been taking place for some time. It wasn't just eye work at all. And even without the experiment I would've soon noticed my eyes regaining their freedom. I'd already been looking away a bit without knowing it.

For instance, after the first few days of intently focusing the ball, I began noticing that my head was inscribing a path that followed its passage as well. So tightly glued to the ball's route, I was now nodding through the TV court as if it were a full-scale hand-ball game seen from above. I look at my index finger held a foot and a half in front of my eyes, my head perfectly still, no sideway movement at all. Quickly tracing the finger a couple of feet back and forth from left to right to left to right, I track with only my eyeballs. First, it's strainful. Second, it feels inaccurate. The finger goes by in a blur at times, is hard to hold on to, and at various places the eyes fall out of phase and move in spurts. Now I move my head to track the finger in the natural way, finely synchronizing the scan. Eyeball movement proportionately lessens, the finger is seen clearly throughout, and even appears to move slower. Eyes don't sense their movements' pace, so to coordinate motions in tight alignment with a visible object's rate, we must follow with other moving parts. As we watch race-horses cross the finish line, our full upper torsos synchronize a pan to follow the heads in sharp focus and feel the winner's nose touch the ribbon.

After a few sessions gluing my gaze on the ball, the eyes were bringing the feet into play. I caught myself tapping tempos along with the bleeps. And several days later still, I found I was hitting fast shots with the slightest little upbeat twist, a zestful flick of the fingers, stylistically accenting this one, then that one, then this one, then that. A slight waist pivot had been joining in too. Day by day the fast Breakout rates were more and more systemically acquired. So the test for peripheral vision confirmed what my body was learning all along. Gluing my eyes to the ball had brought the rest of me along, and my look then gained some freedom.

At the instant the pace changes when the ball strikes that band, you at first watch intently for the onset of the slam. But when it shoots down and the eyes try to grab it, they can't possibly hold on not knowing how fast it'll go. That's why we need a "get ready, get set, and then go" should we specially care to coordinate an action at some pace.

As the Breakout ball heads toward the critical band, there's no "get ready, get set, and then go." Just a "go." So to grab a firm hold you must possess the game's rates, and supply the "ready, set, go" missing on screen. Your eyes beckon you within range of the pace, but till you more thoroughly learn to feel how fast upcoming slams go in relation to how fast slow shots rise, there's no way at all to ride on the wave.

Playing Breakout again and again and again, through the slow phase and fast, from the one to the other to the other, I hit slam after slam after slam after slam, and was nodding, and bobbing, and tapping. I was learning to feel it go fast and go slow, to feel how fast fast is from this slow and that. And just as I may move into a song at the remembered same tempo day after day, I've been going back and then forth and then back and then forth, and it's ready, and get set, and go *wooosh* into this, that, this, that, this, that.

Cathexis

Last ball out of five. Three bricks left on screen. The farthest I'd ever come. After a minute's break to gather composure, I serve. For some twenty seconds the ball floats off the boards around the empty space of the nearly vacant terrain. A no man's ball, I feel the attempted seduction of the long lobbing interim, a calm before the storm, the action so laid back that I'm consciously elaborating a rhythm to be ready, set, go for a slam. Then! It hits the high brick, shoots down like a whip and I'm right there on time to return. Forget about placement. Just hold on, don't miss, keep the time right, and watch like a hawk for added rhythmic protection. The phone rings. Return, back, return, back. Another one's gone. The caller hangs up and maybe two seconds later I get the last, by God. Can't say who or what else could've mattered at that point. And who knows what I would've done had someone walked between me and the TV during one of the most tense half minutes I've known.

I'd been playing Breakout each day, but not all that much, by no means yet your typical video addict. Nobody was around, no competition, just me and Atari on a rainy night. Over the past weeks I regularly stopped in the midst of the action, and suffered no grief for poor showings. I sometimes played sloppily, at other times well, and I couldn't yet explain the inconsistency. About all I could sense was a need for competition, and could especially see a real gain to be had if I could witness Breakout played well. What if I'd exaggerated the potential for careful shot placement all the way through? I wanted to see, even hear, the elegance of the game, and lacking a model, it was almost like buying a piano having never heard music.

Maybe I needed an expert. How about a Video Athletes Hotline. "Thanks for calling. Try going for the left side if you're right handed. It's been working wonders." Then the phone incident. Down to three bricks, the closest I'd come, a serve yet to go, the thing rings and I let it. Unbelievable. At my age. To remove one lousy remaining inch-long pastel rectangle from a TV screen, and hear a final inane sine wave bleep.

Atari had me hooked. I've said that before, but this was a whole different business, nothing like I'd known in the silo, or when breaking through, or in handling slams. Like night and day. Thirty seconds of play, for three bricks, and I'm on a whole new plane of being, all synapses wailing as I'm poised there with paddle, ball, a few remaining lights on screen, and a history that made this my first last brick.

Forget about placement, a score, elegance as an end in its own right. Forget about a model of good play to motivate practice. Here's all the motivation you'd ever want: get that action again, those last few bricks left and that eery lobbing interim as the ball floats about so you never know when it'll hit and you dont' dare try placing a shot because you're more than happy just to hold on with your eyes glued to the ball. Please don't miss, come on, do it, get that brick, easy does it, no surprises, now stay cool, don't panic, take it in stride, get it now. Get that closure. Video-game action. You know when you've got it like you know your first drunk.

For two weeks I'd watched that barricade eaten away and then reconstituted with a flick of the reset button, the move from everything to nothing never consummated, the gesture left dangling. In the past I'd look at the leftovers, cocky Atari bricks standing invulnerably there. In the first days their looks had no special significance. Not doing anything with them, their appearance was in the horizon of my interest and gaze, with paddle and ball in the fore-ground. I didn't notice how many got left each time, just the blurred and colorful swatch of a bunch still there. But as I gradually ate my way more and more into the upper reaches, the remaining bricks tempted a more discerning inspection. I'd notice their features, notice the amount of them in general. Not a brick count, just "a whole bunch" left or "a getting sort of close bunch" left or "a hazardously arranged bunch" left. But here, at the end, there were three! Right there, there, and there.

Serve. There's barely anything to interfere with a long end-to-end volley. The ball lofts to the far wall from a slight angle off the paddle and reflects off a side wall back down. Hit it back. It retraces exactly the same trajectory. Fingers tautly poised on the edge of a neurological breakdown, I go through ten or fifteen slowly drawn triangular tracings over the same path without moving. And one of those bricks is right nearby, *oooooooh* missing by a fraction. I'd love to redirect the shot just a touch right now, but that feels unbearably risky and I'm too scared to move. I want that closure, ache for it, know I'd literally hit that reset switch if I missed now. Come on, go all the way, undress that screen after two weeks of dating. I'm figuring at a thousand miles a second that the trajectory is bound to loosen a bit, or maybe there's enough movement in the paddle from nerves alone to slightly change course. Please do one of your dumb programmed deflections right now, damn it, and get us both out of here. I'd gladly forgive you for acting like that kind of a computer. Come on already, deflect off and stop the endless lobbing, do your thing right now while I've got hold of the long rhythm and I'm geared to move double speed if the ball hits a brick that makes it change tempo. For the first time I'm expressly aware of caring about the color of fast bricks. Uh-oh, is orange a fast color? Watch out. Can't let your eyes see just what's what, must be especially careful because the rhythms are so elongated and the full-court distance so deceptively slow. Now out in the open, drawn by the eyeballs along an ascending two-dimensional roller coaster, I'm locked on a course over which I dare not exert will. I wait for a hopefully reasonable change in the value of some variable, as I'm moved under strict mathematic control with literally calculated suspense, having one monstrous geometrical high, trigonometric upper, topological chip trip. Is this what they mean by the pleasures of mathematics, when numbers electrically tickle, torment, and torture your nerve endings?

I'd been intellectualizing the game and its skills to engage interest and time. But now here I am with my first authentic video experience, going for the last brick like any kid in an arcade, palms wet, pulse racing, mouth dry, nerve endings interfaced in nanoseconds, the knob itself throbbing, electronic reflections going straight for my spinal cord. I mean way up there with the bottom of *the* ninth, the ninth, and it's a long fly ball to left field, it's going, going.... Answer the phone before it's gone? Are you kidding? And it was worse and better than that.

Hollywood gets you to cry, TV cop serials flip your blood pressure up and down along with the best that Parke Davis and UpJohn can offer. A few hours in front of the tube any night of the week and you had to jog the next morning to recover. But now Atari had it, the ultimate adrenaline. Lay out a half-dozen lines for just a couple of bucks? A bargain.

Was I hooked? "I've been trying to reach you all day, were you out?" they'll be asking. No way. Not me. Not for that kind of thrill. Not a chance. Maybe at sixteen for a couple of hours. But now? No way. Meanwhile, next morning I was back at it. As soon as I got out of bed I glanced at the darkened TV set and flashed on an image of those last three bricks. Whacky though it is to admit, the very thought of the screen in that state of final tension, just saying the word "Breakout" to myself, and I had to fight the temptation to drop everything and make for the paddle, for those last few bricks with one remaining serve, for that supersaturated last lousy square and its intense beckoning desire. I woke up not eight hours later and I wanted a fix, so I plugged myself right in with the first cup of coffee, stuffed to the gills with electric anticipation. Object cathexis, I think it's called. Come on, Atari bricks you. I'm gonna gobble you.

I serve, and break all the way down to about ten bricks on the first ball. Never did that before, and I sure hadn't picked up new skills sleeping. Forget the opponent. When the history is just right, all the intensity you need to motivate practice is right there in the action, one on one. Just hook up, plug yourself in till you reach the right dosage. Breakout starts taking effect in about two weeks, a hookup per day.

Perhaps they called them video "games" only to avoid troubles with the Food and Drug Administration. Then, too, there'd be problems with South Americans over coffee, for at fifty cents a cup Atari could take over that market, what with a long-lasting quarter at Missile Command worth three double espressos loaded with sugar. How about some straight talk, Atari Pharmaceuticals, tell the whole story. Have you conducted the necessary blood-sugar tests? What about E.K.G. and E.E.G. changes? Pulse rates? "The Surgeon General has ascertained that when used in excess the final stages of Breakout are hazardous to your health."

All the while I figured I'd been fashioning a skill. I found a solution for how to handle the fast slams. I practiced. Got to where I could breakout. But now I breakout on my first ball, playing ten times better than the day before, motivated by a scheduled, packaged up, guaranteed-to-thrill Skinnerian payoff from a box they call a "game" for promotional purposes.

I started thinking about these so-called skills. They were odd, even scary. They took place a little too fast for comfort. It was five years at the piano before I looked down and saw my hands appearing to make music all by themselves. But within two weeks at Breakout, I watch them handling fast slams, with no consciousness of guiding their movements. And they look elaborate as all get out. Amazing. But what honest basis have I got for taking anything you'd call "credit" for the achievement? I look down at my piano keyboard hands, and a history of struggle lets me appreciate the natural accomplishment they now reveal, the result of a lifelong interaction between a biography and social settings that were frequented, yielding a particular path toward a unique style with its merits and deficiencies. Acquiring such a skill, I have an ongoing conversation with these hands, an elaborate interchange of advice, complaint, and cooperation born of years of collective effort. Here I look down at a knob-holding hand and watch it go through what seem like altogether complex little calibrations. I look at the screen. It so impersonates a real world setting, tennis, say, that I'm taken in by the illusion of adept motion, running all around that court, perfectly skilled at returning shots every which way coming at all angles. I never had such athletic skill before, not to that high a level, and I'd played a fair share of sports in my day. But two weeks? Take credit for that?

The fact is I didn't have to tell myself to keep my eye to the ball. If I kept putting in quarters, or hitting a reset switch, playing the strictly scheduled arrangement of tasks Atari engineered, this calibrating hand would've gotten to the same place pretty much without respect for anything I tried or tried not to do. What "effort" had I made? Strategic problem solving? How to learn this and that? Simply ways to make it interesting. Give the folks a little consciousness so they'll figure there's more to them than just bundles of programmable nerve pathways.

I hadn't forged a skill. Any blackjack player with a night's experience learns the right gesture for a "hit me" flick of the cards on the felt when the dealer's look invites a choice. How much more "skill" was here? Holding your cards a certain way isn't a skill intrinsic to success at blackjack, but a social skill at gambling. And all you need to know on that score here is to keep your body upright and hold on to the knobs at a TV screen, with your clothes on in a public place. If you're too smashed to stand up, they make sit-down models. I couldn't even take credit for "good reflexes," since it looked like nearly anybody who played for not too many hours got to roughly the same level.

A part in an animated movie? Sure, with a script automatically memorized for you. The full caressing potentials of the human hand realized in creative action on screen? Wait a minute. Fooling around with TV graphics and computational manipulations, Atari comes on a surprising discovery. If you engage a human body through eyes and fingers in a precisely scripted interaction with various sorts of computer-generated events, what seem like quite complex skills are rapidly acquired by regular repetition. Sequences of events can be scheduled into readily mastered routines of progressive difficulty, and a program of timed transitions can be organized, programming you, in turn, at an economically desirable rate.

They meant no harm. They were exploring a frontier. We modern humans had become increasingly fascinated with the notion that all things wonderful come from the smallest elements of matter: genes, molecules, proteins, atoms. Now electricity was finally carved down to its littlest bits and pieces and pressed into the service of science, industry, defense, business, government, medicine, exploration, and video games. The folks at Atari had only to use their microscopes to study the chip, that roadmap for bringing electricity into the eyeballs.

How could we not play these "games"? How could we not stand in awe of the computer, the ultimate rational tool, that device that the most influential brands of reason for a hundred years could announce as their perfect piece of auxiliary equipment? How not to be enthralled by the lights, sounds, and colors, knowing they result from the purest modes of human thought—adding, subtracting, subdividing, and the like? No teams of draftsmen laboring frame by frame to create Bambi, but simply fingered instructions creating fantastic microcosms, the entire syntax of thinking engraved on a sliver of silicon, our most perfected thought mirroring itself back in a visually moving display. How utterly irresistible, at first, to applaud the marvelous variety of it all: talking clocks, Missile Command, word processing, robots, digital displays, spread sheets, pie charts, networks, light pens, missile guidance systems, satellites, airplanes that fly themselves. You can do just everything with computers.

Of course they had a kick at Atari, varieties of kicks. Who in his right brain wouldn't? With a set of instructions you tell the electrons where to go: "Take a left here, go four blocks down there, then make a forty-five-degree turn to the left, take four steps and blow up." With written instructions you tell other electrons to form themselves up into the neighborhood itself, with its shapes, colors, and sounds. You talk with your programmed programming fingers into the TV tube and out comes PAC-MAN. No paintbrushes, except in the planning stages. Just instructions. Of course they had kicks when movements could be designed, and counter-movements made with the fingers, and that interaction coordinated by instructions as well. Particular kicks could be fashioned, as two instructions head for a collision, say. You could play around with the variables and with the body, stimulate little bundles of nerve-teasing action and emotion. Thrills. They were thinking up thrills and found that they worked.

There were varieties of kicks, like the Breakout kind, an electromathematic version of an ancient dramatic format with its hour-long minute of tantalizing perceptual closure, the pause before punch lines, the javelin floating through air as the Romans held their breath, the dead calm as a motionless deer is lined in the hunter's sight and the body stills itself for perfection. Some kicks felt new, all seemed much heightened by the electric intensity here. Elicited by programmable events, the enhanced kicks stimulated the development of more varied attempts at their own enrichment. Build them up, pack them with maximum density, program them to the tolerable limit for the allocated time and attention span. Now package them into gloriously graphic little fantasy worlds to disguise their real intent and result, throw in some scoring procedures to tide you through the learning plateaus, and call them "games." People like games, after all.

They weren't sure how and why such seemingly complex maneuvers as slam handling were acquired so fast. Nor did they know why such neat boundaries could be fashioned to lay out apparently marked shifts in skill at critical yet short-lived stages along the way. Add on a slam shot and it'll take several hours to get to handle that. Add on something else, and a week is needed. Build in dramatic moments where the action rises to a certain sort of crescendo. The little skill routines reach a new degree of synchronization, a new stage is attained, and a new excitement seduces further incentive to play.

Maybe it all has to do with the fact that when interfaced on the TV screen, the human body is in an altogether unaccustomed setting, as holistic three-dimensional movements are graphed onto a two-dimensional plane. The Breakout hand doesn't move a paddle freely along all facets of bodily space and surroundings. It encircles the knob, to be sure, but all actions transmit back and forth between the mere surface of things. I look down and watch my fingers quickly adjusting the control, the shot made to happen with superrapid, flexible-looking motion. But it's as if the fullness of things, and of myself, has been strangely halved. I could even say that I wasn't so much interfaced on screen as I was "interpictured" there. The potentials for bodily movement and the display lined up point for point as on a graph, eyes and hands in an altogether novel world of action.

Draw a figure on the two-dimensional surface of a blackboard, and you must stretch to reach areas in the far upper corners. The amount of pressure exerted on the chalk further adds the palpable touch of a third dimension. But on the screen a magical intervention destroys all consequences of pressure and perspective. Play Breakout with your face two inches to the side and six inches in front of the TV. While the ball is a lot farther away for the eyes, it's the "same distance" away for the hand, with a new burden for movement created along only one dimension.

In the video game, eye-hand coordination occurs in a radically delimited, even surrealistic milieu, all action taking place as though from a third party bird's-eye view. The space of mobility flattened to the nondepth of an electron, eyes and hands needn't attend the forward coming and backward going of things. There is no such motion here. Even should objects be made to grow in size to afford an illusion of three-dimensional movement, that's quite beside the eye's point as regards its task with the hand. Were the Breakout paddle mobile along a vertical as well as horizontal axis, like the Missile Command cursor, you could move in closer to field a slam shot, say. That would undoubtedly add a significant, if not insurmountable, increment in the skill level needed for the game. On the other hand, if missiles slammed down like Breakout balls, and you had to bring a cursor beneath them on time, Missile Command would require an altogether different format of events. In either modification, the third dimension would still be missing. You can't move both in and out, side to side, and up and down to field balls, missiles, asteroids, what have you. With movements instantaneously converted onto a flat grid, it's no wonder the little skills are quickly attained. Their size isn't the issue, but the fact that they're embedded in a strictly linear plane.

Isn't it neat how everything fits together? Invent such a game and put it out into the social world. Make it dazzling, no tough task here, so remarkable the achievement in its own right. People wander up, put in quarters, and soon get themselves hooked. A half-dozen lunch hours. A few days after or during school. Two rank amateurs buy tennis rackets to teach themselves the game, and spend the whole summer chasing balls. Two hours in an arcade and you're a gamesman, getting a small dose of bona fide action right off. Perfectly patient opponent, this Atari fellow. It's as though you could be given a violin, seated in the midst of the Julliard String Quartet, and there'd be a way of playing the music that allowed you to do your part altogether perfectly for a little while before they left you behind.

Put such a game on the market and instantly stratify almost the entire population of the country into dozens of slightly different skill categories. Two players meet, one has a few more hours of game time under his money belt, and you've got a score spread. Any two players and one's the teacher, the other a pupil: "No, don't do that, watch out for that city, you're running out of ammo, remember smart missiles, keep your eye on the ball, there, you're getting it...."

You've got all the resources you'd ever want for guaranteeing massive social interest: the neurological and cardiovascular kick, and among the most perfect social arrangements for generating interaction. Bless you, Atari et al, you've resocialized us after thirty years of being vaguely with each other during prime time. So what if we're claiming ownership to skills actually accrued quite independent of our conscious selves.

Frames and Games

Gary Alan Fine

Context

*"Frames and Games" is a chapter from my book **Shared Fantasy: Role-Playing Games as Social Worlds** (University of Chicago Press, 1983), which was based on ethnographic observations and in-depth interviews conducted between 1977 and 1979 in Minneapolis. It was likely the first scholarly observation study of Dungeons & Dragons and similar games. Thus, the book represents a description of role-playing games at a particular historical moment. By the end of the research there was some talk of using computers to play such games, but few had attempted such technological innovations. The book owes much to the analysis of sociologist Erving Goffman in its analysis of how small groups create cultural traditions. The book argues that although fantasy may seem personal and idiosyncratic, fantasies are often socially constructed and are transformations of collective norms and values.*

Player and Character

Games and Narrative

Cultural Representation

Gary Alan Fine is John Evans Professor of Sociology at Northwestern University. Fine received his Ph.D. in Social Psychology from Harvard University in 1976. He is the author of numerous ethnographic studies, examining Little League baseball, restaurant kitchens, mushroom collecting clubs, high school debate squads, folk art collectors and dealers, and government meteorologists, as well as fantasy-role playing gamers.

I have conceived of fantasy gaming as a social world, a universe of discourse. In this chapter I will examine the implications of this view for understanding the players' interpretations of their experiences. Central to this approach is the assertion that human beings reside in finite worlds of meaning, and that individuals are skilled in juggling these worlds. I will use fantasy gaming data to explore some implications of Erving Goffman's discussion of frame analysis.

Sociologists and philosophers have long recognized the existence of finite worlds of meaning that have the potential for allowing human beings to become encapsulated in them. William James (1950; orig. 1890:287–93) addressed the existence of "various orders of reality" grounded in the paramount reality of the "world of 'Practical Realities'." Similarly, Alfred Schutz asserted that people make sense of their perceptions through multiple realities:

> All of these worlds—the world of dreams, of imageries and phantasms, especially the world of art, the world of religious experience, the world of scientific contemplation, the play world of the child, and the world of the insane—are finite provinces of meaning. [Schutz 1971:232]

According to Schutz these worlds have a particular cognitive style, are internally consistent, and have a "specific accent of reality" (Schutz 1971:232). Goffman describes social worlds as constituting frames of experience. He defines a frame as a situational definition constructed in accord with organizing principles that govern both the events themselves and participants' experiences of these events (1974:10–11). Extending the work of Schutz and James, Goffman examines the linkages among frames of involvements, how individuals pass from one frame to another, and how they become entangled and involved in frames, which are grounded in the social order. *Frame Analysis* is original in its invocation of the social organization of interaction to uncover perceptions of experience.

Games seem particularly appropriate to the application of frame analysis because they represent a bounded set of social conventions, namely a social world. Goffman's 1961 essay "Fun in Games," with its concern for the boundaries of play, can be seen as the logical precursor to *Frame Analysis,* which also relied upon gaming examples to depict the foundations of experience. This choice of topic is significant because it reminds us that frames of experience may be conscious. Unlike dreams or madness, these worlds have a logical structure, recognizable as parallel to the mundane world.

579

Games are quintessential examples for frame analysis because of their capacity for inducing engrossment. That is, voluntarily cutting oneself off from other realms of experience distinguishes this world of meanings from those primary frameworks (or the paramount reality) that individuals "naturally" inhabit. Games—at least those that are judged as successful—provide alternative social worlds in which individuals can become involved. The significance of gaming resides in the shared nature of the engrossment (see Riezler 1941) and in the supportive recognition that others are equally engrossed:

> As far as gaming encounters and other focused gatherings are concerned, the most serious thing to consider is the fun in them. Something in which the individual can become unselfconsciously engrossed is something that can become real to him. Events that occur in his immediate physical presence are ones in which he can become easily engrossed. *Joint* engrossment in something with others reinforces the reality carved out by the individual's attention, even while subjecting this entrancement to the destructive distractions that the others are now in a position to cause. [Goffman 1961:80; italics in original]

Yet Goffman does not here recognize the oscillating character of such engrossment. Although perhaps contrary to common sense, people easily slip into and out of engrossment. Frames succeed each other with remarkable rapidity; in conversations, people slip and slide among frames. Engrossment, then, need not imply a permanent orientation toward experience. This point is consistent with Goffman's discussion of talk as a "rapidly shifting stream of differently framed strips" (Goffman 1974:544).

A weakness in *Frame Analysis* is its insistent shifting of examples. The reader never learns enough about any one social world to understand the dynamics of the frames embedded in that world and the dynamics of keying in that "universe of experience." Through a discussion of fantasy gaming I intend to examine several issues that Goffman suggests are characteristic of all human experience. It is not my intention to use my ethnography of fantasy gaming to explicate Goffman's approach point for point. Rather, I will attempt to ground these data in my own rendering of frame analysis. My analysis, then, is heavily influenced by Goffman's writing, but is not an exegesis of it. I wish to expand two features of frame analysis that, I believe, have not received sufficient attention: the extent to which different frames of experience are stable, and the relations among the framed selves of the individual—in other words the extent of awareness allowed between frames.

Fantasy Games and Frame Analysis

Like many social worlds (acting, storytelling), fantasy games produce a "make-believe" world set apart from the everyday world. By playing fantasy games, participants implicitly agree to "bracket" the world outside the game. Yet ultimately all events are grounded in the physical world. As Goffman notes:

> Fanciful words can speak about make-believe places, but these words can only be spoken *in* the real world. [Goffman 1974:247; italics in original]

Furthermore, our understanding of the rules of framing and of organizing game experiences are acquired in the "outside" world, and are required for the structuring of a play world. [Goffman 1974:249]

Every play world has a set of transformation rules that indicates *what* is to be treated as real and *how* it is to be treated as real within the make-believe framework. In acting, the what and how are typically bounded by the footlights. For games, such as bridge, meaning-relevant actions have a particularly artificial patina:

> [Players] do not treat the fact that the other player withdraws a card from his hand and places it on the table as the event "putting down a pasteboard" or "effecting a transla-tion of position of a card," but rather through the translation of the card's position the player signalizes that "he has played the ace of spades as the first card of the trick." [Goffman, 1961:26, quoting Garfinkel, unpublished paper, n.d.:7]

The rules of the game and the meaning of these rules imbue the game with its meaning (Riezler 1941). Games, through the transformation of events embedded in natural interaction, constitute world-building activities (Goffman 1961:27).

This assignment of meaning through transformation applies to fantasy gaming, but because of the attempt to simulate a world of interaction, the properties of this transforma-tion are somewhat more complicated than those of other games, such as bridge, chess, or backgammon. In those games the simulated actions have an arbitrary relation to naturally occurring events. Putting down a card has symbolic meaning in the game world, but it has no regularly expected meaning in the nongame world. In fantasy gaming the relationship between the meaning of an action within the game and natural interaction is closer.

In board games, such as backgammon, dice determine the outcome of sequential action, but in fantasy games, unlike in backgammon, the dice generate actions that *could* occur in the real world. A roll of six in backgammon means that the player's piece gets to advance six spaces on the board: that same six in fantasy gaming means that a player's character successfully bashes an opponent. While both of these actions are unreal, they are unreal in different ways. In backgammon, the pieces do move six spaces—a physical movement of a material object—but the spaces have no inherent meaning. No physical movement occurs in fantasy gaming, since the actions of characters are internally represented; however, within the framework of the game the bash is a real one, and the character who is bashed is really injured. The world of fantasy gaming and the rules that structure that world do not have physical effects, but the consequences are close simulations of natural interaction. The action is a direct simulation of a hypothetical world rather than, as in backgammon, an indirect simulation enacted in a physical world.

Because fantasy gaming does not have winning as a clearly defined goal, what is the reason for playing? In some ways fantasy gaming represents a pure game in that engrossment in the game world is the dominant reason for playing. One can play bridge to win and not really care about the cards. Even in a semi-role-playing game such as *Diplomacy* one may have no interest in the scenario of the game; however, the structure of fantasy gaming requires such engrossment in the created fantasy world. If the player doesn't care about his character then the game is meaningless. Thus players can incorporate anything into the game world provided that it increases their engrossment in the fantasy. Additional frames beyond the players' primary framework must be seen as desirable alternatives in order for the game to continue.

Frame Levels in Fantasy Gaming

It is neither realistic nor useful to provide an exhaustive list of the types of frames available to individuals. As Goffman notes, frames are embedded within frames, and the structure of these framing devices, either keyings or fabrications,[1] may be complex. In fantasy gaming, there are keyings (and sometimes fabrications)[2] nestled within the original frame. Characters sometimes find it necessary to trick others by pretending that they (the characters) are someone other than who they "really" are. This can be achieved by invoking a magical spell ("Transmorph," "Disguise"[3]) or by playing one's character as if he were someone else. Characters pretend to be weary strangers while they are actually the foes of those they attempt to deceive.

In one *EPT* [Empire of the Petal Throne] scenario, our party visited a dungeon in which several characters were trapped in a magical mural that contained "fantasy" figures with whom our "real" characters had to deal in order to escape. Our characters were doing this at the same time that other characters were in the room watching us trying to escape from the enchanted mural. The activity in the mural was a keying from our status as characters, which in turn rested on the keyings of the gaming framework, further based upon a keying of the primary framework of the players.

It is not important to present a list of the schemas of belief that are possible in the gaming world. What *is* important is that transformations of realms of action do occur, and vary greatly in content and structure. I shall simplify matters by focusing on three levels of meaning, drawing on the vast tangle of other possible keyings and fabrications only when necessary for explication.

First, gaming, like all activity, is grounded in the "primary framework," the common-sense understandings that *people* have of the real world. This is action without laminations. It is a framework that does not depend on other frameworks but on the ultimate reality of events.

Second, players must deal with the game context; they are *players* whose actions are governed by a complicated set of rules and constraints. They manipulate their characters, having knowledge of the structure of the game, and having approximately the same knowledge that other players have. Players do not operate in light of their primary frameworks—in terms of what is physically possible—but in light of the conventions of the game.

Finally, this gaming world is keyed in that the players not only manipulate characters; they *are* characters. The *character* identity is separate from the *player* identity. In this, fantasy gaming is distinct from other games. It makes no sense in chess to speak of "black" as being distinct from Karpov the player (although one can speak of Karpov the player as different from Karpov the man). The pieces in chess ("black") have no more or less knowledge than their animator. However, Sir Ralph the Rash, the doughty knight, lacks some information that his player has (for example, about characteristics of other characters, and spheres of game knowledge outside his ken such as clerical miracles) and has some information that his player lacks (about the area where he was raised, which the referee must supply when necessary). To speak of a chess knight as having different knowledge from its animator might make for good fantasy but not for meaningful chess.

Each of these three levels has its own structure of meaning (and its own shared understandings). Thus in chapter 4 I discussed the friendship culture of players, which corresponds to their primary understandings, and their gaming culture, which corresponds to the player's information about the game. I might have pushed the point and argued that the characters in the game (like characters in a play) have their own "culture," but that analysis would have had the effect of pushing culture far from its behavioral moorings—although in theory such an analysis might have been justified.

Awareness Contexts

Every frame has meanings associated with it, but these meanings are not necessarily shared with figures (persons, players, characters) operating in other frames. Building on Glaser and Strauss's article, "Awareness Contexts and Social Interaction" (1964), I wish to extend the construct of awareness to the understanding of levels of meaning and experience. Contours of awareness coupled with engrossment permit us to speak of frames as being different from each other. Thus a joke is considered funny even though its content is "seriously" known to be false. The joke provides a circumstance in which the shared awareness of the "true" falsity is set aside to permit engrossment in the joke. Engrossment implies the setting aside or ignoring of alternative awarenesses.

Glaser and Strauss (1964) distinguish four structural types of awareness contexts (examined through dyadic relations). An open awareness context is present when each interactant is aware of the other's identity and his own identity as seen by the other. A closed awareness context occurs when one interactant does not know either the other's identity or his own identity in the eyes of the other. A suspicion awareness context emerges when one individual suspects the identity of the other or one's own identity in the eyes of the other. Finally, a pretense awareness context applies when both parties are aware but pretend that they are not. Glaser and Strauss's analysis is limited to the awareness of *others* and does not examine the awareness of *selves* and the knowledge of selves in other frames.

Numerous activities involve the enactment of several selves by the same individual. Actors, storytellers, spies, experimental confederates, con men, and of course fantasy gamers all have multiple selves lodged within the same body. These would seem to require open awareness, since both "figures" are the same physical being. However, this reasonable assumption is misleading about the nature of frames of experience. In few cases is there open awareness between frames, because open awareness entails denying the existence of the other frames as realms of experience. Open awareness denies the engrossing character of fantasy. Closed awareness contexts and suspicion awareness contexts seem equally rare; split personalities or recovering split personalities are examples of these states, but these psychotic states gain their clinical significance by their rarity. Dreaming, hallucinating, or hypnotic trances represent temporary closed awareness contexts. More characteristic of framing is the pretense awareness context; the existence of frames outside of primary frameworks depends on the individual's being willing to *assume* an unawareness of his other selves. The actor's character pretends to know nothing of the actor's self and knowledge, but it is only a pretense of ignorance for nondissociated individuals. In the game structure players must play by the rules and refrain from using other devices that are illegitimate. Likewise, the character must *know* only that information which is available within the game frame and not what the player or the person knows.

The character is supposed to operate under the constraints of a closed awareness context with regard to his animator, although this of course is a pretense. Because player, person, and character share a brain, this separation of knowledge on occasion is ignored. Characters do draw on their animator's knowledge of contemporary reality when their character could not have this knowledge, or they can draw on their player's knowledge of game events outside of their own knowledge. Also players and persons are unaware of the specialized knowledge that their characters have. These problems arise when one upkeys from one's primary framework. That is, it is not considered a problem when persons admit knowledge of the game structure or actions of characters, and no dispute arises because players know what their characters know. Only in situations that in theory are closed awareness contexts but in reality are pretense awareness contexts (in which advantages are to be gained in the application of awareness) do difficulties occur. I shall examine each of these problematic components of awareness contexts, and then discuss their implications for frame analysis.

Character awareness of person reality

Characters use knowledge of late twentieth century America to select and evaluate game options. Technically this is considered poor role-playing, but it is functional within the game context because it gives the character an advantage not otherwise available. This issue is most relevant to the two games based on medieval Europe, *C & S [Chivalry and Sorcery]* and *D & D [Dungeons and Dragons]*. For a character to know about advanced weapon design or the laws of physics gives him an advantage, unless all in that situation (including nonplayer characters) share that knowledge. The slippage of awareness poses a problem for the referee, who must distinguish the character's legitimate knowledge from his animator's knowledge of a more technologically advanced age (see Ward 1979:7). Referees sometimes allow this tainted knowledge in the game in order to expedite game events, but they may exclude information if characters seem to know too much:

> Sometimes they'll try to apply twentieth-century knowledge to a medieval situation.... They love to invent the airplane.... A lot of people want to be clever; they'll invent the cannon. And I'll say, "Fine, what metallurgical processes do you wish to apply to refine the iron ore to this quality?" and they go, "Huh? Doesn't somebody know?" They don't really know themselves how to do it.... You know, you're acting out of character, so I'm not going to give you the benefit of the doubt. [Personal interview]

Players' incomplete knowledge allows referees to restrict the awareness of characters, and to prevent the pretense awareness context from shifting too obviously to an open awareness context. Referees can merely disallow knowledge, but this raises questions when the character does "in fact" know what he claims to know. In these situations the referee and player must determine the extent of the character's knowledge. This is complicated by the fact that referees create worlds that are *not* historical replicas of the European Middle-Ages. In fantasy, it is *possible* for the characters to know *anything.* Despite this flexibility of fantasy, both players and referees recognize that medieval characters should not have too much information gleaned from contemporary scholarship and technical training.

Character awareness of player reality

Typically, a player does not leave the gaming area when other players' characters are adventuring outside of the physical presence of that player's character. It is expected that a player can shield the information he receives from his character. Here again players operate in a pretense awareness context—the characters must pretend not to know something the players know. It is in the interest of characters to use this information, although it contaminates the role-playing.

When the information gained might directly influence the game (often when some characters are attempting to devise a fabrication to trap others), the referee or other players may insist that players leave the gaming area:

> Howard (the referee) tells our party to leave the table while he is refereeing another spaceship which misjumped into a planet controlled by our enemies, fearing that we would find out too much about their military system. [Field notes]

The integrity of the distribution of information precludes participation by all players. In this instance, our group waited for forty-five minutes while Howard resolved the scenario.

Referees typically do not insist that players leave the gaming area, but they do try to prevent players from using the information. Enforcement is difficult because a character may act in a legitimate fashion but do so because of information he has acquired "illegitimately." If a player discovers that a particular dungeon room contains a very hungry dragon with a very small treasure, the player's character might choose another door. The character *might* have done that anyhow, but this information makes the possibility a certainty. Similarly, if a player learns that another's character plans to steal his treasure, he will take precautions to protect his wealth—precautions that he might not have taken otherwise. Players often use information this way, and referees can do little about a player who makes cynical use of his pretense awareness context.

However, referees have some power in controlling the spread of information among frames when the source of that information is obvious. Thus we find the following debate among players about a character's personal knowledge of another character:

> Barry: *I'm going to see my father in the Great White Lodge* [a magical lodge that other characters have mentioned, and which he knows about as a player—but not as a character—of which his father is the leader].
>
> George: *You don't know anything about the Great White Lodge.*
>
> Barry: *I've heard about it.*
>
> George: *Well, you might have heard about it.*
>
> Barry: *In mythology, you know.*
>
> George: *That's about all you've heard. You don't even know there is a leader there.*
>
> Barry: *Yes, I do.*
>
> GAF: *You certainly don't know it's your father.*

> Barry: *No, but I always wanted to see him.*
>
> George: *Well, but everybody wants to see somebody important. That doesn't mean anything.* [Field notes]

Although Barry as a player knows of the Great White Lodge, this information must be shielded from his character; he is forced to adopt a pretense awareness context, even though some leeway is allowed. This slippage in awareness is also seen in the following example from *EPT*:

> Roger has been informed by other players that a party his character was not in had met some Ru'un[4] in the dungeon of his castle, but his character, Lord Ahanbasrim, had not been told. Roger keeps making reference to these creatures, and finally the referee tells him (Lord Ahanbasrim): "You don't know these Ru'un are there, so stop pretending that you do." [Field notes]

Some referees extend their concern with the degree of players' awareness and suggest that, as in "real life," characters should not know the probabilities in the game world (the rules of the game with their percentages of success). This secretiveness—keeping the player ignorant so that his character will be ignorant—adds to the verisimilitude of the simulation according to some referees:

> I have long felt it best for the players *not* to know all the rules of the game they are playing. Even if a [referee] utilizes a particular set of [role-playing] rules, she or he should change the rules (characteristics of "monsters" or magical items, etc.) just to keep things interesting. [Sustare 1979:21; italics in original]

Most referees find this approach cumbersome; it's easier to give in to players' demands for complete awareness. As one player commented in an adventure in which this rule was enforced, "Don't you just hate not knowing what's going on?" As a result, many referees permit slippage between character and player knowledge.

Slippages of awareness indicate the fragility of the role-playing enterprise—it can easily be subverted. I emphasize, however, that although this subversion damages the nature of the role-playing, it does not destroy the game. This extra information gives the characters an advantage that they would not have if the fantasy situation were the primary framework for their characters—it tarnishes the illusion of the "real fantasy" world, but it doesn't make the game less of a game.

Player unawareness of character reality

The game illusion is that players are enacting the roles of personages who lived during the Middle Ages or who will live in the far distant future. This implies that the player must play the character. Yet the player is portraying this character *in a world*—a world created by the referee, of which the player knows little. Thus a character who is a knight would know many of the nuances of armed battle with which the player is totally unfamiliar; the Tsolyani priest would be aware of the details of his religion; and the starship commander would know how to command a starship. This means that players and referees must *assume* the details of existence within the worlds that the characters occupy. Down-keying from the character to the player involves a closed awareness context. In game terms it is assumed that the character exists independently of the player—the player only animates his character. In practice, the character must rely either on the knowledge of the player or on the assumption of the referee that the character does know the nuances of "mundane" fantasy life. However, in addition to ensuring that the character does not fail because of the player's lack of "obvious" knowledge, the referee must ensure that the players are aware of things that the character would definitely know:

> Our *EPT* party is thinking of going to M'relu, the regional capital, to trick the regional commander into giving us permission to hunt for treasure. The referee suggests that our characters probably couldn't deceive him, saying, "he's a man who's not stupid," but he suggests that we might be able to bribe someone in his entourage. He adds, "You'd know this; this isn't telling you anything." [Field notes]

This is significant in that the players did *not* know this, and had no way of knowing it; the referee is providing advice to the players and through his advice is opening the closed awareness context. The claim of legitimate knowledge is also used by a referee to justify giving a player special treatment:

> Barry: [when George (the referee) and Jerry are exchanging notes] *Back and forth with the notes.*
>
> George: *He's not asking me anything really important to tell the truth.*
>
> Jerry: *Just for my own information.*
>
> George: *Which he would actually know; he would know anyway.*
>
> Jerry: *My character would know, but I wouldn't.* [Field notes]

This not only represents the opening of a closed awareness context (by down-keying information from the character to the player) but also indicates the boundaries of information between one character (for whom this information was central to the plot) and the other characters in the game. Unlike the previous examples of awareness contexts, which were influenced by the simultaneous operation of frames and in which the problem was too much information in the system (the character knew more than he ought), here the problem is too little information (the player does not know enough). Generally, roles that have fewer keyed laminations are "legitimately" aware of up-keyed roles; roles with more laminations are less "legitimately" aware of down-keyed roles. Simultaneously, portrayers of roles with more laminations have less information about their keyed roles than those who portray roles with fewer laminations. Put simply, the closer one is to one's primary framework, the wider one's pool of knowledge is, and the more one can draw upon all the other worlds of knowledge.

Awareness context of the referee

Although the referee has created a world, it is a world that he does not know well. Typically, the referee creates a bare outline of the world. Thus the fantasy world the referee has created is very different in scope from the world he inhabits. As referee, he is not the same as God, despite the metaphorical linkage. If we think of "God" as being a keying of the game organizer's role, we can see that he is in a somewhat similar position to players who find that their characters know more than they do. The referee has a world to run, yet it is an opaque world, and he has no one to consult to give it form except himself, although at times he may become so engrossed in his world that he temporarily forgets that only he can create it (Holmes 1980:93).

This means that the referee must create the world as the game proceeds, according to the needs of the characters. Since referees can't plan the details of their world too far in advance, they may have nonplayer characters give the player-characters less information than might reasonably be expected:

> Our party in *Traveller* runs into several Gilgemeshers (huge merchant ships). Although the commanders of these ships are friendly, they (as portrayed by Howard, the referee) refuse to give us any information about neighboring planets. The reason for this becomes clear when we see Howard's map of space. Although he has the planets located, he has not yet given them any characteristics, and therefore does not know enough about them to answer our questions. [Field notes]

The referee as animator of nonplayer characters is not aware of all of the information that he implicitly has by being "God." This structure of awareness has implications for the operation of any universe.

Awareness context and frames

In examining relationships among the roles that individuals adopt while interacting, I have suggested that there are difficulties in the awareness that persons have of other keyed roles. My interest is in the relations among an individual's selves (and the information controlled by selves) in different frames. This suggests that there are different contours of knowledge, and participants must ensure, if they are to stay within frame, that the pretense of awareness is maintained—for it is the pretense of awareness coupled with the possibilities for engrossment that comprise the basis of behavior within a frame.

I have suggested that three basic frames operate in fantasy gaming and that each of these has a world of knowledge associated with it—the world of commonsense knowledge grounded in one's primary framework, the world of game rules grounded in the game structure, and the knowledge of the fantasy world (itself a hypothetical primary framework). The individual has the right and responsibility to know about the first two, and typically can learn about them if he wishes. The third world is in theory known only through the character and in practice is known through the referee and through action in the game. This knowledge is, then, often inaccessible. This situation is not unique to gaming, but applies to all role-playing—acting, spying in disguise, or doing comic impressions. While the person *is* the person he is playing, he only knows a limited amount of information about that person and is unable to generate more knowledge. Further, if the role-playing is effective, he is limited to knowing *only* what that individual knows. This is what makes role-playing difficult: the player must block information about the game and the contemporary world that the character would not know, while simultaneously not letting his own ignorance of the fantasy world affect the successful action of the character. Using awareness effectively is intimately connected to the keying of social worlds.

Every social world has its own structure of meaning. It is my contention that although the specific structure of fantasy role-play gaming is unique, the processes being examined here characterize other social worlds as well. Consider spying. Here we find espionage agents acting under cover, portraying the roles of other (real or fictitious) individuals. At least two levels of awareness operate here: the spy in his "real" identity and the spy in his "assumed" identity (see Goffman 1969). The spy knows only those details about his "assumed" self that he is told and cannot recall other "biographical facts." Thus the spy is like the player portraying a fantasy character. Likewise, the "assumed identity" cannot know those things that the spy would know (as the medieval character cannot know about modern technology). The spy-in-disguise can be uncovered if he knows things that the person he is portraying couldn't know—as well, of course, as not knowing things he would surely have known.

Acting and storytelling provide similar instances of several personae being enacted by a single individual in different frames. The actor and storyteller must make sure that the character doesn't learn what the animator knows, and in turn the animator can't peek into the character's world to learn just a little bit more (other than through the use of imagination, grounded in the "real" world). Yet the "assumed" persona must be real to the audience. Whenever we step out of our primary frameworks into new "selves" for extended periods (even in dreams, reveries, or the like), the issue of "self"-awareness must be addressed.

The examples presented represent the actions of professional keyers and fabricators, but what about everyday life? The dramaturgical analogy suggests that we are all keyers and fabricators. The person consists of a bundle of identities that are more or less compatible, but which when enacted must presume a lack of awareness that other identities are possible. The identity enacted is grounded in the assumption that that is the "real" identity, although often the enactor is well aware that this identity is chosen for purposes of impression management. The task of self-presentation does not merely involve manifesting an appropriate and coherent identity, but also involves concealing those other identities that are either incompatible or differently keyed. Even when awareness of the impression management is not wholly conscious, the structural relationship between selves is still present. Admittedly, the identities enacted in everyday interaction are less distinct from each other than those found in the more dramatic examples.

Switching Frames

Frames have different levels of stability. By that I mean that some frames oscillate rapidly—up-keying or down-keying frequently—while other frames are comparatively stable. The actor must remain in the part of his character continuously while onstage; similarly, the spy-in-disguise cannot switch frames without some danger. In other situations (e.g., put-ons, playfulness, fantasy gaming), frame switching typically poses no substantial problem for participants.

The extent of frame switching can be seen as a function of engrossment (Goffman 1974:345). Games are designed to provide "engrossable" systems of experience in which participants can become caught up. In fact, individuals do get "caught up" in fantasy gaming; however, this engrossment is a flickering involvement—it depends on events that occur in the game world. Players do become involved when they face a monster; but once this encounter is completed, they may return to "mundane" discussions about politics, girlfriends, or the latest science fiction novel, even though the game continues.

In addition to the recognition that engrossment is essential for the stability of the fantasy frame, one should consider the effect of the voluntary nature of the frame and the "fun" that is embedded in it. Voluntary frames, i.e., frames in which persons are not constrained to stay, are more likely to be rapidly keyed than are mandatory frames—although this is, of course, a matter of degree. It is not only the amount of engrossment that the actor finds in his character's role that stabilizes the play, but the consequences of breaking frame. In voluntary activities, such as fantasy gaming, there are few aversive consequences for breaking frame. Frame switching is considered legitimate as long as it does not overly affect the continuation of the game:

> When one player takes time out to answer the telephone, the play may be stopped in mid-air, being transfixable for any period of time, but not the social affair, the gaming encounter, for this can be threatened and even destroyed if the absent player is held too long on the telephone or must return with tragic news. (Goffman 1961:36)

Because it is voluntary, fantasy gaming permits side involvements to take precedence—a point structurally different from how engrossed one can become in the game.

A third point relevant to the nature of frame breaking within the gaming encounter concerns "fun." "Fun" would seem to be a *sine qua non* for gaming, but "fun" is a flickering experience, and along with it flickers engrossment and the stability of the frame. When other side-involvements are perceived to have greater rewards in terms of "enjoyment," the game will be put aside—temporarily or permanently. The search for fun also leads to players' "toying" with their play (Goffman 1961:36–37). Side-involvements, if frequent and enjoyable enough, may be incorporated as regular parts of games (such as inserting gambling with real coins within the structure of fantasy games). Both voluntary involvement and fun are related to the nature and extent of engrossment—but these are analytically separable constructs that affect engrossment while increasing or decreasing the likelihood of frame-shifting.

Mundane shifts of levels occur when the fantasy is interrupted by the pressures of the real world—the ringing telephone, the ordering (and then eating) of a pizza, or the biological needs of participants. These activities generate breaks in the game—and down-key the interaction to the "real world." The "real world" will always intrude, for the gaming structure is not impermeable to outside events. However, the extent to which this down-keying occurs is also a consequence of interest in the game. One player comments:

> From a theoretical standpoint I would guess that as the game gets more and more interesting people do less and less talking out of character.... I'm sure that there are times when [talking out of character] can be very, very, frustrating to referees, cause like I was reffing a game once, and the players kept making comments about the room and how the water didn't taste very good.... I would suspect that as the game got more and more intense, people would stick more and more to the game itself. [Personal interview]

Just as games can be down-keyed, so too can reality be up-keyed to the level of fantasy, which occurs when one's primary reality proves frustrating:

> At the convention banquet the food service is very slow, and diners joke about the speed of the meal, banging their utensils on the table in imitation of rugged adventurers waiting to be served at a tavern. One diner commented: "We should have brought along dungeon rations." [Field notes]

Games may also involve the up-keying of reality. As discussed in chapter 3 in another context, a referee may take a comment made by a player outside his game role and incorporate it into the action of the game:

> We are trying to find the materials for a cabalist charm for Lewis's character. At one point Lewis's character enters a butcher shop to purchase cow's blood for the charm. The referee (Don) says that the butcher looks at him suspiciously when he asks for it, and Don, speaking as the butcher, says: "What do you want it for?" Lewis jokes out of frame: "I'm thirsty." Don says the butcher scowls, "Get out of my shop." After leaving the butcher we head back to the inn where we meet six Knights Templar who insist that Lewis's character comes with them to talk to the priest. Lewis agrees, and, while at the church, his character is killed, because they think this blood-drinker is demonic. [Field notes]

However, there is a complication. Unlike the example of the hungry convention gamers, these up-keyed comments (that is, comments given an additional meaning or lamination) are themselves grounded in the game events. They add a level to the game events by satirically giving game events relevance in the everyday world; these are then further up-keyed by the referee back to the gaming frame. Thus the referee's action is a mocking of a mocking, which is accepted as part of the gaming world:

> GAF: *I notice in playing at the Golden Brigade that some referees will incorporate what people say out of character into the game structure.*

> Barker: *I do this as a joke. For instance, somebody will make a smart crack. Like he'll say, "Bullshit," whereupon I have one of the Tekumel characters say "What's a bull?" or they'll use some particularly American idiom, say "He kicked the bucket," and so the Tekumel character says "Why did he do that?" and "What was this bucket doing there in the first place?" Just to tease them and embarrass them sort of and make them realize that you must not shift out of character.* [Personal interview]

By speaking out of character, players up-key the structure of the game, and Barker up-keys it further by incorporating this talk humorously in the context of the game.

By up-keying, players and referees transform game-relevant statements into remarks that are not defined in terms of the game context but are based upon it. These remarks are distinct from secondary involvements and out-of-frame activities, which are viewed as separate and subsidiary to the game. These remarks use the game framework and can only be understood in this context, although they do not presuppose an extended framed self. As a consequence, players can make an up-keyed joke, get a laugh, and immediately return to character as if nothing had happened (if the referee or other players don't up-key the remark further). For example, a player who has a "haste" spell placed on his character will himself (as a player) talk rapidly. Or a dungeon pool of bubbling water is referred to as "Mountain Dew" or "7-Up." These comments are not disattended by *players* in that they draw laughter, but are disattended by the *characters* whose actions are being mocked. Only rarely is there confusion about the level on which a jocular statement is to be taken.

Is such fooling with frames unique to fantasy gaming? Assuredly not, although there seems not to be any generic name for its parallel in the real world, except perhaps what we might call an extended put-on or informal joking. Friends often "put-on" characters when gabbing with others, and the others in turn have the opportunity to engage in conversations with other personae or reground the joking remarks back into the primary framework, as gamers do. These gambits have the same evanescent quality as fantasy interludes, and perhaps for this reason have been little studied (see Goffman 1974:87–89; Hall 1974).

Despite the possibilities for engrossment in fantasy gaming, frame shifting occurs frequently—both up-keying (adding laminations to the game world) and down-keying (returning to players' primary frameworks or to a discussion of the gaming rules). These keyings may be stable, chaining the frame for a considerable period of time, but often are evanescent. The implications of this are consistent with seeing interactants negotiating reality with each other—a reality that is continually in dynamic tension, subject to shifts in interpersonal definitions.

Problems in Frame Interpretation

As Goffman notes, ambiguity in the interpretation of events is not uncommon, and this produces difficulty in determining which frame of reference to use to respond to an event:

> What is ambiguous is the meaning of an event, but what is at stake is the question of what framework of understanding to apply and, once selected, to go on applying, and the potential frameworks available often differ quite radically one from the other. [Goffman 1974:304]

Although such radical shifts do not occur in fantasy gaming, we still find ambiguities of frame. We can imagine such gaming statements as "Did you kill James?" being taken in two ways, but this confusion did not occur, partly because context and paravocal clues indicated that no "real" crime was being discussed, even though "real" names were used. The misunderstandings between frames are relatively minor—more suitable to a chuckle than to a blush—and they center around those aspects of the game that have counterparts in the primary frameworks of players: name, place, age, and time. Usually the nature of the speaker (in terms of which keyed identity is talking) and the keyed identity of the audience can be reasonably well determined. However, we do find some briefly confused situations:

> George asks me: *"How old are you?"* Thinking of my character, I say, *"Twenty-three."* George: *"No, in real life."* I say, *"Twenty-seven."* He comments, *"I'm twenty-six."* [Field notes]

A group of players were discussing various games that they had participated in. Sandy was explaining an event in a game he had recently played.

Ron: *Where were you?*

Sandy: *In Detroit.*

Ron: *No, in the game.*

Sandy: *Over by some huts.* [Field notes]

These ambiguities are resolved quickly, because the speaker will typically provide a corrective account (Goffman 1974:480) which has the effect of protecting the other from embarrassment as well as gaining the information originally desired. Indeed, if such a corrective is not given, it may well be impossible to know that a misframing has occurred.

Audiences must determine *who* the speaker is. They must discover not only the source of the words, but which of the speaker's selves is doing the talking—the person or the referee, the player or the character. The following is one of the more complex confusions of this genre:

Jerry said that "I" [my character] had gone over to the king's capital city, and on the docks "I" [my character] had met "Barry" [Barry's character]. "Barry" [the person] shakes my hand [my real hand] and says, "Nice to meet you [the character]." "I" [in character] say, "Nice to meet you [Barry's character]" to him. Jerry seems surprised and asks: "Don't the two of you know each other?" Barry comments, "Not in this game." [Field notes]

In the game context, players or characters often refer to a character by the person's "real" name, and this practice produces a potential confusion. The "source" of the greeting becomes unclear. This was especially likely in the above example, because Barry and I had not gamed together often, and our characters had not yet met in the game. The ambiguity in this instance arose in the physical act of the two persons shaking hands. Only persons or players physically act, not characters—unless these characters are up-keying, by pantomiming their statements. Thus, had "Barry" said, "I say 'nice to meet you' and shake his hand," Jerry would not have become confused.

Another example of confusion derives from the all-encompassing culture of Tekumel:

Doug: *What be the date?*

Barker: *It's the end of Langala.*

Doug: *No, in this world.*

Barker: *This world doesn't exist.*

Doug: *I know, but anyway.*

Barker: *August tenth.* [Field notes]

This encounter is the reverse situation of the previous example. In that situation players assumed they were talking as persons; in this situation, players assumed the character was the source. Confusion may arise either from attributing an action to the primary framework or to one of its keyed alternatives. Doug's comment, "I know, but anyway," testifies to the fact that he is switching from one frame to another in mid-sentence—his character says "I know," and his person says "but anyway."

When a linkage can be made between the two worlds of being that coexist in the gaming encounter, tension (and joking) is found (Goffman 1974:77). Through humorous up-keying of game encounters participants connect the game to a version of the "natural world"—expressed unnaturally through humor. Joking happens when people are faced with a situation in which alternate perspectives can apply, or in which a sharp dichotomy exists between the player's publicly given impression and the character's attitude expressed within the context of the game. Topics in which ambiguity of attribution may be present, and hence implicit tension, are sexuality and aggression—and these are topics in which there is much humorous up-keying, as if to deny the seriousness of the topics:

Jack (the referee) reports that one soldier in Larry's character's army reports feeling ill.

Larry: *Remove your clothes. Not him, you.* (To Jack) Jack smiles and gives Larry the finger. [Field notes]

Hal: *What's a bash?*

Sam: [joking] *That means I bash you if I die.*

George: *This guy's [Sam's] a psychopath, he chokes people for the fun of it.* (Sam playfully chokes Hal.) [Field notes]

In these examples joking occurs when players make distinctions between the character's orientation and that of the player or referee. Each example involves a play on words in which the parties to the humor are portrayed simultaneously as persons and as characters. It is this juxtaposition, in conjunction with the very different attitudes toward sex and violence between free-wheeling characters and rather repressed (nonaggressive, nonsexual) persons, that provides the tension that results in humor.

Fantasy and Other "Realities"

The world of fantasy gaming as a framed world is both typical and unique. It is unique in the particular experiences it creates and the rules necessary to create these experiences. At the same time it is typical of other forms of social life in that it permits the rapid shifting of frames and requires the enactment of several framed selves. While not every situation is characterized by both oscillation of frames and pretense awareness, the former is found in many situations of play and informality and the latter is found in situations in which the person "acts" a role other than the one to which he feels entitled (not only acting and espionage, but many forms of impression management). In other words, the performer recognizes the existence of several selves that must be juggled, hidden, or exhumed when appropriate. Both, then, characterize "everyday life" as well as this pastime.

The point, of course, is not that we can generalize directly from the description of fantasy gaming; rather, fantasy gaming provides a setting in which the dynamics of framing are particularly central to the enterprise and are evident to the participants. In this chapter I have attempted to extend Goffman's argument by specifying two components of frame analysis: (1) the relationship among identities generated in different frames, and (2) the stability of frames. If we assume, as I do, that these issues transcend the narrow social scene I have described, they open the way for further investigations of the relationships among frames, engrossment, and identities, which Goffman only hints at.

Specifically, I have argued that frames have different stabilities. Some, such as in fantasy gaming, mock fighting, and informal talk, are flexible, while others, such as the dramatic frame or malicious fabrications, typically are more stable. Central to the stability of frames are the level of engrossment possible within them and the external (social or political) consequences of up-keying and down-keying. The possibility of the rapid oscillation of frames suggests that frame stability and change should be conceptualized as an interactional achievement of members rather than as a function of stable situated meaning. Since participants commonly and cooperatively shift frames in the same situation, frames are not merely a shared individual schema that is triggered by the objective properties of a situation: rather, they are part of a dynamic consensus that can be bracketed, altered, or restored through the collective action of the participants.

The other focus of this chapter is related to the first. On occasions in which some frame switching occurs, actors must deal with the knowledge that adheres to each of the "nested" identities they present. In some cases, as in fantasy gaming, this may pose interactional difficulties, particularly when up-keyed figures know both more and less than their down-keyed counter-parts. This leads the actor to adopt a pretense awareness context *among his own selves.* The implications and generality of this "inner espionage" remain to be explored in depth, although it would not be unreasonable to assume that regular pretenders have distinctly different interactional styles than those who engage in such activities less frequently. Following interactionst theory I have conceived of persons as collections of selves or identities. However, such selves typically are seen as operating sequentially and in isolation from each other; frame analysis suggests that we need to examine the effects of simultaneously activated selves on worlds of meaning.

Notes

1. By a "key" Goffman means the "set of conventions by which a given activity, one already meaningful in terms of some primary framework, is transformed into something patterned on this activity but seen by the participants to be something quite else" (Goffman 1974:43–44; see p. 45 for a more complete and formal definition). A fabrication for Goffman involves the attempt by one party to induce another party to have a false understanding of what is going on (Goffman 1974:83), in essence a keying in which there is incomplete information and a closed awareness context.

2. Although "make-believe" is keyed from one's primary framework, within this make-believe fabrications are possible—as in the content of drama and stories.

3. The "Disguise" spell provides an illusion that causes others to believe that the character is someone or something else. "Transmorph" involves actually transforming the "physical" existence of the character into another size or shape.

4. The Ru'un are animated, humanoid, bronze demon-automatons, about seven feet tall. These creatures have high intelligence, although they refuse to talk to humans. Their bodies are covered with a fine network of thin wires that give off a powerful shock to those who touch them.

Bibliography

James, William. 1950. *The principles of psychology.* Volume one. New York: Dover (orig. 1890).

Schutz, Alfred. 1971. *Collected papers I: the problem of social reality.* The Hague: Martinus Nijhoff.

Reizler, Kurt. 1941. Play and seriousness. *Journal of philosophy* 38 (Sept.): 505–17.

Goffman, Erving. 1961. *Encounters.* Indianapolis: Bobbs-Merrill.
_____. 1969. *Strategic interaction.* Philadelphia: University of Pennsylvania Press.
_____. 1974. Alarums and excursions. *Different Worlds* 1:21–22.
_____. 1976. Replies and responses. *Language and society* 5 (Dec.): 257–313.

Garfinkel, Harold. N.d. Some conceptions of and experiments with 'trust' as a condition of stable and concerted action. Unpublished paper.

Glaser, Barney and Anselm Strauss. 1964. Awareness contexts and social interaction. *American Sociological Review.* 29:669–79.

Sustare, B. Dennis. 1979. The design and solution of puzzles. *Different Worlds* 1:18–21.

Hall, Frank. 1974. Conversational joking: a look at applied humor. *Folklore Annual of the University Folklore Association* 6:26–45.

Bow, Nigger

always_black

Context

*I wrote "Bow, Nigger" as an experimental piece for the now-defunct games webzine **State Magazine**. It was spotted, bought and published by the UK edition of **PC Gamer (2004)** and subsequently held up as an example of less conventional (but importantly still commercially viable) games journalism by Kieron Gillen in his "New Games Journalism" manifesto. It's a true account of one night's play at multiplayer Jedi Knight II: Jedi Outcast, although thought by many to be fictional. To those people I would say: if I could make this stuff up, I'd be rich by now.*

Player and Character

Cultural Representation

"always_black" is British writer and amateur games journalist Ian Shanahan, published sometimes by the UK edition of *PC Gamer* and on his own website at www.alwaysblack.com.

"Bow, nigger." he typed.

I kind of hunched uncomfortably over the keyboard at that point. Not that I should've taken offence, really.

For one thing, my screen name has nothing to do with my ethnicity and for another, it's only a game and the fascist doing the typing is probably hundreds of miles away and far beyond anything you could call an actual influence on my life.

But still... It's not very nice is it?

What to do?

I circled around him warily.

JKII: Jedi Outcast does one thing very, very well, and that's lightsabres. In fact, it's probably more accurate to say George Lucas et al did lightsabres very well in the *Star Wars* films and Outcast does a good job of recalling the memory of those flashing contests. The emulation is near perfect, from the initial hiss as it slowly rises from the handle, the sweeping motion-blurred visuals to the pitch-shifting, threatening hum.

Throughout the game you can choose which perspective you choose to view the action from. The game defaults to first-person for projectile weapons but drawing your lightsabre switches to third-person ass-cam and this is by far the best configuration. Leave it alone.

Third-person allows you to fully-appreciate the acrobatics of the sabre fighting animations. You can swing away in one of three "styles," fast, medium and heavy, all of which allow you wrestle mouse movement and direction key presses to produce jaw-dropping combinations of slashes, chops and stabs that risks you forgetting any question of your actual opponent as you stare in disbelief and whisper "Did I just do that?".

"Bow," he types.

Hmm. Problem. For all of the excellent sword-play animations, Raven seems to have omitted any of the more mundane actions you could envisage your avatar performing. There is no "bow" button.

What my socially retarded friend is being so insistent about is something else, and that's a form of "physical" expression that grew up out of the enthusiasm of some of the more ardent *Star Wars* fans who play JKII online. Some people take their fiction VERY seriously and wannabe Jedi Knights are among the most serious. The faithful, in order to be more true to the "Jedi Code of Honour," crouch before each other and duck their "heads" down as a mark of respect before enjoining battle. Some people think that's silly.

603

I thought it was silly, the first time I saw it. Then I saw everybody was doing it. And then I felt silly not doing it. It's strange how much weight the actions of your peers can bring to bear, even when your social medium is only a bunch of really fast maths on a German server.

I'm currently in "heavy" style. This affords me the most damaging attacks at the expense of much slower swings. When you're not attacking it also provides the best defence, parrying is handled automatically. The best defence is wise while I'm facing off with this wanker. We've been engaged in our duel for two or three minutes and neither of us has come close enough to hit each other yet. This is a period of "sizing up".

Sometimes rash, headlong attacks can be exploited by a player of a reasonable skill level and you'll find yourself ghosting and waiting for another turn before you know what hit you. If you've never played a particular opponent before it pays to feel him out a bit.

First, though, there are the formalities. I crouch and duck my head, a "bow". Vulnerable. Stupid? Yeah.

But you know what? I entered in to it willingly and "Why?" is a very interesting question.

I'm a big boy now and I don't want to be a Jedi Knight when I grow up. The *Star Wars* films are great, but they're also just that, films, a form of entertainment to be enjoyed during breaks from my very real and financially challenging life (mortgage, two cats, a broken gutter and a car that needs some attention. Cheers.)

So I didn't bow because I wanted to "role-play" the Jedi of the game. It was an act of defiance.

Dueling is not new. Any multiplayer game can leave you with one opponent on either side and I've played that scenario out in many games. The difference with lightsabre dueling, Outcast-style, is that it's so very personal. These aren't detached sniping matches across the width of the map or rocket-spamming blast-fests to see who can respawn the least. JKII duel is "winner-stays-on" and you can be floating around for anything up to half-an-hour on a busy server waiting for a game. This makes your game "life" actually worth something and it makes it worth fighting for.

Into this potent mix you can toss in the fact that while you're a ghosting spectator you have time to chat and actually get to know the people you're playing, even on that usually most impersonal of beasts, the public server. Even during actual fights, play can swing from bouts of thrust, slash and parry to more distanced, wary sizing-up, searching for an opening that will allow you to get a sucker-hit in before your opponent can counter, time to talk and taunt.

But perhaps most personal of all is the close proximity you have to come to damage your opponent. I'm an avoidant player at the best of times, but JKII lightsabre duels just don't allow you to hit and fade from range. You have to be right in there trying to give the other guy a laser enema if you're going to avoid watching the show for another six games.

So I bowed. Not because I was naive enough to think he'd give any significance to the gesture. Not because he was commanding me to from his pillar of arrogance. I bowed *despite* his taunts. For all his goading I did "the right thing", to show him I wasn't going to come and meet him down on his level.

Blammo.

SONOFABITCH! Jesus, all my shields and forty health from one big heavy-stance overhead chop before he spun away, back to the other side of the map.

"LOL! Nigger"

He goes into a "blender". Every style has a selection of "special moves" that can activated by combination key presses, set pieces taken from notable moments of the films. Unfortunately, because JKII is based on the Quake III engine, the macro scripting of that seminal of all first-person shooters is easily migrated across. This means that all skill or effort can be eliminated from the execution of these moves by a few simple scripts that can be readily downloaded and bound to a key. A "blender" is the heavy-stance "backsweep" move, or several rather, chained together, causing the model to spin unrealistically like a top. Fatal if you get too near it, but very difficult to use in an actual fight, as you're unable to do anything until the animation has finished. It's a shame that exploits like this would eventually lead to the ultimate downfall of the multiplayer game.

He's showboating. He's demonstrating how 1337 he is.

"Are you really black nigger?," he types.

"Why?," I replied.

"Because it matter." he says.

I ignored that and edged closer by a circuitous route. Don't want to get caught out by one of his lame keybinds. I switched down to medium stance, my favourite and the best balance between speed and damage.

"I know I hurt you by the things I say," he says.

I hit "T" to talk and the chat icon appears above my head. But I hesitate. I wanted to say something, but with the little underscore blinking away there my fingers stopped over the keys. Say what? "No, you don't," "No, you aren't," "How can you when your insults are meaningless?" "Fuck you, asshole?"

And SLASH. Bastard.

In chat mode you're powerless, like most other games, your typing fingers can't do much about an assault by a conscienceless typekiller. In all my years of twitch-gaming my fingers have never moved so fast across the keyboard, escaping the trap of chat mode and rallying my defences against his lightning fast slashes.

Almost too late I put distance between us. Almost too late but not quite. Five health points remain and I know I haven't even hit him yet. Five health means you're nearly dead. A brush from the tip of a sabre that is just held idly will remove five health points from you and take you out of the game. Shit.

It's really, really unfair. I mean, alright, I've asked for it, haven't I? I was aware from the outset what kind of player I am facing, and still I insisted on performing the ritual courtesies and still I fell for the oldest trick in the book, cut to ribbons while I answer a pointless taunt. I've only myself to blame.

But for the most part JKII multiplayer isn't like that. Mostly, JKII players are like players everywhere, they just want to have a blast and enjoy the competition. They'll show each other a degree of respect that is just absent from most other multiplayer games and they express that respect in a variety of ways, from the odd little emergent bow to ad hoc lessons from complete strangers to clans adopting the padawan/master relationship outlined in the films. Most of the players are good guys.

This is why it's unfair. The game allows "bad behaviour", this is a good thing. It means that by avoiding "bad" behaviour you can demonstrate how "good" you are. Virtuous. A lack of virtue is unfairness in the unofficial "rules" of the game but the only answer you have is to fight back. You too can be "unfair," but, um, some people don't like to play that way... They make a choice.

This one does. This one is a bad guy, and he isn't messing about anymore. I guess he must've run out of tricks, or perhaps he'd done a few quick mental calculations and realised that I'm probably on the ropes, because he starts spamming the heavy-stance finishing move informally termed "Death From Above". This begins with a long flat leap and ends with an overhead chop, get caught under it and it's fatal no matter how many shield or health points you have remaining.

Which is a mistake on his part. It's total overkill, even though he doesn't know I have only five points left, and I happen to know that the very end of the move leaves you very vulnerable indeed. He has underestimated me and who can blame him? I've hardly been the epitome of laser swordsmanship thus far. I'll rectify that impression just now.

A quick swap down to fast style and a crouch-forward-attack puts me into a lunge, catching him with the uppercut. By no means fatal, but I rocked his world there for a moment. He thought he was dominating and now he's lost a whole lot of health and he wasn't ready for that.

He actually "reeled". There's always scope for projecting a little extra personification onto a computer generated character, but I swear to god he had shock on his face. Entirely too rash for my current health level, I went into a little whirlwind of fast-style slashes and probably dinged him a little more in the process as he beat a hasty retreat.

No chatting now. No more insults. Collision detection in JKII is a little flaky. Sometimes hits do far more damage than you'd have thought. I can hope. He comes at me and we have at it.

The lightsabres hiss and fizz when they come into contact with each other. I rolled and dodged and parried for all I was worth. Five health only. Nearly dead.

A little something personal about myself: I don't sweat. Never have. Not under normal, sat-at-the-computer, circumstances anyway. Obviously, physical exertion makes me sweat, running, jumping, swimming etc. But not just sat in a chair.

We spun around each other, bouncing off the furniture of the map. My concentration was absolutely intense and never before have I tried so hard to "be the mouse". I felt a trickle of wet run down from under my right armpit.

You see what this has become? It's not just a trivial game to be played in an idle moment; this is a genuine battle of good versus evil. It has nothing to do with *Star Wars* or Jedi Knights or any of the fluff that surrounds the game's mechanics. I played by the "rules" and he didn't, that makes me the "good" guy and him the "baddie", but this is real, in the sense that there's no telling who's going to win out here. There's no script or plot to determine the eventual triumph of the good guy (that's me, five health), there's no "natural order" of a fictional universe or any question of an apocryphal ultimate "balance". There's just me and him, light and dark, in a genuine contest between the two.

607

And there it is. I don't even know what it was. Some chance slash or poke in all of the rolling and jumping around and his lifeless avatar, with all his racist stabs and underhand duplicity, goes tumbling to the floor vanquished by the guy who even in the face of all of that, played by the "rules". Only one health point remains but I win.

I'm a fucking hero. A real one.

A beep and a server message: Wanker has disconnected.

I can only dream of the howls of anguish so far away.

My next opponent spawns. And bows. A chat icon appears.

"Awesome," he types.

Cultural Models:
Do You Want to Be the
Blue Sonic or the Dark Sonic?

James Gee

Context

This essay is a chapter from my book, **What Video Games Have to Teach Us About Learning and Literacy,** *(Palgrave/Macmillan, 2003), which was written because watching my then six-year-old son play video games inspired me to try playing them myself. I was amazed by how hard they were and yet, at the same time, deeply motivating and engaging. When I stuck with them, I also became fascinated by how well they dealt with learning as part of the deep pleasure of playing.*

Speaking of Games

Cultural Representation

James Paul Gee is the Tashia Morgridge Professor of Reading at the University of Wisconsin at Madison. Originally trained as a linguist, he now works on issues related to literacy and learning in and out of schools. His books include: *Social Linguistics and Literacies, The Social Mind, What Video Games Have to Teach Us About Learning and Literacy,* and *Situated Language and Learning.*

Content in Video Games

Chapter 2 discussed a case where a grandfather said that a six-year-old playing *Pikmin* was wasting his time, because he wasn't learning any "content." But, of course, video games *do* have content. *RollerCoaster Tycoon,* for instance, is about building, maintaining, and making a profit from an amusement park. *Medal of Honor Allied Assault* is about World War II and includes an absolutely hair-raising invasion of Omaha Beach, reminiscent of the opening scenes of the movie *Saving Private Ryan. Civilization III* is about world history and the dynamics of building and defending a society from the ground up. A great many video games, such as *Half-Life, Deus Ex,* and *Red Faction,* are about conspiracies where powerful and rich people or corporations seek to control the world through force and deception. In fact, the content of video games is nearly endless.

One of the things that makes video games so powerful is their ability to create whole worlds and invite players to take on various identities within them. When players do this, two things can happen: On one hand, their presupposed perspectives on the world might be re-inforced. For example, if someone thinks war is heroic, *Return to Castle Wolfenstein* will not disabuse him or her of this viewpoint. If someone thinks that the quality of life is integrally tied to one's possessions, *The Sims* (a best-selling game where you build and maintain whole families and neighborhoods) will not disabuse him or her of this perspective, either.

On the other hand, through their creation of new and different worlds and characters, video games can challenge players' taken-for-granted views about the world. Playing through the invasion of Omaha Beach in *Medal of Honor Allied Assault* gives one a whole new perspective on what a full-scale battle is like. The movie *Saving Private Ryan* did this as well, but the game puts the player right in the midst of the action, pinned to the ground, surrounded by deafening noise and wounded, sometimes shell-shocked, soldiers, and facing the near certainly of a quick death if he or she makes one wrong move. As players make choices about people, their relationships, and their lives in *The Sims* (and sometimes players have made real people, such as their friends, into virtual characters in the game), they may come to realize at a conscious level certain values and perspectives they have heretofore taken for granted and now wish to reflect on and question.

This chapter is about the ways in which content in video games either reinforces or challenges players' taken-for-granted perspectives on the world. This is an area where the future potential of video games is perhaps even more significant than their current instantiations. It is also an area where we enter a realm of great controversy, controversy that will get even more intense as video games come to realize their full potential, for good or ill, for realizing worlds and identities.

Sonic the Hedgehog and Cultural Models

Sonic the Hedgehog—a small, blue, cute hedgehog—is surely the world's fastest, most arrogant, and most famous hedgehog. Originally Sonic was the hero in a set of games for the Sega Dreamcast game platform. However, now that the Dreamcast has been discontinued, he has shown up on the Nintendo GameCube in the game *Sonic Adventure 2 Battle.* Sonic can run really really fast. He can go even faster—like a blurry blue bomb—when he rolls into a ball. Either way, he can race around and through obstacles, dash into enemies, and streak through the landscape, leaping high in the air over walls and barriers.

The back story for *Sonic Adventure 2 Battle* is that the sinister Dr. Eggman, while searching the remnants of his grandfather's laboratory, uncovers a dark form of his arch-nemesis, Sonic, namely a black hedgehog named Shadow. Together the two conspire to unleash the Eclipse Cannon, a weapon of mass destruction. The government, unable to tell the blue Sonic from the dark Shadow (they look alike) arrests Sonic for Shadow's evil doings. Sonic escapes and has to free the world of Dr. Eggman and Shadow's evil to clear his name.

Players can play *Sonic Adventure 2 Battle* in two different ways. They can be "good" and play as the blue Sonic, or they can be "bad" and play as Sonic's look-alike, Shadow. If they choose Sonic, they play as Sonic, together with his friends Knuckles (a boy echidna) and Tails (a boy squirrel), trying to stop Dr. Eggman and Shadow from taking over the world. If they choose Shadow, they play as Shadow, together with his friends Rouge (a girl bat) and Dr. Eggman, trying to destroy the world. Players can switch back and forth, playing part of the Sonic quest and then changing to play part of the Shadow quest.

The six-year-old from chapter 2 also plays *Sonic Adventure 2 Battle.* When he originally got the game, he first played a few episodes from the Sonic quest and then started playing episodes from the Shadow quest. When he was playing as Shadow, he commented on the fact that "the bad guy was the good guy"—an odd remark. What he meant, of course, is that when you are playing as a virtual character in a video game, that character (you) is the hero (center) of the story and in that sense the "good guy" no matter how bad he or she might be from another perspective. This boy had never before played a game where the hero (himself) was, in terms of the story behind the virtual world, a bad or evil character.

Of course, video games are just as easy to design to allow you to play a sinner as a saint. Indeed, this fact has generated a good deal of controversy. While the video game world is replete with heroes who destroy evil, it also contains games where you can be a mob boss, a hired assassin, or a car thief. For example, in the notorious *Grand Theft Auto 2,* you play a budding young criminal, striving to make a name for yourself in a near-future world filled with drugs, guns, and gang wars. Your city is populated by three different gangs, each of which runs a different section of the city. Each gang has a set of pay phones that you can use to take on odd jobs stealing cars. The problem is that a gang will assign you work only if it respects you. You earn this respect by driving over to a rival gang's turf and shooting as many of their members as you can. Here you are certainly not a "good guy" in any traditional mainstream sense. (*Grand Theft Auto 2* was followed by the highly successful sequels *Grand Theft Auto III* and *Grand Theft Auto: Vice City.*)

What our six-year-old discovered was that there are (besides still others) two different models of what counts as being or doing "good." In one model, what counts as being or doing good is determined by a character's own goals, purposes, and values, as these are shared with a particular social group to which he or she belongs. Shadow and his group (Rouge and Dr. Eggman) have a set of goals, purposes, and values in terms of which destroying the world is their valued goal.

If you want to play *Sonic Adventure 2 Battle* from Shadow's perspective you must act, think, and value (while playing) from this perspective, a perspective that makes Shadow "good" or "the hero." After all, you are fighting numerous battles as Shadow and feel delight when winning them and dismay when losing them. It would be absolutely pointless to play as Shadow but purposely lose battles because you disapprove of his value system. If you played that way, Shadow would die quickly in the first episode and you'd never see anything else in the Shadow part of the game.

In the other model, what counts as being and doing good is determined by a wider perspective than just a character's own goals, purposes, and values, as these are shared with a particular social group. Rather, what counts is determined by the values and norms of a "wider society" that contains multiple, sometimes competing, groups as well as more or less generalized rules and principles about behavior. In terms of this model, Sonic is fighting for social order and the survival of the majority, things that are considered good from the perspective of many different groups and in terms of rather general principles of right and wrong.

By "models" of what it means to be and do good, I do not mean "professional" philosophical positions on ethics or theological ones on morality. I just mean "everyday" people's conceptions. The first model, which we might call the group model, can be captured by something like the following: "I am acting like a good person when I am acting in the interests of some group of which I am a member and which I value." The second model, which we might call the general model, can be captured by something like this: "I am acting like a good person when I am acting according to some general conception of what is good and bad, a conception that transcends my more narrow group memberships."

These two models regularly come into conflict in real life and cause all sorts of interesting issues and questions to arise. Some people readily believe that their group interests and values are or ought to be the general good. Others think that general conceptions of good really just hide the narrow interests of particular groups in a society that has cloaked them as general goods. Yet other people believe their interests and values represent future, rather than present, general conceptions of good and may see going against current conceptions of good as a necessary evil for a greater future good. And, of course, there are multiple ideas about what general conceptions of good and bad are.

The six-year-old, in playing *Sonic Adventure 2 Battle,* has been confronted with these two models. He has realized that when you act in (or think in terms of) the role of someone else (even a hedgehog), this involves not merely taking on a new identity but sometimes thinking and valuing from a perspective that you or others may think "wrong" from a different perspective. He also has learned that experiencing the world from that perspective (in one's mind or in a video game) does not mean that he accepts it in the sense that he wants, in his real-world identity, to adopt the values and the actions that this perspective underwrites.

These two models of what it means to be good are examples of what I will call *cultural models.* Cultural models are images, story lines, principles, or metaphors that capture what a particular group finds "normal" or "typical" in regard to a given phenomenon. By "group" here I mean to single out anything ranging from small groups to the whole of the human race with everything in between. Cultural models are not true or false. Rather, they capture, and are meant to capture, only a partial view of reality, one that helps groups (and humans in general) go about their daily work without a great deal of preplanning and conscious thought. After all, if many things were not left on "automatic pilot," we would spend all our time thinking and never acting.

So, for example, something like "People are good people when they are acting so as to help their group (family, church, community, ethnic group, state—pick your group)" is a cultural model for many different groups. It is a version of what I called the group model of good. Something like "People are good when they are acting according to general principles of morality (pick your principles)" is another cultural model that many groups use, though they may accept different cultural models about what are typical general principles of morality. This is a version of what I called the general model of good. And, of course, the two models can and sometimes do come into conflict.

Since cultural models are usually not conscious for people and since people rarely, if ever, try to formulate them definitively and once and for all in words, there is no exactly right way to phrase them. If forced to formulate them, people will put them into different words in different situations. The best researchers can do, then, is study people's behavior and words when they are acting as members of a certain sort of group and acting within certain sorts of situations and eventually conclude that, given what they do and say, they must accept a certain cultural model for a given phenomenon, a cultural model we formulate in words the best we can. Of course, when they are acting as members of different groups in different situations they may not act according to the cultural model we have hypothesized but in terms of another one.

Social groups do not usually pay much overt attention to their cultural models, unless one is threatened. Of course, when cultural models are challenged or come into conflict with other such models, then they can come to people's conscious awareness (even to the conscious awareness of the group as a whole). If someone comes to think that the actions he or she is taking for the family's good conflict with general conceptions of morality (not even necessarily the person's own general conceptions), this can give rise to discomfort and conflict, discomfort and conflict that can be resolved in various ways.

A number of pervasive cultural models about gender have become conscious to people thanks to the fact that these models have been openly challenged in society. For example, a cultural model that holds that unmarried women are unfulfilled "spinsters" because they do not have families has long been challenged by feminists, single women with children, lesbian couples with children, and perfectly fulfilled single women with good careers with which they are satisfied. Of course, all these people existed before, but as long as they did not speak out and make themselves visible, they were easily rendered invisible and marginal by traditional cultural models. Once they did speak out, those models and the social work they did came to people's consciousness and had to be overtly defended or changed.

The world is full of an endless array of ever-changing cultural models. For example, what do you think of a teenage child who tells his or her parents to "F___ off?" Perhaps you apply a model like "Normal teenagers rebel against their parents and other authority figures" and are not too concerned. Perhaps you apply a model like "Normal children respect their parents" and conclude the teenager is out of control. Who is to say what a "normal" or "typical" teenager is or does? Different cultural models hold different implications.

What do you make of a toddler who throws a tantrum when you, in a hurry to get your chores done, open a heavy car door that he or she wants to try to open, no matter how long it takes? Perhaps you apply a cultural model like "Young children go through sometimes-difficult 'stages' in their urge for growing self-reliance and independence" and conclude your child and the situation you are in is quite "normal." Perhaps you even encourage the child. Or perhaps you apply a model like "Young children are naturally willful and selfish and need discipline to learn to get along with and cooperate with others." Again, you would conclude you have a "normal" child, but one in need of discipline.

When you see a beggar on the street, your first reaction might stem from a cultural model like "People are responsible for themselves and when they fail it's their own fault" and go on your way, ignoring the person's pleas for money. Or you might apply a model something like "Down-and-out people are victims of problems that have overwhelmed them in a harshly competitive society" and give the person some money. Or you might apply a model like "Giving people money just encourages them to seek more help from others rather than seek to help themselves" and give the beggar an address of a foundation that can help him or her get a (probably quite bad) job.

When you have an argument with someone, do you apply a model something like "Arguments are a sort of verbal conflict" (helped along in this case by metaphors in our language like "I won the argument" or "I *defeated* her positions")? When you are in a romantic relationship, do you apply a model something like "Relationships are a type of work" (helped along in this case by metaphors in our language like "I've put a lot of *work* into this relationship" or "He has *worked hard* to be a good lover")? When you talk about people's jobs, do you apply a model something like "Working with the mind is more valuable to society than working with one's hands" and find yourself valuing even an academic who debates how many angels can sit on the head of a pin over your plumber? Perhaps the answer is no in all these cases, in which case you operate, at least sometimes and in some places, with different cultural models.

There are several important points to be made about cultural models. They are not just in your head. Of course, you store images and patterns in your head that represent cultural models, but they are also represented out there in the world. For example, the cultural model that said that "Young children go through sometimes-difficult 'stages' in their urge for growing self-reliance and independence" exists in a lot of self-help guides on babies and childrearing. The words and images of the magazines, newspapers, and other media all around us represent many cultural models. The models also are represented and acted out in the words and deeds of the people with whom we interact and share memberships in various groups.

Different cultural models are associated with different groups in the larger society, though some are also shared widely by many, perhaps all, groups in that society. For instance, the cultural model about children going through "stages" toward independence is associated more closely (though not exclusively) with the modern middle class, and the cultural model that said "Young children are naturally willful and selfish and need discipline to learn to get along with and cooperate with others" is associated more closely (though not exclusively) with the traditional working class.

Cultural models, which cannot be stated in one definitive way, are stories or images of experience that people can tell themselves or simulate in their minds, stories and images that represent what they take to be "normal" or "typical" cases or situations. In this sense, they are like theories, theories about things like children, childrearing, relationships, friendship, being and doing good, and everything else. These theories are usually unconscious and taken for granted. However, like all theories, even overt ones in science, they are not meant to be detailed, blow-by-blow descriptions of reality. Reality is too complex to be described accurately in every detail. Rather, cultural models and formal theories both are meant to capture general patterns in such a way that we can do things in and with the world, whether this is to accomplish a goal with others or to make successful predictions in an experiment.

Cultural models are picked up as part and parcel of acting with others in the world. We act with others and attempt to make sense of what they are doing and saying. We interact with the media of our society and attempt to make sense of what is said and done there, as well. Cultural models are the tacit, taken-for-granted theories we (usually unconsciously) infer and then act on in the normal course of events when we want to be like others in our social groups. People who have no cultural models would have to think everything out for themselves minute by minute when they attempt to act. They would be paralyzed. And they certainly would not be social beings, since part of what makes us social beings is the set of cultural models we share with those around us.

Cultural models can be used for many different purposes and they can sometimes conflict with each other. For example, the anthropological psychologist Claudia Strauss found that working-class men she studied behaved in their daily lives according to what she called a bread-winner model. This model can be phrased something like this: "Men take care of their families even if this means sacrificing their own interests." On the other hand, Strauss found that many upper-middle class people operate with a cultural model that stresses their own self-development over the interests of those around them, including their own families. When such people were faced with moving to take a new and better job, they often did so, even if this damaged their families and relationships. The working-class men Strauss studied, when faced with the same choice, gave up the new career opportunity for the benefit of their families.

These working-class men also used what Strauss and others have called the success model to judge their own behaviors. This model says something like "In the United States, anyone can get ahead if they work hard enough." The working-class men saw that they did not hold jobs the wider society considered successful and used this model to condemn themselves, saying they had not worked hard enough or weren't smart enough. They used the success model to judge themselves negatively even though this model exists in some degree of conflict with the bread winner model on which they led their lives in action, a model that would not let them take the "selfish" steps often required by the success model.

Since this conflict did not surface to consciousness for these men, it did not come out into the open. They simply felt bad about themselves, at least when forced to think about themselves in relation to the society as a whole. In other settings, of course, they may have felt quite differently—remember, people take on different identities in different situations and all people are members of many different groups.

Are cultural models, then, "good" or "bad"? They are good in that they allow us to act and be social in the world without having to constantly reflect and think. They are bad when they operate so as to do harm to ourselves or others but go unexamined. Certain circumstances can, however, force us to think overtly and reflectively about our cultural models. We certainly don't want or need to think overtly about all of them. But we do need to think about those that, in certain situations or at certain points in our lives, have the potential to do more harm than good.

Sonic Adventure 2 Battle forced the six-year-old overtly to realize and confront two different, and sometimes conflicting, cultural models of what constitutes being and doing "good." Of course, this realization was only beginning. Many other experiences, not the least in video games, will give this child other opportunities to think more about these two models. And, indeed, they are models that bear a good deal of thinking about, since they have done and have the potential to do a lot of harm in the world.

Under Ash

The sort of thing that the six-year-old experienced can go much further and deeper. Consider the case of Arab children. After the terrorist attacks of September 11, 2001, a number of video games came out, initially on the Internet and thereafter as packaged games, featuring U.S. soldiers killing Arabs and Muslims. These games, for obvious reasons, were not entirely palatable to Arab children. In response, the Syrian publishing house Dar Al-Fikr designed a video game called *Under Ash*. Its hero is a young Palestinian named Ahmed who throws stones to fight Israeli soldiers and settlers. The game, of course, involves the player deeply in the Palestinian cause and Palestinian perspectives.

In the game, Ahmed initially must reach Jerusalem's Al-Aqsa mosque, an important Islamic holy site, avoiding or fighting Israeli soldiers and settlers along the way. Once he reaches the mosque, Ahmed has to help injured Palestinians, find weapons, and expel Israeli soldiers. There are many other episodes to the game, including ones where Ahmed infiltrates a Jewish settlement and where he serves as a guerrilla warrior in southern Lebanon. As is typical of such video games, Ahmed only attacks those he does not consider "civilians." (In this case, occupation forces, settlers, and soldiers do not count as "civilians.") "Civilians" (all others) are left unharmed.

Of course, it is clear that in video games who does and does not count as a "civilian" is based on different perspectives embedded in the game's virtual world. I was originally surprised (which shows I was operating with a different cultural model) that settlers (since they are not in the army) didn't count as civilians. But then I realized that this game accepts a cultural model in terms of which the settlers are seen as the "advance" troops of an occupation army.

The general manager of the company that produced *Under Ash,* Adnan Salim, considers the game, one that is violent in just the way many U.S. shooter games are, "a call for peace." In an Internet site devoted to the game, Salim says that "Slaying and shedding blood have been the worst of the Human's conducts [*sic*] since the beginning of creation." I got Salim's views from Google's (a search engine) cache of www.underash.com/emessage.htm. (A cache is a snapshot that the people at Google took of the page as they "crawled the web.") This site, like several others devoted to *Under Ash,* no longer exits. Opponents of the game have destroyed many sites devoted to it. I have no idea whether this was true of this site or not. Salim goes on to say that "[i]n spite of the Human's endeavor and struggle to get rid of the crime of murder since he appeared on Earth, Israel has been practicing collective killing and eradication."

On the other hand, he claims that:

Under Ash is a call to humanity to stop killing and shedding blood. After all its awful experience and global destructive wars, the whole world has become aware of the fact that wars never solve problems....

Under Ash is a call to dialogue, coexistence and peace. Justice is the deeply-rooted human value that God Almighty enjoined.... On the other hand, nations perish, states stabilize and civilizations collapse according to the amount of aggression, injustice and harm they practice....

Under Ash is a call to justice, realizing truth, preventing wronging [sic] and aggression. God made all mankind as equal to each other as the comb teeth....

Such is the philosophy of *Under Ash*. The idea on which it was based repulses violence, injustice, discrimination and murder, and calls for peace, justice and equality among people.

This idea, accompanied by the best available technology, is still handy to our youth, trying to dry up their tears; heal their wounds; remove all the feelings of humiliation, humbleness and wretchedness from their souls, and draw the smile of hope and the sense of dignity and efficiency on their faces.

If you find these remarks odd in regard to a violent video game (remember that there was no outcry in the United States over shooter games where the enemies were Arabs), that is because these remarks and the game itself take for granted a number of cultural models foreign to many Americans (just as American games and remarks about them take for granted different cultural models). For example, consider that Salim says that, after having experienced the violence of global wars, the world: "turned back to the patient dialogue around the table of negotiation which resulted in the establishment of a *European Union* among nations which previously hated one another and went on fighting for centuries. Then they agreed to co-exist peacefully within a union under whose authority none is harmed and every one benefits."

One cultural model that seems to be at work here is something like this: "The experience of violence will make people seek peace." In terms of this model, we can see the guerrilla fighter as trying to push more powerful entities (i.e., states), entities that the guerrilla cannot defeat outright, to settle their differences through negotiation rather than war. A cultural model something like "The experience of overwhelming violence will make less powerful entities give up and give in to more powerful entities" seems at play in both some U.S. video games and much U.S. media devoted to warfare in the modern world. Note that like all cultural models, these are not "true" or "false." (History is replete with examples and counter-examples to both.) They are meant to help people make sense to themselves and others and to engage in joint activity with others with whom they share these cultural models.

Now, you might very well not want to play *Under Ash*. If you did play the game, you would be placed in a situation where you took on the virtual identity of a character whose cultural models about many things are different from yours. If you not only adopted this virtual identity while you played but took on what I called in chapter 3 a projective identity vis-à-vis your virtual identity (Ahmed), you would surely come to understand what it feels like to be among those angry young people who are "trying to dry up their tears; heal their wounds; remove all the feelings of humiliation, humbleness and wretchedness from their souls, and draw the smile of hope and the sense of dignity and efficiency on their faces."

Would this mean you would, all of a sudden, want to kill Israeli settlers or even that you would support the Palestinian cause over the Israeli one if you had not before? Certainly not. But it would mean that, far more interactively that you could in any novel or movie, you would have experienced the "other" from the inside. Even more interesting, since the cultural models built into the game are not yours, you would be able to reflect on them in a more overtly conscious way than young Arabic players for whom the models are taken for granted (as U.S. game players take for granted different models that fit their own sense of reality). In turn, this might make you contrast these models to ones you have taken for granted and bring them to consciousness for reflection.

What if *Under Ash* allowed you to play through the game twice, once as Ahmed and once as an Israeli settler, just as *Sonic Adventure 2 Battle* allows you to be Sonic or Shadow, or *Aliens vs. Predator 2* allows you to be a Marine fighting off the Aliens and Predator or either an Alien or Predator trying to survive by killing the Marines? My guess is that if you had taken on both the projective identity of you as Ahmed and you as Israeli settler, you would find the whole thing much more complex than you do now and would be a bit more reluctant to take the death of either side for granted. Such complexity is bad, I admit, for people and states trying to wage war.

Video games have an unmet potential to create complexity by letting people experience the world from different perspectives. Part of this potential is that in a video game, you yourself have to act as a given character. As you act quickly, and not just think leisurely, and as you (while playing) celebrate the character's victories and bemoan his or her defeats, you must live in a virtual world and make sense of it. This making sense of the virtual world amid not just thought but also action in the world amounts to experiencing new and different cultural models. Furthermore, you may experience these models much more consciously—and render some of your own previous models conscious by contrast in the process—than is typical of our daily lives in the real world. In the next section I turn to an example that is less esoteric for Americans than *Under Ash*.

I am well aware that this potential of video games—if and when it is more fully realized—is liable to be very controversial. An Israeli or Palestinian who has lost a loved one to violence is not going to want to play both sides of my make-believe *Under Ash* game. Indeed, the Israeli and Palestinian may each revel in playing "their" side and getting virtual revenge. Each may think it immoral to "play" the other side, to take on such a perspective on the world even in play. I, too, think that certain perspectives are so repugnant that we should not take them even in play. But who decides? And if we are willing to take none but our own side, even in play, then violence would seem inevitable.

We do not have to imagine games that most of us would find entirely repugnant, regardless of our political perspectives. Such games actually exist. For example, a game called *Ethnic Cleansing*, put out by the Virginia-based National Alliance, has players killing African Americans, Latinos, and Jews as they run through gritty ghetto and subway environments. The game is quite sophisticated technologically. (It was built using free game development software called Genesis 3D.) Hate groups like the National Alliance have long recruited members through the use of web sites, white-power music, and books and magazines. However, there is concern, for just the reasons we have discussed, that interactive media like video games are a more powerful device than such passive media. But if they are, then they are potentially more powerful for both good and ill.

Whether we like it or not, new technologies make it easy to design realistic and sophisticated video games that allow players to be almost any sort of person or being living in almost any sort of world that any designer can imagine. Eventually this capacity will be used to allow people to live and interact in worlds where violence plays no role and is replaced by conversation and other sorts of social interactions. (*The Longest Journey*, a game whose lead character is an 18-year-old woman named April Ryan, is one such game; *Siberia*, whose protagonist is a female lawyer wandering around a town full of automatons, is another.)

The same capacity that will allow us to enact new identities and learn to act according to new cultural models can also allow us to renew our hate or even learn new models of hate. In the end, who is to decide what identities you or I can enact and whether enacting them will be a good or bad thing for us? Publicly the issue usually is couched in terms of children and teens, where parents surely bear a major responsibility, but the average video-game player is in his or her late 20s or early 30s. I don't want politicians dictating what identities I can enact in a virtual world. At the same time, I worry about people who play *Ethnic Cleansing*. But any attempt to stop the flow of identities that new technologies allow presents the danger of locking everyone into their most cherished identities, and that has brought us a great deal of ethnic cleansing of its own. I have no solid answers to offer, only the claim that video games have the potential to raise many such questions and issues.

Going to War

Both *Return to Castle Wolfenstein* and *Operation Flashpoint: Cold War Crisis* are shooter games played out in military settings. *Castle Wolfenstein* is a first-person shooter. (You see only the weapon you are holding, unless you look in something like a mirror when you then see yourself.) *Operation Flashpoint* can be played either in the first-person or in the third-person (where you see your character's body as if you were just a bit behind him). In *Castle Wolfenstein* you play Major B. J. Blazkowitz in World War II fighting against the Nazis. In *Operation Flashpoint* you start the game as Private David Armstrong, though you (Armstrong) go up in rank during the game. Private Armstrong is involved as a U.S. soldier representing NATO in a war against a resistance movement on an island nation.

While all this makes these two games sound similar, they are in a great many respects entirely different. In *Return to Castle Wolfenstein,* Major William J. "B.J." Blazkowicz is a highly decorated Army Ranger recruited into the Office of Secret Actions (OSA) and given the task of going to Castle Wolfenstein to thwart Heinrich, the reincarnation of a tenth-century dark prince, Henry the Fowler (also known as Heinrich), and an army of genetically engineered super soldiers.

As in most shooter games, your character (B. J. Blazkowitz) can take a great deal of damage before he dies. It takes a number of bullets to kill him, and he can find health kits throughout the game to replenish his health. While he faces tough enemies, the fact that he can dish out a great deal of damage with special weapons (like a Venom Gun, which fires dozens of bullets at once) and sustain a good deal of damage makes you, the player, feel like quite a superhero. Indeed, when you have successfully finished the game, you see a cut scene (video) where Blazkowitz's superiors in Washington are discussing what a great job he has done and how he is currently taking some well-deserved R and R, imagining him relaxing on some tropical isle. But then the video cuts away to a dramatic scene where we see Blazkowitz jumping from a ledge, machine gun in hand, entering the fray in yet another battle against multiple Nazis, a sly grin on his face. This is *his* form of R and R.

Games like *Return to Castle Wolfenstein* trade on several pervasive cultural models that are part of their allure. They play on cultural models that treat heroes as superhuman people and that see warfare (for the "right" cause) as heroic. Also they play on a cultural model that is quite pervasive particularly among males, namely one that sees fighting (and even losing) against all odds—standing alone against the horde no matter what—as romantic (a model often triggered when people watch a bad sports team against a good one). And, of course, they play on cultural models, pervasive particularly in United States, that romanticize the individual against the group.

There is nothing particularly wrong with this. People get pleasure out of seeing their cultural models confirmed and, in the case of video games, actually getting to act them out. After all, a good many of these models have been picked up not so much from one's actual experiences in the world as through experiences with books and the media. However, I believe there is something wrong when these sorts of models are never challenged or overtly reflected on.

Some modern shooter games have begun to play against these sorts of pervasive models in interesting ways. Games like *Thief: The Dark Project* and *Metal Gear Solid 2: Sons of Liberty*, in their entirety, and parts of *Deus Ex* and *No One Lives Forever 2: A Spy in H.A.R.M.'s Way*, and a good many other modern sophisticated shooter games, stress stealth and cunning over fighting. A shooter game like *Anachronox* and many fantasy role-playing games (like *Baldur's Gate II: Shadows of Amin*) stress teamwork. At times *Anachronox* plays to hilarious effect against cultural models about heroism and individuality.

In fact, these trends are strong enough that games like *Duke Nukem* and *Serious Sam* bill themselves as nostalgic returns to the "good old days" of shooters where you just rushed in and shot up everything around you. (Duke Nukem's motto in his more recent game, *Duke Nukem: Manhattan Project*, is "It's my way or ... Hell—it's my way.") In many a modern shooter game that's a strategy that will lead quickly to your death. Finally, we can mention that the very popular *No One Lives Forever* games star a female James Bond figure and parodies (in a very playful way) the conventions of the Bond genrè and 1960s.

But none of this prepares you for a game like *Operation Flashpoint: Cold War Crisis;* a realistic military game that quickly disabused me of all the cultural models about warfare I had picked up from books and movies. Its contrast with games like *Return to Castle Wolfenstein* is so stark that a player cannot help but be confronted consciously with the cultural models heroic shooter games reinforce.

Operation Flashpoint is set in the Cold War period just as Soviet President Mikhail Gorbachev is elected into power. The game follows a fictional story line centered around the battle between a disgruntled rogue Soviet military group that has seized control of an island community and a NATO peace-keeping force, sent in at the request of the Soviets. The player assumes the role of Private David Armstrong in over 30 missions that have you assaulting small towns as a member of a large squad, commandeering vehicles, launching sniper attacks, and, later, serving as a squad leader. In the early parts of the game, you follow a computer AI-controlled leader as you and other squad members try to survive to later missions, where you move up the ranks, eventually becoming a battle-hardened commander.

Operation Flashpoint is fully realistic. One bullet is usually enough to kill or disable you pretty fully. Opposing soldiers can shoot at you from far away, can snipe you from hiding places that are hard to discover, and often appear as small deadly spots on the horizon, not as larger-than-life foes confronting you face-to-face. There are no health kits to be found, only the very occasional medic on the battlefield if you are lucky enough to find one and get to him quickly enough. Very often, if you are not very careful, you get shot and die without even having seen what direction the bullet came from.

Needless to say, if you try to be Rambo in *Operation Flashpoint* and run out heroically firing all guns, you will, as a review on gamezilla.com put it, "find yourself in a black body bag being shipped to the USA, next day air." Cooperation from and with your computer-controlled squadmates is a must for survival. Many times there are more of the enemy than there are of you, and they are well trained. When things go wrong—and they often do—you can hide from enemies, for example, in bushes, especially when you are in camouflage. But once you fire, there's a good chance the enemy will hear it and attack your position, with predictable results. (You die.)

Playing *Operation Flashpoint: Cold War Crisis* let me experience what it would be like to have quite different cultural models about warfare. Early on, I found myself (as Private Armstrong) with my squad following my commander as we skirted the edges of forests and open fields in search of the enemy. I really had no idea how I should move. My inclination as an "everyday" person was to stand up and move forward briskly. I died, shot from afar. In fact, I never saw the enemy soldier who shot me.

Replaying the game, I watched how my (computer-controlled) squadmates moved. Often they moved forward in a crouching position, staying low to the ground. They rarely moved in straight lines and frequently stopped and checked the horizons all around them. When they sensed any danger, they hit the ground and crawled forward for a while. Progress was punishingly slow. You had to develop a sense of possible danger everywhere, knowing that the enemy might very well see you before you saw them. For long periods nothing happened and a sense of boredom overcame me. Then all of a sudden information would come over my radio or the commander would shout out orders and there would be firing and mayhem. Often I barely had time to get excited before I died, having failed to think beforehand of possible avenues of protection or retreat.

During the game's early episodes, as I moved (ever more skillfully and "paranoidly") with my squad, I went into missions with high expectations and optimism. After all, we were the "good guys," weren't we? We were in a well-trained professional army with highly qualified officers (I was, after all, only a private), weren't we? But time and again, things did not go as planned. We had to change plans, retreat and regroup, or even be evacuated in defeat. Winning was no simple matter, and every step forward seemed to portend two possible steps backward. While I often got orders directly from the commander of my squad or over my radio, I didn't always know what the "big plan" was, if there was one, only what my group was supposed to accomplish and that changed under the conditions of the actual battle on the field.

Speaking of orders: As I said, I often got them under conditions where I had to act fast. But many times these orders left me in quandaries. In one case, for example, an officer got killed only moments after ordering me to move in a certain direction and take up a certain position. Should I follow the order now that he just got shot—which, of course, didn't inspire great confidence? In other cases, there were clearly much safer—and sometimes, from my perspective, smarter—things for me to do than follow the order to the T. What to do? How exactly need I follow orders? What room is there for my own judgment? Sometimes when I hesitated, I got yelled at. At other times, I was too far away for the officer to observe the details of my behavior.

When we did accomplish our goals in fine fashion, I did not know how much or how little I had contributed to the "victory." For example, once we assaulted an enemy position on the outskirts of a town. I and others were ordered to move forward under fire, while some of our fellow soldiers stayed behind sniping at the enemy positions from farther back. I moved forward, firing my gun and evading return fire. We "won," but I never knew if I had disabled any of the enemy or contributed to the task (partly because I was not the first soldier over the top—see the next paragraph). The whole squad got praised, but I didn't know how good (or bad) to feel about the matter.

Finally, early on, I discovered an important but very uninspiring principle. I have already pointed out that I learned a good deal by observing my squadmates—for example, how to move. But I also learned that the safest position is to move with but behind other squadmates. The people in front have to make the snap decisions and take the fire first. But it felt very "unmanly" staying behind the others. I particularly liked moving behind (not too close, though) some of the officers on the field who seemed to know the most about how to proceed and often made the best decisions.

Enough said; this is not war as romantic and heroic. Here are some of the cultural models I was beginning to pick up about warfare from playing this game, none of which is remotely part of the experience of playing *Return to Castle Wolfenstein:*

- War is, for the most part, boring.

- Soldiers need to move as if they are constantly paranoid.

- When war is exciting, it is also confusing.

- Following orders is a vexed matter.

- Things don't go as planned.

- Situations on the ground don't resemble people's generalities and plans about them.

- No one really knows what people at the top know and whether they really know what they're doing.

- The guys next to you on the actual battlefield often do know what they're doing. It's hard to know what you can take credit for as an individual.

- "Manly" behavior often gets you dead quickly, Rambo-type behavior even quicker.

These are cultural models, because they are images, principles, or story lines that I don't really "know" are true. I picked them up from my own experience, and one's experience is always limited, local, connected to particular groups and situations, and never scientifically "valid." Such models help organize and make sense of experience and help one move on and get on with the job at hand (in this case, staying alive long enough to go on fighting a war). Of course, people and game players differ. In my case, I have never had the slightest desire to be a real soldier, and playing *Operation Flashpoint* certainly does not inspire me to change my desires in this regard. It does make me worry about media depictions of war and gives me loads of sympathy for anyone who has to fight one, especially bottom up in the ranks. (The U. S. Army has created a massive multiplayer realistic game called *America's Army* but I do not know what effect it has on players, save to say a number have wanted to sign up.)

Cultural Models in School

Cultural models play a crucial role in school. Let me give you a specific example from a science classroom. High school students taking a physics class were having a discussion about whether a ball rolling on a level plane would keep moving at constant speed. They had previously heard from their teacher Galileo's arguments that under ideal conditions (i.e., leaving out friction and assuming no force acts to accelerate or retard the ball's progress) the ball would keep moving at a constant speed.

During the discussion, one student asks, "What's making the ball move?" Another answers, "The forces behind it." The student who asked the question responds, "The force that's pushing it will make it go." Yet another student says, "Where'd that force come from, because you don't have a force" (which, of course, is Galileo's and modern physics' assumption), and another student answers, "No, there is force, the force that's pushing it, but no other force that's slowing it down." The teacher comments that some students say there are no forces on the ball, while others say there is "a force that's moving it." One student now says, "There's an initial force that makes it start, giving it the energy to move."

What is happening here—and it happens in many physics classrooms—is that some (most) of the students are assuming that things in motion stay in motion either because some force is constantly acting on them (they are being "pushed" by this force) or because they have stored up energy from some initial force (a "push") that acted on them, a stored energy that is a kind of "impetus" (which itself is like an internal force acting on the object, one that gradually "runs down"). However, in terms of the semiotic domain of physics, any object stays at rest or in constant motion unless some force acts to change its state. When its state is changed, it stays in the new state (in motion or at rest) until some other force changes this state. In physics, there is no need to explain why things stay in constant motion or at rest. Thus, there is no need to appeal to any "impetus" moving objects have stored up (a "force" that doesn't exist). We only need to explain the situation when things in motion accelerate or slow down or things at rest move. In these cases, we must assume some force has acted on the object.

Of course, in the real world, things rarely stay in constant motion for any length of time, since forces almost always act on them to change (speed up or slow down) their motion. And when things stay at rest in the real world, often it takes a number of forces to keep them that way and oppose forces that are attempting to change them. Galileo was assuming an ideal world, for instance a world with no friction between surfaces and nothing in the environment to perturb the motion of the ball. Furthermore, the ball is assumed to be rolling horizontally on level plane to make the force of gravity irrelevant to the problem. (If the ball were falling down it would be accelerating, thanks to gravity.) He wanted to think about things in a certain ideal-ized way so that the basic pattern or fundamental principle at work would show itself clearly, namely, the principle that things at rest stay at rest and things moving at a constant speed stay moving at a constant speed unless some force acts on them to change their state.

This is a new and different way of looking at the world. In physics, things moving at constant speed or at rest don't need explaining. What needs explaining is change. In the world of our "everyday" experience, since things are always changing, what often has to be explained is how certain things resist these changes to remain in a constant state.

Physicists want to think in terms of such ideal worlds so that they can discover elegant mathematical models that can later be applied to the real world. When they are applied to the real world, we have to think about things that were left out of the model (like friction). Such elegant models, when these other things are added in, make a multitude of correct predictions about the real world.

Most other academic disciplines operate in a similar way. They leave out a myriad of details to formulate a basic pattern that later can be made more complex to apply in dif-ferent ways to different situations. For example, some branches of economics operate with the assumption that people are always rational when they act within free markets. This lets these economists think about and discover principles about how markets work in an ideal sense. Of course, when they want to make predictions about the real world, they have to add in adjustments for different situations where people display different kinds of irrational behavior or where markets are not fully free. Their idealized assumption is good if, when they add back in these different adjustments (different ones for different situations), they are able to make good predictions.

Ironically, this way of proceeding—i.e., leaving out a lot of details to get to the basic pattern—is not all that different from how cultural models work. People form cultural models from their experience by leaving out many of the details to capture what they take to be the typical cases. Scientific models are formed through the socially organized process of scientific investigation (e.g., formal research and peer review), not through largely unconscious encounters with daily life. Furthermore, scientific models and cultural models exist for different reasons. Scientific models attempt to explain how some aspect of the world works as an answer to a formal and consciously formulated question, and sometimes the aspects of the world that they deal with are not ones we experience in our everyday lives (e.g., atoms). Cultural models exist to help us get on with our "everyday," less specialized and often less consciously reflected on social and cultural business and our everyday lives in the material world.

In the high school physics class, the cultural models of some students were in conflict with the scientific models used by physicists. They did not realize this and could not turn off (for the time being) their conflicting cultural models and begin to think and act through the physicists' models. Let me discuss for a moment, then, one of the conflicting cultural models that these students were using.

A number of studies in science education have found that students often bring to the physics classroom, in one form or another, a conception that *motion is caused by force.* They believe that if an object is moving, then there must be a force on it causing that motion. It is common to read in this literature that this is a "misconception," a mistake commonly made by people who don't know physics. The problem is that often students continue to make this "mistake" even after they have taken a good deal of physics and learned that it is a "mistake."

The reason why the idea that motion is caused by force is so hard to remove is that it is not, in reality, a "mistake." Rather, it is a type of cultural model, a model built up from our experiences in the material world. Most or all humans hold a model something like this: "Things keep working because they are continually supplied with some form of power or agency." Like all models, this model is neither wrong nor right. Rather, it works in a lot of situations. Because it does, we usually can get by perfectly well by assuming it without much conscious thought. For example, we assume (correctly in this and the following cases) that a car keeps running because its engine keeps powering its wheels. Lights keep working because electricity keeps flowing into them. Humans move because, at one level, they (continuously) "will" it and, at another level, because the energy reserves from their food fuel their cells and limbs.

While it is fair to say this is a physical model, it applies to social affairs as well and, thus, is also a social model. In fact, it is really just a cultural model that applies both to the physical and the social world. We assume that students keep working because something is motivating them or that relationships last because people put effort into them. In general, people do what they do and keep doing it, when they do keep doing it, because they are "agents" empowering themselves (through will or desire or whatever) to do and keep doing. The model that says, "things keep working because they are continually supplied with some form of power or agency" is deeply rooted in our physical and social experience. Of course, different cultural groups have different cultural models about what sorts of things can or cannot be sources of power or agency (e.g., spirits).

This cultural model—in its specific physical instantiation as *motion is caused by force*—happens to be wrong in physics, no matter how accurate it may be in a great many other areas. However, you do not get people to realize it is wrong in physics and then pick up other models that work better in physics, if you don't realize the power of this model or if you abuse people for holding it (e.g., tell them they are stupid or misguided). You must bring the model to consciousness and juxtapose it to other ways of thinking appropriate for the new situation, without implying that the model is wrong in all situations.

You must also make the way physicists think—a way that does not use this cultural model, at least when they are doing physics—sensible and clear by letting students under-stand it not just as words but in terms of embodied thought and action in the same physical world in which they got their original model. After all, just as people's cultural models come from their everyday experience of the world, physicists' scientific models come from their experiences (in problem solving, thinking, dialoging, and carrying out experiments in and on the world) within the semiotic domain of physics as it applies to the world. This domain, like all specialized domains, looks at and operates on the world in a different way from "everyday" people do, but it operates in and on the material world nonetheless.

Students bring to their classes a great many cultural models. For example, cultural models about what counts as "good English" (e.g., something like "Educated people speak good or correct English") cause lots of trouble when students are trying to learn linguistics and discover that, to a linguist, a dialect of English that says things like "My puppy be following me everywhere I go" is just as rule governed and "good" as a dialect that doesn't say such things. (In fact, this sort of construction, using a form like "be" to mean that something happens repeatedly or habitually, is not at all uncommon across the world's languages.)

However, students also bring to classrooms cultural models about school subject matter (e.g., what "physics" as a school subject is) and about learning (e.g., what learning is or should be like in school). For example, in regard to physics or other academic domains, many students bring with them a cultural models that says: "Learning is a matter of mastering a set of facts." They may bring, as well, a model that says: "Learning is a matter of memorizing information from teachers and books."

These models are not "wrong"—indeed, a great many schools operate so as to reinforce them daily. Nonetheless, if you have gotten this far in this book, you know that I believe they are in many situations unfortunate models of learning. However, if students are to adopt different models of content learning in school, teachers need to know that these unfortunate models exist. Students need to think about them, why they have them, where they do and do not work, and new and different models and why they might want to adopt these in word and deed. Of course, the newer models I am advocating involve the sorts of active and critical learning I have been stressing throughout this book.

Cultural Models of Learning and Video Games

Good video games have a powerful way of making players consciously aware of some of their previously assumed cultural models about learning itself. In fact, good video games expose a whole set of generational models of what constitutes typical ways of learning. Since the baby-boomer models are still quite prevalent in schools as teachers, administrators, and parents, children today are most certainly exposed to them and often adopt these models uncritically and unconsciously, at least when they are at school.

Consider, for instance, the famous game *Metal Gear Solid* (a game that has a sequel called *Metal Gear Solid 2: Sons of Liberty*). In this game you are Solid Snake (one of the most famous video game characters of all time), a genetically enhanced antiterrorist, who has been called on to infiltrate an Alaskan military base that has been taken over by terrorists. The terrorists are also genetically enhanced and some are foes Solid Snake has confronted in the past (in earlier games), such as his brother Liquid Snake. The terrorists have fitted a massive robot called "Metal Gear" with nuclear warheads and are threatening to fire them at the United States if their demands are not met. As Solid Snake goes about infiltrating the military base and ultimately trying to destroy Metal Gear, he finds out a great deal about himself and about love and loyalty. In fact, in the middle of the game, if Solid Snake does not give in under torture, his great love and fellow warrior, Meryl, survives, and they eventually head off into the sunset together at the end of the game. (If he does give in and ask for the torture to stop, Meryl does not survive and the game has a different ending.)

Early in the game, you (as Solid Snake in a third-person view) are standing in the shadows looking at a massive building with many doors and balconies, fronted by a courtyard with many additional rooms coming off it. There are searchlights fixed atop the building and guards everywhere. You must sneak past the searchlights, staying in the shadows, get into the building, and move unseen through it to your goal.

If the player is inclined to move as straightforwardly and efficiently as possible toward the goal, this game and almost all other video games, will punish this inclination. The player needs to take the time to explore, even if this means moving off the main line toward the goal and delaying getting there. If Snake does not head right to his goal of entering the main building but instead moves carefully into a side room off the courtyard, he finds important items (e.g., weapons, ammunition, tools). When he sneaks into the back of a truck parked in the courtyard, he not only avoids the searchlights, he also finds more good things. As he sneaks around the perimeter of the courtyard and the edges of the building, he can check out less obvious ways into the building.

Even when he gets in, lingering over grates in the floor of an overhead duct he is moving through allows him to overhear important information and see various things (including Meryl in a cell with not too many clothes on). Sneaking to other nooks and crannies in the building allows him to gain crucial information. All the while Snake is receiving, via a communication device that only he can hear, orders to move forward and information about how to do so.

When I played the game, I was tempted to rush guards, guns firing, to clear my path, since they seemed like such clear and straightforward targets. But, of course, if there were more of them than there was of me, I usually died or took too much damage. Even when there was only one and he seemed an obvious and easy target, often an alarm sounded, set off by a hidden camera triggered when I had snuck out into the open behind the guard, an alarm that quickly brought a good many other guards to his rescue.

This and other games have brought home to me that I hold cultural models about learning something like this: "The final goal is important, defines the learning, and good learners move toward it without being distracted by other things" and "Good learners move quickly and efficiently toward their goal." I also hold other models: "There is one right way to get to the goal that the good learners discover (and the rest of us usually don't)" and "Learning is a matter of some people being better or worse than others, and this is important."

These models all get entrenched in school repeatedly. They are linear models that stress movement ever forward toward greater skill until one has mastered one's goal. They are competitive models, as well, that stress better and worse and sorting people into categories along the lines of better and worse.

Video games tend not to reward these models. They stress both nonlinear movement—exploring all around without necessarily moving forward toward one's ultimate goal and the mastery defined by that goal—as well as linear movement, which, of course, eventually happens, greatly deepened, sometimes transformed, by the horizontal movement. They stress multiple solutions judged by a variety of different standards, some of which are internal to the game (different things happen when you take different tacks) and some of which are set by the player (who wants to solve the problem on his or her own terms and may play scenes over to solve problems in different ways).

Unless segments of games are timed, and they usually are not (save for special problems or races within certain games or in some aspects of real-time strategy games), how quickly you proceed is not a big value, unless you choose to make it one. (And then you may well miss some of the best stuff in a game.) Finally, while there are certainly better and worse video-game players, and players can and do play competitively with each other via the

Internet, games are most certainly playable by a wide variety of people who set their own standards and worry about how well they are doing by those standards, not by who out there in the world is better or worse than they are at defeating Liquid Snake in the fight atop the tank.

Video games challenged a number of other cultural models I held about learning. For one last example, I held a model something like: "When faced with a problem to solve, good learners solve it quickly, the first time they try or soon thereafter. If you have to try over and over again, this is a sign that you are not very good at what you are attempting to learn." All good shooter games have "bosses," particularly strong opponents with far more life than your character. Players regularly spend lots of time and effort trying to kill these bosses. They have to discover new strategies in their various failed attempts and not give up.

When players do succeed at killing the bosses, some (after they have played the game through) set the difficulty level higher, to make getting the bosses even harder. (Many games can be played at a relatively easy, normal, hard, or even harder level; the difficulty level determines things like how many enemies there are and how strong they are.) I once watched a younger lawyer refight a final boss from a PlayStation 2 version of *Baldur's Gate* at the highest level of difficulty. He was a real expert. His character ran up to and away from the boss (a dragon) repeatedly, moving all around a complex dungeon space, hiding here and there, coming out to attack and running away, coaxing the boss into tight corners or close spaces where it could be better attacked. All the while, the player used various potions and healing spells to gain stronger arrows and more health. The battle lasted 20 intense minutes. In the end, with the dragon on its last legs, the lawyer ran out of both magical arrows and healing potions and he died.

Far from being dismayed at his failure (as a school learner might after such a struggle), he responded with some nasty language as he died but also with a big smile on his face. In video games, losing is not losing, and the point is not winning easily or judging yourself a failure. In playing video games, hard is not bad and easy is not good. The six-year-old mentioned earlier was once asked whether easy or hard was better in a video game. Without a pause, he said hard is always good, easy is not. Would that children said such things about learning science in school.

There is a wonderful moment in *Metal Gear Solid*, which is a quite difficult game, where Solid Snake, as he infiltrates the military base, is talking via his built-in communication system to a young Asian woman who is an expert on mapping and radar systems. She and Solid Snake joke with each other, and she usually ends each talk session with him with a Chinese proverb that applies both to his situation in the virtual world of the game and to the player in the real world. At one point she says to Solid Snake something that is not a proverb, of course, but is meant to have much the same effect: "Aren't you glad that you have the time to play a video game? Relax and enjoy yourself."

When players hear this, they might very well realize that they are intensely involved in solving quite hard problems and often failing. Yet they are playing, having fun, enjoying themselves. Wouldn't it be great if we could say to children in school when they were struggling mightily with hard problems in physics: "Aren't you lucky you have the time and opportunity to do science?" and have them smile and nod?

Learning Principles

A variety of learning principles are built into good video games, yet there is still immense potential for future developments. Certain areas—for example, the ways in which video games allow for the free creation of virtual identities and worlds—cause a great deal of controversy and will undoubtedly cause a great deal more in the future.

Some of the learning principles this chapter has implicated follow. Again, each principle is relevant to both learning in video games and learning in content areas in classrooms. The cultural models about the world principle says that learners should have the opportunity to think reflectively about their cultural models about the world (e.g., the ways in which *Operation Flashpoint* made me rethink my cultural models of warfare). The cultural models about learning principle says that learners should have the opportunity to think reflectively about their cultural models about learning and themselves as learners (e.g., the ways in which *Metal Gear Solid* and a great many other games made me rethink the values of exploration and delaying getting to the major goal). The cultural models about semiotic domains principle says that learners should have the opportunity to think reflectively about their cultural models regarding the nature of semiotic domains they are trying to learn—for instance, about what a given type of video game is or should be like, or what makes something a game in the first place (e.g., Is *Under Ash* a video game or terrorist training? What about *Ethnic Cleansing*?) or what physics is (e.g., A set of facts? A way of thinking about and acting on the world? A set of social practices in which certain sorts of people engage?).

30. Cultural Models about the World Principle

Learning is set up in such a way that learners come to think consciously and reflectively about some of their cultural models regarding the world, without denigration of their identities, abilities, or social affiliations, and juxtapose them to new models that may conflict with or otherwise relate to them in various ways.

31. Cultural Models about Learning Principles

Learning is set up in such a way that learners come to think consciously and reflectively about their cultural models of learning and themselves as learners, without denigration of their identities, abilities, or social affiliations, and juxtapose them to new models of learning and themselves as learners.

32. Cultural Models about Semiotic Domains Principle

Learning is set up in such a way that learners come to think consciously and reflectively about their cultural models about a particular semiotic domain they are learning, without denigration of their identities, abilities, or social affiliations, and juxtapose them to new models about this domain.

Bibliographic Note

Major sources in the literature on cultural models include D'Andrade 1995; D'Andrade & Strauss 1992; Holland, Lachicotte, Skinner, & Cain 1998; Holland & Quinn 1987; Shore 1996; and Strauss & Quinn 1997.

The example from the high school physics class comes from Hammer (1996a). For the relationships between everyday ways of understanding the world and scientific ways, and how to bridge between them, see diSessa 2000; Hammer 1996a, b; and Minstrell 2000.

The review of *Operation Flashpoint* is dated March 18, 2002 at www.gamezilla.com/reviews/o/ofp.asp.

References

D'Andre, R. (1995). *The development of cognitive anthropology.* Cambridge: Cambridge University Press.

D'Andre, R. & Strauss, C., Eds. (1992). *Human motives and cultural models.* Cambridge: Cambridge University Press.

diSessa, A. A. (2000). *Changing minds: Computers, learning, and literacy.* Cambridge, Mass: MIT Press.

Hammer, D. (1996a). More than misconceptions: Multiple perspectives on student knowledge and reasoning, and an appropriate role for educational research. *American Journal of Physics* 64 1316–1325.

Hammer, D. (1996b). Misconceptions of p-prims: How many alternative perspectives of cognitive structure influence instructional perceptions and intentions? *Journal of the Learning Sciences* 5: 97–127.

Holland, D., Lachicotte, W., Skinner, D., & Cain, C. (1998). *Identity and agency in cultural worlds.* Cambridge: Mass.: Harvard University Press.

Holland, D., & Quinn, N. Eds. (1987). *Cultural models in language and thought.* Cambridge: Cambridge University Press.

Minstrell, J. (2000). Student thinking and related assessment: Creating a facet-based learning environment. In N. S. Raju, J. W. Pelligrino, M. W. Bertenthal, K. J. Mitchell, & L. R. Jones, Eds., *Grading the nation's report card: Research from the evaluation of NAEP.* Washington, D.C.: National Academy Press, pp. 44–73.

Shore, B. (1996). *Culture in mind: Cognition, culture, and the problem of meaning.* New York: Oxford University Press.

Strauss, C., & Quinn, N. (1997). *A cognitive theory of cultural meaning.* Cambridge: Cambridge University Press.

Seriously though. Why are we out here? As far as I can tell it's just a box canyon in the middle of nowhere. No way in or out.

The only reason that we set up a red base here is because they have a blue base over there. And the only reason they have a blue base over there is because we have a red base here.

redVSblue

presents

Yeah. But that's because we're fighting each other.

No, but I mean even if we were to pull out today, and they were to come take our base...they would have two bases in the middle of a box canyon. Whoop-de-fuckin-do.

Interaction and Narrative

Michael Mateas and Andrew Stern

Context

"Interaction and Narrative" *is a chapter from Michael's Ph.D. dissertation on Expressive AI (AI-based art and entertainment). A significant portion of the dissertation describes his collaborative work with Andrew Stern on the interactive drama* **Façade;** *the purpose of this chapter was to provide a theoretical framework for interactive drama, particularly addressing the problem of agency. The neo-Aristotelian theory described here is Michael's work, the rest is our joint work.*

Player and Character

Games and Narrative

Exploring the intersection between art and artificial intelligence, academic Michael Mateas has forged a new art practice and research discipline called "Expressive AI." He is currently a faculty member at the Georgia Institute of Technology, where he holds a joint appointment in the College of Computing and the School of Literature, Communication and Culture. At Georgia Tech, Michael is the founder of the Experimental Game Lab, whose mission is to push the technological and cultural frontiers of computer-based games.

Andrew Stern is a designer, researcher, writer, and engineer of personality-rich, AI-based interactive characters and stories. With Michael Mateas, he developed the interactive drama *Façade*, a 4-year art/research project, completed in Spring 2005. Previously, Andrew was a lead designer and software engineer at PF.Magic, developing Virtual Babyz, Dogz, and Catz, which sold over 2 million units worldwide. He is now a member of the creative and technical staff of Zoesis, and blogs at www.grandtextauto.org.

Approaches

A number of approaches are currently being pursued in the theorizing and building of interactive narratives. Each of these approaches foregrounds a different aspect of the problem, focusing on a different point within the design space of interactive narrative.

Before continuing, a note about terminology. When speaking generally about interactive story, I will sometimes use the word story and sometimes the word narrative. I use story when talking about experiences that have a tightly organized plot arc, progression towards a climax, beginning, middle and end, etc., that is, experiences such as "mainstream" novels and movies, which are understood as "stories" by the general population. I use *narrative* when talking about the abstract properties or qualities of stories, and more loosely structured, "experimental," story-like experiences.

Commercial Computer Games

The relationship between narrative and game is a hot topic within the computer game design community. The contemporary gaming scene, perhaps driven by the ever-increasing capabilities of computer graphics, and the resulting inexorable drive towards real-time photo-realism, is dominated by mimetic representations of physical scenes, objects and characters. With mimetic representation approaching the richness of animated movies, and with the increasing use of cinematic techniques, such as virtual cameras implementing automated shot vocabularies, comes the desire to provide a narrative explaining who these characters are and why they are in the situation they're in. Contrast this with classic arcade games such as *Pac Man* or *Tempest,* in which the more iconic mode of representation led to games where the proto-narrative was completely dominated by gameplay, and in fact could be safely ignored.

But with this increased interest in narrative, game designers also experience a deep ambivalence. The ephemeral quality of gameplay, the experience of manipulating elements within a responsive, rule-driven world, is still the raison d'être of games, perhaps the primary phenomenological feature that uniquely identifies the computer game as a medium. Where gameplay is all about interactivity, narrative is all about predestination. There is a pervasive feeling in the game design community that narrative and interactivity are antithetical:

> I won't go so far as to say that interactivity and storytelling are mutually exclusive, but I do believe that they exist in an inverse relationship to one another.... Interactivity is almost

the opposite of narrative; narrative flows under the direction of the author, while interactivity depends on the player for motive power.... [Adams 1999a]

This tension is reflected in the decline of the most story-based game genre, the commercial adventure game. Text adventures were a highly successful form in the 1980s, giving way to the graphic adventures of the early and mid 1990s. And through the mid 1990s, with the release of critically acclaimed titles such as *Myst* and *Grim Fandango,* the adventure game remained a vibrant form. But by the late 1990s the form was in trouble, with reviewers and critics pronouncing the death of the adventure game [Adams 1999b; OMM 2001]. But while early declarations of the death of the adventure game sometimes ended with hope (e.g. "Adventure games appeal to a market which is unimpressed by the size of the explosions or the speed of the engine, a market that for the most part, we're ignoring. But those people want to play games too. It's time to bring adventure games back." [Adams 1999b]), the decline continues to this day, with a recent review in the *New York Times* declaring "So far, 2002 has been the worst year for adventure games since the invention of the computer." [Herold 2002]. While adventure elements continue to live on in action adventures such as *Luigi's Mansion,* the *Resident Evil* franchise, and the *Tomb Raider* franchise, action adventures emphasize physical dexterity (e.g. shooting, running, jumping) over puzzle solving and plot progression.

In contemporary game design, narrative elements are primarily employed to provide an explanatory background against which the high-resolution mimetic action of the game takes place. Thus characters and situations may make reference to well known linear narratives (e.g. *Star Wars*), or nuggets of backstory may be revealed as the game progresses, or the game action may occur within an inexorably progressing narrative. But strongly authored stories whose path and outcome depend on player interaction are not currently an active line of exploration in commercial game design.

Emergent and Player Constructed Narrative

Rather than viewing narratives as highly structured experiences created by an author for consumption by an audience, emergent narrative is concerned with providing a rich framework within which individual players can construct their own narratives, or groups of players can engage in the shared social construction of narratives. Autonomous characters may be designed in such a way that interactions among autonomous characters and between characters and the player may give rise to loose narratives or narrative snippets [Stern 2002; Stern 1999; Aylett 1999]. Multi-user online worlds, including text-based Multi-User Dungeons (MUDs), avatar spaces, and massively multiplayer games such as *Everquest* and *Ultima Online*, create social spaces in which groups co-construct ongoing narratives. And simulation environments such as *The Sims* may be used by players to construct their own stories. Using the ability to capture screen shots and organize them into photo albums, plus the ability to construct new graphical objects and add them to the game, players of *The Sims* are constructing and posting online thousands of photo album stories.

Narrative and New Media Art

In fine art practice, narrative is understood as one, rather powerful, form of representation. Much of contemporary art practice involves self-consciously questioning representational modes, exploring the boundaries, breaking the representation, questioning whose power is being preserved by a representational mode, and hybridizing modes in order to create new ones. Thus, when engaging in narratively-based work, artists rarely tell straightforward narratives employing the standard narrative tropes available within their culture, but rather ironize, layer, and otherwise subvert the standard tropes from a position of extreme cultural self-consciousness. For example, *Terminal Time* constructs ideologically-biased documentary histories based on audience responses to psychographic profiles. The narrative structure of the traditional documentary form is made visible through endless replication [Domike, Mateas & Vanouse 2002, Mateas, Vanouse & Domike 2000]. *The Dr. K—Project* creates a narrative landscape that, rather than having a mimetic, independent existence, is created in response to audience interaction [Rickman 2002]. In these and similar works, interaction is used to open the narrative, to make its internal structure visible.

A highly active area in new media interactive narrative is net art. Such work, while employing multi-media elements such as sound, still and moving imagery as in Mark Amerika's *Grammatron,* or making use of interaction tropes from classic video games as in Natalie Bookchin's *Intruder,* often makes heavy use of textual presentation and literary effects, and thus is also a form of electronic literature.

Electronic Literature

Electronic literature is concerned with various forms of interactive reading, that is, interactive literary textual narratives. While there is certainly much exploration in this area combining multi-media elements, kinetic text, and novel interfaces, the canonical forms of electronic literature are hypertext and interactive fiction.

A hypertext consists of a number of interlinked textual nodes, or lexia. The reader navigates these nodes, selecting her own path through the space of lexia, by following links. Links may be dynamic, appearing and disappearing as a function of the interaction history, the contents of nodes may dynamically change, and navigation may make use of spatial mechanisms and metaphors rather than relying purely on link following [Rosenberg 1998]. However, a static node and link structure is the skeleton upon which such effects are added; many hypertext works consist solely of static node and link structures. The production of hypertext literature is intimately connected with the production of hypertext theory. Early theorists saw hypertext as the literal embodiment of postmodernist theories of deferred and intertextual signification [Landow 1992]. Like new media artists, hypertext authors tends to engage in theoretical explorations of the limits of narrative. Interactivity is seen as enabling rhizomatic stories that avoid the authorial imposition of a preferred viewpoint. Every story event can be viewed from multiple points of view, with closure indefinitely deferred.

Interactive fiction is a generalized term for "text adventure," the form inaugurated with the 1976 creation of *Adventure*, a textual simulation of a magical underground world in which the player solves puzzles and searches for treasure. *Adventure*, and all later interactive fictions, makes use of a conversational interface in which the player and the computer exchange text; the player types commands she wishes to perform in the world and the computer responds with descriptions of the world and the results of commands. While text adventures have not been commercially viable since the early 90's, there remains a very active non-commercial interactive fiction scene producing many literary interactive fictions, holding a number of yearly competitions, and actively theorizing the interpretation and production of interactive fiction [Montfort 2003].

Interactive Drama

Interactive drama per se was first conceived in Laurel's 1986 dissertation [Laurel 1986], an extended thought experiment involving dramatic stories in which the player enters as a first-person protagonist. While based most closely on the genres of the text and graphic adventure, interactive drama distinguishes itself from these and other conceptions of interactive narrative in a number of ways.

- Interactive drama takes *drama*, rather than literature, fine art, or game interaction tropes, as the guiding narrative conception. With this focus on drama comes a concern with intensity, enactment, and unity.

- Interactive drama wants player interaction to deeply shape the path and outcome of the story, while maintaining a tight, author given story structure. Thus interactive drama confronts head-on the tension between interactive freedom and story structure.

- Interactive drama seeks first-person immersion as a character *within* the story. *Façade* continues in the tradition of interactive drama.

A Neo-Aristotelian Theory of Interactive Drama

This section describes a neo-Aristotelian theory of interactive drama, continuing a specific thread of discussion first begun by Laurel's adoption of an Aristotelian framework for interactive drama [Laurel 1986], and then more generally for interactive experiences [Laurel 1991], and continued by Murray's description of the experiential pleasures and properties of interactive narratives [Murray 1998]. As an interactive narrative approach, interactive drama foregrounds the tension between interaction and story: how can an interactive experience have the experiential properties of classical, Aristotelian drama (identification, economy, catharsis, closure) while giving the player the interactive freedom to have a real effect on the story? This section provides a theoretical grounding for thinking about this question by developing a theory of interactive drama based on Aristotle's dramatic theory [Aristotle 330BC] but modified to address the interactivity added by player agency. This theory provides both design guidance for maximizing player agency within interactive dramatic experiences (answering the question "What should I build?") and technical direction for the AI work necessary to build the system (answering the question "How should I build it?").

As described above, interactive drama is one approach among many in the space of interactive narrative. The neo-Aristotelian poetics developed here is not intended to be a superiority argument for interactive drama, isolating it as the preferred approach in interactive narrative; rather, this poetics informs a specific niche within the space of interactive narrative and provides a principled way of distinguishing this niche from other interactive narrative experiences.

Defining Interactive Drama

In interactive drama, the player assumes the role of a first person character in a dramatic story. The player does not sit above the story, watching it as in a simulation, but is immersed in the story. Following Laurel, Table 1 lists distinctions between dramatic and literary narratives.

Dramatic narratives	Literary narratives
Enactment	Description
Intensification	Extensification
Unity of Action	Episodic Structure

Table 1. Distinctions between dramatic and literary narratives

Enactment refers to action. Dramas utilize action rather than description to tell a story. Intensification is achieved by arranging incidents so as to intensify emotion and condense time. In contrast, literary forms often "explode" incidents by offering many interpretations of the same incident, examining the incident from multiple perspectives, and expanding time. Unity of action refers to the arrangement of incidents such that they are all causally related to a central action. One central theme organizes all the incidents that occur in the story. Literary narratives tend to employ episodic structure, in which the story consists of a collection of causally unrelated incidents.

Though the model developed in this paper will provide design guidance on how to generate a sense of user agency in any interactive experience, it is primarily designed to illuminate interactive drama, that is, an interactive experience with the properties of dramatic stories.

Though interactive drama is strongly related to interactive fiction, it is interesting to note that a major trope of interactive fiction, the puzzle, is in conflict with the dramatic properties of enactment, intensification, and unity of action. Puzzles disrupt enactment, breaking immersion in the action and forcing reflection on the action as a problem to be solved. As the player thinks about the puzzle, action grinds to a halt. Solving puzzles invariably involves trial-and-error problem solving. All the dead ends involved in solving a puzzle introduce incidents that expand time and reduce emotion, thus disrupting intensification. Each puzzle can be thought of as having a "halo" consisting of all the failed attempts to solve the puzzle. These "halos" are extensive; they expand the experience rather than focus it. Puzzle-based experiences tend to be episodic; individual puzzles are loosely related by virtue of being in the same world, but are not strongly related to a central action. Puzzles have an internal logic that makes them self sufficient and internally consistent, but disrupts unity of action across the entire experience.

This is not to say that puzzles lack any aesthetic value or are a uniformly "bad" idea in interactive experiences. Montfort convincingly argues that puzzles in interactive fiction are related to the literary figure of the riddle, " ...inviting the riddlee to awaken to a new vision of the world" [Montfort 2003]. It is only to say that the form of engagement demanded by the puzzle is disruptive of dramatic properties.

Murray's Aesthetic Categories

Murray [Murray 1998] proposes three aesthetic categories for the analysis of interactive story experiences: immersion, agency, and transformation.

Immersion is the feeling of being present in another place and engaged in the action therein. Immersion is related to Coleridge's "willing suspension of disbelief"—when a participant is immersed in an experience, they are willing to accept the internal logic of the experience, even though this logic deviates from the logic of the real world. A species of immersion is telepresence, the feeling of being physically present (from a first person point of view) in a remote environment.

Agency is the feeling of empowerment that comes from being able to take actions in the world whose effects relate to the player's intention. This is not mere interface activity. If there are many buttons and knobs for the player to twiddle, but all this twiddling has little effect on the experience, there is no agency. Furthermore, the effect must relate to the player intention. If, in manipulating the interface elements, the player does have an effect on the world, but they are not the effects that the player intended (perhaps the player was randomly trying things because he didn't know what to do, or perhaps the player thought that an action would have one effect, but it instead had another), then there is no agency.

Transformation is the most problematic of Murray's three categories. Transformation has at least three distinct meanings.

- Transformation as masquerade. The game experience allows the player to transform themselves into someone else for the duration of the experience.
- Transformation as variety. The game experience offers a multitude of variations on

a theme. The player is able to exhaustively explore these variations and thus gain an understanding of the theme.

- Personal transformation. The game experience takes the player on a journey of personal transformation.

Transformation as masquerade and variety can be seen as means to effect personal transformation.

Integrating Agency into Aristotle

Murray's categories are phenomenological categories of the interactive story experience, that is, categories describing what it *feels* like to participate in an interactive story. Aristotle's categories (described below) are structural categories for the analysis of drama, that is, categories describing what *parts* a dramatic story is made out of. The trick in developing a theoretical framework for interactive drama is integrating the phenomenological (that is, what it feels like) aspect of a first person experience with the structural aspect of carefully crafted stories. In attempting this integration, I will first discuss the primacy of the category of agency. Second, I will briefly present an interpretation of the Aristotelian categories in terms of material and formal cause. Finally, agency will be integrated into this model.

Primacy of Agency

From an interactive dramatic perspective, agency is the most fundamental of Murray's three categories. Immersion, in the form of engagement, is already implied in the Aristotelian model. Engagement and identification with the protagonist are necessary in order for an audience to experience catharsis. Transformation, in the form of change in the protagonist, also already exists in the Aristotelian model. Murray's discussion of transformation as variety, particularly in the form of the kaleidoscopic narrative that refuses closure, is contrary to the Aristotelian ideals of unity and intensification. To the extent that we want a model of interactive *drama,* as opposed to interactive narrative, much of Murray's discussion of transformation falls outside the scope of such a model. While immersion and transformation exist in some form in non-interactive drama, the audience's sense of having agency within the story is a genuinely new experience enabled by interactivity. For these reasons, agency will be the category integrated with Aristotle.

Aristotelian Drama

Following Laurel [Laurel 1991], Aristotle's theory of drama is represented in *Figure 2.1.*

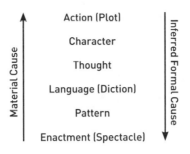

Figure 2.1. Aristotelian theory of drama

Aristotle analyzed plays in terms of six hierarchical categories, corresponding to different "parts" of a play. These categories are related via material cause and formal cause. The material cause of something is the material out of which the thing is created. For example, the material cause of a building is the building materials out of which it is constructed. The formal cause of something is the abstract plan, goal or ideal towards which something is heading. For example, the formal cause of a building is the architectural blueprints.

In drama, the formal cause is the authorial view of the play. The author has constructed a plot that attempts to explicate some theme. The characters required in the play are determined by the plot; the plot is the formal cause of the characters. The characters' thought processes are determined by the kinds of characters they are. The language spoken by the characters is determined by their thought. The patterns (song) present in the play are determined, to a large extent, by the characters' language (more generally, their actions). The spectacle, the sensory display presented to the audience, is determined by the patterns enacted by the characters.

In drama, the material cause is the audience view of the play. The audience experiences a spectacle, a sensory display. In this display, the audience detects patterns. These patterns are understood as character actions (including language). Based on the characters' actions and spoken utterances, the audience infers the characters' thought processes. Based on this understanding of the characters' thought processes, the audience develops an understanding of the characters, the characters' traits and propensities. Based on all this information, the audience understands the plot structure and the theme. In a successful play, the audience is then able to recapitulate the chain of formal causation. When the plot is understood, there should be an "ah-ha" experience in which the audience is now able to understand how the characters relate to the plot (and why they must be the characters they are), why those type of characters think they way do, why they took the actions they did and said what they did, how their speech and actions created patterns of activity, and how those patterns of activity resulted in the spectacle that the audience saw. By a process of interpretation, the audience works up the chain of material cause in order to recapitulate the chain of formal cause.

Interactive Drama

Adding interaction to the Aristotelian model can be considered the addition of two new causal chains at the level of character as depicted in *Figure 2.2.* The [dashed] arrows are the traditional chains of material and formal causation. The player has been added to the model as a character who can choose his or her own actions. This has the consequence of introducing two new causal chains. The player's intentions become a new source of formal causation. By taking action in the experience, the player's intentions become the formal cause of activity happening at the levels from language down to spectacle. But this ability to take action is not completely free; it is constrained from below by material resources and from above by authorial formal causation from the level of plot.

The elements present below the level of character provide the player with the material resources (material cause) for taking action. The only actions available are the actions supported by the material resources present in the game. The notion of affordance [Norman 1988] from interface design is useful here. In interface design, affordances are the opportunities for action made available by an object or interface. But affordance is even stronger than

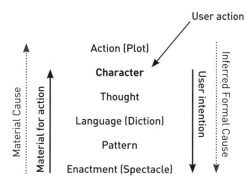

Figure 2.2. Neo-Aristotelian theory of interactive drama

implied by the phrase "made available"; in order for an interface to be said to afford a certain action, the interface must in some sense "cry out" for the action to be taken. There should be a naturalness to the afforded action that makes it the obvious thing to do. For example, the handle on a teapot affords picking up the teapot with your hand. The handle cries out to be grasped. In a similar manner, the material resources in an interactive drama afford action. Thus these resources not only limit what actions can be taken (the negative form of constraint) but cry out to make certain actions obvious (the positive form of constraint). Several examples of the material affordances in interactive drama are provided below.

The characters in an interactive drama should be rich enough that the player can infer a consistent model of the characters' thought. If the characters' thought can be understood (e.g. goals, motivations, desires), then this thought becomes a material resource for player action. By reasoning about the other characters' thoughts, the player can take actions to influence these characters, either to change their thoughts, or actively help or hinder them in their goals and plans.

The dialog (language) spoken by the characters and the opportunities for the player to engage in dialog are another material resource for action. Dialog is a powerful means for characters to express their thoughts, thus instrumental for helping the player to infer a model of the characters' thoughts. Conversely, dialog is a powerful means to influence character behavior. If the experience makes dialog available to the player (and most contemporary interactive experiences do not), this becomes a powerful resource for expressing player intention.

The objects available in the experience (I place the presence of interactive objects somewhere between spectacle and pattern) are yet another material resource for player action.

Finally, the mechanics of interaction (spectacle) provide the low-level resources for player actions. The mechanics provide the interface conventions for taking action.

In addition to the material affordances (constraints) from below, the player experiences formal constraints from above. Of course, these constraints are not directly perceived by the player, but, just as in non-interactive drama, are understood by recapitulating the author's chain of formal causation by making inferences along the chain of material causation. In non-interactive drama, understanding the formal chain of causation allows the audience to appreciate how all the action of the play stems from the dramatic necessity of the plot and theme. In interactive drama, the understanding of the formal causation from the level of plot to character additionally helps the player to have an understanding of what to do, that is, why they should take action within the story world *at all*. Just as the material constraints can be considered as affording action from the levels of spectacle through thought, the formal constraints afford *motivation* from the level of plot. This motivation is conveyed as dramatic probability. By understanding what actions are dramatically probable, the player understands what actions are worth considering.

Agency

We are now ready to propose a prescriptive, structural model for agency. *A player will experience agency when there is a balance between the material and formal constraints.* When the actions motivated by the formal constraints (affordances) via dramatic probability in the plot are commensurate with the material constraints (affordances) made available from the levels of spectacle, pattern, language, and thought, then the player will experience agency. An imbalance results in a decrease in agency. This will be made clearer by considering several examples.

Many puzzle-based adventures suffer from the imbalance of providing more material affordances than formal affordances. This results in the feeling of having many things to do (places to go, objects to fiddle with) without having any sense of why any one action would be preferable to another. For example, *Zork Grand Inquisitor* offers a rich world to navigate and many objects to collect and manipulate. Yet, since there is no unity of action, there is no way to relate current actions to the eventual goal of defeating the Grand Inquisitor. This leaves the player in the position of randomly wandering about trying strange juxtapositions of objects. This detracts from the sense of agency—though the player can take action, this action is often not tied to a high-level player intention. Notice that adding more material opportunities for action would not help the matter. The problem is not a lack of options of things to do, the problem is having insufficient formal constraint to decide between choices.

First-person shooters such as *Quake* induce agency by providing a nice balance between material and formal constraints. The proto-plot establishes the following formal constraints (dramatic probabilities):

1. Everything that moves will try to kill you.

2. You should try to kill everything.

3. You should try to move through as many levels as possible.

From these three principles, all the rest of the action follows. The material affordances perfectly balance these formal affordances. The player can run swiftly and smoothly through the space. The player can pick up a wide array of lethal weapons. The player can fire these weapons at monsters and produce satisfying, gory deaths. The monsters' behavior is completely consistent with the "kill or be killed" ethos. Everything that one would want to try and do given the formal constraints is doable. There are no extraneous actions available (for example, being able to strike up a conversation with a monster) that are not dictated by the formal constraints.

Note that though these example games are not specifically interactive drama, the model can still be used to analyze player agency within these games. Though the model is motivated by interactive drama, it can be used to analyze the sense of agency in any interactive experience by analyzing the experience *in terms of the dramatic categories* offered by the model. For example, though *Quake* has neither plot nor characters in the strict sense, there are top-down player expectations established by a "proto-plot." This "proto-plot" is communicated by the general design of the spectacle (e.g. the design of the creepy industrial mazes) as well as the actions of the characters, even if these characters do have primitive diction and thought.

In order to invoke a sense of agency, an interactive experience must strike a balance between the material and formal constraints. An experience that successfully invokes a sense of agency inhabits a "sweet spot" in design space. Trying to add additional formal constraints (more plot) or additional material constraints (more actions) to a balanced experience is likely to move it out of the sweet spot.

I would like to conclude this section with a brief clarification of my use of Aristotle's causal terminology (this clarification will appear in [Mateas 2003c]). Laurel notes that my statements "formal cause is the authorial view of the play" and "material cause is the audience view of the play" are, strictly speaking, a misuse of the Aristotelian causal nomenclature [Laurel 2003]. The actual work of authoring is correctly understood as an efficient cause, while Aristotle proposes no causal role for the audience. But what I mean to highlight by these statements is not the author or audience viewed as a cause, but rather what sort of information is directly available to author vs. audience. The author, through the act of authoring (efficient cause), arranges the elements both materially and formally. But while the material arrangement of the elements is more or less available to the audience, the formal arrangement is not. The author knows things about the play, such as why a character must be *this* character for *this* whole action (formal cause), that the audience does not. The audience must work from what is directly available to the senses, and hopefully, by following the chain of material causation, eventually recapitulate the chain of formal causation. So in referring to the "authorial view" and "audience view," I am attempting to highlight this asymmetry in knowledge between author and audience. The chain of formal cause is available to the author in a way that it is not available to the audience. And the chain of material cause is in some sense designed *for the audience* as it is the ladder they must climb in order to understand the whole action.

Similarly a player in an interactive drama becomes a kind of author, and thus, as an efficient cause, contributes both materially to the plot and formally to elements at the level of character on down. But these contributions are constrained by the material and formal causes (viewed as affordances) provided by the author of the interactive drama. Hopefully, if these constraints are balanced, the *constrained freedom* of the player will be productive of agency. In these discussions, I elided efficient cause and went straight for a discussion of the material and formal causes that the act of authoring puts in place.

Clarification of the Conceptual Experiment

This neo-Aristotelian theory clarifies the conceptual experiment we are undertaking with *Façade*. The goal is to create an interactive dramatic experience with the experiential properties of traditional drama, namely enactment, intensity, catharsis, unity and closure (these experiential properties are not independent; for example, intensity and unity are related to each other as are catharsis and closure). The Aristotelian analytic categories describe the structure (parts and relationships) of a story experience that induces these experiential properties. The way in which interaction has been incorporated into this model clarifies what is meant by *interactive* dramatic experience. Here, interaction means *first person* interaction as a character within the story. Further, the essential experiential property of interactivity is taken to be agency. The interactive dramatic experience should be structured in such a way as to maximize the player's sense of agency within the story. The model provides prescriptive structural guidance for maximizing agency, namely, to balance material and formal constraints. So the conceptual experiment of *Façade* can now be more precisely stated as follows: build a first-person, interactive dramatic world that, in addition to the classical experiential properties of Aristotelian drama, also provides the player with a strong sense of agency.

Relationship to Immersion and Transformation

Agency was taken as the fundamental Murray category to integrate with Aristotle. In this section, I examine what the new, integrated model has to say about the other two categories, immersion and transformation.

Immersion

Murray suggests three ways of inducing immersion: structuring participation with a mask (an avatar), structuring participation as a visit, and making the interaction conventions (the interface mechanics) seamless. These three mechanisms can be viewed in turn as a way to provide material and formal constraints, as a design suggestion for balancing the constraints, or as a design suggestion for providing effective material constraints at the level of spectacle. Agency is a necessary condition for immersion.

An avatar can provide both material and formal constraints on a player's actions. The avatar can provide character exposition through such traits as physical mannerisms and speech patterns. This character exposition helps the player to recapitulate the formal, plot constraints. Through both input and output filtering (e.g. the characters in *Everquest*, [Mateas 1997]), the avatar can provide material constraints (affordances) for action.

A visit is one metaphor for balancing material and formal constraints when the material opportunities for action are limited. From the formal side, the conventions of a visit tell the player that they won't be able to do much. Visits are about just looking around, possibly being guided through a space. Given the limited expectations for action communicated by the formal constraints, the game designer can get away with providing limited material means for action (and in fact, must *only* provide limited means).

The mechanics provide the material resources for action at the level of spectacle (the interface can be considered part of the spectacle). Providing a clean, transparent interface insures that agency (and thus immersion) will not be disrupted.

Transformation

Most of Murray's discussion of transformation examines transformation as variety, particularly in the form of kaleidoscopic narratives, which can be reentered multiple times so as to experience different aspects of the story. Agency, however, requires that a plot structure be present to provide formal constraints. An open-ended story without a clear point of view may disrupt the plot structure too much, thus disrupting agency. However, transformation as variety is necessary to make interaction really *matter*. If, every time a player enters the dramatic world, roughly the same story events occur regardless of the actions taken by the player, the player's interaction would seem inconsequential; the player would actually have no real effect on the story.

One way to resolve the apparent conflict between transformation and agency is to note that agency is a first-person experience induced by making moment-by-moment decisions within a balanced (materially and formally) interactive system, while transformation as variety is a third-person experience induced by observing and reflecting on a number of interactive experiences. Imagine an interactive drama system that guides the player through a fixed plot. As the player interacts in the world, the system, through a number of clever and subtle devices, moves the fixed plot forward. Given that these devices are clever and subtle, the player never experiences them as coercive; the player is fully engaged in the story, forming intentions, acting on them, and experiencing agency. Then imagine an observer who watches many players interact with this system. The observer notices that no matter what the players do, the same plot happens (meaning that roughly the same story events occur in the same order, leading to the same climax). By watching many players interact with the system, the observer has begun to discern the devices that *control* the plot *in the face of* player interaction. This observer will conclude that the player has no true agency, that the player is not able to form any intentions that actually matter within the dramatic world. But the first-time player within the world *is* experiencing agency. The designer of the dramatic world could conclude that since they are designing the world for the player, not for the observer, that as long as the player experiences a true sense of interactive freedom, that is, agency, transformation as variety is not an important design consideration.

The problem with this solution to the agency vs. transformation dilemma becomes apparent as the player interacts with the world a *second* time. On subsequent replays of the world, the player and the observer become the same person. The *total* interactive experience consists of both first-person engagement within the dramatic world and third-person reflection across multiple experiences in the world. In order to support the total experience, the system must support both first-person engagement and third-person reflection; must provide agency *and* transformation as variety.

A dramatic world supporting this total experience could provide agency (and the concomitant need to have a plot structure providing formal constraints) and transformation by actively structuring the player experience such that each run-through of the story has a clean, unitary plot structure, but multiple run-throughs have different, unitary plot structures. Small changes in the player's choices early on result in experiencing a different unfolding plot. The trick is to design the experience such that, once the end occurs, any particular run-through has the force of dramatic necessity. The story should have the dramatic probabilities smoothly narrowing to a necessary end. Early choices may result in different necessary ends—later choices can have less effect on changing the whole story, since the set of dramatically probable events has already significantly narrowed. Change in the plot should not be traceable to distinct branch points; the player should not be offered an occasional small number of obvious choices that force the plot in a different direction. Rather, the plot should be smoothly mutable, varying in response to some global state that is itself a function of the many small actions performed by the player throughout the experience. The *Façade* architecture, and the accompanying authorial idioms for character behavior and story sequencing offers one approach for supporting this variety within unity.

Technical Agenda

In addition to clarifying conceptual and design issues in interactive drama, the neo-Aristotelian model informs a technical agenda of AI research necessary to enable this kind of experience.

The primary heuristic offered by the model is that to maintain a sense of player agency in an interactive experience, material and formal constraints must be balanced. As the sophistication of the theme and plot of an experience increases, maintaining this balance will require characters whose motivations and desires are inferable from their actions. In addition, these characters will have to respond to the player's actions. Believable agents, that is, computer controlled characters with rich personality and emotion, will be necessary to provide these characters. In a domestic drama like *Façade,* in which the plot centers around relationships, trust, betrayal, infidelity, and self-deception, language is necessary to communicate the plot. In order to convey the formal constraints provided by the plot, the characters must have a rich repertoire of dialog available. In addition, the player must be able to talk back. One can imagine a system in which the characters can engage in complex dialog but the player can only select actions from menus or click on hotspots on the screen; this is in fact the strategy employed by character-based multimedia artwork and contemporary adventure games. But this strategy diminishes agency precisely by unbalancing material and formal constraints. The characters are able to express complex thoughts through language.

However, the player is not able to influence these thoughts except at the coarse level provided by mouse-click interactivity. Since part of the conceptual experiment of *Façade* is to maximize agency in interaction, *Façade* must support player dialog and thus must provide an AI solution for a limited form of natural language dialog.

The function of interactive characters is primarily to communicate material and formal constraints. That is, the player should be able to understand why characters take the actions they do, and how these actions relate to the plot. Sengers [Sengers 1998a] provides a nice analysis of how this focus on agents as communication vs. agent as autonomous, independent entities, results in changes in agent architectures. When the focus changes from "doing the right thing" (action selection) to "doing the thing right" (action expression), the technical research agenda changes [Sengers 1998b]. The neo-Aristotelian model indicates that action expression is exactly what is needed. In addition, an interactive drama system must communicate dramatic probability (likely activity given the plot) while smoothly narrowing the space of dramatic probability over time. This means that story action must be coordinated in such a way as to communicate these plot level constraints. Thus it is not enough for an individual character's actions to be "readable" by an observer. Multiple characters must be coordinated in such a way that their joint activity communicates both formal and material (plot and character level) affordances. This focus on communicating affordances changes the standard architectural assumptions regarding the relationship between plot and character.

Critiques of Interactive Drama

Interactive drama, in its Aristotelian conception, currently inhabits a beleaguered theoretical position, caught in the cross-fire between two competing academic formations: the narrativists and the ludologists. The narrativists generally come out of literary theory, take hypertext as the paradigmatic interactive form, and use narrative and literary theory as the foundation upon which to build a theory of interactive media. Ludologists generally come out of game studies (e.g. [Avedon & Sutton-Smith 1971]), take the computer game as the paradigmatic interactive form, and seek to build an autonomous theory of interactivity (read: free of the English department), which, while borrowing from classical games studies, is sensitive to the novel particularities of computer games (this is sometimes described as a battle against the colonizing force of narrative theory [Eskelinen 2001]). Both camps take issue with an Aristotelian conception of interactive drama, finding it theoretically unsophisticated, an impossible combination of game and narrative (though of course the camps disagree on whether this should be decided in favor of game or narrative), and technically impossible. Gonzalo Frasca, an able proponent of ludology, offers three specific objections to the neo-Aristotelian conception of drama in [Frasca 2003], namely: neo-Aristotelian interactive drama creates an impossible-to-resolve battle between the player and the system, confuses first and third-person perspectives, and is technically impossible. My responses to Frasca's comments here will appear in [Mateas 2003b]. Frasca's critique is representative of ludological critiques of neo-Aristotelian interactive drama, with similar critiques appearing in [Aarseth 1997].

A Specific Ludological Critique

Frasca argues that a conception of interactive drama that attempts to create a strong sense of closure with a well-formed dramatic arc introduces a battle for control between the player and system. If the system decides the ending, we have guaranteed closure without interactive freedom; if the user decides the ending we have guaranteed freedom but possibly no closure. Further, if the player is playing a prescribed role, such as Gandhi, we either have to limit interactive freedom to maintain the player's role (and story arc) or provide interactive freedom at the expense of the role (and story arc). Both these arguments have the following form: story means fate, interactivity means freedom (doing whatever you want), therefore interactivity and story can't be combined. However, the whole point of the neo-Aristotelian theory presented in this chapter is to replace the vague and open-ended term *interactivity* with the more specific term *agency,* and to then argue the conditions under which a player will experience agency: a player will *experience agency when material and formal constraints are balanced.* This is not the same as "a player will experience agency when they can take arbitrary action whenever they want." So in the case of choosing the ending of an interactive story, the player does not need the ability to make arbitrary endings happen in order to feel agency. A small number of authorially-determined ending configurations can still produce a strong feeling of player agency if reached through sequences of player actions within a materially and formally balanced system. Similarly, a Gandhi story can still produce a sense of agency without providing Gandhi with a chain gun or rocket launcher. If an interactive Gandhi story left weapons and power-ups lying about, but used some heavy handed interaction constraint (like the cursor turning red and beeping) to prevent the player from picking them up, then the experience would certainly be offering material affordances ("here's a gun for you to pick up—oops, not really") not balanced by the formal affordances (the dramatic probabilities of the Gandhi story), resulting in a decrease in the feeling of player agency. If, however, the Gandhi world never provided access to such weapons, and given the plot it never made sense to think of using such weapons, the player would still experience agency, even in the absence of access to plasma cannons. Interactive story designers do not have to be saddled with the impossible task of allowing the player to do whatever they want while somehow turning it into a well-formed story; creating a sense of both story and agency (interactivity) requires "merely" the hard task of balancing material and formal constraints.

Note that the neo-Aristotelian theory does not *prove* that if you build a system that materially balances more complex formal affordances, the player will experience both agency and "storyness." But neither do Frasca's arguments *prove* that this combination of agency and "storyness" is impossible. This is an empirical question. But the neo-Aristotelian theory has the advantage of providing a constructive plausibility argument that can inform the technical research agenda required to search for an empirical answer.

Frasca also argues that neo-Aristotelian interactive drama confuses the first-person gaming situation with the third-person narrative situation. A narrative is an already accomplished structure that is told to a spectator. A game is an evolving situation that is being accomplished by an interactor. Since an already accomplished static structure is not the same thing as an evolving, dynamic situation, then the argument goes, narrative and game are fundamentally dichotomous. What this argument denies, however, is the possibility for hybrid situations, such as the storytelling situation, in which a storyteller constructs a specific story through interaction with the audience. In this situation, the audience is both spectator and interactor, and the evolving story only becomes an already accomplished structure at the end, yet still has story properties (e.g. interpreted in accord with narrative conventions) in its intermediate pre-completed forms. Aristotelian interactive drama is similar to this storytelling situation; through interaction the player carves a story out of the block of narrative potential provided by the system.

Finally, Frasca argues against neo-Aristotelian interactive drama on the grounds of technical impossibility. It is very difficult for a human author to write a single drama. It would be even more difficult to write multiple dramas, in real-time, in response to player interaction. Since the current state of AI is nowhere near the point of producing systems that can write good linear plays on their own, then certainly interactive drama is not possible. This argument, however, assumes that an interactive drama system must have the capability to construct stories out of whole cloth, denying human authorship of the AI system itself. But any AI system consists of knowledge (whether represented symbolically, procedurally, or as learned probability distributions) and processes placed there by human authors, and has a circumscribed range of situations in which the system can function. The "only" thing an interactive drama system must be able to do is represent a specific space of story potential and move appropriately within this space of story potential in response to player interaction. As argued above, the system doesn't need to handle arbitrary player actions, but only those that are materially and formally afforded by the specific story space. While still hard, this becomes a much easier problem than building a system that can do everything a human playwright can do and more.

Frasca has proposed an interesting alternative conception of interactive drama based on the dramatic theory of Augusta Boal [Boal 1985]. Frasca's "video games of the oppressed," rather than attempting to immerse the player in a seamless dramatic world, instead invite the player to reflect on and critique the rules of the world, and to communicate this critique to other players by authoring their own behaviors and adding them to the game [Frasca 2001]. For example, someone dealing with alcoholism in their family may create an alcoholic mother character for a *Sims*-like environment and make the character publicly available. Others may download the character, play with it, and offer their own comments and commentary on alcoholic families by posting new alcoholic family member characters. This is certainly a provocative direction to pursue. However, Frasca notes that this Boalian conception of interactive drama provides both a better theoretical *and practical* framework for constructing interactive pieces. But the Boalian technical agenda of building powerful social simulation environments in which non-programmers can use easy-to-learn languages to simulate complex social phenomena is as challenging a technical project as the neo-Aristotelian technical agenda of building dramatic guidance systems. If one is inclined towards making technical impossibility arguments, it is unclear which agenda should be labeled more impossible.

Narrativist Critiques of Interactive Drama

Narrativist[1] critiques of interactive drama, inherited from their critiques of interactive fiction, are concerned that the interactive freedom resulting from making the player a protagonist *in* the world disrupts narrative structure to the point that only simple-minded, "uninteresting" stories can be told. This position is often held by hypertext theorists, who feel that the proper function of interaction in narrative is to engage in structural experiments that push the limits of narrative form, resulting in the "...resolutely unpopular (and often overtly antipopular) aesthetics promoted by hypertext theorists" [Jenkins 2003]. This overtly antipopulist stance can be seen in hypertext theorists' reactions to interactive fiction:

> Digital narratives primarily follow the trajectory of *Adventure,* a work considered venerable only by the techies who first played it in the 1970s, cybergaming geeks, and the writers, theorists, and practitioners who deal with interactivity. Hypertext fiction, on the other hand, follows and furthers the trajectory of hallowed touchstones of print culture, especially the avant-garde novel. [Douglas 2000:6–7] (quoted in [Montfort 2003])

Bernstein specifically places *Façade* within the category of interactive fiction and makes similar arguments to Frasca's, specifically that a first person story inevitably introduces a disruptive battle between the system and the player, and that no AI system will ever be able to respond to the space of actions a player will want to take within a story [Bernstein 2003] (see also Stern's response with respect to *Façade* [Stern 2003]). Of course Berstein's conclusions are the opposite of Frasca's. Rather than remove all narrative structure to open up the space of interaction, Berstein wants to limit interaction by making the reader a witness, a minor character on the periphery of the action. My response to this is similar to my response to Frasca. While I find hypertextual experiments in narrative structure conceptually and aesthetically interesting, I reject any attempt to establish such experiments as the only "culturally legitimate" approach to interactive narrative. And *Façade* is precisely a theoretical, technical, and story design experiment in the problems and potentials of building a first-person dramatic story that is about adult relationships, not the heroic travel narrative that narrativists believe first-person interaction inevitably produces.

Middle Ground Positions

A number of theorists have assumed middle ground positions, attempting to find a place for both game elements and narrative elements in the study of games.

Jenkins [Jenkins 2003] argues that while not all games tell stories, a number of strategies are available for weaving narrative elements into a game world, including:

- evoked narratives, in which elements from a known linear narrative are included in the spatial design of the game (e.g. *Star Wars Galaxies*)

- enacted narratives, organized around the player's movement through space (e.g. adventure games),

- embedded narratives, in which narrative events (and their consequences) are embedded in a game space such that the player discovers a story as they progress through the game (e.g. *Half-Life*)

- emergent narratives, narratively pregnant game spaces enabling players to make their own stories (e.g. *The Sims*).

Interestingly, perhaps purposely restricting himself to the current technical state of the art in commercial game design, he does not mention the strategy of actively weaving a player's activity into a story.

Ryan [Ryan 2001], while acknowledging that not all games are productive of narrative, defends the use of narrative as an analytic category in game studies:

> The inability of literary narratology to account for the experience of games does not mean that we should throw away the concept of narrative in ludology; it rather means that we need to expand the catalog of narrative modalities beyond the diegetic and the dramatic, by adding a phenomenological category tailor-made for games.

Ryan's proposal hinges on the relationship between the diagetic and mimetic mode. What allows us to bring narrative analysis to bear on movies and plays is that they are virtually diagetic: audience members, were they to reflect on and describe their experience, would produce a diagetic narrative. Ryan proposes extending this virtuality one step further, in which game players, were they to reflect on their action in the game, would produce a dramatic plot. Thus gameplay is virtually mimetic, which is itself virtually diagetic.

Both the ludological and narrativist critiques of interactive drama open up interesting conceptual spaces. I find Frasca's conception of Boalian "videogames of the oppressed" extremely interesting, and hope that he pursues this idea. And the structural experiments of the hypertext community continue to create new modes of literary expression. I certainly don't believe that the conception of interactive drama described in this chapter is the only proper conception of interactive story-like experiences. Nor do I believe that all interactive experiences must be assimilated to the concept of narrative. The ludologists commonly use examples such as chess, *Tetris* or *Space Invaders* in their analyses, and I agree that such games are most profitably studied using non-narrative analytic tools (but conversely, denying any story-like properties to games such as *The Last Express, Grim Fandango,* or *Resident Evil* also does not seem profitable). However, I reject the notion that games and stories are fundamentally irreconcilable categories, that providing the player with an experience of both agency and story structure is impossible. The neo-Aristotelian theory, and the concrete system that Andrew and I are building, are a theoretical and empirical investigation within this hybrid space of interactive story.

Note

I use the term "narrativist" as opposed to the more natural "narratologist" to refer to a specific, anti-game, interactive narrative position. While the narrativist position is often informed by narratology, this is not to say that all narratologists are anti-game or that narratology is intrinsically opposed to game-like interaction.

References

Aarseth, E. 1997. *Cybertext: Perspectives on Ergodic Literature.* Baltimore: The Johns Hopkins University Press.

Adams, E. 1999b. It's Time to Bring Back Adventure Games. *Designer's Notebook Column, Gamasutra,* November 9, 1999. http://www.gamasutra.com/features/designers_notebook/19991109. htm

Aristotle, 330 BC. *The Poetics.* Mineola, N.Y.: Dover, 1997.

Avedon, E., and Sutton-Smith, B. 1971. *The Study of Games.* New York: Wiley.

Aylett, R. 1999. Narrative In Virtual Environments: Towards Emergent Narrative. *Working notes of the Narrative Intelligence Symposium,* AAAI Spring Symposium Series. Menlo Park: Calif.: AAAI Press.

Boal, A. 1985. *Theater of the Oppressed.* New York: Theater Communications Group.

Domike, S.; Mateas, M.; and Vanouse, P. 2002. The recombinant history apparatus presents: Terminal Time. Forthcoming in M. Mateas and P. Sengers (Eds.), *Narrative Intelligence.* Amsterdam: John Benjamins.

Douglas, J. Y. 2000. *The End of Books—Or Books Without End?: Reading Interactive Narratives.* Ann Arbor: University of Michigan Press.

Eskelinen, M. 2001. Towards Computer Game Studies. In *Proceedings of SIGGRAPH 2001, Art Gallery, Art and Culture Papers,* 83–87.

Frasca, G. 2003. Frasca response to Mateas. In N. Wardrip-Fruin and P. Harrigan. (Eds.), *First Person: New Media as Story, Performance and Game.* Cambridge, MA: MIT Press.

Frasca, G. 2001. *Videogames of the Oppressed: Videogames as a Means for Critical Thinking and Debate.* Masters Thesis, Interactive Design and Technology Program, Georgia Institute of Technology. Available at: www.ludology.org.

Herold, C. 2002. A Streak of Glamour but a Lack of Lifeblood. *New York Times, Game Theory Column,* Sept. 5, 2002.

Jenkins, H. 2003. Game Design as Narrative Architecture. In N. Wardrip-Fruin and P. Harrigan. (Eds.), *First Person: New Media as Story, Performance and Game.* Cambridge, MA: MIT Press.

Landow, G. 1992. *Hypertext: The convergence of contemporary critical theory and technology.* Baltimore, MD: John Hopkins University Press.

Laurel, B. 2003. Laurel response to Mateas. In N. Wardrip-Fruin and P. Harrigan. (Eds.), *First Person: New Media as Story, Performance and Game.* Cambridge, MA: MIT Press.

Laurel, B. 1991. *Computers as Theatre*. Reading, MA: Addison-Wesley.

Laurel, B. 1986. *Towards the Design of a Computer-Based Interactive Fantasy System*. Ph.D. dissertation, Ohio State University.

Mateas, M. 2003b. Mateas response to Frasca. In N. Wardrip-Fruin and P. Harrigan. (Eds.), *First Person: New Media as Story, Performance and Game*. Cambridge, MA: MIT Press.

Mateas, M. 2003c. Mateas response to Laurel. In N. Wardrip-Fruin and P. Harrigan. (Eds.), *First Person: New Media as Story, Performance and Game*. Cambridge, MA: MIT Press.

Mateas, M. 1997. Computational Subjectivity in Virtual World Avatars. *Working notes of the Socially Intelligent Agents Symposium, AAAI Fall Symposium Series*. Menlo Park, Calif.: AAAI Press.

Mateas, M., Vanouse, P., and Domike S. 2000. Generation of Ideologically-Biased Historical Documentaries. In *Proceedings of AAAI 2000*. Austin, TX, pp. 236–242.

Montfort, N. 2003. *Twisty Little Passages: An Approach to Interactive Fiction*. Cambridge, MA: MIT Press.

Murray, J. 1998. *Hamlet on the Holodeck*. Cambridge, MA: MIT Press.

Norman, D. 1988. *The Design of Everyday Things*. New York: Doubleday.

OMM 2001. Who Killed Adventure Games? *Old Man Murray*. http://web.archive.org/web/20010417025123/www.oldmanmurray.com/features/doa/page1.shtml.

Rickman, B. 2002. The Dr. K—Project. In M. Mateas and P. Sengers (Eds.), *Narrative Intelligence*. Amsterdam: John Benjamins.

Rosenberg, J. 1998. Locus Looks at the Turing Play: Hypertextuality vs. Full Programmability. In *Hypertext 98: The Proceedings of the Ninth ACM Conference on Hypertext and Hypermedia*, ACM, New York, 152–160.

Ryan, M. 2001. Beyond Myth and Metaphor—The Case of Narrative in Digital Media. *Game Studies: The International Journal of Computer Game Research*, Vol. 1, Issue 1. Available at: http://www.gamestudies.org/0101/.

Sengers, P. 1998a. *Anti-Boxology: Agent Design in Cultural Context*. Ph.D. Dissertation. School of Computer Science, Carnegie Mellon University.

Sengers, P. 1998b. Do the Thing Right: An Architecture for Action-Expression. In *Proceedings of the Second International Conference on Autonomous Agents*. pp. 24–31.

Stern, A. 2003. Stern response to Bernstein. In N. Wardrip-Fruin and P. Harrigan. (Eds.), *First Person: New Media as Story, Performance and Game*. Cambridge, MA: MIT Press.

Stern, A. 2002. Virtual Babyz: Believable Agents with Narrative Intelligence. Forthcoming in M. Mateas and P. Sengers (Eds.), *Narrative Intelligence*. Amsterdam: John Benjamins.

Stern, A. 1999. Virtual Babyz: Believable Agents with Narrative Intelligence. In M. Mateas and P. Sengers (Eds.), *Working Notes of the 1999 AAAI Spring Symposium on Narrative Intelligence*. AAAI Press.

Game Design as Narrative Architecture

Henry Jenkins

Context

*"Game Design as Narrative Architecture" was written for Noah Windrip-Fruin and Pat Harrigan (eds.) **First Person: New Media as Story, Performance, and Game** (MIT Press, 2004). I was specifically asked to write an essay addressing what narrative theory might contribute to our understanding of games. When I presented this essay at the Bristol Games Conference, it provoked strong reactions from the so-called Ludologists and resulted in my being falsely (in my opinion) identified as a Narratologist in many accounts of that conference. In practice, I see most of my work on games as developing a more space-centered theory of the medium. Each essay adds another layer to our understanding of games space and this one happened to be exploring what, if anything, game space contributes to our perception of games as a storytelling medium.*

Games and Narrative

Game Spaces

Henry Jenkins is the founding director of the Comparative Media Studies Program and the de Florez Professor of Humanities at MIT. He is one of the leaders of the Education Arcade, a joint MIT-University of Wisconsin effort to promote the pedagogical uses of computer and video games. He is the editor and author of a dozen books on various aspects of popular culture, including *Textual Poachers: Television Fans and Participatory Culture*, *From Barbie to Mortal Kombat: Gender and Computer Games*, and *Convergence Culture: Where Old and New Media Intersect*.

The relationship between games and story remains a divisive question among game fans, designers, and scholars alike. At a recent academic Games Studies conference, for example, a blood feud threatened to erupt between the self-proclaimed Ludologists, who wanted to see the focus shift onto the mechanics of game play, and the Narratologists, who were interested in studying games alongside other storytelling media.[1] Consider some recent statements made on this issue:

> *"Interactivity is almost the opposite of narrative; narrative flows under the direction of the author, while interactivity depends on the player for motive power"*—Ernest Adams[2]

> *"There is a direct, immediate conflict between the demands of a story and the demands of a game. Divergence from a story's path is likely to make for a less satisfying story; restricting a player's freedom of action is likely to make for a less satisfying game."*—Greg Costikyan[3]

> *"Computer games are not narratives....Rather the narrative tends to be isolated from or even work against the computer-game-ness of the game."*—Jesper Juul[4]

> *"Outside academic theory people are usually excellent at making distinctions between narrative, drama and games. If I throw a ball at you I don't expect you to drop it and wait until it starts telling stories."*—Markku Eskelinen[5]

I find myself responding to this perspective with mixed feelings. On the one hand, I understand what these writers are arguing against—various attempts to map traditional narrative structures ("hypertext," "Interactive Cinema," "nonlinear narrative") onto games at the expense of an attention to their specificity as an emerging mode of entertainment. You say narrative to the average gamer and what they are apt to imagine is something on the order of a choose-your-own adventure book, a form noted for its lifelessness and mechanical exposition rather than enthralling entertainment, thematic sophistication, or character complexity. And game industry executives are perhaps justly skeptical that they have much to learn from the resolutely unpopular (and often overtly antipopular) aesthetics promoted by hypertext theorists. The application of film theory to games can seem heavy-handed and literal minded, often failing to recognize the profound differences between the two media. Yet, at the same time, there is a tremendous amount that game designers and critics could learn through making meaningful comparisons with other storytelling media. One gets rid of narrative as a framework for thinking about games only at one's own risk. In this short piece, I hope to offer a middle ground position between the Ludologists and the Narratologists, one that respects the particularity of this emerging medium—examining games less as stories than as spaces ripe with narrative possibility.

Let's start at some points where we might all agree:

1) Not all games tell stories. Games may be an abstract, expressive, and experiential form, closer to music or modern dance than to cinema. Some ballets (*The Nutcracker* for example) tell stories, but storytelling isn't an intrinsic or defining feature of dance. Similarly, many of my own favorite games—*Tetris, Blix, Snood*—are simple graphic games that do not lend themselves very well to narrative exposition.[6] To understand such games, we need other terms and concepts beyond narrative, including interface design and expressive movement for starters. The last thing we want to do is to reign in the creative experimentation that needs to occur in the earlier years of a medium's development.

2) Many games *do* have narrative aspirations. Minimally, they want to tap the emotional residue of previous narrative experiences. Often, they depend on our familiarity with the roles and goals of genre entertainment to orientate us to the action, and in many cases, game designers want to create a series of narrative experiences for the player. Given those narrative aspirations, it seems reasonable to suggest that some understanding of how games relate to narrative is necessary before we understand the aesthetics of game design or the nature of contemporary game culture.

3) Narrative analysis need not be prescriptive, even if some Narratologists—Janet Murray is the most oft cited example—do seem to be advocating for games to pursue particular narrative forms. There is not one future of games. The goal should be to foster diversification of genres, aesthetics, and audiences, to open gamers to the broadest possible range of experiences. The past few years have been one of enormous creative experimentation and innovation within the games industry, as might be represented by a list of some of the groundbreaking titles. *The Sims, Black and White, Majestic, Shenmue;* each represents profoundly different concepts of what

makes for compelling game play. A discussion of the narrative potentials of games need not imply a privileging of storytelling over all the other possible things games can do, even if we might suggest that if game designers are going to tell stories, they should tell them well. In order to do that, game designers, who are most often schooled in computer science or graphic design, need to be retooled in the basic vocabulary of narrative theory.

4) The experience of playing games can never be simply reduced to the experience of a story. Many other factors which have little or nothing to do with storytelling per se contribute to the development of a great game and we need to significantly broaden our critical vocabulary for talking about games to deal more fully with those other topics. Here, the Ludologist's insistence that game scholars focus more attention on the mechanics of game play seems totally in order.

5) If some games tell stories, they are unlikely to tell them in the same ways that other media tell stories. Stories are not empty content that can be ported from one media pipeline to another. One would be hard-pressed, for example, to translate the internal dialogue of Proust's *In Remembrance of Things Past* into a compelling cinematic experience and the tight control over viewer experience which Hitchcock achieves in his suspense films would be directly antithetical to the aesthetics of good game design. We must, therefore, be attentive to the particularity of games as a medium, specifically what distinguishes them from other narrative traditions. Yet, in order to do so requires precise comparisons   not the mapping of old models onto games but a testing of those models against existing games to determine what features they share with other media and how they differ.

Much of the writing in the Ludologist tradition is unduly polemical: they are so busy trying to pull game designers out of their "cinema envy" or define a field where no hypertext theorist dare to venture that they are prematurely dismissing the use value of narrative for understanding their desired object of study. For my money, a series of conceptual blind spots prevent them from developing a full understanding of the interplay between narrative and games. First, the discussion operates with too narrow a model of narrative, one preoccupied with the rules and conventions of classical linear storytelling at the expense of consideration of other kinds of narratives, not only the modernist and postmodernist experimentation that inspired the hypertext theorists, but also popular traditions which emphasize spatial exploration over causal event chains or which seek to balance between the competing demands of narrative and spectacle.[7] Second, the discussion operates with too limited an understanding of narration, focusing more on the activities and aspirations of the storyteller and too little on the process of narrative comprehension.[8] Third, the discussion deals only with the question of whether whole games tell stories and not whether narrative elements might enter games at a more localized level. Finally, the discussion assumes that narratives must be self-contained rather than understanding games as serving some specific functions within a new transmedia storytelling environment. Rethinking each of these issues might lead us to a new understanding of the relationship between games and stories. Specifically, I want to introduce an important third term into this discussion—spatiality—and argue for an understanding of game designers less as storytellers and more as narrative architects.

Spatial Stories and Environmental Storytelling

Game designers don't simply tell stories; they design worlds and sculpt spaces. It is no accident, for example, that game design documents have historically been more interested in issues of level design than plotting or character motivation. A prehistory of video and computer games might take us through the evolution of paper mazes or board games, both preoccupied with the design of spaces, even where they also provided some narrative context. *Monopoly*, for example, may tell a narrative about how fortunes are won and lost; the individual Chance cards may provide some story pretext for our gaining or losing a certain number of places; but ultimately, what we remember is the experience of moving around the board and landing on someone's real estate. Performance theorists have described RPGs as a mode of collaborative storytelling, but the Dungeon Master's activities start with designing the space—the dungeon—where the players' quest will take place. Even many of the early text-based games, such as *Zork*, which could have told a wide array of different kinds of stories, centered around enabling players to move through narratively-compelling spaces: "You are facing the north side of a white house. There is no door here, and all of the windows are boarded up. To the north a narrow path winds through the trees." The early Nintendo games have simple narrative hooks—rescue Princess Toadstool—but what gamers found astonishing when they first played them were their complex and imaginative graphic realms, which were so much more sophisticated than the simple grids that *Pong* or *Pac-Man* had offered us a decade earlier. When we refer to such influential early works as Shigeru Miyamoto's *Super Mario Bros.* as "scroll games," we situate them alongside a much older tradition of spatial storytelling: many Japanese scroll paintings map, for example, the passing of the seasons onto an unfolding space. When you adopt a film into a game, the process typically involves translating events in the film into environments within the game. When gamer magazines want to describe the experience of gameplay, they are more likely to reproduce maps of the game world than to re-count their narratives.[9] Before we can talk about game narratives, then, we need to talk about game spaces. Across a series of essays, I have made the case that game consoles should be regarded as machines for generating compelling spaces, that their virtual playspaces have helped to compensate for the declining place of the traditional backyard in contemporary boy culture, and that the core narratives behind many games center around the struggle to explore, map, and master contested spaces.[10] *Communications in Cyberspace* (New York: Sage, 1994); Henry Jenkins, "'Complete Freedom of Movement': Video Games as Gendered Playspace," in Justine Cassell and Henry Jenkins (Ed.) *From Barbie to Mortal Kombat: Gender and Computer Games* (Cambridge: MIT Press, 1998). Here, I want to broaden that discussion further to consider in what ways the structuring of game space facilitates different kinds of narrative experiences.

As such, games fit within a much older tradition of spatial stories, which have often taken the form of hero's odysseys, quest myths, or travel narratives.[11] The best works of J.R.R. Tolkien, Jules Verne, Homer, L. Frank Baum, or Jack London fall loosely within this tradition, as does, for example, the sequence in *War and Peace* which describes Pierre's aimless wanderings across the battlefield at Borodino. Often, such works exist on the outer borders of literature. They are much loved by readers, to be sure, and passed down from one generation to another, but they rarely figure in the canon of great literary works. How often, for example, has science fiction been criticized for being preoccupied with world-making at the expense of character psychology or plot development? These writers seem constantly to be pushing against the limits of what can be accomplished in a printed text and thus their works fare badly against aesthetic standards defined around classically-constructed novels. In many cases, the characters—our guides through these richly-developed worlds—are stripped down to the bare bones, description displaces exposition, and plots fragment into a series of episodes and encounters. When game designers draw story elements from existing film or literary genres, they are most apt to tap those genres—fantasy, adventure, science fiction, horror, war—which are most invested in world-making and spatial storytelling. Games, in turn, may more fully realize the spatiality of these stories, giving a much more immersive and compelling representation of their narrative worlds. Anyone who doubts that Tolstoy might have achieved his true calling as a game designer should reread the final segment of *War and Peace* where he works through how a series of alternative choices might have reversed the outcome of Napoleon's Russian campaign. The passage is dead weight in the context of a novel, yet it outlines ideas which could be easily communicated in a god game like *Civilization*.

Don Carson, who worked as a Senior Show Designer for Walt Disney Imagineering, has argued that game designers can learn a great deal by studying techniques of "environmental storytelling" which Disney employs in designing amusement park attractions. Carson explains, "The story element is infused into the physical space a guest walks or rides through. It is the physical space that does much of the work of conveying the story the designers are trying to tell....Armed only with their own knowledge of the world, and those visions collected from movies and books, the audience is ripe to be dropped into your adventure. The trick is to play on those memories and expectations to heighten the thrill of venturing into your created universe."[12] The amusement park attraction doesn't so much reproduce the story of a literary work, such as *The Wind in the Willows,* as it evokes its atmosphere; the original story provides "a set of rules that will guide the design and project team to a common goal" and which will help give structure and meaning to the visitor's experience. If, for example, the attraction centers around pirates, Carson writes, "every texture you use, every sound you play, every turn in the road should reinforce the concept of pirates," while any contradictory element may shatter the sense of immersion into this narrative universe. The same might be said for a game like *Sea Dogs* which, no less than *The Pirates of the Caribbean,* depends on its ability to map our pre-existing pirate fantasies. The most significant difference is that amusement park designers count on visitors keeping their hands and arms in the car at all times and thus have a greater control in shaping our total experience, whereas game designers have to develop worlds where we can touch, grab, and fling things about at will.

Environmental storytelling creates the preconditions for an immersive narrative experience in at least one of four ways: spatial stories can evoke pre-existing narrative associations; they can provide a staging ground where narrative events are enacted; they may embed narrative information within their mise-en-scene; or they provide resources for emergent narratives.

Evocative Spaces

The most compelling amusement park attractions build upon stories or genre traditions already well known to visitors, allowing them to enter physically into spaces they have visited many times before in their fantasies. These attractions may either remediate a pre-existing story (*Back to the Future*) or draw upon a broadly shared genre tradition (Disney's *Haunted Mansion*). Such works do not so much tell self-contained stories as draw upon our previously existing narrative competencies. They can paint their worlds in fairly broad outlines and count on the visitor/player to do the rest. Something similar might be said of many games. For example, *American McGee's Alice* is an original interpretation of Lewis Carroll's *Alice in Wonderland*. Alice has been pushed into madness after years of living with uncertainty about whether her Wonderland experiences were real or hallucinations; now, she's come back into this world and is looking for blood. McGee's wonderland is not a whimsical dreamscape but a dark nightmare realm. McGee can safely assume that players start the game with a pretty well-developed mental map of the spaces, characters, and situations associated with Carroll's fictional universe and that they will read his distorted and often monstrous images against the background of mental images formed from previous encounters with storybook illustrations and Disney movies. McGee rewrites Alice's story, in large part, by redesigning *Alice's* spaces.

Arguing against games as stories, Jesper Juul suggests, "you clearly can't deduct the story of *Star Wars* from *Star Wars* the game," whereas a film version of a novel will give you at least the broad outlines of the plot.[13] This is a pretty old fashioned model of the process of adaptation. Increasingly, we inhabit a world of transmedia story-telling, one which depends less on each individual work being self-sufficient than on each work contributing to a larger narrative economy. The *Star Wars* game may not simply retell the story of *Star Wars,* but it doesn't have to in order to enrich or expand our experience of the *Star Wars* saga. We already know the story before we even buy the game and would be frustrated if all it offered us was a regurgitation of the original film experience. Rather, the *Star Wars* game exists in dialogue with the films, conveying new narrative experiences through its creative manipulation of environmental details. One can imagine games taking their place within a larger narrative system with story information communicated through books, film, television, comics, and other media, each doing what it does best, each a relatively autonomous experience, but the richest understanding of the story world coming to those who follow the narrative across the various channels. In such a system, what games do best will almost certainly center on their ability to give concrete shape to our memories and imaginings of the storyworld, creating an immersive environment we can wander through and interact with.

Enacting Stories

Most often, when we discuss games as stories, we are referring to games that either enable players to perform or witness narrative events—for example, to grab a lightsabre and dispatch Darth Maul in the case of a *Star Wars* game. Narrative enters such games on two levels—in terms of broadly defined goals or conflicts and on the level of localized incidents.

Many game critics assume that all stories must be classically constructed with each element tightly integrated into the overall plot trajectory. Costikyan writes, for example, that "a story is a controlled experience; the author consciously crafts it, choosing certain events precisely, in a certain order, to create a story with maximum impact."[14] Adams claims, "A good story hangs together the way a good jigsaw puzzle hangs together. When you pick it up, every piece locked tightly in place next to its neighbors."[15] Spatial stories, on the other hand, are often dismissed as episodic—that is, each episode (or set piece) can become compelling on its own terms without contributing significantly to the plot development and often, the episodes could have been reordered without significantly impacting our experience as a whole. There may be broad movements or series of stages within the story, as Troy Dunniway suggests when he draws parallels between the stages in the Hero's journey as outlined by Joseph Campbell and the levels of a classic adventure game, but within each stage, the sequencing of actions may be quite loose.[16] Spatial stories are not badly constructed stories; rather, they are stories which respond to alternative aesthetic principles, privileging spatial exploration over plot development. Spatial stories are held together by broadly defined goals and conflicts and pushed forward by the character's movement across the map. Their resolution often hinges on the player's reaching their final destination, though, as Mary Fuller notes, not all travel narratives end successfully or resolve the narrative enigmas which set them into motion.[17] Once again, we are back to principles of "environmental storytelling." The organization of the plot becomes a matter of designing the geography of imaginary worlds, so that obstacles thwart and affordances facilitate the protagonist's forward movement towards resolution. Over the past several decades, game designers have become more and more adept at setting and varying the rhythm of game play through features of the game space.

Narrative can also enter games on the level of localized incident, or what I am calling micronarratives. We might understand how micronarratives work by thinking about the Odessa Steps sequence in Sergei Eisenstein's *Battleship Potempkin.* First, recognize that, whatever its serious moral tone, the scene basically deals with the same kind of material as most games—the steps are a contested space with one group (the peasants) trying to advance up and another (the Cossacks) moving down. Eisenstein intensifies our emotional engagement with this large scale conflict through a series of short narrative units. The woman with the baby carriage is perhaps the best-known of those micronarratives. Each of these units builds upon stock characters or situations drawn from the repertoire of melodrama. None of them last more than a few seconds, though Eisenstein prolongs them (and intensifies their emotional impact) through crosscutting between multiple incidents. Eisenstein used the term "attraction" to describe such emotionally-packed elements in his work; contemporary game designers might call them "memorable moments." Just as some memorable moments in games depend on sensations (the sense of speed in a racing game) or perceptions (the sudden expanse of sky in a snowboarding game) as well as narrative hooks, Eisenstein used the word "attractions" broadly to describe any element within a work which produces a profound emotional impact and theorized that the themes of the work could be communicated across and through these discrete elements. Even games which do not create large-scale plot trajectories may well depend on these micronarratives to shape the player's emotional experience. Micronarratives may be cut scenes, but they don't have to be. One can imagine a simple sequence of preprogrammed actions through which an opposing player responds to your successful touchdown in a football game as a micronarrative.

Game critics often note that the player's participation poses a potential threat to the narrative construction, whereas the hard rails of the plotting can overly constrain the "freedom, power, self-expression" associated with interactivity.[18] The tension between performance (or game play) and exposition (or story) is far from unique to games. The pleasures of popular culture often center on spectacular performance numbers and self-contained set pieces. It makes no sense to describe musical numbers or gag sequences or action scenes as disruptions of the film's plots: the reason we go to see a kung fu movie is to see Jackie Chan show his stuff.[19] Yet, few films consist simply of such moments, typically falling back on some broad narrative exposition to create a framework within which localized actions become meaningful.[20] We might describe musicals, action films or slapstick comedies as having accordion-like structures. Certain plot points are fixed where-as other moments can be expanded or contracted in response to audience feedback without serious consequences to the overall plot. The introduction needs to establish the character's goals or explain the basic conflict; the conclusion needs to show the successful completion of those goals or the final defeat of the antagonist. In commedia del arte, for example, the masks define the relationships between the characters and give us some sense of their goals and desires.[21] The masks set limits on the action, even though the performance as a whole is created through improvisation. The actors have mastered the possible moves or lassi associated with each character, much as a game player has mastered the combination of buttons that must be pushed to enable certain character actions. No author prescribes what the actors do once they get on the stage, but the shape of the story emerges from this basic vocabulary of possible actions and from the broad parameters set by this theatrical tradition. Some of the lassi can contribute to the plot development, but many of them are simple restagings of the basic oppositions (the knave tricks the master or gets beaten). These performance or spectacle-centered genres often display a pleasure in process—in the experiences along the road—that can overwhelm any strong sense of goal or resolution, while exposition can be experienced as an unwelcome interruption to the pleasure of performance. Game designers struggle with this same balancing act—trying to determine how much plot will create a compelling framework and how much freedom players can enjoy at a local level without totally derailing the larger narrative trajectory. As inexperienced storytellers, they often fall back on rather mechanical exposition through cut scenes, much as early film makers were sometimes overly reliant on intertitles rather than learning the skills of visual storytelling. Yet, as with any other aesthetic tradition, game designers are apt to develop craft through a process of experimentation and refinement of basic narrative devices, becoming better at shaping narrative experiences without unduly constraining the space for improvisation within the game.

Embedded Narratives

Russian formalist critics make a useful distinction between plot (or Syuzhet) which refers to, in Kristen Thompson's terms, "the structured set of all causal events as we see and hear them presented in the film itself," and story (or fabula), which refers to the viewer's mental construction of the chronology of those events.[22] Few films or novels are absolutely linear; most make use of some forms of back story which is revealed gradually as we move through the narrative action. The detective story is the classic illustration of this principle, telling two stories—one more or less chronological (the story of the investigation itself) and the other told radically out of sequence (the events motivating and leading up to the murder). According to this model, narrative comprehension is an active process by which viewers assemble and make hypothesis about likely narrative developments on the basis of information drawn from textual cues and clues.[23] As they move through the film, spectators test and reformulate their mental maps of the narrative action and the story space. In games, players are forced to act upon those mental maps, to literally test them against the game world itself. If you are wrong about whether the bad guys lurk behind the next door, you will find out soon enough—perhaps by being blown away and having to start the game over. The heavy-handed exposition that opens many games serves a useful function in orienting spectators to the core premises so that they are less likely to make stupid and costly errors as they first enter into the game world. Some games create a space for rehearsal, as well, so that we can make sure we understand our character's potential moves before we come up against the challenges of navigating narrational space.

Read in this light, a story is less a temporal structure than a body of information. The author of a film or a book has a high degree of control over when and if we receive specific bits of information, but a game designer can somewhat control the narrational process by distributing the information across the game space. Within an open-ended and exploratory narrative structure like a game, essential narrative information must be redundantly presented across a range of spaces and artifacts, since one can not assume the player will necessarily locate or recognize the significance of any given element. Game designers have developed a variety of kludges which allow them to prompt players or steer them towards narratively salient spaces. Yet, this is no different from the ways that redundancy is built into a television soap opera, where the assumption is that a certain number of viewers are apt to miss any given episode, or even in classical Hollywood narrative, where the law of three suggests that any essential plot point needs to be communicated in at least three ways.

To continue with the detective example, then, one can imagine the game designer as developing two kinds of narratives—one relatively unstructured and controlled by the player as they explore the game space and unlock its secrets; the other pre-structured but embedded within the mise-en-scene awaiting discovery. The game world becomes a kind of information space, a memory palace. *Myst* is a highly successful example of this kind of embedded narrative, but embedded narrative does not necessarily require an emptying of the space of contemporary narrative activities, as a game like *Half Life* might suggest. Embedded narrative can and often does occur within contested spaces. We may have to battle our way past antagonists, navigate through mazes, or figure out how to pick locks in order to move through the narratively-impregnated mise-en-scene. Such a mixture of enacted and embedded narrative elements can allow for a balance between the flexibility of interactivity and the coherence of a pre-authored narrative.

Using *Quake* as an example, Jesper Juul argues that flashbacks are impossible within games, because the game play always occurs in real time.[24] Yet, this is to confuse story and plot. Games are no more locked into an eternal present than films are always linear. Many games contain moments of revelation or artifacts that shed light on past actions. Carson suggests that part of the art of game design comes in finding artful ways of embedding narrative information into the environment without destroying its immersiveness and without giving the player a sensation of being drug around by the neck: "Staged areas...[can] lead the game player to come to their own conclusions about a previous event or to suggest a potential danger just ahead. Some examples include...doors that have been broken open, traces of a recent explosion, a crashed vehicle, a piano dropped from a great height, charred remains of a fire."[25] Players, he argues, can return to a familiar space later in the game and discover it has been transformed by subsequent (off-screen) events. *Clive Barker's The Undying,* for example, creates a powerful sense of back story in precisely this manner. It is a story of sibling rivalry which has taken on supernatural dimensions. As we visit each character's space, we have a sense of the human they once were and the demon they have become. In Peter Molyneux's *Black and White,* the player's ethical choices within the game leave traces on the landscape or reconfigure the physical appearances of their characters. Here, we might read narrative consequences off mise-en-scene the same way we read Dorian Grey's debauchery off of his portrait. Carson describes such narrative devices as "following Saknussemm," referring to the ways that the protagonists of Jules Verne's *Journey to The Center of the Earth*, keep stumbling across clues and artifacts left behind by a sixteenth Century Icelandic scientist/explorer Arne Saknussemm, and readers become fascinated to see what they can learn about his ultimate fate as the travelers come closer to reaching their intended destination.

Game designers might study melodrama for a better understanding of how artifacts or spaces can contain affective potential or communicate significant narrative information. Melodrama depends on the external projection of internal states, often through costume design, art direction, or lighting choices. As we enter spaces, we may become overwhelmed with powerful feelings of loss or nostalgia, especially in those instances where the space has been transformed by narrative events. Consider, for example, the moment in *Doctor Zhivago* when the characters return to the mansion, now completely deserted and encased in ice, or when Scarlet O'Hara travels across the scorched remains of her family estate in *Gone With the Wind* following the burning of Atlanta. In Alfred Hitchcock's *Rebecca,* the title character never appears, but she exerts a powerful influence over the other characters—especially the second Mrs. DeWinter who must inhabit a space where every artifact recalls her predecessor. Hitchcock creates a number of scenes of his protagonist wandering through Rebecca's space, passing through locked doors, staring at her overwhelming portrait on the wall, touching her things in drawers, or feeling the texture of fabrics and curtains. No matter where she goes in the house, she can not escape Rebecca's memory.

A game like Neil Young's *Majestic* pushes this notion of embedded narrative to its logical extreme. Here, the embedded narrative is no longer contained within the console but rather flows across multiple information channels. The player's activity consists of sorting through documents, deciphering codes, making sense of garbled transmissions, moving step by step towards a fuller understanding of the conspiracy which is the game's primary narrative focus. We follow links between websites; we get information through webcasts, faxes, e-mails, and phone calls. Such an embedded narrative doesn't require a branching story structure but rather depends on scrambling the pieces of a linear story and allowing us to reconstruct the plot through our acts of detection, speculation, exploration, and decryption. Not surprisingly, most embedded narratives, at present, take the form of detective or conspiracy stories, since these genres help to motivate the player's active examination of clues and exploration of spaces and provide a rationale for our efforts to reconstruct the narrative of past events. Yet, as my examples above suggest, melodrama provides another—and as yet largely unexplored—model for how an embedded story might work, as we read letters and diaries, snoop around in bedroom drawers and closets, in search of secrets which might shed light on the relationships between characters.

Emergent Narratives

The Sims represents a fourth model of how narrative possibilities might get mapped onto game space. Emergent narratives are not pre-structured or pre-programmed, taking shape through the game play, yet they are not as unstructured, chaotic, and frustrating as life itself. Game worlds, ultimately, are not real worlds, even those as densely developed as *Shenmue* or as geographically expansive as *Everquest.* Will Wright frequently describes *The Sims* as a sandbox or dollhouse game, suggesting that it should be understood as a kind of authoring environment within which players can define their own goals and write their own stories. Yet, unlike Microsoft Word, the game doesn't open on a blank screen. Most players come away from spending time with *The Sims* with some degree of narrative satisfaction. Wright has created a world ripe with narrative possibilities, where each design decision has been made with an eye towards increasing the prospects of interpersonal romance or conflict. The ability to design our own "skins" encourages players to create characters who are emotionally significant to them, to rehearse their own relationships with friends, family or coworkers or to map characters from other fictional universes onto *The Sims.* A quick look at the various scrapbooks players have posted on the web suggests that they have been quick to take advantage of its relatively open-ended structure. Yet, let's not underestimate the designers' contributions. The characters have a will of their own, not always submitting easily to the player's control, as when a depressed protagonist refuses to seek employment, preferring to spend hour upon hour soaking in their bath or moping on the front porch. Characters are given desires, urges, and needs, which can come into conflict with each other, and thus produce dramatically compelling encounters. Characters respond emotionally to events in their environment, as when characters mourn the loss of a loved one. Our choices have consequences, as when we spend all of our money and have nothing left to buy them food. The gibberish language and flashing symbols allow us to map our own meanings onto the conversations, yet the tone of voice and body language can powerfully express specific emotional states, which encourage us to understand those interactions within familiar plot situations. The designers have made choices about what kinds of actions are and are not possible in this world, such as allowing for same sex kisses, but limiting the degree of explicit sexual activity that can occur. (Good programmers may be able to get around such restrictions, but most players probably work within the limitations of the program.)

Janet Murray's *Hamlet on the Holodeck* might describe some of what Wright accomplishes here as procedural authorship.[26] Yet, I would argue that his choices go deeper than this, working not simply through the programming, but also through the design of the game space. For example, just as a doll house offers a streamlined representation which cuts out much of the clutter of an actual domestic space, *The Sims'* houses are stripped down to only a small number of artifacts, each of which perform specific kinds of narrative functions. Newspapers, for example, communicate job information. Characters sleep in beds. Bookcases can make your smarter. Bottles are for spinning and thus motivating lots of kissing. Such choices result in a highly legible narrative space. In his classic study, *The Image of the City,* Kevin Lynch made the case that urban designers needed to be more sensitive to the narrative potentials of city spaces, describing city planning as "the deliberate manipulation of the world for sensuous ends."[27] Urban designers exert even less control than game designers over how people use the spaces they create or what kinds of scenes they stage there. Yet, some kinds of space lend themselves more readily to narratively memorable or emotionally meaningful experiences than others. Lynch suggested that urban planners should not attempt to totally predetermine the uses and meanings of the spaces they create: "A landscape whose every rock tells a story may make difficult the creation of fresh stories."[28] Rather, he proposes an aesthetic of urban design which endows each space with "poetic and symbolic" potential: "Such a sense of place in itself enhances every human activity that occurs there, and encourages the deposit of a memory trace."[29] Game designers would do well to study Lynch's book, especially as they move into the production of game platforms which support player-generated narratives.

In each of these cases, choices about the design and organization of game spaces have narratological consequences. In the case of evoked narratives, spatial design can either enhance our sense of immersion within a familiar world or communicate a fresh perspective on that story through the altering of established details. In the case of enacted narratives, the story itself may be structured around the character's movement through space and the features of the environment may retard or accelerate that plot trajectory. In the case of embedded narratives, the game space becomes a memory palace whose contents must be deciphered as the player tries to reconstruct the plot and in the case of emergent narratives, game spaces are designed to be rich with narrative potential, enabling the story-constructing activity of players. In each case, it makes sense to think of game designers less as storytellers than as narrative architects.

End Notes

1. The term, Ludology, was coined by Espen Aarseth, who advocates the emergence of a new field of study, specifically focused on the study of games and game play, rather than framed through the concerns of pre-existing disciplines or other media.

2. Ernest Adams, "Three Problems for Interactive Storytellers," *Gamasutra.com*

3. Greg Costikyan, "Where Stories End and Games Begin," *Game Developer,* September 2000, pp. 44–53.

4. Jesper Juul, "A Clash between Games and Narrative," paper presented at the Digital Arts and Culture Conference, Bergen, Finland, November 1998, http://www.jesperjuul dk/text/ DA%20Paper%201998.html. For a more recent formulation of this same argument, see Jesper Juul, ""Games Telling Stories?" *Game Studies,* http://cmc.uib.no/gamestudies/0101/juul-gts

5. Markku Eskelinen, "The Gaming Situation," *Game Studies,* htttp:cmc.uib.no/gamestudies/ 0101/Eskelinen

6. Eskelinen, op cit., takes Janet Murray, *Hamlet on the Holodeck: The Future of Narrative in Cyberspace* (Cambridge: MIT Press, 1997) to task for her narrative analysis of Tetris as "a perfect enactment of the over tasked lives of Americans in the 1990s—of the constant bombardment of tasks that demand our attention and that we must somehow fit into our overcrowded schedules and clear off our desks in order to make room for the next onslaught." Eskelinen is correct to note that the abstraction of Tetris would seem to defy narrative interpretation, but that is not the same thing as insisting that no meaningful analysis can be made of the game and its fit within contemporary culture. *Tetris* might well express something of the frenzied pace of modern life, just as modern dances might, without being a story.

7. "A story is a collection of facts in a time sequenced order that suggests a cause and effect relationship." Chris Crawford, *The Art of Computer Game Design,* chapter one, http://members. nbci.com/kalid/art/art.html. "The story is the antithesis of game. The best way to tell a story is in linear form. The best way to create a game is to provide a structure within which the player has freedom of action." Costikyan, op cit.

8. "In its richest form, storytelling—narrative—means the reader's surrender to the author. The author takes the reader by the hand and leads him into the world of his imagination. The reader has a role to play, but it's a fairly passive role: to pay attention, to understand, perhaps to think...but not to act." Adams, op. cit.

9. As I have noted elsewhere, these maps take a distinctive form—not objective or abstract top-down views but composites of screenshots which represent the game world as we will encounter it in our travels through its space. Game space never exists in abstract, but always experientially.

10. Henry Jenkins and Mary Fuller, "Nintendo and New World Narrative," in Steve Jones (Ed.)

11. My concept of spatial stories is strongly influenced by Michel de Certeau, *The Practice of Everyday Life* (Berkeley: University of California Press, 1988) and Henri LeFebvre, *The Production of Space* (London: Blackwell, 1991).

12. Don Carson, "Environmental Storytelling: Creating Immersive 3D Worlds Using Lessons Learned from the Theme Park Industry," *Gamasutra.com,* http://www.gamasutra.com/features/20000301/carson_pfv.htm

13. Juul, op. cit.

14. Costikyan. For a fuller discussion of the norms of classically constructed narrative, see David Bordwell, Janet Staiger, and Kristen Thompson, *The Classical Hollywood Cinema* (New York: Columbia University Press, 1985).

15. Adams, op. cit.

16. Troy Dunniway, "Using the Hero's Journey in Games," *Gamasutra.com,* http://www.gamasutra.com/features/20001127/dunniway_pfv.htm.

17. Fuller and Jenkins, op. cit.

18. Adams, op. cit.

19. For useful discussion of this issue in film theory, see Donald Crafton, "Pie and Chase: Gag, Spectacle and Narrative in Slapstick Comedy," in Kristine Brunovska Karnick and Henry Jenkins (Eds.) *Classical Hollywood Comedy* (New York: Routledge/American Film Institute, 1995); Henry Jenkins, *What Made Pistachio Nuts?: Early Sound Comedy and The Vaudeville Aesthetic* (New York: Columbia University Press, 1991); Rick Altman, T*he American Film Musical* (Bloomington: Indiana University Press, 1999); Tom Gunning, "The Cinema of Attractions: Early Film, Its Spectator and the Avant Garde" in Thomas Elsaesser with Adam Barker (Eds.), *Early Cinema: Space, Frame, Narrative* (London: British Film Institute, 1990); Linda Williams, *Hard Core: Power, Pleasure and 'The Frenzy of the Visible'* (Berkeley: University of California Press, 1999).

20. "Games that just have nonstop action are fun for a while but often get boring. This is because of the lack of intrigue, suspense, and drama. How many action movies have you seen where the hero of the story shoots his gun every few seconds and is always on the run? People loose interest watching this kind of movie. Playing a game is a bit different, but the fact is the brain becomes over stimulated after too much nonstop action." Dunniway, op. cit.

21. See, for example, John Rudlin, *Commedia Dell'Arte: An Actor's Handbook* (New York: Routledge, 1994) for a detailed inventory of the masks and lassi of this tradition.

22. Kristen Thompson, *Breaking the Glass Armor: Neoformalist Film Analysis* (Princeton: Princeton University Press, 1988), p.39–40.

23. See, for example, David Bordwell, *Narration in the Fiction Film* (Madison: University of Wisconsin, 1989) and Edward Branigan, *Narrative Comprehension and Film* (New York: Routledge, 1992).

24. Juul, op cit.

25. Carson, op. cit.

26. Murray, op. cit.

27. Kevin Lynch, *The Image of the City* (Cambridge: MIT Press, 1960), p. 116.

28. Ibid, p. 6.

29. Ibid, p. 119.

Adventure as a Video Game: Adventure for the Atari 2600

Warren Robinett

Context

*This essay is a revised version of Chapter 3 from my unpublished book manuscript **Inventing the Adventure Game,** which I wrote in 1983–'84. I had designed the games Adventure for the Atari 2600 videogame console (developed during 1978–'79) and Rocky's Boots for the Apple II personal computer (developed during 1980–'82). **Inventing** was a design history of these two commercial games. For **The Game Design Reader,** I added a brief introduction.*

Game Design Models

Game Spaces

Warren Robinett in 1979 designed the first action-adventure video game, Adventure, for the Atari 2600 video game console. He cofounded the Learning Company, and there designed the educational simulation Rocky's Boots. He did research in virtual reality at NASA and University of North Carolina, and now works at Hewlett-Packard Labs on fault-tolerant computing for nano-electronics.

Introduction

Game designers decide what ideas to develop based on the milieu of the time they live in—the hit games, the cool new ideas, the technical tricks for exploiting the hardware, the user interface techniques, and so on. The art of interactive game design was evolving as new ideas were discovered, and these two games of mine were links in the chain. Adventure for the Atari 2600 was directly inspired by the original text game Adventure created by Willie Crowther and Don Woods. (Chapter 2 of Inventing the Adventure Game was about this game.) Rocky's Boots (Chapter 4 of Inventing) was, for me, a logical further development of the ideas in the Atari 2600 Adventure. Many subsequent designers found the concept of the adventure game worthy of further exploration and development, producing what we now recognize as the genre of adventure games. Chapter 3 is thus a contemporaneous report, from the dawn of the video game era, on the creation of the adventure game genre. My website <WarrenRobinett.com> has more information on the design of Adventure, including the complete text of the book manuscript.

*For Chapter 3 to make sense in isolation, it is necessary to know something about the game that preceded and inspired my version of Adventure. Crowther and Woods's wonderful text adventure game (see <www.rickadams.org/adventure>) used no graphics at all—it was **entirely** text. Text described where you were:* `You are in a debris room filled with stuff washed in from the surface. A low wide passage with cobbles becomes plugged with mud and debris here, but an awkward canyon leads upward and west. A note on the wall says "MAGIC WORD XYZZY."` *Text described objects you could carry:* `A three-foot black rod with a rusty star on an end lies nearby.` *And text commands were typed by the player to move around and do things:* `GO WEST` *or* `TAKE ROD` *or* `SAY XYZZY.` *Chapter 3 describes how I adapted the adventure game concept from its birth medium (text descriptions of places and objects, typing text commands on a keyboard) to the video game medium (graphics, motion, animation, color, sounds, and joystick input).*

The process of creating video games has changed almost beyond recognition in the 25 years since Adventure was created. It has morphed from an act of individual authorship, similar to that of a novelist, to the coordinated effort of a large team of specialists, similar to that of making a movie. The resources available to the game de-signer (memory, computing power) have also changed enormously during this period, increasing by a factor of 1000 or more. It is therefore difficult nowadays to imagine the world that we game designers lived in back then.

The Atari 2600 was the first widely distributed video game console. After the success of Pong—the first mass-market video game—the Atari 2600 was the first home videogame machine meant to play more than one game. Different cartridges let you play different games. Today's Playstation, Xbox, and GameCube are direct descendants of the Atari 2600.

*Back at Atari in the late 1970s, each game cartridge for the Atari 2600 console was created by one person. You had the idea, wrote the program, created the graphics, did the sound effects, chased down bugs, tested the game on kids, revised it until you were satisfied, and wrote a draft of the game manual. This made sense at that time, because with only 4K of ROM memory available to hold the game program, it took only a few months of programming to fill up the ROM. RAM memory was even more limited, with only 128 bytes available. (Current personal computers typically have 256 **million** bytes of RAM.) And not only was the memory extremely limited, but the processing power was also very limited—the Atari 2600 had an 8-bit processor with a 1.2 MHz clock speed. (Current personal computers typically have 1000 MHz clocks.) To top it off, the display hardware, although flexible, was also extremely limited, providing only two decent sprites for displaying moving objects on the screen. So you needed to start out with a game concept that was simple enough, in both graphics and gameplay, to fit into the tiny memory available. You programmed the game in assembly language. You counted bytes and machine cycles. You had to make every bit and every machine cycle carry its weight. Your job was to make the trade-offs, and come up with an interesting game, given these resources. The adventure game concept appeared to be too complex in fit into a 4K game cartridge. At least, my boss at Atari thought so. After all, Crowther and Woods's text adventure game ran on mainframe computers and required more than 100K of memory. But I thought I could do it.*

Although Chapter 3 of my book is mostly about the intellectual aspect of Adventure—how I juggled the ideas and technical limits to make the game—behind the intellectual is the emotional: the motivation, the driving force. In my case, it was a combination of passion and stubbornness, taking root in the Atari culture of that period, where designer/programmers were encouraged to have their own game ideas and then code them up. The passion came from perceiving new possibilities that demanded to be explored. The stubbornness was just one of my traits. I had to fight to create Adventure. And yes, it **was** a good idea. It **did** fit into 4K. The Adventure cartridge was marketed, and one million copies were sold.

I am proud of Adventure. I'm glad I was lucky enough to be there at Atari at that time, and to have played Crowther and Woods's game. I'm glad I had the idea of an adventure game as a video game, and that I had what it took—guts, training, tools, luck in navigating the political currents—to stay with it. I hope I've steered a middle course between false modesty and arrogance. In truth, it takes a certain amount of arrogance **to even try.**

When **you** come up with your own good idea for a game, think about it for a while. Not every idea is earth-shaking. If you really feel you have a good one, don't let the Big Guys stop you. (If, on the other hand, your big idea is another DOOM clone, please go stick your head in the toilet now, and flush.) The field of interactive games is still pretty young, and I believe there are many interesting directions that are still completely unexplored. After you read my story, get busy and make something cool.
—*Warren Robinett, November 2004*

Description of the Game

Adventure, a video game cartridge for the Atari 2600 video game console, was the first action-adventure video game. It was published by Atari Inc. in 1978, and sold 1 million copies.

Adventure introduced the idea of movable objects (represented by visible icons) that could be picked up by the player (using a joystick) and moved from place to place in the game world. It was also one of the first video games to allow the player to explore a large multi-screen game world. As the first action-adventure game, it inspired the current genre of action-adventure video games, including *Legend of Zelda*, the *Ultima* series, and many others. Adventure also contained the first Easter Egg (hidden surprise) in a video game, which in this case was the author's signature hidden in a secret room.

I had played the new sensation, the original text game Adventure, when I finished designing my first video game. The time was June l978, I worked for Atari, and my next order of business was to begin working on another game cartridge for the Atari 2600 home video game. I had a scheme for adapting the text dialogue of Adventure into a video game: use the joystick to move around, show one room at a time on the video screen, and show objects in the room as little shapes. I hoped the program to do this might somehow fit into the tiny (4K) memory available in a game cartridge, so, despite my boss's skepticism, my infatuation with Adventure swept me into a mad frenzy of programming.

A month later, I had a prototype: the player could move a small square "cursor" from screen to screen, picking up the little colored shapes to be found on some of the screens, which were connected edge to edge. And there was a pesky dragon that chased the cursor around, trying to eat it. Exhausted, I went on vacation, and found, on my return, that Atari upper management had decided that I should turn my fledgling adventure game into a video game about Superman. Atari's parent corporation, Warner Communication, owned the soon-to-be-released Superman movie, and a Superman video game could ride on the wave of "hype." I squirmed, and soon wriggled out of that assignment: my coworker John Dunn agreed to take over and turn the program into a Superman videogame, leaving me free to develop the same program in a different direction, namely, to continue with Adventure. (This sort of contrariness later caused Atari executives to label their video game designers "a bunch of high-strung prima donnas.") I moved forward, discovering how ideas from the text adventure game could be made to work as moving shapes in a video game, and discovering what the young tradition of video games could contribute to the new genre of adventure games. The program took eight months to complete start to finish; Atari marketed the cartridge, and since Woods' game was in the public domain, the video game, too, could be called Adventure.

This new videogame version of Adventure was a quest: the player started out beside the Yellow Castle with the goal of retrieving the Enchanted Chalice, which was out there some-where in the network of thirty rooms. (See *Figure 1*). To make things difficult, three dragons infested the game, chasing the player from room to room, and trying to eat him. A giant bat also caused trouble, moving objects around and stealing things from the player. There were a number of useful objects. The sword killed dragons. The bridge let the player cross walls in the maze. The magnet sucked out objects that were stuck in the walls. The black, white, and yellow keys each unlocked a castle of matching color. (See *Figure 2*).

Adventure as a Video Game: Adventure for the Atari 2600   Warren Robinett

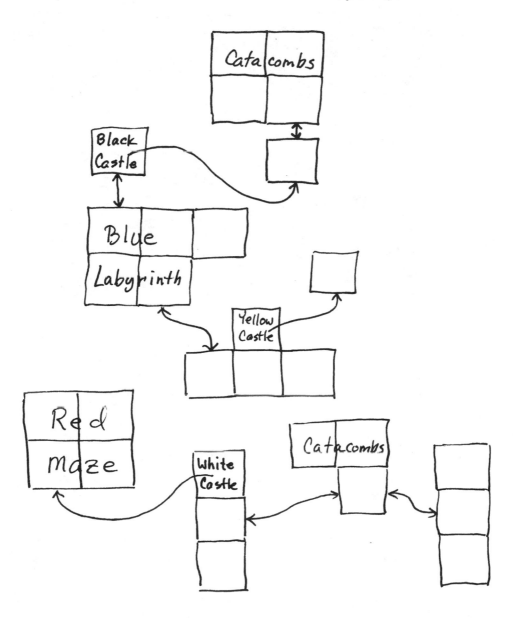

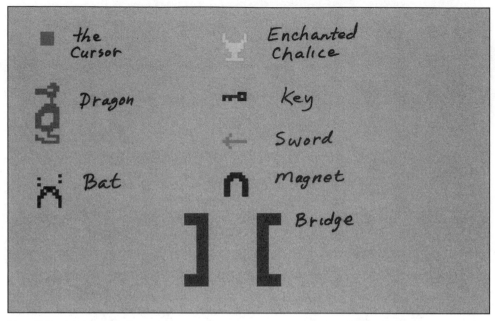

Figure 2: Creatures and Objects

Each of the three castles in Adventure had interiors composed of one or more rooms. The player entered a castle by moving through a doorway equipped with a portcullis, which could be raised or lowered with a key. When the portcullis was down, the castle was locked, and entering or leaving the locked castle was impossible. Each of the three castles had its own key object, and all the castles were locked when the game began.

This video game, Atari 2600 Adventure, was inspired directly by Crowther and Woods' text game, Adventure. I tried at first to create video game counterparts of features in the text game. The magic rod can create a crystal bridge to span an impassable crevasse in the text version; I tried a rod shape which that when it touched a maze wall, caused a bridge shape to appear. The "maze of twisty little passages, all alike" became a very confusing 8-room video maze. These direct transliterations from text to video format didn't work out very well. While the general idea of a video game with rooms and objects seemed to be a good one, the graphic language of the video game and the verbal language of the text dialogue turned out to have significantly different strengths. Just as differences between filmed and live performance caused the art form of cinema to slowly diverge from its parent, drama, differences between the medium of animated graphics and the medium of text have caused the animated adventure game to diverge from the text adventure game.

Player Input

The adaptation of the adventure game to the video game medium required a radical change in the form of the player's commands to the game. Typing was not possible on the Atari 2600 video game console: the standard input was a joystick with one "fire" button on it. The video game player could push the joystick lever in one of four directions, or press the button. The text game player, on the other hand, typed in a two-word command, composed of an action verb and a noun. There were dozens of words in the text game's vocabulary, both for nouns and for verbs; in two-word combinations, there were thousands of possible commands. How could the video game player initiate the wide variety of actions that were possible in the text game?

The joystick was a natural for north-south-east-west movement. There is something satisfyingly responsive about shoving the joystick lever and having a shape on the screen move in the same direction. It is important that players can hold onto the single lever and move it in any of several different directions. The lever itself fades out of consciousness, and players feel that they are propelling the cursor with their own muscles, as if they were scooting a brick around on a sidewalk.

Indeed, players identify themselves with the shape they move around on the video screen. When they say, "I ran into a wall." they mean the shape they moved ran into a wall; they *are* that shape. In Atari 2600 Adventure, this self shape is a little solid-colored square. It can be called a "cursor," since its function, as a position indicator is similar to the rectangular blinking cursor found on word processing screens. I originally called it "the man."

Besides movement, picking up and dropping objects are the most important player actions in an adventure game. With the joystick lever assigned to movement, the single button on the base of the Atari joystick was the clear candidate for grappling with objects, although it wasn't clear exactly how the button should control taking and dropping objects. If the function of "take," for instance, was to be invoked when the button was pressed, which object should be taken? The graphical nature of the video game provided a solution to this. In the world of video games, objects on the screen usually interact only when they run into each other. This is called a "collision," and is defined as an overlap of one shape with another. The object shape to be taken could be specified by moving the cursor to touch it. In fact, the collision itself could invoke the pick-it-up action, which left the button free for dropping. But dropping what? If several objects had been picked up, a selection was again needed. And how should the carried objects be shown? Although pushing the button could have called up an "inventory" screen, and the cursor could have been steered into the object to be dropped, a simpler solution was adopted. Only one object could be carried at a time, and that object was shown besides the cursor on the screen. Pushing the button dropped it.

This approach had several advantages. It was simpler, so the program was shorter. The screen always showed the room players were in, and what they carried; players didn't have to worry about their cursor being eaten by a dragon that came by while they were examining inventory. Of course, time could have been suspended during inventory view, but that didn't seem right for a real-time game. The limitation of being able to carry only one object gave players some interesting strategic choices: which object should they carry—the treasure or the weapon?

Since the object being carried was shown on the screen, it had a position relative to the cursor. Players could adjust the positioning of their held object. When exploring unknown dragon-infested territory, it usually made sense to have your sword out front, because simply holding a sword did not prevent a dragon from eating you—but poking the sword into the dragon did. For a dragon that was scared of the sword, it worked better to loiter near a room boundary, with a behind-the-back sword dangling into the next room, ready to make a swift stroke when the dragon came into striking range.

What about all the other actions that players might want to initiate in an adventure game? These, too, could be specified by touching objects together. For example, in a text game, one might command "KILL DRAGON." The corresponding action in the video game was to pick up a sword and touch it to the dragon. In a sense, the held object and the touched object were the analogues of the action verb and noun from the text adventure game.

A great variety of "commands" might be given if players had the right verb objects at hand. Placing the bridge object across a maze wall and going across it was equivalent to "CROSS WALL." Touching a key to a castle's portcullis commanded, "UNLOCK CASTLE." Bringing the magnet into a room to retrieve a sword stuck in the wall was like "ATTRACT SWORD." Thus the syntax of nouns and verbs in the text adventure had an analogue in a video adventure—a "syntax" of overlapping shapes.

Objects

Objects that could be picked up, carried from place to place, and used for various tasks, were described with a phrase in the original text game Adventure:

```
A three-foot black rod with a rusty star on the end lies nearby.
```

Such an object became, in the graphic language of the video adventure game, a little colored shape that appeared at some location on the screen. Each object had a location, which consisted of a room and an (X, Y) position within that room.

Each object in Atari 2600 Adventure does something. The keys open castles; the sword kills dragons; the bridge crosses walls; the magnet retrieves lost objects; and the chalice wins the game. Although it would of course be possible to have useless objects in a game, to serve as decoys or decorations, in Adventure every object has a function. The objects are really tools since players can use them to cause things to happen in the game world.

Whereas the goal of the original text game Adventure was treasure gathering, the video game Adventure is defined as a quest. One single treasure, the Enchanted Chalice, must be located and brought home. Thus, the tool objects must contribute somehow to the overall goal of the quest. For example, if the chalice is locked inside the Black Castle, then finding the Black Key becomes a subgoal, subordinated to the primary goal of getting to the chalice. If the Black Key is found, but is inaccessible because of the dragon guarding it, then another subgoal is spawned—find the sword so as to get past the dragon. Each tool object is a means of getting past a certain kind of barrier. Since needed objects may be behind barriers that, in turn, require other objects, a hierarchy is created of goals and subgoals. *Figure 3* shows the arrangements of some obstacles and their solutions.

Creatures

A creature in an adventure game is an object that moves around on its own, initiating actions. It is best to consider a creature as a special type of object so that the creature can inherit the traits already defined for objects: shape, color, location, and ability to be picked up. Each type of creature has some special rules that specify how it behaves, what it responds to, and what actions it can take. These special rules are defined by a part of the game program, usually a subroutine that corresponds to the creature type. There are two species of creature in Adventure: dragon and bat.

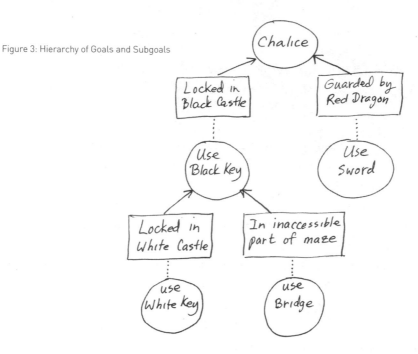

Dragons are the main villains in the game. There are three of them, and they chase the player's cursor around, trying to eat it. If players' reflexes are too slow, or if they get cornered, the dragon swallows their cursor. Once eaten, a player's cursor can be "reincarnated" to get out of the dragon's belly, but as a penalty is sent back to the starting location, losing whatever it was carrying, and any dragons it may have killed are reincarnated, too. (Having already killed some dragons is like being vulnerable in the game of bridge. There is more to lose in the battle with the third dragon. Getting eaten means that the two dead dragons will come back to life.)

There are four states that a dragon can be in, each shown on the screen by a different dragon image: chasing a player's cursor, biting it, having swallowed it, and being dead. The state diagram of *Figure 4* shows the conditions in the game that cause transition from one dragon state to another. In a typical interaction between player's cursor and dragon, the dragon goes back and forth between the biting and chase states several times as it tries to eat the player's cursor, and then the cursor either gets away, gets eaten, or kills the dragon with the sword. The dragon graphics change rapidly, mirroring the state changes. Not only is this interesting animation, but it also gives players valuable visual feedback about which state the dragon is in at any given moment.

Adventure as a Video Game: Adventure for the Atari 2600   Warren Robinett

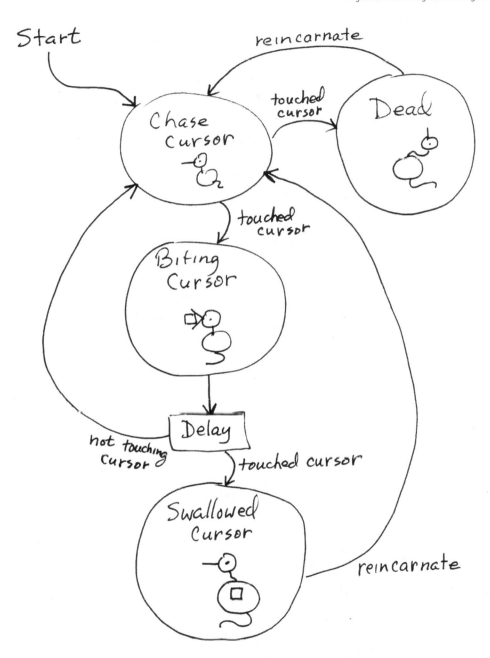

For the dragon to succeed in swallowing a player's cursor, it must collide once with the cursor (entering biting state), and after a fraction of a second, collide again. This brief delay gives players time to recoil, and if their reflexes are fast enough, then they avoid having their cursor swallowed and the dragon resumes chasing it. As a player's cursor and dragon go repeatedly through this chase-bite cycle, neither has the advantage. The dragon wins the battle if it can swallow the player's cursor; the player wins if he or she can get to a sword and use it to kill the dragon.

It is significant that it takes two collisions with the dragon, not one, for the cursor to be swallowed. Merely colliding with the dragon is not fatal. Thus the interesting chase-bite cycle is made possible. Most video games define simple one-time collision with enemies as fatal and irrevocable, and thereby miss a chance to create a more interesting interaction.

The length of the recoil interval between biting and swallowing is quite important. If it is too long, it is trivial to avoid being eaten, and players can ignore the dragon and do whatever they want. If the interval is too short, players never succeed in recoiling, and their cursors get eaten every time. There is a middle ground between "trivial" and "impossible" called "challenging." Trying out the game with various players and watching how well they do is the best way to adjust a game's timing. This process is called "tuning" the game. Varying the length of the recoil interval turned out to be an effective means of varying the game's difficulty. It ranges from around a tenth of a second at the most difficult, to about three seconds at the easiest.

The bat is the second species of creature in Adventure. As it flaps from room to room carrying along an object, periodically the bat tires of its current trinket, and discards it in favor of a new object to carry off. Without the bat, non-creature objects would never move from the spots where the player dropped them. The effect of the bat is to move objects around, to disturb the predictability of the game. The bat is the game's confusion factor.

As detailed in *Figure 5,* the bat has two states: seeking a new object to pick up, and carrying off a newly acquired object, ignoring all other objects. This ignore state, which lasts for about ten seconds after a new object is picked up, was needed to make sure the bat would carry its new trinket off to another room. In an early version of the game, the bat reentered the seek state immediately after picking up a new object; in a room containing two objects (plus the one carried by the bat) the bat would ferry objects back and forth between the two positions forever, never leaving the room.

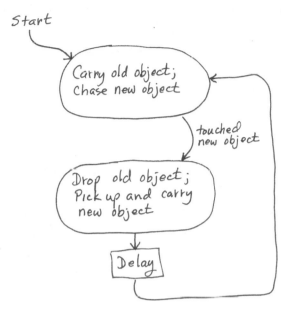

The bat can carry dragons. It sometimes happens that the bat will appear carrying a dragon, steal the player's sword and fly off with it, leaving the disarmed player to deal with the left-behind dragon.

Mazes

In a text adventure game, a room is a single location. Although there are passages to other rooms, the room itself has no internal structure. A video adventure game, by comparison, allows the player to have a position within a room, shown on the screen by the cursor's position. A single room can show a simple maze on the screen, with passages going off the screen to other (as yet unseen) maze rooms. The walls of the maze, of course, block the cursor's movement. A 4- or 5-room maze can be quite complicated.

Besides forming mazes, walls prevent the player from leaving a room in certain directions, and thus help form the overall layout of the network of rooms. In some rooms in Crowther and Woods's text adventure game, typing "GO EAST" would produce this response:

> There is no way to go that direction.

Walls perform the analogous function in a graphical adventure game.

A maze is a geometric construction in space; the positioning of its walls defines a maze. Video graphics do an excellent job of capturing the geometry of a maze. By contrast, using sentences to describe a maze is inefficient and piecemeal. Players lost in the maze of "twisty little passages" in Crowther and Woods's text adventure game invariably draw a map if they want to get out by understanding the maze, rather than by just the luck of random wandering. The verbal representation of a maze is abstract, whereas the graphical representation is concrete and therefore less confusing. Five-year-olds learn the path to the Black Castle through the five maze rooms of the Blue Labyrinth in Adventure. Moving through the visual depiction of each room lets children remember their path in the same way that they remember the route from living room to bathroom in a friend's house.

One leaves a room in video Adventure by driving off the edge of the screen. Since the screen has four edges (top, bottom, left, and right), every room has four links to other rooms (to the north, south, east, and west). Going from one room to another in an adventure game is like using a Star Trek transporter. ("Beam me up, Scottie!") The player vanishes from one place and materializes in another place. The two places are not necessarily "near" each other: they are merely connected. It is often impossible to draw a map of an adventure game's network of rooms so that all linked rooms are side by side. The map of Adventure (*Figure 1*) is an example of that: although small groups of rooms can show links among each other by adjacency, there are leftover links that must be shown explicitly with lines running between the two connected places. If a map, which is a shrunken replica of a region's geometry, cannot be constructed, then that region cannot be built full-sized, either. In other words, these places are impossible. Adventure games simulate spaces that can't exist in the physical world. But it doesn't really matter that a map or scale model of these places cannot be built; players can still move from room to room in the game. As in the Bugs Bunny cartoon with the vast volume inside the tiny tent, these impossible spaces have surprising properties.

A network of rooms, depending on how the rooms are interconnected, can have inconsistent geometry. One might assume that a lot of square screens connected edge to edge could be thought of as a big array of screens, arranged as rows and columns in a plane, just like the square tiles on a kitchen's linoleum floor. However, rooms can be interconnected in a way that is inconsistent with plane geometry, and with commonsense expectations about moving through space. Three inconsistencies that occur are non-retraceable paths, nonunique diagonal rooms, and wrap-around paths. (See *Figure 6*).

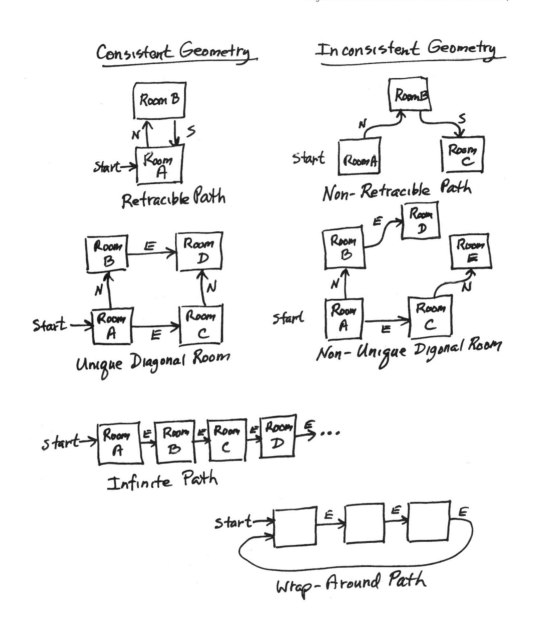

In moving through space, common sense suggests that the space passed through is still there, and that, if necessary, one should be able to turn around and retrace one's path back through that space. Of course, this is not always true in real life: there are one-way doors that swing shut and lock, and trapdoors that one can fall through and not be able to climb out of. If players can go one room north, then go south from that room and be back where they started, they have retraced their path. If the room-to-room south link doesn't take them back to where they started, there is no backing up—they are on a one-way, non-retraceable path. This non-retracibility is a device the designer may use to construct a trickier, more confusing maze. Because it is essential that a game be challenging, confusing players to a certain degree is a quite proper objective for the game designer. Too much illogical trickiness, however, can frustrate and irritate players. In the video game Adventure, I chose to let players always be able to retrace their path.

Figure 7: Comparison of the Room Topologies of the Four Mazes

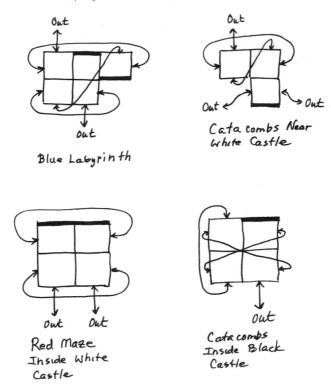

Does going one room north, then one room east get to the same place as east then north? The answer is either yes or no, depending on how the rooms are linked. Although on a perfectly flat plane, going east forever will never bring one back to his starting point, the surface of the earth, which seems pretty flat, wraps around to meet itself eventually . So, too, in a finite network of rooms, the limited memory of a computer would have difficulty representing an infinite number of rooms, any path must eventually return (wrap around) to some previously encountered room, assuming walls never block the path.

The pattern of interconnection within a network of rooms is called "topology." Topology has to do with what is connected to what. The four mazes of Adventure are all unrealizable in the flat. They wrap around in various strange ways (See *Figure 7*), and thus have interesting topologies.

The Blue Labyrinth

The Blue Labyrinth in Adventure has two features that make it different from mazes printed on paper: inconsistent geometry and partial view. *Figure 8* shows how the five rooms are interconnected to form the Blue Labyrinth. The maze is more confusing than the diagrams suggest because only a part of the maze (one room) can be seen at any one time. Viewing the diagram, the eye can rapidly follow maze paths and identify dead ends; but in playing the game, the cursor must move along each path to explore it, and laboriously retrace from dead ends. Not only is exploring slower, but explorers must rely on their memory of the maze rooms they have passed through in order to form a mental model of the whole maze. Players find the Blue Labyrinth quite confusing at first—more so than would be expected from the number of its forks and different passages—and the principal source of this confusion is that players get only a partial view of the maze, never seeing the whole. One is reminded of the story of four blind men examining an elephant, forming different conclusions about what kind of beast it was from feeling its trunk, tusk, foot, and tail. It is hard to reconcile several partial views of something into a coherent global picture.

To add to the confusion, unless normal assumptions about spaces are abandoned, no coherent model of the Blue Labyrinth exists. This is because the Blue Labyrinth has several wraparound paths and nonunique diagonal rooms. One player remarked that he could learn paths through the maze from place to place, but could never get a picture of the whole thing in his mind.

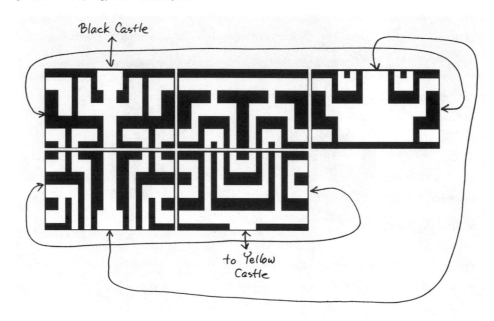

These inconsistent maze geometries are confusing because players' experience with mazes (usually printed on flat pages) leads them to expect more flat mazes. They attempt to make a mental model that incorporates the maze rooms they have seen into a flat map. Even though the players explore, contradictions occur in their mental flat map; the assumption that maps are flat surfaces is a deep-seated one and hard to challenge. Experience exploring real-world mazes when surfaces are not flat at least offers a clue. But the Blue Labyrinth offers no such clue.

The Red Maze

Inside the White Castle lies the Red Maze. (See *Figure 9*). The distinguishing feature of this maze is that it is composed of two disjointed sets of passages that are intertwined but do not connect. Players enter Section 1 of the maze through the door to the castle; to get into Section 2, they must bring the bridge object into the castle and use it to cross one of the maze-walls that separate the two sections.

Figure 9: Room Topology of the Red Maze Inside the White Castle

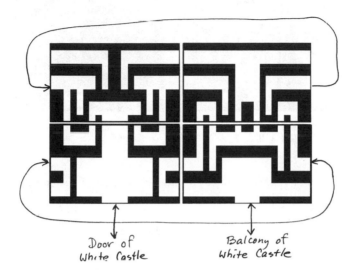

Door of
White Castle

Balcony of
White Castle

Section 1 extends through only three of the four rooms of the Red Maze; without using the bridge, players cannot get a glimpse of the fourth room and whatever useful objects it might contain. In Game 2 of Adventure, the key to the Black Castle starts out in this hard-to-get-to place.

The topology of the Red Maze is simpler than that of the Blue Labyrinth: wrapping around in the horizontal dimension, it goes down from either of the two lower rooms to exit from the castle. One of these exits is the normal one through the door of the castle, but the other exit, from the hard-to-get-to room in Section 2, leads to the "balcony" of the White Castle. The link from the Red Maze to the balcony is one-way, however; it is not possible to go back into the Red Maze from the balcony. This violates my principle of making all paths retraceable, and was a mistake—an earlier idea that was rejected but never expunged. (Once a product is released, harmless bugs like this one are often redefined by the marketing people as "features." The manual for Adventure explains away its bugs under the heading "Bad Magic.")

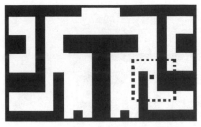

(10a) diagram of invisible part of maze   (10b) actual screen image

Catacombs

In the original text game Adventure, once players had moved a couple of rooms into the cave, they got this message:

```
It is now pitch dark. If you proceed you will likely fall into
a pit.
```

The solution was to light the "shiny brass lamp" picked up earlier. Atari 2600 Adventure has a maze that works in analogous fashion: orange lamp glow penetrates a short distance into the surrounding gloom to expose nearby maze walls. Mazes of this type are called catacombs. *Figure 10a* diagrams the walls of a typical maze room in the catacombs, and the dotted line around the cursor shows how far the lamp glow reaches. This illuminated area around the cursor is equivalent to the circle of radiance thrown out by a lantern, but a smooth circle being impossible, in this case, the circle of radiance is square. Beyond the illuminated area near the cursor, walls cannot be distinguished from passages. *Figure 10b* shows the screen image resulting from the maze position diagrammed above it. The static image does a poor job of conveying the feel of being in the catacombs; the cursor can move about the screen, bumping into unsuspected walls, and the orange firelight surrounds the cursor wherever it goes. It is like shining a flashlight around in a cave.

Just as seeing a single room of the Blue Labyrinth is a partial view of its 5-room entirety, the image of the maze walls near the cursor is a partial view of a single catacomb room. The lamp glow covers about a tenth of the screen. The two catacomb mazes in the game consist of three rooms and four rooms. So, in the catacombs, a partially viewed room, if the player could imagine it entire, is itself only a partial view of a multiroom maze. The smaller

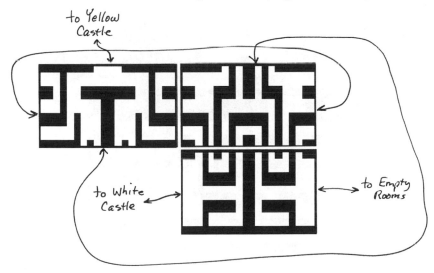

the individual views are relative to the whole, the greater the difficulty in assembling them into an overall picture. The Blue Labyrinth, with its five rooms viewed one at a time, has a fractional view ratio of 1:5. By comparison, the 3-room catacombs near the White Castle, with each room seen a tenth at a time, compounds fractional views of 1:3 and 1:10 to yield an overall ratio of 1:30. Thirty different images must be remembered (or sketched) and joined together correctly to get a picture of the entire maze. The interconnections among the three rooms of this maze are shown in *Figure 11*.

The Catacombs Inside the Black Castle

The maze inside the Black Castle is a tricky one. It is a catacomb-type maze, with the lamp glow surrounding the cursor allowing only a partial view of each room. Four rooms compose the maze, yielding a view ratio of 1:40. In addition, the topology of the maze is complicated. (See *Figure 12*.) Like the Red Maze, the Black Castle maze has two disjointed parts: the bridge is needed to get from one section to the other. But unlike the Red Maze, where the two sections were of similar size, in this maze the isolated section is a tiny little chamber at the bottom of one room. The existence of this chamber is not obvious because when the player's cursor is beside the chamber, but not in it, the orange lamp glow does not extend far enough for the

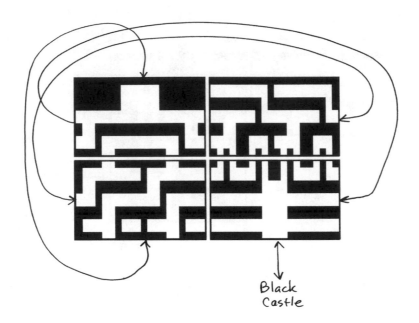

Black
Castle

player to see that the chamber is surrounded by maze walls on four sides. The chamber (partially viewed) seems to be just the dead end of one of the other passages. And yes, there is an interesting object—the Gray Dot—hidden within this chamber.

The dot was not needed in the normal play of the game. Being gray, it was invisible until it was picked up. It was not mentioned in the game's manual because Steve Harding, who wrote the manual, didn't know it existed. The dot's purpose, which had to be discovered by trial and error, was to allow passage through a certain sidewall into a secret room. In this deviously hidden secret room, I affixed my signature, in flashing lights: "Created by Warren Robinett."

I did this in the tradition of artists, down through the centuries, identifying themselves as the authors of their own works. Atari imposed an irksome anonymity upon its designers, so subterfuge was required to put one's mark upon a game. I kept the secret of the signature room to myself for a year (not an easy thing to do) in order to avoid being forced to expunge it from the program, and also to test experimentally whether players could, on their own, discover such an obscure thing. I really wasn't sure that it would be discovered, but thought that if several hundred thousand cartridges were manufactured, then someone, somewhere, would find the dot and the secret room. I remembered, from when I was in high school, the rumors that Paul McCartney was dead, and how people played Beatle records backward, searching for secret messages.

The Adventure cartridge was manufactured and marketed, and the secret room was discovered. A fifteen-year-old from Salt Lake City wrote to Atari, explaining with a detailed diagram how to get into the secret room. By then, I no longer worked for Atari, so they had a couple of their designers track down the part of the game program that produced the secret room. Brad Stewart, who located the offending code, said that if he were assigned to change the program, he would replace "Created by Warren Robinett" with "Fixed by Brad Stewart." Ultimately, Atari blessed the whole idea, referring to hidden surprises in their games as "Easter eggs."

The major innovation of Atari 2600 Adventure is the idea of moving a cursor through a network of screens connected edge to edge. This idea made it possible to make a video game that was at the same time an adventure game, by identifying the network of screens with the adventure game's network of rooms. The action of the game could therefore take place in a much larger and more interesting space than the single screen of most of the then-current video games. It was natural to adopt the small movable shapes provided for in the video game hardware to be adventure game objects. Crowther and Woods had established in their text adventure game that objects were tools for getting past obstacles. My idea for a sequel to Adventure was to allow tools to be combined in order to solve more complex problems. I thought of this as building machines. The idea evolved as I worked on it. The end result, three years later, was a game in which tool objects (sensors, logic gates, and others) could be combined to make machines that made things happen in the game in response to conditions detected by the sensors. This game was called Rocky's Boots.

Eastern Front (1941)

Chris Crawford

Context

Eastern Front (1941) was my first big hit, which came as a surprise to everybody. I designed it in defiance of all marketing wisdom, as a renegade project to satisfy my own values. It's this sort of renegade design that advances a medium. This essay is taken from my book **Chris Crawford on Game Design** *(New Riders Games, 2003), which presents the design narratives of each of my games.*

The Game Design Process

Game Spaces

Chris Crawford sold his first computer game in 1978. He has designed and programmed fourteen published games, written seven books, and patented technology for interactive storytelling. He founded and led the Game Developers' Conference for many years. He has lectured and taught on game design issues all over the world.

Chris Crawford, Preface from *Art of Computer Game Design*, 1982. Reprinted by permission of McGraw-Hill Osborne Media.

In August of 1980, I saw a wonderful bit of software (I believe it was written by Ed Logg) for the Atari Home Computer System (HCS) that set up a huge map and smoothly scrolled through it. The map was done with character graphics, but the HCS had the ability to change character sets, so it was not difficult to use graphic character sets to assemble a map or larger image. I realized that this opened up a world of possibilities for wargames. No longer would we need to squeeze the entire map onto a single 320 x 192 screen; now we could have huge maps. I sat down and wrote a routine that duplicated the functions of the original demo, then designed a custom character set for map use, and finally assembled a map using that custom character set. The result was astounding: a smooth-scrolling map that was four screens wide by four screens high.

It may be difficult for designers brought up with modern PCs to appreciate just how exciting this was. We had been confined to single-screen, low-resolution displays; the best we could do to add more information was to jump from one display to the next. This smooth scrolling map was absolutely revolutionary!

The Scrolling Map

I was busy working on Scram at that time, so progress on the scrolling map was slow. I was also helping outside software developers with their needs for technical support for the Atari hardware. In November of 1980, I was promoted and given the task of setting up a group that would provide technical support for external software developers. I immediately began approaching software developers in the Bay Area, giving them photocopied documentation, software demonstrating how to take advantage of various features of the Atari computers, and so forth. Despite the clear superiority of the HCS, many programmers had a strong emotional attachment to the trusty old Apple II, which they knew inside and out. The scrolling map demo was the most powerful demo I had. Programmers' eyes would bug out when they saw that. Even then, though, some people just wouldn't budge from their loyalties. I especially remember a visit to a wargames company. As the piece de resistance, I dangled the scrolling map demo in front of their eyes, and enticingly suggested all the new possibilities this could open up for wargaming. But no, they were too wedded to the Apple II. They were building real wargames, not childish videogames.

I was deeply disappointed by their rejection; it seemed that nobody was willing to develop this wonderful technology into a game. Very well, I decided, if nobody else will accept this challenge, then I shall have to do it myself. I would build a wargame using scrolling map technology.

During December 1980, I began serious design work. I refrained from putting fingers to keyboard or pencil to paper; I wanted to get a clear vision of the game before I plunged in. I took many long walks alone at night, considering the fundamental properties of the game. Above all, I concentrated on the player's experience. What should it feel like to play the game? Would it be a complex logical problem? A matter of recognizing weak spots in the enemy line and exploiting them? What should the pace be like: fast and clean, or slower and more deliberate? All through December I mused over the game, and then in early January, I put my ideas down on paper in a single-page design document.

Eastfront Game Preliminary Description

Map: 64×64 squares

Unit count: 32 German corps, up to 64 Russian armies

Time scale: "Semi-time" of one week/turn. German enters moves for the next week (meanwhile, computer figures Russian move). When player is ready, play proceeds in real time.

Human interface: Map window on screen. Joystick input scrolls map and players. Putting unit under crosshairs activates it and orders arrows show. Then holding down button while twiddling joystick enters next order. Arrows (player-missile graphics) pop onto screen showing orders. Space bar clears orders. Releasing button resumes scrolling.

START button starts turn.

Colors:

Background:	Brown
PF0:	Green (forests)
PF1:	Blue (rivers, lakes, seas)
PF2:	Grey (German units, cities)
PF3:	Red (Russian units)
P0–P3:	Pink (orders arrows)

[Not enough color! Use DLI's or time-multiplexed color.]

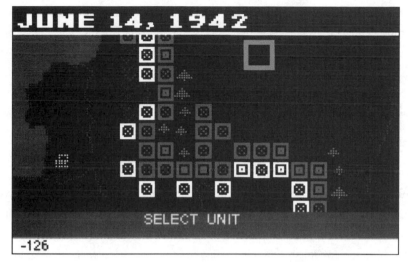

JUNE 14, 1942

SELECT UNIT

-126

Figure 42.2

I worked on my game at home on nights and weekends; I enjoyed the work because my work at Atari involved less and less programming and more and more management issues. It was pleasant to concentrate on the simpler problems of programming rather than the messy personnel issues that crowded my days at work.

The end result of this work was a beautiful scrolling map (see *Figure 42.2*).

Once I had a scrolling map, I needed some military units that could move around on the map, so I went to work on those. After a month's time, I had units that I could select with the joystick and give orders to; not much later they were executing those orders, marching all over the map.

I had all the mechanics necessary for a wargame, but this program was by no means a wargame yet. It needed two major components: a combat system and AI for the computer player.

The Combat System

Combat was no big deal; having worked with combat systems for board games, I knew most of what I needed to do. Terrain considerations were the least of my concerns: I'd just double defensive strength in dense terrain and behind rivers. Facing considerations were important: Units being attacked from the flanks or, worse, from the rear, would suffer a loss of effective defensive strength. What I really wanted to focus on was the disruption element. When units fought, they would suffer both casualties and disruption. The casualties were never replaced, but the units would slowly recover from their disruption. This meant that there were two forms of combat strength: muster strength and combat strength. The former was the full strength of the unit based on the number of men and weapons it possessed. Combat strength was the actual working strength at any given moment, based on how badly disrupted the unit was.

Here I made a classic mistake: I allowed old ways of thinking to influence my design. In boardgames, combat was always resolved in a single roll of the dice. I built my combat resolution algorithms to do the same thing, never realizing that there were plenty of other possibilities opened up by the computer. I thought that being able to do simple arithmetic was a big enough improvement. However, I quickly ran into a fatal problem: My combat system was unable to take proper advantage of disruption. Since each combatant got exactly one crack at its opponent, the disruption it inflicted would not be of any significance unless another unit also attacked the enemy unit immediately after the first battle. This kind of one-two punch had been an important part of Legionnaire, but that game had an open battlefield in which units could freely maneuver. In this game, the units were packed together more tightly and so arranging a one-two punch was more difficult.

I wasted far too much time on this problem before the solution came to me: break the battle up into a series of micro-battles. When Unit A attacks Unit B, don't resolve the combat with one formula based on their relative strengths; instead, fight a series of tiny battles, each of which inflicts casualties and disruption onto both units. The advantage of this scheme was that the benefits of disruption of the defender could be enjoyed by the attacker. On the very first micro-battle, the defender would likely suffer some tiny disruption, which, in turn, would make it slightly weaker in the next micro-battle. In this way, two closely-matched units would not batter each other into splinters; one would gain the upper hand sooner and break the morale of the weaker, forcing it to retreat. This scheme for multiple micro-battles worked much better than the old-style, single-step battle system.

AI

Although Eastern Front (1941) is remembered primarily for its scrolling map, I can take no credit for that; it was built into the hardware. The design element of which I am most proud is the AI for the game. At a time when many wargames were still being written in BASIC, my design boasted two major innovations.

The first of these was the threaded execution. All of the I/O was executed during the Vertical Blank Interrupt (VBI), a routine that executed once each 60th of a second, synchronized with the vertical blank period of the television set. This was the only good time to mess with the display, as changes to the display while the beam was drawing it were likely to yield irritating rips or tears in the image. So I set up all I/O through the VBI routine, which meant in turn that the mainline program—the one that executed in the absence of interrupts—could operate in the background while the player worked in the foreground. In other words, even as the player was entering his own orders, the program was figuring the Russian move.

The more important innovation, of course, was the algorithm for planning the Russian move. This time, I told myself, I was going to solve the problem of figuring a front line. My initial plan had been to start at one edge of the map, select the closest Russian unit to begin the line, and then somehow trace a line through other Russian units to the opposite edge of the map. This idea broke to pieces against a nasty problem: what to do if the line were broken? If the Germans achieved a complete breakthrough, would my algorithms break down and lead to a total collapse of the Russian position?

This led me to think of the line from the point of view of individual units. Since they might be operating in some isolation, it would be necessary to think of each unit as a fragment of a line; my algorithm then needed only to find a way to link together such fragments.

At the time I was designing the AI, there were no zones of control (ZoC) in the movement system. The concept of the zone of control was developed for board wargames way back in the 1950s. In such games, each unit projected a zone of control into each of the squares (or hexes) adjacent to it. Movement from one ZoC square into another ZoC square was forbidden. With ZoCs, you didn't need a solid front line; you could hold the line with a thin string of units. Yet you could still concentrate lots of units in the spaces to mount an offensive. It was a winning idea, and most board wargames used it. Yet I chose not to use this design construct in Eastern Front (1941). I had initially believed that my unit densities were so high that it would not be difficult to trace a continuous line.

All this meant that my algorithms should be directed toward gap-filling in the line. The overall course of the line, I expected, would remain intact through the game; I needed only find a scheme for plugging holes that might develop.

One of the big questions that bedevil many designers is the problem of whether to design the AI to be bottom-up or top-down. In a top-down design, the AI system starts off by looking at the grand strategic situation, figuring out what needs to be done, and then trickles these decisions down to the individual units. In a bottom-up design, the AI is applied to the individual units without any central coordinating authority. Each unit follows its own nose in planning its move. This type of AI, when it works, yields what is called emergent behavior. When it doesn't work, it yields what is termed a turkey.

I decided on the latter course because I expected that Russian units might face chaotic situations where they would need to think for themselves. Besides, this allowed me to break the problem down into smaller steps that could be addressed in increments, so that the program would not need to complete some monstrous calculation before it could begin the turn.

For this discussion, I will present the system I used in the final version, which used a 5-wide square for analysis. In the initial design, I used only a 3-wide square; later on, it occurred to me that I could improve the overall quality of the AI by simply extending the 3-wide square notions into a 5-wide square. I am proud to say that my code had been so cleanly written that the conversion from 3-wide squares to 5-wide squares went smoothly. So here is what my 5-wide square might look like under analysis (*See Figure 42.3*).

The five rectangular symbols with crosses in them are standard military symbols for infantry units.

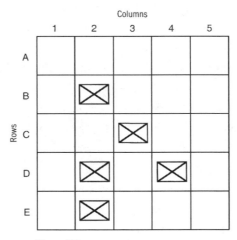

Figure 42.3

The first problem to tackle is, what is the direction of the front line? Does the line trace right to left, or up and down? Given the fluidity of the Eastern Front, I could not assume some standard direction; German units sometimes found themselves attacking toward the west. My answer to this problem was simple and clean: danger is a vector, not a scalar. When evaluating its tactical situation, each unit must first evaluate how much danger it finds itself in and the overall direction from which that danger emanates. The algorithm calculates the overall danger coming from each of the four cardinal directions, and then evaluates the strength of the defensive position against that danger. This is done for each of the four cardinal directions, so the 5-wide square above is, in effect, rotated through each of its four possible orientations.

The details of the algorithm are quite messy, especially because I didn't have hardware multiplication and division. I made use of doubling and halving by the simple expedient of shifting a byte to the right or left, but if I wanted 16-bit precision, I had to carry the bits between the low byte and the high byte. The thrust of the algorithm is to assign points for each column that is occupied, with adjustments for the straightness of the line. This is done by looking at vertical offsets between pairs of units; in a good line, those vertical offsets are minimal. Thus, points are assigned to each square, representing the overall utility of the unit positioning itself there. The unit simply selects the best square and plots a path to it.

The algorithm had a nicely convergent behavior: Each unit determined its objective square, taking into consideration the objective squares of every other unit. As the algorithm ran through more and more iterations, it converged on an ideal move for the Russian player. "No plan survives contact with the enemy"—so goes the military adage. Such was the case with the behavior of units in Eastern Front (1941). Their carefully laid plans were based on the assumptions that the Germans would all cooperatively remain in their original positions. The fact that those Germans did in fact move wrought havoc with the Russian plans—but then again, the Russian moves did exactly the same thing to German plans. It's an unavoidable problem in war. My AI made no attempt to anticipate German plans.

Looking back at this old assembly language code from the vantage point of twenty additional years of experience, I see only a few improvements to make. The code ran fast, so I could have stepped up to a 7-wide square to get even better coordination of behavior. The code was insufficiently documented, although I was able to figure out its workings even after twenty years have passed. In particular, I should have given more labels to my constants. The incidence of mysterious values ("LDX #$97," for example) detracts considerably from the cogency of the code.

Tuning

When I first tried it out as a game rather than a program, I instantly realized that I had created a turkey of the highest order. The game was slow and tedious; the Germans slogged through the Russian line with all the excitement of a World War I infantry offensive. I was heartbroken; I had expected that the game would need tuning, but I didn't expect it to be so terribly bad.

At this point, my design instincts served me well. First, I took a long walk to think about the design in the largest possible terms. I refused to start throwing patches at the problem; I wanted to characterize the problem precisely, to put my finger on exactly what was wrong with the design. Some good ideas came to me, but I still refused to act on them; I wanted to be sure of my next move. After two days of intense cogitation. I had my answers.

Four related problems turkified my game:

· There were too many units for the player to handle.

· It took too long to play.

· There was little opportunity to maneuver.

· The Russian AI was too stupid.

I resolved upon three solutions. First, I would introduce zones of control into the game. This dramatic change would have no effect on the Russian AI, and it would permit the second change: a drastic reduction in the unit count. With zones of control, fewer units would be needed to hold a solid line. My third solution was merely a decision to proceed with a feature I had already determined to put into the game: logistics. Units were required to trace a clear line of supply back to their home edge of the map; if not, they were "out of supply" and their combat strength was halved. This would make encirclements an attractive ploy.

After carefully considering all possible implications of these changes, I set to work. It took me just three weeks to complete these changes. When I brought the new game up for the first time in mid-June, I knew that I had a winner. The game still had plenty of rough spots, but as a designer I could see that they were blemishes, not structural defects.

It required another eight weeks of playtesting and tuning to get the game just right. I spent much of that time expunging trivial bugs, juggling the reinforcement schedules for the

Russians, and fine-tuning the AI algorithms. I also had a number of friends playtest the game. They all had lots of suggestions; I rejected the great majority of these suggestions and eagerly embraced a minority of them. My playtesters were mystified by my reactions to their ideas. Some suggestions I dismissed instantly without any further discussion, it seemed that I was a stubborn ass. But other suggestions I would pounce upon enthusiastically. "What was the difference?," one of them asked me.

Most suggestions are additions; some are embellishments, some are corrections, and some are consolidations. The additions are new features; those I dumped instantly. You don't add new features to a game during playtesting. If the game needs major improvement, then it should be redesigned; if it doesn't need major improvement, you shouldn't go adding features this late in the design cycle. Embellishments are improvements on existing elements in the game; these got a few seconds' consideration. Again, the burden of proof falls on the embellishment; if I can't see a compelling reason for adding the embellishment, then I don't want to mess around with it. Corrections fix clumsy aspects of the design; these I relish. My only concern in hearing such suggestions is that they constitute genuine corrections, that they really do fix a problem in the design. If they do, then there's nothing to discuss; it's a go. Lastly, consolidations are ways of bringing two dissonant aspects of the game into harmony; these I also embrace. It's rare that a playtester sees some deeper connection that escaped me, but when they do, I grab the idea and run with it as if it were my own.

Herein lies a small lesson concerning open mindedness and the ownership of ideas. Some people think that open mindedness requires a designer to hear out every idea, to give every suggestion its day in court. This isn't noble; it's stupid. Seriously considering every idea that drifts by isn't a sign of open mindedness; it's an indicator of indecisiveness. A good designer has already thought through all the basics of the design and so should be able to reject a great many ideas without much consideration, knowing that they are incompatible with the heart of the design. To put it another way, you should already have considered most of the ideas that are put to you; if somebody surprises you with an idea you didn't think of, you should consider it a warning sign that you haven't thought through the design carefully enough. If the great majority of ideas that are offered you have already gone through your mill, you should have no problem rejecting them without much consideration. So; let them. Your job is to build a great design, not gratify your co-workers. Be courteous, but concentrate on doing your job.

Conclusion

Eastern Front (1941) was released in August of 1981. It was an immediate hit, sold very well, and garnered a number of awards. It propelled me into the forefront of the gaming industry; I was suddenly Mr. Big Shot. None of this, of course, served to inflate my ego, which was already at maximum inflation. I handled it all with a graciousness derived from my utter certainty that this was the natural and proper order of things. The game also earned impressive royalties (for the time); I think that total royalties amounted to some $40,000, which was more than my salary.

In 1982, we published the source code for the game, including detailed explanations of how it all worked. I am confident that this was the first time anybody had published source code for a major game. I wanted to show people how it was done. The source code, although rather expensive, sold well.

Eastern Front (1941) was one of my best works. It incorporated bold innovations, technical excellence, and a clear design vision. What more can we ask of a great game?

VELVET-STRIKE

COUNTER-MILITARY GRAFFITI FOR CS

16

17

CAPE FROM
OOMERA

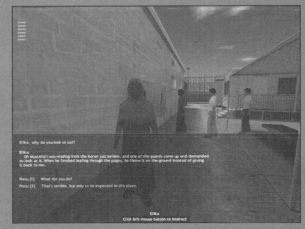

Elika, why do you look so sad?

Elika.
Oh Mustafa! I was reading from the Koran just before, and one of the guards came up and demanded to look at it. When he finished leafing through the pages, he threw it on the ground instead of giving it back to me.

Press [1]   What did you do?
Press [2]   That's terrible, but only to be expected in this place.

Elika
Click left mouse button to interact

The Lessons of Lucasfilm's Habitat

F. Randall Farmer and Chip Morningstar

Context

This paper was presented at The First Annual International Conference on Cyberspace in 1990. It was published in **Cyberspace: First Steps,** *Michael Benedikt (ed.) (MIT Press, 1990).*

Gaming the Game

The Game Design Process

Game Communities

For more than 30 years, F. Randall Farmer has been connecting people with each other using computers as the mediating technology. He has co-created the following: one of the first online forums, the first Trek MUD, the first graphical MMOG with the first avatars, the first virtual MMOG currency, the first virtual information marketplace, the first fully distributed virtual world platform, the first no-plugin web session platform, and more. He continues to publish on these topics.

Chip Morningstar was one of the founders of Electric Communities, a cyberspace design and development company. He was also heavily involved in the initial development of Fujitsu's WorldsAway service, for which Electric Communities provided creative and technical oversight. Morningstar worked at Lucasfilm Ltd where he was the designer and project leader for Lucasfilm's Habitat, the world's first large scale commercial multiperson online graphical virtual world.

Introduction

Lucasfilm's *Habitat* was created by Lucasfilm Games, a division of LucasArts Entertainment Company, in association with Quantum Computer Services, Inc. It was arguably one of the first attempts to create a very large scale commercial multi-user virtual environment. A far cry from many laboratory research efforts based on sophisticated interface hardware and tens of thousands of dollars per user of dedicated compute power, *Habitat* is built on top of an ordinary commercial online service and uses an inexpensive—some would say "toy"—home computer to support user interaction. In spite of these somewhat plebeian underpinnings, *Habitat* is ambitious in its scope. The system we developed can support a population of thousands of users in a single shared cyberspace. *Habitat* presents its users with a real-time animated view into an online simulated world in which users can communicate, play games, go on adventures, fall in love, get married, get divorced, start businesses, found religions, wage wars, protest against them, and experiment with self-government.

The *Habitat* project proved to be a rich source of insights into the nitty-gritty reality of actually implementing a serious, commercially viable cyberspace environment. Our experiences developing the *Habitat* system, and managing the virtual world that resulted, offer a number of interesting and important lessons for prospective cyberspace architects. The purpose of this paper is to discuss some of these lessons. We hope that the next generation of builders of virtual worlds can benefit from our experiences and (especially) from our mistakes.

Due to space limitations, we won't be able to go into as much technical detail as we might like; this will have to be left to a future publication. Similarly, we will only be able to touch briefly upon some of the history of the project as a business venture, which is a fascinating subject of its own. Although we will conclude with a brief discussion of some of the future directions for this technology, a more detailed exposition on this topic will also have to wait for a future article.

The essential lesson that we have abstracted from our experiences with *Habitat* is that a cyberspace is defined more by the interactions among the actors within it than by the technology with which it is implemented. While we find much of the work presently being done on elaborate interface technologies—Data Gloves, head-mounted displays, special-purpose rendering engines, and so on—both exciting and promising, the almost mystical euphoria that currently seems to surround all this hardware is, in our opinion, both excessive and somewhat misplaced. We can't help having a nagging sense that it's all a bit of a distraction from the really pressing issues. At the core of *our* vision is the idea that cyberspace is necessarily a *multiple-participant environment.* It seems to us that the things that are important to the inhabitants of such an environment are the capabilities available to them, the characteristics of the other people they encounter there, and the ways these various participants can affect one another. Beyond a foundation set of communications capabilities, the technology used to present this environment to its participants, while sexy and interesting, is a peripheral concern.

What Is *Habitat?*

Habitat is a "multi-player online virtual environment" (its purpose is to be an entertainment medium; consequently, the users are called "players"). Each player uses his or her home computer as a front end, communicating over a commercial packet-switching data network to a centralized backend system. The front end provides the user interface, generating a real-time animated display of what is going on and translating input from the player into requests to the backend. The backend maintains the world model, enforcing the rules and keeping each player's front end informed about the constantly changing state of the universe. The backend enables the players to interact not only with the world but also with each other.

Habitat was inspired by a long tradition of "computer hacker science fiction", notably Vernor Vinge's novel, True Names[1], as well as many fond childhood memories of games of make-believe, more recent memories of role-playing games and the like, and numerous other influences too thoroughly blended to pinpoint. To this we add a dash of silliness, a touch of cyberpunk,[2, 3] and a predilection for object-oriented programming.[4]

The initial incarnation of *Habitat* uses a Commodore 64 for the frontend. One of the questions we are asked most frequently is, "Why the Commodore 64?" Many people somehow get the impression that this was technical decision, but the real explanation has to do with business, not technology. *Habitat* was initially developed by Lucasfilm as commercial product for QuantumLink, an online service (then) exclusively for owners of the Commodore 64. At the time we started (1985), the Commodore 64 was the mainstay of the recreational computing market. Since then it has declined dramatically in both its commercial and technical significance. However, when we began the project, we didn't get a choice of platforms. The nature of the deal was such that both the Commodore 64 for the front end and the existing Quantum Link host system (a brace of Stratus fault-tolerant minicomputers) for the backend were givens.

A typical *Habitat* scene

The largest part of the screen is devoted to the graphics display. This is an animated view of the player's current location in the *Habitat* world. The scene consists of various objects arrayed on the screen, such as the houses and tree you see here. The players are represented by animated figures that we call "Avatars." Avatars are usually, though not exclusively, humanoid in appearance. In this scene you can see two of them, carrying on a conversation.

Avatars can move around, pick up, put down and manipulate objects, talk to each other, and gesture, each under the control of an individual player. Control is through the joystick, which enables the player to point at things and issue commands. Talking is accomplished by typing on the keyboard. The text that a player types is displayed over his or her Avatar's head in a cartoon-style "word balloon".

The *Habitat* world is made up of a large number of discrete locations that we call "regions." In its prime, the prototype *Habitat* world consisted of around 20,000 of them. Each region can adjoin up to four other regions, which can be reached simply by walking your Avatar to one or another edge of the screen. Doorways and other passages can connect to additional regions. Each region contains a set of objects which define the things that an Avatar can do there and the scene that the player sees on the computer screen.

Some of the objects are structural, such as the ground or the sky. Many are just scenic, such as the tree or the mailbox. Most objects, however, have some function that they perform.

For example, doors transport Avatars from one region to another and may be opened, closed, locked and unlocked. ATMs (Automatic Token Machines) enable access to an Avatar's bank account. Vending machines dispense useful goods in exchange for *Habitat* money. *Habitat* contained its own fully-fledged economy, with money, banks, and so on. *Habitat's* unit of currency is the Token, owing to the fact that it is a token economy and to acknowledge the long and honorable association between tokens and video games.

Object Class	Function
ATM	Automatic Token Machine; access to an Avatar's bank account
Avatar	Represents the player in the *Habitat* world
Bag, Box	Containers in which things may be carried
Book	Document for Avatars to read (e.g., the daily newspaper)
Bureaucrat-in-a-box	Communication with system operators
Change-o-matic	Device to change Avatar gender
Chest, Safe	Containers in which things can be stored
Club, Gun, Knife	Various weapons
Compass	Points direction to West Pole
Door	Passage from one region to another; can be locked
Drugs	Various types; changes Avatar body state, e.g., cure wounds
Elevator	Transportation from one floor of a tall building to another
Flashlight	Provides light in dark places
Fountain	Scenic highlight; provides communication to system designers
Game piece	Enables various board games: *backgammon, checkers, chess,* etc.
Garbage can	Disposes of unwanted objects
Glue	System building tool; attaches objects together
Ground, Sky	The underpinnings of the world
Head	An Avatar's head; comes in many styles; for customization
Key	Unlocks doors and other containers
Knick-knack	Generic inert object; for decorative purposes
Magic wand	Various types, can do almost anything
Paper	For writing notes, making maps, etc.; used in mail system
Pawn machine	Buys back previously purchased objects
Plant, Rock, Tree	Generic scenic objects
Region	The foundation of reality
Sensor	Various types, detects otherwise invisible conditions in the world
Sign	Allows attachment of text to other objects
Stun gun	Non-lethal weapon
Teleport booth	Means of quick long-distance transport; analogous to phone booth
Tokens	*Habitat* money
Vendroid	Vending machine; sells things

Many objects are portable and may be carried around in an Avatar's hands or pockets. These include various kinds of containers, money, weapons, tools, and exotic magical implements. Listed here are some of the most important types of objects and their functions. The complete list of object types numbers in the hundreds.

Implementation

The following, along with several programmer-years of tedious and expensive detail that we won't cover here, is how the system works:

At the heart of the *Habitat* implementation is an object-oriented model of the universe.

The front end consists of a system kernel and a collection of objects. The kernel handles memory management, display generation, disk I/O, telecommunications, and other "operating system" functions. The objects implement the semantics of the world itself. Each type of *Habitat* object has a definition consisting of a set of resources, including animation cels to drive the display, audio data, and executable code. An object's executable code implements a series of standard behaviors, each of which is invoked by a different player command or system event. The model is similar to that found in an object-oriented programming system such as Smalltalk,[5] with its classes, methods and messages. These resources consume significant amounts of scarce front end memory, so we can't keep them all in core at the same time. Fortunately, their definitions are invariant, so we simply swap them in from disk as we need them, discarding less recently used resources to make room.

When an object is instantiated, we allocate a block of memory to contain the object's state. The first several bytes of an object's state information take the same form in all objects, and include such things as the object's screen location and display attributes. This standard information is interpreted by the system kernel as it generates the display and manages the run-time environment. The remainder of the state information varies with the object type and is accessed only by the object's behavior code.

Object behaviors are invoked by the kernel in response to player input. Each object responds to a set of standard verbs that map directly onto the commands available to the player. Each behavior is simply a subroutine that executes the indicated action; to do this it may invoke the behaviors of other objects or send request messages to the backend. Besides the standard verb behaviors, objects may have additional behaviors which are invoked by messages that arrive synchronously from the backend.

The backend also maintains an object-oriented representation of the world. As in the front end, objects on the backend possess executable behaviors and in-memory state information. In addition, since the backend maintains a persistent global state for the entire *Habitat* world, the objects are also represented by database records that may be stored on disk when not "in use". Backend object behaviors are invoked by messages from the front end. Each of these backend behaviors works in roughly the same way: a message is received from a player's front end requesting some action; the action is taken and some state changes to the world result; the backend behavior sends a response message back to the front end informing it of the results of its request and notification messages to the front ends of any other players who are in the same region, informing *them* of what has taken place.

The Lessons

In order to say as much as we can in the limited space available, we will describe what we think we learned via a series of principles or assertions surrounded by supporting reasoning and illustrative anecdotes. A more formal and thorough exposition will have to come later in some other forum where we might have the space to present a more comprehensive and detailed model.

We mentioned our primary principle above:

A multi-user environment is central to the idea of cyberspace.

It is our deep conviction that a definitive characteristic of a cyberspace system is that it represents a multi-user environment. This stems from the fact that what (in our opinion) people seek in such a system is richness, complexity and depth. Nobody knows how to produce an automaton that even approaches the complexity of a real human being, let alone a society. Our approach, then, is not even to attempt this, but instead to use the computational medium to augment the communications channels between real people.

If what we are constructing is a multi-user environment, it naturally follows that some sort of communications capability must be fundamental to our system. However, we must take into account an observation that is the second of our principles:

Communications bandwidth is a scarce resource.

This point was rammed home to us by one of *Habitat's* nastier externally imposed design constraints, namely that it provide a satisfactory experience to the player over a 300 baud serial telephone connection (one, moreover, routed through commercial packet-switching networks that impose an additional, uncontrollable latency of 100 to 5000 milliseconds on each packet transmitted).

Even in a more technically advanced network, however, bandwidth remains scarce in the sense that economists use the term: available carrying capacity is not unlimited. The law of supply and demand suggests that no matter how much capacity is available, you always want more. When communications technology advances to the point were we all have multi-gigabaud fiber optic connections into our homes, computational technology will have advanced to match. Our processors' expanding appetite for data will mean that the search for ever more sophisticated data compression techniques will *still* be a hot research area (though what we are compressing may at that point be high-resolution volumetric time-series or something even more esoteric).[6]

Computer scientists tend to be reductionists who like to organize systems in terms of primitive elements that can be easily manipulated within the context of a simple formal model. Typically, you adopt a small variety of very simple primitives which are then used in large numbers. For a graphics-oriented cyberspace system, the temptation is to build upon bit-mapped images or polygons or some other *graphic* primitive. These sorts of representations, however, are invitations to disaster. They arise from an inappropriate fixation on display technology, rather than on the underlying purpose of the system.

However, the most significant part of what we wish to be communicating is human behaviors. These, fortunately, can be represented quite compactly, provided we adopt a relatively abstract, high-level description that deals with behavioral concepts directly. This leads to our third principle:

An object-oriented data representation is essential.

Taken at its face value, this assertion is unlikely to be controversial, as object-oriented programming is currently the methodology of choice among the software engineering cognoscenti. However, what we mean here is not only that you should adopt an object-oriented approach, but that the basic objects from which you build the system should correspond more-or-less to the objects in the user's conceptual model of the virtual world, that is, people, places, and artifacts. You could, of course, use object-oriented programming techniques to build a system based on, say, polygons, but that would not help to cope with the fundamental problem.

The goal is to enable the communications between machines to take place primarily at the behavioral level (what people and things are doing) rather than at the presentation level (how the scene is changing). The description of a place in the virtual world should be in terms of what is there rather than what it looks like. Interactions between objects should be described by functional models rather than by physical ones. The computation necessary to translate between these higher-level representations and the lower-level representations required for direct user interaction is an essentially local function. At the local processor, display-rendering techniques may be arbitrarily elaborate and physical models arbitrarily sophisticated. The data channel capacities required for such computations, however, need not and should not be squeezed into the limited bandwidth available between the local processor and remote ones. Attempting to do so just leads to disasters such as NAPLPS.[7, 8]

Once we begin working at the conceptual rather than the presentation level, we are struck by the following observation:

The implementation platform is relatively unimportant.

The presentation level and the conceptual level cannot (and should not) be *totally* isolated from each other. However, defining a virtual environment in terms of the configuration and behavior of objects, rather than their presentation, enables us to span a vast range of computational and display capabilities among the participants in a system. This range extends both upward and downward. As an extreme example, a typical scenic object, such as a tree, can be represented by a handful of parameter values. At the lowest conceivable end of things might be an ancient Altair 8800 with a 300 baud ASCII dumb terminal, where the interface is reduced to fragments of text and the user sees the humble string so familiar to the players of text adventure games, "There is a tree here." At the high end, you might have a powerful processor that generates the image of the tree by growing a fractal model and rendering it three dimensions at high resolution, the finest details ray-traced in real-time, complete with branches waving in the breeze and the sound of wind in the leaves coming through your headphones in high-fidelity digital stereo. And these two users might be looking at the same tree in same the place in the same world and talking to each other as they do so. Both of these scenarios are implausible at the moment, the first because nobody would suffer with such a crude interface when better ones are so readily available, the second because the computational hardware does not yet exist. The point, however, is that this approach covers

the ground between systems already obsolete and ones that are as yet gleams in their designers' eyes. Two consequences of this are significant. The first is that we can build effective
cyberspace systems today. *Habitat* exists as ample proof of this principle. The second is that it is
conceivable that with a modicum of cleverness and foresight you could start building a system
with today's technology that could evolve smoothly as the tomorrow's technology develops.
The availability of pathways for growth is important in the real world, especially if cyberspace
is to become a significant communications medium (as we obviously think it should).

Given that we see cyberspace as fundamentally a communications medium rather
than simply a user interface model, and given the style of object-oriented approach that we
advocate, another point becomes clear:

Data communications standards are vital.

However, our concerns about cyberspace data communications standards center
less upon data transport protocols than upon the definition of the data being transported. The
mechanisms required for reliably getting bits from point A to point B are not terribly interesting
to us. This is not because these mechanisms are not essential (they obviously are) nor because
they do not pose significant research and engineering challenges (they clearly do). It is because
we are focused on the unique communications needs of an object-based cyberspace. We are
concerned with the protocols for sending messages between objects, that is, for communicating behavior rather than presentation, and for communicating object definitions from one
system to another.

Communicating object definitions seems to us to be an especially important problem, and one that we really didn't have an opportunity to address in *Habitat*. It *will* be necessary
to address this problem if we are to have a dynamic system. The ability to add new classes of
objects over time is crucial if the system is to be able to evolve.

While we are on the subject of communications standards, we would like to make
some remarks about the ISO Reference Model of Open System Interconnection.[9] This multi-
layered model has become a centerpiece of most discussions about data communications
standards these days. Unfortunately, while the bottom 4 or 5 layers of this model provide a
more or less sound framework for considering data transport issues, we feel that the model's
Presentation and Application layers are not so helpful when considering cyberspace data
communications.

We have two main quarrels with the ISO model: first, it partitions the general data communications problem in a way that is a poor match for the needs of a cyberspace system; second, and more importantly, we think it is an active source of confusion because it focuses the attention of system designers on the wrong set of issues and thus leads them to spend their time solving the wrong set of problems. We know because this happened to us. "Presentation" and "Application" are simply the wrong abstractions for the higher levels of a cyberspace communications protocol. A "Presentation" protocol presumes characteristics of the display are embedded in the protocol. The discussions above should give some indication why we feel such a presumption is both unnecessary and unwise. An "Application" protocol presumes a degree of foreknowledge of the message environment that is incompatible with the sort of dynamically evolving object system we envision.

A better model would be to substitute a different pair of top layers: a Message layer, which defines the means by which objects can address one another and standard methods of encapsulating structured data and encoding low-level data types (e.g., numbers); and a Definition layer built on top of the Message layer, which defines a standard representation for object definitions so that object classes can migrate from machine to machine. One might argue that these are simply Presentation and Application with different labels, but we don't think the differences are so easily reconciled. In particular, we think the ISO model has, however unintentionally, systematically deflected workers in the field from considering many of the issues that concern us.

World Building

There were two sorts of implementation challenges that *Habitat* posed. The first was the problem of creating a working piece of technology—developing the animation engine, the object-oriented virtual memory, the message-passing pseudo operating system, and squeezing them all into the ludicrous Commodore 64 (the backend system also posed interesting technical problems, but its constraints were not as vicious). The second challenge was the creation and management of the *Habitat* world itself. It is the experiences from the latter exercise that we think will be most relevant to future cyberspace designers.

We were initially our own worst enemies in this undertaking, victims of a way of thinking to which we engineers are dangerously susceptible. This way of thinking is characterized by the conceit that all things may be planned in advance and then directly implemented according to the plan's detailed specification. For persons schooled in the design and construction of systems based on simple, well-defined and well-understood foundation principles, this is a natural attitude to have. Moreover, it is entirely appropriate when undertaking most engineering projects. It is a frame of mind that is an essential part of a good engineer's conceptual tool kit. Alas, in keeping with Maslow's assertion that, "to the person who has only a hammer, all the world looks like a nail", it is a tool that is easy to carry beyond its range of applicability. This happens when a system exceeds the threshold of complexity above which the human mind loses its ability to maintain a complete and coherent model.

One generally hears about systems crossing the complexity threshold when they become very large. For example, the Space Shuttle and the B-2 bomber are both systems above this threshold, necessitating extraordinarily involved, cumbersome and time-consuming procedures to keep the design under control—procedures that are at once vastly expensive and only partially successful. To a degree, the complexity problem can be solved by throwing money at it. However, such capital intensive management techniques are a luxury not available to most projects. Furthermore, although these dubious "solutions" to the complexity problem are out of reach of most projects, alas the complexity threshold itself is not. Smaller systems can suffer from the same sorts of problems. It is possible to push much smaller and less elaborate systems over the complexity threshold simply by introducing chaotic elements that are outside the designers' sphere of control or understanding. The most significant such chaotic elements are autonomous computational agents (e.g., other computers). This is why, for example, debugging even very simple communications protocols often proves surprisingly difficult. Furthermore, a special circle of living Hell awaits the implementors of systems involving that most important category of autonomous computational agents of all, groups of interacting human beings. This leads directly to our next (and possibly most controversial) assertion:

Detailed central planning is impossible; don't even try.

The constructivist prejudice that leads engineers into the kinds of problems just mentioned has received more study from economists and sociologists[10–15] than from researchers in the software engineering community. Game and simulation designers are experienced in creating virtual worlds for individuals and small groups. However, they have had no reason to learn to deal with large populations of simultaneous users. Since each user or group is unrelated to the others, the same world can be used over and over again. If you are playing

739

an adventure game, the fact that thousands of other people elsewhere in the (real) world are playing the same game has no effect on your experience. It is reasonable for the creator of such a world to spend tens or even hundreds of hours crafting the environment for each hour that a user will spend interacting with it, since that user's hour of experience will be duplicated tens of thousands of times by tens of thousands of other individual users.

Builders of online services and communications networks are experienced in dealing with large user populations, but they do not, in general, create elaborate environments. Furthermore, in a system designed to deliver information or communications services, large numbers of users are simply a load problem rather than a complexity problem. All the users get the same information or services; the comments in the previous paragraph regarding duplication of experience apply here as well. It is not necessary to match the size and complexity of the information space to the size of the user population. While it may turn out that the quantity of information available on a service is a function of the size of the user population, this information can generally be organized into a systematic structure that can still be maintained by a few people. The bulk, wherein the complexity lies, is the product of the users themselves, rather than the system designers—the operators of the system do not have to create all this material. (This observation is the first clue to the solution to our problem.)

Our original specification for *Habitat* called for us to create a world capable of supporting a population of 20,000 Avatars, with expansion plans for up to 50, 000. By any reckoning this is a large undertaking and complexity problems would certainly be expected. However, in practice we exceeded the complexity threshold very early in development. By the time the population of our online community had reached around 50 we were in over our heads (and these 50 were "insiders" who were prepared to be tolerant of holes and rough edges).

Moreover, a virtual world such as *Habitat* needs to scale with its population. For 20,000 Avatars we needed 20,000 "houses", organized into towns and cities with associated traffic arteries and shopping and recreational areas. We needed wilderness areas between the towns so that everyone would not be jammed together into the same place. Most of all, we needed things for 20,000 people to do. They needed interesting places to visit—and since they can't all be in the same place at the same time, they needed a *lot* of interesting places to visit—and things to do in those places. Each of those houses, towns, roads, shops, forests, theaters, arenas, and other places is a distinct entity that someone needs to design and create. We, attempting to play the role of omniscient central planners, were swamped.

Automated tools may be created to aid the generation of areas that naturally possess a high degree of regularity and structure, such as apartment buildings and road networks. We created a number of such tools, whose spiritual descendents will no doubt be found in the standard bag of tricks of future cyberspace architects. However, the very properties which make some parts of the world amenable to such techniques also make those same parts of the world among the least important. It is really not a problem if every apartment building looks pretty much like every other. It is a big problem if every enchanted forest is the same. Places whose value lies in their uniqueness, or at least in their differentiation from the places around them, need to be crafted by hand. This is an incredibly labor intensive and time consuming process. Furthermore, even very imaginative people are limited in the range of variation that they can produce, especially if they are working in a virgin environment uninfluenced by the works and reactions of other designers.

Running the World

The world design problem might still be tractable, however, if all players had the same goals, interests, motivations and types of behavior. Real people, however, are all different. For the designer of an ordinary game or simulation, human diversity is not a major problem, since he or she gets to establish the goals and motivations on the participants' behalf, and to specify the activities available to them in order to channel events in the preferred direction. *Habitat,* however, was deliberately open-ended and pluralistic. The idea behind our world was precisely that it did not come with a fixed set of objectives for its inhabitants, but rather provided a broad palette of possible activities from which the players could choose, driven by their own internal inclinations. It was our intent to provide a variety of possible experiences, ranging from events with established rules and goals (a treasure hunt, for example) to activities propelled by the players' personal motivations (starting a business, running the newspaper) to completely free-form, purely existential activities (hanging out with friends and conversing). Most activities, however, involved some degree of pre-planning and setup on our part—we were to be like the cruise director on an ocean voyage, but we were still thinking like game designers.

The first goal-directed event planned for *Habitat* was a rather involved treasure hunt called the "D'nalsi Island Adventure". It took us hours to design, weeks to build (including a 100-region island), and days to coordinate the actors involved. It was designed much like the puzzles in an adventure game. We thought it would occupy our players for days. In fact, the puzzle was solved in about 8 hours by a person who had figured out the critical clue in the first

15 minutes. Many of the players hadn't even had a chance to get into the game. The result was that one person had had a wonderful experience, dozens of others were left bewildered, and a huge investment in design and setup time had been consumed in an eye blink. We expected that there would be a wide range of "adventuring" skills in the *Habitat* audience. What wasn't so obvious until afterward was that this meant that most people didn't have a very good time, if for no other reason than that they never really got to participate. It would clearly be foolish and impractical for us to do things like this on a regular basis.

Again and again we found that activities based on often unconscious assumptions about player behavior had completely unexpected outcomes (when they were not simply outright failures). It was clear that we were not in control. The more people we involved in something, the less in control we were. We could influence things, we could set up interesting situations, we could provide opportunities for things to happen, but we could not dictate the outcome. Social engineering is, at best, an inexact science (or, as some wag once said, "In the most carefully constructed experiment under the most carefully controlled conditions, the organism will do whatever it damn well pleases").

Propelled by these experiences, we shifted into a style of operations in which we let the players themselves drive the direction of the design. This proved far more effective. Instead of trying to push the community in the direction we thought it should go, an exercise rather like herding mice, we tried to observe what people were doing and aid them in it. We became facilitators as much as we were designers and implementers. This often meant adding new features and new regions to the system at a frantic pace, but almost all of what we added was used and appreciated, since it was well matched to people's needs and desires. We, as the experts on how the system worked, could often suggest new activities for people to try or ways of doing things that people might not have thought of. In this way we were able to have considerable influence on the system's development in spite of the fact that we didn't really hold the steering wheel—more influence, in fact, than we had had when we were operating under the illusion that we controlled everything.

Indeed, the challenges posed by large systems are prompting some researchers to question the centralized, planning dominated attitude that we have criticized here, and to propose alternative approaches based on evolutionary and market principles.[16–18] These principles appear applicable to complex systems of all types, not merely those involving interacting human beings.

The Great Debate

Among the objects we made available to Avatars in *Habitat* were guns and various other sorts of weapons. We included these because we felt that players should be able to materially effect each other in ways that went beyond simply talking, ways that required real moral choices to be made by the participants. We recognized the age old story-teller's dictum that conflict is the essence of drama. Death in *Habitat* was, of course, not like death in the real world! When an Avatar is killed, he or she is teleported back home, head in hands (literally), pockets empty, and any object in hand at the time dropped on the ground at the scene of the crime. Any possessions carried at the time are lost. It was more like a setback in a game of "Chutes and Ladders" than real mortality. Nevertheless, the death metaphor had a profound effect on people's perceptions. This potential for murder, assault and other mayhem in *Habitat* was, to put it mildly, controversial. The controversy was further fueled by the potential for lesser crimes. For instance, one Avatar could steal something from another Avatar simply by snatching the object out its owner's hands and running off with it.

We had imposed very few rules on the world at the start. There was much debate among the players as to the form that *Habitat* society should take. At the core of much of the debate was an unresolved philosophical question: is an Avatar an extension of a human being (thus entitled to be treated as you would treat a real person) or a *Pac-Man*-like critter destined to die a thousand deaths or something else entirely? Is *Habitat* murder a crime? Should all weapons be banned? Or is it all "just a game"? To make a point, one of the players took to randomly shooting people as they roamed around. The debate was sufficiently vigorous that we took a systematic poll of the players. The result was ambiguous: 50% said that *Habitat* murder was a crime and shouldn't be a part of the world, while the other 50% said it was an important part of the fun.

We compromised by changing the system to allow thievery and gunplay only outside the city limits. The wilderness would be wild and dangerous while civilization would be orderly and safe. This did not resolve the debate, however. One of the outstanding proponents of the anti-violence point of view was motivated to open the first *Habitat* church, the Order of the Holy Walnut (in real life he was a Greek Orthodox priest). His canons forbid his disciples to carry weapons, steal, or participate in violence of any kind. His church became quite popular and he became a very highly respected member of the *Habitat* community.

Furthermore, while we had made direct theft impossible, one could still engage in indirect theft by stealing things set on the ground momentarily or otherwise left unattended. And the violence still possible in the outlands continued to bother some players. Many people thought that such crimes ought to be prevented or at least punished somehow, but they had no idea how to do so. They were used to a world in which law and justice were always things provided by somebody else. Somebody eventually made the suggestion that there ought to be a Sheriff. We quickly figured out how to create a voting mechanism and rounded up some volunteers to hold an election. A public debate in the town meeting hall was heavily attended, with the three Avatars who had chosen to run making statements and fielding questions. The election was held, and the town of Populopolis acquired a Sheriff.

For weeks the Sheriff was nothing but a figurehead, though he was a respected figure and commanded a certain amount of moral authority. We were stumped about what powers to give him. Should he have the right to shoot anyone anywhere? Give him a more powerful gun? A magic wand to zap people off to jail? What about courts? Laws? Lawyers? Again we surveyed the players, eventually settling on a set of questions that could be answered via a referendum. Unfortunately, we were unable to act on the results before the pilot operations ended and the system was shut down. It was clear, however, that there are two basic camps: anarchy and government. This is an issue that will need to be addressed by future cyberspace architects. However, our view is that a virtual world need not be set up with a "default" government, but can instead evolve one as needed.

A Warning

Given the above exhortation that control should be released to the users, we need to inject a note of caution and present our next assertion:

You can't trust anyone.

This may seem like a contradiction of much of the preceding, but it really is not. Designers and operators of a cyberspace system must inhabit two levels of virtual world at once. The first we call the "infrastructure level", which is the implementation, where the laws that govern "reality" have their genesis. The second we call the "percipient level", which is what the users see and experience. It is important that there not be "leakage" between these two levels. The first level defines the physics of the world. If its integrity is breached, the consequences can range from aesthetic unpleasantness (the audience catches a glimpse of the scaffolding behind the false front) to psychological disruption (somebody does something "impossible", thereby violating users' expectations and damaging their fantasy) to catastrophic failure (somebody crashes the system). When we exhort you to give control to the users, we mean control at the percipient level. When we say that you can't trust anyone, we mean that you can't trust them with access to the infrastructure level. Some stories from *Habitat* will illustrate this.

When designing a piece of software, you generally assume that it is the sole intermediary between the user and the underlying data being manipulated (possibly multiple applications will work with the same data, but the principle remains the same). In general, the user need not be aware of how data are encoded and structured inside the application. Indeed, the very purpose of a good application is to shield the user from the ugly technical details. It is conceivable that a technically astute person who is willing to invest the time and effort could decipher the internal structure of things, but this would be an unusual thing to do as there is rarely much advantage to be gained. The purpose of the application itself is, after all, to make access to and manipulation of the data easier than digging around at the level of bits and bytes. There are exceptions to this, however. For example, most game programs deliberately impose obstacles on their players in order for play to be challenging. By tinkering around with the insides of such a program—dumping the data files and studying them, disassembling the program itself and possibly modifying it—it may be possible to "cheat." However, this sort of cheating has the flavor of cheating at solitaire: the consequences adhere to the cheater alone. There is a difference, in that disassembling a game program is a puzzle-solving exercise in its own right, whereas cheating at solitaire is pointless, but the satisfactions to be gained from it, if any, are entirely personal.

If, however, a computer game involves multiple players, delving into the program's internals can enable one to truly cheat, in the sense that one gains an unfair advantage over the other players of which they may be unaware. *Habitat* is such a multi-player game. When we were designing the software, our "prime directive" was, "The backend shall not assume the validity of anything a player computer tells it." This is because we needed to protect ourselves against the possibility that a clever user had hacked around with his copy of the front end program to add "custom features." For example, we could not implement any of the sort of "skill and action" elements found in traditional video games wherein dexterity with the joystick determines the outcome of, say, armed combat, because you couldn't guard against someone modifying their copy of the program to tell the backend that they had "hit," whether they actually had or not. Indeed, our partners at QuantumLink warned us of this very eventuality before we even started—they already had users who did this sort of thing with their regular system. Would anyone actually go to the trouble of disassembling and studying 100K or so of incredibly tight and bizarrely threaded 6502 machine code just to tinker? As it turns out, the answer is yes. People have. We were not 100% rigorous in following our own rule. It turned out that there were a few features whose implementation was greatly eased by breaking the rule in situations where, in our judgment, the consequences would not be material if people "cheated" by hacking their own systems. Darned if people didn't hack their systems to cheat in exactly these ways.

Care must be taken in the design of the world as well. One incident that occurred during our pilot test involved a small group of players exploiting a bug in our world database which they interpreted as a feature. First, some background. Avatars are hatched with 2000 Tokens in their bank account, and each day that they login they receive another 100T. Avatars may acquire additional funds by engaging in business, winning contests, finding buried treasure, and so on. They can spend their Tokens on, among other things, various items that are for sale in vending machines called Vendroids. There are also Pawn Machines, which will buy objects back (at a discount, of course).

In order to make this automated economy a little more interesting, each Vendroid had its own prices for the items in it. This was so that we could have local price variation (i.e., a widget would cost a little less if you bought it at Jack's Place instead of The Emporium). It turned out that in two Vendroids across town from each other were two items for sale whose prices we had inadvertently set lower than what a Pawn Machine would buy them back for: Dolls (for sale at 75T, hock for 100T) and Crystal Balls (for sale at 18,000T, hock at 30,000T!). Naturally, a couple of people discovered this. One night they took all their money, walked to the Doll Vendroid, bought as many Dolls as they could, then took them across town and pawned them. By shuttling back and forth between the Doll Vendroid and the Pawn Shop for *hours,* they amassed sufficient funds to buy a Crystal Ball, whereupon they continued the process with Crystal Balls and a couple orders of magnitude higher cash flow. The final result was at least three Avatars with hundreds of thousands of Tokens each. We only discovered this the next morning when our daily database status report said that the money supply had quintupled overnight.

We assumed that the precipitous increase in "T1" was due to some sort of bug in the software. We were puzzled that no bug report had been submitted. By poking around a bit we discovered that a few people had suddenly acquired enormous bank balances. We sent Habitat mail to the two richest, inquiring as to where they had gotten all that money overnight. Their reply was, "We got it fair and square! And we're not going to tell you how!" After much abject pleading on our part they eventually did tell us, and we fixed the erroneous pricing. Fortunately, the whole scam turned out well, as the nouveau rich Avatars used their bulging bankrolls to underwrite a series of treasure hunt games which they conducted on their own initiative, much to the enjoyment of many other players on the system.

Keeping "Reality" Consistent

The urge to breach the boundary between the infrastructure level and the percipient level is not confined to the players. The system operators are also subject to this temptation, though their motivation is expediency in accomplishing their legitimate purposes rather than the gaining of illegitimate advantage. However, to the degree to which it is possible, we vigorously endorse the following principle:

Work within the system.

Wherever possible, things that can be done within the framework of the percipient level should be. The result will be smoother operation and greater harmony among the user community. This admonition applies to both the technical and the sociological aspects of the system.

For example, with the players in control, the *Habitat* world would have grown much larger and more diverse than it did had we ourselves not been a technical bottleneck. All new region generation and feature implementation had to go through us, since there was no means for players to create new parts of the world on their own. Region creation was an esoteric technical specialty, requiring a plethora of obscure tools and a good working knowledge of the treacherous minefield of limitations imposed by the Commodore 64. It also required a lot of behind-the-scenes activity that would probably spoil the illusion for many. One of the goals of a next generation *Habitat*-like system ought to be to permit far greater creative involvement by the participants without requiring them to ascend to full-fledged guru-hood to do so.

A further example of working within the system, this time in a social sense, is illustrated by the following experience. One of the more popular events in *Habitat* took place late in the test, the brainchild of one of the more active players who had recently become a QuantumLink employee. It was called the "Dungeon of Death".

For weeks, ads appeared in *Habitat's* newspaper, The Rant, announcing that that Duo of Dread, DEATH and THE SHADOW, were challenging all comers to enter their lair. Soon, on the outskirts of town, the entrance to a dungeon appeared. Out front was a sign reading, "Danger! Enter at your own risk!" Two system operators were logged in as DEATH and THE SHADOW, armed with specially concocted guns that could kill in one shot, rather than the usual.[12] These two characters roamed the dungeon blasting away at anyone they encountered. They were also equipped with special magic wands that cured any damage done to them by other Avatars, so that they wouldn't themselves be killed. To make things worse, the place was littered with dead ends, pathological connections between regions, and various other nasty and usually fatal features. It was clear that any explorer had better be prepared to "die" several times before mastering the dungeon. The rewards were pretty good: 1000 Tokens minimum and access to a special Vendroid that sold magic teleportation wands. Furthermore, given clear notice, players took the precaution of emptying their pockets before entering, so that the actual cost of getting "killed" was minimal.

One evening, one of us was given the chance to play the role of DEATH. When we logged in, we found him in one of the dead ends with four other Avatars who were trapped there. We started shooting, as did they. However, the last operator to run DEATH had not bothered to use his special wand to heal any accumulated damage, so the character of DEATH was suddenly and unexpectedly "killed" in the encounter. As we mentioned earlier, when an Avatar is killed, any object in his hands is dropped on the ground. In this case, said object was the special kill-in-one-shot gun, which was immediately picked up by one of the regular players who then made off with it. This gun was not something that regular players were supposed to have. What should we do?

It turned out that this was not the first time this had happened. During the previous night's mayhem the special gun was similarly absconded with. In this case, the person playing DEATH was one of the regular system operators, who, used to operating the regular Q-Link service, simply ordered the player to give the gun back. The player considered that he had obtained the weapon as part of the normal course of the game and balked at this, whereupon the operator threatened to cancel the player's account and kick him off the system if he did not comply. The player gave the gun back, but was quite upset about the whole affair, as were many of his friends and associates on the system. Their world model had been painfully violated.

When it happened to us, we played the whole incident within the role of DEATH. We sent a message to the Avatar who had the gun, threatening to come and kill her if she didn't give it back. She replied that all she had to do was stay in town and DEATH couldn't touch her (which was true, if we stayed within the system). OK, we figured, she's smart. We negotiated a deal whereby DEATH would ransom the gun for 10,000 Tokens. An elaborate arrangement was made to meet in the center of town to make the exchange, with a neutral third Avatar acting as an intermediary to ensure that neither party cheated. Of course, word got around and by the time of the exchange there were numerous spectators. We played the role of DEATH to the hilt, with lots of hokey melodramatic shtick. The event was a sensation. It was written up in the newspaper the next morning and was the talk of the town for days. The Avatar involved was left with a wonderful story about having cheated DEATH, we got the gun back, and everybody went away happy.

These two very different responses to an ordinary operational problem illustrate our point. Operating within the participants' world model produced a very satisfactory result. On the other hand, what seemed like the expedient course, which involved violating this model, provoked upset and dismay. Working within the system was clearly the preferred course in this case.

Current Status

As of this writing, the North American incarnation of Lucasfilm's *Habitat*, QuantumLink's "Club Caribe," has been operating for almost two years. It uses our original Commodore 64 front end and a somewhat stripped-down version of our original Stratus backend software. Club Caribe now sustains a population of some 15,000 participants.

A technically more advanced version, called *Fujitsu Habitat*, has recently started pilot operations in Japan, available on Nifty Serve. The initial front end for this version is the new Fujitsu FM Towns personal computer, though ports to several other popular Japanese machines are anticipated. This version of the system benefits from the additional computational power and graphics capabilities of a newer platform, as well as the Towns' built-in CD-ROM for object imagery and sounds. However, the virtuality of the system is essentially unchanged and Fujitsu has not made significant alterations to the user interface or to any of the underlying concepts.

Future Directions

There are several directions in which this work can be extended. Most obvious is to implement the system on more advanced hardware, enabling a more sophisticated display. A number of extensions to the user interface also suggest themselves. However, the line of development most interesting to us is to expand on the idea of making the development and expansion of the world itself part of the users' sphere of control. There are two major research areas in this. Unfortunately, we can only touch on them briefly here.

The first area to investigate involves the elimination of the centralized backend. The backend is a communications and processing bottleneck that will not withstand growth above too large a size. While we can support tens of thousands of users with this model, it is not really feasible to support millions. Making the system fully distributed, however, requires solving a number of difficult problems. The most significant of these is the prevention of cheating. Obviously, the owner of the network node that implements some part of the world has an incentive to tilt things in his favor there. We think that this problem can be addressed by secure operating system technologies based on public-key cryptographic techniques.[19,20]

The second fertile area of investigation involves user configuration of the world itself. This requires finding ways to represent the design and creation of regions and objects as part of the underlying fantasy. Doing this will require changes to our conception of the world. In particular, we don't think it will be possible to conceal all of the underpinnings to those who work with them. However, all we really need to do is find abstractions for those underpinnings that fit into the fantasy itself. Though challenging, this is, in our opinion, eminently feasible.

Conclusions

We feel that the defining characteristic of cyberspace is the shared virtual environment, not the display technology used to transport users into that environment. Such a cyberspace is feasible today, if you can live without head-mounted displays and other expensive graphics hardware. *Habitat* serves as an existence proof of this contention.

It seems clear to us that an object-oriented world model is a key ingredient in any cyberspace implementation. We feel we have gained some insight into the data representation and communications needs of such a system. While we think that it may be premature to start establishing detailed technical standards for these things, it is time to begin the discussions that will lead to such standards in the future.

Finally, we have come to believe that the most significant challenge for cyberspace developers is to come to grips with the problems of world creation and management. While we have only made the first inroads onto these problems, a few things have become clear. The most important of these is that managing a cyberspace world is not like managing the world inside a single-user application or even a conventional online service. Instead, it is more like governing an actual nation. Cyberspace architects will benefit from study of the principles of sociology and economics as much as from the principles of computer science. We advocate an agoric, evolutionary approach to worldbuilding rather than a centralized, socialistic one.

We would like to conclude with a final admonition, one that we hope will not be seen as overly contentious:

Get real.

In a discussion of cyberspace on Usenet, one worker in the field dismissed Club Caribe (*Habitat's* current incarnation) as uninteresting, with a comment to the effect that most of the activity consisted of inane and trivial conversation. Indeed, the observation was largely correct. However, we hope some of the anecdotes recounted above will give some indication that more is going on than those inane and trivial conversations might indicate. Further, to dismiss the system on this basis is to dismiss the users themselves. *They* are paying money for this service. They don't view what they do as inane and trivial, or they wouldn't do it. To insist this presumes that one knows better than they what they should be doing. Such presumption is another manifestation of the omniscient central planner who dictates all that happens, a role that this entire article is trying to deflect you from seeking. In a real system that is going to be used by real people, it is a mistake to assume that the users will all undertake the sorts of noble and sublime activities which you created the system to enable. Most of them will not. Cyberspace may indeed change humanity, but only if it begins with humanity as it really is.

Notes

Note 1: One of the questions we are asked most frequently is, "Why the Commodore 64?" Many people somehow get the impression that this was a technical decision, but the real explanation has to do with business, not technology. *Habitat* was initially developed by Lucasfilm as commercial product for QuantumLink, an online service (then) exclusively for owners of the Commodore 64. At the time we started (1985), the Commodore 64 was the mainstay of the recreational computing market. Since then it has declined dramatically in both its commercial and technical significance. However, when we began the

751

project, we didn't get a choice of platforms. The nature of the deal was such that both the Commodore 64 for the frontend and the existing QuantumLink host system (a brace of Stratus fault-tolerant minicomputers) for the backend were givens.

Note 2: Habitat contains its own fully-fledged economy, with money, banks, and so on. *Habitat's* unit of currency is the Token, reflecting the fact that it is a token economy and to acknowledge the long and honorable association between tokens and video games. Incidently, the Habitat Token is a 23- sided plastic coin slightly larger than an American quarter, with a portrait of Vernor Vinge and the motto "Fiat Lucre" on its face, and the text "Good for one fare" on the back; these details are difficult to make out on the Commodore 64 screen.

Acknowledgements

We would like to acknowledge the contributions of some of the many people who helped make *Habitat* possible. At Lucasfilm, Aric Wilmunder wrote much of the Commodore 64 frontend software; Ron Gilbert, Charlie Kelner, and Noah Falstein also provided invaluable programming and design support; Gary Winnick and Ken Macklin were responsible for all the artwork; Chris Grigg did the sounds; Steve Arnold provided outstanding management support; and George Lucas gave us the freedom to undertake a project that for all he knew was both impossible and insane. At Quantum, Janet Hunter wrote the guts of the backend; Ken Huntsman and Mike Ficco provided valuable assistance with communications protocols. Kazuo Fukuda and his crew at Fujitsu have carried our vision of *Habitat* to Japan and made it their own. Phil Salin, our boss at AMiX, let us steal the time to write this paper and even paid for us to attend the First Conference on Cyberspace, even though its immediate relevance to our present business may have seemed a bit obscure at the time. We'd also like to thank Michael Benedikt, Don Fussell and their cohorts for organizing the Conference and thereby prompting us to start putting our thoughts and experiences in writing.

References

Alber, Antone F., *Videotex/Teletext: Principles and Practices* (McGraw-Hill, New York, 1985).

American National Standards Institute, *Videotex/Teletext Presentation Level Protocol Syntax,* North American PLPS (ANSI, December 1983).

Drexler, K. Eric, *Engines of Creation* (Anchor Press, Doubleday, Garden City, New York, 1986).

Drexler, K. Eric, and Miller, Mark S., "Incentive Engineering for Computational Resource Management", in Huberman, B.A., ed., *The Ecology of Computation* (Elsevier Science Publishers, Amsterdam, 1988).

Gibson, William, *Neuromancer* (Ace Books, New York, 1984).

Goldberg, Adele, and Robson, David, *Smalltalk-80: The Language and Its Implementation* (Addison-Wesley, Reading, Mass, 1983).

Hayek, Friedrich A., *Law Legislation and Liberty*, Volume I: Rules and Order (University of Chicago Press, Chicago, 1973).

Hayek, Friedrich A., *New Studies in Philosophy, Politics, Economics, and the History of Ideas* (University of Chicago Press, Chicago, 1978).

Hayek, Friedrich A., *The Fatal Conceit* (University of Chicago Press, Chicago, 1989).

International Standards Organization, *Information Processing Systems—Open System Interconnection—Transport Service Definition*, International Standard number 0072 (ISO, Switzerland, June 1986).

Miller, Mark S., Bobrow, Daniel G., Tribble, Eric Dean, and Levy, David Jacob, "Logical Secrets", in Shapiro, Ehud, ed., *Concurrent Prolog: Collected Papers* (MIT Press, Cambridge, 1987).

Miller, Mark S., and Drexler, K. Eric, "Comparative Ecology: A Computational Perspective", in Huberman, B.A., ed., *The Ecology of Computation* (Elsevier Science Publishers, Amsterdam, 1988a).

Miller, Mark S., and Drexler, K. Eric, "Markets and Computation: Agoric Open Systems", in Huberman, B.A., ed., *The Ecology of Computation* (Elsevier Science Publishers, Amsterdam, 1988b).

Popper, Karl R., *The Open Society and Its Enemies* (fifth edition) (Princeton University Press, Princeton, New Jersey, 1962).

Popper, Karl R., *Objective Knowledge: An Evolutionary Approach* (Oxford University Press, Oxford, 1972).

Rivest, R., Shamir, A., and Adelman, L., "A Method for Obtaining Digital Signatures and Public-Key Cryptosystems", in *Communications of the ACM*, Vol. 21, No. 2 (February 1978).

Sowell, Thomas, *A Conflict of Visions* (William Morrow, New York, 1987).

Sterling, Bruce, ed., *Mirrorshades: The Cyberpunk Anthology* (Arbor House, New York, 1986).

Sussman, Gerald Jay, and Abelson, Harold, *Structure and Interpretation of Computer Programs* (MIT Press, Cambridge, 1985).

Vinge, Vernor, "True Names", *Binary Star* #5 (Dell Publishing Company, New York, 1981).

Hearts, Clubs, Diamonds, Spades: Players Who Suit MUDs

Richard Bartle

Context

The essay grew from a long discussion between senior players of MUD2 regarding why people play virtual worlds. It appeared in embryonic form in several places before the definitive version appeared in the first issue of the (now moribund) **Journal of MUD Research.** *Since then, it has been translated into several languages, and republished in Mulligan and Patrovsky's book* **Developing Online Games.** *The themes that the essay explores have been extended further in my book,* **Designing Virtual Worlds.**

The Player Experience

Game Communities

Game Economies

Richard Bartle co-wrote the first virtual world, MUD, in 1978. His book, *Designing Virtual Worlds* (New Riders Games, 2003), has already established itself as a foundation text for researchers and developers of virtual worlds alike. He is currently Visiting Professor of computer game design at the University of Essex, England.

Preface

Most MUDs can trace their lineage directly back to Trubshaw's 1978 game (Bartle, 1990b; Burka, 1995) and, perhaps because of this heritage, the vast majority are regarded as "games" by their "players". For the convenience of its readers, this paper continues to view MUDs in this tradition; however, it should be noted that MUDs can be of considerable value in non-game (i.e. "serious") applications (Bruckman, 1994a; Kort, 1991; Bruckman & Resnick, 1993; Curtis & Nichols, 1993; Evard, 1993; Fanderclai, 1995; Riner & Clodius, 1995; Moock, 1996). Indeed, the thrust of this paper emphasizes those factors which should be borne in mind when attempting to create a stable MUD in general, whatever the application; it is only the terminology which is that of "fun" MUDs, not the subject matter. In any case, even those MUDs which are built, from the ground up, to be absolutely straight are still treated by users as if they were games in some respects, e.g. by choosing whimsical names rather than using their real ones (Roush, 1993).

It is worthwhile considering for a moment whether MUDs (as they are generally played) really are games, or whether they are something else. People have many recreational activities available to them, and perhaps MUDs fit some other category better? Looking up the word "game" in a dictionary of synonyms (Urdang & Manser, 1980) elicits three related nouns: "pastime," "sport" and "entertainment" (a fourth, "amusement," is the general class of which the others are all examples). So it might be useful to ask:

Are MUDs

- Games? Like chess, tennis, AD&D?

- Pastimes? Like reading, gardening, cooking?

- Sports? Like huntin', shootin', fishin'?

- Entertainments? Like nightclubs, TV, concerts?

Or are they a combination of all four? Perhaps individual players even see the *same* MUD differently from each another?

These questions will be returned to at the end of this paper, along with some proposed answers.

A Simple Taxonomy

This work grew out of a long, heated discussion which ran from November 1989 to May 1990 between the wizzes (i.e. highly experienced players, of rank wizard or witch) on one particular commercial MUD in the UK (Bartle, 1985). The debate was sparked by the question "What do people want out of a MUD?", and comprised several hundred bulletin-board postings, some of considerable length, typically concerning what the players liked, what they didn't like, why they played, and changes they would like to see to "improve" the game. Some 15 individuals took a major part, with perhaps another 15 adding their comments from time to time; this comprised almost the entire set of active wizzes during that period. Although at times the debate became quite intense, never did it lapse into flaming, which typically ends most open-ended, multi-speaker, online discussions.

The fact that the people contributing to this argument were the most advanced players in a MUD, which allowed player-killing might, on the face of it, be taken as evidence that they would probably prefer more "gamelike" aspects over "social" ones. However, this was not the case: the MUD in question had players of all types in it, even at wiz level. (Later in this paper, an analysis is given as to how such a MUD can come to be).

When the participants had finally run out of new things to say, it became time for me (as senior administrator) to summarize. Abstracting the various points that had been raised, a pattern emerged; people habitually found the same kinds of thing about the game "fun," but there were several (four, in fact) sub-groupings into which opinion divided. Most players leaned at least a little to all four, but each tended to have some particular overall preference. The summary was generally well received by those who had participated in the debate.

Note that although this MUD was one in which player-killing was allowed, the taxonomy which is about to be described does (as will be explained later) apply equally to "social" MUDs. The advice concerning changes which can be made to affect the player make-up of a MUD is, however, less useful to social MUDs, or to ones with a heavy role-playing component. Also, the original discussion concerned only non-administrative aspects of MUDding; people who might play MUDs to learn object-oriented programming, for example, are therefore not addressed by this paper.

The four things that people typically enjoyed personally about MUDs were:

i) Achievement within the game context.

Players give themselves game-related goals, and vigorously set out to achieve them. This usually means accumulating and disposing of large quantities of high-value treasure, or cutting a swathe through hordes of mobiles (i.e. monsters built in to the virtual world).

ii) Exploration of the game.

Players try to find out as much as they can about the virtual world. Although initially this means mapping its topology (i.e. exploring the MUD's breadth), later it advances to experimentation with its physics (i.e. exploring the MUD's depth).

iii) Socializing with others.

Players use the game's communicative facilities, and apply the role-playing that these engender, as a context in which to converse (and otherwise interact) with their fellow players.

iv) Imposition upon others.

Players use the tools provided by the game to cause distress to (or, in rare circumstances, to help) other players. Where permitted, this usually involves acquiring some weapon and applying it enthusiastically to the persona of another player in the game world.

So, labeling the four player types abstracted, we get: achievers, explorers, socializers and killers. An easy way to remember these is to consider suits in a conventional pack of cards: achievers are Diamonds (they're always seeking treasure); explorers are Spades (they dig around for information); socializers are Hearts (they empathize with other players); killers are Clubs (they hit people with them).

Naturally, these areas cross over, and players will often drift between all four, depending on their mood or current playing style. However, my experience having observed players in the light of this research suggests that many (if not most) players do have a primary style, and will only switch to other styles as a (deliberate or subconscious) means to advance their main interest.

Looking at each player type in more detail, then:

i) Achievers regard points-gathering and rising in levels as their main goal, and all is ultimately subservient to this. Exploration is necessary only to find new sources of treasure, or improved ways of wringing points from it. Socializing is a relaxing method of discovering what other players know about the business of accumulating points, that their knowledge can be applied to the task of gaining riches. Killing is only necessary to eliminate rivals or people who get in the way, or to gain vast amounts of points (if points are awarded for killing other players).

Achievers say things like:

"I'm busy."

"Sure, I'll help you. What do I get?"

"So how do YOU kill the dragon, then?"

"Only 4211 points to go!"

ii) Explorers delight in having the game expose its internal machinations to them. They try progressively esoteric actions in wild, out-of-the-way places, looking for interesting features (i.e. bugs) and figuring out how things work. Scoring points may be necessary to enter some next phase of exploration, but it's tedious, and anyone with half a brain can do it. Killing is quicker, and might be a constructive exercise in its own right, but it causes too much hassle in the long run if the deceased return to seek retribution. Socializing can be informative as a source of new ideas to try out, but most of what people say is irrelevant or old hat. The real fun comes only from discovery, and making the most complete set of maps in existence.

Explorers say things like:

"Hmm..."

"You mean you *don't know* the shortest route from *obscure room 1* to *obscure room 2*?"

"I haven't tried that one, what's it do?"

"Why is it that if you carry the uranium you get radiation sickness, and if you put it in a bag you still get it, but if you put it in a bag and drop it then wait 20 seconds and pick it up again, you don't?"

iii) Socializers are interested in people, and what they have to say. The game is merely a backdrop, a common ground where things happen to players. Inter-player relationships are important: empathizing with people, sympathizing, joking, entertaining, listening; even merely observing people play can be rewarding—seeing them grow as individuals, maturing over time. Some exploration may be necessary so as to understand what everyone else is talking about, and points-scoring could be required to gain access to neat communicative spells available only to higher levels (as well as to obtain a certain status in the community). Killing, however, is something only ever to be excused if it's a futile, impulsive act of revenge, perpetrated upon someone who has caused intolerable pain to a dear friend. The only ultimately fulfilling thing is not how to rise levels or kill hapless drips; it's getting to *know* people, to understand them, and to form beautiful, lasting relationships.

Socializers say things like:

"Hi!"

"Yeah, well, I'm having trouble with my boyfriend."

"What happened? I missed it, I was talking."

"Really? Oh no! Gee, that's terrible! Are you sure? Awful, just awful!"

iv) Killers get their kicks from imposing themselves on others. This may be "nice", i.e. busybody do-gooding, but few people practice such an approach because the rewards (a warm, cosy inner glow, apparently) aren't very substantial. Much more commonly, people attack other players with a view to killing off their personae (hence the name for this style of play). The more massive the distress caused, the greater the killer's joy at having caused it. Normal points-scoring is usually required so as to become powerful enough to begin causing havoc in earnest, and exploration of a kind is necessary to discover new and ingenious ways to kill people. Even socializing is sometimes worthwhile beyond taunting a recent victim, for example in finding out someone's playing habits, or discussing tactics with fellow killers. They're all just means to an end, though; only in the knowledge that a real person, somewhere, is very upset by what you've just done, yet can themselves do nothing about it, is there any true adrenalin-shooting, juicy fun.

Killers says things like:

"Ha!"

"Coward!"

"Die!"

"Die! Die! Die!"

(Killers are people of few words).

How many players typically fall within each area depends on the MUD. If, however, too many gravitate to one particular style, the effect can be to cause players of other persuasions to leave, which in turn may feed back and reduce the numbers in the first category. For example, too many killers will drive away the achievers who form their main prey; this in turn will mean that killers will stop playing, as they'll have no worthwhile victims (players considered by killers to be explorers generally don't care about death, and players considered to be socializers are too easy to pose much of a challenge). These direct relationships are discussed in more detail towards the end of this paper.

For the most part, though, the inter-relationships between the various playing styles are more subtle: a sharp reduction in the number of explorers for whatever reason could mean a gradual reduction in achievers, who get bored if they're not occasionally told of different hoops they can jump through for points; this could affect the number of socializers (the fewer players there are, the less there is to talk about), and it would certainly lower the killer population (due to a general lack of suitable victims).

Making sure that a game doesn't veer off in the wrong direction and lose players can be difficult; administrators need to maintain a balanced relationship between the different types of player, so as to guarantee their MUD's "feel." Note that I am not advocating any particular form of equilibrium: it is up to the game administrators themselves to decide what atmosphere they want their MUD to have, and thus define the point at which it is "balanced" (although the effort required to maintain this desired state could be substantial). Later, this paper considers means by which a MUD can be pushed in different directions, either to restore an earlier balance between the player types, to define a new target set of relationships between the player types, or to cause the interplay between the player types to break down entirely. However, first a means is required of formally linking the four principal playing styles into aspects of a unified whole; this helps account for different degrees of adherence to particular styles, and aids visualization of what "altering the balance" of a MUD might actually *mean*.

Interest Graph

Consider the following abstract graph:

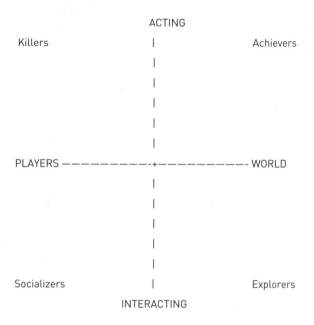

The axes of the graph represent the source of players' interest in a MUD. The x-axis goes from an emphasis on players (left) to an emphasis on the environment (right); the y-axis goes from acting with (bottom) to acting on (top). The four extreme corners of the graph show the four typical playing preferences associated with each quadrant. To see how the graph works, it is appropriate to consider each of the four styles in detail:

i) Achievers are interested in doing things to the game, i.e. in ACTING on the WORLD. It's the fact that the game environment is a fully-fledged world in which they can immerse themselves that they find compelling; its being shared with other people merely adds a little authenticity, and perhaps a competitive element. The point of playing is to master the game, and make it do what you want it to do; there's nothing intrinsically worthwhile in rooting out irrelevant details that will never be of use, or in idling away your life with gossip.

Achievers are proud of their formal status in the game's built-in level hierarchy, and of how short a time they took to reach it.

ii) Explorers are interested in having the game surprise them, i.e. in INTERACTING with the WORLD. It's the sense of wonder that the virtual world imbues that they crave for; other players add depth to the game, but they aren't essential components of it, except perhaps as sources of new areas to visit. Scoring points all the time is a worthless occupation, because it defies the very open-endedness that makes a world live and breathe. Most accomplished explorers could easily rack up sufficient points to reach the top, but such one-dimensional behavior is the sign of a limited intellect.

Explorers are proud of their knowledge of the game's finer points, especially if new players treat them as founts of all knowledge.

iii) Socializers are interested in INTERACTING with other PLAYERS. This usually means talking, but it can extend to more exotic behavior. Finding out about people and getting to know them is far more worthy than treating them as fodder to be bossed around. The game world is just a setting; it's the characters that make it so compelling.

Socializers are proud of their friendships, their contacts and their influence.

iv) Killers are interested in doing things to people, i.e. in ACTING on other PLAYERS. Normally, this is not with the consent of these "other players" (even if, objectively, the interference in their play might appear "helpful"), but killers don't care; they wish only to demonstrate their superiority over fellow humans, preferably in a world which serves to legitimize actions that could mean imprisonment in real life. Accumulated knowledge is useless unless it can be applied; even when it is applied, there's no fun unless it can affect a real person instead of an emotionless, computerized entity.

Killers are proud of their reputation and of their oft-practiced fighting skills.

The "interest graph" is a representational structure that can chart what players find of interest in a MUD. The axes can be assigned a relative scale reflecting the ratio of an individual's interest between the two extremes that it admits. Thus, for example, someone who thinks that the people who are in the world are maybe twice as important as the world itself would lie on a vertical line intersecting the x-axis at a point 1/6 of the distance from the origin to the left edge; if they had little interest in bending the game to their will, preferring their actions to have some give and take, then they would also lie on a horizontal line at the bottom of the y-axis. The intersection of the two lines would put them in the socializer quadrant, with leanings to explorer.

It is, of course, possible to analyze the behavior of individual players quantitatively by processing transcripts of their games. Unfortunately, this is very difficult to do except for very limited domains (e.g. forms of communication (Cherny, 1995a; Cherny, 1995b)). An alternative approach might simply be to ask the players what they themselves like about a particular MUD: even a short questionnaire, completed anonymously, can give a fair indication of what players find enjoyable (Emert, 1993). Such information can then be used to determine the make-up of the MUD's player base, so that in times of falling player numbers the current composition could be compared against some earlier ideal, and remedial action taken to re-dress the imbalance. This "ideal" configuration would, however, be specific to that particular MUD, and its precise form is therefore not addressed here. Instead, the more general issue of how to alter the balance between player types is considered, along with the gross effects that can be expected to follow from having done so.

Changing the Player Type Balance

A stable MUD is one in which the four principal styles of player are in equilibrium. This doesn't imply that there is the same number of players exhibiting each style; rather, it means that over time the proportion of players for each style remains roughly constant, so that the balance between the various types remains the same. Other factors *are* important, to do with the rate at which new players arrive and overall player numbers, but their consideration is not within the brief of this paper; the interaction between players of different types *is* within its brief, however, and is discussed in some detail later.

The actual point of balance (i.e. whereabouts in the interest graph the centre of gravity of the individual players' points lies) can vary quite enormously; it is up to individual administrators to determine where they want it to lie, and to make any programming or design changes necessary to ensure that this is where it actually does. What kind of strategies, though, can be employed to achieve this task?

In order to answer this question, consider the interest graph. If it is regarded as a plane in equilibrium, it can be tilted in a number of ways to favor different areas. Usually, this will be at the expense of some other (opposite) area, but not necessarily. Although tilting can in theory occur along any line in the plane, it makes sense (at least initially) to look at what happens when the tilt lines coincide with the x and y axes of the graph.

What follows, then, is a brief examination of means by which a MUD can be adjusted so as to favor the various extremes of the interest graph, and what would happen if each approach were taken to the limit.

Players

Putting the emphasis on players rather than the game is easy—you just provide the system with lots of communication commands and precious little else. The more the scales are tipped towards players, though, the less of a MUD you have and the more of a CB-style chatline. Beyond a certain point, the game can't provide a context for communication, and it ceases to be a viable virtual world: it's just a comms channel for the real world. At this stage, when all sense of elsewhere-presence is lost, you no longer have a MUD.

World

Tilting the game towards the world rather than its inhabitants is also easy: you simply make it so big and awkward to traverse that no-one ever meets anyone in it; alternatively, you can ensure that if they do meet up, then there are very few ways in which they an interact. Although this can result in some nice simulations, there's a loss of motivation implicit within it: anyone can rack up points given time, but there's not the same sense of achievement as when it's done under pressure from competing players. And what use is creating beautifully-crafted areas anyway, if you can't show them to people? Perhaps if computer-run personae had more AI a MUD could go further in this direction (Mauldin, 1994), but it couldn't (yet) go all the way (as authors of single-player games have found (Caspian-Kaufman, 1995)). Sometimes, you just *do* want to tell people real-world things—you have a new baby, or a new job, or your cat has died. If there's no one to tell, or no way to tell them, you don't have a MUD.

Interacting

Putting the emphasis on interaction rather than action can also go a long way. Restricting the freedom of players to choose different courses of action is the mechanism for implementing il, so they can only follow a narrow or predetermined development path. Essentially, it's MUD-as-theatre: you sit there being entertained, but not actually participating much. You may *feel* like you're in a world, but it's one in which you're paralyzed. If the bias is only slight, it can make a MUD more "nannyish," which newcomers seem to enjoy, but pushing it all the way turns it into a radio set. Knowledge may be intrinsically interesting (i.e. trivia), but it's meaningless unless it can be applied. If players can't play, it's not a MUD.

Acting

If the graph is redrawn to favor doing-to over doing-with, the game quickly becomes boring. Tasks are executed repeatedly, by rote. There's always monotony, never anything new, or, if there is something new, it's of the "man versus random number generator" variety. People do need to be able to put into practice what they've learned, but they also need to be able to learn it in the first place! Unless the one leads to the other, it's only a matter of time before patience is exhausted and the players give up. Without depth, you have no MUD.

From the above list of ways to tilt the interest graph, a set of stratagems can be composed to help MUD administrators shift the focus of their games in whatever particular direction they choose. Some of these stratagems are simply a question of management: if you don't tell people what communication commands there are, for example, people will be less likely to use them all. Although such approaches are good for small shifts in the way a MUD is played, the more powerful and absolute method is to consider *programming* changes (programming being the "nature" of a MUD, and administration being the "nurture").

Here, then, are the programming changes that administrators might wish to consider in order to shape their MUD:

Ways to emphasize PLAYERS over WORLD:

- add more communication facilities
- add more player-on-player commands (e.g. transitive ones like TICKLE or CONGRAT-ULATE, or commands to form and maintain closed groups of personae)
- make communication facilities easy and intuitive
- decrease the size of the world
- increase the connectivity between rooms
- maximize the number of simultaneous players

- restrict building privileges to a select few
- cut down on the number of mobiles

Ways to emphasize WORLD over PLAYERS:

- have only basic communication facilities
- have few ways that players can do things to other players
- make building facilities easy and intuitive
- maximize the size of the world (i.e. add breadth)
- use only "rational" room connections in most cases
- grant building privileges to many
- have lots of mobiles

Ways to emphasize INTERACTING over ACTING:

- make help facilities produce vague information
- produce cryptic hints when players appear stuck
- maximize the effects of commands (i.e. add depth)
- lower the rewards for achievement
- have only a shallow level/class system
- produce amusing responses for amusing commands
- edit all room descriptions for consistent atmosphere
- limit the number of commands available in any one area
- have lots of small puzzles that can be solved easily
- allow builders to add completely new commands

Ways to emphasize ACTING over INTERACTING:

- provide a game manual
- include auto-map facilities
- include auto-log facilities
- raise the rewards for achievement
- have an extensive level/class system
- make commands be applicable wherever they might reasonably have meaning
- have large puzzles that take over an hour to complete
- have many commands relating to fights
- only allow building by top-quality builders

These strategies can be combined to encourage or discourage different styles of play. To appeal to achievers, for example, one approach might be to introduce an extensive level/class system (so as to provide plenty of opportunity to reward investment of time) and to maximize the size of the world (so there is more for them to achieve). Note that the "feel" of a MUD is derived from the position on the interest graph of the MUD's players, from which a "centre of gravity" can be approximated. It is therefore sometimes possible to make two changes simultaneously which have "opposite" effects, altering how some individuals experience the MUD but not changing how the MUD feels overall. For example, adding large puzzles (to emphasize ACTING) and adding small puzzles (to emphasize INTERACTING) would encourage both pro-ACTING and pro-INTERACTING players, thereby keeping the MUD's centre of gravity in the same place while tending to increase total player numbers. In general, though, these stratagems should not be used as a means to attract new players; stratagems should only be selected from one set per axis.

The effects of the presence (or lack of it) of other types of player are also very important, and can be used as a different way to control relative population sizes. The easiest (but, sadly, most tedious) way to discuss the interactions which pertain between the various player types is to enumerate the possible combinations and consider them independently; this is the approach adopted by this paper. First, however, it is pertinent to discuss the ways that players generally categorize MUDs today.

The Social Versus Gamelike Debate

Following the introduction of TinyMUD (Aspnes, 1989), in which combat wasn't even implemented, players now tend to categorize individual MUDs as either "social" or "gamelike" (Carton, 1995). In terms of the preceding discussion, "social" means that the games are heavily weighted to the area below the x-axis, but whether "gamelike" means the games are weighted heavily above the x-axis, or merely balanced on it, is a moot point. Players of social MUDs might suggest that "gamelike" means a definite bias on and above the x-axis, because from their perspective any explicit element of competitiveness is "too much." Some (but not most) players of gamelike MUDs could disagree, pointing out that their MUDs enjoy rich social interactions between the players despite the fact that combat is allowed.

So strongly is this distinction felt, particularly among social MUDders, that many of their newer participants don't regard themselves as playing "MUDs" at all, insisting that this term refers only to combat-oriented games, with which they don't wish to be associated. The rule-of-thumb applied is server type, so, for example, LPMUD =→ gamelike, MOO =→ social; this is despite the fact that each of these systems is of sufficient power and flexibility that it could probably be used to implement an interpreter for the other one!

Consequently, there are general Internet-related books with chapter titles like "Interactive Multiuser Realities: MUDs, MOOs, MUCKs and MUSHes" (Poirier, 1994) and "MUDs, MUSHes, and Other Role-Playing Games" (Eddy, 1994). This fertile ground is where the term "MU*" (Norrish, 1995) originates—as an attempt to fill the void left by assigning the word "MUD" to gamelike (or "player-killing") MUDs; its deliberate use can therefore reasonably be described as a political act (Bruckman, 1992).

This attitude misses the point, however. Although social MUDs may be a major branch on the MUD family tree, they are, nevertheless, still on it, and are therefore still MUDs. If another overarching term is used, then it will only be a matter of time before someone writes a combat-oriented surver called "KillerMU*" or whatever, and cause the wound to reopen. Denial of history is not, in general, a wise thing to do.

Besides, social MUDs do have their killers (i.e. people who fall into that area of the interest graph). Simply because explicit combat is prohibited, there is nevertheless plenty of opportunity to cause distress in other ways. To list a few: virtual rape (Dibbell, 1993; Reid, 1994); general sexual harassment (Rosenberg, 1992); deliberate fracturing of the community (Whitlock, 1994a); vexatious litigancy (Whitlock, 1994b). Indeed, proper management of a MUD insists that contingency plans and procedures are already in place such that antisocial behavior can be dealt with promptly when it occurs (Bruckman, 1994b).

Social MUDs do have their achievers, too: people who regard building as a competitive act, and can vie to have the "best" rooms in the MUD (Clodius, 1994), or who seek to acquire a large quota for creating ever-more objects (Farmer, Morningstar & Crockford, 1994). The fact that a MUD might not itself reward such behavior should, of course, naturally foster a community of players who are primarily interested in talking and listening, but there nevertheless will still be killers and achievers around—in the same way that there will be socializers and explorers in even the most bloodthirsty of MUDs.

Researchers have tended to use a more precise distinction than the players, in terms of a MUD's similarity to (single-user) adventure games. Amy Bruckman's observation that:

> there are two basic types [of MUD]: those which are like adventure games, and those
> which are not (Bruckman, 1992)

is the most succinct and unarguable expression of this dichotomy. However, in his influential
paper on MUDs, Pavel Curtis states:

> Three major factors distinguish a MUD from an Adventure-style computer game, though:
>
> A MUD is not goal-oriented; it has no beginning or end, no 'score,' and no notion of
> 'winning' or 'success.' In short, even though users of MUDs are commonly called players,
> a MUD isn't really a game at all.
>
> A MUD is extensible from within; a user can add new objects to the database such as
> rooms, exits, 'things,' and notes. [...]
>
> A MUD generally has more than one user connected at a time. All of the connected
> users are browsing and manipulating the same database and can encounter the new
> objects created by others. The multiple users on a MUD can communicate with each
> other in real time. (Curtis, 1992)

This definition explicitly rules out MUDs as adventure games—indeed, it claims that
they are not games at all. This is perhaps too tight a definition, since the very first MUD was
most definitely programmed to be a game. (I know, because I programmed it to be one!) The
second point, which states that MUDs must involve building, is also untrue of many MUDs; in
particular, commercial MUDs often aim for a high level of narrative consistency (which isn't
conducive to letting players add things unchecked), and, if they have a graphical front-end,
it is also inconvenient if new objects appear that generate no images. However, the fact that
Curtis comes down on the side of "social" MUDs to bear the name "MUD" at least recognizes
that these programs are MUDs, which is more than many "MU*" advocates are prepared to
admit.

This issue of "social or gamelike" will be returned to presently, with an explanation
of exactly *why* players of certain MUDs which are dubbed "gamelike" might find a binary distinction counter-intuitive.

Player Interactions

What follows is a brief explanation of how players predominantly of one type view those other
players whom they perceive to be predominantly of one type. Warning: these notes concern

stereotypical players, and are not to be assumed to be true of any individual player who might otherwise exhibit the common traits of one or more of the player classes.

The effects of increasing and decreasing the various populations are also discussed, but this does *not* take into account physical limitations on the amount of players involved. Thus, for example, if the number of socializers is stated to have "no effect" on the number of achievers, that disregards the fact that there may be an absolute maximum number of players that the MUD can comfortably hold, and the socializers may be taking up slots which achievers could otherwise have filled. Also, the knock-on effects of other interactions are not discussed at this stage: a game with fewer socializers means the killers will seek out more achievers, for example, so there is a secondary effect of having fewer achievers even though there is no primary effect. This propagation of influences is, however, examined in detail afterwards, when the first-level dynamics have been laid bare.

Achievers vs. Achievers

Achievers regard other achievers as competition to be beaten (although this is typically friendly in nature, rather than cut-throat). Respect is given to those other achievers who obviously are extraordinarily good, but typically, achievers will cite bad luck or lack of time as reasons for not being as far advanced in the game as their contemporaries are.

That said, achievers do often co-operate with one another, usually to perform some difficult collective goal, and from these shared experiences can grow deep, enduring friendships which may surpass in intensity those commonly found among individuals other groups. This is perhaps analogous to the difference between the bond that soldiers under fire share and the bond that friends in a bar share.

Achievers do not need the presence of any other type of player in order to be encouraged to join a MUD: they would be quite happy if the game was empty but for them, assuming it remained a challenge (although some do feel a need to describe their exploits to anyone who will listen). Because of this, a MUD cannot have too many achievers, physical limitations excepted.

Achievers vs. Explorers

Achievers tend to regard explorers as losers: people who have had to resort to tinkering with the game mechanics because they can't cut it as a player. Exceptionally good explorers may be elevated to the level of eccentric, in much the same way that certain individuals come to be regarded as gurus by users of large computer installations: what they do is pointless, but they're useful to have around when you need to know something obscure, fast. They can be irritating, and they rarely tell the whole truth (perhaps because they don't know it?), but they do have a place in the world.

The overall number of explorers has only a marginal effect on the population of achievers. In essence, more explorers will mean that fewer of the really powerful objects will be around for the achievers to use, the explorers having used their arcane skills to obtain them first so as to use them in their diabolical experiments... This can cause achievers to become frustrated, and leave. More importantly, perhaps, the number of explorers affects the *rate of advancement* of achievers, because it determines whether or not they have to work out all those tiresome puzzles themselves. Thus, more explorers will lead to a quicker rise through the ranks for achievers, which will tend to encourage them (if not overdone).

Achievers vs. Socializers

Achievers merely tolerate socializers. Although they are good sources of general hearsay on the comings and goings of competitors, they're nevertheless pretty much a waste of space as far as achievers are concerned. Typically, achievers will regard socializers with a mixture of contempt, disdain, irritation and pity, and will speak to them in either a sharp or a patronizing manner. Occasionally, flame wars between different cliques of socializers and achievers may break out, and these can be among the worst to stop: the achievers don't want to lose the argument, and the socializers don't want to stop talking!

Changing the number of socializers in a MUD has no effect on the number of achievers.

Achievers vs. Killers

Achievers don't particularly like killers. They realize that killers as a concept are necessary in order to make achievement meaningful and worthwhile (there being no way to "lose" the game if any fool can "win" just by plodding slowly unchallenged), however they don't personally like being attacked unless it's obvious from the outset that they'll win. They also object to being interrupted in the middle of some grand scheme to accumulate points, and they don't like having to arm themselves against surprise attacks every time they start to play. Achievers will, occasionally, resort to killing tactics themselves, in order to cause trouble for a rival or to reap whatever rewards the game itself offers for success; however, the risks are usually too high for them to pursue such options very often.

Increasing the number of killers will reduce the number of achievers; reducing the killer population will increase the achiever population. Note, however, that those general MUDs which nevertheless allow player-killing tend to do so in the belief that in small measure it is good for the game: it promotes camaraderie, excitement and intensity of experience (and it's the only method that players will accept to ensure that complete idiots don't plod inexorably through the ranks to acquire a degree of power which they aren't really qualified to wield). As a consequence, reducing the number of killers *too* much will be perceived as cheapening the game, making high achievement commonplace, and it will put off those achievers who are alarmed at the way any fool can "do well" just by playing poorly for long enough.

Explorers vs. Achievers

Explorers look on achievers as nascent explorers, who haven't yet figured out that there's more to life than pursuing meaningless goals. They are therefore willing to furnish them with information, although, like all experts, they will rarely tell the full story when they can legitimately give cryptic clues instead. Apart from the fact that they sometimes get in the way, and won't usually hand over objects that are needed for experiments, achievers can live alongside explorers without much friction.

Explorers' numbers aren't affected by the presence of achievers.

Explorers vs. Explorers

Explorers hold good explorers in great respect, but are merciless to bad ones. One of the worst things a fellow explorer can do is to give out incorrect information, believing it to be true. Other than that, explorers thrive on telling one another their latest discoveries, and generally get along very well. Outwardly, they will usually claim to have the skill necessary to follow the achievement path to glory, but have other reasons for not doing so (e.g. time, tedium, or having proven themselves already with a different persona). There are often suspicions, though, that explorers are too theoretical in most cases, and wouldn't be able to put their ideas into practice on a day-to-day basis if they were to recast themselves in the achiever or killer mould.

Explorers enjoy the company of other explorers, and they will play more often if they have people around them to whom they can relate. Unfortunately, not many people have the type of personality that finds single-minded exploring a riveting subject, so numbers are notoriously difficult to increase. If you have explorers in a game, hold on to them!

Explorers vs. Socializers

Explorers consider socializers to be people whom they can impress, but who are otherwise pretty well unimportant. Unless they can appreciate the explorer's talents, they're not really worth spending time with. There *are* some explorers who treat conversation as their specialist explorer subject, but these are very rare indeed; most will be polite and attentive, but they'll find some diversion if the conversation isn't MUD-related or if their fellow interlocutor is clearly way below them in the game-understanding stakes.

The explorer population is not directly affected by the size of the socializer population.

Explorers vs. Killers

Explorers often have a grudging respect for killers, but they do find their behavior wearisome. It's just *so* annoying to be close to finishing setting up something when a killer comes along and attacks you. On the other hand, many killers do know their trade well, and are quite prepared to discuss the finer details of it with explorers. Sometimes, an explorer may try attacking other players as an exercise, and they can be extremely effective at it. Explorers who are particularly riled by a killer may even decide to "do something about it" themselves. If they make such a decision, then it can be seriously bad news for the killer concerned: being jumped and trashed by a low-level (in terms of game rank) explorer can have a devastating effect on a killer's reputation, and turn them into a laughing stock overnight. Explorers do not, however, tend to have the venom or malice that true killers possess, nor will they continue the practice to the extent that they acquire a reputation of their own for killing.

The affect of killers on the explorer population is fairly muted, because most explorers don't particularly care if they get killed (or at least they profess not). However, if it happens too often then they will become disgruntled, and play less frequently.

Socializers vs. Achievers

Socializers like achievers, because they provide the running soap opera about which the socializers can converse. Without such a framework, there is no uniting cause to bring social-izers together (at least not initially). Note that socializers don't particularly enjoy talking *to* achievers (not unless they can get them to open up, which is very difficult); they do, however, enjoy talking *about* them. A cynic might suggest that the relationship between socializers and achievers is similar to that between women and men... .

Increasing the achiever/socializer ratio has only a subtle effect: socializers may come to feel that the MUD is "all about" scoring points and killing mobiles, and some of them may therefore leave before matters "get worse." Decreasing it has little effect unless the number of active achievers drops to near zero, in which case new socializers might find it difficult to break into established conversational groups, and thus decide to take their play elsewhere.

Note: although earlier it was stated that this paper does not address people who play MUDs for meta-reasons, e.g. to learn how to program, I believe that their empirical behavior with regard to the actions of other players is sufficiently similar to that of socializers for the two groups to be safely bundled together when considering population dynamics.

Socializers vs. Explorers

Socializers generally consider explorers to be sad characters who are desperately in need of a life. Both groups like to talk, but rarely about the same things, and if they do get together, it's usually because the explorer wants to sound erudite and the socializer has nothing better to do at the time.

The number of explorers in a MUD has no effect on the number of socializers.

Socializers vs. Socializers

A case of positive feedback: socializers can talk to one another on any subject for hours on end, and come back later for more. The key factor is whether there is an open topic of conversation: in a game-like environment, the MUD itself provides the context for discussion, whether it be the goings-on of other players or the feeble attempts of a socializer to try playing it; in a non-game environment, some other subject is usually required to structure conversations, either within the software of the MUD itself (e.g., building) or without it (e.g., "This is a support MUD for the victims of cancer."). Note that this kind of subject-setting is only required as a form of ice-breaker: once socializers have acquired friends, they'll invariably find other things that they can talk about.

The more socializers there are in a game, the more new ones will be attracted to it.

Socializers vs. Killers

This is perhaps the most fractious relationship between player group types. The hatred that some socializers bear for killers admits no bounds. Partly, this is the killers' own fault: they go out of their way to rid MUDs of namby-pamby socializers who wouldn't know a weapon if one came up and hit them (an activity that killers are only too happy to demonstrate), and they will generally hassle socializers at every opportunity simply because it's so easy to get them annoyed. However, the main reason that socializers tend to despise killers is that they have completely antisocial motives, whereas socializers have (or like to think they have) a much more friendly and helpful attitude to life. The fact that many socializers take attacks on their personae personally only compounds their distaste for killers.

It could be argued that killers do have a positive role to play from the point of view of socializers. There are generally two defenses made for their existence: 1) without killers, socializers would have little to talk about; 2) without evil as a contrast, there is no good. The former is patently untrue, as socializers will happily talk about anything and everything; it may be that it helps provide a catalyst for long conversations, but only if it isn't an everyday occurrence. The second argument is more difficult to defend against (being roughly equivalent to the reason why God allows the devil to exist); however, it presupposes that those who attack other players are the only example of nasty people in a MUD. In fact, there is plenty of opportunity for players of all persuasions to behave obnoxiously to one another; killers merely do it more openly, and (if allowed) in the context of the game world.

Increasing the number of killers will decrease the number of socializers by a much greater degree. Decreasing the number of killers will likewise greatly encourage (or, rather, fail to discourage) socializers to play the MUD.

Killers vs. Achievers

Killers regard achievers as their natural prey. Achievers are good fighters (because they've learned the necessary skills against mobiles), but they're not quite as good as killers, who are more specialized. This gives the "thrill of the chase" which many killers enjoy—an achiever may actually be able to escape, but will usually succumb at some stage, assuming they don't see sense and quit first. Achievers also dislike being attacked, which makes the experience of attacking them all the more fun; furthermore, it is unlikely that they will stop playing after being set back by a killer, and thus they can be "fed upon" again, later. The main disadvantage of pursuing achievers, however, is that an achiever can get so incensed at being attacked that they decide to take revenge. A killer may thus innocently enter a game only to find a heavily armed achiever lying in wait, which rather puts the boot on the other foot...

Note that there is a certain sub-class of killers, generally run by wiz-level players, who have a more ethical point to their actions. In particular, their aim is to "test" players for their "suitability" to advance to the higher levels themselves. In general, such personae should not be regarded as falling into the killer category, although in some instances the ethical aspect is merely an excuse to indulge in killing sprees without fear of sanction. Rather, these killers tend to be run by people in either the achievement category (protecting their own investment) or the explorer category (trying to teach their victims how to defend themselves against *real* killers).

Increasing the number of achievers will, over time, increase the number of killers in a typically Malthusian fashion.

Killers vs. Explorers

Killers tend to leave explorers alone. Not only can explorers be formidable fighters (with many obscure, unexpected tactics at their disposal), but they often don't fret about being attacked—a fact which is very frustrating for killers. Sometimes, particularly annoying explorers will simply ignore a killer's attack, and make no attempt whatsoever to defend against it; this is the ultimate in cruelty to killers. For more long-term effects, though, a killer's being beaten by an explorer has more impact on the game: the killer will feel shame, their reputation will suffer, and the explorer will pass on survival tactics to everyone else. In general, then, killers will steer well clear of even half-decent explorers, except when they have emptied a game of everyone else and are so desperate for a fix that even an explorer looks tempting...

Increasing the number of explorers will slightly decrease the number of killers.

Killers vs. Socializers

Killers regard socializers with undisguised glee. It's not that socializers are in any way a challenge, as usually they will be pushovers in combat; rather, socializers feel a dreadful hurt when attacked (especially if it results in the loss of their persona), and it is this which killers enjoy about it. Besides, killers tend to like to have a bad reputation, and if there's one way to get people to talk about you, it's to attack a prominent socializer...

Increasing the number of socializers will increase the number of killers, although of course the number of socializers wouldn't remain increased for very long if that happened.

Killers vs. Killers

Killers try not to cross the paths of other killers, except in pre-organized challenge matches. Part of the psychology of killers seems to be that they wish to be viewed as somehow superior to other players; being killed by a killer in open play would undermine their reputation, and therefore they avoid risking it (compare killers vs. explorers). This means that nascent or wannabe killers are often put off their chosen particular career path because they themselves are attacked by more experienced killers and soundly thrashed. For this reason, it can take a very long time to increase the killer population in a MUD, even if all the conditions are right for them to thrive; killer numbers rise grindingly slowly, unless competent killers are imported from another MUD to swell the numbers artificially.

Killers will occasionally work in teams, but only as a short-term exercise; they will usually revert to stalking their victims solo in the next session they play.

There are two cases where killers might be attacked by players who, superficially, look like other killers. One of these is the "killer killer," usually run by wiz-level players, which has been discussed earlier. The other is in the true hack-and-slash type of MUD, where the whole aim of the game is to kill other personae, and no-one particularly minds being killed because they weren't expecting to last very long anyway. This type of play does not appeal to "real" killers, because it doesn't cause people emotional distress when their personae are deleted (indeed, socializers prefer it more than killers do). However, it's better than nothing.

The only effect that killers have on other killers is in reducing the number of potential victims available. This, in theory, should keep the number of killers down, however in practice killers will simply attack less attractive victims instead. It takes a very drastic reduction in the number of players before established killers will decide to stop playing a MUD and move elsewhere, by which time it is usually too late to save the MUD concerned.

Dynamics

From the discussion in the previous section, it is possible to summarize the interactions between player types as follows:

To increase the number of achievers:

- Reduce the number of killers, but not by too much.
- If killer numbers are high, increase the number of explorers.

To decrease the number of achievers:

- Increase the number of killers.
- If killer numbers are low, reduce the number of explorers.

To increase the number of explorers:

·   Increase the number of explorers.

To decrease the number of explorers:

·   Massively increase the number of killers.

To increase the number of socializers:

·   Slightly decrease the number of killers.

·   Increase the number of socializers.

To decrease the number of socializers:

·   Slightly increase the number of killers.

·   Massively increase the number of achievers.

·   Massively decrease the number of achievers.

·   Decrease the number of socializers.

To increase the number of killers:

·   Increase the number of achievers.

·   Massively decrease the number of explorers.

·   Increase the number of socializers.

To decrease the number of killers

·   Decrease the number of achievers.

·   Massively increase the number of explorers.

·   Decrease the number of socializers.

What are the dynamics of this model? In other words, if players of each type were to trickle into a system, how would it affect the overall make-up of the player population?

The following diagram illustrates the flow of influence. Each arrow shows a relationship, from the blunt end to the pointed end. Ends are marked with a plus or minus to show an increase or decrease respectively; the symbols are doubled up to indicate a massive increase or decrease. Example: the line

```
killers + ———> - achievers
```

means that increasing the number of killers will decrease the number of achievers.

A graphical version of the figure appears at the end of the paper.[2]

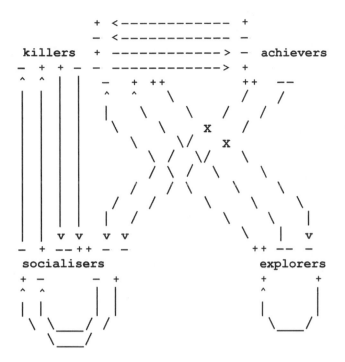

From this, it can be seen that the numbers of killers and achievers is basically an equilibrium: increasing the number of achievers will increase the number of killers, which will in turn dampen down the increase in the number of achievers and thereby reduce the number of excess killers.

The explorer population is almost inert: only huge numbers of killers will reduce it. It should be noted, however, that massively increasing the number of explorers is the *only* way to reduce the number of killers without also reducing the player numbers in other groups. Because increasing the number of explorers in a MUD generally encourages others to join (and non-explorers to experiment with exploration), this gives a positive feedback which will eventually reduce the killer population (although recall the earlier point concerning how few people are, by nature, explorers).

The most volatile group of people is that of the socializers. Not only is it highly sensitive to the number of killers, but it has both positive and negative feedback on itself, which amplifies any changes. An increase in the number of socializers will lead to yet more socializers, but it will also increase the number of killers; this, in turn, will reduce the number of socializers drastically, which will feed back into a yet greater reduction. It is possible for new socializers to arrive in large enough quantities for a downward spiral in numbers not to be inevitable, but it is unlikely that such a system could remain viable in over a long period of time.

This analysis of the dynamics of the relationships between players leads naturally to a consideration of what configurations could be considered stable. There are four:

1) Killers and achievers in equilibrium. If the number of killers gets too high, then the achievers will be driven off, which will cause the number of killers to fall also (through lack of victims). If there aren't enough killers, then achievers feel the MUD isn't a sufficient challenge (there being no way to "lose" in it), and they will gradually leave; new killers could appear, attracted by the glut of potential prey, however this happens so slowly that its impact is less than that of the disaffection among achievers. Socializers who venture out of whatever safe rooms are available eventually fall prey to killers, and leave the game. Those who stay find that there aren't many interesting (to them) people around with whom to talk, and they too drift off. Explorers potter around, but are not a sufficient presence to affect the number of killers.

2) A MUD dominated by socializers. Software changes to the MUD are made which prevent (or at least seriously discourage) killers from practicing their craft on socializers; incoming socializers are encouraged by those already there, and a chain reaction starts. There are still achievers and explorers, but they are swamped by the sheer volume of socializers. The number of socializers is limited only by external factors, or the presence of killers masquerading as socializers. If the population of socializers drops below a certain critical level, then the chain reaction reverses and almost all the players will leave, however only events outside the MUD would cause that to happen once the critical mass had been reached.

3) A MUD where all groups have a similar influence (although not necessarily similar numbers). By nurturing explorers using software means (i.e. giving the game great depth or "mystique," or encouraging non-explorers to dabble for a while by regularly adding new areas and features), the overall population of explorers will gradually rise, and the killer population will be held in check by them. The killers who remain do exert an influence on the number of socializers, sufficient to stop them from going into fast-breeder mode, but insufficient to initiate an exodus. Achievers are set upon by killers often enough to feel that their achievements in the game have meaning. This is perhaps the most balanced form of MUD, since players can change their position on the interest graph far more freely: achievers can become explorers, explorers can become socializers, socializers can become achievers—all without sacrificing stability. However, actually attaining that stability in the first place is very difficult indeed; it requires not only a level of game design beyond what most MUDs can draw on, but time and player management skills that aren't usually available to MUD administrators. Furthermore, the administrators need to recognize that they are aiming for a player mix of this kind in advance, because the chances of its occurring accidentally are slim.

4) A MUD with no players. The killers have killed/frightened off everyone else, and left to find some other MUD in which to ply their trade. Alternatively, a MUD structured expressly for socializers never managed to acquire a critical mass of them.

Other types could conceivably exist, but they are very rare if they do. The dynamics model is, however, imprecise: it takes no account of outside factors, which may influence player types or the relationships between then. It is thus possible that some of the more regimented MUDs (e.g. role-playing MUDs, educational MUDs, group therapy MUDs) have an external dynamic (e.g. fandom interest in a subject, instructions from a teacher/trainer, tolerance of others as a means to advance the self) which adds to their cohesion, and that this could make an otherwise flaky configuration hold together. So other stable MUD forms may, therefore, still be out there.

It might be argued that "role-playing" MUDs form a separate category, on a par with "gamelike" and "social" MUDs. However, I personally favor the view that role-playing is merely a strong framework within which the four types of player still operate: some people will role-play to increase their power over the game (achievers); others will do so to explore the wonder of the game world (explorers); others will do so because they enjoy interacting and co-operating within the context that the role-playing environment offers (socializers); others will do it because it gives them a legitimate excuse to hurt other players (killers). I have not, however, undertaken a study of role-playing MUDs, and it could well be that there is a configuration of player types peculiar to many of them which would be unstable were it not for the order imposed by enforcing role-play. It certainly seems likely that robust role-playing rules could make it easier for a MUD to achieve type 3) stability, whatever.

At this point, we return to the social/gamelike MUD debate.

Ignoring the fourth (null) case from the above, it is now much easier to see why there is a schism. Left to market forces, a MUD will either gravitate towards type 1) ("gamelike") or type 2) ("social"), depending on its administrators' line on player-killing (more precisely: how much being "killed" annoys socializers). However, the existence of type 3) MUDs, albeit in smaller numbers because of the difficulty of reaching the steady state, does show that it is possible to have both socializers and achievers co-existing in significant numbers in the same MUD.

It's very easy to label a MUD as either "hack-and-slash" or "slack-and-hash," depending on whether or not player-killing is allowed. However, using player-killing as the only defining factor in any distinction is an over-generalization, as it groups together type 1) and type 3) MUDs. These two types of MUD should *not* be considered as identical forms: the socializing which occurs in a type 3) MUD simply isn't possible in a type 1), and as a result, the sense of community in type 3)s is very strong. It is no accident that type 3) MUDs are the ones preferred commercially, because they can hold onto their players for far longer than the other two forms. A type 1) MUD is only viable commercially if there is a sufficiently large well of potential players to draw upon, because of the much greater churn rate these games have. Type 2)s have a similarly high turnover; indeed, when TinyMUD first arrived on the scene it was almost slash-and-burn, with games lasting around six months on university computers before a combination of management breakdown (brought on by player boredom) and resource hogging would force them to close down—with no other MUDs permitted on the site for perhaps years afterwards.

This explains why some MUDs perceived by socializers to be "gamelike" can actually be warm, friendly places, while others are nasty and vicious: the former are type 3), and the latter are type 1). Players who enter the type 3)s, expecting them to be type 1)s, may be pleasantly surprised (Bruckman, 1993). However, it should be noted that this initial warm behavior is sometimes the approach used by administrators to ensure a new player's further participation in their particular MUD, and that, once hooked, a player may find that attitudes undergo a subtle change (Epperson, 1995).

As mentioned earlier, this paper is not intended to promote any one particular style of MUD. Whether administrators aim for type 1), 2) or 3) is up to them—they're all MUDs, and they address different needs. However, the fact that they are all MUDs, and not "MU*s" (or any other abbreviation-of-the-day), really should be emphasized.

To summarize: "gamelike" MUDs are the ones in which the killer-achiever equilibrium has been reached, i.e. type 1); "social" MUDs are the ones in which the pure-social stability point has been reached, i.e. type 2), and this is the basis upon which they differ. There is a type 3) "all round" (my term) MUD, which exhibits both social and gamelike traits, however such MUDs are scarce because the conditions necessary to reach the stable point are difficult or time-consuming to arrange.

Overbalancing a MUD

Earlier, the effect of taking each axis on the interest graph to its extremes was used to give an indication of what would happen if a MUD was pushed so far that it lost its MUDness. It was noted, though, that along the axes was not the only way a MUD could be tilted.

What would happen if, in an effort to appeal to certain types of player, a MUD were overcompensated in their favor?

Tilting a MUD towards achievers would make it obsessed with gameplay. Players would spend their time looking for tactics to improve their position, and the presence of other players would become unnecessary. The result would be effectively a single-player adventure game (SUD?).

Tilting towards explorers would add depth and interest, but remove much of the activity. Spectacle would dominate over action, and again there would be no need for other players. The result of this is basically an online book.

Tilting towards socializers removes all gameplay, and centers on communication. Eventually, all sense of the virtual world is lost, and a chatline or IRC-style CB program results.

Tilting towards killers is more difficult, because this type of player is parasitic on the other three types. The emphasis on causing grief has to be sacrificed in favor of the thrill of the chase, and bolstered by the use of quick thinking and skill to overcome adversity in clever (but violent) ways. In other words, this becomes an arcade ("shoot 'em up") type of game.

It's a question of balance: if something is added to a MUD to tilt the graph one way, other mechanisms will need to be in place to counterbalance it (preferably automatically). Otherwise, what results is a SUD, book, chatline or arcade game. It's the combination that makes MUDs unique—and special. It *is* legitimate to say that anything, which goes too far in any direction, is not a MUD; it is *not* legitimate to say that something, which doesn't go far enough in any direction, is not a MUD. So long as a system is a (text-based) multi-user virtual world, that's enough.

Summary

To answer the questions posed in the preface:

> Are MUDs

- games? Like chess, tennis, D&D?
  Yes, to achievers.

- pastimes? Like reading, gardening, cooking?
  Yes, to explorers.

- sports? Like huntin', shooting', fishin'?
  Yes, to killers.

- entertainments? Like nightclubs, TV, concerts?
  Yes, to socializers.

End Notes

1. This paper is an April 1996 extension of an earlier article, "Who Plays MUAs" (Bartle, 1990a). As a result of this, and of the fact that I am not a trained psychologist, do not expect a conventionally rigorous approach to the subject matter.

2. In the figure below, green indicates increasing numbers and red indicates decreasing numbers. A red line with a green arrowhead means that decreasing numbers of the box pointed from lead to increasing numbers of the box pointed to; a red line with a red arrowhead would mean that a decrease in one leads to a decrease in the other, and so on. The thickness of the line shows the strength of the effect: thin lines mean there's only a small effect; medium lines mean there's an effect involving roughly equal numbers of players from both boxes; thick lines means there's a great effect, magnifying the influence of the origin box.

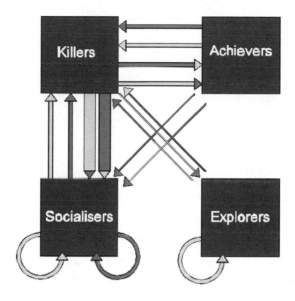

References

Aspnes, J. (1989). TinyMUD [C] http://ftp.tcp.com/ftp/pub/mud/TinyMUD/tinymud-pc.1.0.tar.gz

Bartle, R. A. (1985). MUD2 [MUDDLE] MUSE Ltd, Colchester, Essex, UK.

Bartle, R. A. (1990a). Who Plays MUAs? *Comms Plus!,* October/November 1990 18-19.

Bartle, R. A. (1990b). Interactive Multi-Player Computer Games. MUSE Ltd, Colchester, Essex, UK ftp://ftp.lambda.moo.mud.org/pub/MOO/papers/mudreport.txt

Bruckman, A. S. (1992). *Identity Workshop: Emergent Social and Psychological Phenomena in Text-Based Virtual Reality.* MIT Media Laboratory, Cambridge, Massachusetts. ftp://media.mit.edu/pub/asb/papers/identity-workshop.ps

Bruckman, A. S. (1993). Gender Swapping on the Internet Proc. INET-93 ftp://media.mit.edu/pub/asb/papers/gender-swapping.txt

Bruckman, A. S. & Resnick, M. (1993). Virtual Professional Community: Results from the MediaMOO Project. MIT Media Laboratory, Cambridge, Massachusetts. ftp://media.mit.edu/pub/asb/papers/convergence.txt

Bruckman, A. S. (1994a). Workshop: "Serious" Uses of MUDs? *Proc. DIAC-94* ftp://media.mit.edu/pub/asb/papers/serious-diac94.txt

Bruckman, A. S. (1994b). Approaches to Managing Deviant Behavior in Virtual Communities. MIT Media Laboratory, Cambridge, Massachusetts. ftp://media.mit.edu/pub/asb/deviance-chi94.txt

Burka, L. P. (1995). The MUDline. http://www.ccs.neu.edu/home/lpb/mudline.html

Carton, S. (1995). *Internet Virtual Worlds Quick Tour: MUDs, MOOs and MUSHes: Interactive games, Conferences and Forums.* Ventana Press, Chapel Hill, North Carolina.

Caspian-Kaufman, J. (1995). *Sid Meier's CivNET: Instruction Manual Microprose,* Hunt Valley, Maryland.

Cherny, L. (1995a). The Modal Complexity of Speech Events in a Social MUD. *Electronic Journal of Communication,* Summer 1995. ftp://bhasha.stanford.edu/pub/cherny/ejc.txt

Cherny, L. (1995b). The Situated Behaviour of MUD Back Channels. Dept. Linguistics, Stanford University, California. ftp://bhasha.stanford.edu/pub/cherny/aaai.ps

Clodius, J. A. (1994). Concepts of Space in a Virtual Community. http://tinylondon.ucsd.edu/~jen/space.html

Curtis, P. (1992). Mudding: Social Phenomena in Text-Based Virtual Realities. *Proc. DIAC-92* ftp://ftp.lambda.moo.mud.org/pub/MOO/papers/DIAC92.txt

Curtis, P. & Nichols, D. A. (1993). MUDs Grow Up: Social Virtual Reality in the Real World. Xerox PARC, Palo Alto, California. ftp://ftp.lambda.moo.mud.org/pub/MOO/papers/MUDsGrowUp.txt

Dibbell, J. (1993). A Rape in Cyberspace. *The Village Voice,* December 21, 1993. ftp://ftp.lambda.moo.mud.org/pub/MOO/papers/VillageVoice.txt

Emert, H. G. (1993). "X" Marks the Spot. East Stroudsburg University, Pennsylvania. http://www-f.rrz.uni-koeln.de/themen/cmc/text/emert.n01.txt

Eddy, A. (1994). Internet After Hours Prima, Rocklin, California.

Epperson, H. L. (1995). Patterns of Social Behaviour in Computer-Mediated Communications. Dept. Sociology, Rice University. http://www.eff.org/pub/Net_culture/Misc_net_culture/ web_social_behaviour.paper

Evard, R. (1993). Collaborative Networked Communication: MUDs as System Tools. *Proc. LISA-93.* http://www.ccs.neu.edu/home/remy/documents/cncmast.html

Fanderclai, T. F. (1995). MUDs in Education: New Environments, New Pedagogies. *Computer-Mediated Communication Magazine,* 2(1), 8.

Farmer, F. R., Morningstar, C. & Crockford, D. (1994). From Habitat to Global Cyberspace. *Proc. CompCon-94*, IEEE. http://www.communities.com/paper/hab2cybr.html

Kort, B. (1991). The MUSE as an Educational Medium BBN Labs, Cambridge, Massachusetts. ftp://musenet.bbn.com/pub/micromuse

Mauldin, M. L. (1994). Chatterbots, TinyMUDs and the Turing Test: Entering the Loebner Prize Competition. *Proc. AAAI-94.* http://fuzine.mt.cs.cmu.edu/mlm/aaai94.html

Moock, C. (1996). Virtual Campus at the University of Waterloo. http://arts.uwaterloo.ca:80/~camoock/virtual_classroom.htm

Norrish, J. (1995). MU*s. http://www.vuw.ac.nz/~jamie/mud/mud.html

Poirier, J. R. (1994). Interactive Multiuser Realities: MUDs, MOOs, MUCKs, and MUSHes. *The Internet Unleashed, 1192-1127.* SAMS Publishing, Indianapolis, Indiana.

Reid, E. (1994). Cultural Formations in Text-Based Virtual Realities. Dept. English, University of Melbourne, Australia. ftp://ftp.lambda.moo.mud.org/pub/MOO/papers/CulturalFormations.txt

Riner, R. D. & Clodius, J. A. (1995). Simulating Future Histories: The NAU Solar System Simulation and Mars Settlement. *Anthropology & Education Quarterly 26(1):95-104.* http://tinylondon.ucsd.edu/~jen/solsys.html

Rosenberg, M. S. (1992). Virtual Reality: Reflections of Life, Dreams and Technology. An Ethnography of a Computer Society. ftp://ftp.lambda.moo.mud.org/pub/MOO/papers/ethnography.txt

Roush, W. (1993). The Virtual STS Centre on MediaMOO: Issues and Challenges as Non-Technical Users Enter Social Virtual Spaces MIT Media Laboratory, Cambridge, Massachusetts. ftp://media.mit.edu/pub/MediaMOO/Papers/STS-Centre

Urdang, L. & Manser, M. (1980). *The Pan Dictionary of Synonyms and Antonyms Pan Reference,* London, UK.

Whitlock, T. D. (1994). Fuck Art, Let's Kill!: Towards a Post Modern Community. gopher://actlab.rtf.utexas.edu/00/art_and_tech/rtf_papers/pmc.terrorism

Whitlock, T. D. (1994b). Technological Hierarchy in MOO: Reflections on Power in Cyberspace http://www.actlab.utexas.edu/~smack/papers/TechHier.txt

Declaring the Rights of Players

Raph Koster

Context

Back in 2000, I was thinking a lot about the issues surrounding good customer service in online games. It struck me that really, what I was pondering was governance more than the traditional customer-provider relationship. The original form of the declaration was posted to the MUD-Dev mailing list, and the ensuing discussion is what led to the full form of the article as you read it here. Since it was first published, it has attracted a fair amount of attention from the legal community. There are even a handful of online worlds that have signed one form or another of the document.

The Rules of a Game

Game Communities

Raph Koster is the Chief Creative Officer at Sony Online Entertainment. He was the creative director on Star Wars Galaxies and the lead designer on Ultima Online, and writes and speaks frequently on issues surrounding online worlds. His website is www.legendmud.org/raph/.

Do players of virtual worlds have rights?

One of those questions that given my position, I shouldn't write about. No matter what, any answer I give is bound to be wrong, either from the perspective of my employers or my customers. Heck, even over on the non-commercial side of the fence, it's likely to raise some hackles among hardworking mud admins.

The pesky thing about rights is that they keep coming up. Players keep claiming that they have them. Admins keep liberally applying the word like some magic balm ("oh, you have every right to be upset...), in every circumstance except the ones where the players want the notion of rights taken seriously. Of course, administrators of any virtual space are loathe to "grant players rights" because it curbs their ability to take action against people, restricts their ability to walk away from it all, holds them to standards they may not be able to live up to.

Here's a great example of a mud rights document from IgorMUD that I had to include, well, because:

===

```
HELP RIGHTS
Igor has adopted this bill of unalienable player rights, written by
Jacob Hallen aka Tintin:

PARAGRAPH 1
Every player has the right to be a frog.

PARAGRAPH 2
Should the system the player is on fail to implement the "being frog"
functionality, the player has a right to pretend he/she/it/Garlic is
a frog.

PARAGRAPH 3
If a player does not exercise the right to be a frog, or to pretend
to be one, other players have a right to pretend it/she/Garlic/he is
a frog.
```

===

There's at least one theory of rights, which says that rights aren't "granted" by anyone. They arise because the populace decides to grant them to themselves. Under this logic, the folks who rose up in France weren't looking for some king with a soon-to-be-foreshortened head to tell them, "You've got the right to live your lives freely." They told themselves that they had that right, and because they had said so, it was so. The flip side of this is that unless you continually fight to make that claim true, then it won't stick. The battleground is not a military one: it's a perception one; as long as everyone is convinced that people have rights, they do. They're inalienable only as long as only a minority does the, uh, aliening. And, of course, especially as long as they are enshrined in some sort of law. In other words, the guys in charge sign away a chunk of power, in writing, that the populace expects them to sign away.

There's another theory of rights which holds them to be intrinsic to people. Under this far more rigid standard, all those cultures which fail to grant them are benighted bastions of savagery. The harder part here is agreeing on what rights are intrinsic to all people everywhere—cultural differences tend to make that hard.

Many mud admins are of the belief that their muds are their private playgrounds. That they have discretion on who enters and who gets to stay. That they can choose to eject someone on any grounds whatsoever, can delete a character at a whim, can play favorites and choose to grant administrative favors to their friends. Even in pay-for-play circles, it is always made very clear who owns the data, who has to sign Terms of Service, etc. There's a bunch of this that is antithetical to the notion of rights.

Now, it's pretty clear that there are some rights which leak over from the real world into the virtual. If your local pay-for-play mud operator isn't providing adequate service, you can report them to the Better Business Bureau; there are probably sexual discrimination laws and harassment laws and slander laws that apply equally well in both kinds of space. But rights (and much less legislation) have not caught up to the notion of virtual spaces very well. Which makes for an interesting thought experiment.

What if we declared the rights of avatars?

I've based what follows on a couple of seminal documents: The Declaration of the Rights of Man and of the Citizen approved by the National Assembly of France on August 26 of 1789; and the first ten amendments to the Constitution of the United States, perhaps better known as the Bill of Rights. This is, perhaps, not the best basis from which to begin a stab at this hypothetical exercise, given our multicultural world today; some have suggested that a better starting point might be the United Nations Charter of Rights and Freedoms. I admit that one reason for choosing the version I did was its language, not its content per se.

So let's give it a whirl. This is all still hypothetical, OK?

A Declaration of the Rights of Avatars

When a time comes that new modes and venues exist for communities, and said modes are different enough from the existing ones that question arises as to the applicability of past custom and law; and when said venues have become a forum for interaction and society for the general public regardless of the intent of the creators of said venue; and at a time when said communities and spaces are rising in popularity and are now widely exploited for commercial gain; it behooves those involved in said communities and venues to affirm and declare the inalienable rights of the members of said communities. Therefore herein have been set forth those rights which are inalienable rights of the inhabitants of virtual spaces of all sorts, in their form henceforth referred to as avatars, in order that this declaration may continually remind those who hold power over virtual spaces and the avatars contained therein of their duties and responsibilities; in order that the forms of administration of a virtual space may be at any time compared to that of other virtual spaces; and in order that the grievances of players may hereafter be judged against the explicit rights set forth, to better govern the virtual space and improve the general welfare and happiness of all.

Therefore this document holds the following truths to be self-evident: That avatars are the manifestation of actual people in an online medium, and that their utterances, actions, thoughts, and emotions should be considered to be as valid as the utterances, actions, thoughts, and emotions of people in any other forum, venue, location, or space. That the well-established rights of man approved by the National Assembly of France on August 26th of 1789 do therefore apply to avatars in full measure saving only the aspects of said rights that do not pertain in a virtual space or which must be abrogated in order to ensure the continued existence of the space in question. That by the act of affirming membership in the community within the virtual space, the avatars form a social contract with the community, forming a populace which may and must self-affirm and self-impose rights and concomitant restrictions upon their behavior. That the nature of virtual spaces is such that there must, by physical law, always be a higher power or administrator who maintains the space and has complete power over all participants, but who is undeniably part of the community formed within the space and who must therefore take action in accord with that which benefits the space as well as the participants, and who therefore also has the rights of avatars and may have other rights as well. That the ease of moving between virtual spaces and the potential transience of the community does not limit or reduce the level of emotional and social involvement that avatars may have with the community, and that therefore the ease of moving between virtual spaces and the potential transience of the community does not in any way limit, curtail, or remove these rights from avatars on the alleged grounds that avatars can always simply leave.

Articles:

1. Avatars are created free and equal in rights. Special powers or privileges shall be founded solely on the common good, and not based on whim, favoritism, nepotism, or the caprice of those who hold power. Those who act as ordinary avatars within the space shall all have only the rights of normal avatars.

2. The aim of virtual communities is the common good of its citizenry, from which arise the rights of avatars. Foremost among these rights is the right to be treated as people and not as disembodied, meaningless, soulless puppets. Inherent in this right are therefore the natural and inalienable rights of man. These rights are liberty, property, security, and resistance to oppression.

3. The principle of all sovereignty in a virtual space resides in the inalterable fact that somewhere there resides an individual who controls the hardware on which the virtual space is running, and the software with which it is created, and the database which makes up its existence. However, the body populace has the right to know and demand the enforcement of the standards by which this individual uses this power over the community, as authority must proceed from the community; a community that does not know the standards by which the administrators use their power is a community which permits its administrators to have no standards, and is therefore a community abetting in tyranny.

4. Liberty consists of the freedom to do anything which injures no one else including the weal of the community as a whole and as an entity instantiated on hardware and by software; the exercise of the natural rights of avatars is therefore limited solely by the rights of other avatars sharing the same space and participating in the same community. These limits can only be determined by a clear code of conduct.

5. The code of conduct can only prohibit those actions and utterances that are hurtful to society, inclusive of the harm that may be done to the fabric of the virtual space via hurt done to the

hardware, software, or data; and likewise inclusive of the harm that may be done to the individual who maintains said hardware, software, or data, in that harm done to this individual may result in direct harm done to the community.

6. The code of conduct is the expression of the general will of the community and the will of the individual who maintains the hardware and software that makes up the virtual space. Every member of the community has the right to contribute either directly or via representatives in the shaping of the code of conduct as the culture of the virtual space evolves, particularly as it evolves in directions that the administrator did not predict; the ultimate right of the administrator to shape and define the code of conduct shall not be abrogated, but it is clear that the administrator therefore has the duty and responsibility to work with the community to arrive at a code of conduct that is shaped by the input of the community. As a member of the community himself, the administrator would be damaging the community itself if he failed in this responsibility, for abrogation of this right of avatars could result in the loss of population and therefore damage to the common weal.

7. No avatar shall be accused, muzzled, toaded, jailed, banned, or otherwise punished except in the cases and according to the forms prescribed by the code of conduct. Any one soliciting, transmitting, executing, or causing to be executed, any arbitrary order, shall be punished, even if said individual is one who has been granted special powers or privileges within the virtual space. But any avatar summoned or arrested in virtue of the code of conduct shall submit without delay, as resistance constitutes an offense.

8. The code of conduct shall provide for such punishments only as are strictly and obviously necessary, and no one shall suffer punishment except it be legally inflicted according to the provisions of a code of conduct promulgated before the commission of the offense; save in the case where the offense endangered the continued existence of the virtual space by attacking the hardware or software that provide the physical existence of the space.

9. As all avatars are held innocent until they shall have been declared guilty, if detainment, temporary banning, jailing, gluing, freezing, or toading shall be deemed indispensable, all harshness not essential to the securing of the prisoner's person shall be severely repressed by the code of conduct.

10. No one shall be disquieted on account of his opinions, provided their manifestation does not disturb the public order established by the code of conduct.

11. The free communication of ideas and opinions is one of the most precious of the rights of man. Every avatar may, accordingly, speak, write, chat, post, and print with freedom, but shall be responsible for such abuses of this freedom as shall be defined by the code of conduct, most particularly the abuse of affecting the performance of the space or the performance of a given avatar's representation of the space.

12. The security of the rights of avatars requires the existence of avatars with special powers and privileges, who are empowered to enforce the provisions of the code of conduct. These powers and privileges are therefore granted for the good of all and not for the personal advantage of those to whom they shall be entrusted. These powers and privileges are also therefore not an entitlement, and can and should be removed in any instance where they are no longer used for the good of all, even if the offense is merely inactivity.

13. A common contribution may, at the discretion of the individual who maintains the hardware, the software, and the data that make up the virtual space, be required in order to maintain the existence of avatars who enforce the code of conduct and to maintain the hardware and the software and the continued existence of the virtual space. Avatars have the right to know the nature and amount of the contribution in advance, and said required contribution should be equitably distributed among all the citizens without regard to their social position; special rights and privileges shall never pertain to the avatar who contributes more except insofar as the special powers and privileges require greater resources from the hardware, software, or data store, and would not be possible save for the resources obtainable with the contribution; and as long as any and all avatars are able to make this contribution and therefore gain the powers and privileges if they so choose; nor shall any articles of this declaration be contingent upon a contribution being made.

14. The community has the right to require of every administrator or individual with special powers and privileges granted for the purpose of administration, an account of his administration.

15. A virtual community in which the observance of the code of conduct is not assured and universal, nor the separation of powers defined, has no constitution at all.

16. Since property is an inviolable and sacred right, and the virtual equivalent is integrity and persistence of data, no one shall be deprived thereof except where public necessity, legally determined per the code of conduct, shall clearly demand it, and then only on condition that the avatar shall have been previously and equitably indemnified, saving only cases wherein the continued existence of the space is jeopardized by the existence or integrity of said data.

17. The administrators of the virtual space shall not abridge the freedom of assembly, save to preserve the performance and continued viability of the virtual space.

18. Avatars have the right to be secure in their persons, communications, designated private spaces, and effects, against unreasonable snooping, eavesdropping, searching and seizures, no activity pertaining thereto shall be undertaken by administrators save with probable cause supported by affirmation, particularly describing the goal of said investigations.

19. The enumeration in this document of rights shall not be construed to deny or disparage others retained by avatars.—*January 26th, 2000*

*   *   *   *   *

(Yes, I've had this knocking around my desk for that long.)

Lofty, eh? And I don't doubt that there's some folks out there right now seizing on this as an important document. For all I know, maybe it is.

But there's also some other folks who think that this exercise is plain dangerous. As an example, let me take a co-worker of mine to whom I showed an early draft. He pointed out that virtual world servers run on somebody's hardware. And that most declarations of rights give rights over personal property. By declaring that avatars have rights, we're abrogating that administrator's right to personal property.

Others point out that it's superfluous. After all, if virtual worlds are just extensions of the real world, then surely all the rights we already have apply?

What if the virtual space in question is a game? Doesn't it, by its nature, obviate some of these rights?

And the biggie: what if you don't accept the basic premises in the prefatory paragraphs?

And that's where it gets interesting: in the details. I basically posted the document to a mailing list with a collection of the smartest virtual world admins and designers I know. Here's some of the various comments from admins from various walks of life, who got to see the original draft of this document (names hidden to protect the innocent, and remarks vastly paraphrased, because many of the objections were hypothetical ones).

A Declaration of the Rights of Avatars

> *Rights of **avatars**? Why not of "chess pieces"? Maybe the players have rights, but avatars are just representations.*

When a time comes that new modes and venues exist for communities, and said modes are different enough from the existing ones that question arises as to the applicability of past custom and law;

> *Come now, we're not **that** beyond current law, are we?*

> *It's been convincingly argued (by Dr. Barry Wellman among others) that the only difference that the Internet makes to communities is the speed of information transmission. So what's really new here?*

and when said venues have become a forum for interaction and society for the general public regardless of the intent of the creators of said venue; and at a time when said communities and spaces are rising in popularity and are now widely exploited for commercial gain; it behooves those involved in said communities and venues to affirm and declare the inalienable rights of the members of said communities. Therefore herein have been set forth those rights which are inalienable rights of the inhabitants of virtual spaces of all sorts, in their form henceforth referred to as avatars, in order that this declaration may continually remind those who hold power over virtual spaces and the avatars contained therein of their duties and responsibilities; in order that the forms of administration of a virtual space may be at any time compared to that of other virtual spaces; and in order that the grievances of players may hereafter be judged against the explicit rights set forth, to better govern the virtual space and improve the general welfare and happiness of all.

> *Poppycock. I have not signed any agreement to keep the mud running, and I have no responsibility towards the players. In fact, I might have made **them** sign an agreement saying so!*

> *What if the players don't want to accept their rights?*

> *If admins see themselves as above the community, rather than part of it, this whole thing is for nothing.*

Therefore this document holds the following truths to be self-evident: That avatars are the manifestation of actual people in an online medium, and that their utterances, actions, thoughts, and emotions should be considered to be as valid as the utterances, actions, thoughts, and emotions of people in any other forum, venue, location, or space.

> *Plainly incorrect; for one thing, the legal standards for expression in other media vary wildly from country to country and, in fact, from medium to medium. Bandwidth is arguably a commodity rare enough to fall under the same sort of regulation as the FCC in the US imposes upon use of the airwaves; certainly **my** bandwidth is a precious resource.*

> *Doesn't the fact that we have psychological disinhibition in virtual spaces argue against this?*

> *There's no consequences to online actions, as there are to real world actions. In fact, you could arguably consider online actions merely speech, and therefore bound by those standards.*

> *Don't tell me that you are going to consider AI avatars people too.*

That the well-established rights of man approved by the National Assembly of France on August 26th of 1789 do therefore apply to avatars in full measure saving only the aspects of said rights that do not pertain in a virtual space or which must be abrogated in order to ensure the continued existence of the space in question.

> *Uh, the rights of man approved by the National Assembly in France didn't last very long (only until Napoleon!) and I don't think anybody lives under them today.*

> *With your escape hatch in this clause, you've left all sorts of abuses available by justifying them as "necessary for the world's survival." Sort of like the "national security" exception real world governments use.*

That by the act of affirming membership in the community within the virtual space, the avatars form a social contract with the community, forming a populace which may and must self-affirm and self-impose rights and concomitant restrictions upon their behavior.

> *I don't believe in the notion of a social contract. Rights are granted explicitly by those in power.*

> *How do you affirm membership in a free text mud anyway?*

That the nature of virtual spaces is such that there must, by physical law, always be a higher power or administrator who maintains the space and has complete power over all participants, but who is undeniably part of the community formed within the space and who must therefore take action in accord with that which benefits the space as well as the participants, and who therefore also has the rights of avatars and may have other rights as well.

In many cases, the admins and the people with fingers on the power switch aren't the same people. What do you do then?

In fact, the person with a finger on the power switch is probably beholden to others —network service providers, maybe. What about them?

That the ease of moving between virtual spaces and the potential transience of the community does not limit or reduce the level of emotional and social involvement that avatars may have with the community, and that therefore the ease of moving between virtual spaces and the potential transience of the community does not in any way limit, curtail, or remove these rights from avatars on the alleged grounds that avatars can always simply leave.

"Why should the creator of an online community—especially one which is created explicitly for the purpose of entertainment—be bound to do certain things simply because others have chosen to make an emotional or social investment in his/her construct?" (A direct quote.)

Articles:

1. Avatars are created free and equal in rights. Special powers or privileges shall be founded solely on the common good, and not based on whim, favoritism, nepotism, or the caprice of those who hold power. Those who act as ordinary avatars within the space shall all have only the rights of normal avatars.

You know, we deny avatars the right to exist pre-emptively sometimes, by not approving them as new players.

Are you arguing that inequality within society is only justified if it improves the standing of the lowest common denominator? How Rawlsian. (No, I don't know who Rawls is either.)

2. The aim of virtual communities is the common good of its citizenry, from which arise the rights of avatars. Foremost among these rights is the right to be treated as people and not as

disembodied, meaningless, soulless puppets. Inherent in this right are therefore the natural and inalienable rights of man. These rights are liberty, property, security, and resistance to oppression.

> *There are literally muds out there intended for psychological experimentation. Muds where they **ask** for people banned elsewhere so they can test-to-destruction new game notions. What about those?*
>
> *What about orcs storming in and oppressing the players? Or NPC thieves?*
>
> *You just defined "the aim of virtual communities." That's not liberating, that's severely limiting! The beauty of virtual communities is their ability to be whatever we want them to be.*
>
> *What if I **want** you to treat me like a dog?*
>
> *Property, freedom from oppression—these are pretty Western rights, you know. Are we dragging Western ideology into primacy in the virtual setting here?*
>
> *Proudhon in his classic essay "What is Property? An Inquiry into the Principles of Right and Government" argues that property is inimical to liberty, you know. (No, I didn't.)*

3. The principle of all sovereignty in a virtual space resides in the inalterable fact that somewhere there resides an individual who controls the hardware on which the virtual space is running, and the software with which it is created, and the database which makes up its existence. However, the body populace has the right to know and demand the enforcement of the standards by which this individual uses this power over the community, as authority must proceed from the community; a community that does not know the standards by which the administrators use their power is a community which permits its administrators to have no standards, and is therefore a community abetting in tyranny.

> *It might not be an individual who controls the hardware. It could be a consortium too.*
>
> *But the players only have whatever powers the admins give them anyway.*

4. Liberty consists of the freedom to do anything which injures no one else including the weal of the community as a whole and as an entity instantiated on hardware and by software; the exercise of the natural rights of avatars is therefore limited solely by the rights of other avatars

sharing the same space and participating in the same community. These limits can only be determined by a clear code of conduct.

> *What if there are two muds on the same machine? According to this article, each can feel free to do whatever to starve the other of CPU and memory.*
>
> *I dare you to define injury!*
>
> *Arbitrary imposed rule sets are not the only way to define rights, you know.*

5. The code of conduct can only prohibit those actions and utterances that are hurtful to society, inclusive of the harm that may be done to the fabric of the virtual space via hurt done to the hardware, software, or data; and likewise inclusive of the harm that may be done to the individual who maintains said hardware, software, or data, in that harm done to this individual may result in direct harm done to the community.

> *What about a game? We might explicitly **want** Buffy to blast Bubba with a fire-ball spell.*
>
> *What about a virtual world for psych experiments? Or one which is not open to the public? Or one which is solely for the admin's amusement?*
>
> *Who gets to define hurtful? (me! me!)*
>
> *You just made admins immune from harm. This means that they are not part of the community and subject to the same things as everyone else. This means this document vanishes in a poof of logic and doesn't exist. QED.*

6. The code of conduct is the expression of the general will of the community and the will of the individual who maintains the hardware and software that makes up the virtual space. Every member of the community has the right to contribute either directly or via representatives in the shaping of the code of conduct as the culture of the virtual space evolves, particularly as it evolves in directions that the administrator did not predict; the ultimate right of the administrator to shape and define the code of conduct shall not be abrogated, but it is clear that the administrator therefore has the duty and responsibility to work with the community to arrive at a code of conduct that is shaped by the input of the community. As a member of the community himself, the administrator would be damaging the community itself if he failed in this responsibility, for abrogation of this right of avatars could result in the loss of population and therefore damage to the common weal.

Pfft. The one real right they incontrovertibly have is the right to log off.

Can guests contribute?

Who decides what contributions are worthy?

Do you automatically become a citizen, or is there some hurdle there?

So admins have to listen, not act. Big whoop-te-do.

7. No avatar shall be accused, muzzled, toaded, jailed, banned, or otherwise punished except in the cases and according to the forms prescribed by the code of conduct. Any one soliciting, transmitting, executing, or causing to be executed, any arbitrary order, shall be punished, even if said individual is one who has been granted special powers or privileges within the virtual space. But any avatar summoned or arrested in virtue of the code of conduct shall submit without delay, as resistance constitutes an offense.

What about games where arbitrary orders are part of the rules? As a simple example, what about "Simon Says"?

What about the notion that anything an admin orders you to do is by definition, the law?

*This isn't even a right, it's a law. Rights are trumps **against** laws. This says you have the right not to be banned unless the law says you can be banned. That's just window-dressing.*

8. The code of conduct shall provide for such punishments only as are strictly and obviously necessary, and no one shall suffer punishment except it be legally inflicted according to the provisions of a code of conduct promulgated before the commission of the offense; save in the case where the offense endangered the continued existence of the virtual space by attacking the hardware or software that provide the physical existence of the space.

What about games where the evil king arrests characters?

This really curtails the freedom admins have to police things. I have better things to do than try to anticipate everything a player might do.

According to this clause, the majority can establish a Code of Conduct that systematically removes all the rights, and the populace can't do anything about it.

801

9. As all avatars are held innocent until they shall have been declared guilty, if detainment, temporary banning, jailing, gluing, freezing, or toading shall be deemed indispensable, all harshness not essential to the securing of the prisoner's person shall be severely repressed by the code of conduct.

> *What if the game is harsh in its rules?*

> *In France the burden of proof rests on the accused, not the accuser. This is very North American.*

10. No one shall be disquieted on account of his opinions, provided their manifestation does not disturb the public order established by the code of conduct.

> *What about a game where no freedom of speech is part of the fictional game setting?*

11. The free communication of ideas and opinions is one of the most precious of the rights of man. Every avatar may, accordingly, speak, write, chat, post, and print with freedom, but shall be responsible for such abuses of this freedom as shall be defined by the code of conduct, most particularly the abuse of affecting the performance of the space or the performance of a given avatar's representation of the space.

> *What about a game where no freedom of speech is part of the fictional game setting?*

12. The security of the rights of avatars requires the existence of avatars with special powers and privileges, who are empowered to enforce the provisions of the code of conduct. These powers and privileges are therefore granted for the good of all and not for the personal advantage of those to whom they shall be entrusted. These powers and privileges are also therefore not an entitlement, and can and should be removed in any instance where they are no longer used for the good of all, even if the offense is merely inactivity.

> *What about a game where a corrupt government (even one that players can take on significant roles in) is part of the fictional game setting?*

> *Who removes these powers, and who grants them?*

13. A common contribution may, at the discretion of the individual who maintains the hardware, the software, and the data that make up the virtual space, be required in order to maintain the existence of avatars who enforce the code of conduct and to maintain the hardware and the software and the continued existence of the virtual space. Avatars have the right to know the

nature and amount of the contribution in advance, and said required contribution should be equitably distributed among all the citizens without regard to their social position; special rights and privileges shall never pertain to the avatar who contributes more except insofar as the special powers and privileges require greater resources from the hardware, software, or data store, and would not be possible save for the resources obtainable with the contribution; and as long as any and all avatars are able to make this contribution and therefore gain the powers and privileges if they so choose; nor shall any articles of this declaration be contingent upon a contribution being made.

You mean I can't discontinue someone's account because they didn't pay the bill?

*In combination with Article 16, does this mean if I delete a character I have to **pay** them for it?*

Doesn't this prevent a community from selectively appointing admins, coders, whatever, since it requires that anyone who can make the contribution be allowed to?

Does this mean that the game admins cannot sell a superpowered item for cash money to players? Because that seems to me to be a valid business model in use today by several companies.

In fact, if no rights are contingent upon a contribution, does that mean that you should not have to pay for your avatar or your access?

14. The community has the right to require of every administrator or individual with special powers and privileges granted for the purpose of administration, an account of his administration.

*What **sort** of statement?*

15. A virtual community in which the observance of the code of conduct is not assured and universal, nor the separation of powers defined, has no constitution at all.

No community can do the assuring—that requires admins.

What powers need to be separated and how?

*And do these really apply to the guy with his finger on the power button? He is unbannable, after all. If you did ban him, then there are **no** rules left because there is no ultimate enforcement. And then what?*

IMHO, bad customers or players have less rights than good ones!

Who are we to determine what is and is not a constitution?

"I think we have to acknowledge that any participation in this kind of Charter would be strictly voluntary. Therefore, in the interests of diplomacy, we shouldn't include statements that are going to alienate people from signing on to the document."

16. Since property is an inviolable and sacred right, and the virtual equivalent is integrity and persistence of data, no one shall be deprived thereof except where public necessity, legally determined per the code of conduct, shall clearly demand it, and then only on the condition that the avatar shall have been previously and equitably indemnified, saving only cases wherein the continued existence of the space is jeopardized by the existence or integrity of said data.

You mean monsters can't loot or break equipment? Or characters die?

This has too many exceptions. All you're saying is that players have the right to be pissed off if it happens.

17. The administrators of the virtual space shall not abridge the freedom of assembly, save to preserve the performance and continued viability of the virtual space.

What about a game setting where the right to assembly is not recognized?

18. Avatars have the right to be secure in their persons, communications, designated private spaces, and effects, against unreasonable snooping, eavesdropping, searching and seizures, no activity pertaining thereto shall be undertaken by administrators save with probable cause supported by affirmation, particularly describing the goal of said investigations.

On a lot of muds, eavesdropping on players is considered a perk (repellent, I know).

Worse yet, a lot of **countries** *don't grant their citizens this right when using the Internet. How are you going to resolve the discrepancy?*

What about all the other privacy issues? Depending on the mud, the admins may know a heck of a lot about you and your lifestyle.

19. The enumeration in this document of rights shall not be construed to deny or disparage others retained by avatars.

Then what is it supposed to do? This negates the whole exercise!

> *You know, in Canada, the Charter of Rights and Freedoms allows provincial governments to ignore the rulings of the Supreme Court and do whatever they want anyway. What about something like that?*

And a final comment, because it's priceless:

> *"If I were the United States Secretary of Virtual Worlds and I were shopping around for an administration policy for USMud I would start with something like this. If I were Joe Businessman, I might pay lip-service to this, but I sure as heck wouldn't put it in my user contract and leave myself open to lawsuits."*

*   *   *   *   *

There are a lot of interesting points raised above. One of the most interesting is, why should an admin feel bound by the fact that others have made an emotional investment in their work?

A sense of responsibility?

A coworker and I got into an argument over this. Let's say you publicly say, "Hey, my empty lot is now open to the public, anyone can squat there!" In the real world, you can actually get in trouble for not providing adequate sanitation. You'd certainly be reviled as an insensitive slob for kicking the squatters off. The sense here is that by making the invitation, you are entering into a social contract with the people who may or may not come by and use the empty lot.

We can argue endlessly whether this is fair or not. It's not, in my opinion (but what is?). But it's still the case. If I personally invite people to squat in my empty lot and then some of them die because I failed to cover the open mineshaft, well, I'd feel a sense of responsibility. It'd sure be nice not to, but I will because I have developed a certain level of personal ethics that entail feeling that way.

Plenty of mud admins do not have this particular ethic—nor am I arguing that they must. But I think arguing whether they should *is* a good debate to have.

I *would* argue that if your goal is to have a thriving empty lot that develops into a small town, then you probably *want* to feel this sense of responsibility, because the squatters are not likely to thrive unless someone with authority over the lot does have that personal ethic.

In the real world, we actually go further than that—we can be held responsible for things that happen to *trespassers* on our property.

Now, you may have different intentions for your virtual space—or your property. You may have just invited people there for the evening. So shutting down (as long as you announced it in advance) is still fine. There was an expectation established, after all.

It's also been pointed out by my panel of mud-*cum*-rights experts that technically, the property is intangible, which means we're actually in the realm of Group Intellectual Property Law, which is a nebulous construct even in the real world, much less the virtual. Here there be dragons.

On the point that the document as a whole restricts admins too much in managing the virtual spaces, I'd point out that having a clear code of conduct for both players *and* admins has been shown to make running the space go much smoother overall. Some argue that having unposted rules, or relying purely on community norms, helps curb the idiots or anarchists who find ways to skirt the posted rules. But we can reference the Minnie case (and the Finn case come to think of it) described in *My Tiny Life* for what can happen if unwritten rules are used against such a person and then others start to fear that it could be used against them with less cause. It's a very slippery slope.

Of course, having good tracking of patterns of behavior will mean that these people will likely get taken care of anyway. People who break any given rule repeatedly tend to break several of them repeatedly. So concrete advice to admins is, have a history of infractions for every avatar. It doesn't say anything in the document about not keeping records, establishing more severe penalties for repeated infractions, curtailing the freedoms of players with long admin records, etc. Presumably someone who has a long admin record isn't going to be considered a "good customer" anymore, right?

In a commercial endeavor, it makes sense to include money as a factor. Good customers may well get permitted more infractions, because the definition of an admin record is "things that cost us money (via admin time spent)." As long as this is in the code of conduct, and applies equally well to two different good customers who have paid the same amount, then you're fulfilling the letter of the article.

I'd submit that the enhanced recordkeeping alone from doing that would probably streamline your costs and make for better business decisions when the time comes to punish someone.

Perhaps the most interesting thing about all the admin commentary on the document is that the biggest concerns boil down to just a few things:

1. I don't want to surrender control. I hate the notion of "rights" for players.

2. I may not be making this sort of virtual world. Maybe it's a game. (Which is largely easily answered by saying, "these rights apply out of character, not in character, of course.")

3. By the way, I *really* don't want to surrender control.

The second is interesting. What about virtual meeting places for businesses, or online universities? I'd argue that the need for rights applies even *more* in such environments. But it is clear that there's a sliding scale of applicability here. It raises the question of what a mud is for, and what lifecycle it has. Common wisdom has it that "a mud must grow, or stagnate and die." If so, then the common good means anything that works against increasing the population of a mud. However, a mud that grows into something which all of its members despise is not developing towards the common good. So a better definition might be, the common good is that which increases the population of a mud without surrendering core social tenets or mores. But that word "stagnate" is in that bit o' common wisdom too. So it may be good for a mud to evolve its core social tenets in order to adapt to the changing population. Free immigration means that this will be accelerated—note that nowhere does the document say that you can't simply not accept people into the mud who aren't aligned with the mud's key social tenets.

Then there are the mud admins who don't give a flip about population growth...

When all is said and done, though, I am clearly defending something completely implausible on one key level:

- As a document for players, it's a waste of time. They may trumpet it, but who cares? They have zero power, and the document actually states that several times over.

- As a document for admins, however, it's pretty much all common sense. Whether or not you believe in *any* of the principles that lead to calling these articles rights, or whether or not you believe in rights at all, I'd bet that you probably subscribe to most of these. In many cases, out of sheer, ruthless practicality and business horse sense.

What happens if we remove the word rights, and in fact remove all the high-flown language? If we just phrase this as suggestions instead? If we just phrase it in modern English? I'll present just the plain language version this time.

Advice to Virtual World Admins

Mud players are people. They don't stop being people when they log on. Therefore they deserve to be treated like people. This means they have the rights of people. By joining a mud, they join a community of people. Rights arise from the community. But there's always someone with his or her finger on the power switch. But he's part of the community too, and should use his powers for the common good and the survival of the community. The fact that you can easily move to another mud doesn't mean that these rights go away.

Articles:

1. All mud players get the same rights. Special powers on the mud are given out for the good of the mud, not because some guy is the friend of a wizard.

2. Mud players are people, and therefore they have the rights of people: liberty, property, security, and freedom from oppression.

3. Somewhere, there's a guy with his finger on the power button. What he says ultimately goes. The mud players have the right to know the code of conduct he is going to enforce over them, and what rules and standards he's going to use when he makes a decision. Otherwise, they are suckers and deserve what mistreatment they get.

4. You can do whatever you want as long as it doesn't hurt others. "Hurting others" needs to be defined in the code of conduct.

5. The code of conduct shouldn't be capricious and arbitrary. The rules should be based on what is good for the mud (and for the good of the mud's hardware, software, and data).

6. The code of conduct should evolve based on the way the mud culture evolves, and players should get a say in how it evolves. The mud admins get to write it however they want, but they have an obligation to listen or else the players might leave.

7. You can't punish someone for something that isn't the code of conduct. Abusing your wiz powers is a serious crime. If you are caught in a violation of the code of conduct, fess up.

8. You can't punish someone in a way not in the code of conduct, and you the admin don't get to rewrite the code of conduct after the fact to make it legal. The only exception is action taken to keep the mud from going "poof."

9. Players are innocent until proven guilty. Treat them decently until guilt is proven.

10. As long as they aren't spamming or breaking the code of conduct, players should be free to believe whatever they want.

11. As long as they aren't spamming or breaking the code of conduct, players should be free to yell, chat, gossip, post, or otherwise say whatever they want.

12. You're probably going to want admins. Admins get special powers for the good of the mud, not to make them feel cool. They aren't an entitlement because the imp is your cousin, and if you're not using them for the good of all (which includes not using them at all and shirking your admin duties) they should get yanked.

13. Players might have to pay to keep the mud running. They should know how much they would have to pay beforehand. You shouldn't have different pay scales for different players unless those other players actually involve more costs. If you do let people buy greater privileges, then you should allow ANY player to buy these privileges, and not bar some people from it because you don't like them. Also, payment doesn't mean they get to have godlike powers to fry other people with—they still have to obey these rights.

14. Players have a right to know why the admins did things the way they did, like why they playerwiped or moved an area or whatever. In particular, why a given immort banned one guy for spamming but let the other off the hook. (Note that given the circumstances, you may not be able to for legal reasons.)

15. No exceptions to the code of conduct—it applies to everyone.

16. Don't playerwipe/data wipe unless the mud can't survive unless you do. If you do have to wipe someone, make it up to him or her somehow.

17. Let people hang out wherever they want with whomever they want in the mud, unless it's causing mud slowdowns or something.

18. Players have a right to privacy. Don't snoop them or spy on them or rifle through their mail unless you are investigating a code of conduct violation.

19. There's probably stuff missing in this doc.

*   *   *   *   *

The interesting thing is that mud admins find the second doc much more palatable. Phrased in this way, it's not an abrogation of their power. It's concrete advice that will help you retain your playerbase. In fact, some even said they'd be willing to sign to it as a "declaration" because it would make them look good as admins to adhere to such a standard. There are damn few justifiable reasons to deny any of the things in the above version—and if you did, likely you'd be considered a jerk for doing it—or a power-hungry admin with a god complex. (Is there a difference?)

If admins see themselves as above the community, do they have any responsibilities towards the community whatsoever?

If they do, can they be articulated?

If they can be articulated and generally agreed upon, are they players' rights or are they merely good ethics on the part of a mud administrator?

One camp is going to argue that it's their mud, by god, and therefore they have the right to do whatever they want with it (and with the people in it). Some might temper this by saying that they don't have the right to violate RL law in the process, but I think a sizable faction would argue that even that doesn't curtail their power in any way.

Another camp is going to argue that with great power comes great responsibility, *a la* Spiderman. And that clear guidelines and the rule of law is the only way to handle a responsibility of such magnitude.

Both sides will agree that they still have their finger on the power button, and that this changes the landscape of "rights" considerably. And if you do feel that you are ethically bound to act responsibly, then you may have to violate some of your ethical principles in order to keep the mud running.

And if it's a commercial environment:

- Is it bad business to be a part of the community?

- Is it bad business NOT to be?

This is one of the self-contradictions built into the document. The logic goes like this:

- Of paramount importance is the survival of the community.

- Somebody who has his finger on the power switch can make the community go poof.

- Ergo, keeping this guy happy is of paramount importance.

- But if keeping him happy means letting him psychologically torture you, well, that means the community isn't likely to survive.

- And survival of the community is of paramount importance...

The logical answer is for the community to move wholesale—in essence, picking another guy with a power switch who hopefully is made happy by other sorts of pleasures. Virtual communities often do this, as we have seen. And they always seem to feel that they were betrayed by the previous admin—which indicates the self-assignation of a right by the community.

The irony is that it's all probably moot. The reason why players hold admins to this standard is because they have assumed that this standard is what should be there regardless. In other words, the advice works because it's what players expect and say they want. Which is no different from self-affirmed rights. This is probably why players scream that their rights have been violated when one of the above articles is violated (even if the admins are not signatories to any such document).

So the real point of a document like this would be to see how many admins would sign, not how many players. As an admin, yes, I'd probably sign, in the sense that I'd agree that these are solid administrative principles *in terms of practical effect.*

The question then becomes, if we subscribe in terms of practical effect, and as long as there are sufficient loopholes present that we can exercise power when we need to, who *cares* whether players think these are rights, laws, doohickeys, or power fantasies? (Welcome to the Machiavellian world of player relations!)

Why do you want freedom to do things that are *bad* admin or business practice? (Even considering that "freedom" and so on are total mirages in this whole situation...)

Especially since "rights" in the real world already have zero power?

(Note that I am not suggesting that all the muds or commercial endeavors should run out and implement this list of "rights," nor am I suggesting that if they don't that they are run by power-hungry maniacs. This is too complex an issue to reduce to that level.)

The last step that would be required to actually make such a document into a Bill of Rights for players would be for it to be codified into "law," (which is probably a Code of Conduct or Terms of Service agreement signed by all players, account holders, and admins) and thus be something that admins would be bound to. Admins are, by and large, not going to do this, even though some of the commercial MMORPG companies *do* require their game masters to sign documents saying that they will behave in a manner surprisingly similar to what the document espouses. But there's an interesting forward-thinking pie-in-the-sky reason for admins to contemplate doing so someday...

Someday there won't *be* any admins. Someday it's gonna be your bank records and your grocery shopping and your credit report and yes, your virtual homepage with data that exists nowhere else. Someday it's gonna be *Snow Crash* and *Neuromancer* and *Otherland* all wrapped up into one, and it may be a little harder to write to Customer Service. Your avatar profile might be your credit record and your resume and your academic transcript, as well as your XP earned.

On the day that happens, I bet we'll all wish we had a few more rights in the face of a very large, distributed server, anarchic, virtual world where it might be very, very *hard* to move to a different service provider. Heck, I would bet that those folks who plan to play Bioware's forthcoming *Neverwinter Nights* might very well want their admins to sign such a doc. The future is already almost here.

So in the end, all the Declaration of the Rights of Avatars is, is a useful tool for players and admins alike: admins who don't know what they are doing can use it as a blueprint, and players can use it to evaluate mud administrations in search of one they like.

So yeah. I'm not seriously proposing that we declare the rights of avatars. The doc is, as has been shown, riddled with gotchas and logical holes. It's a hypothetical exercise.

For now.

Acknowledgments

This essay could not have been written without the help of:

Christopher Allen

Paul Schwanz

David Bennett

John Bertoglio

Par Winzell

Eli Stevens

Phillip Lenhardt

Erik Jarvi

Justin Randall

and most especially:

Geoffrey A. MacDougall

Jon A. Lambert

Matt Mihaly

Jeff Freeman

Travis S. Casey

Jame Scholl

and extra especially Kristen Koster, who helped draft the original version.

Raph Koster, August 27th, 2000

Virtual Worlds: A First-Hand Account of Market and Society on the Cyberian Frontier

Edward Castronova

Context

*I wrote "Virtual Worlds" at a low point in my career as an academic economist. Nothing I'd written seemed to be having an effect on anyone's thinking. All along, though, I had been an avid gamer, and at that time I happened to be playing EverQuest. Given my frustrations at writing serious papers, I thought I might thumb my nose at the hierarchy by writing a tongue-in-cheek paper about the economy of a videogame. Yet after I set to work on the project, its implications came to look more important than I had thought. It dawned on me that I was exploring not a videogame but humanity's next and possibly final frontier. The paper evolved from a scholarly jest into a personal journey. I posted the paper in January 2002 to **SSRN,** the world's top site for papers in economics, law, finance, and management. Within a few months it had become the top economics paper in the history of the site and the third-ranked in all fields. As I write this, the paper has had over 27,000 downloads. And it still has not been published in a stodgy economics journal.*

Game Communities

Game Economies

Edward Castronova is an Associate Professor of Telecommunications at Indiana University, Bloomington. From 1991 to 2004 he held university professorships in Public Policy, Political Science, and Economics, while his research focus shifted from social policy, to social norms, to theories of society as an evolving game, to the study of persistent online societies. In 2003 he co-founded the academic blog Terra Nova. Castronova regularly consults on the implications of synthetic worlds with leaders in business, government, education, and software design, and he is currently preparing a book on the topic for the University of Chicago Press with the tentative title *Synthetic Worlds: The Business and Culture of Online Games.*

Abstract

In March 1999, a small number of Californians discovered a new world called "Norrath", populated by an exotic but industrious people. Having just returned from a dangerous exploratory journey through this new world, I can report a number of interesting findings about its people and economy. About 12,000 people call it their permanent home, although some 60,000 are present there at any given time. The nominal hourly wage is about $3.42 per hour, and the labors of the people produce a GNP per capita somewhere between that of Russia and Bulgaria. A unit of Norrath's currency is traded on exchange markets at $0.0107, higher than the Yen and the Lira. The economy is characterized by extreme inequality, yet life there is quite attractive to many. The population is growing rapidly, swollen each each day by hundreds of émigrés from various places around the globe, but especially the United States. Perhaps the most interesting thing about the new world is its location. Norrath is a virtual world that exists entirely on 40 computers in San Diego. The entire dollar-based economy is underground, since the owning company, Sony, considers everything created in the world to be its intellectual property. Unlike many internet ventures, virtual worlds are making money—with annual revenues expected to top $1.5 billion by 2004—and if network effects are as powerful here as they have been with other internet innovations, virtual worlds may be the next step in the evolution of internet (and possibly human) culture.

This report is based primarily on the author's personal experiences while traveling and gathering data in Norrath from April to September, 2001. Other sources include data made publicly available by Verant Interactive, data available for free or by fee from public websites, and data collected by the author from surveys. No one affiliated with Verant Interactive, Sony, or any private companies have sponsored the report or bear any responsibility for its contents. Any avatar names used in the report have been changed to protect the privacy of their owners. All errors in the report are mine.

I. A New World

Journal entry, 18 April. I have called my avatar 'Alaniel.' I land in Norrath for the first time, in a town called Freeport. I am standing in a stone courtyard behind a gate. I see several lean-tos and a firepit. All around I hear the sounds of footsteps and I see humanoids of various shapes and sizes running back and forth, names like "Zikon" and "Sefirooth" over their heads, wearing odd costumes, carrying strange implements. Are they people? Or merely beings created by the software?

Statements flow into my chat box at a rapid rate. "Galadriel shouts: Looking for bind at gate." I see a being with the name Galadriel. Is he talking to me? What is he saying? "Friitz says out of character: brt - omwb." What? No sign of anyone named Friitz. "Ikillu auctions: WTS bone chips." An auction. What should I do? I feel the presence of humanity, but I suddenly feel like a stranger in a very foreign culture. I become afraid of breaking some taboo, of making a fool of myself. Clumsily, I maneuver Alaniel toward the nearest lean-to and hide behind it. No one can see me here.

On March 16, 1999, Verant Interactive, a holding of Sony, launched an on-line computer game called EverQuest on five servers in San Diego, California, USA.[1] With that act the company called into existence a new world named "Norrath" that has become a meeting place, a market place, and even a home, to tens of thousands of people. This paper offers a first-hand look at the people, the customs, and especially the economy of this New World.

Why bother? Isn't Norrath just part of a silly game? Perhaps it is, on an abstract level. But economists believe that it is the practical actions of people, and not abstract arguments, that determine the social value of things. One does not study the labor market because work is holy and ethical; one does it because the conditions of work mean a great deal to a large number of ordinary people. By the same reasoning, economists and other social scientists will become more interested in Norrath and similar virtual worlds as they realize that such places have begun to mean a great deal to large numbers of ordinary people. Almost 1 million people already have active accounts in Virtual Worlds. At a time when many ecommerce concerns are going under, revenues from on-line gaming will grow to over $1.5 billion in 2004. Some 60,000 people visit Norrath in any given hour, paying for the privilege, around the clock, every day, year-round. Nearly a third of the adults among them—perhaps some 93,000 people out of Norrath's 400,000 person user base—spend more time in Norrath in a typical week than they do working for pay. The exchange rate between Norrath's currency and the US dollar is determined in a highly liquid (if illegal) currency market, and its value exceeds that of the Japanese Yen and the Italian Lira. The creation of dollar-valued items in Norrath occurs at a rate such that Norrath's GNP per capita easily exceeds that of dozens of countries, including India and China. Some 20 percent of Norrath's citizens consider it their place of residence; they just commute to Earth and back. To a large and growing number of people, virtual worlds are an important source of material and emotional well-being.

Virtual worlds may also be the future of ecommerce, and perhaps of the internet itself. The game designers who created thriving places like Norrath have unwittingly discovered a much more attractive way to use the internet: through an avatar. The avatar represents the user in the fantasy 3D world, and avatars apparently come to occupy a special place in the hearts of their creators. The typical user devotes hundreds of hours (and hundreds of dollars, in some cases) to develop the avatar. These ordinary people, who seem to have become bored and frustrated by ordinary web commerce, engage energetically and enthusiastically in avatar-based on-line markets. Few people are willing to go web shopping for tires for their car, but hundreds of thousands are willing to go virtual shopping for shoes for their avatar.

The business potential of this interest in avatar shopping is not lost on everyone. Mindark, a private Swedish company, hopes to use avatar-based shopping to build a global network monopoly in internet interface. The strategy: start a virtual world in a game of truly massive scale, so that millions can use it at any time. Make the game free. Allow people to use their credit cards to make transactions. Then wait for the society and markets to develop, and invite Earth retailers to open 3D stores in the virtual space. At that point, your Lara Croft looka-like avatar will be able to follow up her tough day of adventuring with a run into the nearby virtual JC Penney—to buy her owner a new suit, for real money. The commercial potential of the new virtual worlds is impressive, and makes them well worth a first look.

In the past, the discovery of new worlds has often been an epochal event for both the new world and the old. The new world typically has a herald, a hapless explorer who has gotten lost and has wandered aimlessly about in strange territory, but has had the wit and good fortune to write down what he has seen, his impressions of the people, and the exciting dangers he has faced, for an audience far away. In similar fashion, I stumbled haplessly into Norrath in April 2001, and then spent four months wandering around there. It took me about six weeks to get my bearings. I began recording data in May. And I assure you, I faced many dangers, and died many, many times, in order to gather impressions and bring them back for you. In the end I have been able to include only a small fraction of what I have learned, indeed only enough to give a flavor of what is happening. I apologize to anyone reading this who thinks that I have left out something of great importance.

My report is structured as follows. Section II, below, describes the universe of virtual worlds of which Norrath is a member, and gives an overview of the economic and social impact these worlds have already generated. Section III, focusing on Norrath alone, describes the organization of society and economy and provides some indicators of macroeconomic health, such as the exchange rate, the inflation rate, GNP per capita, and the poverty rate. Finally,

Section IV sketches the forseeable near-term future of virtual worlds, with some thoughts on the broader implications of virtual worlds for everyday human life. For those interested in doing research on Norrath, Appendix A offers a list of potential projects that came to mind during my tour. Appendix B describes the weighting method behind the main survey data in the report. Appendix C specifies how GNP figures are calculated. Finally, Appendix D discusses specific economic and policy issues that will be of most interest only to those with a fairly deep involvement in Norrath.

II. Virtual Worlds

A. The Market for Virtual Worlds

Journal entry, 18 April. A new avatar on a different server. Same world, different people. First steps outside the gate of Freeport. Bustling activity all around, but I feel ignored, which is good—my first conversations went poorly as I had trouble speaking the language. Suddenly my chat box lights up with message from a Being named "Deathfist Pawn" to the effect that I will not be allowed to ruin his land. Then: "Deathfist Pawn hits YOU for 2 points of damage." I hear myself grunt in pain. Flustered, I peer out and see no one. "Deathfist Pawn hits YOU for 3 points of damage." He is behind me of course. I learn that you can be attacked here. Why is this person attacking me? What have I done? I guess I have to fight. "Deathfist Pawn hits YOU for 5 points of damage." A sickening gashing sound is heard—my flesh. I fumble for my sword. The chat box reports "You have been slain by Deathfist Pawn." The screen freezes. I am dead.

A *virtual world* or VW is a computer program with three defining features:

> **Interactivity:** it exists on one computer but can be accessed remotely (i.e. by an internet connection) and simultaneously by a large number of people, with the command inputs of one person affecting the command results of other people.

> **Physicality:** people access the program through an interface that simulates a first-person physical environment on their computer screen; the environment is generally ruled by the natural laws of Earth and is characterized by scarcity of resources.

> **Persistence:** the program continues to run whether anyone is using it or not; it remembers the location of people and things, as well as the ownership of objects.[2]

A VW is the product of combining the graphical 3D environment of games like Tomb Raider with the chat-based social interaction systems developed in the world of Multi-User

Domains (MUDs). In Tomb Raider, you run a little person around on your screen and do things; in a VW, other people are running around in the same virtual space as you are, and they can talk to you. VWs can trace their history back to on-line games on the ARPA-Net in the 1980s. The game that started the recent explosion of VWs was Meridian 59, or M59 (Colker, 2001), begun in 1995 by Andrew and Chris Kirmse, two Microsoft interns. They made a town and an open field and let users manipulate the environment by issuing keyboard and mouse commands to a graphical representation of themselves. This virtual persona, now known as an 'avatar,' could be told to walk here and there, pick up a sword, look behind a bush, and hit whatever was there.[3] To make things interesting, you could chat with others, and there were biots in the world: computer-driven beings, also known as mobile objects or MOBS. In essence, biots were either monsters who would attack and kill an avatar on sight, or merchants who would talk to the avatar from a script and buy and sell things.[4] Given the circumstances presented by the objective functions of the biots, the avatar's survival and success depended on its ability to deal with merchants and defend itself from monsters. The avatar could join with other avatars to kill powerful monsters, and loot the corpse to become the new owner of whatever the monster held. Items could be traded back and forth between avatars. All of these events unfolded on the user's computer screen like a moving picture, and communication went back and forth via text-based messages. When the user left the world and came back hours later, their avatar was returned to the spot they left, still possessing whatever she had held before. M59 made its debut in October 1996 and survived until August 2000, when competitive pressure from much larger VWs forced its closure. At its closing, hundreds of people mourned its loss. They felt that the world had been a significant part of their lives in the few years it had existed. People had made friends there and were loathe to leave.[5]

M59 was quite small by contemporary standards; current VWs can support several thousand users simultaneously on a single server. The first VW on this scale was Ultima Online (UO), launched in Fall 1997. UO is owned by Electronic Arts, a California-based publicly-traded software company with 3,600 employees and $1.3 billion in annual revenues.[6] Its popularity led to the development of other VWs, especially Sony/Verant Interactive's EverQuest, launched in Spring 1999 and now the industry leader in terms of subscriptions. Microsoft entered the competition in Spring 2000 with Asheron's Call. Recent major additions have been Anarchy Online, released in June 2001 by Funcom, a 120-employee Norwegian company; World War II Online, by Cornered Rat Software, a small Texas company; and Dark Age of Camelot, by

Mythic Entertainment, a small Washington DC company. The first VW *not* based on killing and adventuring will appear in 2002, when Electronic Arts releases The Sims Online.

The market is quite competitive at the moment, but since VWs are human networks, there is reason to believe that only a few VWs will eventually dominate the market.[7] The tendency to network monopoly is enhanced by the fact that most people seem to be willing to "live" in at most one fantasy world at a time, and switching is costly as it can take weeks to become familiar with a new world.

The growth in the number of VWs has been spurred by a growth in user base and revenues; VWs stand out as one area of internet commerce that actually seems to be profitable. With most software game titles, the user pays a one-time fee to purchase the game. With VW-based games, the user purchases the game software and then pays additional monthly fees (from $10 to $20) to access the VW on an ongoing basis. This revenue stream seems to be stable and growing. While most firms do not publish these figures regularly, there are estimates from March 2001 putting the combined subscriber base for VWs at about 800,000, 360,000 subscribing to EverQuest and another 230,000 to UO (Harris, 2001; Zito, 2001). By late summer 2001 the subscriber base to EverQuest was said to be over 400,000 (according to off-hand remarks by developers on discussion boards), a growth of over 10 percent in two quarters. And this is for a computer game that is ancient by industry standards, already over two years old. Sony's monthly revenues from EverQuest are about $3.6 million; revenues from online gaming were $208 million in 2000 and are estimated to grow to $1.7 billion in 2004 (Zito, 2001).[8] A site maintained by VW programmer Patrik Holmsten (hem.passagen. se/ulkis/) estimates that there are currently 18 VWs running and publicly available, with 40 others in development.[9] At a time when many ecommerce ventures are struggling, VWs have become a flourishing sector of the economy.

The business success of VWs derives from their ability to attract customers who are willing to pay an ongoing fee to visit the world, and that requires VWs to offer a form of entertainment that is persistently more attractive than the competition. As it turns out, VWs seem to be able to offer entertainment that is attractive enough to many people that they sacrifice major portions of their time to it. A survey of EverQuest users conducted by Nicholas Yee, an undergraduate psychology major at Haverford College, indicates that the typical user spends about 22 hours per week in the game (Yee, 2001). My own survey of EverQuest users (see Section III below) indicates that the median user devotes 4 hours per day and more than 20 hours per week to the game. In Yee's study, many people used the term 'addiction' to describe their own behavior, perceiving their time in the VW as a source of serious conflict with various Earth activities and relationships.[10] If we take the economist's view, however, and see their behavior as rational choice, we must conclude that VWs offer something that is perhaps a bit more than a mere entertainment to which the players have become addicted. Rather, they offer an alternative reality, a different country in which one can live most of one's life if one so chooses. And it so happens that life in a VW is extremely attractive to many people. A competition has arisen between Earth and the virtual worlds, and for many, Earth is the lesser option.

B. An Avatar's Life

Journal entry, 20 April. I have made my first kills, mostly rats. They did me a great deal of damage and I have been killed several times. I do return to life but it is a pain to go through. Nonetheless, I have to attack the rats. I need money to buy edible food and water, and rat fur, and other similar junk, is about the only thing I can get my hands on that the vendors will pay money for. I was hoping to do more exploring and less work, but a woman named "Soulseekyre" told me that beyond Freeport lie biots so powerful they could kill me instantly. My problem is that I am under-equipped. Soulseekyre was wearing an elaborate suit of armor and she had impressive weapons. I have been basically naked, carrying only a simple club, a caveman in a world of cavaliers. My poverty is oppressive—no amount of rat fur is sufficient to buy even a simple tunic at the ludicrously high prices of the merchant biots. Fortunately I just killed enough rats to gain a "level" of experience, and I seem to have become a much more effective rat killer.

What features of the virtual worlds give them this competitive edge? An overview of the conditions of existence in VWs will provide some obvious answers. To enter a VW, the user is first connected to the server via the internet. Once the connection is established, the user enters a program that allows them to choose an avatar for themselves. In all of the major VWs, one can spent an extraordinarily long time at this first stage, choosing the appearance of the avatar as well as its abilities. Always wondered what it is like to be tall? Choose a tall avatar. Want to be one of the smart people in society? Make your avatar a brilliant wizard. Need to get out your aggressions? Give your avatar immense strength and a high skill in wielding a mace. Think it would be fun to be a beautiful dark-skinned woman? Go for it. These choices occur under a budget constraint that ensures equality of opportunity in the world: Your mace-wielding ogre will be dumb, and your brilliant wizard will have a glass jaw. At the same time, the budget constraint ensures equality among avatars along dimensions that most people think should not matter for social achievement. In particular, male and female avatars have the same initial budget of skills and attributes. Avatars whose physical characteristics (i.e. skin tone, size) are associated with any benefit in the game must accept some compensating disadvantage. Any inequality in the VW can only be due to one of two things: a) a person's choices when creating the avatar, or b) their subsequent actions in the VW.

Once the avatar is created, it is deposited at some place in the VW. Because most of the laws of Earth science apply, most of the time, it is quite easy to "become" the avatar as you perceive the world through its eyes. You cannot run through walls; you can only see where you are looking; if you are at Point A and want to get to point B, you will have to walk your avatar in that direction. If you jump off a roof, you will fall and hurt yourself. When the sun goes down, it gets darker and you will need a light. If you do something over and over, you will get better at it. If you hold things, you might drop them; if you drop them, someone else may pick them up. You can give things to another avatar if you wish. You can hit other avatars and biots. You can kill them if you wish. And they can kill you.

Of course the natural laws of Earth need not apply in a world that exists entirely as software, and much of what defines an avatar's uniqueness is its ability to bend or break some of these laws and not others. Depending on the skills chosen, an avatar might be able to fly, see for miles, hypnotize, heal wounds, teleport themselves, or shoot great flaming fireballs at other avatar's heads. Again a budget constraint applies: those who can heal or hypnotize often have difficulty summoning a fireball worthy of mention. As a result, avatars come to view themselves as specialized agents, much as workers in a developed economy do. The avatar's skills will determine whether the avatar will be a demander or supplier of various goods and services in the VW. Each avatar develops a social role.

Social roles are defined through communication with other avatars. When an avatar is launched into the VW, it is granted a limited ability to communicate with other avatars. The communication is in the form of a clipped written English ("chat").[11] An avatar may approach another avatar, type a message out on the keyboard, and send that message to the other avatar. Depending on the nature of the laws of sound in the VW, an avatar may also be able to overhear the conversations of others, as well as hold conversations with avatars hundreds of virtual miles away. These communications allow social interactions that are *not* a simulation of human interactions; they *are* human interactions, merely extended into a new forum. As with any human society, it is through communication that the VW society confers status and standing.

As it turns out, the social standing of the avatar has a powerful effect on the entertainment value of the VW. Having specialized in certain skills, an avatar may find the accomplishment of certain goals much easier with the assistance of an avatar who has a complementary skill. For example: When traveling from A to B, the monsters must be killed and so skills in destruction are needed; when traveling from B to C, the monsters must be evaded and so skills in deception are needed; when traveling from A to C, one should form a party consisting of a destroyer and a deceiver, rather than travel alone. An avatar who does not form social relationships on at least an ad hoc basis will generally have a more difficult time doing things in the VW. In some VWs, it is a matter of survival—an avatar acting alone will eventually starve or be killed by a biot.

These social relationships are essential, and they emerge under the same kinds of circumstances as required in Earth societies: two people with complementary abilities or resources have an incentive to engage in mutually beneficial trade. It follows that an avatar must have skills to do and see much in the world. However, developing the avatar's skills takes time; monsters must be killed, axes must be forged, quests must be completed. The result of all this effort, which can take hundreds of hours, is "avatar capital": an enhancement of the avatar's capabilities through training. In most VWs, capital is given by a number called the "level," so that an avatar at level 6 who kills 100 kobolds is given an increase to level 7. With that increase comes an enhancement of the avatar's abilities, which then makes the avatar a more attractive social contact.

In sum, activity in the VW requires social integration, but social integration requires activity: the avatar faces the same sort of social reward systems as are found in Earth society. The leveling and integration system also draws on the basic human tendency to get self-esteem from the opinions of others, and the result is that users are powerfully motivated to increase their avatars' abilities. Like the humans who imbue them, avatars find themselves on something of a treadmill of social success through avatar capital accumulation: they must work to advance, but each advancement raises the aspiration level and spurs them to still greater work (Easterlin, 2001). It is the success and standing of avatars that makes people devote hundreds of hours to virtual worlds, indeed so many hours that one can almost believe that many people do live *there,* wherever it is, and not on Earth.

C. Scarcity is Fun

Journal entry, 22 April. I have killed enough rats to have earned the title "Ratslayer of Freeport." But powerful orcs lurk in the beyond, and I need a better mace. To get a better mace, I have to go from Freeport to the hobbit village of Rivervale. If I go on my own, I will be killed by bears. I walk as far as I can safely go, and then make my first ever general appeal for help. Thinking that an Elizabethan tone would be helpful, I shout "Brave adventurers! I seek safe conduct to Rivervale! I can only compensate you with my eternal gratitude!" The woods and fields erupt in guffaws and insults: "ne1 want to hold the newbie's hand?" and "geteth a clueth you noobeth." then I get eaten by a bear.

The avatar seems so entertaining that it generates hundreds of millions of dollars in annual revenue for gaming companies. Why? Certainly, one can understand why many people would prefer existence in a VW to existence in the "real world." Unlike Earth, in VWs there is real equality of opportunity, as everybody is born penniless and with the same minimal effectiveness.[12] In a VW, people choose their own abilities, gender, and skin tone instead of having them imposed by accidents of birth. Those who cannot run on Earth can run in a VW. On Earth, reputation sticks to a person; in VWs, an avatar with a bad reputation can be replaced by one who is clean.

Yet VWs are only one of many different ways of constructing an avatar space; other approaches have not had the same commercial success. Before the explosion in VWs, there were a number of virtual reality avatar spaces that offered similar forms of entertainment, for free.[13] Users could create their own avatars and chat with other avatars. They could build rooms and wander about, looking at other people's houses. Some of these user-built avatar spaces became extremely large; Alpha World began as a virtual plain and was built, byte by byte, into a vast city by hundreds of thousands of users (Damer, 2001). There were a number of ways to amuse one's self in these places: one could look around at pretty virtual landscapes, or simply talk to others, or show off your avatar's skills ("Look what happens when I shoot a fireball at my head!"). However, these first generation avatar spaces failed to sustain any interest from private companies; most have folded or are maintained by private contributions (Damer, 2001).

Their failure helps identify the source of the success of VWs, because there really is only one major difference between these avatar spaces and VWs: Scarcity. Nothing was scarce in the avatar space. A user could create as many avatars as desired; all avatars had equal abilities; the user could build without limit, as long as the desire to write code persisted.

The activities of one avatar posed no real obstacle and imposed no significant cost on any other avatar's activities.

In a VW, conversely, the user faces scarcity along a number of dimensions. First, not all avatars are the same: the user faces constraints on the creation of avatars and, through leveling, on the development of their abilities. An avatar may die, and death may rob it of some or all of its powers. Second, the avatar is constrained by the physicality of the VW in that a large percentage of important goods and services can only be obtained from other avatars or from biots, always at a price or by risking death. No free lunches. Third, the avatar is constrained by society in the VW, in that social roles are not open to everyone; an avatar must compete against other avatars to fill a role. In a sentence, avatars in avatar spaces could do no work and still do anything that any other avatar could do; avatars in VWs *must* work to do anything interesting at all.

And, somewhat shockingly, scarcity is what makes the VW so fun. The process of developing avatar capital seems to invoke exactly the same risk and reward structures in the brain that are invoked by personal development in real life. The idea is shocking because it seems to suggest that utility and well-being are not the same thing. Utility always rises when constraints are relaxed, yet people seem to prefer a world *with* constraints to a world *without* them.[14] Constraints create the possibility of achievement, and it is the drive to achieve something with the avatar that seems to create an obsessive interest in her well-being. Moreover, since the VWs are inherently social, the achievements are relative: it is not having powerful weapons that really makes a difference in prestige, but in having the most powerful weapons in the world. In a post-industrial society, it is social status, more than anything else, that drives people to work so diligently all their lives. In this respect, VWs are truly a simulacrum of Earth society.

But the rules are different in important ways, making VWs more popular, for many, than both Earth society and the avatar spaces that preceded them. VWs offer the essential human story of challenge, maturity, and success, but played out on a more level playing field. They offer life with an escape clause, because if things go wrong and you cannot walk or talk and everyone hates you, you can just start over. And they give you a freedom that no one has on Earth: the freedom to be whomever you want to be. Already, a large number of people seems willing to pay an ongoing monthly fee to enjoy this privilege, and the numbers are growing. For many, the best world is one with scarcity but perfect equality of opportunity. VWs provide such a world and, as a result, they seem to be growing in importance as a forum of human interaction.

III. The Norrath Economic Report, 2001

journal entry, 25 april. after the rivervale fiasco, i feel that my second avatar is socially dead. i could wait for my reputation to improve, but i just feel too stupid. so i started a third avatar, a halfling, basically a midget. i made him a healer. it turns out that healers are in high demand. i've been playing him two nights and people i don't know keep coming up and saying "heal me." im making a little money at it, which is good. and i am learning which biots to kill and how to kill them. i've also learned there's a whole world of trade skills you can learn, baking, tailoring, blacksmithing. to do all these things you need skill, which means you need to train and develop the avatar. meanwhile, im seeing more of the world. i realize i have only seen about 5 percent of it so far. it is big.

VWs are amusing and profitable, that much is certain. Are they "real" societies in any sense?[15] From an economist's point of view, any distinct territory with a labor force, a gross national product, and a floating exchange rate has an economy. By this standard, the new virtual worlds are absolutely real.[16] In this section I will document the existence of an economy in Norrath, the VW of the game EverQuest. My report on Norrath will cover four areas:

A. Data and methods

B. Population of Norrath

C. Microeconomic conditions in Norrath: the main markets

D. Macroeconomic indicators for Norrath

A. Data and Methods

journal entry 25 april. new avatar, new server. ive started to "group," basically team up with other players to kill monsters. my unique effectiveness is to heal, so i spend my time healing warriors so they can go back and fight. it turns out that grouping is essential to advancement, and people can quickly get bad reputations from cheating on the group. it's just a 6-person prisoner's dilemma. so i try to keep playing 'cooperate' even after someone has defected. and, lo, i have had no trouble be re-invited for groups.

I choose Norrath because its mother game, EverQuest, is the industry leader in terms of subscriptions and revenues.[17] My attention was first drawn to this topic by news articles in January 2001 reporting that dollar-denominated trade in Norrathian goods had become so extensive that Sony, the owning corporation, had pressured auction sites like eBay and Yahoo to forcibly close down any Norrath-related auctions on the site (Sandoval, 2001).[18] Its economy seems as extensive as the other economies, although Ultima Online is also extremely well-developed and has been the subject of media scrutiny as well.[19] However, there are more dollar-based trade and currency transactions involving Norrath than the other VWs.

If there were extensive prior research on these VWs, of course, it would be possible to report about them all. However, it seems that virtually no academic attention has been devoted to VWs to date, judging from a search of 8 major research databases covering public affairs (PAIS), economics (Econlit), humanities (Arts and Humanities Search, Humanities Abstracts), sociology (Sociological Abstracts), communications (ComAbstracts), and mainstream media (Lexis-Nexis). The search covered the words MMORPG, EverQuest, Ultima Online, Asheron's Call, Anarchy Online, Persistent State World, and Persistent Online World. ("Virtual World" was too general and yielded thousands of hits; those I examined were all unrelated to VWs as understood here.) These searches produced 66 hits, all of them newspaper and magazine articles, many of those being tongue-in-cheek "EverQuest wrecked my marriage" human interest stories. In the end, the report will focus on Norrath only because there is not enough time to report more broadly on all the virtual economies in existence. I have had experience in the four major economies, however, and I believe that my impressions of Norrath are typical of them all.

The following sections report data of three kinds. First, as a person who has participated directly in Norrath's markets, I will report my own observations. Second, I will make use of publicly-available websites. These consist primarily of official support sites and various fan sites. Last, I will use information from a survey of Norrathians that I conducted via the internet.

I posted the "Norrath Economic Survey" (NES) on my website on August 17, 2001, and sent a message to two popular EverQuest bulletin boards announcing the survey's existence and asking for respondents. The survey was open for about 48 hours and yielded 3,619 responses. Since it is not random, this cannot be a representative survey of Norrath's population. However, the direction of bias is fairly easy to identify. The respondents are those who take the time to read fan site discussion boards, and therefore they are more serious EverQuest users.[20] It seems likely that the more serious user has been involved with the game for a longer time; therefore, her avatars should be at a higher level. It follows that the survey will be biased in favor of the experiences of high-level avatars. To correct this bias, I conducted population counts on EverQuest servers at various times in order to measure the true distribution of avatars. I then developed weights for the survey data so that the distribution of avatars in the survey accurately reflected the distribution of avatars in Norrath. As expected, the weight for low-level avatars is much higher than for high-level avatars. There is a good reason to believe, however, that the weighted data actually underrepresent the high-level avatars (*see Appendix B*). As it turns out, the weighting seems to make little difference in the results. *See Appendix B for an extended discussion of weighting.*[21]

B. The Population of Norrath

journal entry 26 april. i made a killing in misty acorns. you can pick these up from the ground in misty thicket. i was in rivervale one day and some lady was paying 8 pp per acorn. that's a lot of money. she told me it was for halfling armor. ok, whatever. so i started making a habit of picking them up whenever i saw one, then walking into rv and selling them to rich people. they would rather spend that kind of money than wander around looking for acorns. classic economics—my comparative advantage in foraging leads to exchange. and now i can buy a nice hat.

The overall population of Norrath is distributed on 40 different servers. A user can log on to any server, but an avatar created on Server X must live out its life on that server.[22] The basic geography and biotic population is the same on each server. Thus, the 40 servers represent repeated trials, 40 versions of Norrath with 40 different populations of users and avatars. Moreover, the rules of play differ slightly among servers, allowing some interesting policy impacts to be identified.

In order to get some understanding of the nature of populations on these servers, the Norrath Economic Survey (NES) asks respondents a series of questions about their participation in Norrath and Earth society. Table 1 reports some of the results. Perhaps the most striking finding is that a significant fraction, 20 percent, view themselves as people who "live in" Norrath. A similar fraction, 22 percent, express the desire to spend all of their time there. About 40 percent indicate that if a sufficient wage (self-defined) were available in Norrath, they would quit their economic activity on Earth (work or school, as the case may be) and devote their labor hours to the Norrathian economy. If we take the responses at face value, suppose that 20 percent of the people in Norrath at any one time consider themselves permanent residents. Until August 31, 2001, it was possible to observe overall population counts for Norrath,

Table 1. Participation in Norrath and Earth Society

Question	Agree or Strongly Agree	Disagree or Strongly Disagree	Don't know / NA
I live outside Norrath but I travel there regularly.	84	12	4
I live in Norrath but I travel outside of it regularly.	20	74	6
I wish I could spend more time in Norrath than I do now.	58	34	8
If I could make enough money selling things from Norrath, I would quit my current job or school and make my money there instead.	39	57	4
If I could, I would spend all of my time in Norrath.	22	74	4

N = 3,353 to 3,365. **Source:** NES 2001. The data are weighted so that the distribution of avatar levels in the data is comparable to the distribution of avatar levels in Norrath.

and these counts indicate that the average population at any given time is 60,381, or about 60,000.[23] This would indicate that 12,000 of those present in Norrath at any time consider themselves residents.

Table 2 reports some basic demographic characteristics of respondents to the Norrath Economic Survey. Judging from the means, the typical Norrathian is a well-educated single US man in his 20s, working full time, earning about $20 per hour. A significant fraction of the respondents are students (35 percent).

Interestingly, those who consider themselves residents of Norrath are not radically different from those who do not. The residents do tend to have lower education, fewer work hours, and lower wages, and they are less likely to have major Earth obligations (spouses, children). Like all emigrants, they are more likely to leave for the new world if the old world seems less promising, and if they have few obligations to stay.

Table 3 reports the typical Norrath activity of NES respondents, including an overview of their avatars. Since most people who play EverQuest have more than one avatar (the mean is 2.72 avatars per person), these figures are for the "main" avatar, which I take as the avatar with the highest level, which can go as high as level 60. The average respondent devotes a substantial amount of time to Norrath, especially considering that these figures have been weighted to correct for an over-representation of more-serious players.[24] Norrath consumes

Table 2. Population Characteristics

Characteristics	All Respondents	Residents[a]	Visitors[a]
Age (years)	24.3	22.4	24.8
Female (%)	7.8	10.1	7.2
Region: US (%)	81.3	82.4	81.1
Region: Canada (%)	6.6	7.5	6.4
Region: Western/Southern Europe (%)	8.9	7.1	9.4
Number of adults in HH	2.1	2.1	2.1
Married or cohabiting (%)	22.8	15.9	24.5
Single (%)	60.0	68.0	58.1
Have children to care for daily (%)	15.0	11.4	15.9
Education: less than High School (%)	12.4	19.4	10.6
Education: High School degree only (%)	35.6	41.7	34.1
Education: College degree or more (%)	31.0	18.6	34.1
Employment status: Working full time (%)	53.4	41.5	56.4
Employment status: Student, working (%)	19.4	22.3	18.6
Employment status: Student, not working (%)	15.6	21.1	14.3
Weekly work hours[b]	39.0	36.5	39.5
Monthly earnings ($)[b]	3,154.12	2,621.85	3,268.96
Hourly wage ($)[c]	20.74	17.57	21.42

Source: NES 2001. N = 3,619. The smallest cell count is 401, for resident hourly wage. The data are weighted so that the distribution of avatar levels in the data is comparable to the distribution of avatar levels in Norrath.

Notes:

[a] Residents agree or strongly agree that they "live in Norrath and travel outside of it regularly"—see Table 1. Visitors are all others.

[b] Work hours less than 5 per week were set to 'missing.' Earnings less than $5 per month or more than $100,000 per month were also set to 'missing.' Thus, these are averages among those who work for pay, excluding those earning more than $1.2 million per year. Monthly earnings are after tax ("take home pay"). Non-US respondents converted earnings to $US using prevalent exchange rates. Many respondents refused to answer the income question on grounds of privacy. Still, there were 2,853 valid responses to the question, a 79 percent response rate.

[c] The hourly wage divides monthly earnings by four times weekly hours.

Table 3. Norrath Characteristics

Norrath Characteristics	All Respondents	Residents[d]	Visitors[d]
Hours in Norrath over the past 24 hours	4.5	5.4	4.24
Hours in Norrath in a typical 24-hour period	4.7	6.0	4.43
Hours in Norrath in the past 7 days	26.3	32.5	24.8
Hours in Norrath in a typical 7-day period	28.9	36.1	27.1
Percent of the adult respondents devoting more hours in a typical week to Norrath than to work[a]	31.5	44.7	28.9
Main avatar[b]: Age (months)	12.6	12.3	12.7
Main avatar[b]: Level	38.3	38.4	38.3
Main avatar[b]: Hours devoted to	792.0	797.6	790.6
Main avatar[b]: Cash holdings (PP)[c]	7,678	5,413	8,232
Main avatar[b]: Value of equipment (PP)[c]	199,088	293,296	176,066

Source: NES 2001. N ranges from 2,809 (adult respondents only) to 3,467 (whole sample). The smallest cell count is 451, for residents in row 5. The data are weighted so that the distribution of avatar levels in the data is comparable to the distribution of avatar levels in Norrath.

Notes:

[a] Adults are those older than 18. The percentage is calculated for the adult population only.

[b] The main avatar is the avatar with the highest level. In case of a tie, the older avatar is taken. Levels can be as low as 1 and as high as 60.

[c] "PP" are "platinum pieces," the currency of Norrath. Respondents can observe their avatar's cash in a bank. As for equipment, they estimated the value of the equipment in Norrath markets. Many had difficulty with this, because some extremely valuable items cannot be traded. Still, both of these questions had 3,467 valid responses, a 96 percent response rate.

[d] Residents agree or strongly agree that they "live in Norrath and travel outside of it regularly"—see Table 1. Visitors are all others.

Table 4. Exchange Rates Against the Dollar, Summer 2001

Earth currencies observed on July 31

Country and Currency	Exchange Rate
Swedish Krona	0.09282
Indian Rupee	0.02122
Norrathian Platinum Piece	0.01072
Japanese Yen	0.00800
Spanish Peseta	0.00527
Korean Won	0.00077
Italian Lira	0.00045

Source: moneycentral.msn.com

more than 4 hours a day for visitors, more than 6 hours for those considering themselves residents. Among *adults,* more than a quarter of the visitors and almost one-half of the residents spend more time in Norrath in a typical week than they do working for pay. A typical avatar is about one year old and has seen almost 800 hours of development. The payoff is that the avatar has achieved 38 levels of experience, well on the way to the maximum of 60. Moreover, the typical avatar has banked thousands of platinum pieces—PP, Norrath's currency—in cash and assembled hundreds of thousands of platinum pieces worth of equipment. If we use the black market exchange rate of about 0.01 dollar per PP (more on this below), these wealth holdings range from $1,800 for visitors to $3,000 for residents. This does not account for the market value of the avatar itself, nor of the value of the other avatars (usually more than one) the person owns. The mean net worth of US families headed by a person younger than 35 years old was $66,000 in 1998, the most recent year for which data are available; the median was only $9,000.[25] It seems that for the typical Norrathian, avatars constitute a non-trivial stock of wealth.

C. Microeconomic Conditions in Norrath: The Main Markets

journal entry, 27 april. i notice that every time i enter the area called 'east commons,' the chat box lights up with buy and sell offers broadcast over the auction chat channel. the offers stream by so rapidly i can hardly follow them. since i am here to explore markets, and have finally collected a little cash, about 50pp, i respond to someone offering a pair of 'golden efreeti boots' for sale. golden boots—sounds nice. i ask the vendor where he is. 'come to tunnel.' i find 'the tunnel,' a connecting tunnel that effectively skirts the city of freeport. it is filled with perhaps 50 to 100 people, all of them shouting. looks basically like a pit at the chicago board of trade. i find the vendor and ask for a price. its 8,000pp. 'omg,' i say, 'how much money do people have here?' the reply: 'millions. lemme know when u get more pp :).'

In this section, I will describe Norrath's markets in general terms. Appendix D contains a discussion based on simple supply-and-demand theory; I do not include it here because it requires the reader to be fairly knowledgeable about the details of Norrathian existence. That appendix also has a discussion of local policy issues that are of interest primarily among Norrath's citizens and not the general reader.

There are two modes of buying and selling in Norrath, avatar-to-avatar (a2a) and avatar-to-biot (a2b). The former is much more cumbersome than the latter. In a2b commerce, the avatar can simply walk up to any biot merchant and examine the merchant's wares and buy/sell prices for any length of time. In a2a commerce, avatars on the supply side must constantly shout out what they have, and avatars on the demand side must hear the offer, find the seller, and then haggle over price. It is a bazaar.

Given the much higher transactions costs of a2a trade, it is a wonder that it exists at all. Yet it does exist to some extent, mostly because Norrath's designers encourage it through the prices offered by merchant biots. The typical buy offers of merchant biots are very low and their sell offers are very high. The difference leaves considerable space for an avatar to make money buying and selling a good, despite the difficulties involved in connecting to other avatars.

The biots end up serving two roles in the economy. First, they are the only source of certain important items, such as ore, gems, and spells. Second, merchant biots will buy any good in limitless quantitites, meaning that even if a good has no value in the a2a markets, it can still be turned into cash. As a result, the hunter who takes items from killed monsters can always find a cash outlet for them: if no avatars want them, merchant biots will always pay something. In this, the merchant biots act effectively as employers, and the pattern of their buy offers set the wage for different activities. Unfortunately, the pattern of these buy offers seem to encourage 'farming' over adventuring, because the special items that require risky adventures do not command a sufficiently high price premium from the biots.[26]

The a2a market is apparently expected to provide the price premia for special items. If special items are scarce, then the a2a market will keep the price high. Unfortunately, another unusual feature of the economy prevents the a2a market from sustaining a price above the biot buy price for very long, and it is this: items do not decay. As a result, the stock of these infinitely-durable goods rises continually as more and more people enter the world and hunt their way to the highest levels. Inevitably, the demand for new items falls, and with it, the a2a price. The general pattern is that a new item commands a significant price in the a2a market for some time, then gradually its price declines until the a2a price is as low as the merchant buy price. At that point, the item is just loot: anyone who gets it just sells it to a biot for the quick cash.

The only reason a2a markets persist at all is that the authorities continue to introduce new items, whose initial scarcity sustains them in the a2a market for a time. Nonetheless, the economy is marked by a steady and ongoing deflation (which will be documented below). The fall in goods prices means a gradual but chronic rise in real wages, and hence a decline in the challenge level of the game. This is taken to be a serious problem by many, but it is not clear that it is, or what can be done given the constraints set by history and by the need to keep the citizens happy.

The structure of a2a commerce leads to an interesting geographical phenomenon involving the formation of markets in space. In Norrath, there is an auction channel devoted to commerce, allowing anyone with goods to sell to broadcast their wares over a very wide region. The broadcast range is not unlimited however. The world is divided into zones and auction chat can only be broadcast within a zone. As a result, shrewd avatars do most selling in zones where demand for their goods is likely to be high. Shrewd buyers travel to zones where the goods they seek are abundant. At the same time, the bazaar-like nature of the haggling requires that trade be concentrated in space.

The result is a pattern of markets in predictable places. In every zone, one will often hear demanders shouting their buy offers for goods that are abundant there. Yet general trade for items from far-flung corners of the world occurs only in a few zones, actually usually in just one zone. Interestingly, the specific zone differs across the 40 different servers on which Norrath exists. It can be easily identified; the NES asks respondents where they would go to sell an item at a fair price, if they had to do so quickly and could travel anywhere in the world. On every server, users overwhelmingly indicate just one zone, although the zone that they indicate is not uniform across servers.[27] The most frequent is the East Commons tunnel (described in the vignette above), on 27 of the 40 servers. Next most frequent is a zone named

Greater Faydark (also referred to as "Faymart"), on 9 servers. The city of Freeport, which is very close to the EC tunnel, is the main market on the remaining 4 servers. On 36 of the 40 servers, there is at least 80 percent agreement on the identity of the main market—and this is an open-ended, unstructured question.[28] Appendix A speculates on possible reasons why markets arose in these spots and not others in the vast expanse of the Norrathian world.

Roughly speaking, then, Norrath is characterized by two main markets, an a2b labor market where hunters gain their wages by killing monster biots and selling their loot to merchant biots, and an a2a goods market, existing in all zones but heavily concentrated in just one, where merchants and hunters engage in a cumbersome trade in certain scarce items.

D. Macroeconomic Indicators for Norrath

journal entry, 15 june. i start yet another avatar, this one a tall, beautiful, dark-skinned woman. what the heck, it's becoming more common these days. i wont try to act like a woman, let's just see what happens when i act like me but in a woman's body. well. within 24 hours, i have been repeatedly whistled at, examined, "protected" from biots i could easily kill myself, given rings, and asked to "go on dates in this game." more ominously, i have been having more difficulty getting into groups than usual; there seems to be some question about my understanding of tactics.

Is the aggregate economic activity of the 40 versions of Norrath worthy of mention? To answer this question, I collected whatever macroeconomic data about the world I could find. The main limitation was the need to protect the independence of the study, and therefore I have made no effort to contact Verant Interactive to obtain in-house data. As a result, all of the information reported here is either available to the public at large through various channels, or has been obtained directly from users through the NES. It is important to stress that the external market for Norrathian goods is underground. Sony has stated that Norrathian items are its intellectual property (Sandoval, 2001). Trading these items for US currency is considered theft.[29] Nonetheless, trade goes on.[30]

The foreign trade market and exchange rates. Several dollar-based markets for platinum pieces, avatars, and items exist on web auction sites. Trade occurs as follows. In the Earth market, two earthlings agree to trade US dollars for some Norrathian item. Earthling A gives Earthling B the money. Then they both create avatars in Norrath and meet at an agreed-upon spot, where Norrathian B gives Norrathian A the item.[31]

Trade in platinum pieces seems to be nothing more than an ordinary foreign exchange market. Trade in goods is a little harder to categorize as either imports or exports; it is a trade where Swedes travel to Germany to buy and sell Swedish goods for Deutschmarks, with all the goods remaining in Sweden. It only happens because the dollar markets offer much lower transactions costs than the Norrath markets. Perhaps the best metaphor for this trade is in terms of tourism exports. In the tourism industry, members of country X use X's currency to obtain goods and services that are created in and remain in country Y. In Norrath's foreign trade markets, Earthlings use US dollars to obtain goods that are created in and remain in Norrath.

Without a broad survey of participants, it is impossible to estimate the gross volume of this trade. However, records at one web site show that on an ordinary weekday (Thursday, September 6, 2001), the total volume of successfully completed auctions (N = 112) was about $9,200.[32] A further $3,700 in currency transactions (N = 32) were conducted. At an annual pace, these figures put the gross exports of goods and currency at more than $5 million, about 3.5 percent of gross annual output (see below). This underestimates the volume of trade, of course, because there are many more avenues of exchange than just this one website. Some 45 percent of NES respondents indicated that they knew someone who had purchased Norrathian items for US dollars.

The currency market gives direct information about exchange rates. I collected data on 616 auctions, at random, from various sites, over the period from May to September 2001. This sample represents a small fraction of the universe of ongoing currency auctions. I treated an auction as a valid observation only if it had been completed and there was an obvious winning bid. Across these auctions, the average price of a platinum piece in terms of US dollars was 0.01072, or a little more than a penny. The dollar exchange rates of various currencies are listed in Table 4. Most Norrathians would fix the exchange rate at about 0.0125. The rate was, in fact, 0.0133 in May but had slipped to 0.0098 by September, a decline of over 25 percent in a quarter.

GNP per capita. The market for avatars can be used to develop an estimate of Norrath's GNP per capita. From this market, I obtained data on 651 avatar auctions, using the same selection rules and sites as for the currency auctions. Most accounts are auctioned as if they were sales of the main avatar on the account, that being the avatar with the highest level. However, the billing and login structure of EverQuest means that a person cannot sell an avatar by itself; to give control of one avatar to another person, you must give them access to your entire account, including all of the other avatars. Nonetheless, the contents of auctions are usually a few basic descriptors about the main avatar, such as her level and type (warrior, wizard, etc.). Most accounts sell for between $500 and $1,000. Since the exchange rates indicate that typical avatars have more than $1,000 in Norrathian wealth, the avatars on the auction market are apparently being sold at a discount. The source of the reduced value is fairly apparent however: one of the most attractive features of life in Norrath is the power to choose your avatar's appearance, abilities, and even name. When your purchase a ready-made avatar, that freedom is lost. Moreover, the auctioned avatar already has a well-developed social role on its server, and it is not apparent whether that is a good role or not. For these reasons, we can take the auction market value as an underestimate of the true dollar value of an avatar.

My strategy is to use the avatar auction market to develop the shadow price of an avatar's level, then use the NES data to determine how many levels Norrathians create in a hour of game time; this yields a measure of gross value creation per hour in terms of dollars. The idea is that the avatar's level generally determines its amount of equipment and platinum pieces as well, so that a user who adds a level to an avatar increases Norrath's stock of avatar capital, equipment, and platinum pieces. When someone buys an avatar on the auction market, they buy the avatar with these bells and whistles. This means that the total value of the added level, including all three sources of value, is priced by the auction market.

There are a number of ways of developing the shadow prices. I describe three methods in Appendix C. Using the most direct method, the auction market puts the shadow price of an avatar level at about $13 per level, and data from the NES show that Norrath's avatars create about $15,000 in avatar capital in an hour. This makes the gross national product of Norrath about $135 million. Per capita, it comes to $2,266. Table 5 shows the gross national product per capita of 171 countries, as measured by the World Bank. Norrath is the 77th richest country in the world, roughly equal to Russia. The table also shows the result of two other methods that give a lower GNP per capita, the lowest making Norrath equivalent to Bulgaria. By all measures, Norrath is richer than many important countries, including China and India.

Inflation. A true price index would require a broad-based survey of avatars to determine what items they had recently purchased, and at what prices. Given that there are tens of thousands of items, the survey would have to be quite extensive to generate a reasonably large amount of data about all the items in the market basket of typical avatars. In lieu of undertaking such an enterprise, instead I made informal notes of the kinds of items that seemed often traded in the main markets. There are also a number of web sites that publish platinum piece prices of various goods. Using these data, I developed a price index based on a selection of 29 different goods. The goods were chosen to be representative of the different kinds of items (chest armor, boots, helmets, weapons, etc.). Also, I purposely tried to avoid very high-end items and very low-end items. Finally, unlike real world price indices, I could not weight the items' prices by their contribution to the 'market basket,' since I could not determine what the standard bundle of items really is. Therefore, each item is given equal weight. I also record whether an item is looted from biots or crafted by avatars, as well as whether the item is part of the original EverQuest game or one of the later expansions of the game ("The Ruins of Kunark" was released in April 2000, "The Scars of Velious" in December 2000.)

Having selected the items, I took price data from one site, Allakhazam's Magical Realm (EverQuest.allakhazam.com). This site is one of the more popular fan sites and, importantly, the price data are entered by users and then left untouched.[33] Prices are available beginning in December 2000.

Table 6 reports these indices. The overall price index fell from 100 in Q4 2000 to 71 in Q3 2001, a 29 percent deflation in one year. The individual item indices indicate that much of this disinflation was caused by a price collapse in items from the expansions, which lost 59 percent of their value. However, even the old world items experienced a substantial deflation, with their value falling by 17 percent. Note that if nominal wages (i.e. loot from biots per hour of hunting) remained constant in this period, the deflation represents a rapid rise in the real wage. This is a good thing on Earth, but has led to some dissatisfaction in Norrath as the challenge level of the world, and hence its entertainment value, has fallen.

Nominal wages. Hourly wages in Norrath are substantially below wages on Earth. We can derive an estimate of the wage in platinum pieces by regressing the total value of an avatar's equipment and cash by the number of hours that avatar has been active. The 3,619 NES respondents gave valid information on 7,397 of their avatars. Regressing the PP value of their holdings on hours of time input yields a coefficient of 319, meaning that the average avatar makes 319 PP per hour. At the market exchange rate of 0.01072 PP per dollar, this amounts to about $3.42 an hour. The average Earth wage for those who work in the NES is $20.74, and among the self-identified residents of Norrath it is $17.57. If we treat the conditions of life in Norrath as a compensating differential, this suggests that for the average Norrath

Table 5. Gross National Product Per Capita, Various Countries, 1995

Country	GNP per capita	Country	GNP per capita	Country	GNP per capita	Country	GNP per capita
Luxembourg	43680	Seychelles	6460	Jamaica	1680	Pakistan	500
Switzerland	41350	St. Kitts|Nevis	5460	Jordan	1600	Mauritania	450
Japan	39720	Uruguay	5210	Algeria	1590	Comoros	440
Denmark	31810	Oman	4940	El Salvador	1570	Azerbaijan	410
Norway	31500	Czech Republic	4420	Romania	1410	Bhutan	390
United States	28150	Hungary	4140	Ecuador	1400	Equatorial Guinea	390
Germany	27920	Malaysia	4010	Guatemala	1400	Ghana	370
Austria	26930	Chile	4000	Dominican Republic	1390	India	370
Belgium	25520	Trinidad and Tobago	3870	Swaziland	1380	Lao PDR	370
Netherlands	25360	Gabon	3850	Bulgaria	1370	Nicaragua	360
Sweden	25180	Mexico	3800	*NORRATH III*	*1350*	Benin	350
France	24700	South Africa	3740	Kazakhstan	1280	Central African	350
Iceland	24650	Brazil	3690	Vanuatu	1250	Gambia, The	350
Brunei	24400	St. Lucia	3570	Iran, Islamic Rep.	1220	Sao Tome	340
Hong Kong	23120	Mauritius	3420	Cape Verde	1210	Zambia	340
Singapore	23060	Botswana	3360	Syrian Arab Republic	1210	Bangladesh	330
Finland	21050	Costa Rica	3350	Papua New Guinea	1150	Mongolia	330
Kuwait	20200	Slovak Republic	3110	Samoa	1130	Togo	310
Canada	19880	Croatia	3100	Morocco	1120	Haiti	300
Australia	19790	Venezuela, RB	3070	Philippines	1040	Yemen, Rep.	270
UAE	19340	Estonia	3010	Indonesia	1000	Kenya	260
United Kingdom	19120	Panama	2940	Egypt, Arab Rep.	990	Cambodia	250
Italy	19090	Dominica	2910	Kiribati	960	Mali	250
New Caledonia	17790	Grenada	2840	Ukraine	950	Uganda	250
French Polynesia	17560	Turkey	2810	Maldives	920	Vietnam	250
Macao, China	16640	Poland	2770	Suriname	880	Angola	240
Ireland	16130	Thailand	2760	Bolivia	870	Madagascar	240
Qatar	15570	Belize	2630	Uzbekistan	870	Burkina Faso	220
Israel	14960	Lebanon	2590	Solomon Islands	840	Guinea-Bissau	220
Spain	14370	Fiji	2410	Moldova	820	Chad	210
New Zealand	14240	St. Vincent	2320	Kyrgyz Republic	710	Nepal	210
Bahamas, The	11700	*NORRATH I*	*2260*	Armenia	700	Nigeria	210
Cyprus	11520	Russian Federation	2250	Sri Lanka	700	Niger	190
Greece	10900	Latvia	2160	Lesotho	690	Rwanda	190
Korea, Rep.	10250	Namibia	2160	Albania	660	Eritrea	180
Portugal	10070	Peru	2060	Cameroon	660	Sierra Leone	180
Bahrain	8660	Micronesia	2010	Cote d'Ivoire	650	Malawi	160
Malta	8400	Colombia	2000	Honduras	650	Tanzania	160
Slovenia	8300	Belarus	1980	Guyana	630	Burundi	150
Puerto Rico	7650	*NORRATH II*	*1820*	Zimbabwe	630	Mozambique	140
Argentina	7380	Tunisia	1820	Guinea	560	Congo, Dem. Rep.	130
Antigua	7250	Paraguay	1790	Senegal	550	Ethiopia	110
Saudi Arabia	7180	Tonga	1760	China	520		
Barbados	6850	Lithuania	1690	Congo, Rep.	510		

Source: World Bank

resident, an hour in Norrath produces utility worth $14.15. This figure is more than the fee of $10 per *month* that users pay to access Norrath. Norrathians gain a substantial consumer surplus from the world's existence.

A wage of $3.42 an hour is sufficient to sustain Earth existence for many people. Many users spend upwards of 80 hours per week in Norrath, hours of time input that are not unheard of in Earth professions. In 80 hours, at the average wage, the typical user generates Norrathian cash and goods worth $273.60. In a month, that would be over $1,000, in a year over $12,000. The poverty line for a single person in the United States is $8,794. Economically speaking, there is little reason to question, on feasibility grounds at least, that those who claim to be living and working in Norrath, and not Earth, may actually be doing just that.

Poverty and inequality. Inequality is significant. Certainly, higher level avatars have vastly more wealth than lower-level avatars, but this is intended as part of the structure of the world. It is more striking that significant inequality exists within levels, a fact that seems to trouble many Norrathians. Using avatar wealth holdings, we can calculate two statistics of interest. First, define the poverty rate as the percentage of avatars whose wealth falls below 50 percent of the median wealth in their level. By this measure, about 33 percent of the avatars are poor. If instead we set the poverty line according to the mean wealth, not the median, the poverty rate is 68 percent. Evidently the distribution is extremely long in the upper tail. In any case, the distribution of wealth in Norrath is apparently significantly less equal than its distribution in post-industrial societies on Earth.

IV. Norrath: Its Future and Meaning

journal entry, 20 june. i started a loner, an asocial avatar on a deadly server where all avatars hunt, kill, and loot one another. anyone studying hobbes should come here and have a look at the state of nature.

Why should economists and other social scientists have an interest in places like Norrath? One reason is that these places provide a fascinating and unique laboratory for research on human society; Appendix A lists a number of research projects that seem to be uniquely feasible in Norrath. The second and more significant is that VWs may soon become one of the most important forums for human interaction, on a level with telephones. Moreover, in that role, they may induce widespread changes in the organization of Earth society.

Table 6. Price Indices For Norrathian Items

INDICES	Q4 2000	Q1 2001	Q2 2001	Q3 2001
Armor - Arms - Gatorscale Sleeves	100.00	69.25	88.12	53.04
Armor - Back - Kunzar Cloak (Kunark)	100.00	83.53	57.61	43.06
Armor - Chest - Robe of the Oracle	100.00	103.38	64.51	47.12
Armor - Ear - Forest Loop Earring (Kunark)	100.00	77.05	50.66	35.66
Armor - Ear - Orc Fang Earring (Velious)	100.00	28.75	13.38	12.09
Armor - Face - Silver Ruby Veil (crafted)	100.00	89.30	84.32	87.25
Armor - Feet - Dwarven Work Boots	100.00	85.96	70.20	52.19
Armor - Fingers - Jagged Band	100.00	79.03	80.98	74.70
Armor - Fingers - Platinum Jasper Ring (crafted)	100.00	86.26	81.17	75.91
Armor - Hands - Dark Mail Gauntlets	100.00	44.78	49.21	70.33
Armor - Head - Executioner's Hood	100.00	107.11	61.78	78.07
Armor - Legs - Gatorscale Leggings	100.00	91.96	84.54	71.34
Armor - Neck - Black Iron Medallion	100.00	141.37	158.20	173.61
Armor - Shield - Charred Guardian Shield	100.00	112.50	96.59	103.85
Armor - Shoulders - Drolvarg Mantle (Kunark)	100.00	91.94	59.78	51.81
Armor - Waist - Braided Cinch Cord	100.00	58.21	70.98	71.79
Armor - Wrist - Runed Mithril Bracer	100.00	80.51	66.63	49.36
Armor - Wrist - Chipped Bone Bracelet	100.00	80.00	79.38	63.07
Weapon - 1HB - Enamelled Black Mace	100.00	81.34	57.99	47.90
Weapon - 2HB - Runed Totem Staff	100.00	106.77	120.31	126.95
Weapon - 1HS - Short Sword of the Ykesha	100.00	97.00	55.76	42.51
Weapon - 2HS - Runic Carver (Kunark)	100.00	140.00	143.64	73.65
Weapon - Bow - Trueshot Longbow	100.00	169.41	161.32	172.83
Weapon - Piercing - Harpoon of the Depths (Kunark)	100.00	85.50	60.38	28.80
Miscellaneous Items - Sarnak Ceremonial Dagger (Kunark)	100.00	80.00	107.50	42.05
Miscellaneous Items - Stein of Moggok	100.00	121.73	120.37	106.71
Miscellaneous Items - Fine Plate Breastplate (crafted)	100.00	91.73	97.76	97.34
Miscellaneous Items - Fine Plate Vambraces (crafted)	100.00	71.38	82.34	71.38
Miscellaneous Items - Cone of the Mystics (Kunark)	100.00	50.00	54.17	39.58
Overall Item Index - Weights each item equally	100.00	89.85	82.05	71.17
Loot Index - Items not made by avatars	100.00	90.68	81.36	69.28
Old World Index - Items before Kunark and Velious	100.00	93.76	87.26	82.73
New World Index - Items from Kunark and Velious	100.00	79.60	68.39	40.84
Craftwork Index – Items crafted by avatars	100.00	84.67	86.40	82.97
Old World Loot Index - Looted old world items only	100.00	95.90	87.46	82.67

Source: Price data from Allakhazam's Magical Realm price database (everquest. allakhazam.com). Prices are entered by users and are in no sense "official." Obviously frivolous prices were ignored. Each item has at least five legitimate price entries in each quarter.

Virtual Worlds are flourishing and their growth seems likely to continue. They already represent an area of internet commerce that is booming when other sectors are having difficulty surviving. The attraction of the VW lies in its ability to replicate the physical and economic world of Earth, with slight but significant changes in the rules. These changes—such as granting people the freedom to have whatever appearance and skills they wish—are sufficient to generate a society and a flavour of daily life that is so attractive that many thousands of people apparently consider themselves permanent residents. Tens of thousands of adults now devote more time to VWs than to paid employment. Similar numbers use their Earth money to buy things in VWs. Almost one million seem willing to pay a monthly fee to at least see what VWs are all about. And these numbers are growing.

What does the future look like? The Next Big Thing appears to be Project Entropia, expected to be launched sometime in early 2002. Where Norrath considers the infusion of Earth dollars and Earth markets a problem, Project Entropia embraces them. The game (which is apparently not really a game at all, according to its owners) is being developed by a private Swedish company, Mindark. According to materials on the company website (www. mindark.com), the ultimate goal of the project is a worldwide network monopoly in virtual reality 3D commerce, replacing all existing internet browsers and web interfaces with a single virtual world of millions of users. The "game" will be distributed for free, and access will be free; it is assumed that a seedling VW market and society, along the lines of Norrath, will rapidly emerge. Unlike Norrath, however, users in Project Entropia will be able to buy things for their avatars using real currency and credit cards, and they will get real cash from the VW by selling loot.

The company hopes that success in the gaming world will be a beachhead to broader commercial success. Free software and free access to the VW will encourage more and more people to come to Project Entropia to socialize with one another, and then to shop with their avatars while they socialize. Network effects will kick in; if you and your friends spend 800 hours developing avatars in Project Entropia, no single person in your group will want to incur a friendless 800-hour start-up cost to switch to a competing world. At some point the Project will encourage brick-and-mortar companies to establish virtual 3D stores in the world, where a person could go to buy a hat for the avatar, and then a hat for themselves. Mindark envisions the emergence of virtual jobs. For example, Walmart might pay a user (in which currency?

does it matter?) to use her avatar to sell avatar clothes in the virtual Walmart. By the economics of network monopolies, the Project Entropia VW may become "the internet" for most people: you turn on your computer, wake up your avatar in Project Entropia, and teleport her to some spot where you meet your old college friend's avatar, chat for awhile, then go shopping.

Much argues for the viability of Mindark's strategy, and the company will probably not be alone in this niche for long. Indeed, there is already evidence in existing VWs that the inclusion of Earth-style markets and marketing would be profitable. Microsoft's virtual world of "Dereth" has markets that are clumsier than Norrath's, and Dereth's population is smaller and not as wealthy. That is exactly what development economists would predict. Transactions costs slow down economic growth. It follows that modernized markets would allow a new VW to rapidly eclipse Norrath in population and wealth, brushing aside its quaint bazaar economy like the anachronism it was designed to be. The future of avatar spaces, and perhaps internet commerce and the internet itself, may belong to highly commercialized VWs.

The impact on Earth society is hard to overestimate. With the development of voice technology, communication in VWs will move from cumbersome chat to telephone-like conversation, thus greatly enhancing the VW as a place of social interaction. Already one can conduct chat-based a2a meetings and classes in places like Norrath, and soon such meetings will not seem much different from actual face-to-face meetings. Telecommuting, which now involves working on the home computer and emailing reports to the boss, will eventually become "going to work" in a virtual office and holding face to face meetings with the avatars of coworkers. Families living thousands of miles apart will meet every day for a few hours in the evening, gathering their avatars around the virtual kitchen table and catching up. And the day of driving to the store may well be over. Earth roads will be empty because, instead of using them, everyone will be sailing across the azure heavens on their flying purple horses, to shimmering virtual Walmarts in the sky.

journal entry, 14 july. someone just told me that the name of my favorite city, qeynos, is just "sony eq" backwards.

Appendices

Appendix A. Norrath as a laboratory of human society

journal entry, 28 may. i started a new avatar, just so i could look at a different continent. this guy is a dwarf. dwarves hate water, now i know why. i took a boat across an ocean. at an island stop, some idiot fellow-traveler provoked a local biot pirate, who came onto the ship and started attacking me. near death, i took my only recourse and jumped off the boat. too bad it had long since left the dock. i watched it sail off into the mist, leaving me desperately paddling about, far at sea, a very lonely dwarf indeed.

In the course of preparing this report, I was struck by the number of research projects that would be uniquely feasible in Norrath. Here I will list a few.

Utopia. What is the ideal society? Philosophers and theologians debate it in the abstract, while politicians, journalists, and social scientists attempt to remold Earth societies in what they presume are good directions. But when business people actually design fee-based societies, we discover in the most popular ones the kind of world that ordinary people want the most. If ordinary people actually wanted a world of equality, peace, relaxation, freedom from want, then Norrath would be an equal, peaceful, relaxing, free world. But the Norrath that makes money is not a cyberpolynesia at all. It is a world of grotesque inequality, of incessant warfare and struggling, a world with bitter wants and unmet needs, where rising real wages make people *complain*. It is much like Earth, except for two elements that are quite utopian and have been impossible to implement here: freedom to start over, and equality of opportunity. It would seem that Utopia is just Earth with an escape clause and a level playing field.

Social norm studies. In the NES, 7.7 percent of the respondents are female, but 18.7 percent of the main avatars are female. It turns out that 12.6 percent of males are playing females as their main avatar, while 11.2 percent of females are playing male avatars. That some people switch gender is a well-known fact in Norrath, and it is also well-known that sex does not have any impact on the avatar's skills and abilities. Nonetheless, it appears that male and female avatars are treated differently. (See two essays on economics and gender in Norrath by Mindy Basi (PhD, Library and Information Sciences, at www.angelfire.com/journal/kwill/).

One could conduct endless studies on the impact of various features of the avatars on the avatar's outcomes and social standing. As a research method, one could have study participants do various specific things with the avatar and then record the avatar's success at accomplishing various tasks. Since social activity involves repeating N-player prisoner's dilemmas with a fluid population, it is an ideal environment for studying cooperation. It would be relatively easy to hold experiments and provide meaningful payoffs, since PP—which have a great deal of value in Norrath—can be purchased for only about a penny apiece.

Market studies. The world has flourishing central markets in goods. It would be a simple matter to conduct auctions in a number of ways and record their outcomes. Again, the items for sale are really quite valuable to the people there; there is a high likelihood that the auction or experiment would be taken seriously.

Social conventions. There are many conventions in Norrath, and variation in them can be directly observed because of the way that the world exists on 40 different servers. This variation can be exploited to allow comparative studies of the emergence of conventions and focal points. For example, there is one main marketplace on each of the 40 servers, and on most, but not all, servers it is located in the East Commons Tunnel. Now it so happens that sometimes Verant will create a new server as a "split" from an old one; the new server is launched and then any avatars on certain old servers may transfer to the new server. A brief examination of the server-split patterns reveals that a new server is far more likely to have its market somewhere *besides* the EC tunnel if, and only if, at least one of its mother servers had its market somewhere else. In other words, there is strong evidence of path dependence in the geographical location of the main market.

Law and economics. Many of the servers have different rules about who can kill whom and how much loot an avatar can take. The most Hobbesian server, Rallos Zek, does not yet have a sovereign. It also has weak and splintered markets and a low population. Other servers divide the avatars into warring races or continents. One could learn much by tracing the status of markets to legal conditions.

Poverty. Norrath is marked by an extremely unequal distribution of wealth. Thus, if the question is "If we could construct any world we wished, in order to make ourselves happy, would we choose one with equality?" the answer from Norrath seems to be a clear NO. Most people in Norrath seem to believe that the world and its reward system are basically just. Rather, there is some concern about the practice of twinking, by which the wealth of a powerful avatar is used to give a new avatar extraordinary equipment. This reveals that the one ethical norm that dominates social politics in Norrath is not equality of outcomes but equality of opportunity.

Spontaneous order and endogenous government. Most servers have an elaborate political order based on guilds of avatars. The guild system regulates access to certain scarce items and imposes punishments on asocial behavior. Guilds can war with one another. An exploration of guild behavior could produce useful insights about the emergence of governing structures.

Urban location. Why is the main market in the EC tunnel in most cases? That particular spot is somewhat in the center of Norrath, but it has only one biot merchant, no conveniences (ovens, forges, etc.), no protecting biot guards, and no bank. The nearby city of Freeport has many vendors, a bank, all the major conveniences, and it is a walled city protected by guards. Why not Freeport instead? The main reason would appear to be that a percentage of the avatars in Norrath have a faction identity ('evil') that prevents them from entering Freeport. They can, however, cut around the city by using the tunnel. And it would seem that this is the only reason the tunnel is preferred to the city: it has a slightly greater amount of through traffic. Of course it would take a geographer to give a more solid answer. Still, the distribution of Norrath's population in space, and the endogenous emergence of urban areas that were not designed to be urban, can provide useful research materials for those interested in the economics of location.

These are only a few of many other projects that might lend themselves to an application in Norrath. The primary difficulty for the researcher would be the costs involved in becoming familiar with what is, at first, a very strange world indeed.

Appendix B. Weights and weighting

journal entry, 28 may, continued. as i paddle, my stamina dwindles towards zero, at which point i will presumably drown. no sign of land. 'help!' i shout. but no one can help me—too far away, and who could find me in this mist anyway. then, like a miracle, i see land. i paddle over to it. step ashore. then i hear a sound, like giant footsteps...i look around..it IS giant footsteps, a cyclops, and coming my way. does it see me? maybe. then run. but it will catch me. maybe i should turn, face the music, fight. no way. therefore: "HELP!!" this time i am in luck—there's a wizard nearby. 'hang on ill tp u.' a teleport! gods be praised. he arrives and conducts the teleport spell, and in a flash i am back home.

The Norrath Economic Survey (NES) was conducted by posting notices to internet discussion boards frequented by EverQuest players. Thus, the sample is entirely self-selected. However, there is a clear direction of selection, in that those who respond are more likely to be an avid player of the game. Thus, the NES sample contains avatars whose levels will be higher than the levels of avatars in the game's population. While in game, one cannot observe anything about an avatar's users, so correcting for the bias on the basis of user information is not possible. However, it was possible (until August 31, 2001) to observe the distribution of avatars by level on a given server.

I used actual distributions of avatar levels on EverQuest servers to assign weights to NES respondents. The weights ensure that the distribution of avatar levels in the NES corresponds to the distribution of levels in the game. It seems likely that the weights reduce (although they may not eliminate) the corresponding bias in the NES towards more avid players.

My method for weighting was as follows. I observed avatars by distribution on two servers, Tarew Marr and Tholuxe Paells, over a 72-hour time period. The first is one of the oldest servers in the game, the second is one of the newest. Since newer servers are likely to have less advanced avatars, the two servers put bounds on the likely range of level distributions. As it turned out, the distributions were surprisingly similar. I broke the distributions down into groups of five levels, so that in the end I had 12 numbers indicating the percentage of Norrath's avatar population having levels from 1 to 5, 6 to 10, 11 to 15, and so on. Call these percentages $p1$, $p2$, $p3$, etc. In the NES sample, the corresponding percentages by level can be labeled $q1$, $q2$, $q3$, and so on. If the NES sample size is $N1$ and the Norrath population is $N2$, the weight applied to a level 1 avatar in the NES was $(N2/N1)*(p1/q1)$. Thus, the weighted percentage of level 1 to 5 avatars in the NES would become $p1$.

I made these weight calculations for Tarew Marr and Tholuxe Paells separately and then averaged them to derive a single weight.

I then used these avatar weights to derive a person weight for the NES respondents. Each respondent had been asked to indicate what percentage of time he played each of his avatars. I used these percentages to make a weighted average of the weights on each of his avatars. Thus, a person who uses a level 1 avatar frequently and a level 30 avatar less frequently would receive a higher weight. This is because EverQuest population has more level 1 avatars than the NES sample.

Table A1 below lists the avatar weights by level. The table reflects that N1, the sample size of the NES is 3,619 and N2, the population of Norrath round the clock, is 60,381. Thus N2/N1 = 16.68, and the weights are distributed around this figure. Interestingly, the biggest deviation of the NES from Norrath is not at the top but at the bottom. Low-level avatars are quite under-represented, but high-level avatars are not heavily over-represented. Instead, it is the mid-level avatars who mostly selected themselves into the NES. Perhaps this reflects the possibility that highest-level avatars know the game so well that they no longer spend time at 'spoiler' web sites.

Table A1. Avatar Weights for the NES sample

Level	Weight
1–5	99.72
6–10	30.16
11–15	22.11
16–20	15.41
21–25	13.51
26–30	12.21
31–35	12.38
36–40	12.14
41–45	11.72
46–50	14.52
51–55	16.32
56–60	17.48

Appendix C. Methods of calculating GDP per capita

journal entry, september 24. i investigate another server—it happens to be the one where i started my first avatar, alaniel. i haven't been back since. so i load him into the world. arriving, i smile to myself—he is still hiding behind the lean-to at freeport west gate.

The first method is simplest. A regression of price on level in the auction market yields the following equation:

Price = -319.625 + 13.297*Level

This implies that the shadow price of a level is about $13.30.

The NES asks respondents how much time they have devoted to each avatar. A regression of hours of time for the highest-level avatar (which is always the avatar that is the subject of the auction market) on the avatar's level yields this equation:

Hours = -568.129 + 51.440*Level

This implies that it takes about 51.4 hours to add a level to an avatar on average. The 60,381 users present in Norrath in a given hour are therefore adding about (60381/51.440) = 1,173.81 levels to their avatars in that hour. Each level being valued on the market at $13.297, we have a gross creation of value that amounts to (1,173.81)*(13.297) = $15,608.15 per hour. Now because the 60,381 average user population is an average over all times of day and all days of the week, it reflects an avatar-building workforce that is present round the clock, all year long. The average, in other words, indicates that there are typically 60,381 people actively building avatar capital at any time of day or night, weekends, holidays, whenever. This goes on all day long, 365 days a year. There are no weekends or vacations in Norrath; 60,381 represents not full-time equivalents but "all-time equivalents." This means that the annual creation of value for this economy is found by taking the hourly creation of value and multiplying by the number of hours in a year, which is 8,766. This makes the gross national product of Norrath equal to about (8766)*(15608.15) = $136.821 million. Dividing by the population of 60,381, we estimate the annual GNP per capita as $2,266.

This is the most straightforward approach but not perhaps the most plausible. An examination of scatterplots of the avatar auction data (see *Figure A1*) suggests that the simple approach is biased in some significant ways. Mostly, it does not take into account that there is almost no market for avatars below level 20. Second, it ignores the fact that levels above 50 are given a much higher price by the auction market. Third, it ignores that fact that adding levels becomes much harder after level 50, something that is apparent to anyone active in Norrath for any length of time.

To correct for these aspects, first of all, I will assume that avatar-building below 20 adds nothing to the GNP.

Second, the scatterplots suggest that between level 20 and level 50, the dollar value of an avatar rises moderately, and after level 50 it rises more rapidly. A linear spline regression

Figure A1. Predicted Avatar Prices by Level

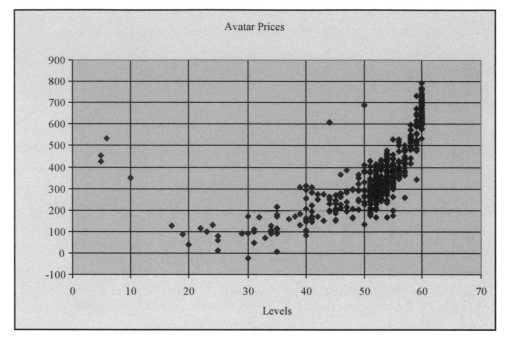

Source: N = 639. Data from completed web auctions. Prices are the fitted values of regressions of winning bid price on the main avatar level up to the 6th power, plus dummy variables for the avatar's class (warrior, wizard, etc.) and server.

of prices on levels reveals that the price of an avatar rises by about $5.33 per level between levels 20 and 50, and by about $37.37 per level above level 50. I will use these figures as the shadow prices of adding a level to avatars at the corresponding levels.

As for the creation of levels, what is needed is some measure of how long it takes to add a level to an avatar. This in turn requires a regression of the hours devoted to an avatar on the level the avatar has attained. The NES asks respondents directly how many total hours they have spent on a given avatar, but it is not clear how accurate such responses would be. A typical avatar is more than one year old—how many could accurately estimate how many hours they spent on a given activity over the past year? On the other hand, there is reason to believe that these responses might be extremely accurate. For players of EverQuest, it is actually possible to observe exactly how many hours an avatar has been active, simply by typing a command. But we cannot know how many NES respondents did this before entering their responses. (Some were actually confused about whether the question wanted earth hours or Norrath hours, which are much shorter. For many people, Earth's position as sole locus of Reality is really quite unstable.) So perhaps the figures are inaccurate.

In anticipation of such accuracy problems, the NES also asks respondents what percent of their total time they devote to each of their avatars, as well as the month that the avatar was born. It seems fairly likely that both of these responses are more accurate than the gross hours estimate. The NES then asks respondents how many hours they spend in Norrath in a typical week. The total hours per avatar can be measured as total hours = (months avatar has been alive)*(4 weeks per month)*(X hours in Norrath per week)*(percent of time on this avatar).

It turns out that the direct estimate of hours per avatar average 798 hours in the NES sample, while the indirect method averages 1,443 hours per avatar.

I estimated two spline regressions of hours on levels, estimating the number of hours necessary to add a level between levels 20 and 50 and above level 50, with these two measures of time input. For the direct method, the regression indicated an input of 21 hours per level between 20 and 50, and 152 per level above 50. For the indirect method, the inputs were 31 hours per level between 20 and 50, and 183 hours per level above 50.

Of the 60,000 avatars present in Norrath at any one time, 27,600 are between 20 and 50, and the remaining 22,200 are above 50. Recall that these figure have been weighted to reflect the fact that the NES over-represents high-level avatars, and that the weighting method probably makes than under-represented. These figures indicate that, in a given hour, the middle group is responsible for 27,600 hours of avatar level creation, and the higher group is responsible for 22,200 hours of avatar level creation.

Using the direct time figures, the middle group produces an aggregate of 27,600/21 = 1,314 levels per hour, valued at $5.33 each. The higher group produces 22,200/152 = 146 levels per hour, valued at $37.37 each. Thus each hour, Norrathians generate 1314*5.33 + 146*37.37 = $12,460 worth of avatar capital. In the course of a year, this is $109 million in new avatar value, about $1,820 per user. This would make Norrath the 84th richest country in the world, equivalent to Tunisia. See *Table 5*.

Using the indirect time figures, the middle group produces an aggregate of 27,600/31 = 890 levels per hour. The higher group produces 22,200/183 = 121 levels per hour. Using the shadow prices of levels, aggregate hourly production is valued at $9,265.47. Annually, this comes to $81 million, or $1,350 per capita. That would make Norrath the 97th richest country in the world—Bulgaria.

Note that all of these figures are based on the avatar auction market, which is based on avatars whose features are already fixed. They are likely to be sold at a discount relative to avatars whose features could be freely chosen.

Appendix D. Economic policy issues specific to Norrath

This appendix will describe the principle markets of Norrath in terms of supply and demand and will use an abstract model of their functioning to explain the price and behavioral dynamics discussed in the main body of the paper. Some policy issues will be raised at the end. The abstract modeling is based on some technicalities that will not be easy to understand if you have never had economics. At the same time, the items and practices being discussed will not be easy to understand if you have never been to Norrath. This material is therefore targeted at a fairly unique reader: Norrathians who are comfortable with introductory college-level economic theory.

Labor market. The labor market in Norrath is essentially the hunters market. It determines the amount of hunting/farming that goes on, as well as the compensation for an hour's hunting. We will take the relevant quantity in this market as "Hours of hunting level X MOBs by all avatars, during the current month." The relevant price, or wage, will be "Platinum pieces earned per hour of hunting level X MOBs, during the current month."

Looking at supply first, avatars differ in the cost of undertaking hunting activity at a given level. The higher the return to hunting, the more hunting hours avatars will undertake. Therefore the supply of hunting hours rises with the wage.

The demand side of the market indicates how much compensation is available for avatars as they work more. Standard economic theory says that an increase in the total number of hours of hunting will a) increase the total amount of loot, but b) will decrease the marginal loot from an additional hour. As more and more avatars hunt MOBs of a given level, they create congestion and crowding, and this lessens the amount of loot that can be gained by hunting for an extra hour. Let H be the total hours of hunting labor for MOBs of a given level. If TP is the total product of hunting labor (the total loot per hour of all avatars combined), and MP is the marginal product of hunting labor (the extra loot for an extra hour of hunting), production theory says that TP rises as H rises, but MP eventually falls as H rises. Now the relevant decision for every avatar, in deciding whether or not to hunt an extra hour, is to compare her opportunity cost of hunting for that extra hour to the compensation she would get. That compensation comes from selling the extra loot she would get to the merchant biots, who, we assume, pay price R-B; the real value of those platinum pieces also depends on their purchasing power, which is a function of the overall price level. If the overall price level in Norrath is P, the value of an extra hour's hunting is given by the function

$$D = (RB/P)*(MP)$$

This compensation is essentially the demand curve in the labor market, and it slopes downward. The market is depicted in Figure S-1.

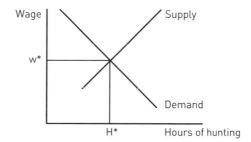

S-1 Labor Market

In this market, the equilibrium hours of hunting is given by H*. The equilibrium compensation is w*, which is equal to (RB/P)*(MP at H*). For the rest of the analysis we will hold the supply curve as fixed. The demand curve can shift, however. For example, if merchant biots pay more for the loot provided by these MOBs, then RB rises, meaning that demand shifts to the right. Both hunting and wages increase. If, however, all merchant biots pay more for all goods, then the general price level P rises, and demand shifts to the left. Both hunting and wages decrease.

Goods markets. As for goods, it will be useful to consider two kinds of goods; I will call them 'prizes' and 'loot' for reasons that will become apparent. First, consider an amazing magic helmet that has just been discovered. On its first day, the helmet counts as a prize good: demand is heavy, and avatars will pay much more than any merchant biot's buy price (call this PB) in order to have the helmet. Still, the higher the price, the fewer avatars will want the helmet, so its demand is downward sloping. The supply of the helmet is dictated by the willingness of avatars to hunt the MOBs who drop it. From the labor market, we know that hunting hours rise with the level of compensation. Therefore, if the price of a good rises, there will be more hunting of its MOBs and therefore a greater supply of the good in the market. Therefore supply slopes upward. And finally, since this good is in demand by avatars, we know that the market equilibrium price is above the price that merchant biots will pay to buy the good. That price, in terms of real purchasing power, would be PB/P. Also, since avatars rarely end up buying prize items from merchants, we can also assume that the market equilibrium price is below the merchant sell price, PS (which in real terms is PS/P). The situation is shown in S-2 below.

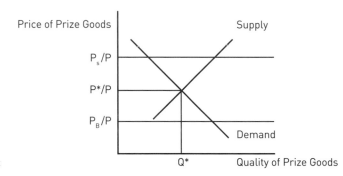

S-2 Prize Market

The prize market determines an equilibrium price (P*/P) and quantity (Q*) of the good. The market is entirely in the hands of avatars. Merchant biots play no role because they are offering to buy at a price below the market equilibrium, and offering to sell at a price above it.

Note that these markets are defined within periods of time, so that Q* is the quantity of helmets bought and sold this month. In Norrath, these items never decay, and, unless their owner retires or destroys them, the items never leave the economy. This means that, over time, the demand for new helmets—ones newly looted this month—falls. As demand falls, the price of the helmets declines. Eventually, the price in the avatar market is close to or even below the price that biot merchants will pay.

At that point the prize item becomes a loot item: a good that avatars sell immediately to the nearest biot merchant for cash. They do this because the good has low or no value in the avatar market and is not worth the trouble of selling there. Therefore they are willing to accept the biot merchant price (RB) even though it is quite low. The loot market looks like Figure S-3.

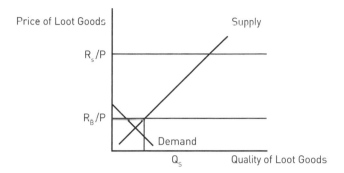

S-3 Loot Market

In the loot market, the real purchasing power of the merchant biot buy price RB/P determines the quantity that avatars hunt for, loot, and sell (QS). Generally, there is no a2a market for loot.

Anyone who has observed the launch of a server is aware that, for a certain time, there is an active market for patchwork armor. That market eventually collapses as demand for the cheap armor falls. Eventually, patchwork items become loot; if one ever acquires it, one simply sells it to the next merchant. Indeed, the permanent nature of goods in Norrath assures that every item will eventually become loot. The only way this would not happen is if a) enough new low-level avatars keep entering the server so that demand for newly-looted items remains, or b) higher-level avatars regularly retire or destroy their goods. Either phenomenon keeps the demand for new goods from sliding. However, recent experience in Norrath is that demand cannot be sustained in this fashion.

Thus, the general trend has been for goods prices to fall as prize goods become loot. When they become loot, the goods' prices stabilize. Returning to the labor market, we have that PB remains constant through time while the general price level, P, constantly falls. The effect is to shift demand rightward, which results in higher hourly compensation and an increase in hunting hours. The increase in hunting has well-known side effects in Norrath: an increase in crowding at spawn points, an increase in kill-stealing, and a tilt in the loot balance in favor of the higher-level avatars who can shoulder lower-level avatars away from good spots. Also, once the merchant biot prices become the price of goods, the market tends to strongly encourage farming over hunting. This is because the biot merchant prices do not put enough value on magic items. When Split Paw Gloves can be sold to a merchant for the same amount as a cracked staff, avatar incentives are strongly tilted in favor of farming the cracked staff instead of hunting the Split Paw Gloves.

Policy problems. These dynamics in the Norrath economy are taken as troublesome by many. There are three basic problems:

First, Norrath must be entertaining. To be entertaining, it must be challenging. To be challenging, valuable items must be hard to get. A general decline in prize item prices makes it easier to get valuable items. Ultimately, it waters down the Norrath experience.

Second, Norrath must be fair, in the sense that avatars who make similar efforts and take similar risks at similar levels should get similar rewards. A general decline in prize item prices means that later-arriving cohorts of avatars get higher rewards for their efforts than early-arriving avatars.

Third, Norrath must provide avatars with interesting activities and give them the proper incentives to undertake them. When loot and magic items can be sold for about the same amount to biot merchants, the merchant economy is signaling to players that farming is more lucrative than adventuring. They respond in a rational way to that incentive and spend more time camping easy spawn points instead of hunting down dangerous MOBs. This degrades the hunting experience for all. With low prize item prices, many avatars will decide that, rather than attack risky and dangerous MOBs to obtain an item, it would be easier to simply farm lower-level MOBS and get enough cash to go buy it. If, conversely, prize items were extremely expensive, hunting the dangerous MOB for the prize would seem more attractive than farming the weak MOB for money.

Policy discussion. Over the long run, a general decline in prices creates problems for the entertainment value of Norrath. Declining prices means declining challenges and a shift toward farming, and two recent VWs (Anarchy Online and WWII Online) have struggled because avatars have too quickly run out of challenging things to do.

The direct policy recommendation would be to find some way to keep prize item prices high. One way would be to keep demand high. On discussion boards, various ways of creating 'sinks' of items have been proposed, such as item decay. This would essentially force avatars to renew their stocks of prize items from time to time, and would keep the demand higher. But it is unlikely that users will be happy with any system that makes them lose their prize items; any of the proposed systems seem tedious or unfair. And the sink would have to function on an ongoing basis at very high volumes to have any effect.

Other proposals involve making more items simply untradeable. This seems to go against the authorities' stated desire to encourage functioning and lively avatar markets.

Another option is to keep offering expansions and new items, so that at any time there will be a large number of prize items whose prices are still determined in the avatar markets. This creates something of an arms race, however. To be of interest to the avatar market, new items must be better than old items. Old prize items will continually trickle down the levels, enhancing the power of lower level avatars relative to the MOBs they face. To keep the challenge level equal, those MOBs would have to be enhanced in power. As the authorities gradually increase the power of avatars, the power of MOBS has to go up. This process can continue without end, in principle. Yet it requires a great deal of developer time to invent and code new items and new MOBs.

The authorities have undertaken some policies to address some of the symptoms of the price decline, notably the trivial loot code. This prevents high-level avatars from looting low-level MOBs; it ends farming by brute force. It certainly does encourage avatars to take risks and attack MOBs at their own level, and that is a good thing. But again, the policy attacks a symptom, not a cause.

The core problem of price decline will probably have to be addressed at some point, though it is not clear right now what to do. Ongoing discussions about it may very well lead to valuable policy proposals.

Other policy issues: Twinking. A final policy issue worth discussing involves "twinking," whereby users with high-level avatars transfer vast wealth to low-level characters they have created. This is perceived as unfair; it allows the rich level 1 avatar to avoid many of the struggles and difficulties of starting out that the poor ones face. One answer would be to not allow users to have more than one character on a server, and Verant seems to be implementing that rule on all new servers. The problem is deeper than this, however, because twinking can also be done simply by purchasing thousands of PP for the character directly from dollar auction markets. Indeed, the existence of the avatar auction markets makes it possible for two level 60 avatars to be controlled by users with radically different amounts of time input to the avatar, and this is perceived as grossly unfair. In effect, it transfers the circumstances of Earth to the world of Norrath. This seems to be a very important problem, since the value of

Norrath as an alternative world depends to a large extent on its ability to allow users opportunities to succed in ways that they do not have on Earth. Norrath must allow some re-writing of the rules of Earth in order to be viable.

It is not clear how the authorities might end the phenomenon of twinking. They seem intent on limiting the number of avatars per server, which is a good policy in that it would at least eliminate twinking between one user's avatars. Yet it would not stop twinking from Earth markets. The severest challenge to future quality of life in Norrath would thus appear to be the probable continuing influx of Earth-based marketing and commerce into Norrath's pleasant and fun bazaar economy. Perhaps the only feasible strategy involves preventing material gift-giving, since every Earth-to-Norrath transaction involves a transaction that looks like a material gift in Norrath. One avatar gets something from another, for absolutely nothing. One approach might be to simply prevent such trade: all exchanges must involve items of roughly equal value on both sides. (The rules on dropping items would have to be changed too, since that would be another way to trade.) Another approach would be to have avatars of a certain level strictly limited in what they can have; the low-level avatar who uses a high-level item will soon break it, and the one with a great store of wealth will soon lose much of it. In effect this imposes level-based upper limits on the wealth of avatars. A second advantage of this policy is that it would reduce the severe within-level inequality that now dominates the social world.

In any case, twinking from Earth is a phenomenon that invites Earth-based markets and commerce into Norrath, and this can only degrade the world's entertainment value over time. Again, it is not clear what can or should be done, but ongoing discussions are certainly warranted.

Notes

1. I date Norrath's birth by EverQuest's public launch date. A few of the servers were used as beta tests of the game for months before the public launch. Some of the citizens of Norrath have been living there continuously since beta.

2. 'Virtual World' is a term used by the creators of the game *Ultima Online*, though they seem to prefer 'persistent state world' instead (www.uo.com). Neither is a universally accepted term. Perhaps the most frequently used term is 'MMORPG,' which means 'massively multi-player on-line role-playing game,' apt since VWs were born and have grown primarily as game environments. However, virtual worlds probably have a future that extends beyond this role. Moreover, MMORPG is impossible to pronounce. Other terms include 'MM persistent universe,' with 'MM' meaning 'massively-multiplayer;' also, there is Holmsten's term, 'persistent online world.' 'Virtual worlds' captures the essence of these terms in fewer words, with fewer syllables and a shorter acronym; by Occam's Razor, it is the better choice. J.R.R. Tolkien, perhaps the cultural

and intellectual father of these worlds, used the term 'Secondary World' to describe his fantasy universe (Tolkien, 1939). What might amaze Tolkien is how completely un-secondary his fantasy worlds have become. I would argue that virtual worlds are neither fantasy (constructions of the mind) nor reality (impositions of nature). They are Artistry: mental constructs expressed by their creators in whatever media the physical world allows. At the 20th annual Ars Electronica Festival, a Golden Nica was given to Team chman for their development of the game Banja (Kettman, 2001). The award apparently horrified many purists of electronic arts. Yet anyone who has wandered in worlds like Norrath has experienced the art of other people at an unprecedentedly deep psychological and social level. You are not looking at a painting. You are *in it*. And it is not a painting at all, but an immersive scenary that induces you and thousands of other people to play parts in what becomes an evolving and unending collective drama.

3. This usage of the term was coined in 1985 by Chip Morningstar, a user of the first avatar environment (Damer, 2001). According to Encarta: *Avatar* [Sanskrit]: **1. incarnation of Hindu deity:** an incarnation of a Hindu deity in human or animal form, especially one of the incarnations of Vishnu such as Rama and Krishna. **2. embodiment of something:** somebody who embodies, personifies, or is the manifestation of an idea or concept. **3. image of person in virtual reality:** a movable three-dimensional image that can be used to represent somebody in cyberspace, for example, an Internet user.

4. A "biot" is a biological bot. A "bot" is a shortening of the term robot and refers to code in multi-user domains that performs some function; a bot may be programmed to say "hello, this is the economics 201 chat room" to whomever enters the chat; in a VW, a standard bot is the door that opens and closes when double-clicked. A biological bot is a bot with the features of a biological life form: it generally looks and acts like an avatar, but it is being commanded not by a person but by coded instructions. New visitors to a VW often have difficulty at first determining which beings are avatars and which are biots.

5. As a VW, however, Meridian 59 is not dead. Black market versions are currently maintained in Germany, South Korea, and Russia.

6. There is often very little public information about the subscriber base of the different VWs. EverQuest's base was public information until August 31, 2001, when Verant stopped publishing the data. The official reasons for the decision were openly strategic: why help competitors by releasing data on the customer base? UO has said that it has 230,000 users in 120 countries (Harris, 2001). EverQuest is said to have over 400,000 users.

7. On internet and network economics, see Varian and Shapiro (1998) and a symposium on the subject in the *Journal of Economic Perspectives* (Katz and Shapiro, 1994; Besen and Farrell, 1994; Liebowitz and Margolis, 1994).

8. Games are big business. According to the Game Developer's Conference (www.gdconf.com/aboutus/), game industry revenues have exceeded box office revenues since 1999.

9. Holmsten has some claim to expertise, being the lead programmer for Project Entropia, a game that appears to be the next generation in VWs.

10. Anecdotal evidence abounds that time in VWs puts significant strain on life in Earth (see "EverQuest Creates a Trail of Cyberwidows," Salkowski, 2001; "Father Guilty in Death of Son," Karp, 2001). I have spoken to several people who claim to have terminated relationships because of their partner's devotion of time to VWs. At the same time, there are people who get married in ceremonies in VWs. And when a real person dies, sometimes his avatar is given a funeral.

11. Given that people are trying to speak by writing in real time, chatspeak is infused with extensive abbreviations and there is little punctuation. "omwb – brt" means "I am on my way back, and I will be right there." Voice interfaces are in development.

12. Unfortunately the equality of opportunity is beginning to erode as import and export markets for VW goods and currency have evolved. It has become possible to start a new avatar and use US currency to instantly endow it with vast virtual riches and expensive equipment.

13. The first virtual reality avatar environments had apparently been designed as early as 1985 (Damer, 2001). In Spring 1995, Worlds Chat became the first internet-based avatar environment.

14. VWs are worlds that are *designed* to be appealing. Their features tell us much about what the ideal society really looks like, in the minds of ordinary people. It is evident that the ideal society to ordinary people is very different from the ideal society as described by Great Thinkers. More on this in Appendix A.

15. According to the 11th U.S. Circuit Court in Atlanta, virtual places are geographically distinct from Earth places. In the "Voyeur Dorm" case, the court ruled that zoning laws of the city of Tampa do not apply to activities taking place in a Tampa home but broadcast on the internet. The internet activity is not considered part of the public space of Tampa; it occurs in its own "virtual space" (Kaplan, 2001).

16. Norrath has another feature that is common in healthy Earth economies: get rich quick schemes. At some sites, there are auctions urging you to pay $200 to obtain materials that will supposedly teach you how to make $100,000 a year by gleaning and selling Norrath items. And then there's "Khalidorr's Guide to Uber Platinum," for only $12, delivering five ways to make over 1,000 platinum pieces per hour.

17. Among its fans: Curt Schilling, baseball player; Jacques Villeneuve, race car driver; and Edward Castronova, obscure economist.

18. My impression is that the ban has had little impact on trading. Sony, effectively the government of Norrath, is fighting a war of trade restrictions that no government has ever won.

19. Elizabeth Kolbert (2001) gives a fascinating overview of the economy of UO. That world has apparently experienced its share of hyperinflations, hoarding, land shortages, and mass protest. The in-game economy of UO seems more developed also; avatars in UO have more opportunities to simply be merchants and craftmakers, whereas in EverQuest there is a much heavier emphasis on hunting. (See www.geocities.com/faramir_uo/ for some thoughts on UO's economy by Scott Salmon, a long-time player.) Avatars in UO can build and own houses, and it is possible to buy and sell these houses online at Ebay (Electronic Arts has not tried to suppress dollar-based trading of UO items). The one feature that weakens UO as a competitor to games like EverQuest is its visual perspective, which is 3rd person, not 1st. In UO, you see your avatar doing things; in EverQuest, you see things happen through the eyes of your avatar. Nonetheless, the UO economy is so rich that it is well worthy of a study of its own.

20. Lest there be any doubt about the "seriousness" of the entire enterprise here, I can report that of the over 3,000 responses to the NES, only one was identifiably frivolous. When I publicized the survey, I received dozens of emails, making various economic policy suggestions and commending me for undertaking the project. The reader who doubts the real economic value of items created in the Norrath economy, and hence the utility concerns of the people who spend time there, is invited to go to Norrath, steal something, and observe reactions.

21. Yee's study (Yee, 2001) also used an internet survey. According to his report, the demographics of his sample seem representative of the game's population data, which he has obtained from Verant. I have not made an effort to obtain official data from Verant, preferring instead to protect the independence of the report and its conclusions.

22. Recently, Verant has allowed some character transfers across servers, for a fee. The refugee avatar loses all of her cash and equipment, however. To date, avatar transfer has not had a noticeable impact on the world.

23. I took population counts at various times from May to August 2001, then regressed the count on the time of the day and day of the week. The fitted value of this regression at the mean hour (assigning 1/4 to each of four six-hour spans) and day (assigning 1/7 to each day) is 60,381. In essence this is the average population after removing cyclical weekly and hourly fluctuations. The raw average over my observations is 56,682 (N = 48).

24. The figures in Tables 1–3 are not seriously affected by weights in any case.

25. See www.census.gov/prod/2001pubs/statab/sec14.pdf. 91 percent of the respondents to the NES are 35 or younger.

26. Since monsters often spawn at the same place in the world over and over, an avatar can simply wait nearby and kill the monster every time it reappears. Aptly, this practice is referred to not as hunting but as farming. The problem with merchant biot prices is that they offer only a little more money for very useful magic items than they do for useless loot items.

27. Many respondents took this to be an obvious and, ultimately, stupid question. A typical response was "EC Tunnel—duh." Of course they overlooked the fact that the next respondent, playing on a different server, was responding "Greater Faydark—duh." One infers that the main market zone is a very powerfully established focal point on the servers, in that *everyone* knows that is where you go to sell. More on this in the appendix.

28. The other four servers are player-killer servers, where, because of the frequency of murder and robbery, property rights are feeble. Predictably, markets on these servers are poorly developed.

29. To protect the innocent, I have not recorded the identities of any individuals involved in such activities, and I will not reveal the sources of these data. My direct survey of users, the NES, did not obtain any information regarding the user's participation in black markets. The interested reader should have little difficulty, as I did, in finding open markets for Norrathian goods.

30. See Patrizio, 2001.

31. The meeting place is typically shady, such as an abandoned building. This is a black market, after all.

32. The standards for judging an auction as "successfully completed" were as follows. If there was more than one bid, I assumed the auction had generated a transaction. If there were no bids, I assumed it had not. If there was only one bid, I assumed it reflected a transaction only if the auction was listed as a "Buy It Now" or a "First Bid Wins" auction. Of course, the researcher cannot know whether a transaction actually took place. NES survey data and anecdotal evidence suggest that real transactions occur. The author personally knows someone who bought an item at auction and successfully collected it moments later in Norrath.

33. On most price-reporting sites, the admins go to great lengths to purge the data of 'incorrect' old prices. For this exercise, however, the old prices are of most interest.

References

Besen, Stanley M., and Joseph Farrell (1994), "Choosing How to Compete: Strategies and Tactics in Standardization," *The Journal of Economic Perspectives,* Vol. 8, No. 2, pp. 117–131.

Colker, David (2001), "The Legend Lives On: Fans of 'Meridian 59' are Flocking to Revival Sites to Resurrect a Game World That Started Six Years Ago," *Los Angeles Times,* May 17, p. T1.

Damer, Bruce (2001), "Global Cyberspace and Personal Memespace," *kurzweilai.net,* http://www.kurzeilai.net/meme/frame.html?main=articles/art0096.html.

Easterlin, Richard A. (2001), Income and Happiness: Towards a Unified Theory, *Economic Journal,* v. 111 no. 473, pp. 465–84.

Harris, Lyle V. (2001), "A New Species of Online Gamers Is Swarming the Net," *Atlanta Journal and Constitution,* March 21, p. 1G.

Kaplan, Carl S. (2001), "Florida Community Can't Shut Down 'Voyeur Dorm,'" *New York Times,* October 5.

Karp, David (2001), "Father Guilty in Death of Son," *St. Petersburg Times,* January 3, p. 3B.

Katz, Michael L., and Carl Shapiro (1994), "Systems Competition and Network Effects," *The Journal of Economic Perspectives,* Vol. 8, No. 2, pp. 93–115.

Kettman, Steve (2001), "Gamers Score at Arts Festival," *wired.com,* www.wired.com/news/print/0,1294,46598,00.html, September 7.

Kolbert, Elizabeth (2001), "Pimps and Dragons: How an Online World Survived a Social Breakdown," *The New Yorker,* May 28.

Liebowitz, S. J., and Stephen E. Margolis (1994), "Network Externality: An Uncommon Tragedy," *The Journal of Economic Perspectives,* Vol. 8, No. 2, pp. 133–150.

Patrizio, Andy (2001), "Virtual Baggage, Real Bucks," *Wired News,* October 1, www.wired.com/news/print/0,1294,47181,00.html.

Salkowski, Joe (2001), "EverQuest Creates a Trail of Cyberwidows," *Chicago Tribune,* February 5.

Sandoval, Greg (2001), "eBay, Yahoo Crack Down on Fantasy Sales," *CNET Tech News,* http://news.cnet.com/news/0-1007-200-4619051.html, January 6.

Shapiro, Carl and Hal R. Varian (1998), *Information Rules: A Strategic Guide to the Network Economy,* Cambridge: Harvard Business School.

Tolkien, J.R.R. (1939), "On Fairy-Stories," lecture, reprinted in *Poems and Stories,* London: Harper-Collins, 1992.

Yee, Nicholas (2001), *"The Norrathian Scrolls: A Study of EverQuest"* (version 2.5), http://www.nickyee.com/eqt/report.html.

Zito, Kelly (2001), "PC Games Battle the Consoles by Going Online," *San Francisco Chronicle,* March 20, p. C1.

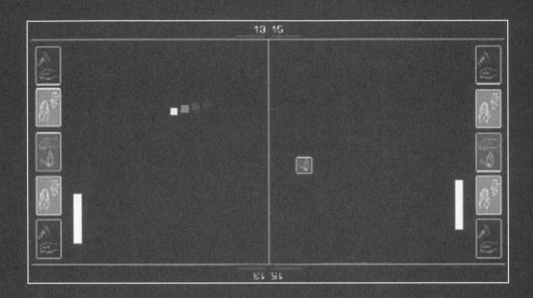

13 15

15 13

PainStation 2.5

Willi
Series: 1 of 5
Built: March 2004
Location: Norway
Owner: //////////fur////
→ Details

Rudi
Series: 2 of 5
Built: April 2004
Location: Zurich, Switzerland
Owner: etoy.CORPORATION
→ Details

Harri
Series: 3 of 5
Built: May 2004
Location: Cologne, Germany
Owner: //////////fur////
→ Details

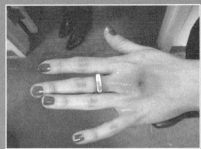

PainStation 2

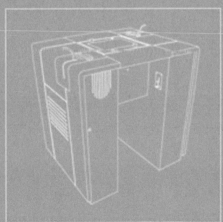

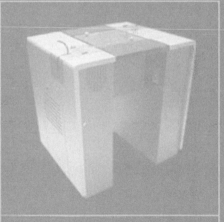

Unnamed 4
Series: 4 of 5
Built: under construction
Location: Cologne, Germany
Owner: ////////fur////
→ Details

Unnamed 5
Series: 5 of 5
Built: under construction
Location: Cologne, Germany
Owner: //////////fur////
→ Details

PS 2
Series: 1 of 1
Built: June 2003
Location: Cologne, Germany
Owner: //////////fur////
→ Details

Coda: Piercing the Spectacle

Brenda Laurel

The spectacle is not a collection of images, but a social relation among people, mediated by images.—Guy Debord, *The Society of the Spectacle*

In today's media-saturated world, the Spectacle provides a glittering array of substitutes for the experience of personal agency. Fewer and fewer opportunities for action outside the Spectacle present themselves to us. We must seek them out; a hike in open country may require several hours of travel to the trailhead, passing fast-food joints and gas stations clumped along the highway like fungi on rotting logs. The same junk sprouts out of all the screens in our lives—televisions, computers, PDAs, and cell phones. Commercials and brands, spam and flickering web ads, friendly text messages from your cellular service provider, product placements in movies and computer games, all reminding—or rather un-minding—us of the web of politico-consumerism in which we are enmeshed like spiders' snacks, stashed for hungry marketers and politicians. The spectacle holds us fast.

"You have a mighty low opinion of us, Dr. Laurel," you might say. "We are free people. We aren't passive consumers; we're *players.*" And you would have a valid point. Interactivity as we constructed it back in the days of early PCs and console games was a very hopeful thing. How not-TV it was to play a game of Star Raiders! But read the texts of our games, examine the roles of our player-characters, and see how we *enact* the spectacle—of wars and fast cars, of crimes and disasters and other fare of the evening news, of heroic acts in magical worlds so far from the actual agency in our daily lives as to engage us wholly in alternate universes of possibility.

I used to be fond of saying that people will always know the difference between media and reality. What I have come to understand is that, while we may know the difference well enough, we are rarely called by representations of choice and action to enact our power more robustly in the real world. No, games are not rehearsals for life. Through fantasies of agency we are entrained to satiate our needs for personal power in a realm where we can create no real disturbance to the web of control that entangles us.

What of those innocent games that simply occupy our time with pleasurable interaction? In an interview about Digital Chocolate, a company that builds games for web phones, EA founder Trip Hawkins said: "The first products we put out at Digital Chocolate to be honest [don't] do very much. And yet what [they] do is addictive and compelling....The games are geared to help you win. People get hooked." [*USA Today*, 9/13/04] You heard the man. The philosophy of games as business—to get people hooked—hasn't changed much since Trip first started his trip. And while it may be all innocent fun, I wonder how it changes us.

A key premise of the mobile technology game industry is that the pleasure of interactivity is preferable to boredom. Who of us would choose simply to sit on a train or wait in a line when we could be distracting our brain and hands with a game? Idleness, slowness, contemplation, being mentally present in a situated context has no place in this wired world. But for those who were alive before this hyperactive culture grew up around us, it was during those interstices of life's activities that we breathed, relaxed, observed, thought things over. Listen up—even the smallest fragments of your idle time have now been colonized with meaningless, addictive junk. Junk that is part of the fabric of the Spectacle.

Likewise, for thirty years, a key premise of the educational game industry has been that the magic of gaming could serve as a hook for engagement. Why, when we are willing to learn so much detailed stuff to play a computer game, can't we simply design games in which that detailed stuff has some educational value? Why, for thirty years, have we failed at this? One reason comes immediately to mind: educational software is built on a representation of *education*. Give me a game with mathematical concepts as its content and I'll show you a game that reminds me of sitting in a classroom, learning and doing things with no demonstrable personal relevance. Educational games typically fail to populate the dimension of action with choices that are personally relevant, creative, or powerful. That's because contemporary education fails in exactly the same way.

The construction of public education in America is very much about the Spectacle. School imparts basic principles, information, and skills. The information is not to be questioned. Now more than ever, the skills are about passing tests. School embodies an authority structure in which the rules are predetermined and transgressions are punished. Team sports in school subvert a sense of play by reinforcing a notion of ritual competition within a status hierarchy. Students pass from the arms of education into the arms of consumerism with virtually no change in the construction of power and personal agency. Yes, we can vote when we come of age. But that is rather like choosing between red and blue in today's America. Those students who emerge from high school with good critical thinking skills are an endangered species. Of course, those are the very skills that give power to the notion of citizenship. In the absence of critical thinking or the knowledge that one may intervene in the Way Things Are through the exercise of citizenship or personal choice, we become a nation of consumers, participating smoothly within the spectacle like parts in a well-oiled machine.

The reason we have not succeeded in building good games for education is that to do so would entail reconstructing the notion of education itself. In particular, we would need to redefine what it means to be a good learner. Instead of receiving information, we might construct understanding. Instead of giving the right answer, we might think of taking an appropriate action. Instead of obeying the rules, we might question authority. These are the sorts of rehearsals for living that games could be offering us.

Games about language or math, science or sociology, economics or geopolitics lack luster because neither the activity they model (education) nor the activity for which education itself intends to prepare us (life in the Spectacle) offers little in terms of significant interaction. With no models of ourselves as agents of change in the "real" world, how can we envision such possibilities within a representation of it? In Middle Earth I can kick ass, but I am a helpless speck compared to the interests and institutions that define the realities of my life. That is what both games and schools are teaching us. And both of them are wrong.

The Spectacle is not all there is, and there are representations that pierce the Spectacle by inviting us to have a look at the person (or web of relations) behind the curtain. Each of us can think of images or stories that have powerfully revealed to us a hidden or unsanctioned truth. Such representations can also take interactive form, and are perhaps more powerful when they do. Just as games can entrain us to enact the Spectacle, they may enable us to enact its converse. Situationists call this sort of reversal a reconstruction. Game designers have it in their power to reconstruct notions of personal awareness, choice, and agency in ways that might seriously disturb the consumerist ethos that has been prepared for us. Now, *that* could be really fun.

Brenda Laurel is a designer, writer, researcher, and performer. She chairs the graduate Media Design Program at the Art Center College of Design in Pasadena, CA. She also serves as a Distinguished Engineer at Sun Microsystems Laboratories. Since 1976, her work has focused on the intersection of culture and technology at Atari, Apple, Interval, and other companies. She edited *The Art of Human-Computer Interface Design* (Addison-Wesley, 1990) and authored *Computers as Theatre* (Addison-Wesley, 1991 and 1993) and *Utopian Entrepreneur* (MIT Press, 2001). Her latest book is *Design Research: Methods and Perspectives* (MIT Press, 2004).

Photo: www.le-parkour.com

19

Interstitial Credits

1   **How to Win "Super Mario Bros"**
Conceptual game art, 2003
Alex Galloway
Game: *Super Mario Bros.*
http://artport.whitney.org/gatepages/april03.shtml

2   **Cosplay**
Game fan creativity, 2004
Dragon*Con 2004
www.cosplay.com

3   **Urban Invasion**
Game art intervention, 1998+
Space Invader
Game: *Space Invaders*
www.space-invaders.com
Invasions to date: *Paris, London, Aix en Provence, Anvers, Montpellier, Tokyo, Amsterdam, Grenoble, Los Angeles, New York, Bern, Avignon, Lausanne, Geneve, Pau, Lyon, Hong Kong, Rotterdam, Berlin, Barcelone, Australia, Dhaka, Manchester, Marseille.*

4   **Collateral Romance**
Conference presentation, GDC 2004
Wil Wright
The Game Design Challenge: The Love Story
Game: *Battlefield 1942*

5–7   **Urban Games**
Alternate reality games (ARGs) & big games

         5   **I Love Bees (2004)**
              Elan Lee, Sean Stewart, Jim Stewartson, Jane McGonigal,
              4orty 2wo Entertainment in collaboration with Microsoft and Bungie,
              Game: *Halo 2*
              ww.ilovebees.com

         6   **Conqwest (2005)**
              Frank Lantz, Mattia Romeo, SS+K in collaboration with Qwest
              www.conqwest2004.com

         7   **Big Urban Game (2003)**
              Nick Fortungo, Frank Lantz, Katie Salen in collaboration with the Design Institute,
              University of Minnesota
              http://design.umn.edu/go/project/TCDC03.2.BUG

8–9   DDR Step Charts
         Level walkthroughs
         Game: *Dance Dance Revolution*
         www.ddrfreak.com

   8   GOTCHA (The Theme from Starsky and Hutch): Andy's G's Magic Disco Machine
             Basic Double
             117 BPM: Max Combo: 90

   9   Silent Hill (3rd Christmas Mix): Thomas Howard
             Maniac2 Double
             125 BPM; Max Combo: 234

10–12   Indie Game Jam
         Annual game design event, IGJ1, 2003
         www.indiegamejam.com
         Hosted by Chris Hecker and Sean Barrett at the definition six code barn
         Game technology: *Shadow Garden (Zack Simpson et al.)*

   10   Supermodel Shootout
             Sean Barrett, Mike Linkovich, Michael Sweet

   11   Paris Plague Dodging
             Ken Demarest, Ryan Ellis, Michael Sweet

   12   Stealth Game
             Chris Carrollo, Brian Sharp

13–14   Blast Theory
         Pervasive gaming
         Led by Matt Adams, Ju Row Farr and Nick Tandavanitj, in collaboration with the Mixed Reality
         Lab, University of Nottingham.
         www.blasttheory.co.uk

   13   Can You See Me Now? (2001)

   14   Uncle Roy All Around You (2003)

15   Red vs. Blue
         Machinima, 2003+
         Rooster Teeth Productions: Burnie Burns, Matt Hullum, Joel Heyman, Gustavo Sorola, Geoff
         Fink, Dan Godwin, Jason Saldana
         Game: *Halo*
         www.redvsblue.com

16–17   Serious Games
Educational and activist game mods

16   **Velvet Strike (2002)**
Anne-Marie Schleiner, Joan Leandre, Brody Condon
Game: *Counter-Strike*
www.opensorcery.net/velvet-strike

17   **Escape from Woomera (2003)**
Ian Malcom, Andrea Blundell, Justin Halliday, Matt Harrigan, Darren Taylor, Chris
Markwart, Kate Wild, Stephen Honegger
Game: *Half-Life*
www.escapefromwoomera.org

18   **Painstation**
Game art intervention, 2001+
Volker Morawe, Tilman Reiff
Game: *Pong*
www.painstation.de

19   **Le Parkour**
Urban play
Invented by David Belle and Sebastian Foucan
www.le-parkour.com; www.parkour.com

Index

Aarseth, E., 37, 667, 687n1

Abelson, H., 753

abstractions

    in communication, 315

    and game spaces, 687n9

    in Go, 204

    models as, 53–55

    of real-life, 502

accelerators, 451

achievement, 145, 757, 825

achievers

    vs. achievers, 770

    description, 6, 757, 761

    and levels, 767

    vs. other player types, 770–783

    proportion of, 760, 777

    in social MUDs, 768

action(s)

    in adventure games, 697

    discrete *vs.* continuous, 418, 688n20

    extraneous, 654, 657, 765

    feedback, 214, 373

    in games, 421, 654, 657

    opportunities, 648, 652–655, 657, 660

active learning, 238, 254–263

Adams, E., 644, 667, 671, 678

Adams, M. J., 265

adaptations, 677

added features, 723, 742, 744–746

addiction

    to Breakout, 570–577

    and marketing, 868

    vs. meeting goals, 340

    to virtual worlds, 821, 823

Adelman, L., 753

Adkison, P., 540

administrators

    documentation, 804

    future role, 812

    MUD stability, 763–767, 777–784

    and player rights, 796, 798, 800–809

    responsibilities, 805, 810

adults

    and Magic, 555

    and video games, 342, 344

    and virtual worlds, 830t, 832

Adventure

    catacomb, 711–713

    creatures, 699–703

    description, 693–697

    game spaces, 66, 68, 703–713

    hierarchical model, 55

    and interactive fiction, 646

    objects, 699, 713

    precursor, 691, 694–697

    prototype, 694

    screens, 713

    sequel, 713

adventure, 338–346, 349, 352–357

adventure games

    action types, 697

    and consequence, 375

    and information, 201

    vs. MUDs, 769

    and narrative, 654, 664

    and plot, 195

    text adventures, 644, 646, 691

Figures are indicated by "f"; tables are indicated by "t," and footnotes by "n".

advice
 to admins, 808–809
 on Summoner, 269–295
 vs. tips, 257
aesthetics
 and change, 649, 657–659
 definition, 441
 and dynamics, 4, 55, 441
 and masks, 118
 and play, 102, 105
affinity groups, 242, 247–250, 253, 257–259
 See also game communities
affordances, 652–655, 657, 660
African Americans, 74, 623
agency
 vs. immersion, 29, 649
 in Jedi Knights II, 30
 model, 654–656, 661
 reconstructed, 869
 vs. transformation, 658
agôn, 5, 131–133, 148t
 and *ludus,* 143, 144
 and slot machines, 153
 See also competition
airplane models, 143
Alber, Antone F., 752
alea, 5, 133–135, 137, 148t
 and *ludus,* 143
 and *paidia,* 144
 and slot machines, 153
 See also chance
Alexander, C., 54, 436
algorithms, 272
Alice in Wonderland, 677
alliances, 202, 406
Alpha World, 824
always_black, xviii, 30, 39, 74, 602–608

ambiguity
 and frame analysis, 596–599
 in on-line interactions, 74
 and play, 85, 297–311
 and Rooie Rules, 16
 and RPGs, 72, 596–599
 See also uncertainty
American Gladiators, 451, 452
America Online, 208
America's Army, 629
Amerika, M., 645
amusement parks, 127, 140, 676
anachronism, 585
Anachronox, 272, 625
anagrams, 143, 144
anarchism, 356
Anarchy Online, 819
Animal Crossing, 163
animals
 and *agôn,* 132
 birds, 136, 139, 318
 communication, 84
 dolphins, 482
 and games, 134, 496
 and girl culture, 349–352
 insects, 135, 149n5
 and mimicry, 135, 149n5
 monkeys, 84, 142, 152n12, 316, 318
 play, 99, 101, 297, 316–320
 race horses, 484
 and religion, 118
 and vertigo, 139
anticlimax, 209
antisemitism, 623
antisocial behavior, 768
appetites, 104
Apple II, 715

Arabs, 619–621

arcade games, 261, 462–473

    See also Battlezone; Defender; Sinistar; Tempest

Arcanum, 272

archaic man, 108–118

Aristotle, 101, 236, 655

    See also agency

Arneson, D., 205

art

    interactivity, 645

    trompe l'oeil, 319

artificial intelligence

    in Eastern Front, 718–722

    and neo-Aristotelian model, 659, 662

    Summoner, 282, 286–288

    and virtual worlds, 741

artwork, 542

Asheron's Call, 819

Aspnes, J., 785

assembly language, 721

Asteroids, 432, 463

Atari, 692, 712, 715

    See also Adventure; Breakout

atmosphere

    and amusement parks, 676

    in Magic, 542, 549, 550

    in Monopoly, 203

    in MUDs, 766, 782

    in Pikman, 256

    and role-play, 207

attitude

    of adults, toward video games, 342

    in games of chance *vs.* games of skill, 129, 133, 137

    in games of chance *vs.* mimicry, 137

    for learning, 259

    of mothers, toward video games, 343

    and player types, 769–777

    toward repetition, 249

    toward women, 341, 343

    of Western societies, 302, 304–306

    See also lusory attitude; seriousness

auctions

    bidding games, 131

    and Everquest, 827, 834, 836, 848, 857, 862n32

    and Magic, 61

audience. *See* spectators

Audobon, J., 139

authority

    and game change, 500, 531

    in MUDs, 790, 794, 808

    in schools, 868

    See also administrators

avatars

    definitions, 859n3

    as game element, 421

    guilds, 846

    in Habitat, 731, 740

    and immersion, 657

    infractions, 806

    research on, 844

    and resources, 430, 836

    rights, 42, 791–805

    and servers, 858, 861n22

    in virtual worlds, 816, 819, 821–823, 836

        transactions, 833, 836

        worker metaphor, 822, 835, 838, 852

Avedon, E. M., 81, 516, 667

awareness

    of enemy (Summoner), 282

    of fantasy, 28

    of game, 484–486, 495, 584–596

    of make-believe, 103

    at metalevel, 256

    of play, 35, 85, 99, 114–116, 127, 128, 320–323

vs. seriousness, 112, 116
of signals, 315–318
Axis & Allies, 202, 203
Aylett, R., 667

baccara, 127, 133
backend, 734, 744–747, 749
backgammon, 134, 581, 582
backyards, 332–335, 675
Bakhtin, M., 301
Baldur's Gate II, 625
bandwidth, 734–736
Banja, 859n2
Barker, C., 682
Bartle, R., 6, 25, 41, 43, 61, 754–784
Barwood, H., 53, 57, 413
baseball
    cashing out, 452
    and game theory, 403
    mechanics, 440
    Strat-o-matic™, 540, 542
    umpire disputes, 498
basketball
    game state, 447
    hidden energy, 450
    hoop height, 489
    mechanical bias, 448
    NBA Live, 375
    semiotic domain, 230, 232, 236
    time limits, 479
    unwritten rules, 483
Bates, B., 265
Bateson, Geoffrey, 297
Bateson, Gregory, 28, 35, 84, 314–327, 516
Battlefield 1942, 71
    battles, 71, 73, 272, 717, 719
Battleship Potempkin, 679

Battlezone, 465
Beck, U., 265
behavior, 18, 39, 300
    See also etiquette
belief systems, 45–49, 72
Bereiter, C., 265
Berg, Richard, 206
Bernstein, 664
Besen, S. M., 862
Best Buy, 157–161
bias, 448
Big Mitch, 359
billiards, 131
biots, 819, 833, 859n4
Bioware, 812
Birdwell, K., xviii, 22, 212–225
Bit, 548
Björk, S., 10–11, 54, 57, 79, 80, 410–436
Black and White, 75, 672, 682
blackjack, 574
Blade Masters, 272
blame, 215, 770
Blix, 672
bluffing, 404, 541
Boal, A., 663, 667
board games
    Carolus Magnus, 428
    combat, 718
    Go, 204
    Lord of the Rings, 21
    Monopoly, 203, 419, 421, 674
    sessions, 415
    and socializing, 208
    Space Hulk, 428
    vs. trading card games, 553
    zone of control, 719
Bolter, J. D., 31

Bomberman, 452
Bookchin, N., 645
books, 337, 345–355, 357–360
    See also literature
Booth, A., 362
borderwork, 360
boredom
    and action, 688n20
    and change, 521
    and DOOM 3, 166
    vs. interactivity, 868
    and *ludus*, 144
    and mastery, 535
    and Operation Flashpoint, 428
    and randomness, 205
    and Zero Zero, 354
Borel, E., 386
borrowed rules, 523
bounding components, 415
boys and men
    and avatars, 822, 844
    books, 345–347, 358
    boy culture, 338–347
    in Foursquare game, 511–515
    and game spaces, 68
    gap between, 342
    going against odds, 625
    play spaces, 336–340, 346
    primitive ceremonies, 115
    and videogames, 6, 74
bragging, 464, 483
brainstorming, 215, 224
Bransford, J. D., 265
bravery, 105
Breakout
    game spaces, 67
    pleasure, 3

skill, 559–569, 561, 573, 576
social aspects, 561, 577
tension, 4
bridge
    and *agôn*, 131, 143
    on America Online, 208
    frame analysis, 581
    and *ludus*, 143
    network version, 208
    seriousness, 178
    socializing, 208
Brotchie, A., 86
Bruckman, A. S., 768, 785, 786
Bruer, J. T., 265
bugs, 709, 739, 746
builders, 766
Burka, L. P., 786
Burke, K., 297, 307
Burnett, F. H., 348–352, 362
Burns, M. S., 266
Buzzwords, 59, 62

Cabal process, 23, 215–225
Cage, J., 195
Caillois, R., 5–6, 28, 78, 80, 84, 123–155
Cain, C., 639
Calhammer, A., 202
Campaigns for North Africa, 206
Campbell, J., 678
canasta, 326
Candyland
    and decisions, 209
Can You See Me Now?, 68
Carcassone, 421
card games
    canasta, 326
    individually-owned decks, 541

Magic antecedent, 540

merit *vs.* destiny, 134

tokens, 200

trading card games, 550

uncertainty, 126

See also bridge; Buzzwords; Magic: The Gathering; solitaire

Carmack, J., 5

Carnap, R., 315

carnaval, 107, 136, 306

carnaval rides, 127

Carolus Magnus, 428

Carson, D., 676, 682–683

cashing out, 33

Caspian-Kaufman, J., 786

Cassell, J., 75

Castronova, E., 40, 60, 63, 814–862

Catin, C., 545

causality, 651–655

Cavallo, D., 362

Centipede, 466f, 472f

exemplary design, 4, 55, 466–473

interconnectedness, 55

scoring, 464

ceremonies. *See* rituals

Chadwick, F., 203

chain combos, 288

Chall, J. S., 265

challenges

Adventure, 702

arcade games, 463

and boy culture, 339

Centipede, 471

and children, 141

to cultural models, 625

EverQuest, 856

obstacles, 451

Pikman, 254, 258

of rules, 498

Summoner, 274

tennis, 536

types, 444

to viewpoints, 611

chance

in fantasy games, 582

fate *vs.* free choice, 304

in game definition, 78, 124

as pleasure, 5

in poker, 385

and slot machines, 153

strategy, 399–405, 408n3

See also games of chance

change

aesthetics, 649, 657–659

and balance, 525–530

behavioral approach, 736

in cultural models, 616

and game community, 520–526

in Magic, 551–555

nonreversibility, 454

physics, 630

in play mood, 114

recommendations, 531

in repetition, 143

in rules, 12–18, 500, 515, 531

and socializers, 42, 779

of source code, 221

chaos, 139, 141

characters

and AI, 659

Arabs/Muslims, 619–621

Aristotelian drama, 651

bosses, in shooter games, 636

Castle Wolfenstein, 624

Centipede, 467–469
in daydreams, 299
and emergent narrative, 644
identification with (*see* identification)
in interactive drama, 653
Metal Gear Solid, 634
metaphors, 216f, 219f, 224f
real people as, 75, 611, 663, 684
in role playing games, 195, 200
Saturn's Night, 359
The Sims, 684
Summoner, 273, 277, 279, 281, 284, 294
vs. technology, 729
traits, 134, 154
women, 341, 355
See also avatars; player-character construct
charades, 144, 208
chaturanga, 383
cheating
by cleverness, 746–749
by code change, 745, 750
and game change, 531
and game design, 15
hidden *vs.* open, 524
and play, 106
and rules, 126, 417, 522
and slot machines, 154
solitaire, 522
Summoner, 291
and winning, 175
checkers, 131, 447, 533
Cherny, L., 786
chess
action type, 418
and *agôn,* 143
appeal, 209
computerized, 481, 484, 496

cultural model, 71
decisions, 196
distractions, 481
framework, 417, 421, 584
and game theory, 389
as *ludus,* 143
mechanics, 440
mirroring battle, 383
opposition, 131, 198
and player-character, 72
rationality, 392
for real, 127
strategy, 393
tie rules, 391
time limits, 479
variety, 205
winning, 183
Chi, M. T. H., 265
Chick, T., 5, 156–169
children
competition, 133, 141, 142
computer expertise, 253
and destruction, 142
dressing-up, 107
and games of chance, 134
and handicapping, 535
hyperactivity, 223
identity formation, 258
learning hatred, 623
make-believe in, 28, 103
and mazes, 704
and outdoors, 332–336
performances, 108
and play, 103, 304
and rules, 16, 142, 511
seriousness, 112
threat and histrionics, 318

and vertigo, 138
and video games, 6, 235–237, 258–262, 332, 613
and wagers, 142
China, 108, 145, 154n16
Chivalry and Sorcery, 585
Chkhenkeli, M., 546
choices, 304
    See also decisions
Chomsky, N., 242, 244
Chop Suey, 354
ChronoTrigger, 376
Chudowsky, N., 266
Church, D., 53, 366–380, 413, 436
city spaces, 685, 846
civilization, 100
Civilization, 197, 431, 451
Civilization III, 73, 457, 611
Clodius, J. A., 786, 787
closed awareness, 584–590
closure, 419, 449, 463
clowns, 101
Club Caribe, 749, 751
Clue, 454
coalitions, 406
cock fights, 131, 132
Cocking, R. R., 363
code. See source code
code of conduct, 792–794, 800–809
    See also etiquette
cognition, 134, 299, 495, 520
    See also learning; thinking
Cold War, 625–629
Coles, G., 265
Colker, D., 862
collecting, 145, 299, 551
collisions, 697

color
    Adventure, 712
    Breakout, 560
    Eastern Front (1941), 716
    Magic, 60, 544
    Monopoly, 207
    Saturn's Night, 359
    Secret Paths, 349
    See also environment
comedy, 101
    See also humor
comic books, 230
commands
    Habitat, 733
    in MUDs, 765, 766
    text games, 697, 698
Commodore, 730, 738, 749, 751n1
communication
    about games, 43–50
    abstraction levels, 315
    between avatars, 822, 833
    and Cabal process, 221
    cryptography, 750
    of data, 734, 737, 750
    design vocabulary, 367–370
    evolution, 84, 315
    in interactive drama, 653
    metacommunication, 28–30, 35, 84, 323–326
    and MUDs, 734, 759, 764, 769
    play as, 302
    between players, 319, 418
    of play intent, 315–318, 325
    of plot constraints, 660
    secret codes, 340
    situated meaning, 239–241, 252, 254–256
    and virtual worlds, 840
        See also semiotic domains

communities. *See* cultural status; game communities
competition
    boys and girls, 358
    and chance, 129, 134, 137
    in children, 132
    in courtesy, 487, 491, 606
    equal adversaries, 131
    between games, 434
    game type, 5, 131–133, 148t
    JKII, 603–608
    and *ludus,* 144
    in MMORPGs, 61
    with non-opponents, 499
    vs. opposition, 198
    as pleasure, 5
    slot machines, 153
    social context, 49
    social MUDs, 768
    spectator role, 137
    team sports, 868
    and uncertainty, 126
complexity threshold, 739
component framework
    actions, 418, 421
    closures, 419
    end conditions, 419
    evaluation functions, 419, 421
    events, 418
    extra-game activities, 416
    facilitator, 420
    game elements, 421, 431
    goals and subgoals, 417
    instance, 415
    interactions, 422–434
    interface, 420
    modes of play, 417

    players, 420
    rules, 416 (*see also* rules)
    sessions, 415
    set-up/set-down, 416
    time, 421
    without design pattern, 436
computer games
    characteristics, 250
    and diplomacy, 203
    documentation, xviii
    and information, 200
    vs. platform games, 250
    and plot, 195
    post-mortems, 457
    racing games, 418
    realism, 643
    role-playing, 415, 417
    saves, 249
    single-player, 207, 209
    tension, 209
    triggering events, 418
    computer role-playing games. *See* massively
    multiplayer on-line role-playing games
computers
    and children, 253
    vs. game platforms, 248
    as game players, 481, 484, 485, 496
    as play, 299
conflict
    about games, 498
    and Cabal process, 223
    and community, 43
    between cultural models, 628, 631, 638
    between design patterns, 426, 427
    between design tools, 375
    and drama, 444
    and game theory, 385

and goodness, 615
Habitat, 743
Half-Life, 222f
narrative vs. interactivity, 643
player vs. system, 661, 664, 758
rhetoric of play, 305
between rule-sets, 500
transformation vs. agency, 658
unproductive, 33
in virtual world, 821
consensus, 500, 502, 524
consequences
design patterns, 427, 430, 432
embedded narrative, 664, 682
perceivable, 373–377, 413
The Sims, 684
consistency
in fighting games, 377
Habitat, 747–749
in interacttive drama, 653
Mario, 371
in MUDs, 766, 769
constitutive rules, 187
constraints, 653–661, 825
bandwidth as, 734
construction games, 143, 145
consumerism
and education, 868
and game journalism, 49
of resources, 431–433
and video games, 344
and virtual worlds, 817, 819
contagion, 136, 137, 139
content
in real life, 251
social practices, 236, 241–246
video games, 262, 334, 343, 611

contests, 144, 300, 444
context, 480, 584
See also frames and contexts; situated meaning
control
in amusement parks, 676
and arcade games, 466
of design project, 473
in game vs. play, 519
and MUDs, 742, 743–750, 807
of narrative, 444, 687n8
by parents vs. others, 344
player vs. player, 757, 762, 765
player vs. system, 661, 664, 744–7490, 758
vs. power need, 867
in RPGs, 374
self-control, 144, 339
of source code, 221
control, sense of
design for, 372, 433
and game community, 525
and girls, 345
in Half-Life, 214
and Mario 64, 371
and producer-consumer, 433
and tokens, 200
controls
commands vs. joystick, 697
in Habitat, 733
and learning curve, 377
in Mario 64, 371
conventions
for Goffman, 600n1
for immersion, 657
no takebacks, 534
social, 845
Conway, J. H., 204
Cook, K. V., 363

cooperation
    between achievers, 770
    in design, 23, 215–225
    vs. opposition, 198
    research on, 845
Cope, B., 265
cops and robbers, 126
Cornered Rat Software, 819
Cosmic Encounter, 539
Costikyan, G., 10, 78, 192–211, 436, 671, 678
costumes, 107, 124
Cotton, Charles, 3
Counterstrike, 421
courtesy
    in games (*see* etiquette)
    player rights, 792
    in playtesting, 623
crabs, 136
Crawford, C., xv, 22, 25, 65, 81, 193, 210, 436, 687n7, 714–724
creativity, 110, 305, 435, 741
critical learning, 238, 254–263, 849
critical thinking, 868
croquet, 131
crosswords, 143, 144
Crowther, W., 691, 713
cruelty, 133
cryptography, 750
Csikszentmihalyi, M., 7
Cubism, 68
cultural models
    change in, 616
    China, 145–147
    definition, 45, 614, 617
    and design, 73–75
    in Habitat, 744–749

juxtaposition of, 638
and learning, 629–633
linearity, 635
Operation Flashpoint, 628
The Sims, 45, 71, 611
Sonic Adventure II, 612–619
and space, 67
of terrorism, 619–623
video games, 613–619, 633–637
and Wolfenstein, 45, 611, 624–629
See also values
cultural status
    and Breakout, 577
    of games, 79, 124, 485–487, 491
    of play, 46, 84, 99–119, 141
    rhetorics of play, 309
    semiotic domains, 251–253
    of spectacles, 867–869
cup-and-ball, 143, 144
cursors, 351, 697, 700–703
Curtis, P., 769, 786
cybernetic feedback, 446–449

Damer, B., 863
dance, 138, 140, 151n8, 672
D'Andre, R., 639
danger. *See* risk
Dark Age of Camelot, 819
data communication, 735, 737
data wiping, 809
Davidsson, O., 436
Davis, M., 540
day-dreaming, 299
death. *See* arcade games; killers
Debord, G., 69, 867
decals, 215

deceit
    in fantasy games, 582
    in monkeys, 318
    in poker, 385, 404
    in shooter games, 625
decelerators, 55, 451
De Certeau, M., 69, 688n11
decisions
    and agency, 658
    and design, 21, 427
    and game definition, 196, 209
    and game theory, 54
    and information, 200
    in Mario 64, 370
    of MUD admins, 763–767
    narrowing choices, 659
    Operation Flashpoint, 627
    vs. plot, 194
    and resources, 10, 59–63, 199
    to rework game, 213
    and rules, 10
    The Sims, 684
    by voting, 744
    War and Peace, 676
decision trees, 54
Deep Blue, 481, 484
Defender, 465
DeKoven, B., 15, 17, 24, 518–537
demeanor, 510
demographics
    of Norrath, 816, 828–832, 859n6
    of players, 623, 830t, 860n10
denouments, 457
Dereth, 843
Derrida, J., 301

design
    Adventure, 693–697
    Centipede, 466–473
    and cheating, 15
    concept, 434
    consistency, 218
    fine-tuning, 219
    for game community, 41
    graphing, 220
    Half-Life, 23, 213–218
    for involvement, 369–380, 430, 443
    for learning, 260
    Magic, 539–550, 552–553
    and means, 180
    player role, 18, 22–24, 34, 62, 195, 742–750
    redundancy, 681
    reusability, 225
    and semiotic domains, 48
    side-quests, 293
    strength factors, 194–201
    by team, 23, 215–225, 344
    tools, 54
    triggering fun, 4
    Twenty-One, 454–457
    video games, 256, 263
    See also component framework; design patterns;
        documentation; iterative design
designers
    as cruise director, 741
    experience(s), 21
    open-mindedness, 723
    signatures, 693, 712
design grammar, 48, 245–250, 255
design models, 53–56, 442–444
    See also aesthetics; dynamics

design patterns
    defined, 424, 426
    and Easter Eggs, 429
    examples, 427
    interrelationships, 425, 427
    and mechanics, 423
    template, 426
    uses, 54, 428, 430–435
    without framework, 436
design tools, 54, 366–380
destruction, 142
detail, 203
detective stories, 143, 403, 681
Deus Ex, 611, 625
development stage
    problem-solving, 434
    saves, 220
    See also Cabal; iterative design; playtesting
dexterity, 143, 340, 559–569, 576
diabolo, 129, 143, 144
diagetic mode, 665
dialectical vertigo, 185
dialog, 653, 659
Diamond, D., 27
Dibbel, J., 43, 786
dice, 133, 718
Die By the Sword, 333
Dietz, J., 63
Digital Chocolate, 867
digital games. See Summoner
diguise
    as play, 107
diplomacy, 202, 219f
Diplomacy (game), 202, 582
disbelief, suspension of, 29, 649
discipline, 340
diSessa, A. A., 639

disguise
    as aesthetic category, 649
    costumes, 107, 124
    in espionage, 591
    in fantasy games, 582
    in insect world, 135
    vs. transmorph, 600n3
    See also masks
disinterestedness, 103
Disneyworld, 676
disorder, 139, 141, 718
disputes, 408
disruption, 139, 141, 718
Doctor Zhivago, 683
documentation
    of code, 721
    of computer game, xviii
    of design, 215, 218, 223, 224, 426
    game manual, 692
    of infractions, 806
    of player rights, 790–795
dodgeball, 40, 519
Dogon, 143
doll-play, 126, 142
dolphins, 482
Domike, S., 667, 668
dominoes, 134
Donaldson, F., 335, 362
DOOM 3, 5, 39, 157–169
The Dr. K–Project, 645
drama
    aesthetic model, 33, 442–444
    animals, 318
    competitions, 137
    and fantasy RPGs, 592
    interactivity, 646–656, 660–666
    and mechanics, 440, 444–457

and mimicry, 136, 144
    as play, 100
    uncertainty, 34, 445–453
    See also Aristotle; sacred performances
dramatic arc, 33, 442–444, 449, 457, 661
dramatic probability, 660
dreams, 299, 321, 359
Dresher, M., 382
Drexler, K. E., 752, 753
driving fast, 140
dromenon, 109
Duke Nukem, 625
Duncan, M., 307
Duncan, T., 354–356
Dungeons and Dragons
    anachronisms, 585
    player-character construct, 35
    semiotic domains, 262
    as subjective play, 299
    in Summoner, 295
    variety, 205
Dunnigan, J., 210
Dunniway, T., 678
dynamics
    and aesthetics, 4, 55, 441
    defined, 440
    and mechanics, 441
    in MUDs, 777–784
    tension, 446
    tools, 33, 55, 446
Dyson, F., 308

Easter Eggs, 257, 340, 429
    early examples, 693, 712
Easterlin, R. A., 863

Eastern Front (1941)
    AI, 718–722
    combat system, 717
    preliminary description, 716
    release, 724
    Russian move, 719
    scrolling map, 22, 715–717
    source code, 724
    tuning, 722
eavesdropping, 804, 809, 822
E-Bay, 61, 827, 861
ecommerce, 816
economic policies, 334
economics
    game theory, 387–389, 406
    Habitat, 746, 751
    (ir)rationality, 630
    Magic, 551–555
    meta-rules, 497
    network monopolies, 843
    on-line gaming revenue, 816, 860n8
    research projects, 845
    revenues, 816, 820, 868n8
    scarcity, 61, 824–826, 834, 846
    supply/demand, 833, 852, 856
    See also game economies
Eddy, A., 786
Edge, 49
editing, 220, 223
educational games, 868
    See also learning
Egyptians, 439
Eisenstein, S., 679
election, 744
Electronic Arts, 819, 820
Elias, S., 542, 547–549

email, 164
Emert, H. G., 786
emotions
    and aesthetics, 441
    and Centipede, 472
    and gender, 351, 357, 359
    joy, 114, 125, 142
    See also fear
Empire of the Petal Throne, 583
Empson, W, 297
end conditions, 419
endings, 661
endurance, 133
engagement, moments of, 5
engrossment, 580, 593–596, 599
entertainment
    mistakes, 219f
    virtual worlds, 821, 823, 825, 856
environment
    Disney techniques, 676
    fantasy RPGs, 585, 590
    interactive drama, 663
    Magic, 549, 550
    tension, 222f
    virtual world, 818
environmental storytelling, 674–679
Eon Products, 539
Epperson, H. L., 786
equality
    chess, 131
    and competition, 134
    games of chance, 134, 135
    and virtual worlds, 822, 824, 844, 855
    See also inequality
equipment, 301
Erasmus, 101
Erector sets, 143

Erikson, E., 310
Erikson, F., 516
Eriksson, D., 436
escalation, 55, 449, 469–472
escape, 305
Eskelinen, M., 667, 671, 687n6
espionage, 591
ethical norms, 845
ethical value, 105
Ethnic Cleansing, 623, 637
ethos, 483
etiquette
    competition in, 487, 491
    and cultural context, 480
    in Foursquare, 510
    in informal game, 489
    in JKII, 606
    and tradition, 483
evaluation, 419, 421
Evard, R., 786
EverQuest
    economies, 61, 63
    immersion, 657
    narrative, 645
    social culture, 40
    subscribers, 820, 859n6
    See also Norrath
evil
    Black and White, 75
    JKII, 607
    and play, 102
    Sonic Adventure, 612
evolution, 84, 298, 302, 316
expectations
    of following rules, 501
    Quake, 655
    room connections, 704

experience(s)
 components, 378
 and cultural models, 619–622, 629, 631
 density, 214, 220
 of game purchase, 157–161
 immersion (*see* immersion)
 involvement (*see* involvement)
 memorable moments, 679
 of outdoors, 335–340
 and play definition, 84, 310
 of player, 3–7, 49
 of player types, 769–777
 and pleasure types, 442
 puzzle-based, 649
 repetition, 659
 semiotic domains, 238
 of set-up/set-down, 416
 in spectacles, 680
 See also agency
exploration
 and boy culture, 338–346
 and girls, 349–352, 359
 vs. linearity, 635
 links, to narrative, 646
 Magic, 550
 Mario, 370
 in MUDs, 757
 of new media, 435
 and player types, 758
 Saturn's Night, 359
 Secret Paths, 349–352
 spatiality, 675
 in town games, 354–356
 of virtual world, 817
explorers
 vs. other explorers, 772
 vs. other types, 770, 772–776

 as player type, 6, 61, 758, 762
 proportion of, 778
Expressive AI, 642
extra-game factors, 416, 480

Façade, 34, 656, 659, 664
facilitator, 420
FADT. See formal abstract design tools
Fagen, R., 83, 297
fairness
 and avatars, 822, 857
 equal opportunity, 131, 135
 handicapping, 532–535
 minimax principle, 388, 396–398
 and MUD admins, 808–812
 and unwritten rules, 481, 486, 496, 509
 as value, 49
Falstein, N., 53, 57, 413, 436
family life, 334, 343
Fandango, 644
Fanderclai, T. F., 786
fantasy
 in amusement parks, 676
 awareness of, 28
 in girl books, 349
 Habitat, 750
 of niceness, 354
 as play, 299
 role, 315–327
 in RPGs, 35, 72, 506
 Saturn's Night, 359, 361
 and virtual worlds, 859n2
 fantasy games, 581–591
 See also role-playing games (RPGs)
FAQs, 17, 62, 269–295
Far Cry, 164
Farley, W., 346, 362

Farmer, F. R., 18, 23, 41, 728–752, 787
Farrell, J., 862
fashions, 144, 152n15
fate, 85, 304
Fatsis, S., 43
fear
    amusement parks, 140
    and children, 142
    and exploration, 357
    and mimicry, 135
    and movies, 319
feedback
    for actions, 214, 373
    Adventure, 700
    from backend, 734
    from playtesters, 22, 723
    pseudo-feedback, 449
    and socializers, 779
    sound, 215
    and uncertainty, 446–449
Feinstein, K., 332, 362
Feltovich, P. J., 265
festivals, 107, 114, 300
Feyerabend, P., 301
fiction, 127, 195, 198, 206
    short story, 156–169
fighting games, 377
    See also war games
films
    Battleship Potempkin, 679
    David and Bathsheba, 319
    Gone with the Wind, 683
    Hans Christian Anderson, 319
    kung fu, 680
    Rebecca, 683
    Star Wars, 75, 664, 676
    Wargames, 485

film theory, 671, 673, 688n19
Final Fantasy, 376
Fine, G. A., xviii, 29, 35, 72, 506, 515, 516, 578–600
fire walls, 279
first-person, 861n19
first-person shooter games
    agency, 654
    bosses, 636
    end conditions, 419
    game state, 447
    individualism, 625
    resources, 428
    as semiotic domain, 241, 261
    See also Operation Flashpoint: Cold War Crisis;
    Return to Castle Wolfenstein; Wolfenstein 3D
Fischer, Bobby, 481
Fitzhugh, L., 352–354, 362
Five Magics, 540
flackbacks, 681, 682
flame wars, 771
Flood, M., 382
Fluxus, 68
Flynn, E. A., 363
fog of war, 33, 55, 446, 451
folly, 101
Fontaine, T., 545
football, 484
force, 444
formal abstract design tools, 369–380, 413
Formanek-Brunnel, M., 362
Foucault, M., 307
400 Rules Project, 53, 413
Foursquare
    description, 507
    rules, 16, 43, 508–516
    social culture, 40, 43, 509–516

frame analysis, 579
    of fantasy games, 581–591
frames and contexts, 320–327, 485, 515, 582–596
frame switching, 593–596, 600
framework. *See* component framework
Frasca, G., 33, 51, 661–663, 667
free choice, 304
freedom
    of admins, 810–812
    to change game, 525–531
    and fantasy RPGs, 593
    vs. narrative, 647, 661, 663, 679
    and play, 102, 126
    player rights, 792, 794, 799, 802–809
    vs. rules, 141–147
    self-liberation, 136
    and video games, 344
    and virtual worlds, 825, 837, 844
freeforms, 201
Freeman, D., 7
Freire, P., 265
Freitag, W., 210
Frequency and Amplitude, 65
Friedman, T., 362
frivolity, 85, 305
Frobenius, L., 109–111, 117
Fujitsu Habitat, 749
Fuller, M., 678
Fullerton, T., 13, 25, 437
fun
    aesthetics, 442
    analysis, 98
    density, 214
    in fantasy RPGs, 593
    and learning, 637
    and meta-game, 498
    and rules, 514
    types, 4
Funcom, 819

Galileo, 629
Gamasutra, 49
gambling. *See* games of chance
game(s)
    analysis (*see* component framework; design patterns)
    change recommendations, 531
    classification, 129–147, 148t, 435, 612
    definitions, 77–81, 184–191, 196, 477
    elements of, 185–191, 196–209
    instance, 415, 506, 658
    instance of, 415, 506, 658
    multiple run-throughs, 658
    narrative hybrids, 662
    nonlinearity, 194
    non-narrative, 672 (*see also* narrative)
    oldest, 439
    vs. play, 519, 525–530
    vs. puzzles, 193
    and real life, 506, 579
    session, 415
    as social contract, 11–18, 796–805
    speaking about, 43–50
game communities
    antisocial activity, 768
    and change, 520–526
    and conflict, 33
    and cyberspace, 730, 734, 750
    design for, 41
    and first-person shooters, 241, 247
    Foursquare, 17
    Habitat, 23, 39–43, 746–749
    Jedi Knights II, 603–608
    magic, 554
    and narrative, 645
    and platform *vs.* computer games, 250
    player rights, 796–812
    and player types, 61

purchase, 39, 157–161

and spoilsports, 106

See also multiuser domains (MUDs)

GameCube, 248, 692

Game Developer, 49

game development software, 623

game economies

defined, 59

in design patterns, 55, 430–433

in Habitat, 746, 751, 752n2

in Magic, 60, 63, 547–549, 551

in MMORPGs, 61

in Norrath, 59–63, 816, 826–840, 846–858

of Ultima Online, 861n19

game mechanics. *See* mechanics

game models, 505

games of chance

cultural status, 124

and fate, 304

social ambiguity, 302

and threat, 318

transformations to, 129

See also alea; baccara

games of patience, 143

game spaces, 65–69

adventure island, 346

arcade games, 462

catacombs, 710–713

evocative spaces, 34

experiential nature, 687n9

and framework, 421

and gender, 74, 346–361

Habitat, 731, 740, 743, 750

Joust, 463

mazes, 66, 68, 703–713

in MUDs, 765

multiscreen, 66

narrative, 65, 68, 664, 674–682

property rights, 794, 795, 860n15

for rehearsal, 681

in Saturn's Nights, 359

scrolling map, 65, 715–717

secret gardens, 348–352

secret room, 712

The Sims, 685

single screen, 463

towns, 352–356

in virtual worlds, 834, 846, 860n15, 862n27

Gamespot, 49

game state, 447

game theory

and chess, 392

and component framework, 414

and economics, 387–389

and genetics, 404

minimax principle, 54, 388, 396–398, 405

mixed strategy, 399–405, 408n3

N-person games, 406

origins, 383–386

table of outcomes, 392–395

tic-tac-toe, 389–392

zero-sum games, 54, 395

gaming, 506, 580, 746–749

gaming mind, 520

Gamma, E., 437

Gandhi, 661

Gardner, H., 265

Garfield, R., xviii, 22, 23, 60, 63, 205, 538–555

Garfinkel, H., 601

Gee, J., 45, 47, 73, 228–264, 265, 610–638

Geertz, C., 86

gender

in avatars, 822, 844

books, 337, 345–355, 357–360

boy culture, 338–347
cultural models, 616, 618, 625
and cursor, 351
Foursquare, 511–514
misogyny, 341, 343, 358 (see also girls and women)
playthings, 151n6
and representation, 71, 74
and spaces, 69, 74, 336–338, 346–352
spoilsports, 106
Genesis 3D, 623
genetics, 298, 404
genres, 412, 435, 679, 867–869
Gibson, W., 752
Gillen, K., 49, 51, 602
girls and women
and avatars, 822, 844
in books, 348, 352–357
and boy culture, 341
exploration-oriented game, 349
game movement, 344
and male games, 358
misogyny, 341, 343, 358
in rituals, 116
and spaces, 68, 336, 348–356
and video games, 6, 74, 355
Glaser, B., 584
Glaser, R., 265, 266
Go, 204, 383, 453
goals
and action, 654
and addiction, 340
Adventure, 699
adventure games, 375
Breakout, 560
in Cabal process, 215
chess, 183
in component framework, 417

and diplomacy, 202
in freeforms, 201
as game element, 186, 191
in game vs. work, 173
golf, 174
Habitat, 740
levels of, 372
and linearity, 635
Mario, 370, 372
Operation Flashpoint, 627
prelusory, 186, 191
resource collection, 430
and resources, 430
and RPGs, 197
and rules, 174–177
Sim City, 197
subgoals, 417
and toys, 194
god games, 430
Godzilla, 160
Goffman, E., 510, 516, 579–581, 582, 596, 601
Goldberg, A., 753
Goldberg, E., 210
Goldstein, J., 51
Goldstein, K., 15, 19, 505, 506, 515, 516
golf, 174, 178
Gooding, M., 86
goodness, 607, 612, 614
gothic romances, 349
Gould, S. J., 298
Grammatron, 645
Grand Theft Auto, 65, 75, 439
graphics, 542, 696, 735
greed. See minimax principle
Greenberg, E. R., 479
Greenfield, P. M., 363
Griffin, P., 266

Groos, K., 132, 139, 142

Grossman, A., 25

Grusin, R., 31

GTA San Andreas, 75

Guardini, R., 112

Gygax, G., 9, 205

Habbo Hotel, 41

Habermas, J., 265

Habitat

    current status, 749

    election, 744

    future directions, 750

    incipient *vs.* percipient level, 744–746

    in Japan, 749

    lessons learned, 734–747

    object-orientation, 733

    player contribution, 18, 22

    precursors, 730

    regions, 731–733

    scaling, 740

    social culture, 41

    violence, 743

hackers, 291, 744–746

Haiti, 138

Hale, R.-E., 63

Haley, J., 326

Half-Life, 23, 213–220, 611, 682

Hall, F., 601

Halmos, P., 386, 407

Hammer, D., 639

handicapping, 448, 532–535

hard drives, 248

harmony, 105

Harré, R., 516

Harrigan, P., 37

Harris, L., 202, 203

Harris, L. V., 863

Harris, R., 199

Hart, R., 335, 336, 362

Haslam, F., 200

hate groups, 623

Hayek, F. A., 753

Hays, J., 540

hazing, 133, 318

heads or tails, 133, 399–402, 405, 408n3

Heath, S. B., 265

hedgehog. *See* Sonic Adventure 2 Battle

Helm, R., 437

heroes, 624

Herold, C., 667

HeroQuest, 207

Herron, R. E., 86

Herz, J. C., 19

Hickey, D., 51

hidden energy, 33, 450

hide and seek, 142

high-jumper, 179, 182

Hill, C., 265

history

    Adventure, 691, 694–697

    Apple II, 715

    Eastern Front, 715

    of infractions, 806

    Magic, 539–543

    of virtual worlds, 818–820, 824, 860n13

    of war games, 383

hobbies, 145, 299

hockey, 506

Hoffman, S., 13, 25, 437

holidays, 114

holistic components, 415

Holland, D., 639

Holland, N. N., 349, 362

Holmsten, P., 858n2, 860n9

Holopainen, J., 10–11, 54, 57, 79, 80, 436

Homo Ludens, 83, 96–119, 123

horse races, 131, 132

hot cockles, 139

Houser, N., 266

Hudson, 136

Hughes, L., 16, 43, 504–516

Huhtamo, E., 19

Huizinga, J., 46, 83, 97–119, 123, 417

    critique of, 123–124

human nature, 751

humor, 625, 766

    See also joking

hyperactivity, 334

hypertext, 195, 646, 663, 671

Ice Age, 552

identification, 27–31

    and agency, 650

    in fantasy RPGs, 35, 72

    in Mideast game, 622

    as mimicry, 28, 137

    with moving shape, 697

    in races and contests, 137

    and simulation, 204

    and tokens, 206

identity(ies)

    Under Ash, 621–623

    in fantasy RPGs, 592–599

    of on-line players, 74

    as problem-solver, 258, 262

    in religions, 117

    and representations, 109

    as rhetoric of play, 85, 305

    in society, 258, 262

    three-layer, 29

    See also player-character construct

ideology, 43–50, 73, 309

idleness, 146, 154n16

ilinx, 5, 138–140, 148t

    and *ludus,* 144

    in slot machines, 153

    See also vertigo

illusion

    of closeness, 446

    in fantasy RPGs, 589

    fog of war, 446, 451

    trompe l'oeil, 319

    and uncertainty, 449

I Love Bees, 68

imagination

    and myth, 100

    respresentations as, 99, 108

    and rhetorics of play, 85, 305

    and seizure, 110

    See also make-believe

immersion

    disbelief suspension, 649

    environmental storytelling, 674–676, 682

    in experience, 29

    in Jedi Knights II, 30

    mechanisms, 657

    and narrative, 34

immersive fallacy, 29

    See also lusory attitude; magic circle

improvisation, 126

individualism, 625

inefficiency

    and game definition, 78

    of play, 124

    of rules, 9, 173–184, 188

inequality
  and pleasure, 61
  and virtual worlds, 840, 845, 858, 860n12
  See also equality
inevitability
  destiny, 133
  in fantasy RPGs, 506
  and interactivity, 660–664
  sources, 453–456, 459n2
  and transformation vs. agency, 458
  vs. uncertainty, 33, 55, 445
infinite play, 463
infinite regression, 492–494, 501
information
  as content, 236
  game analysis, 434
  and game design, 217f, 421
  and game theory, 390
  and player types, 772
  relevance, 200–202
  See also knowledge
information availability
  about resources, 429
  about score, 451
  in arcade games, 463, 465
  in Aristotelian drama, 656
  backstory revelation, 681–683
  Clue, 454
  in fantasy RPGs, 586–590
  Majestic, 683
  outcome, 126
  See also deceit; fog of war
instinct, 103, 118, 141, 145
intellectual property, 434, 805–807, 815, 835
intention
  in adventure games, 654
  of changing game, 531

description, 372–377
  in interactive drama, 652
  of playing well, 527
  and Rooie Rules, 509
interactive fiction, 646, 648, 663
interactivity
  in arts, 645
  vs. boredom, 868
  and cyberspace, 730, 734, 750
  in drama, 646–656, 660–666
  as game trait, 194, 196
  in literature, 645
  in MUDs, 764, 767
  vs. narrative, 439, 643, 664–666, 671
  and player types, 769–777
  theories of, 660
  in virtual world, 818
  See also agency; involvement; social interaction
interconnectedness, 467–469, 737
interfaces. *See* user interfaces
Internet
  Under Ash, 620
  as learning tool, 253, 257
  Magic, 554
  multiplayer games (see multiuser domains; virtual worlds)
  Project Entropia, 843
interpretation, 71–75, 547, 553
interstitials, xxiii, 873–875
Intruder, 645
involvement
  and agency, 650
  design for, 369–380, 430, 443
  fantasy RPGs, 580, 593, 599
  and frame analysis, 579
  Habitat, 746–748
  and narrative, 376–380, 643, 659, 662
  puzzles, 649and rules, 495

ISO Model, 737
Israelis, 73, 619–623
iterative design, 21–24, 55, 213, 218–225

James, W., 579, 601
Japan, 152, 749
Järvinen, A., 436, 437
Jedi Knights II: Jedi Outcast
    identity
    of on-line player, 74, 604
    player-character, 30, 603–608
    lightsabre dueling, xviii, 603–605
    and Quake III, 605
    as social culture, 40
Jenkins, H., 6, 33, 34, 51, 67, 69, 74, 75, 330–361, 362, 664, 667, 668–689
Jensen, A. E., 115–117
Jeopardy, 449, 450
Jewitt, C., 266
Johnson, D., 362
Johnson, R., 437
Johnson, S., 63
joking, 595, 598
Jones, J., 75
Jones, K., 476
journalists, 49, 433
        See also always_black
Journey to the Center of the Earth, 683
Joust, 463
joy, 114, 125, 142
joysticks, 248, 697
Junta, 207
Just Grandma and Me, 194
Juul, J., 33, 37, 57, 80, 81, 671, 677, 682

Kalantzis, M., 265
Kant, I., 524
Kaplan, C. S., 863

Karp, D., 863
Katz, J., 339, 362
Katz, M. L., 863
Kaufman, D., 210
Kennedy, H. W., 75
Kent, S., 362
Kerényi, K., 114
Kessen, W., 308
Kettman, S, 863
keyboards, 248
killers
    vs. other killers, 776
    and other types, 757, 762, 765, 771–783
    as player type, 6, 42, 61, 759, 762
    proportion, 778
    in social MUDs, 768
Kinchloe, J. L., 362
Kinder, M., 51, 363
King, T., 210
Kirmse, A., 819
Kirmse, C., 819
kites, 127, 142, 143, 154n16
Kloesel, C., 266
kludges, 681
Knizia, R., 21, 437
knowledge
    anachronisms, 585, 591
    content orientation, 236–239
    and decisions, 200–202
    and fantasy, 583–591
    of outcome, 126
    of player vs. character, 72
    as power, 303
    and producers, 231
    from simulation, 204
    See also information; information availability
Kolbert, E., 861n19, 863

Kort, B., 787
Korzybski, A, 317
Koster, R., 7, 11, 42, 788–812
kredati, 141
Kreimeier, B., 57, 436, 437
Kress, G., 266
Kriegspiel, 383
Kuhn, T. S., 307
Kuittinen, J., 436
Kushner, D., 25

Lachicotte, W., 639
Landow, G., 667
language
    about games, 43–50, 412
    abstraction levels, 315
    assembly language, 721
    BASIC, 718
    capitalizations, 211
    in card game, 59
    Chinese, 141, 146, 154n16
    critical language, 193
    design vocabulary, 367–370
    and "fun," 98
    ludus, 141–147
    metaphors, as play, 100, 299
    meta-rules, 497
    "play" definitions, 126
    play rhetorics, 48, 85
    recognition, 34
    and rules, 492, 547
    The Sims, 684
    for structuralists, 242–247
    in tennis game, 490
    See also dialog; linguistics; software
lapsed players, 555
LARPs, 195, 198
Larsen, E., 265

lassi, 680
Latinos, 623
laughing, 101
launch activities, 5, 62
Laurel, B., 25, 29, 33, 37, 349, 647, 655, 667, 668, 867–869
lawsuits, 768, 805
leapfrog, 139, 142
learning
    about real life, 502
    of arcade games, 465
    by contemporary children, 253, 259
    critical and active, 237, 254–263
    and critical thinking, 156, 253, 256–259
    and cultural models, 629–637
    educational games, 868
    from failures, 636
    for future work world, 344
    and girls, 352, 356, 358
    Half-Life, 611
    and MUDs, 765
    and Norrath, 843
    (not)counting, 487
    play as, 304
    to play Breakout, 569–579
    and videogames, 236–239, 263, 358, 611–613, 633–637
learning curve, 377
learning principles, 263
LeBlanc, M., 4, 33, 55, 438–459
The Legend of Zelda, 421, 439, 693
Legionnaire, 718
Lemke, J., 266
Lemmings, 430
levels
    of abstraction, 315
    and achievers, 767
    in arcade games, 463

of avatars, 849–851, 857, 858
behavior vs. presentation, 736
Breakout, 577
of cognition, 495
of constraints, 660
in data communication, 737
of difficulty, 220, 471
in fantasy gaming, 582–584
frame analysis, 579, 582–584, 592–596
of game change, 525
of goals, 372
in MUDs, 766
of narratives, 679
of rules, 493
Summoner, 274
of virtual world, 744–748
Levy, D. J., 753
Lewis, E., 548
Lieberman, J., 334
Liebowitz, S. J., 863
Life, 204
lifeworlds, 251–259
limits
and animals, 132
in Atari Adventure, 698
and competition, 131
of culture, 253
gender, 360
of human nature, 751
of play, 104, 113, 125
rules *vs.* means, 177–183
on sexual activity, 685
in spectacles, 680
on twinking, 858
See also rules; time limits
Lin, Jim, 546

Lineage, 40
linearity, 194, 635, 644, 687n7
See also narrative(s)
linguistics, 242–247, 317
literacy, 47, 229–235, 345, 357
literature
Alice in Wonderland, 677
electronic, 645
spatial exploration, 675
War and Peace, 676
See also books
Logg, E., 473, 715
logic
asymmetrical relations, 321
frames and contexts, 320–327
and game spaces, 66
and game theory, 388
and psychotherapy, 327
and resources, 430
See also frames and contexts; paradoxes
Logical Types, 317, 327
logistics, 722
London, J., 346
The Longest Journey, 623
The Lord of the Rings, 21
losing, 498
lotteries, 133
Lucasfilm Games, 729
Lucey, P., 459
ludology, 411, 422, 660, 673, 687n1
ludus, 141–147
Luigi's Mansion, 644
Lundgren, S., 436, 437
lusory attitude
and game, 78, 185, 188–190
and make-believe, 137

and religious feasts, 115–117
and rules, 501
and spoilsports, 106, 127
lusory goals, 186
lusory means, 187
lusory rules, 187
Lynch, K., 685

Mackay, D., 31
Magic: The Gathering
    antecedents, 539
    appeal, 209
    deck types, 545, 550
    design, 539–550, 553
    economies, 60, 63, 547–549, 551
    formats, 553
    and Ice Age, 552
    inevitability, 453
    iterative design, 22, 23
    playtesting, xviii, 542–546, 550
    Pro Tour, 554
    releases, 541–543
    resource management, 459n1
    role play, 549
    tension, 445
    variety, 205, 541, 544
magic circle, 106, 113
Magic Online, 554
mail games, 415
mais d'or, 138
Majestic, 68, 672, 683
make-believe
    awareness of, 103
    and characters, 27–31
    in children, 136
    dressing-up, 107
    fabrications within, 600n2

in game definition, 78
pleasure in, 5, 136
and rules, 126, 137, 501
The Sims2, 71
societal view, 262
    See also fantasy; simulations
Malinowski, B., 116
Manning, F. E., 504
Manser, M., 787
maps, 317–321, 705f, 758, 766
    scrolling, 715–717
marbles, 129, 134, 540
Marett, R. R., 116
Margolis, S., 863
Mario Bros., 347, 371, 463
    See also Super Mario Bros.
Mario Golf, 169
Mario Golf Advance, 163
Mario 64
    consequences, 374
    design, 370–372
    design tool model, 372–380
marketing
    and addiction, 868
    and bugs, 709
    and design patterns, 434
    and infinite play, 463
    key premise, 868
    potential research, 845
    of source code, 724
Martins, I., 266
masculinity, 340
    See also boys and men
masks, 118, 124, 135, 680
    See also disguise

massively multiplayer on-line role-playing games
(MMORPGs)
    admins, 812 (*see also* rights)
    economies, 61
    and narratives, 645
    and planning, 738–741
    play mode, 417
    and role-playing, 207, 757
    sessions, 415
    See also virtual worlds
mastery
    and boredom, 535
    and gender, 339, 345, 347
    handicapping, 532–535
    and pleasure, 142
    undoing, 258
matching pennies, 399–402
Mateas, M., 29, 33, 34, 642–669
mathematics, 143, 302, 322
    and game theory, 385
    See also Life
Matthews, M. H., 335
Matthews, R. C., 363
Mauldin, M. L., 787
Mayer, R. E., 266
Mayfair Games, 539
mazes, 182
    Adventure, 66, 68, 703–711
McConville, R., 500
McCulloch, W. W., 321
McEnany, L., 343
McGillicuddy, K., 266
McGilvray, J., 266
McGonigal, J., 69
MdLuhan, M., 45
meaning, 581
    See also fantasy games; goals; resource management;
    semiotic domains

means, 9, 179–184, 187, 188
mechanical bias, 448
mechanics
    in arcade games, 465
    defined, 413
    and design patterns, 423
    and drama, 440, 444–457
Medal of Honor Allied Assault, 611
medieval games, 585
meditation, 146
Mega Man, 347
Meier, S., 197
melodrama, 683
memories, 676–679
men. *See* boys and men
merchants, 819, 833, 853–856
Meridian 59 (M59), 819
Merkle, B., 479
merry-go-rounds, 129
messaging, 418
metacommunication, 28–30, 35, 84, 323–326
metalevel thinking, 256, 263
Metal Gear Solid, 634, 636
Metal Gear Solid 2: Sons of Liberty, 625
metaphors
    avatar/worker, 822, 835, 838, 852
    flags, 319
    games as, 506, 579
    psychopathology, 326, 327
    visual, 216f, 219f
meta-rules, 489, 493, 497–4500
Mexico, 138
Microsoft, 248–250, 819, 843
    See also Xbox
military barracks, 139
Miller, M. S., 752, 753
mimetic mode, 665

mimicry
    in animals, 136, 149n5
    and *ludus,* 143
    play type, 5, 28, 135–137, 148t
    scale models, 143
    Secret Paths, 350
    in slot machines, 153
Mindark, 817, 840
minimax principle, 54, 388, 396–398, 405
Minnie case, 806
Minstrell, J., 639
Mirage, 552
mischief, 142, 152n12, 300
misogyny, 341, 343, 358
Missile Command, 576
mixed-reality games, 68
mixed strategy, 399–405, 408n3
MMORPGs. *See* massively multiplayer on-line
role-playing games
mobile objects (MOBs), 819, 853–857, 859n4
Mochan, xviii, 27, 63, 269–295
models
    to scale, 143, 145, 299
    See also cultural models; design models
Molyneux, P., 682
money
    and *alea,* 149n4
    games of chance, 134
    monetary system, 497
    from on-line gaming, 816, 860n8
    payment issues, 803, 806, 809
    and poker, 173
    virtual world profit, 820
    in virtual worlds, 832, 835, 838, 842, 857, 860n12
    zero-sum games, 395
Monopoly, 203, 419, 421, 674
monsters, 819, 862n26

Montfort, N., 649, 668
Moock, C., 787
Moore, R. C., 335, 338
morality
    goodness, 615
    play, 47, 102
    rules, 176, 181–183, 483, 496
    vertigo, 139
    video games, 613
Morganstern, O., 387, 437
    See also game theory
Morningstar, C., 18, 23, 41, 728–752, 859n3
Morrowind, 272
Mortal Kombat, 341
Mortensen, T., 69
motivation, 654
motorcycles, 140
mountain climbing, 144
movies. *See* films
MUDs. *See* multiuser domains
multiculturalism, 253
multimodal texts, 229
multiuser domains (MUDs)
    cheating, 745
    commercial viability, 782
    and community, 40–42
    cyberspace use, 730, 734, 750
    elections, 744
    extensibility, 769
    game spaces, 765
    game status, 755, 769, 784
    game *vs.* social, 767–769, 782
    interest, 761f, 763–767, 783
    narratives, 645
    player rights, 789
    player types, 6, 756–763
    stability, 763–767, 777–784, 790–795

See also Habitat; massively multiplayer on-line role-playing games; rights

Murphy, P., 208

Murray, J., 29, 33, 37, 647, 649, 668, 672, 685, 687n6

music, 256, 300, 347

Muslims, 619–621

Myst, 644, 682

mystery, 112, 114, 118, 124

myth, 100

Mythic Entertainment, 820

NAPLPS, 736

Napoleon's Last Battles, 204

narrative(s)
    and Cabal process, 216
    embedded, 34, 664, 681–684, 686
    emergent, 34, 644, 665, 684–686
    enacted, 34, 664, 685–686
    evoked, 664, 685
    and exploration, 646
    vs. freedom, 647, 661, 663, 679
    and games, 664–666, 671–674
    adventure games, 375
    arcade games, 465
    MUDs, 645, 769
    RPGs, 33–36, 375–377
    spaces, 65, 68, 664, 674–680
    Ultima Online, 645
    Half-Life, 682
    keeping track of, 218
    linearity, 194, 635, 644, 687n7
    and links, 646
    micronarratives, 679
    and multiple run-throughs, 658
    Pac-Man, 643
    vs. player involvement, 376–380, 643, 659, 662
    rhetorics as, 310

The Sims, 645, 665, 684
    vs. simulation, 204
    structured *vs.* episodic, 678
    Summoner, 294
    in town games, 355
    traditional forms, 439
    See also tension

narratologists, 666n1, 670, 672

National Alliance, 623

nature
    equal opportunity, 131
    mimicry, 135
    and rituals, 108–111
    Secret Paths, 350

navigation, 65

NBA Live, 375, 378

negotiation, 12, 30, 43

neo-Aristotelianism, 647–649, 656, 660–666

Neo-platonism, 100

network games, 201, 343

network monopolies, 843

networks
    of screens, 713
    social, 343

Neverwinter Nights, 812

New Games Foundation, 518

New London Group, 266

Newson, E., 363

Newson, J., 363

NHL 99, 377
    niceness, 509–516, 543

Nichols, D. A., 786

Nifty Serve, 749

Nintendo, 248, 612, 674

nonreversible processes, 454

nonviolence, 623

No One Lives Forever II, 625

Norman, D., 21

Norrath

    demographics, 816, 828–832, 859n6

    economy, 826–840

        goods markets, 853–856

        inflation, 837

        labor market, 852, 855

        per capita GNP, 836, 849

    meetings and classes, 843

Norrish, J., 787

no takebacks, 534

novices, 465

N-person games, 406

Nussbaum, M., 437

objectivity, 307

object-oriented programming, 730, 733, 735, 750

objects

    Adventure, 699, 713

    in design, 735–737

    Habitat, 731–733, 743, 748, 750

    in MUDs, 766, 769

    The Sims, 685

    in virtual worlds, 819, 833, 853–857

obsession, 178

Ogborn, J., 266

Old Man Murray, 49

olorhymes, 143, 152n14

OMM, 668

on line board game lounges, 420

online sites, 49

open awareness, 584

open-endedness, 741

Operation Flashpoint: Cold War Crisis, 625–629, 637

order, 105, 110, 139

    disorder, 139, 141

orgies, 107

outdoors, 332–336, 675

pacing

    Centipede, 469–472

    decelerators, 451

    denouement, 457

    of difficulty (*see* challenges)

    of engineering, 224

    in fine-tuning, 220

    of girl game, 351

    in racing games, 448

    Summoner, 289

    and tension, 4, 208, 218

Pac-Man

    framework, 417, 421

    game spaces, 65, 463

    graphics, 675

    producer-consumer, 432

    story, 643

pageantry, 203

paida, 141–147, 148t

Palestinians, 73, 619–623

Paper-Rock-Scissors, 415

paradoxes

    awareness, 317, 319

    Foursquare rules, 514

    frames and contexts, 324, 515

    necessity, 327

Parlett, D., 437

parody, 625

participation

    and cyberspace, 730, 734, 750

    significance, xii, 195

    and tokens, 200

    See also interactivity; involvement

patience, 143, 146

patience (game). *See* solitaire

Patrizio, A., 863

patterns
    and architecture, 54
    and cultural models, 631
    and fun, 4
    and game definition, 79
    See also design patterns
payment, 803, 806, 809, 816
PC Gamer, 5, 49, 160, 602
Pearson, P. D., 266
Pechuel Loesche, E., 116
Peitz, J., 436
Pelligrino, J. W., 266
penalties
    Foursquare, 510, 512
    player rights, 793, 801, 806, 808
    for rule violation, 188, 506
    Twenty-One, 457
pen pals, 299
Pepper, S., 307
perceivable consequences, 373–377, 413
perceptions
    Breakout, 576
    of goodness, 614
    of inevitability, 449, 454
    of intentionality, 509–511
    and reality, 449, 454, 579
    in virtual world, 744–747
persistence, 104, 143, 636, 818
personality
    Cabal process, 221, 224
    and poker, 134
    transformation, 650
    See also player types
perspective
    first- vs. third-person, xviii, 861n19
    political, 73
Peterson, S., 210

Petrik, P., 363
Phantom Menace, 160
physical sensations
    and multimodality, 229
    See also vertigo
physical strength, 358
physical surrender, 84
physics, 629–631, 744, 818, 822
Piaget, J., 13
Piccione, P. A., 459
Pictionary, 208
Pikmin, 235, 254–259, 262, 430
pinball games, 463
Ping Pong, 535
Pirates of the Caribbean, 676
place, sense of, 203
.plan, 5
Planetquake, 49
planning
    Centipede, 467
    Mario, 371
    for MMORPGs, 738–742
    platform games
    characteristics, 250
    vs. computer games, 248–250
    design patterns, 435
    RPGs, 376
    saves, 248
    semiotic domains, 248
    Sonic Adventure 2 Battle, 612
    web phones, 867
    See also Xbox
Plato, 112, 119, 236
play
    awareness, 35, 85, 99, 114–116, 127, 128, 320–323
    characteristics, 102–107, 124, 128
    as communication, 28, 316–320

and culture, 46, 84, 99–119, 141
definitions, 83–87, 97–100, 123–128, 310
diversity, 298–301
extrinsic/intrinsic, 310
forms, 5, 129–147
functions, 97, 104, 108, 111
vs. game, 519, 525–530
and game models, 505
and limits, 104, 113, 125
and morality, 47, 102
over time, 104, 125
and progress, 304
vs. rules, 126, 505
sacredness, 119
scholarship, 301–311
seriousness, 101, 103, 114
vs. table of outcomes, 394
theories, 309
vertigo examples, 138
play-by-mail games, 415
player-character construct
in Under Ash, 621
avatars, 42, 85, 420
and core beliefs, 611
description, 27–31
in Dungeons & Dragons, 35
and emergent narrative, 644
in interactive drama, 648, 660
in JKII, 30, 603–608
real people, as characters, 611, 663
in RPGs, 35, 72, 583–599
in Sonic Adventure 2 Battle, 612
See also agency
player experience. *See* experience(s)
player identity. *See* identification

players
acknowledgement of, 214
as allies, 202, 406
assumptions about, 742
attitude (see attitude; lusory attitude; seriousness)
and characters (see player-character construct)
as component, 420
demographics, 301, 623, 828–832, 860n10
design awareness, 256
design role, 18, 22–24, 34, 62, 195, 742–750
as focus, 41
and game spaces, 67
in game theory, 388
involvement, 369–380, 430, 443, 495
in fantasy RPGs, 580, 593, 599
lapsed, 555
messaging between, 319, 418
mistakes, 219f
and narrative, 34, 644
novices, 465
position, 131
predictability, 18, 39
professionals, 125
rights of (see rights, of players)
and rules, 188
and sessions, 415
subjectivity, 71, 449, 454, 547, 554
three-layer identity, 29
types (see player types)
video game benefits, 236–239, 263, 358, 611–613, 633–6.
See also avatars
player types, 6, 41, 61, 756–763
interactions, 769–777
and MUDs, 777–784
playerwiping, 809
playful behaviors, 300

playgrounds
    backyards, 332–335
    demarcation, 105, 113, 125
    as game spaces, 68
playing mind, 520
playing well, 527
play session, 415
play spaces
    gender differences, 336–338, 358
    outdoors, 68, 332–335
Playstation, 248, 692
playtesting
    crashes, 220
    Eastern Front, 722
    feedback, 22, 723
    Habitat, 746
    Half-Life, 218–220
    Magic, xviii, 542–546, 550
    and new games, 21–24, 543
pleasure
    analysis, 3–7, 98, 442
    and artifice, 29
    in make-believe, 5, 136
    in pain, 142
    in process, 680
    and rules, 9
    and scarcity, 61, 824–826, 834
    and vertigo, 140
    plot, 375, 651, 657–660, 681
    See also narrative(s)
Plucky Little England, 198
poetry, 143
Poirier, J. R., 787
Pokèmon, 71, 550
poker
    bluffing, 404
    and chips, as signals, 319

    and game theory, 385
    goal, 173
    network version, 208
    player traits, 134
    and socializing, 208
politics, 73, 181, 744
polo, 127, 482
Pong, 675, 692
pool, 450
Poole, S., 75
Popper, K. R., 753
post-mortems, 457
Poundstone, W., 54, 382–408
power
    of administrator, 798–812
    of agency, 649
    and cashing out, 452
    and casual tennis game, 491
    and consensus, 500, 502
    of cultural models, 632
    and game change, 525
    and girls, 358
    of interactive vs. passive media, 623
    and Jedi Knights II, 606
    and knowledge, 303
    learning about, 611
    Magic, 60, 445, 543, 552
    need satiation, 867
    and player rights, 794
    of referees, in fantasy RPGs, 587
    and rhetoric of play, 305
    Sim City, 353
powerlessness, 349
predictability
    and boredom, 205, 535
    and Mario 64, 371
    of players, 18, 39

and rules, 500
of situation, 126
See also variety
Preece, J., 437
prelusory goals, 186, 191
prelusory means, 187
prelusory rules, 187
presentation, 203
primitives, 108–118
prisoner's base, 127
privacy, 804, 809
privileges, 809
probability, 399–402, 408n3, 660
problem-solving
and design patterns, 423, 433
in development, 434
in interactive drama, 648
Pikmin, 258, 262
for pleasure, 142
and puzzles, 193
in simulations, 204
in video games, 635
productivity, 124, 231
profit, 124
progress, 85, 145, 304
Project Entropia, 842
property rights
intellectual, 434, 805–807
virtual, 794, 795, 819
prototypes, 21–23, 694
Prussia, 383
psychology, 134, 799
psychotherapy, 325–327
purchase, 5, 60, 157–161, 433
purpose, 111
put-ons, 595

puzzles
actions and goal, 654
crosswords, 127, 143, 144
DOOM 3, 168
vs. games, 127, 193
and girl culture, 349
and interactive drama, 648
and ludus, 143, 144
in MUDs, 767
rings, 143, 155n16
Secret Paths, 350, 352

Qix, 432
Quake, 654, 655, 682
quake girls, 358
Quake III, 605
quality, 223
Quantum Computer, 730, 746
quests. *See* Adventure
quickslots, 278, 282
Quinn, N., 639

races, 137, 178, 180, 300
racial terms, 74
racing games, 418, 448, 450, 454
Raessens, J., 51
RAM, 692
randomness, 205
random numbers, 459n3
rapture, 110
rationality
game theory, 388, 392, 398, 405
and play, 99, 111, 113
realism, 626, 643
reality
abstractions, 502
and ambiguity, 72
Club Caribe, 751

and cultural models, 73, 618
vs. game, 506, 579
Habitat, 747–749
interlude from, 103, 107, 114
Jedi Knights II, 607
mixed-reality, 68
vs. perceptions, 449, 454, 579
and physics, 629–631
and player rights, 802–805
and psychotherapy, 326
real people, as charactars, 75, 611, 663, 684
and representations, 109
rhetorics in, 306
and RPGs, 585–591, 593–599
rules in, 189, 515
Saturn's Night, 359
semiotic domains, 251–259
The Sims 2, 71
vs. spectacle, 867
in town games, 354
and vertigo, 138
vs. virtual worlds, 61, 622, 821, 824, 844, 858, 860nn10,15
vs. perceptions, 579
See also society
real-time, 368, 421, 698
real-time strategy (RTS) games, 368, 428, 431
rebuses, 144
reconstructions, 849
recovery, 718
Red Faction, 611
red queen dilemma, 430
redundancy, 681
referees, 586–591, 594
rehearsal, 681
Reid, E., 787
Reizler, K., 601

relationships
    producer-consumer, 55, 431–433
    See also social interaction
relativism, 500–502
relaxation, 104, 146, 305
religion, 109, 112–114, 117–119
repetition, 104, 143, 249
representations, 71–75, 108
research, 411–413, 422
    in AI, 659
    virtual worlds, 840, 844–846
Resident Evil, 644
resource management
    bandwidth, 734–736
    design patterns, 55, 427–430
    Eastern Front, 722
    Habitat, 746
    and inevitability, 454, 459n2
    and interactive drama, 652
    Magic, 459n1
    producer/consumer, 55, 431–433
    profitabiliIy, 124
    scarcity, 61, 824–826, 834, 846
    time, 453
    tokcns, 200
    uses, 10, 59–63, 105, 199
    in virtual worlds, 818
respect, 506, 606, 770, 772
Return to Castle Wolfenstein, 45, 611, 624–629
reusability, 225
Reversi, 453
rewards, 215, 766, 823, 825
Rheingold, H. L., 363
rhetorics
    defined, 302
    of everyday life, 306
    of play, 46, 85, 302–311

Rickman, B., 668
Rifkin, J., 266
rights, of players
    comments, 796–805
    in ordinary language, 808–812
    reality *vs.* game, 802–804
    social contract, 11–18, 42, 796–805
    theories, 790–795
    See also intellectual property
Riner, R. D., 787
ring-around-a-rosy, 80
risk
    in *alea,* 133
    and gender, 346, 348, 353
    and player types, 771
    strategy, 399–405, 408n3
    Super Mario Brothers, 347
    and threat, 318
    in town games, 356
    types, 126, 301
    in virtual worlds, 825
rituals, 100, 107–118, 124, 318
    voladores, 138, 151n8
Rivest, R., 753
Robinett, W., 55, 66, 690–725
RoboRally, 540
Robson, D., 753
Rocky's Boots, 691, 713
Rogers, Y., 437
role-play
    in boy culture, 342, 347
    and fiction, 195
    and insects, 135
    and knowledge, 591
    Magic, 549
    in MUDs, 207, 757, 781

    and rules, 126
    and socializing, 207
    subversion, xviii
    as technique, 207
role-playing games (RPGs)
    characters, 29, 206
    consequences, 373–378
    fantasy, 35, 72, 506, 582–586
    framework, 419, 421
    goals, 197
    on-line (*see* massively multiplayer on-line role-playing games)
    opposition, 198
    Pikmin, 235
    and real-time strategy, 368
    referees, 586–591, 594
    resources, 428
    social interaction, 208
    and spaces, 674
    SquareSoft, 376
    Star Wars, 204
    time-out, 593
    tokens, 200
Roller Coaster Tycoon, 611
Rolston, K., 210
Romanes, G. J., 142
Rosas, R., 437
Rosenberg, J., 668
Rosenberg, M. S., 787
Rotundo, E. A., 337, 341, 347, 363
roulette, 133, 209
Rouse III, R., 4, 56, 266, 450–473
Roush, W., 787
rules
    bending, 188, 520–523
    by the book, 488

borrowing, 523

change, 12–18, 500, 515, 531

and children, 142, 509–516

consitutive, 11, 187

cultural context, 73

and decisions, 10

and ends, 9, 174–177

explicit vs. implicit, 48, 500, 511, 515 (see also unwritten rules)

and facilitator, 420

and framework, 414, 583, 591

vs. freedom, 141–147

vs. fun, 514

game definition, 80, 173–184

Habitat, 743

ideal and real, 15, 507

incomplete, 126, 492–495

interpretation, 492, 547, 553

linguistics, 48, 317

lusory, 187

Magic, 546, 553

and meaning, 581

vs. mechanics, 413

and morality, 181–183

and MUD admins, 806, 808

and order, 105

and play, 106, 125

and psychotherapy, 326

in real life, 189

vs. rulings, 479

self-defeating, 478

and seriousness, 178, 483, 495

of skill, 187

and tension, 9, 15

for tournaments, 554

and trading cards, 553

violations, 126, 175–184, 188, 500, 524

Russell, B., 315, 317, 321, 324

ruthlessness, 543

Ryan, M., 665, 668

Ryan, M.-L., 37

Rydenhag, T., 436

sacred performances, 107–118, 124

saddle point, 398–402

St. Louis Court Brief, 51

Salim, A., 620

Salkowski, J., 863

Sandoval, G., 863

saturnalia, 107

Saturn's Nights into Dreams, 359

saves

    by developers, 220

    game state metaphor, 447

    by players, 248

    Summoner, 294

Saving Private Ryan, 611

scale models, 143, 145, 740

scapegoating, 509, 512

scarcity, 60, 824–826, 834, 846

Scardamalia, 265

scatological images, 341

Schechner, R., 297

schizophrenia, 325, 327

Schmittberger, R. W., 13

Scholder, A., 13, 63

Schon, D. A., 266

schools, 232, 629–633, 868

    See also learning

Schutz, A., 579, 601

Schwartz, D. L., 265

Schwartzman, H., 307, 505, 516

Schweickart, P. P., 363

science
    critical learning, 238, 254–263
    cultural models, 629
    rhetorics of, 306–308
Scollon, R., 266
Scollon, S. B. K., 266
scoring
    in arcade games, 463
    cashing out, 452
    and change, 535–537
    function, 447
    hiddenness, 451
    and player types, 757
    lies, 391, 448
    Twenty-One, 456
screens, network of, 713
scripts, 282, 286–288
scrolling, 465
scrolling map, 65, 715–717
Sea Dogs, 676
Searles, H., 363
Second Life, 41
secrecy, 107, 124, 349, 352
secret codes, 340
The Secret Garden, 348–352
Secret Paths in the Forest, 349–352
see-saws, 127
Sega, 343, 359
Segel, E., 345, 348, 357, 358, 363
Seiter, E., 343
Seitzer, E., 363
seizure, 110, 138
self. rhetoric of, 85, 305
self-control, 144, 339
self-esteem, 215, 464, 483
self-interest, 388, 396–398

self-pity, 318
semiotic domains
    carryover, 261
    and cultural models, 632, 638
    description, 47, 233, 239–250
    design grammars, 245–250, 255
    external and internal views, 241–244, 251
    and learning, 238, 254–261
    in real life, 251–259
    situated meaning, 239–241, 252, 254–256
Senet, 439
Sengers, P., 660, 668
seriousness
    vs. awareness, 112, 116
    and play, 101, 103, 114–116
    and ritual, 111
    and rules, 178, 483, 495
    and virtual world, 861n20
Serious Sam, 625
servers, 845, 855, 858, 861n22, 862n27
session, 415
set-up/set-down, 416
sexual activity
    in films, 319
    orgies, 107
    as play, 299, 300
    The Sims, 685
    virtual rape, 768
sexual harassment, 768
Shamir, A., 753
Shanahan, I. See always_black
Shapiro, C., 863
Sharp, H., 437
Shelley, B., 197
Shenmue, 672
Sherman, L. F., 349, 362

shooter games. *See* first-person shooter games

shopping, 817, 819, 827, 832

    virtual stores, 842

    See also consumerism; game economies; purchase

Shore, B., 639

Shultz, J., 516

Siberia, 623

Siegal, J., 154

signals, 315–318

signatures, 693, 712

Sim City, 194, 197, 353

Sim Earth, 200

Simon says, 493

The Sims, 684, 685

The Sims II

    cultural model, 45, 71, 611

    as innovation, 672

    and narrative, 645, 665

    precursor, 41

The Sims Online, 684

simulations

    of battle, 383

    classification, 148t

    and narrative, 645

    in slot machines, 153

    of social environment, 663

    uses, 204–207

single-player games

    computer games, 207, 209

    and diplomacy, 203

    and ludus, 144

    opposition, 195

    solitary play, 299, 305

Sinistar, 464f, 465

situated meaning, 239–241, 252, 254–256

Situationist Texts (Web site), 86

skill

    acquisition, 142

    of avatars, 822

    Breakout, 561, 573, 576

    critical thinking, 868

    and disputes, 498

    rules, 187

    Summoner, 274–278, 280, 284, 287

Skinner, D., 639

sliding, 138

slot machines, 143, 152n15, 154

Smalltalk, 733

Smarty, 354

Sniderman, S., 11, 15, 47, 48, 476–502

Snood, 672

Snooze, 175, 180

Snow, C. E., 266

social contract, 11–18, 42, 796–805

social engineering, 742

social interaction

    Breakout, 561, 577

    Foursquare, 16

    friendship adventures, 349, 352–357

    and fun, 514

    game metaphor, 506, 580

    and girl culture, 354, 356

    Habitat, 23

    and killing, 772

    in MUDs, 757, 767–769

    predominance, 208

    in purchase, 39, 157–161

    and RPGs, 207

    rule disputes, 499

    sportsmanship, 487, 491

    tennis game, 16, 484–489, 492

    virtual worlds, 822, 840–843

socializers
    increasing/decreasing, 778
    and other player types, 771–780
    vs. other socializers, 774, 779
    as player type, 6, 41, 61, 758, 762
social networking, 343
social practices
    vs. content, 236, 241–246
    and learning, 238
    and literacy, 230–232
    and rhetorics of play, 309
    and semiotic domains, 258
    See also affinity groups
social standing, 823, 844
social structures, 48, 106
    See also game communities
society
    family life, 334, 343
    and game spaces, 67
    gender roles, 357
    ideal, 860n14
    and play, 104
    play-communities, 106
    representations, 71–75
    research topics, 844–846
    rituals, 110
    semiotic domains, 258
    virtual world effect, 840–843
    in virtual worlds, 823
socioeconomic class
    and cultural models, 618
    Everquest players, 830t
    and fate, 302
    GTA San Andreas, 75
    in Norrath, 840, 845
    software
    for game development, 623, 663

object-oriented, 730, 733, 735, 750
    Smalltalk, 733
solitaire, 143, 205, 522, 523
solitary play. *See* single-player games
Sonic Adventure 2 Battle, 612–619
Sony, 248, 816, 819, 820, 827, 861n18
sound
    Breakout, 564
    as feedback, 215
    multimodality, 229
    Super Mario Brothers, 347
    in town game, 254
source code
    control of, 221
    decrementing functions, 459n2
    documentation, 721
    of Eastern Front, 724
    emphasis on, 220
    marketing, 724
    reusing, 225
Sowell, T., 753
Space 1899, 203
Space Hulk, 428
Space Invaders, 332, 417, 432, 467
spam, 164, 809
Spariosu, M., 297, 307
spatiality
    and cultural model, 67
    and inevitability, 454
    limits, 105
    and narrative, 34, 674–680
    sacred performances, 108, 113
    and tracks, 131
    See also game spaces
spectacles, 679, 867–869
spectators
    drama, 651, 655, 662, 665

and mimicry, 137
and play, 300
and threat, 318
traditional artforms, 195
of vertigo, 140
Spector, W., ix–xiii
speed
Centipede, 469
and girl game, 351
Summoner, 289, 294
and vertigo, 138, 140
spies, 591
spin the bottle, 85
spoil-sports, 106, 126, 499
sports, 300, 479, 868
sports games
characters, 206
equal adversaries, 131
intention, 377
power, 305
semiotic domains, 230, 232, 236
statistics, 377
tokens, 200
tradition, 489
sportsmanship, 482, 487, 491
spoil-sports, 106, 126
SquareSoft, 376
Squire, K., 69
standards
for admins, 792, 808–812
data communication, 737, 750
StarCraft, 432
Star Wars, 75, 664, 677
Star Wars: The Roleplaying Game, 204
Star Wars Galaxies, 664
stealing, 543, 743
stealth. *See* deceit

Steinberg, S. R., 362
Sterling, B., 753
Stern, A., 29, 33, 34, 642–666, 668, 669
story, 375, 681, 687n7
about DOOM 3, 157–169
See also narrative; plot
strategy
and chance, 399–405, 408n3
chess, 393
minimax principle, 396–402
mixed, 399–405, 408n3
resource management, 430
Summoner, 278
tic-tac-toe, 392
Strat-o-matic™ Baseball, 540, 542
Stratus, 749
Strauss, A., 584
Strauss, C., 618, 639
Street, B., 267
strength, 358
structural components, 419–422
structuralists, 242–246
subjective play, 299
Sudnow, D., 3, 67, 558–571
Suits, B., 9, 11, 78, 172–191
Summoner, 269–295
algorithms, 272
bugs, 290
chain combo, 288
characters, 273, 277, 279, 281, 284, 294
cheating, 291
economies in, 62
FAQ, 17, 269–295
firewalls, 279
gameplan, 278
quickslots, 278, 282, 286
releases, 271

saves, 294
scripts, 282, 286–288, 293
side-quests, 293
skills, 274–278, 284, 287
speed, 289, 294
storyline, 294
tactics, 279, 282, 286
time to finish, 293
Super Mario Bros., 68, 347, 675
Super Mario Sunshine, 440
Super Metroid, 341
surprise, 205
suspension of disbelief, 496, 649
suspicion, 499, 584
Sussman, G. J., 753
Sustare, B. D., 601
Sutton-Smith, B., 46, 81, 85, 86, 296–311, 516, 667
Swain, C., 13, 25, 437
Syria, 73, 619
systems
    complexity threshold, 739
    as discourse universe, 71
    and flexibility, 15
    games as, 80, 499–502
    learning about, 263
    and patterns, 54
    and rhetorics of play, 85
    of spaces, 67
    See also game economies
System Shock, 164

table of outcomes, 392–395
tactics, 279, 282, 286
Talisman, 199
Tapscott, D., 339, 363
Taylor, C., 267
Team Fortress II, 221

teamwork, 625, 691
    See also Cabal process
technology
    and Atari 2600, 692
    bandwidth, 734–736
    vs. characters, 729
    vs. community, 41
    cryptography, 750
    data communication, 737
    as emphasis, 220
    evolution, 737
    and game spaces, 65
    and journalists, 59
    platform/computer, 248–250
    reusability, 225
    servers, 845
    and slot machines, 154
    standards, 737, 750
    timeliness, 224
    See also artificial intelligence
teetotum, 138, 142
Tekken, 377
telepresence, 648
television
    networks, 203, 208
    quiz shows, 449, 450, 454–457
    watching, 299
Tempest, 464f, 643
tennis
    Breakout, 577
    extra-game activities, 414
    McEnroe antics, 498
    scoring, 536
    unwritten rules, 16, 484–492
tension
    and aesthetics, 105
    Centipede, 4, 55, 469–472

components, 33, 55, 445
and contests, 444
and dynamics, 446
and environment, 222f
and joy, 114
and *ludus,* 143
and mistakes, 219f
pacing, 4, 208, 218
playing *vs.* gaming mind, 520
play *vs.* story, 679
and plot, 195
resolution, 457
in RPGs, 593–596, 598
and rules, 9, 15
uncertainty, 445
Terminal Time, 645
terror, 116, 319
terrorism, 619, 634, 637
testing. *See* playtesting
Tetris, 672, 687n6
text adventures, 646, 691, 694–699, 703
thematic structure, 218
Thief: The Dark Project, 625
thinking
all-or-nothing, 320
critical, 868
metalevel, 256, 263
third-person, xviii, 861n19
Thompson, K., 681
Thorne, B., 360, 361, 363
threaded execution, 719
threat, 317
3D
Breakout, 576
development software, 623
and realism, 68, 319
Saturn's Night, 360

and virtual worlds, 818
Wolfenstein 3D, 261
thrills, 573, 575
ticking clocks, 453–457
tic-tac-toe
extra-game factors, 480
game theory, 389–393
rules, 11, 477, 527–530
tie scores, 391, 448
tightrope, 144
time
anachronism, 585, 591
and change, 524
denouement, 457
diversity of, 301
to finish Summoner, 293
and framework, 415, 418, 421
and inevitability, 453–456
infinite play, 463
Jeopardy, 450
Magic, 546
and play, 104
and players
of EverQuest, 820, 831t, 832, 849
lapsed, 555
of MUDs, 763
real-time, 368, 421, 698
as resource, 430
trading card games, 553
video games, 635
time limits
chess, 481
and information, 201
of play, 104, 125
sports, 479
for technology, 224
tic-tac-toe, 477

time-out, 486, 493, 593

TinyMUD, 767, 782

tips
> vs. advice, 257
> on Summoner, 269–295

tokens
> and characters, 206
> and control, 200
> in framework, 420
> Habitat, 746, 752n2

Tolkien, J. R. R., 858, 863

Tomb Raiders, 425, 644, 818

top-spinning, 127

tournaments, 478, 554

Town, 352–356

town games, 352–356
> *See also* urban design

toys, 143, 151n6, 194, 336

trading card games, 550, 553

traditions, 104, 107, 489, 491

transformation, 649, 657–659

transmorph, 582, 600n3

transport, 139

trash-talking, 49, 483, 603–608, 759
> *See also* flame wars

Traveller, 590

travesty, 136

trends, 144, 152n15, 332

Tribble, D. G., 753

triggers, 418

triviality, 751

Trivial Pursuit, 208

trompe l'oeil, 319

troubleshooting, 55

trust
> and minimax principle, 398
> and new games, 499
> in players, 744–747
> and unwritten rules, 497

Tsao, V., 207

Tsatsarelis, C., 266

tug-of-war, 399

tumult, 139, 141, 718

Turkle, S., 7, 31

Turner, V., 297

Twain, M., 337, 346

Twenty-One, 454–457

twinking, 845, 857

Ultima Online
> game economy, 861n19
> narrative, 645
> players, 820, 859n6
> precursor, 693

uncertainty
> and games of chance, 134
> *vs.* inevitability, 33, 55, 445
> and play, 126

Under Ash, 73, 619–621, 637

underdogs, 625

The Undying, 682

units, 430, 432

unwritten rules, 477–502
> consitutive, 11, 187
> of etiquette, 483
> gaming the game, 15–17
> infinite regression, 492–494, 501
> meta-unwritten rule, 489
> and MUD administration, 806
> implicit vs. explicit, 48, 500, 511, 515
> playing fair, 481
> sportsmanship, 482
> tennis example, 16, 484–492
> time out, 486

urban design, 685, 846

Urdang, L., 787

user interfaces
    action opportunities, 652–655, 657, 660
    Breakout, 559–569
    tokens, 420
    and virtual worlds, 818
utility, 395
utopianism, 844, 860n14

Valéry, P., 106, 125
values
    China, 145
    cultural models, 45–48, 75, 618, 636
    fate *vs.* free choice, 304
    gender, 345–352
    individualism, 625
    Metal Gear Solid, 634
    platform *vs.* computer, 250
    prowess testing, 105
    and rhetorics of play, 309
    and rule-breaking, 176
    semiotic domains, 258, 261
    tenacity, 105
    video games, 411, 613
    viewpoints, 614
    See also cultural models; sportsmanship
Valve. *See* Cabal process
van Leeuwen, T., 266
Vanouse, P., 667, 668
van Staden, J. F., 363
Van Vliet, W., 335, 363
Varian, H. R., 863
variety
    as aesthetic, 649, 657–659
    in arcade games, 462
    Cosmic Encounter, 539
    of encounter, 205
    of goals, 197

    Magic, 205, 541, 544
    patience game, 205
Verant Interactive, 816, 819, 845
Vertical Blank Interrupt (VBI), 719
vertigo
    dialectical, 185
    in game definition, 78
    as play type, 5, 138–140, 148t
    ring-around-a-rosy, 80
    in slot machines, 153
vicarious play, 300
Victoria, 428
video arcades, 340, 343
    See also arcade games
video games
    and children, 6, 235–237, 258–263, 332
    and computer careers, 262
    content, 262, 334, 343, 611
    cultural models, 613–619, 633–637
    game spaces, 65–67
    gender, 6, 74, 339, 356–361
    history of, 74, 692
    iterative design, 22
    and learning, 236–239, 358, 611–613, 633–637
    and literacy, 229–235
    morality, 613
    opinions of, 45–48
    and September 11th, 619
    trends, 332
    and violence, 46, 334, 341
Vinge, V., 730, 753
violence
    Under Ash, 619–621
    boy culture, 340
    eradication, 623
    Habitat, 743

The Sims Online, 684
in video games, 46, 334, 341
virtual rape, 768
Virtua Fighter, 453
virtual communities, 791–812
See also game communities
virtual jobs, 842
virtual rape, 768
virtual shopping, 817, 842
virtual worlds
appeal factors, 842, 860n14
definition, 818, 858n2
history, 818–820, 824, 860n13
incipient *vs.* percipient level, 744–746
persistence, 818
profitability, 820
and reality, 821, 822, 824, 844, 858, 860n10, 860n15
research potential, 840, 844–846
utopian elements, 844
and zoning, 860n15
See also Habitat; massively multiplayer on-line role-playing games; Norrath
visual literacy, 229
visual metaphors, 216f, 219f
Vlissides, J., 437
vogues, 144, 152n15
voladores, 138, 151n8
volleyball, 520, 523
voluntariness. See freedom
von Neumann, J., 384, 437
See also game theory
VR Sports, 333

wagers, 124, 127, 134, 142
Waltzer, 267
Walz, S. P., 53, 436

wan, 141, 145
war, 611, 622, 846
See also battles
War and Peace, 676
Warcraft, 449, 451, 453, 457
See also World of Warcraft
Ward, C., 336, 363
Wardrip-Fruin, N., 37
war games, 200, 383, 719
for U.S. army recruiting, 629
Wargames (movie), 485
warp zones, 340
weapons, xviiii, 743, 748, 757
web phones, 867
Weiss, D. B., 65
Wellman, B., 796
West, E., 334, 363
Wheel of Fortune, 453
whirling dervishes, 138
Whitehead, A. N., 315
white supremacists, 623
Whitlock, T. D., 787
Whorf, B. L., 315
winner-take-all, 139
winning
and cheating, 175
chess, 183
desire for, 132
in framework, 419
as goal, 186, 417
winning condition, 419
wiping, 809
Wittgenstein, L., 77–80, 307, 315
Wizards of the Coast, 540, 554
Wolf, M. J. P., 69, 437
Wolf, S., 267
Wolfenstein 3D, 261

women. *See* girls and women

Woods, D., 691, 713

work

 and competition, 132, 199

 vs. game, 173

 and games of chance, 133

 situated meanings, 239–241

 vs. video games, 342

 virtual jobs, 842

World of Warcraft, 29

Worlds Chat, 860n13

World War II Online, 819

Wright, W., 200, 210, 684

Xbox, 160, 248–250, 692

Yee, N., 820, 863

yo-yos, 143, 144

Yu-Gi-Oh, 550

Zagal, J. P., 437

zero-sum games, 54, 124, 395

Zero Zero, 354–356

Zito, K., 863

zone of control, 719, 722

Zork, 193, 439, 654, 674

Zucker, K., 204

The ambience of play is by nature unstable. At any moment "ordinary life" can prevail once again. The geographical limitation of play is even more than its temporal limitation. Any game takes place within the more striking contours of its spatial domain. Around the neighborhood, around its fleeting and threatened immobility, stretched a half-known city where people met only by chance losing their way forever.—Guy Debord

Eric: The end of the book!

Katie: It sure looks that way. So, what's next?

Eric: Another book?

Katie: Please, no. How about a game?

Eric: A rematch. You beat me last time.

Katie: Because you forgot the rules.

Eric: You mean you changed them on me.

Katie: Games are like that.

Eric: If you say so. I'll close my eyes and count to twenty.

Katie: And when you open them, start looking.